W9-AIT-081

Praise for *Best Evidence*:

"*Best Evidence* is a prolix medical thriller that examines every shred of evidence several times over and serves at the very least as a comprehensive narrative of assassination, fact and theory . . . Much of Lifton's evidence is compelling. *Best Evidence* is a disturbing book." —*The Washington Star*

"A blockbuster . . . insistent and inescapable . . . David Lifton just grabs you by the throat and refuses to let you loose." —*The Washingtonian*

BEST
EVIDENCE

DISGUISE AND DECEPTION
IN THE ASSASSINATION OF
JOHN F. KENNEDY

David S. Lifton

Carroll & Graf Publishers, Inc.
New York

Copyright © 1980 by David S. Lifton

Foreword and Afterword Copyright © 1988 by David S. Lifton

All rights reserved

Photo credits: Photo 1, Arthur Shatz; Photo 2, Abraham Zapruder, via LMH Co.; Photo 3, Phil Willis; Photo 4, Mary Moorman; Photo 5A, Wide World Photos; Photo 5B, *Fort Worth Star Telegram*; Photo 6, Orville Nix, via UPI; Photo 7, Wide World Photos; Photo 8, UPI; Photo 9, *Fort Worth Star Telegram*; Photo 10, Phil Willis; Photo 11, Charles Bronson; Photo 12, Marie Muchmore, via UPI; Photo 13, Wilma Bond; Photo 14, *Fort Worth Star Telegram*; Photo 15, Abraham Zapruder, via LMH Co.; Photos 16A through 24, National Archives; Photo 25, Wesley Liebeler; Photo 26A, U. S. Air Force; Photos 26 B and C, Wide World Photos; Photo 27, National Archives; Photo 28, TV broadcast, via Wallace Milam; Photos 29 through 32, National Archives; Photo 33, House Assassinations Committee Report; Photo 34, Wide World Photos; Photo 35, National Archives; Photo 36, Public Broadcasting Service, via Wallace Milam; Photo 37, Paul O'Connor; Photo 38, James Jenkins; Photos 39 and 40, Bob Phillips, *Life* magazine, © 1963 Time, Inc.; Photo 41, National Archives; Photos 42 A, B, and C, Cecil Stoughton; Photos 43 A through F, Cecil Stoughton, via LBJ Library.

ILLUSTRATIONS BY JON NELSON

Published in association with Richard Gallen & Company, Inc.

First Carroll & Graf edition 1988
Ninth Printing 1990

Carroll & Graf Publishers, Inc.
260 Fifth Avenue
New York, NY 10001

ISBN: 0-88184-438-1

Manufactured in the United States of America

To my parents
and
the memory of John F. Kennedy

What you believe happened in Dallas on November 22, 1963, depends on what evidence you believe. Every day, in courtrooms, juries are confronted with conflicting evidence. The usual legal approach is not to seek new information to resolve the conflict; rather, it is to decide which evidence is credible.

Lawyers often call that the "best evidence."

CONTENTS

CONTENTS

Contents

ACKNOWLEDGMENTS

IN THE WEE HOURS of the morning of October 23, 1966, I made a discovery in the Warren Commission's evidence which changed the course of my life. It led to a fifteen-year odyssey, and this book. During that period, I was fortunate enough to have some good and close friends who assisted me with the work.

For eight years, between 1966 and 1974, *Best Evidence* was essentially a research project. At that time I was living in Los Angeles, where I was given invaluable encouragement and support by Bernard Kenton, who served as a sounding board for a developing hypothesis; by Patricia Lambert, who assisted in my documentary research, scouring the Warren Commission's records for data; and by Paul Hoch, who shared his storehouse of files and insights. Steve Bailey was a good friend and helped with technical matters, particularly those relating to the autopsy photographs and X-rays. I owe deep thanks to Al Schweitzer for many valuable discussions and much technical assistance; to William Corrigan and Judith Schmidt for their encouragement and support and for often lending a hand with the research; and to Bruce J. Turner and June Ayling for their friendship.

Beginning in 1975, I produced a draft of this manuscript with assistance from Bernard Kenton, who typed the manuscript and assisted with the technical chapters; and major editorial assistance from Patricia Lambert. Thanks also to Victoria Pasternack, for editorial assistance, and to Linda Valentino for her encouragement and support.

In October 1976, I had the extraordinary good fortune to be introduced to New York literary agent Peter Shepherd, who read that manuscript and agreed to represent me. I came to New York City for what I thought was a brief visit, believing I had a saleable book. We soon learned otherwise. Peter then urged me to recast that manuscript—an abstract evidentiary analysis—into a personal narrative, and offered to assist me in that task. Originally we thought the project would take several months, but it extended nearly four years and involved hundreds of meetings, during which the story of what I had been doing and experiencing became just as much a part of the book as the evidence I had found and the theory I was propounding. Besides convincing me to write the story as a personal narrative and guiding me in that endeavor, Peter also expertly edited the chapters. Without Peter Shepherd, *Best Evidence* would not exist.

During this period, I often felt I had a professional staff at my disposal. I received inestimable help from Bernard Kenton, with whom I was in constant touch, and who made many valuable suggestions, typed several thousand pages of manuscript, and also managed a complex filing system located on the West Coast, while I was in New York City working with Peter Shepherd. Patricia Lambert lent invaluable support, made detailed comments and suggestions, and rendered major editorial assistance in rewriting and cutting the text. Arnon Mishkin offered extremely helpful suggestions during the drafting process, and then reviewed the entire manuscript when it was finished. Throughout, Paul Hoch provided valuable research assistance and insights, and he too reviewed the finished manuscript and made cogent comments and suggestions.

A high point of this activity occurred in December 1978, with the sale of the book to Macmillan Publishing Co., Inc. and I will be forever grateful to Jeremiah Kaplan, the president, who personally decided to publish it.

At Macmillan, my editor George Walsh has been helpful, supportive, and most creative in guiding the book through the complexities of the publication process. Rayanna Simons' encouragement and editorial help are also very much appreciated. I also want to thank Albert Litewka, the president of the General Books Division, for his personal commitment to the project.

I am deeply grateful to those who added particular dimensions to *Best Evidence:* to Robert Ranftel, who spent many an hour in the FBI reading room perusing nearly 100,000 pages of documents, released in 1978 under the Freedom of Information Act, for data pertinent to my research; to Wallace Milam, for many provocative discussions, and for one lead which resulted in a major breakthrough; to Art Smith, for sharing tapes of his 1978 interviews with Bethesda radiologist Dr. John Ebersole; to Gaeton Fonzi, for making available to me tapes of his 1966 interviews with Arlen Specter; to Andrew Purdy and Mark Flanagan, of the House Assassinations Committee, for help in locating key witnesses; to Captain James Albright, of the Military District of Washington, who processed my Freedom of Information Act request and turned up important data from the U.S. Army files; to Sonja Farago, who typed many detailed transcripts

Acknowledgments

and notes of interviews conducted shortly before the book's deadline; to Sarah Holland for valuable research assistance; and to Robert Groden, for most enlightening discussions about the autopsy X-rays and photographs, the Zapruder film, the functioning of the House Assassinations Committee (to which he was a consultant), and for many an evening spent reviewing his outstanding archive of photographs and films.

Thanks to George Barnum, for permission to publish part of a personal memorandum written on November 29, 1963; and to journalist Gil Dulaney, for giving me access to notes of his interview with Dr. Ebersole. Thanks also to Josiah Thompson, for his generosity in putting at my disposal material originally accumulated during the research for his own book, *Six Seconds in Dallas,* published in 1967.

For the past fifteen years, the subject matter of this book was highly confidential. That made life difficult, and friendship counted for a lot. For their encouragement and support, I want to thank: Barbara Kenton, William Lambert, Ellen Starr Schwab, Bea Lebson, Robert Sam Anson, Pat Valentino, Carole Chazin, Robert Blair Kaiser, Caroline Isaacs, Robert Ansell, Francine Klagsbrun, Sam Klagsbrun, Isadore Ziferstein, and the late John Clemente.

I also want to thank Elissa Blaser, George O'Toole, Bob Katz, Fred Webre, Robert Butler, Ed Kabak, Dick Freed, Barbara Landis, Gary Mack, Larry Harris, Jones Harris, Bernard Fensterwald, Yoram Kahana, Peggy Kahana, Hal Verb, Rusty Rhodes, Chris Groden, Roy Lippman, Don Berk, and Marianna Zambeis.

I am indebted to the following researchers for making material available to me: Richard Sprague, Gary Shaw, Jack White, Mary Ferrell, Stewart Galanor, Barbara Bridges, Penn Jones, Earl Golz, Jim Kostman, Harold Weisberg, Tom Stamm, and Ray Marcus.

At the National Archives, Marion Johnson was always helpful, and Les Waffen went out of his way to permit me to study, at length, audio tapes made the weekend of the assassination.

Similar kindness was shown to me by the staffs of the UCLA Research Library and the UCLA Biomedical Library, where much of my research was done.

There are no words that can express my gratitude to my parents Helen and Al Lifton. It was their encouragement and financial support that made this book possible.

DAVID S. LIFTON
Belle Harbor, New York

AUTHOR'S NOTE

Over fifteen years, my search for truth about the assassination of President John Kennedy has taken me down paths with surprising turns. In the pages that follow I have tried to convey to the reader a sense of my journey by relating it chronologically. All the facts that led me to form and discard hypotheses and opinions along the way, therefore, are set forth in the order in which I encountered them.

PROLOGUE

"MY GOD, DAVID, do you realize what you've found? You've found new evidence!"

The speaker: Prof. Wesley J. Liebeler, of the UCLA Law School, former Warren Commission attorney.

The date: October 24, 1966.

Liebeler and I had become sparring partners over the Warren Report. He accepted the Report—or at least said he did. I did not, and devoted months to studying the twenty-six volumes of Hearings and Exhibits—the published evidence of the investigation.

I was a graduate student in engineering at UCLA with a degree from Cornell in engineering physics. My primary interest was the physical evidence. My research culminated with a stint at *Ramparts* magazine in June 1966, where I wrote a thirty-thousand-word article analyzing the medical and ballistic evidence entitled "The Case for Three Assassins."

Liebeler had a contract with a major New York publisher to write a book about the Warren Report, and had asked me to play a part in his project. He invited me to attend the UCLA Law School class he taught on the Warren Report to play devil's advocate and to extend that role in a series of private meetings with him. Liebeler's attitude was: Prove to me we were wrong, and I'll say so in my book.

On October 23, 1966, I discovered a document that astonished and frightened me.

I arranged to meet Liebeler the following day.

I asserted, as I had many times before, that an assassin must have fired from the front. Liebeler made his customary reply, for which, previously, I had had no answer:

"If there's another assassin, where's the bullet?"

Now I responded, "That's simple, Jim." I walked around Liebeler and took up a position behind him, as if I were his barber. I took my right index finger, put it firmly atop his forehead, and drew it from front to back across his scalp, miming the motions of someone cutting into the top of the President's head. "They simply took the bullet out, before the autopsy."

I returned to my seat.

Liebeler stared at me incredulously.

"That is why," I said, "FBI agents Sibert and O'Neill reported that when the President's body arrived at the autopsy room at Bethesda Naval Hospital, there had been, quote, 'surgery of the head area, namely, in the top of the skull,' unquote."

Liebeler's reaction was instantaneous.

"Where does it say that?" he shouted at me.

"Right here," I yelled back, tossing the report across the desk.

As that unforgettable afternoon unfolded, I watched Liebeler follow the path I had traveled twenty-four hours earlier. Here was evidence that someone had altered the President's body prior to the autopsy; evidence that the autopsy report, the source of crucial information about the number and direction of shots, actually described a body no longer in the same condition as it had been immediately after the shooting. If this FBI report were true, the conclusions of the Warren Commission were erected on a foundation of sand.

The next week, Liebeler asked me to assist him in preparing a memorandum to Chief Justice Warren to set forth the questions that ought to be addressed to the autopsy X-rays and photographs which the Kennedy family had just donated to the National Archives. The Warren Commission had never examined the autopsy X-rays and photographs, having relied instead on artist's drawings prepared by the autopsy doctors.

The memorandum quoted the passage about head surgery in the FBI report. "It should be noted that no surgery was performed at Parkland Hospital in the area of the President's head," wrote Liebeler.

"In assessing the probable reaction to the statement concerning surgery in the President's head area, it should be noted that neither the Sibert and O'Neill report nor the comment about head surgery is set forth or discussed anywhere in the Report or 26 volumes of underlying evidence."

Liebeler also said:

Attention was first drawn to the above statement by Mr. David Lifton of Los Angeles. Mr. Lifton is quite familiar with the Report and the underlying evidence. He has agreed not to focus public attention on this matter until an attempt has been made to effect a responsible analysis of the autopsy photographs and X-rays to determine whether or not the Sibert and O'Neill report is accurate.

Prologue

Liebeler sent copies of his memorandum to all former Warren Commissioners, certain members of the staff, Assistant Attorney General Ramsey Clark, and Burke Marshall, the Kennedy family's attorney.

I thought then that Liebeler's memorandum would lead to a reopening of the inquiry, and mark the end of my own eighteen-month interest in the assassination.

It turned out, however, that I had only started a new chapter in a long struggle.

Foreword

In 1966, I was naive enough to believe that if evidence indicating conspiracy in the Kennedy assassination was brought to light, the government would act. The investigation would be reopened. Truth would win out.

It doesn't work that way—at least, not over the short run.

When I first became interested in this case, I was a UCLA graduate student. At this writing, I am 48, and less naive. It seems incredible to me that I was so excited about an idea that it governed and shaped my life for over fifteen years.

I'm still excited about what I discovered—but that excitement is tempered by the knowledge that truth takes a long time to emerge.

Best Evidence went to the printer on October 17, 1980, and almost immediately, I changed gears and embarked on a project to create a filmed record of the testimony of new witnesses I had discovered—the men in the autopsy room who had knowledge of the two caskets, of the body bag, and who had observed the body's arrival without a brain. About six weeks later, as I reviewed the footage back in New York, I was joined by Dan Rather's producer from *60 Minutes*. "Boy, Dan is going to love this!" he said. "Wait till you see the program we're going to do." My publisher began planning my tour assuming a *60 Minutes* kickoff.

As publication date approached, I felt as though I were sitting atop a rocket, moments before liftoff. Where would the journey lead? A close friend, equally ebullient, said: "What's life going to be like after *Best Evidence*?"

We were all excited that I had found so much new evidence. Rather's producer put it this way—the filmed interviews set up a conflict "between the inconceivable and the irrefutable."

My appearance on *60 Minutes,* however, was not to be. In early December, a composite of my filmed interviews was screened for executive producer Don Hewitt. When the lights went up, he barked, with evident hostility: "Did you pay these people?" "Yes," I responded, "A dollar for the release." Then, in the same tone, he asked, "Why did you make this film?" I replied that I wanted to interview the key witnesses on film before they had read the book, and before they realized the implications of their own accounts.

Hewitt eventually calmed down. He even warmed to the idea of doing a show, but at a subsequent screening, Dan Rather said he didn't understand why anybody would want to alter the body. "All you have here" he said, "are witnesses who remember things a bit differently."

Publication date arrived and with it my book tour began. I was on *Good Morning America*. Each day, I found myself in a different city, never having to look at the right-hand side of a menu. But certain things became apparent: first, the difference between the national and the local media.

In city after city, I was given splendid treatment and accorded great respect. This is not to say that everybody agreed with everything I was saying, but I usually got a fair hearing on the local level.

The national media, however, were reluctant to deal with *Best Evidence* at all. This was true not only of the networks, but of the print media as well. (A notable exception was *Time*, which treated *Best Evidence* as a news story and gave it two full pages in the "National Affairs" section.) But the attitude of the majority was better illustrated by a meeting that writer/researcher Pat Lambert and I had with political reporter George Lardner of the Washington *Post* on the day *Best Evidence* was published. After viewing my film and questioning me about how the body was transported from Dallas to Bethesda, he said: "I don't think you'll ever make that palatable to the American public."

This reaction reflects what I have often thought: The difficulty with this material is not logical, but psychological. Truth, as the saying goes, is the daughter of time.

David Lifton
Los Angeles, California
July, 1988

PART 1

The Puzzle

Entering the Labyrinth

Entering the Labyrinth

ON SEPTEMBER 20, 1964, during a recess of UCLA graduate school, I was visiting my parents in New York City. To celebrate my twenty-fifth birthday, they offered to take me out for an evening on the town. We were considering seeing the operetta *The Merry Widow* when I noticed a small advertisement in the *New York Times*: "Mark Lane on Who Killed Kennedy. Jan Hus Theatre. 351 E 74th. Seats $2.00." A friend had heard Lane argue that the official version of the assassination was false and she assured me it would be an interesting evening.

The Warren Commission had not yet issued its Report, but the "official" version was widely reported in the media: President Kennedy's assassin was Lee Harvey Oswald, acting alone. I told my friend that any person with common sense would know a conspiracy was out of the question. Too many people would have to be involved.

I watched Kennedy's funeral on television, but the fact is that I paid scant attention to the assassination or its aftermath. After graduating from Cornell University's School of Engineering Physics in 1962, I went directly to Los Angeles and a job as a computer engineer at the Space and Information Systems Division of North American Aviation, the prime contractor for the Apollo project, the United States program to put a man on the moon. My goal was to obtain an advanced degree in either physics or engineering. I worked at North American by night and attended UCLA by day, where I was taking three physics courses and one math course. I was isolated and preoccupied. To have a quiet place to study, I secluded myself in a hilltop apartment with neither a television nor a telephone. The first eight months of 1964 passed quickly.

The notion that a presidential assassination plot had escaped official detection seemed so absurd that I wanted to attend Mark Lane's lecture simply as entertainment. For similar reasons I might have listened to an eccentric lecture that the earth was flat.

But at the Jan Hus Theatre that night, as Lane flashed slide after slide on the screen and quoted from one *New York Times* account after another, I was disturbed. It seemed clear that something was wrong. He recited data apparently indicating that shots were fired at the President from the front and, even more disturbing, that the authorities were trying to conceal the fact. (See Photo 1.)

[I had been unaware that numerous witnesses thought that shots had come from the "grassy knoll," forward and to the right of the limousine.] Lane emphasized this by quoting from press accounts, including some published in Dallas papers the morning after the assassination, as well as from interviews of his own. He quoted the *New York Times'* accounts reporting that two Dallas physicians who saw the President in the emergency room said that the wound at the front of the President's neck was an entrance wound. These quotations were accompanied by slides showing the actual text from the newspaper. Clearly, he was not fabricating his data. Next came a *New York Times* dispatch, published several days later, that reported the Dallas authorities' explanation reconciling the frontal entry wound with the location of Oswald, who allegedly shot Kennedy from the Texas School Book Depository. Dallas officials explained that Kennedy's limousine was still on Houston Street, approaching the Texas School Book Depository, when the first shot struck him in the neck. But movie films of the assassination proved this explanation was wrong. All shots had been fired after the car made the hairpin turn beneath the alleged sniper's nest and was traveling away from the building. Lane then quoted another "official" explanation—this one published in *Life* magazine—which stated that, although the car had already passed the building, the President had turned around to wave to someone in the crowd, thus exposing the front of his neck toward the rear. But the *Life* issue which carried this explanation also published frames from the Zapruder film, and they demonstrated that during the entire assassination the President was facing forward.

Lane concluded with a flourish. To solve the problem, he announced dramatically, [the throat wound itself had undergone a transformation—it was now the official position that it was an exit, rather than an entrance] But even here there was a mystery. On December 6, 1963, the *New York Times* reported that Dr. James Humes, [the physician who performed the autopsy at Bethesda Naval Hospital on the night of the assassination, had been "forbidden to talk."]

This dizzying presentation of data seemed to indicate that the authorities had been changing the facts to fit a predetermined conclusion. On the plane back to California the next day, I made careful notes on what I had heard. The Warren Report was about to be published. I intended to buy a copy.

The Puzzle

Within days of the release of the Report on September 27, 1964, paperback copies were available everywhere. Just as Lane had said, the official account stated that the throat wound was an exit—indeed, the autopsy report from Bethesda Naval Hospital appeared as Appendix IX. That seemed good enough for me. After all, who was I to argue with the official autopsy report? As for those early news accounts about that wound being one of entrance, the Report said that the Dallas doctors were wrong if they really said that, and strongly suggested they had been misquoted.*

To show that the Dallas doctors had no quarrel with the Commission's conclusion about the throat wound, the Warren Report quoted from a segment of Dr. Perry's testimony:

Q. Based on the appearance of the neck wound alone, could it have been either an entrance or an exit wound?
A. It could have been either.[1]

An ironclad point in Mark Lane's lecture suddenly seemed to dissolve.

In early December 1964 Lane came to Southern California and made a speech to a standing-room-only crowd at the UCLA Student Union. Again he was attacking the "official version," but now the "official version" was the Warren Report itself. The twenty-six volumes of the Warren Commission's Hearings and Exhibits had been released. Lane had one of the first sets. Eager assistants searched through them for ammunition for his assault on the American Establishment. The volumes contained much information mentioned nowhere in the Report itself. One of the earliest discoveries lent still another twist to the throat-wound controversy.

The Report implied that the Dallas doctors' testimony about that wound was ambiguous; it might have been an entrance or an exit. The Commission, relying on the navy autopsy, concluded it was an exit. Now Lane marched to the podium, a large blue volume in hand, and announced to the audience that on page 48 of volume 17 was the following document on the letterhead of Bethesda Naval Hospital:

I, James J. Humes, certify that I have destroyed by burning certain preliminary draft notes relating to Naval Medical School Autopsy Report A63–272 and have officially transmitted all other papers related to this report to higher authority.[3]

---

* "Considerable confusion has arisen," began an explanation offered in the Report, "because of comments attributed to Dr. Perry concerning the nature of the neck wound. Immediately after the assassination, many people reached erroneous conclusions about the source of the shots because of Dr. Perry's observations to the press. . . . At the news conference [held on the afternoon of November 22, 1963], Dr. Perry answered a series of hypothetical questions. . . . Dr. Perry said [in his March 1964 Warren Commission testimony, that] his answers at the press conference were intended to convey his theory about what could have happened, based on his limited knowledge at the time, rather than his professional opinion about what did happen."[2]

This was startling. The Report did not mention that any autopsy documents had been burned.

The debate about the direction of the shots was growing "curiouser and curiouser." I intended to follow it.

Lane's appearance in Southern California was the occasion for several people, intensely interested in the Kennedy assassination, to meet one another, and in March 1965 I was introduced to Raymond J. Marcus.

When the twenty-six volumes were published, Ray Marcus immediately ordered a set, and made a beeline for the frames of the Zapruder film, published two frames to a page in volume 18. Like much else about the event, these reproductions were fuzzy. It required hours of eyestraining concentration to visualize them accurately, to determine even elementary information about movements of people in the car. That the frames were in black and white, and made from a relatively inferior copy of the film, complicated matters further.

In March 1965 Marcus told me that the Zapruder frames showed that President Kennedy's head moved rapidly toward the rear following the fatal shot. I had been a physics major. I appreciated the inviolability of Newton's laws. What I was shown seemed no mere "hypothesis," but absolute proof that Kennedy had been shot from the front.

I could scarcely believe such evidence existed and, skeptical of Marcus' measurements, insisted on verifying them myself. It was easy enough to do. There in volume 18 was the sequence of frames. The bullet which struck the President's head allegedly impacted from the rear. The first film frame after impact was 313. In the following frames, Kennedy's head was clearly visible. Also visible was the rear seat of the limousine, particularly its upholstered edge, a useful reference point against which to measure the movement of his head relative to the automobile. Using an ordinary ruler, it was a simple matter to verify that, starting with frame 313, the President's head moved backward from one frame to the next toward the rear seat of the automobile until, by frame 323 (just a half-second later), his head and upper torso were actually in contact with the rear seat cushion. (See Photo 2.)

I tried to imagine what this must look like when projected in motion. Obviously, the film would show a violent backward thrust of the head and upper torso. Within the space of just ten film frames (approximately one-half second), the President had gone from a relatively upright position to one in which his head and upper torso were momentarily sprawled against the rear seat of the automobile.

My measuring with a ruler was one type of "investigation." The Warren Commission had the motion picture film—in color! Surely, they noticed this backward motion. Why, then, was nothing said about it in the Report?

Two collateral matters gave me the feeling that certain higher authorities were probably aware of the head snap and its potency as evidence. First, Marcus had discovered that, as reproduced in the twenty-six volumes, the two frames immediately following frame 313 were reversed. Anybody unaware of this would get confusing results if he used these reproductions to analyze the film. Several months later, I wrote a letter to the FBI which brought a reply from Director Hoover acknowledging the reversal, and describing it as a "printing error."[4] Second, Marcus showed me that something peculiar had occurred in connection with the publication of the *Life* magazine issue of October 2, 1964, whose cover story was devoted to the Warren Report. That issue carried a selection of ten Zapruder frames, each occupying a full half page. One of them, frame 323, showed Kennedy's head and shoulders, after being driven backward, touching the rear seat of the car. That frame was published along with a caption saying it depicted Kennedy's head "snapping to one side."[5] However, there was another version of *Life* on the stands which differed from the first only in this particular picture and caption. Frame 323 had been withdrawn, frame 313 substituted, and the caption changed to indicate it showed the head exploding "forward," demonstrating that the shot struck from behind. To this day, it is a mystery how that last-minute change came about.

For me, confronting the head-snap evidence was almost a revolutionary experience. For the first time I looked at an official government pronouncement and said: "No, I don't believe that." One of the few absolutes in the world to which I subscribed was the laws of physics. It seemed inconceivable to me that if Kennedy was struck from behind by a bullet traveling at approximately two thousand feet per second, the film which recorded that collision would show that his head moved backward, toward the source of the bullet. The Warren Report must be wrong.

I did not arrive at this conclusion lightly. I had always believed what my government said, and will not easily forget the day in mid-April 1961 when I stood on the steps of the Cornell Student Union and vigorously argued with a man who was handing out leaflets for the Fair Play for Cuba Committee, making the preposterous claim that the Cuban invasion then in the headlines was sponsored by the United States government—specifically, the Central Intelligence Agency. Like many others at the time, I thought the charge was outrageous and that people who made such claims were kooks.

The head-snap issue was also a turning point for me psychologically. Previously, I could play with the idea of conspiracy as an interesting hypothesis, nothing more; now I had to confront it as a certainty.

From Marcus I soon learned about the first published study of the medical evidence. It appeared in the January and March 1964 issues of *Liberation,* a small left-wing periodical of which I had never heard. The articles in *Liberation,* written by Philadelphia lawyer Vincent Salandria, analyzed the medical evidence and the Warren Commission's reconstruction of the crime in detail. One point fairly jumped off the page.

Salandria wrote that of the thirteen doctors and nurses who saw the President at Parkland Memorial Hospital in Dallas, not a single one saw the small wound of entry at the rear of the head reported in the Bethesda autopsy. Doctors at both Dallas and Bethesda had seen a large hole caused by the exit of a missile. But the Bethesda doctors said that just beneath the large hole, on the rear of the head, was a small bullet entrance hole. No one in Dallas saw that wound.

I came away from Salandria's articles with a firm opinion. If the rear entry wound was not seen in Dallas, but was reported in the Bethesda autopsy report, and if the head was thrust backward by an impact from the front, then the Bethesda autopsy report must be false.

From Marcus I learned of the first published study of the testimony of witnesses who believed shots were fired from the grassy knoll. It appeared in another left-wing periodical—the March 1965 issue of *Minority of One*. "Fifty-Two Witnesses: The Grassy Knoll," written by Philadelphia schoolteacher Harold Feldman, was duly reported in the *New York Times,* and is something of a classic. Based entirely on information from the twenty-six volumes, the article paints a vivid picture of the assassination as it appeared to most of the people who were there—and it was not the picture found in the Warren Report. Many witnesses heard the sound of shots from the knoll area. Several people standing on the overpass saw smoke rising from the knoll, and an officer who ran into the railroad yard immediately afterward smelled gunpowder. All this was consistent with the "head-snap" evidence, since the knoll/railroad yard area was forward and to the right of the limousine.

Published with the article was a photograph, taken a half-minute or so after the shooting, showing bystanders running toward the area and a policeman, heading up the hill toward the railroad yard. (See Photo 3.) The Warren Report suggested that many of those running toward the knoll (and from the building) "were fleeing the scene of the shooting."[6] Looking at the picture, that was hard to swallow. But what was everyone looking at? What was going on up there? Were there photographs of the knoll taken during the assassination? If so, what did they show?

A few years later, watching Antonioni's *Blowup,* I had an eerie sense of déjà vu, for I had the experience Antonioni so chillingly portrayed. Enlarging the background of a particular assassination photograph became a twenty-four-hour preoccupation. It all began rather unexpectedly.

In May 1965, while waiting in line in a bookstore, I began to browse through an oversize softcover book titled *Four Dark Days in History,* and I came across a picture I hadn't seen before: an excellent reproduction of a Polaroid photograph taken by Mary Moorman at the instant Kennedy was struck in the head. Mrs. Moorman had been standing on the south side of Elm Street (on Kennedy's left), tracking the President in the viewfinder of her camera. In the space of a few seconds, she heard shots, snapped her picture, and fell to the ground. When Mrs. Moorman clicked her shutter, her camera was pointed at the grassy knoll. In the foreground of her picture, the President is seen slumping to the left toward Jacqueline Kennedy. The background offered the best view of the knoll I had ever seen—showing the wooden fence on the left, the stairs in the center, and the concrete wall going off to the monument on the right. (See Photo 4.)

Mrs. Moorman's picture made me aware that I had a rather distorted idea of Dealey Plaza and was under a false impression regarding the location of the limousine at the time of the fatal shot. Because most news organizations accepted the Dallas Police version of the crime, their articles were illustrated with pictures emphasizing the "commanding view" Oswald allegedly had of Dealey Plaza as he shot the President from the southeast-corner, sixth-floor window of the Texas School Book Depository. (See Photo 5.)

Until I saw the Moorman photo, I had not fully realized that Kennedy was far down Elm Street, well past the Depository building, when he was struck in the head. Indeed, he was much closer to the railroad yard, just behind the fence, fifty feet to his right, than to the "sniper's nest" in the School Book Depository, about 250 feet to the rear. (See Photo 6.)

The Moorman photo was taken immediately after the head shot.* Looking at the picture, I realized that the person who fired it might be in this photograph—somewhere. Studying the photo, I was stunned. There, visible on the printed page, was what appeared to be the puff of smoke the witnesses had spoken of and, just behind it, a human form—someone apparently crouched behind the wall. Were my eyes deceiving me?

I bought the book, went home, and used a magnifying glass to examine the picture carefully. Closer study only reinforced my initial impression. I had to have a copy of the photograph. The book was published by a company on Hollywood Boulevard, and I arranged to obtain a negative.

Within a few hours, I found a photo custom lab in Hollywood willing to let me into the darkroom. I watched the prints come through the development bath; it was an eerie experience. This negative brought me one step closer to the source, and there was a startling increase in clarity. Neither the puff of smoke nor the human form, it seemed, were figments of my imagination, but realities recorded by Mrs. Moorman's camera. It was exciting and frightening. Watching the images come up to full contrast, I felt I was joining the ranks of the eyewitnesses—a year and a half after

---

* Later studies confirmed that the Moorman photo corresponds to frames 313–315 of the Zapruder film (the picture was snapped within one-ninth of a second of the fatal shot).

the event. And perhaps my view was better. Wasn't the Moorman photo like a freeze frame capturing one of the most critical instants of the shooting? None of the eyewitnesses could study their recollections as I could study that picture. As I did so, the idea that the President was struck by an assassin firing from the knoll became less an inference based upon physics than something I could see with my own eyes.* Or so it seemed.

Looking closely at the Moorman photograph, I was surprised to find still another image, an extremely clear one of a man, off to the right side of the picture—just behind Abraham Zapruder. An act of photo interpretation was needed to "see" my first discovery, but this image was quite different. He was definitely there, visible from the waist up, and he was holding something in his hands in a horizontal position.

Had the Warren Commission looked into any of this? Did they really have any idea what had happened on the grassy knoll?

A few months earlier, senior Warren Commission Counsel Joseph Ball had been questioned on a Los Angeles television program about the grassy knoll: "That happens to be the part of the investigation of which I had charge . . ." he blustered. "There were no people there."[9]

Gradually, my excitement was tempered by a growing realization that although photographs were, at some level, representations of reality, in the final analysis what one "saw" in a picture—particularly what one saw in an enlarged picture—was a subjective proposition. I might be convinced of the validity of an image; my interpretation might even prove to be correct, but others did not necessarily see it that way. What people could "see" was not only a function of what was there, but of what they could accept. It was all very psychological.

I remember standing on Hollywood Boulevard, showing the top half of the Moorman photograph to a passerby and asking him to tell me what he saw. He said he saw a wall, and a man behind the wall. I then showed him the bottom half of the picture, showing the Presidential limousine and Kennedy. He recoiled. "Oh, no," he said, "that can't be." "Why not?" I asked. "Because that's not Oswald. Oswald was over here," he said, indicating a position behind the motorcade.

---

* Corroborating evidence was later found on pictures from other cameras. What appeared to be smoke could be seen, in color, on a frame from Orville Nix's film published in the UPI memorial book, *Four Days*. (See Photo 6.) The man was visible, surprisingly enough, in pictures printed in the twenty-six volumes, but which had not yet been published commercially—a sequence of slides taken by Air Force Maj. Phil Willis. A man-size black blob appeared at the corner of the wall in slide 5, taken just as the shooting began, but was not there a minute later when Willis snapped slide 6. (See Photos 3 and 10.) The existence of this image on the Willis slide was confirmed years later by the House Select Committee on Assassinations.[7] The committee, however, disputed the fact that smoke was visible.[8]

It became evident that those who were already in disagreement with the Warren Commission conclusions found it far easier to "see" people on the knoll than those who believed in the Report. I could even apply this reasoning to my own observations: How certain could I be that my basic processes of perception were not hopelessly biased as a result of my belief in, say, the head-snap evidence? I really did not believe that was the case, but I couldn't prove it was not, either. Eventually, I concluded that photographic enlargements had very limited use as evidence.

Nevertheless, the Moorman images, together with the head-snap evidence and the articles I had read analyzing the eyewitness testimony, had deeply aroused my curiosity. For reasons I still do not understand, I found it impossible simply to shrug, say "So what?" and go on with my life. There was an immediacy about the photographic evidence—it demanded attention. Even graduate school did not seem important, or particularly interesting, compared to getting to the bottom of this mystery. For the first time I considered buying a set of the twenty-six volumes.

The twenty-six volumes were the published records of the Warren Commission investigation. Only a few thousand copies were printed, and they have been called "the largest body of source material any armchair student of a crime ever had." They contained what a historian calls "primary source material"—FBI, Secret Service, and CIA reports (as well as the testimony of the Commission's 552 witnesses). Having had no experience with the inner workings of a major criminal investigation, I found them fascinating.

Normally to obtain a set one had to send seventy-six dollars to the U.S. Government Printing Office, and then wait several weeks for its arrival. My purchase was more impulsive. The bookstore where I had found the book with the Moorman photograph had one set of the twenty-six volumes in its window. At first when I wanted to see what a particular assassination eyewitness had told the FBI, I found myself apologizing to the bookstore manager while I took a volume off the shelf for a few minutes.

Given the mass of material in those volumes, it was impossible to complete a search for one item without finding other items, perhaps even more interesting. This was no way to do research. I was making a nuisance of myself. One day, an income tax refund check arrived and I bought the entire set.

I was hooked.

No verbal description really captures the voluminous and disorganized nature of the twenty-six volumes. Numerous side trips were necessary to relate the approximately eight thousand pages of documentary exhibits in the last eleven volumes to the five thousand pages of testimony in the first fifteen. Given a normal schedule and a reasonable curiosity, that task could easily stretch to a year.*

In 1965 the twenty-six volumes lacked an index. They were like a library without a card catalog. One had to plow through everything to find anything. The chaos seemed planned. In 1965, the prevailing climate was one of confusion and a sense of mystery, an uneasy feeling the government was deliberately hiding something.

Volume 18 began with eighty pages containing the Zapruder film and the first mystery: Four frames were missing. A splice appeared across frame 212 with no explanation.[10] Immediately following the Zapruder frames were State Department telegrams concerning the Oswald case. One cable referred to the accused as "Lee Harvey Oswald, former Marine and . . ."[11] And what? Forty-two spaces were blanked out. What was under that excision, asked one wit: ". . . star of stage, screen, and radio"?**

In volume 22 were reports filed by the Secret Service agents who were with Kennedy in Dallas. Why were so many of them dated November 29, 1963?[12]

Volume 23 contained a 216-page FBI transcript of the Dallas Police radio on November 22;[13] but wasn't there a 134-page transcript back in volume 17?[14] Oh, well, there must have been two transcripts. No, in fact there were three—one in volume 17, one in volume 21, and a third in volume 23.[15] What were the differences? To compare them carefully and find out could take one person about two weeks.

One skimmed through the Ruby area, scanning some of the testimony given by police officers on duty in the basement of Police Department Headquarters. The Report assured us that Ruby, and Ruby alone acting without police assistance, shot Oswald. But here was testimony which seemed to indicate that Warren Commission attorney Burt Griffin, investigating the movements of people in the basement where Ruby shot Oswald, was not entirely satisfied with the testimony of one Dallas officer:

> GRIFFIN: You are a d—— l——. [sic] I want you to come back tomorrow night and I want you—I want to question you some more.[16]

* Author Jim Bishop, working full time and with assistants, said he spent two years just reading and annotating the volumes for his book, *The Day Kennedy Was Shot*—a straight chronological narrative of the day which accepted the Warren Commission's version of the event and did not include any detailed analysis disputing the evidence.

** Although this excision strengthened suspicions that Oswald had a secret affiliation with an intelligence agency, this particular item of evidence had an innocent explanation. An unexcised version of the same cable, discovered at the Archives in 1967 by Paul Hoch, revealed that the forty-two spaces contained a reference to another defector. The excised portion read: "Robert Edward Webster, former Navy."

Whatever became of that argument?

Someone took the time to study the entries in Lee Harvey Oswald's diary (volume 16, pages 43 & 90) and, comparing them to Jack Ruby's phone bills (volume 25, page 252), noticed that the same telephone number appeared in both locations. Was that significant?*

Many Ruby-related documents were in volume 22, including dental charts for Jack Ruby's mother's mouth in 1938.[17] What were *they* doing in the twenty-six volumes? Mark Lane remarked they wouldn't be relevant even if Ruby had bitten Oswald to death.

And so it went. The deadly serious mixed with the preposterous.

It was Sylvia Meagher who took upon herself the onerous task of creating an index. It took her over a year to complete, and was an indispensable tool for anyone researching the twenty-six volumes.

My breaking-in period with the volumes lasted about a year, and as I studied them my perspective changed. I saw that there were actually two patterns in the evidence—one supporting the Commission's findings, and a second which did not. For want of better terms, they can be designated the "sniper's-nest" and "grassy-knoll" evidence, respectively.

If one relied on the physical evidence found at the sniper's nest, then Lee Harvey Oswald seemed to be the assassin. The 6.5mm bolt-action rifle found there was traced to Klein's Sporting Goods where records showed that it had been mail-ordered to Oswald's post office box under an assumed name. The name was A. J. Hidell, associated with Oswald's activities on behalf of the Fair Play for Cuba Committee, and the handwriting was Oswald's. Oswald's palmprint was, according to the Dallas Police, on the gun. Finally, according to the FBI, the recovered bullets had been fired from that rifle. Earl Warren once remarked that if he had the case as a prosecutor, he would have gotten a conviction in a few days, and never heard of it again. (See Photos 7 and 8.)[18]

However, there was also all that "grassy-knoll" evidence. Depending upon whether one subscribed to the "sniper's-nest" or the "grassy-knoll" evidence, one could argue that the assassination had happened one way or another. And nowhere was this more apparent than in the medical evidence.

The Warren Report and the "Grassy-Knoll" Evidence

From the day I began studying the twenty-six volumes, I was struck by the fact that two sets of doctors saw President Kennedy on November

---

* Probably not. It was the telephone number of a local TV station.

22, and they arrived at diametrically opposite conclusions as to the direction from which he was shot. After the shooting, the President was rushed to Dallas' Parkland Memorial Hospital, where he was attended by thirteen doctors and nurses. In press interviews that day and in medical reports filed that afternoon, the Dallas doctors expressed the opinion that he had been [shot from the front]

The Dallas doctors did not perform an autopsy. The Warren Commission relied upon the information about bullet trajectories provided in the autopsy performed later that evening at the U.S. Naval Hospital, Bethesda, Maryland. The Bethesda doctors concluded that the President was struck twice—both times from behind—once in the head and once in the neck.

Nevertheless, the fact that the original medical opinion indicated that shots struck from the front caused me to doubt the Commission's central lone-assassin conclusion. The credibility problem arising from conflicting medical reports was exacerbated not only by the "grassy-knoll" witnesses, but by irregularities in the Bethesda autopsy, suggesting it was not to be trusted.

Besides certifying, on November 24, 1963, that he had "destroyed . . . certain preliminary draft *notes* . . . ."[19] Dr. Humes later testified that he had burned an earlier "draft" of the autopsy *report*. "In the privacy of my own home, early in the morning of Sunday, November 24th, I made a draft of this report which I later revised, and of which this represents the revision. That draft I personally burned in the fireplace of my recreation room."[20]

Remarkably enough, neither the Warren Commission attorney conducting the interrogation (Arlen Specter, an Assistant District Attorney from Philadelphia) nor any member of the Commission asked Humes *why* he burned that evidence.

I was surprised to learn of other irregularities surrounding the autopsy. On the handwritten draft were a number of significant changes—without much explanation. For example, the word "puncture" was repeatedly crossed out,[21] and in one case, the throat wound was called a "puncture," but the word "puncture" was deleted from the typewritten version.[22] The Warren Commission's questioning in this area was very skimpy. Humes' commanding officer, Adm. Calvin Galloway, who attended the autopsy, handled the paperwork, and who might have known why such changes were made, was never called to testify.

I felt the testimony of the grassy-knoll witnesses lent great strength to the notion that the Bethesda autopsy should not be taken as the final word on how the shooting occurred. Sixty-four known witnesses indicated that shots originated from forward of the motorcade, from the grassy-knoll. This amounted to approximately two-thirds of the ninety witnesses whose accounts appeared in the twenty-six volumes (or in contemporaneous news accounts), who expressed an opinion as to the source of the shots.*

Statistics, however, do not capture the vivid quality of the grassy-knoll testimony, which made it difficult for me to believe it was the result of collective misperception. Nor do the statistics capture the emotional climate which prevailed in the small community of Warren Report critics at the time this material was originally "discovered." One must understand that the material was not located in one place, but was scattered throughout the twenty-six volumes. Some researchers thought the disorder was deliberate.

The people doing the digging were not, for the most part, experienced in working with government records, but ordinary folk who simply wanted to know what had happened. Perusing the twenty-six volumes, we found accounts of what was seen and heard in Dealey Plaza mentioned nowhere in the Warren Report.

The process was slow and laborious, like learning the names and locations of numerous extras on a huge movie set. Though the FBI could easily have made a complete compilation while memories were fresh, this was not done. Consequently, the historical record was pitifully incomplete. There were photographs of crowds surging toward the grassy knoll taken immediately after the shooting in which the identities of many of the people were not known. Of the four hundred persons present in Dealey Plaza, only about ninety gave testimony. The accounts of many witnesses closest to the grassy knoll were available only because their affidavits were in the Sheriff's Department file which was turned over to the Commission when Sheriff Decker appeared in April 1964.

Some of the grassy-knoll testimony seemed particularly impressive.

The Overpass

Sam Holland, railroad signal supervisor for the Union Terminal, was standing on the triple overpass inspecting signals and switches when he stopped to watch the parade. In a sworn affidavit on November 22, he said:

. . . the President's car was . . . just about to the arcade [when] I heard what I thought for the moment was a firecracker . . . and I looked over toward the arcade and trees and saw a puff of smoke come from the trees . . . the puff of smoke I saw definitely came from behind the arcade and through the trees.[23]

* This tally may not be complete, but is symptomatic of the state of the record. It is based on the numbered list of grassy-knoll witnesses published—along with relevant excerpts from their testimony—in "The Case for Three Assassins" (*Ramparts* magazine; January 1967; reprinted in *The Assassinations: Dallas and Beyond*, edited by Scott, Hoch, and Stetler, Random House, 1976). For a more complete tabulation, see *Six Seconds in Dallas*, by Josiah Thompson.

What Holland called the "arcade"—also called by other witnesses the "monument"—was the white semicircular structure on the grassy knoll. Holland immediately ran to the corner of the fence near the arcade and by the time he arrived, twelve or fifteen policemen and people he surmised were plainclothesmen were already there. He also told the Commission that backed up to the fence was a station wagon with mud on the bumper "as if someone had cleaned their feet, or stood up on the bumper to see over the fence."[24] On the grass by the station wagon was "a spot, I'd say three foot by two foot, looked to me like somebody had been standing there for a long period. I guess if you could count them about a hundred foottracks in that little spot, and also mud up on the bumper of that station wagon. . . ."[25]

Holland's testimony about seeing smoke or hearing shots from the area was corroborated by other men standing on the overpass: Frank Reilly, Austin Miller, James Simmons, and Clemmon Johnson.*

Yet of the thirteen railroad employees on the overpass, only four were questioned by the Commission; the FBI questioned only nine, and those reports were rather sparse. Independent investigators such as Mark Lane, Barbara Bridges, and Stewart Galanor supplemented the record with their own interviews which produced additional information—from witnesses Richard Dodd, Walter Winborn, James Simmons, and Thomas Murphy—about the smoke on the knoll. These interviews made the FBI reports sound suspiciously understated.**

At the depository

Many of Oswald's fellow employees thought the shots came from the knoll. Billy Lovelady was standing in the doorway of the Texas School Book Depository, Steve Wilson was on the third floor, Victoria Adams and Mrs. Alvin Hobson were both on the fourth floor. None thought the shots came from the sixth-floor sniper's nest, and Lovelady and Adams specifi-

---

* Reilly testified: "It seemed to me like the shots come out of the trees. . . ."[26] Miller swore: "I saw something which I thought was smoke or steam coming from a group of trees north of Elm off the railroad tracks."[27] Simmons "thought he saw exhaust fumes or smoke near the embankment. . . ."[28] Johnson "stated that white smoke was observed near the pavilion."[29]

** Simmons said the sounds of shots "came from the left and in front of us, toward the wooden fence, and there was a puff of smoke that came underneath the trees on the embankment."[30] Dodd said that the smoke came from "behind the hedge."[31] Winborn told Barbara Bridges "there was a lot of smoke . . . from out of the trees, to the left." To Galanor, he described it as "a little haze . . . it looked like it was three to ten feet long, and about two or three feet wide . . . right underneath those trees."[32] Murphy told Galanor the shots "come from a tree to the [President's] immediate right" and that he saw smoke "in that tree . . . up there where that concrete facade is located."[33]

cally stated that they thought the shots had come from the direction of the grassy knoll.*

There were three black men on the fifth floor in the window just beneath the "sniper's nest." Despite the fact that two of them testified that the shots came from above, their initial reaction was to run to the west side of the building, not upstairs, and one testified he originally thought the shots came from below, near the motorcade.[38]

Near the president's car at the time of the fatal shot (See Photos 9, 10, and 11.)

As the President's car came abreast of the concrete monument and neared the location where the fatal shot struck, the crowd had thinned out considerably and Kennedy was passing amid a handful of bystanders.** Most of these witnesses were never questioned by the Commission. We had their accounts only because of interviews conducted by the Dallas Sheriff's Department and some news agencies.

Mr. and Mrs. John Arthur Chism were two known witnesses among a cluster of about five persons standing beneath a "Stemmons Freeway" sign, their backs to the knoll. (See Photo 10.) They both thought the shots came from behind them.***

As the car moved past the Stemmons sign, on the President's left was Charles Brehm. (See Photo 12.) The *Dallas Times-Herald* reported on November 22 that Brehm "seemed to think the shots came from in front of or beside the President. He explained the President did not slump forward as he would have after being shot from the rear."[41] Later, in a filmed interview with Mark Lane, Brehm said that there was something which he thought was a piece of the President's skull blasted to the left and rear.[42] Neither the Chisms nor Brehm were called to testify by the Commission.

---

* Lovelady said the sounds came from "right there around that concrete little deal on that knoll. . . ." He told the FBI: "I did not at any time believe the shots had come from the Texas School Book Depository Building."[34] Steve Wilson told the FBI: "The shots really did not sound like they came from above me."[35] One floor up was Victoria Adams. The alleged assassin's window was two floors above her and to her left. Adams testified: ". . . it seemed as if it came from the right below, rather than from the left above."[36] Mrs. Alvin Hopson told the FBI: "it did not sound to her like the sounds were coming from her building." She stated that she thought "they [firecrackers] had been set off on the street below. . . ."[37]

** At that point, the Depository was approximately 250 feet to the rear. The crest of the grassy knoll, behind which was the railroad yard, was just 50 feet to the right.

*** John Chism swore: "I looked behind me, to see whether it was a fireworks display or something."[39] His wife swore: "It came from what I thought was behind us."[40]

At the instant of the fatal shot Bobby Hargis, motorcycle escort riding to the left rear, was splattered with blood and debris.[43] At that same moment the President's automobile had just passed Dallas schoolteacher Jean Hill and her companion Mary Moorman, who was looking in the viewfinder of her Polaroid camera. (See Photo 4.) Hill testified she thought people were "shooting from the knoll."*

To President Kennedy's right, at the instant of the fatal shot, Abraham Zapruder was standing on an abutment to the monument and filming the motorcade (see Photo 10); Mr. and Mrs. William Newman and their two young children were standing at the curb (see Photos 10 and 11); and, just slightly ahead, standing on the stairs which ascended the knoll were three men, one of whom was Emmett Hudson, the caretaker of Dealey Plaza. (See Photo 4.) All these witnesses had their backs to the railroad yard at the instant the fatal shot struck, and the Texas School Book Depository was two hundred feet to their left. Without exception these witnesses believed the shots came from behind them.**

Lee Bowers was at work in a railroad tower fourteen feet high located behind the curving railroad tracks in the yard behind the grassy knoll. (See Photo 1.) He had a splendid view. Bowers reported that during the half hour before the shooting, three cars entered the yard and slowly cruised the area. Two had out-of-state plates and a third, a 1957 black Ford, had "one male in it that seemed to have a mike or telephone. . . . He was very close to the tower. I could see him. . . ."[49]

Bowers was not able to describe exactly what happened at the time of the shooting, but he did make clear that his attention was immediately focused on that grassy-knoll area: ". . . there seemed to be some commotion . . . a sort of milling around, but something occurred in this particular

---

* Hill said: "We were standing on the curb and I jumped to the edge of the street and yelled, 'Hey, we want to take your picture!' . . . The shot rang out. Mary took the picture and fell on the ground and . . . grabbed my slacks and said, 'Get down, they're shooting.' . . . I frankly thought they were coming from the knoll. . . . I thought it was just people shooting from the knoll. . . . I did think there was more than one person shooting—the way the gun report sounded . . . the timing . . ."[44]

** Zapruder testified it was his initial opinion that "it came from back of me."[45] Photographs show that the Newmans fell to the ground, covering their children's bodies with their own. (See Photos 3 and 12.) Newman explained: ". . . it seemed that we were in direct path of fire. . . . I thought the shot had come from the garden directly behind me, that was on an elevation from where I was. . . . I do not recall looking toward the Texas School Book Depository. I looked back in the vicinity of the garden."[46]

Emmett Hudson: "I was . . . on the front steps of the sloping area . . . the shots that I heard definitely came from behind and above me."[47] One of the men standing alongside him (identity unknown) told him: "Lay down, Mister; somebody is shooting the President."[48] (See Photos 3 and 6.)

spot which was out of the ordinary [and] which attracted my eye for some reason, [but] which I could not identify."[50]

Immediately afterward, the railroad-yard area began filling with law enforcement officers. Dallas Patrolman Joe Marshall Smith, who had been directing traffic at Houston and Elm, thought the shots came from that area, and headed up that way. He was approached by a woman yelling: "They're shooting the President from the bushes." When he reached the railroad yard, he later told *Texas Observer* reporter Ron Dugger, he "caught the smell of gunpowder . . . I could tell it was in the air."[51] Sixteen of the twenty Dallas Sheriff's deputies in the Dealey Plaza area (most were outside watching the motorcade, as their office is on the eastern edge of Dealey Plaza) apparently believed the shots came from the grassy knoll and ran in that direction.[52] Upon entering the area, Deputy Sheriff J. L. Oxford encountered "a man who told us he had seen smoke up in the corner of the fence."[53] Deputy Seymour Weitzman told of encountering an unidentified railroad employee who, when asked where the shots came from, "pointed out the wall section where there was a bunch of shrubbery."[54]

These, then, were the accounts of the grassy-knoll witnesses. Almost all of this went unmentioned in the 888-page Warren Report. The Report's entire "discussion" of smoke amounted to the seven words, "where he saw a puff of smoke," tacked onto a sentence describing the testimony of Sam Holland. [55] And ironically the Report cited Holland in support of its conclusion that no shots were fired from the knoll because, when Holland ran back there, he "did not see anyone among the parked cars."[56]

The case for the "grassy-knoll assassin" seemed soundly based upon an interlocking pattern of evidence from: (1) the Dallas medical reports, (2) the accounts of numerous eyewitnesses, and (3) the motion of the President on the Zapruder film. The "grassy-knoll" evidence combined with the "sniper's nest" evidence indicated conspiracy: one assassin firing from behind and a "second shooter" firing from the right front. Indeed, from the "head-snap" evidence, it appeared this "grassy knoll assassin" had actually fired the shot that killed President Kennedy.

Could the Commission have "accidentally" overlooked a second assassin? Or had it deliberately hidden the truth?

I wondered. Although assertions in the Warren Report were ostensibly linked by 6,710 footnotes (often on a sentence-by-sentence basis) to one document or another in the twenty-six volumes, the Report's conclusions correlated poorly with the Commission's published evidence. It was shocking to learn of so much information indicating the assassination might have happened in a way other than the one generally accepted. What provoked suspicion was that so little of the contrary evidence was discussed in the Report. Among researchers, the issue was the simple one of trust between citizens and their government.

Had the Commission functioned so incompetently that it had simply ignored its own evidence? Or was the Report a deliberate lie?

The case for a "grassy-knoll assassin" was just one example—because of the photographic research, it was one in which I was personally most interested. But other critics gave the case against Oswald the same scrutiny. That was how I first learned that the witnesses who saw Oswald carry a paper bag into the Depository swore it was not as big as the one found there.[57] And how I first learned of evidence indicating the rifle ordered by Oswald from Klein's Sporting Goods was not the one found at the sixth floor of the Texas School Book Depository.* All of which opened the door to the idea that a rifle had been planted; and that perhaps Oswald was telling the truth when he denied shooting anyone.** Clearly, had a lawyer representing Oswald's interests been on the staff of the Commission, a rather strong defense brief could have been constructed.

When the Report was published, it was criticized by some as being written in the style of a prosecutor's brief. But the critics, familiar with the twenty-six volumes, did not view the Report in such an academic fashion. They saw it as a rape of that underlying record.

As I read the testimony in the twenty-six volumes, there was one attorney whose questioning particularly annoyed me—Wesley J. Liebeler. He had interrogated several of the grassy-knoll witnesses and in two cases seemed to argue with them about the source of the shots.

Mrs. Donald Baker testified that the sounds seemed to come from the railroad yard. Mr. Liebeler replied: "Now, you have subsequently heard, I'm sure, and from reading in the newspapers and one thing and another, that it appears that the shots actually came from the Texas School Book Depository; is that right?" "Yes," answered Mrs. Baker. "Does that seem possible to you in view of what you heard at the time?" asked Liebeler. "Well," replied Mrs. Baker, "I guess it might have been the wind, but to me it didn't."[64]

Liebeler questioned James Tague in a similar fashion.*** But the most

---

* Oswald ordered from a Klein's advertisement in the February 1963, *American Rifleman,* Klein's item C20-T750, which was 36 inches long.[58] The found rifle was 40.2 inches long. It appears to be the one advertised by Klein's in the November 1963 *Field and Stream* ("only 40″ overall") and identified as catalogue number C20-750.[59]

** Whenever Oswald found himself in front of reporters' microphones, he denied the crime, making statements such as:

> "I'm just a patsy";[60]
> "I didn't shoot anybody, no sir";[61]
> "I don't know what kind of dispatches you people [the reporters] have been given. I have committed no act of violence."[62]
> "I haven't shot anybody."[63]

*** Tague had been standing at the mouth of the triple underpass. (See Photo 1.)

outrageous exchange was with Abraham Zapruder, which occurred toward the end of his interrogation. Zapruder had testified that his initial impression was that the shots "came from back of me." Then, he said: "They claim it was proven it could be done by one man. You know there was an indication there were two?"

Mr. Liebeler replied: "Your films were extremely helpful to the work of the Commission, Mr. Zapruder."[66]

Of everything I read in the volumes, this exchange stuck most in my craw. Among the Southern California critics, it was generally accepted that such questioning was just one aspect of a deliberate Warren Commission coverup and since several grassy-knoll witnesses had been questioned by Liebeler, he seemed to be one of the chief culprits.

In the fall of 1965, it became common knowledge among the critics that Liebeler had recently been appointed Assistant Professor at the UCLA Law School. By now, I was both concerned and angry and, when I heard he was on campus, an idea began to germinate in my mind. Of the thousands of students on campus, I doubted that a single one had read any of the twenty-six volumes of the Commission. Except for a tiny handful of critics, no one seemed to question the findings of the Commission. I thought I had rather specialized knowledge: that a person who had taken part in what I regarded as a highly immoral activity was teaching law at my university in near anonymity! Someone, it seemed, ought to confront the man. Why not I? The Law School was hardly foreign territory—it was near the UCLA Research Library, and I sometimes used the coffee machines in the Student Lounge there at night.

One evening, I checked the Law School building directory. Sure enough, the man whose name had jumped off the pages of volumes 6 and 7 as he questioned the grassy-knoll witnesses, was listed. Once or twice I walked upstairs to see where his office was located. The door on that deserted hallway at night gave no hint of the momentous investigation of which he had been a part, or the type of man he might be. Just a small card posted by his door gave his name and his schedule of classes. To my astonishment, I found that he was teaching Legal Ethics.

On the afternoon of October 12, 1965, I was sitting in the nearby Research Library, turning the matter over in my mind, when I suddenly decided to act. I did it partly out of curiosity, partly out of anger. Entering the Law Building, I ascended the flight of stairs to the hallway I had visited

---

When he testified shots came from the knoll, Liebeler reminded him that ". . . of course . . . we have other evidence that would indicate that the shots did come from the Texas School Book Depository, but see if we can disregard that and determine just what you heard . . ." When Tague persisted, Liebeler volunteered: "There was in fact a considerable echo in that area?" Tague replied: "There was no echo from where I stood. I was asked this question before, and there was no echo."[65]

on previous evenings and walked unannounced into Liebeler's office. I expected some type of ogre—perhaps an acrimonious argument.

Nothing of the sort occurred. It was as if he had been sitting at his desk knowing that, sooner or later, some complete stranger would walk in to demand just what the devil had gone on in the Commission's investigation.

I had the vague feeling that we were both members of the same secret fraternity. Stretching across one of his bookshelves for a distance of about three feet was a set of the twenty-six volumes—a gift from the government for serving on the Commission. Introducing myself, I informed Professor Liebeler that I, too, owned a set of those books and, having studied them, had concluded that the Warren Report was some kind of hoax, a case of the Emperor's New Clothes. I cited page 587 of the Report, with its half-page reproduction "Diagram of a Hair," and scoffed at the false impression being given the American public—fostered by the sheer size of the Report and the inclusion of exhibits like that—that the investigation was massive and thorough. I told Liebeler that I could not understand how an investigation which included, in its published evidence, FBI Laboratory photographs of Oswald's pubic hairs (Warren Commission Exhibit 672), could have failed to take into account the voluminous evidence that someone fired at President Kennedy from the grassy knoll.

Liebeler smiled as if I had become privy to some private joke. I said I had tabulated evidence that more than one assassin was firing, and thought the Commission's extravagant attention to such meaningless detail was part of a deliberate con. Liebeler replied that if the major conclusions of the Commission were wrong, "then either we're lying or we're stupid."[67] He said this with just enough resignation and disgust to imply that a Commission could in fact be that inept. Finding it difficult to accept the "stupidity" hypothesis, I suggested another possibility: that the Commission was hamstrung by their investigating agencies. Liebeler, to my surprise, seemed to reject this. They could have requested the FBI to do anything they wished, he said.

Returning again to the theme of conspiracy, probing for a reaction, I suggested that any lie told was probably for reasons of state. Liebeler rejected any such idea. "We certainly weren't all gathered in one room and told to do this or that. . . ." He termed that "preposterous," and emphatically vouched for his own honesty and integrity.

Indeed, from the way Liebeler talked and from what he said, I sensed that truthfulness was an issue for Liebeler, not in the sense that a Boy Scout swears to tell the truth, but in the sense that conclusions of fact ought to be based on evidence.

Despite my initial suspicions, I found myself tending to believe Liebeler. For one thing, he was rather irreverent about the Commission and its Report. For another, he was astonishingly frank, entertaining hypothetical possibilities that were quite radical. For example, returning to my characterization of the Warren Report as a case of the Emperor's New Clothes, Liebeler said, at that very first meeting: "If you're going to say the emperor isn't wearing any clothes, then you must include our past Vice-President." He did not say this in the manner of one speculating wildly, but as one who had thought about the matter and wanted to let me know that if there was really something wrong with the Commission, the trail could lead to President Johnson.

But he voiced surprise when I expressed the opinion that Oswald might be "totally innocent." He said that talk about witnesses being silenced or hushed up was "bunk." But when I told him I had made blowups of certain photographs of the grassy knoll and they contained manlike images that could very well be assassins, he seemed genuinely eager to see them. "Where do you have them shooting from?" he wanted to know. When I told him the concrete wall to the right of the pergola, he simply grunted, "Uh-huh."

As for the grassy knoll witnesses, Liebeler practically dismissed *all* eyewitness and earwitness testimony with a wave of the hand and the usual generalities, often heard in law classes, I later learned, that such testimony was unreliable. Yet I found it difficult to believe that so many people collectively misperceived the same event. When I asked why he had argued with witnesses as to the source of the shots, he replied that there was nothing illegitimate about interrogating witnesses to test their convictions and to make their answers a matter of record. To hear Liebeler tell it, it had never crossed his mind to get any witness to change testimony.

What about the passage in Zapruder's testimony where the witness seemed on the brink of volunteering information about the existence of a second assassin? That drew a complete blank. Liebeler had no idea what I was referring to. I showed him the passage and he seemed astonished. He said he had absolutely no recollection of it. When a friend walked into his office at a subsequent meeting, he took volume 7 off the shelf, read that passage aloud, and expressed his amazement that he and Zapruder ever had that weird exchange.

The one time during our first meeting that I was frankly disbelieving was when I took volume 18 off the shelf and showed him the head snap. In the notes I made shortly afterward, I wrote: ". . . he leaned back in his chair, and this was the one time I thought he was acting; he said he had never 'noticed' that before."

Then I showed him something that produced a dramatically different reaction. Flipping to the earlier pages of the Zapruder exhibit, I demonstrated that the Warren Commission's copy of the Zapruder film contained an unexplained splice and that four frames were missing between 207 and 212. This was clearly observable on the sequence of individual Zapruder frames published as Exhibit 885. The break in the sequence began just as the President was about to disappear from view behind a highway sign, where the Commission said the first shot struck.*

The splice was clearly visible in frame 212. A thick black horizontal line ran across the center of the frame where the film had been cut, frames removed, and the two ends spliced together.

Liebeler practically did a double take. My suspicions were so profound, however, that I was skeptical. How was it possible that a Warren Commission attorney could be unaware that the film was spliced? The information came from the Commission's own evidence. I turned to Liebeler, who seemed quite taken aback and was studying the frames intently, and asked him if he was acting, adding that it wasn't necessary to put on an act for my benefit. "Honest, no!" he exclaimed, adding that he had definitely not known about the splice before.

I explained my theory about the splice. Perhaps the road sign, a portion of which loomed large in the foreground of the film and obscured Kennedy for about twenty-five frames, had been pierced by a bullet. If that occurred, then the four-frame excision was performed to eliminate from view the left side of the sign until Zapruder had panned far enough to the right so that it no longer appeared in the picture.

I suggested this hypothesis because of a series of curved black lines on the back of the sign in the frames following the one containing the splice. From frame to frame the lengths of these curved lines varied, suggesting they were oscillatory in nature.[69] The curvature of the lines was such that their point of intersection would have appeared on the lower left of the frame, had it been visible. But it was not because the splice had omitted just those frames showing this possible point of intersection.**

The sign in question had been moved, and possibly replaced, shortly after the assassination. Were these two events—the spliced film and the moved sign—related?***

Liebeler followed my explanation closely, and gradually his special

---

* The break was obvious from the captions, which read: . . . 205, 206, 207, 212, 213, etc.[68]

** What caused the lines? If a bullet pierced the sign, it would have imparted a pulse of energy. It was my hypothesis that the surface of the sign might then have reflected light in the manner recorded by Zapruder's film.

*** Later I learned that there were a number of reasons for discarding this hypothesis. First, calculations could be made to see what frequency of light might be reflected. Rough estimates indicated no such pattern would be visible. In the fall of 1967, *Life* magazine released the missing frames: there was no hole visible on the back of the sign.[70] But I was never entirely satisfied. The frames were released almost two full years after the matter was first brought to *Life*'s attention. At this writing, I still wonder why the sign was moved and replaced shortly after the assassination, but must concede that there is no way of proving, from the available data, that there was a hole in it.

brand of cynicism and wry humor surfaced. The splice, he remarked, was a "very unlawyerlike" way of handling evidence, musing that if he were "doing it," he certainly would not have published the frame with the splice but simply omitted that one and renumbered the rest in sequence.

Liebeler announced then and there he would write to J. Lee Rankin, the former U.S. Solicitor General who was the Warren Commission's General Counsel. He seemed genuinely concerned and even took my name and telephone number so he could contact me later, after he had heard from Rankin.

"Yesterday afternoon," began Liebeler's letter of October 13, 1965, to J. Lee Rankin,

a graduate student in the [Engineering] Department here at UCLA walked into my office to discuss some work he [had] been doing on the Report. He had several interesting theories, supporting evidence for which he promised to provide in the future. He did make one point, however, during the course of the conversation that I think deserves some attention.[71]

Liebeler then went into a detailed description of the splice, including a number of other, possibly related, facts I had shown him the day before. "If there is a ready explanation for the omission of the frames," concluded Liebeler's letter to Rankin, "I would certainly be relieved to know what it is. If there is none, I think it would be appropriate for us to raise this matter formally with the FBI."[72]

Liebeler's behavior was clear evidence that he was not part of a deliberate coverup. I began to see that idea for what it was—a crude oversimplification. If any further evidence of this were needed, there was Liebeler's own irreverence toward the working of the Commission. During our meeting a fellow faculty member dropped by for a moment and Liebeler introduced me, saying: "This fellow is showing me that the Report we wrote is a crock of shit,"[73] and laughed loudly.

In a more serious vein, Liebeler asked why I didn't give public talks elucidating the various issues I had raised with him. I remarked that I wouldn't be surprised if I ended up doing so, probably at some expense to my career. "Don't give me that crap," he said. "If you believe what you've told me, do something about it."[74]

I returned to Liebeler's office on November 2, 1965, carrying copies of the earliest articles on the medical evidence written by pioneer Warren Report critic Vincent Salandria. I had no sooner walked in the door when Liebeler tossed several letters at me. "Here, read these," he said, his voice tinged with exasperation. They were the replies to his letter about the splice: a detailed response from Norman Redlich, Rankin's special assistant during the Commission's investigation, to whom Liebeler had sent a copy of his letter, and a brief letter from J. Lee Rankin. Liebeler wanted copies of the Salandria articles and, while he ran off to Xerox them, I studied the letters. For me, the entire experience was fast becoming a crash course on how the Warren Commission had functioned.

Rankin's letter, just five sentences long, said that he had seen Redlich's reply and ". . . [it] seemed to dispose of the matter to me. I confess I am reluctant to dig into the matter further. . . ."[75] How had Redlich "disposed" of it? The sign in the foreground, he wrote, could not have been hit by a bullet. Why was that?

Redlich dealt with each side of the sign separately. A bullet could not have struck the sign from the Depository side, he said, because Oswald had fired just three shots and the Commission had accounted for all of them. A bullet could not have struck from the grassy-knoll side because Oswald was firing from the Texas School Book Depository.[76]

Such circular reasoning seemed comical enough, but Norman Redlich carried it one step further as he addressed the more fundamental issue of the splice and four missing frames. Redlich explained: "I would suspect that the frames you have in mind were deleted . . . because . . . they were of little value because during those frames the Presidential limousine was almost completely hidden by the sign."[77] He concluded that the issues raised in Liebeler's letter did "not warrant any request to the FBI for an investigation, either formal or otherwise."[78] To my surprise Rankin closed his own letter with a gibe at Liebeler: "I am happy to learn that you are enjoying life as a law professor and I am looking forward to seeing some of your writing in the legal periodicals when you find time to make contributions of that kind."[79]

It was clear that Liebeler was annoyed with these replies. Among the deficiencies in Redlich's letter were misstatements of fact. Redlich stated, for example, that the "Stemmons Freeway" sign had not been moved although the record showed that it had.* I pointed this out to Liebeler.

"Look," Liebeler said, "you get all this material together so that I can answer this letter." That was fine with me. Then he remarked that to appreciate what was going on, I had to understand that he and Redlich had had intense personal differences while on the Commission. When I indicated my naive belief that personality disputes could not possibly have interfered with the Commission's fact-finding procedures, Liebeler replied: "My boy, history sometimes turns on petty hates and jealousies."[81]

Besides Salandria's articles, I had brought to Liebeler's office a copy of the first book to be published in this country based upon the twenty-six volumes: *The Unanswered Questions about the Kennedy Assassination*, a small paperback written by Pulitzer Prize–winning journalist Sylvan Fox. "Have you seen this?" I asked, turning the book so that the light would

---

* One could demonstrate that the signs had been moved (and, in the case of the "Stemmons Freeway" sign, probably replaced as well) by comparing pictures taken during the December 1963 reenactment with photographs taken later.[80]

pass through the three bullet holes the publisher had punched through the cover.

No, he hadn't, and he immediately offered to buy my copy. I wanted copies of the three letters about the sign. I had asked Liebeler for them before, and he had hedged. Now, I renewed my request, and we struck a bargain. I would give him my copy of Sylvan Fox's book in return for copies of the three "sign" letters. As we marched off to the Xerox machine, I kept up a running stream of comment that it was only a matter of time now until the entire Warren Report came apart at the seams. To my surprise, Liebeler said if that happened, the various Commission attorneys might try "to hang it on each other."[82] He added that he had urged that the Commission be kept in existence after the Report was published to handle any questions that might come up.

Liebeler's remarks at our November 2, 1965, meeting, and Norman Redlich's letter to Liebeler of October 18, 1965, made a deep impression on me. Redlich's reply exhibited the same obtuse indifference to evidence and probability that ran through the Warren Report. His analytical *tour de force* purporting to prove that the "Stemmons Freeway" sign could not have been struck by a bullet was similar to his remarks about Commission Exhibit 399, the bullet which rolled off a stretcher in Parkland Memorial Hospital about an hour after the shooting. That bullet was relatively clean and unmutilated. Many students, wondering how bullet 399 could possibly have traveled through both the President and the Governor, as required by the Commission's reconstruction, suspected the bullet was planted. Hewing to the line that the only bullets fired on November 22 were the three fired by Lee Harvey Oswald, Redlich had the chutzpah to turn 399's unmutilated condition into a virtue, invoking that to prove it could not have hit the Stemmons sign!*

Liebeler requested I prepare notes for him to use in writing a rebuttal to Redlich's letter. Liebeler did reply but, as far as I know, nothing ever came of the matter.

I came away from our November 2 meeting with the strong impression that Wesley Liebeler stood apart from the other Commission attorneys. He wrote a reasonable letter requesting further investigation and his request was rebuffed. For the first time I began to understand that despite the collective responsibility of the fourteen Commission attorneys for the work produced, they were individuals.

This idea was reinforced when I telephoned Richard Mosk, another

---

* "It is most unlikely (to say the least)," wrote Redlich, that Commission Exhibit 399 "could have fragmented and hit the sign. As you know . . . all the evidence points to the fact that it left the President's body as a whole bullet." Redlich argued that if the sign was not hit from the rear by a bullet fired by Oswald, then it wasn't hit from the rear at all.[83]

attorney on the Commission, who happened to live in Los Angeles. Mosk thought it was really funny that someone like me had bought the twenty-six volumes and would telephone him. "Oh, you're one of those buffs," he said sarcastically. "What's the matter? You worried we didn't catch all the assassins?"

I also began to understand that there was a subsidiary mystery—how had the investigation actually been conducted? If Redlich was unwilling to investigate the fact that the Commission's most basic piece of evidence—indeed, its clock on the event—had an unexplained splice, then what else was overlooked?

This very question—how the Commission had gone about its investigation—was at that time the subject of a master's thesis by Cornell graduate student Edward Jay Epstein. Through the cooperation of the Cornell University Department of Government, Epstein had obtained interviews with ten of the staff attorneys and five of the seven Warren Commissioners. Furthermore, Viking Press planned to publish his master's thesis as a book the following spring.

I learned about Epstein's project from the grapevine and in early November 1965 telephoned him to say hello. Epstein told me he was covering the investigation the way a sportscaster would follow a baseball team and he had come to know Liebeler well, having been an overnight guest at his Vermont farm in late June 1965.

He confirmed my impression that there had been disputes between Liebeler and the other attorneys, and he told me of one such incident. In the closing days of the investigation, when Liebeler was turning up evidence that Oswald might have had contacts hitherto uninvestigated, Rankin reportedly warned him: "At this stage we are supposed to be closing doors, not opening them." Epstein said that Redlich had been Rankin's fair-haired boy and was now his assistant corporation counsel in New York City.

We had a common interest in Wesley Liebeler but Epstein and I parted ways when it came to the assassination. He employed a curious double standard depending upon whether he was judging Lee Harvey Oswald or the Warren Commission. Epstein assured me that anyone reading his book would come away thinking the assassination was the work of more than one man. Nevertheless, he completely accepted the Commission's assessment of Oswald's guilt. I was most curious to see how he would reconcile all this in his forthcoming book.

In the fall of 1965 I crossed a line. My interest in the Kennedy case had developed in stages. After I heard Lane lecture, I studied the Warren Report; then came the labyrinth of the twenty-six volumes followed by a study of photographs, trying to see with my own eyes "what really happened." Now I was impelled to ask direct questions of eyewitnesses.

The Puzzle

On November 1, 1965, I decided to telephone James Altgens.

Altgens was an AP photographer who stood to the south side of Elm, facing the grassy knoll. As soon as the car sped away, he ran across the street and up the grassy knoll, thinking the authorities had an assassin cornered there. But then he realized they were just "chasing shadows," so he returned to Elm Street. Willis slide 7, taken just a minute after the shots were fired, showed how early Altgens got to the railroad yard, because the first policeman to arrive is just ascending the knoll, pistol in hand, while Altgens is scooting back down toward the south side of Elm.

He was friendly on the phone and mentioned quite casually that just before the motorcade came by, a number of people suddenly appeared behind the wall on the knoll.[84] He added that he thought it was an odd place to watch the parade from since the car would speed up right there as it entered the Stemmons Freeway. This was new, exciting information, but I was worried that Altgens might be confusing this recollection with his description of people on the overpass, which was mentioned in his Warren Commission testimony. But he assured me he was talking about the wall on the grassy knoll—to the right of the stairs when one faced the knoll.

When I asked Altgens whether there were any police among the "people" he saw, he replied: "I seem to remember that there were."[85]

Yet the official Dallas Police assignment sheets show the last Dallas policemen stationed at Elm and Houston, with two more on the overpass.[86] No uniformed men were behind the wall, arcade, fence, or anywhere else in the railroad-yard area.[87]

On November 20, I called Jean Hill. She was not specific, but she hinted, melodramatically, that something was being hidden. She stuck by her story that shots came from across the street from where she was standing, and characterized the Warren Report as a fraud and a hoax.[88]

These conversations reinforced my belief that I was not misinterpreting the photographs. Indeed, my telephone call to Altgens produced the first solid indication from any assassination eyewitness I knew of that there *were* people behind the wall on the knoll during the shooting. And the possibility that "police" may have been among them, if true, suggested that disguises might have been used.

Over the summer of 1965 Ray Marcus mailed packets of pictures showing the blowups from the Moorman photographs to various news reporters in the United States and abroad. Domestically, the reaction was noncommittal, but Thomas Buchanan, the author of *Who Killed Kennedy,* took the material and wrote an article, on the second anniversary of Kennedy's assassination, that was widely published in France, Italy, and Spain.

The first one of these I saw was in *Paris Match*—the French equivalent of *Life*. "There was a Second Shooter Behind the Wall,"[89] was the head-line. In late November I telephoned Liebeler and told him that the pictures I had talked about were now the subject of articles being published in the European press. He readily agreed to see them and we set up an appoint-ment for 2:00 P.M. on Tuesday, November 30, 1965.

When I arrived at Liebeler's office, no one was there. On his desk was his oversize "Be Kind to Me or I'll Kill You" button. I took out the Moorman photos and placed them one by one around his desk to create what I termed in a memo written later that day "the deleterious psycho-logical effect akin to 'assassin claustrophobia' when he sits down." Soon I heard voices in the hall.

Liebeler was coming down the hallway accompanied by an extremely attractive blonde. At first, I was rather embarrassed and asked Liebeler if he didn't want me to show him the pictures some other time. "No, go right ahead," he said, introducing me to his friend "Willie," with some poker-faced remark that I was a Warren Report critic, as if bumping into such people armed with pictures of assassins was an everyday experience.

I started by using an aerial photograph to orient them to Dealey Plaza. Then I took out Ray Marcus' photos to demonstrate the backward, left-ward motion of Kennedy's head. Liebeler argued a bit about whether a neuromuscular reaction could have caused this, but he did not press the point. Willie seemed quite impressed with the physics of the argument. "But Osvald," she said, speaking in a thick German accent, "he was shooting from the back?" Liebeler replied: "What this man is saying, Willie, is that there must be someone shooting from up front."[90]

I showed them the recent *Paris Match* story, and began by pointing at the various versions of the unenlarged Moorman photographs that were placed around Liebeler's office. Then, taking out the first of a series of enlargements, I said: "Being reasonable people, we look to see if anything is going on to the right front, since the head snapped back and to the left." As I took out the first enlargements, Willie's response was instantaneous: "Oh, Ves," she groaned. "Look, you can see him, shooting at Kennedy. . . . Oh, Ves . . . you can see him!" And then: "Osvald, Ves? He vas not shooting?"

Liebeler was now lighting his pipe and, with a magnificent puff and a twinkle in his eye, replied: "Oswald is behind, Willie; this man is saying there must be someone up front."

"Ves," she asked a bit hesitantly, "this photograph, you have not seen this photograph?"

She was now beginning to go through the analytical convulsions of mind that occur when someone faces, for the first time, evidence which rebuts the official conclusions and then tries to reason it all out at once.

"The Commission, Ves . . . they did not see this picture?"

"No, Willie, according to him, we didn't admit this into evidence."

Meanwhile, she kept exclaiming: "My God, you can actually see him shooting, Ves. . ."

Suddenly she seemed so skeptical of the Commission that I felt embarrassed for Liebeler's sake. I understood her reaction: If one became convinced that evidence of a second assassin was readily available, the tendency was to conclude that the Warren Commission had deliberately lied.

Looking at the blowups, Willie said: "But who could do such a thing?"

I, being facetious, started to accuse the Chinese Communists, but didn't finish my remark because Liebeler interrupted me, repeating what he had said at our first meeting. "Has anyone considered Lyndon Johnson?" he said.

Unfortunately, the woman replied to my remark, "Oh, that's ridiculous, the Communists had nothing to do with this." I was hoping Liebeler would complete his thought, so I politely agreed with the woman. Liebeler, somewhat annoyed, chimed in: "Well, that's very nice, but *I'm* not so sure." He then proceeded to discuss the possibility of Cubans being involved. He dwelt at great length on a speech Castro had made in September 1963 and the possibility that this speech might have influenced Oswald when he was in New Orleans. He then heaped abuse on the FBI in New Orleans for the investigation they had conducted.

Meanwhile, the woman seemed to give the pictures complete credibility. "But what can be done? What can be done? People all over Europe will laugh at America when they see these pictures." Liebeler, carefully studying the various images, said: "Well, these are certainly going to end up in a book someday." And just as he had previously urged that I give lectures, Liebeler now said: "Why don't you be the person that writes that book?"

I told Liebeler that Willie's reaction was not that unusual. If such photos were published, and if enough people found the images credible, they could have considerable political impact. He replied: "There is an establishment in this country, let's face it . . . you're never going to see *Life* and *Time* publishing photos like those. . . ."

He made another remark that day which struck me with great force. It came after much probing from me for a more specific reaction to the images: "We always knew," he said, "we couldn't exclude the possibility of others being involved in the assassination. You'll find that sort of language running throughout the Report."

One thing I realized for the first time at that meeting was that Liebeler knew there were deficiencies in the investigation, but could do nothing about them. When I pointed out, for example, that there were about twenty-five people on the Plaza facing the grassy knoll, clearly visible in photographs, who had <u>not been called</u> to testify, Liebeler made it clear that <u>he had wanted them all interviewed</u>. <u>But he had been overruled</u>.

"Can you tell me this: Who was responsible for deciding just who was and who was not to be called?" I asked.

"Now that," he replied, "is a question that I definitely refuse to answer." Despite his dissatisfactions with the work of the Commission he was obviously loath to be specific when it came to establishing responsibility.

I told Liebeler that since the appearance of the Sylvan Fox book and the photo blowups, people seemed more willing to talk in Dallas, even on the phone. What should I do, I asked, if I located someone willing to tell me exactly what he saw going on behind the wall on the grassy knoll? "Try bringing it to me," he answered.

He repeatedly said: "I'm not afraid of admitting we were wrong," to which I responded, "That's very unusual; I don't think many of your colleagues feel that way." And Liebeler replied: "I'm sure they don't."

As I look back, I realize that these conversations with Liebeler in 1965 encouraged my involvement and affected the way I looked at the case. They made it clear that <u>investigating the assassination was not a frivolous activity</u>, that it was <u>not unreasonable to disbelieve the Warren</u> Report. Indeed, although he wasn't offering any alternative reconstruction of the crime, it was apparent that <u>even Liebeler had his doubts</u>.

CHAPTER 2

The Head Snap

Allen Dulles and the Head Snap

In December 1965, Allen W. Dulles, former head of the CIA and a Warren Commissioner, visited UCLA as a Regents Scholar. He was paid a princely sum for giving a few speeches and meeting students, informally, in a coffee-klatch atmosphere. This permitted us to rub elbows with someone from the "real world."

Dulles' background was markedly different from that of his fellow Commissioners: Espionage was his major career. After wartime service with OSS, Dulles was Director of Central Intelligence from 1953 to 1961— through the Eisenhower years and almost to the end of Kennedy's first year in office. His last major project as CIA chief was the failed Bay of Pigs invasion. Kennedy replaced him in December 1961, eight months later. Dulles' first return to public service was his appointment to the Warren Commission by Lyndon Johnson.

I called Dulles' student host and asked for a private fifteen-minute interview, thinking that Dulles perhaps wasn't aware of the grassy-knoll evidence or the head snap. I also wanted to show him the Moorman blow-ups. I told the student organizer that I wished to meet privately with Dulles and explained why. The request was relayed to Mr. Dulles, who objected. "Mr. Dulles said if you have information like that, you should take it to the FBI." Mr. Dulles would "gladly" speak with me in front of the other students, but would not meet with me alone. "He thinks that is protection for himself because otherwise you could go out afterward and claim you had a personal interview with him, and misquote him." The student said that the previous night a student in the audience "had that [Sylvan] Fox book . . . and he really badgered Dulles. Please, don't badger him. They were really laughing at this fellow last night. You can come if you want to, but I'm sure they'll laugh at you too." I thought the host relished the idea of seeing mincemeat made of another heckler.

The meeting took place on December 7, 1965, in the Sierra Lounge of Hedrick Hall, one of the UCLA dormitories. Word had spread that someone was going to question Dulles about the Kennedy assassination and about fifty students showed up. I came decorously dressed in a suit, and brought along two of the twenty-six volumes and photographs I thought would be useful.

After a brief delay, Dulles walked in with Mrs. Dulles and the student moderator. He sat down, lit his pipe, and made a few witty remarks. His eyes settled on me several times, and on my two large blue-bound Warren Commission volumes. It was clear that we would be adversaries.

I was recognized by the moderator and there followed the uncomfortable but mandatory introductory remarks necessary, in 1965, to explain how I had all the detailed information I'd be referring to. I was "one of those who owned the twenty-six volumes," I said, explaining what they were, and Dulles chimed in: "I own a set, so you must include me, too."[1] The students laughed, and that broke the ice a bit. I wanted to ask just one question, I said, "and get your comments on it." One of the most important conclusions of the Commission, I began, was that there was no evidence of conspiracy. "Wasn't it," said Dulles, correcting me, and punctuating the air with his finger as he spoke, "we have *found* no evidence of conspiracy?" I proceeded to describe the motion of the President's head on the Zapruder film and some of the grassy-knoll testimony. How could the Commission's Report make a statement like that, in view of all that evidence?

Dulles responded: "We examined the film a thousand times," and he proceeded to deny that the motion I described appeared on the film. As he answered, I retrieved from my briefcase a demonstration panel prepared by Ray Marcus in which the relevant portions of all frames between 313 and 323 were arranged in sequence on one 8½ by 11-inch page. The backward motion was obvious. (See Photo 2.) I walked over to Dulles, and put one of the panels on his lap. "Here," I said, kneeling beside him, "I know these are not the best reproductions, but just look at the President's head and the rear seat of the car, and see if they get closer together or farther apart in successive frames after impact."

"Now what are you saying . . . just what are you saying?" said Dulles, his voice rising.

"I'm saying there must be someone up front firing at Kennedy, and that means a conspiracy," I replied.

"Look," he said, "there isn't a single iota of evidence indicating a conspiracy. . . . no one says there was anything like that. . . ."

As politely as possible I described the statistics in Harold Feldman's

"Fifty-Two Witnesses: The Grassy Knoll," closing with the fact that several people on the overpass saw smoke coming from the area behind the fence, and that a policeman "even smelled smoke there."

"Look," he paused, and then, his voice rising again, angrily, "What *are* you talking about? *Who* saw smoke?" he thundered, sounding as though I had fabricated the information out of whole cloth.

"Sam Holland, for instance," I replied. "He was standing on the overpass." I named a few others, and said that anyone could buy the book *Four Days*, turn to page 21 and see, in color, what was apparently a puff of smoke on the Nix film frame published there.

By now, Dulles had worked himself into a lather.

"Now what are you saying," he roared, "that someone was smoking up there?" His attempt at ridicule was unmistakable. "Are you telling me," he continued, "that there was no one up in that building, that no gun was found there, that no shells were found there?"

"Oh, no, sir," I said, feigning surprise. "I'm sure there was a gun there. I'm sure there were shells there. I think someone was shooting from there.* But I think someone was also shooting from up front. Harold Feldman analyzed all that testimony and quotes witnesses who even heard shots from two locations."

"Just who," asked Dulles in an extremely sarcastic tone, "is Harold Feldman?"

While I was certain Dulles knew who Feldman was, I answered by describing him as "a writer, sir, a freelance writer. . . ."**

"And who does he write for?" inquired Dulles.

". . . He frequently writes for the *Nation*."

Dulles raised his right hand, slapped his knee with a savage intensity, and laughed loudly and derisively.

"The *Nation*! Ha, ha, ha, ha, ha."

There was an embarrassing silence. No one laughed with him.

Politely, I interjected: "I don't think that is so funny, sir. I don't care what magazine the article was printed in—either the right or the left. The article is well written, and it is accurately footnoted."

"You say the *Nation* is accurately footnoted, eh?" replied Dulles.

Dulles now turned to the group and said: "I don't know if you're really all interested in this, and if you're not, we'd just as well . . ." His voice

---

* I wasn't really sure about that, but I didn't want to complicate our discussion with another issue.

** Feldman's "Oswald and the FBI," published in *Nation*, raised one of the thorniest issues the Commission faced: whether or not Oswald was an informant for the CIA or FBI. I later learned that Feldman's article was the subject of Warren Commission staff memos and a topic of discussion at the Commission's secret executive sessions.[2]

trailed off as he was met by anxious murmurs: "Oh, no, we're interested. No, keep going," etc. So he shrugged and we continued sparring.

Dulles looked down at the photographs on his lap and claimed he couldn't see what was there. "Look, there isn't *one iota* of evidence that the shots came from the front. How can you say such a thing?"

"Mr. Dulles," I said, "I'm showing you this evidence, and I've told you about the eyewitness testimony, which was taken under oath and certainly qualifies as evidence. And I'm absolutely amazed to hear you deny the existence of all this. . . ."

Dulles got very angry. "You have *nothing*! Absolutely nothing! The head could be going around in circles for all I can see. You can't see a thing here! I have examined the film in the Archives many times. *This* proves nothing."

This exchange ended with my passing about forty copies of the photo exhibits around the room, and asking the students to see for themselves the movement of the head. Meanwhile Dulles, waving his hand vehemently, simply denied that the head went back at all! "I can't see a blasted thing here. You can't say the head goes back. . . . I can't see it going back . . . it does not go back . . . you can't say that . . . you haven't shown it. . . ."*

At some point during the conversation, Dulles looked at me and said: "You know, I've never heard that argument before, and I've read all those books the experts supposedly are writing." He said it in a very funny way. To the students, I'm sure it sounded as though the argument must be no good because it hadn't been published. But it had the two-edged tone of a disgruntled compliment reluctantly paid.

When the next student recognized from the floor asked another question about the Warren Commission, there was a whispered conference between Dulles and the moderator. Dulles said that if there were no further questions on other subjects he would prefer to go to bed. He said he had had enough of this work when he was on the Commission, that the Commission had settled all these questions a thousand times over.

The student apologized to Dulles, and the moderator asked if there were "other types of questions someone might want to ask Mr. Dulles."

Raising his hand, a starry-eyed student asked a question that returned Mr. Dulles to the role he seemed to like best—that of the wise old raconteur. "Mr. Dulles," he asked, "could you please tell us something

---

* In 1975 when Robert Groden went public with an extremely clear copy of the film, *Boston Globe* Editor Robert Healey published an editorial, describing his impression of the film Allen Dulles acknowledged he had seen repeatedly:

> The visual presentation is far more convincing than all the books and all the magazine articles that have ever been advanced. They make a simple and convincing case that President Kennedy had to be killed by bullets fired from two directions and thus, by more than one person. And no words can make the case better than the Zapruder film. It is as simple as that.[3]

about the methods of torture that are used when spies are captured—especially by foreign governments?"

In November 1965 the UCLA campus was in turmoil. Students found it difficult to understand why the defense of South Vietnam was vital to the national security of the United States, or how the United States had become so deeply involved there in the first place. For somebody just out of high school, nothing concentrated the mind more wonderfully on a difficult issue of foreign policy than the possibility of being shipped off to fight a distant war.

That same month I attended my first UCLA Vietnam teach-in. During the question-and-answer period following an address by Stanley Sheinbaum, an economist with the Center for the Study of Democratic Institutions, I asked a question that was currently the subject of much discussion among critics of the Warren Report: "Do you think the war and the assassination are related?"*

Sheinbaum replied that he did not, and then made an observation which always comes up during a debate of this question—Kennedy's advisers were Johnson's advisers. So was it reasonable to believe Kennedy's policy would have been different?

The only rebuttal to this very sensible argument sounded sophomoric and naive, so I did not articulate it. But I thought it. It came down to believing that Kennedy would have overruled the advisers Johnson had listened to (Dean Rusk, et al.), and taken instead the anti-escalation advice of Mike Mansfield and George Ball. It meant subscribing to the idea that one man—especially if that man is President—can make the difference.

After the teach-in, I cornered Sheinbaum, told him about the critics' research with the twenty-six volumes, and ticked off a number of reasons for disbelieving the Warren Report. Surprisingly, this astute political scientist was virtually unaware of its flaws.

In December 1965, after *Paris Match* published the stories with the photo blowups, Sheinbaum telephoned me and requested that I send him a set of those pictures, and any other research I had done. He had joined the staff of *Ramparts* magazine which, he said, definitely wanted to publish something on the assassination. He suggested that I write an article and submit it for publication. Having no formal training in journalism, the invitation was quite a challenge. Tackling the problem, I found it difficult to communicate my ideas in essay form. So I hit upon the plan of reproducing, as a dialogue, the very conversations and arguments I had been having with friends and acquaintances. Several weeks later, I had put to-

---

* Many Warren Report critics believed events following the assassination represented a reversal of Kennedy's publicly stated intention to withdraw American troops from Vietnam.

gether a 150-page manuscript: "Assassination—1963: The Citizen and the Critic: A Dialogue in Defense of Conspiracy." For epigraphs at both the beginning and end, I used quotes from "The Emperor's New Clothes." Besides Sheinbaum, I sent copies to several critics and gave a copy to Wesley Liebeler.

By the spring of 1966, *Ramparts* was committed to doing *something*. But what? Sheinbaum and David Welsh, the news editor, visited the network of critics scattered about the country and found that everybody had his own theory about the assassination and that the critics often had bitter disagreements with one another. Finally, *Ramparts* organized their "Kennedy project," solicited material from a handful of critics and invited me to San Francisco to write a series of articles.

Those were heady times at *Ramparts*. Every issue, it seemed, broke some new and sensational story about Vietnam or the CIA. At a distance the magazine was slick, professional. Up close the operation was appalling. It was run by two or three people with a flair for public relations, and little genuine commitment to the issues. These people viewed the assassination controversy with derision. The tone was set by the man at the top—Warren Hinckle, Editor in Chief and Associate Publisher.

Hinckle had a genius for persuading well-heeled donors to contribute. The administration of the magazine was chaotic. When they didn't meet their deadlines, they simply skipped an issue. Everyone, including the staff, seemed to have trouble getting paid, and the magazine finally went into bankruptcy with a reduced scale of operations in the late 1960s.

Hinckle was only interested in the assassination if there was some new angle—"so much" had been published already. I told him that *Ramparts* could be first with a new angle on the case. I had seen almost no discussion in the press of the distinction between the evidence suggesting a "second assassin" *behind* the President and that indicating one firing from the *front*. The impression was widespread that when it came to the physical evidence, there were a few loose ends and that was all. I pointed out that the evidence for a "grassy-knoll assassin" was based firmly on physics; that it was solid, it was new, and could be combined with a good critique of the single-bullet theory. Hinckle could be the first to publish a "three-assassin model" of the Kennedy assassination.

Hinckle made fun of the idea. A "third" assassin? Was I sure? He understood there were probably two assassins, but three? Wasn't that a bit extreme? Was the country ready for that? Managing Editor Robert Scheer said the Warren Report critics were obsessed by a ghoulish preoccupation with detail. He could barely control his disdain.

David Welsh and I spent about six weeks writing the article, much of it adapted from my "Dialogue" manuscript. It came to thirty thousand words. As conceived, the chief difference between our article and anything previously published would be the detailed presentation of the head snap. This, we thought, could be decisive in resolving the controversy about the direction of the shots. That controversy, rooted in the contradictory medical and eyewitness testimony, was perceived then in the following terms:

The Dallas/Bethesda Conflict re the Head Wounds: Circa 1965–1966

The Dallas doctors described the large hole in the President's head as being located at the right rear, in the "occipital-parietal area." The Bethesda autopsy report noted: "a large irregular defect [hole] . . . involving chiefly the parietal bone but extending somewhat into the temporal and occipital regions."[4] Both groups of doctors agreed that the large hole was the exit for a missile. Some Dallas doctors provided graphic descriptions of this wound: Dr. Robert McClelland testified:

As I took the position at the head of the table . . . I was in such a position that I could very closely examine the head wound, and I noted that the right posterior portion of the skull had been extremely blasted. It had been shattered, apparently, by the force of the shot. . . . This sprung open the bones . . . in such a way that you could actually look down into the skull cavity itself and see that probably a third or so, at least, of the brain tissue, posterior cerebral tissue and some of the cerebellar tissue had been blasted out.[5]

This hole was first seen by Secret Service Agent Clinton Hill, after he climbed aboard the Presidential limousine just after the fatal shot struck. A large piece of skull had been blasted away. Hill described the damage:

The right rear portion of his head was missing. It was lying in the rear seat of the car. His brain was exposed.[6]

In addition to this large wound of exit, the Bethesda doctors reported that beneath it was a small hole, a bullet entrance wound, approximately a half inch by a quarter inch in size, located "approximately 2.5 cm [1 inch] laterally to the right and slightly above the external occipital protuberance."*[7]

None of the Dallas doctors observed such a wound. Yet it was crucial —the basis for the most fundamental conclusion of the Warren Commission: that the fatal shot struck from behind.**

* The occipital protuberance is the bony point at the bottom of the back of the head, high on the nape of the neck.

** The Warren Report stated: "The detailed autopsy of President Kennedy performed on the night of November 22 . . . led the three examining pathologists to conclude that the smaller hole in the rear of the President's skull was the point of entry and that the large opening on the right side of his head was the wound of exit. . . . Colonel Finck testified: 'President Kennedy was, in my opinion, shot from the rear. The bullet entered in the back of the head and went out on the right side of his skull. . . . he was shot from above and behind.' "[8]

In his original article in *Liberation*, Salandria carefully combed the testimony of all the Dallas doctors and nurses for some confirmation of this small wound. One by one, Salandria quoted the record of the entire Parkland staff. Typical was the questioning of Nurse Diana Bowron:

BOWRON: . . . I saw the condition of his head.
SPECTER: You saw the condition of his what?
BOWRON: The back of his head.
SPECTER: And what was that condition?
BOWRON: Well, it was very bad—you know.
SPECTER: How many holes did you see?
BOWRON: I just saw one large hole.
SPECTER: Did you see a small bullet hole beneath that one large hole?
BOWRON: No, sir.[9]

Again and again Specter asked each doctor and nurse: "Did you observe any other wound or bullet hole below the large area of missing skull?"[10] "Did you notice any holes below the occiput, say, in this area below here?"[11] "Did you notice a bullet hole below the large avulsed area?"[12] ". . . did you observe any other hole or wound on the President's head?"[13] Leading questions in this vein were put to Drs. Jenkins, Peters, Giesecke, Perry, Clark, McClelland, Carrico, and Baxter, and to Secret Service Agent William Greer.

Each answered: "No."[14]

The only support Arlen Specter elicited for the wound was from Dr. Kemp Clark, who stated: ". . . it could have easily been hidden in the blood and hair."[15]

Concluded Salandria: "All the government's proof of this small wound . . . amounts to [is] the statements of the doctors who conducted the autopsy."[16] Indeed, it was clear that what was at stake here was the basic integrity of the Bethesda autopsy report.

Of course the X-rays and photographs taken of the body at the autopsy should indicate exactly where the wounds were, and could have resolved this conflict. But unfortunately the Commission had employed artist's drawings, based on Commander Humes' verbal description, although Humes himself had said: "The complexity of these fractures and the fragments thus produced *tax satisfactory verbal description* [emphasis added] and are better appreciated in photographs and roentgengrams [X-rays] which are prepared."[17]

"It was the Commission's job," Salandria wrote, "to ascertain the nature of the head wounds . . . these wounds which 'tax satisfactory description.' Drawings based on verbal description were inadequate for the Commission's purpose." Salandria pointed out the extraordinary departure from legal procedure this represented. "The Government . . . must recognize that the production of this evidence is the *sine qua non* of credibility in this case."[18]

To most critics, the relationship between the Parkland/Bethesda conflict and the non-availability of the X-rays and photographs was clear. Wrote Salandria: ". . . The Commission concluded, as it had to . . . that there was a small wound of entry in the occiput of the President's skull. It is easy to accept the existence of such a wound. All one requires for such is the willingness to place absolute faith in the Bethesda autopsy doctors. . . ."[19]

In the case of the rear entry in the head, I subscribed to this extremely skeptical view and set the Bethesda autopsy report aside. At best, I thought, it could not be trusted; at worst, it was a pack of lies. So why bother studying it? I turned instead to the information coming from Dallas —the Dallas doctors' testimony, and the eyewitness accounts of those standing close enough to the President to see the bullets strike. This information had the disadvantage of being fragmentary—for example, a Dallas witness, whether a bystander or an emergency-room physician, might have had a view of only one side of the President's body. But the Dallas testimony had this advantage: It was generated immediately. There was no opportunity to tailor it to fit some preconceived notion or strategy.

It fell into three patterns, each providing a different perspective on how the shooting occurred.

Pattern One: In the Throat, out the Back of the Head

The Dallas doctors saw the President for about twenty minutes. According to the clinical summary prepared by Dr. Kemp Clark, the neurosurgeon who pronounced Kennedy dead, the doctors saw only two wounds —one at the front of the throat, and a large head wound at the right rear.*

Because it was small, round, and punctate, most of the Dallas doctors evaluated that throat wound as a point of entrance.** Similarly they judged the large head wound, because of its size alone, as a point of exit. Not having access to the Zapruder film, they had no way of knowing that the wounding of Kennedy's head and neck were caused by separate bullets which struck about five seconds apart. So, many of them combined their observations about the head and neck and initially concluded the President

* According to the Warren Report, they did not observe the entry wound in the back of the neck, because Kennedy was lying on his back, or the entry at the back of the head, because it was obscured by blood and hair.

** The throat wound will be discussed at length in the next chapter.

had been struck only once, from the front, by a bullet which entered the throat, somehow climbed up the spinal column, and then exited out the back of the head.

This "in-the-throat, out-the-head" trajectory appeared in many news accounts published in that weekend's papers because at the Friday afternoon news conference conducted at Parkland Hospital, Dr. Perry told reporters that although he was not certain the shooting happened that way, it was a possible explanation for the two wounds he saw.* The same trajectory also appeared in the Warren Commission testimony, when Counsel Specter asked each Dallas doctor to review his opinion of the throat wound, starting with what he first thought upon seeing the President in the emergency room on November 22, 1963.

For example, Dr. Ronald Jones testified: "With no history as to the number of times that the President had been shot or knowing the direction from which he had been shot, and seeing the wound in the midline of the neck [which Dr. Jones, in his medical report, characterized as an entrance wound] and what appeared to be an exit wound in the posterior [rear] portion of the skull, the only speculation that I could have as . . . to how this could occur with a single wound [bullet] would be that it would enter the anterior [front] neck and possibly strike a vertebral body [the spinal column] and then change its course and exit in the region of the posterior portion of the head. . . . if I accounted for it [both wounds] on the basis of one shot, that would have been the way I [would have] accounted for it."**[20]

However peculiar and incorrect this in-the-throat, out-the-back-of-the-

---

* For example, the main story in the November 23, 1963, *Los Angeles Times,* carrying the byline of Washington Bureau Chief Robert Donovan, offered the following reconstruction, in which all the wounds were accounted for by a single shot fired as the President's car approached the Texas School Book Depository:

Looming in front of the car . . . was the Texas School Book Warehouse. . . . In the bright sunshine three loud shots rang out. . . .
The President was facing the warehouse. In all probability he was hit just once, though doctors did not altogether discount the possibility that two bullets struck him. It appeared that a bullet hit him below the Adam's apple and was deflected up through the brain and then passed out the back of his head.

** Similarly, Dr. McClelland testified:

At the moment . . . it was our impression before we had any other information from any other source at all, when we were just confronted with the acute emergency . . . that this was one bullet, that perhaps [had] entered through the front of the neck and then in some peculiar fashion which we really had . . . to strain to explain to ourselves, had coursed up the front of the vertebra and into the base of the skull and out the rear of the skull."[21]

In the same vein, Dr. Peters explained:

". . . we saw the wound of entry in the throat and noted the large occipital wound, and it is a known fact that high velocity missiles often have a small wound of entrance and a large wound of exit. . . ."[22]

Although not every doctor combined the two wounds along that trajectory, the

head trajectory may appear in light of subsequent information, it was firmly established in the historical record. At the time I was drafting "The Case for Three Assassins," I found it more than an interesting anomaly that the Dallas doctors went to such lengths to provide a frontal entrance for the rear head wound.

If they were correct in their opinion that a bullet exited from the right rear of the head, but wrong in associating that trajectory with the throat wound, then there must have been another entrance wound somewhere on the head. But where?

The answer seemed to be either the right or left temple.

Pattern Two: Right Temporal Entry

When the fatal shot struck, the Texas School Book Depository was almost directly behind Kennedy, and the grassy knoll was off to his right. In 1966 there were a number of pieces of information available indicating that Kennedy was struck in the right temporal area.

Secret Service Reports. Agent Sam Kinney, the driver of the followup car, reported: "I saw one shot strike . . . the right side of the head. The President then fell to the seat to the left toward Mrs. Kennedy."[25]

Agent George Hickey, sitting in the left rear of that vehicle, wrote: "I heard what appeared to be two shots and it seemed as if the right side of his head was hit. . . ."[26]

William Eugene Newman. With his wife and two small children, Newman was standing at curbside, just in front of the wall on the grassy knoll. The President's car was just coming abreast of Newman as Zapruder's camera exposed frame 313. (See Photo 12.) In a television interview conducted by Dallas station WFAA within an hour of the shooting, Newman said: ". . . as the car got directly in front of us . . . a gunshot from apparently behind us hit the President in the side of the temple."*[27]

In November 1966 the Newmans were interviewed by Josiah Thompson and provided a more detailed description of the impact.**

---

predominant medical opinion was that the bullet exited the President's head *from the rear.* Dr. Akin testified: "I assume that the right occipital parietal region [right rear] was the exit. . . ."[23] And Dr. Jenkins, referring to the same wound, testified: ". . . I would interpret it [as] being a wound of exit. . . ."[24]

* In a Sheriff's affidavit filed that afternoon, Newman said the President was struck "in the side of the head."[28]

** Newman said the President was shot "in the side of the head. . . ."[29] He added the shot pushed Kennedy's head back and to the left—"it looked like he had just been hit with a baseball pitch"—and that the shot impacted near the right ear: "In my opinion, the ear went," he told Thompson.[30]

Thinking the shots came from behind them, the Newmans dropped to the ground and covered their children with their own bodies. (See Photos 3 and 13.)

Neither Newman nor his wife testified before the Commission.

Marilyn Sitzman. Another witness with an excellent view of Kennedy's right side at the moment of the fatal shot was Marilyn Sitzman. Sitzman, who stood alongside Zapruder atop the concrete pedestal as he filmed the motorcade (see Photo 10), was not interviewed by either the Dallas authorities or the Warren Commission. In November 1966, she told Josiah Thompson the shot struck Kennedy in the right temporal area: "above the ear and to the front . . . between the eye and the ear."[31]

Impact Debris Reported by Motorcycle Officers and Bystander Charles Brehm. Motorcycle officers B. J. Martin and B. M. Hargis, riding to the *left rear* of the President, both testified they were splattered with debris from the impact of the fatal shot. Hargis testified the debris struck with such force "I thought at first I might have been hit."[32] Hargis told reporters on November 22 the fatal shot struck "the right side of the head."[33] He told the Commission: "I was splattered with blood and brain, and kind of bloody water."[34] Officer Martin testified that bloody matter ended up on his uniform, helmet, and the windshield of his motorcycle.[35]

When the fatal shot struck, the limousine had just passed Charles Brehm, who was standing to the left, at curbside. In a filmed and tape-recorded interview in 1966, Brehm told Mark Lane that he "very definitely saw the effect" of the fatal shot: "That which appeared to be a portion of the President's skull went flying slightly to the rear of the President's car and directly to its left. It did fly over toward the curb to the left and to the rear."[36]

Although only one of this group—Hargis—said he saw Kennedy struck on the right side of the head, the fact that all three reported impact debris being driven to the left rear led me to count them as witnesses providing circumstantial evidence of a shot striking from the right front.

Texas Highway Patrolman Hurchel Jacks. Jacks was at the wheel of Lyndon Johnson's automobile as it squealed to a halt at the Parkland Memorial Hospital emergency entrance, just behind Kennedy's limousine. Jacks' report, filed later that week, provides the only recorded observation in the twenty-six volumes of a right temporal wound by someone who observed the President's body at Parkland Memorial Hospital. Jacks described what he saw when he sprinted to Kennedy's side:

. . . one of the Secret Service agents said he had been hit, put your coat over him. One of the agents removed his suit coat and spread it over the President's body from his chest up. Before the President's body was covered it appeared that the bullet had struck him *above the right ear or near the temple* [emphasis added].[37]

Jacks was not called by the Commission.

News Reporter Seth Kantor. Representing Scripps-Howard newspapers on the Washington press corps, Kantor followed the motorcade to Parkland

Memorial Hospital. His notebook became a Warren Commission exhibit and contained the following entry about the President's head wounds made while he was at Parkland Memorial Hospital: "intered [sic] right temple."[38]

November 22 Statement Transmitted by UPI and Broadcast on NBC-TV. UPI's White House correspondent Merriman Smith arrived at Parkland Memorial Hospital just seconds after the President, and commandeered a hallway telephone. At 1:47, CST, about fifteen minutes after Kennedy's death was announced, UPI transmitted: "President Kennedy was shot in the right temple. 'It was a simple matter of a bullet right through the head,' said Dr. George Burkley, White House Medical Officer." Within minutes, NBC anchorman Chet Huntley repeated the statement to a national television audience.[39]

The Commission did not investigate the source of this report. Merriman Smith was not called as a witness, nor was Dr. Burkley, whose ten-page statement, filed with the Commission, made no mention of the President's wounds.[40]

Pattern Three: Left Temporal Entry

Dr. Robert McClelland, Assistant Professor of Surgery at Southwestern Medical School, affiliated with Parkland Memorial Hospital, concluded his two-page handwritten report filed at 4:45 P.M. on the afternoon of November 22, 1963, with this observation:

The cause of death was due to massive head and brain injury from a gunshot wound of the left temple.[41]

Dr. McClelland was the only Dallas doctor to record the existence of a left temporal wound in a report dated November 22.*

McClelland's observation was later supported by Dr. Marion Jenkins, who volunteered:

---

* When McClelland was questioned by Arlen Specter in March 1964 he did not volunteer the same statement under oath. However, the following exchange did take place:

SPECTER: Dr. McClelland, I show you now a statement or a report . . . identified . . . as Commission Exhibit No. 392 . . . and I would ask you first of all if this is your signature . . . next, whether in fact you did make this report and submit it to the authorities at Parkland Hospital?

MCCLELLAND: Yes.

SPECTER: And are all the facts set forth true and correct to the best of your knowledge, information, and belief?

MCCLELLAND: To the best of my knowledge, yes.[42]

Arlen Specter asked McClelland no question about his observation of a left temporal wound.

". . . I don't know whether this is right or not, but I thought there was a wound on the left temporal area, right in the hairline and right above the zygomatic process.

Specter responded: "The autopsy report shows no such development, Dr. Jenkins."[43] Later, Jenkins brought the matter up again.*

The observations of Drs. McClelland and Jenkins were corroborated by press interviews with Father Oscar Huber, one of two priests who went to the emergency room and gave Kennedy the last rites. The *Philadelphia Sunday Bulletin*, for example, carried an AP report stating that Father Huber

. . . wet his right thumb with holy oil and anointed a cross over the President's forehead, noticing as he did, a "terrible wound" over his left eye.[46]

It will be recalled that by the time the President was struck in the head, his automobile had moved far down Elm Street and the crowd had thinned to but a few bystanders on either side. Nevertheless, as with the right temporal evidence, there was a witness at Dealey Plaza, standing to Kennedy's left, who told reporters on November 22 that he saw a left temporal wound. He was Norman Similas, of Toronto, Canada. Similas, in Dallas on a business trip, said he was standing on the north curb of Elm Street about fifty feet nearer the underpass than Jean Hill and Mary Moorman. Similas' account appeared in the *New York Times* of November 23, 1963, under the headline: 10 FEET FROM THE PRESIDENT. Similas said that as Kennedy passed him,

I could see a hole in the President's left temple and his head and hair were bathed in blood.[47]

Similas was not called as a witness by the Commission.

The evidence for a left temporal entry had one great strength that the right temporal pattern lacked: two Dallas doctors said they saw such a wound, one mentioning it in his report filed on November 22, 1963. Nevertheless, the left temporal evidence presented a bundle of problems for me

---

* One of his initial impressions apparently had been to connect the left temporal wound he thought he saw with the wound at the right rear of the head which, he had said, "I would interpret [as] being a wound of exit."[44]

JENKINS: . . . I asked you a little bit ago if there was a wound in the left temporal area, right above the zygomatic bone in the hairline, because there was blood there and I thought there might have been a wound there [indicating].

SPECTER: Indicating the left temporal area?

JENKINS: Yes; the left temporal, which could have been a point of entrance and exit here [indicating]. [An apparent reference to the large wound at the back of the head.][45]

because it did not lend itself well to a reconstruction of the assassination which fit with the Zapruder film and the accounts of the majority of the Dealey Plaza witnesses.

I remember being perplexed in 1965. The grassy knoll was off to the *right*, yet the strongest evidence of frontal entry was Dr. McClelland's November 22 report of a gunshot wound in Kennedy's left temple. Where was the sniper?

One explanation: Dr. McClelland had reversed right and left. But "left temple," in McClelland's handwriting, stared up from his report, reproduced on page 527 of the Warren Report. Moreover, any such "reversal" hypothesis had to be extended to Dr. Jenkins, another "left temporal" witness, and to the priest as well. Had they all confused right and left, or were they wrong about the wound being there at all? And what about Norman Similas?

Oddly enough Dealey Plaza is symmetric and situated off to the left, on the opposite side, is another "grassy knoll," a mirror image of the first. But I knew of no witnesses who thought shots came from there.

Another question: When could a left temporal hit have occurred? The Zapruder film showed only two major reactions: first, the President grasping at his throat after he came out from behind the Stemmons Freeway sign; then, about three seconds later being struck violently in the head and driven to the left and rear. Neither of these reactions suggested a shot striking the left temple.

So the left temporal evidence, incompatible with both the "head snap" and the accounts of the grassy-knoll witnesses, did not fit into any coherent reconstruction.

Despite the obvious contradictions in this Dallas eyewitness testimony, there was one unifying thread: It all indicated a shot from the front. Indeed, so much of the Dallas information indicated a frontal hit that I found it difficult to believe a Dallas autopsy would have proven all these data incorrect. This reinforced my belief that the Bethesda autopsy could not be trusted, and that the only reliable indicator as to the direction of the shot was the Zapruder film head snap. Clearly, it and the Dallas medical opinion that a bullet exited from the rear of the head were mutually corroborative.

What I hoped to do in "The Case for Three Assassins" was bring to this mix of evidence another element, one which would tip the scales decisively in the critics' favor. I hoped to solicit a famous physicist, someone the public would listen to, who would say that with all due respect to the Chief Justice of the United States and his Commission, the motion observed on the Zapruder film established that the shot came from the front, that there wasn't the slightest doubt about it, that the Commission's conclusion flew in the face of Newton's laws.

At the time a friend of mine, a graduate student at the California

Institute of Technology at Pasadena, had gotten to know Nobel prize-winning physicist Richard Feynman, and told him about my research on the assassination. Dr. Feynman was interested in seeing the Zapruder frames showing the head snap. A meeting was set.

Richard Feynman and the Head Snap

Accompanied by my friend, I walked into Dr. Feynman's office one day in the spring of 1966, hoping to recruit him into the ranks of the Warren Report critics and return to San Francisco with an endorsement that might impress even Warren Hinckle III. Why not? The issue seemed so straightforward—how could I possibly fail?

Using the large aerial photograph, I took Dr. Feynman on a guided tour of Dealey Plaza, explaining that the car almost had reached the stairs on the knoll before the fatal shot struck, pointing to the railroad yard and parking-lot area behind the knoll where fresh footprints had been found and where Officer Smith had smelled gunpowder afterward, and where witnesses had seen smoke and heard the gunfire. Then, after briefly reviewing the Dallas/Bethesda conflict regarding the existence of a rear entry wound in the skull, I concluded with the "head-snap" evidence. Ever interested in fundamentals, Dr. Feynman was skeptical of my unqualified assertion that the President's head went backward in response to a shot allegedly fired from the rear.

I showed him the head-snap panels prepared by Marcus demonstrating that in each frame after 313 the head and the car seat got closer together until, by frame 323, the President was momentarily sprawled against the rear seat. (In 1965 the critics used 323 to show this because it had been published in color in *Life*. Photo 2 shows 321.)

Richard Feynman was not about to take my word for this. He took out a ruler, put my copy of volume 18 on his desk, and began to measure. He was doing the same thing I had done that night in Ray Marcus' home when, disbelieving what Marcus had told me, I insisted on confirming it myself. There was silence as Feynman measured, scribbled, and double-checked his measurements.

Then, looking up, he said: "The head goes forward."

What?!

What was he talking about? Suddenly, I realized that I had forgotten to mention that two frames, 314 and 315, were reversed in volume 18. Marcus had discovered this the year before and I, after writing Lyndal Shaneyfelt at the FBI, had obtained a letter from J. Edgar Hoover confirming that was the case, and stating it was merely "a printing error."

I explained all this to Feynman. That he had to correct for this by reversing 314 and 315, and reading the frames in the sequence: 313, 315, 314, 316, 317, etc.

But no, said Feynman, he wasn't talking about 314 and 315. He was referring to frame 312.

312?

Yes, frame 312, the last frame before impact. Feynman showed me that Kennedy's head went forward by a small, but perceptible, amount between frame 312, the last pre-impact frame, and frame 313, the first frame after impact.

Feynman's response caught me completely by surprise. I knew nothing whatever about the motion between 312 and 313 for the simple reason that I had never measured it. What I had measured was the motion from 313 onward. And there was no question that the head definitely moved to the rear following frame 313.

I felt like a fool, for I instantly realized my error. In applying the laws of physics to a collision (say, between two billiard balls), one compares two situations: "before" impact and "after" impact, the methodology being that while what occurs at the instant of contact may be too difficult to determine with precision, Newton's laws can be applied to the "before" and "after" situations with relative ease. The equations will yield information about the former, if the latter is known precisely, and vice versa. Frames 312 and 313 bracketed the instant of collision.

As the camera exposed frame 312, the bullet was in flight, heading toward the President. That frame represented the last frame before collision. By the time the camera shutter opened and exposed frame 313, the bullet had struck—the instant of collision had passed.*

Measuring the movement between 312 and 313 was not the same as measuring the motion after the collision—after frame 313.**

But I had become so preoccupied with the backward motion after impact that I had made the unwarranted assumption that the entire sequence was continuous, and had not addressed the motion from the proper starting point—frame 312. So I was caught completely off guard by the forward motion between 312 and 313.

According to measurements made subsequently, the President's head traveled about two inches between those two frames before the direction was violently reversed.[48] There was a double motion. Were there two separate causes? Was the President shot from both directions?

---

* Many commentators referred to frame 313 as "depicting" the collision. It gave a fair approximation, but was not precise enough. Precision was essential because the movement of the head between 312 and 313—the initial response to the bullet—was critical in determining the direction from which the bullet came.

** The two motions were not unrelated. Intuitively, one would expect that if the President's head were driven forward by a bullet striking from the rear, it ought to keep moving forward, and not suddenly reverse direction an eighteenth of a second later. Newton's first law says that once an object is in motion, it will continue to move in a straight line at constant speed unless acted upon by an outside force.

On the basis of the film, Feynman declined to give an opinion about the number and direction of the shots.

I was embarrassed. I had walked into the office of one of the world's most famous physicists only to find that he was able to demonstrate, by making a simple measurement with a ruler—a measurement I could and should have made the year before—that I had not yet mastered my own data. I left the Caltech campus that day without any endorsement, but having learned something new.

What did it mean?

Certainly the question still remained: Why was the President's head thrust backward after frame 313? In my gut, I knew it meant the President was shot from the front; there had to be some other explanation for that forward motion. By contrast the backward motion was so violent and sustained. Clearly, *something* impelled the President to the rear. And besides, there was so much other evidence of a grassy-knoll assassin.

Along with my friend, I went to a nearby Pasadena coffee shop. It is difficult to recapture the shock I felt over what might at first appear to be just another evidentiary conflict, more minutiae. For me it was much more than that. The head snap had been the very foundation for my beliefs about the Warren Commission Report, and had provided the framework in which I could evaluate much other evidence.

I had approached the assassination from the standpoint of a scientist. I had a definite hierarchy for evaluating the evidence. I was willing to grant that eyewitnesses could be wrong, but I would not budge when it came to physics.

My deduction, based on Newton's laws, that there was a frontally located assassin initiated a chain reaction which affected my judgments about other closely related areas. Once I was certain that the shot came from the front, there was no longer any need to consider whether echoes came from the grassy knoll. And the Dallas doctors' initial opinion that the throat wound was one of entry became more convincing. All these issues were interlocked; certainty in one area led to certainty in another.

But now, having structured my beliefs in this fashion, I was confronted with the possibility that the motion of the head was more complex than I had realized, that my original analysis was wrong. The motion, as I now understood it, was a double motion—forward for one film frame (an eighteenth of a second), and then a sudden reversal—backward—for ten frames (half a second) as Kennedy was thrown against the rear seat of the car.

Two possibilities came to mind to account for this "double" motion.

Kennedy Was Shot Only from the Rear. This would account for the forward motion but would leave the backward snap unexplained. The only explanation that came to mind was a neuromuscular reaction. A Southern California acquaintance of mine happened to be a neurosurgeon.

I told him about the backward snap of the head after frame 313 of the film and asked whether he thought a neuromuscular reaction of some sort might account for it. He was most skeptical, and went into considerable detail explaining why.

Kennedy Was Struck by Two Shots—One from Each Direction. Was it possible that the President was struck in the head twice—once from the rear pushing his head forward, and then from the front by a bullet which caused the backward snap? I was reluctant to accept this explanation, in part because of my skepticism about the Bethesda autopsy and its rear entry wound.

But I was also aware that the double head hit was mathematically rather improbable. It was highly unlikely that two gunmen, even if both were wearing headsets and responding to the same order, would fire two shots which struck within the same eighteenth of a second. Such things as human reaction time and slight differences in distance from the target would introduce an element of randomness. The odds would be eighteen to one against. This probability argument was intuitive,* but the combination of it with my reluctance to accept the Bethesda autopsy finding of a rear entry wound forced me to look for some other explanation for the double motion, some other trajectory that might cause the motion observed on the film, and yet be consistent with the Dallas medical observations. Pondering the problem, I realized that another explanation was possible, that I had been oversimplifying.

The Forward, High-Angle Shot

At first, it seemed the only way to characterize the 312–313 motion was "forward." But the President's head could pivot about his neck. Consequently, that movement could also be viewed as a clockwise rotation (clockwise when viewed from the right side of the car, the side of Zapruder's camera), that is, a downward movement in which the chin was being driven against the chest. Such clockwise rotation could be imparted to the head by a shot from the front if the angle were steep enough.**

* This assumes both shots being fired within one second, with equal probability of each being fired during any eighteenth of that second.

** At issue was this question: What was the proper model to use in making calculations and, in general, in interpreting the motion observed on the Zapruder film? If one employed a model in which the head could move only forward or backward, then the 312–313 motion had but a single interpretation: It represented a forward motion whose cause must have been an impulse from the rear. If, however, one employed a model in which the head was free to pivot about the neck, then the 312–313 motion could be viewed as a clockwise rotation.

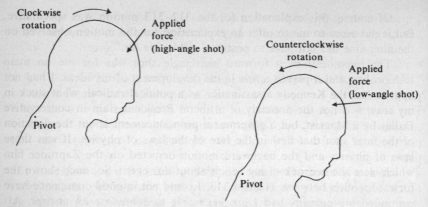

Figure 1.
Effect of shot angle on rotation of head
Above: High-angle forward shot imparts clockwise rotation, driving the chin toward the chest.
Below: Low-angle forward shot imparts counterclockwise rotation, driving the chin up and away from the chest.

A shot from the front fired at a low-angle (practically horizontal) trajectory would drive the head backward and in the process lift the chin up away from the chest (impart to the head a counterclockwise rotation, viewed from the right side). But a high-angle shot, while it would also drive the head backward, would also rotate the head in the opposite direction (drive the chin downward, toward the chest). (See Fig. 1.)

Thus, employing a model which took into account rotation, the entire motion—from frame 312 and on out to frame 323 (when the President is sprawled against the rear seat of the car)—might be explained in terms of a combination of the head pivoting clockwise about the neck (which would cause 312–313), while the head and torso were being propelled toward the rear (313–323). Both these effects would result from one cause— a single strike from the front—as long as the trajectory were steep enough.

How steep was "steep enough"? Since the President was already sagging forward, and the car was on a street which sloped downward, it seemed that the trajectory could be as shallow as 25 degrees and still produce a downward chin-against-chest motion.* (See Fig. 1.)

---

* The angle would be determined by drawing a line from the assumed point of impact to the point at which the head pivots about the neck. As can be seen in Figure 1, any trajectory steeper than that would produce a clockwise (chin-against-chest) rotation, while any trajectory more shallow would produce the opposite effect—a counterclockwise rotation.

Of course, this explanation for the 312–313 motion was speculative. But it did seem to me to offer an explanation for the motion observed on the film. One did not have to postulate a "double hit."

The hypothesis of a forward high-angle shot was for me no mere technicality, and it played a role in the development of my ideas. I had not approached the Kennedy assassination as a political radical; what stuck in my craw was not the anomaly of a liberal President slain in conservative Dallas by a Marxist, but a government pronouncement about the direction of the fatal shot that flew in the face of the laws of physics. It was those laws of physics and the backward motion depicted on the Zapruder film which were the bedrock of my beliefs about this event. So, once shown the forward motion between 312 and 313, I could not in good conscience have continued my pursuits had I not been able to formulate an answer. Although more complex, my hypothesis left my basic beliefs unshaken: I still believed Kennedy was struck in the head only from the front. Most important, I maintained at that time a stubborn belief that Commander Humes, the chief autopsy surgeon, could not have told the truth about that rear entry wound in the head which nobody saw in Dallas.

This hypothesis set me apart from the other critics who, upon learning of the double motion, now tended to believe Commander Humes on this point.

I wanted to check my hypothesis with someone in the Physics Department. A friend of mine, Bernard Kenton, a graduate student pursuing his Ph.D. in physics, introduced me to Dr. James Riddle, a British physicist on the UCLA faculty.

Riddle reviewed my analysis, and agreed with it. He offered to be the consulting physicist for the *Ramparts* article, and even gave a lecture on the head snap at UCLA.

Both Riddle and I would have liked to describe the physics, and the rotation theory which accounted for the "forward" 312–313 motion in detail, but I knew that such an approach would have turned Warren Hinckle off completely. I could just hear him lecturing me, sarcastically, that he was publishing *Ramparts*, not the *Journal of Applied Physics*. So Dr. Riddle drew up a strong statement about the backward motion on the film, and I arranged with Dave Welsh, my co-author and *Ramparts'* News Editor, to insert the statement about 312–313 in a footnote. Which is how we smuggled technical detail into the article.

Riddle's statement concluded: "The motion of Kennedy's body in frames 312–313 is totally inconsistent with the impact of a bullet from above and behind. Thus, the only reasonable conclusion consistent with the laws of physics is that the bullet was fired from a position forward and to the right of the President.

"It is disturbing that this conclusion contradicts the findings of the

Warren Commission, but intellectual honesty compels me to offer the above opinion."[49]

Dr. Riddle's statement was to be the centerpiece for our argument that the President was struck in the head from the grassy knoll. But there was still another reason for believing someone was shooting from the front—the wound at the front of the throat.

CHAPTER 3

The Throat Wound: Entrance or Exit?

ON THE AFTERNOON OF NOVEMBER 22, 1963, millions of Americans heard radio and TV networks report that Dr. Malcolm Perry, a Dallas physician who was with the President in the emergency room when he died, said there was a bullet entrance wound situated on the front of Kennedy's neck.

I wasn't one of those Americans. I was asleep at the time of the assassination; and when awakened by my clock radio about two hours afterward, initially thought the incessant talk about assassination must refer to the Lincoln assassination. Within minutes of learning otherwise, I jumped to another false conclusion: only a lunatic would murder a President. Then, like millions of others, I sat back and waited for the authorities to produce the name of the lunatic.

It never occurred to me to doubt the official pronouncements, to analyze the news reports, or keep track of the statements of the various officials. I never noticed that what the Dallas doctors were saying about the throat wound—that the shot struck from the front—was inconsistent with what the Dallas Police Department was saying about the location of the assassin, who allegedly fired from a building behind the motorcade. I first became aware of that conflict when I attended Mark Lane's lecture in New York City. In 1966, preparing to deal with this issue in detail in the *Ramparts* article, I wanted every scrap of information about it.

I found the throat wound interesting on several levels. It was, of course, important that the first doctors to see the President thought he was struck from the front, but the issue was important for other reasons, as well. The more I probed, the more I learned about the pressures apparently put upon the Dallas doctors to change their initial story, the shadowy role played by the Secret Service, the behavior of the news media, and the unusual way in which the Warren Commission handled all this.

* * *

The source of the November 22 reports describing the throat wound as an entrance was a hospital news conference conducted after President Kennedy's body was removed.[1] In addition to Dr. Perry, neurosurgeon Kemp Clark, who pronounced Kennedy dead, also participated.

At the time of the Warren Commission's investigation, exactly what Dr. Perry said that day in Dallas was a matter of some dispute. Yet it was then, and remains today, a matter of considerable legal and historical interest.

When Dr. Perry entered the emergency room at Parkland Memorial Hospital and took charge of the effort to save President Kennedy, he decided that a tracheotomy—an operation in which an artificial airway is provided by cutting into the throat and inserting a tube directly into the windpipe—was in order. By sheer coincidence the throat wound was at a location suitable for this surgical procedure. Consequently, Dr. Perry made his incision directly through the bullet wound, thus altering its appearance.* Consequently, the only people who saw the actual bullet wound were the doctors and others in Dallas who viewed the body before Dr. Perry made his incision.

Obviously no one had a better opportunity to observe that wound than Dr. Perry himself. And no description of that wound was based on more immediate or direct observation than the comments Dr. Perry made at that first meeting with the press.

At 3:10 P.M., CST, United Press International carried a brief report of that news conference and quoted Dr. Perry directly:

Dr. Malcolm Perry, thirty-four, said "there was an entrance wound below the Adam's apple."[3]

Veteran *New York Times* reporter Tom Wicker, with the White House press in Dallas, rushed to Parkland Memorial Hospital and attended the doctors' press conference. In the next day's *New York Times,* he reported:

. . . Dr. Malcolm Perry, an attending surgeon, and Dr. Kemp Clark, chief of neurosurgery at Parkland Hospital, gave more details. Mr. Kennedy was hit by a bullet in the throat, just below the Adam's apple, they said. This wound had the appearance of a bullet's entry. . . .[4]

The Warren Report had this to say about Dr. Perry: "Considerable confusion has arisen because of comments attributed to Dr. Perry concerning the nature of the neck wound. Immediately after the assassination, many people reached erroneous conclusions about the source of the shots because of Dr. Perry's observations to the press."[5]

---

* Commander Humes testified that when he conducted the autopsy later that evening, he initially diagnosed that hole as a tracheotomy incision because it was "no longer at all obvious as a missile wound."[2]

That was an understatement. Dr. Perry's words, simultaneously transmitted to every subscriber of UPI's primary "A" wire, were reported by radio, TV, and newspapers, and reached an immense audience. In effect, Dr. Perry walked out of the Parkland Memorial Hospital emergency room and delivered his initial medical opinion to the entire world.

When I first began studying the assassination in 1965, I soon realized that the dispute over Dr. Perry's remarks combined two separate issues. First, what did he say? Second, was he right? A tape recording or transcript could answer the first question, but not the second—that was a medical question.

By the spring of 1966, when I was drafting "The Case for Three Assassins," I had come to disagree with the Warren Report's conclusions in both these areas: I believed neither that Dr. Perry was misquoted, nor that he was mistaken. Furthermore, my study of the twenty-six volumes, supplemented by microfilmed records of a number of newspapers, reinforced my suspicions about the way the Commission handled this matter. For Dr. Perry to have been misquoted, all the reporters and news organizations present at his original news conference had to make the same error. The Warren Commission implied that the media had transformed Perry's answer to a hypothetical question about "what could have happened" into a "professional opinion about what did happen." Yet AP, UPI, the *New York Times,* to name but three, all reported Dr. Perry's unqualified opinion that the throat wound was an entrance wound.[6]

Furthermore, in subsequent interviews, Dr. Perry continued to describe the throat wound as one of entrance. It was difficult to believe that Dr. Perry was misquoted on Friday, when he repeated the same thing on Saturday.*

Finally, the opinion attributed to Dr. Perry agreed with that expressed by others who had seen the wound. Dr. Charles Carrico was the first doctor to see the President and, before Perry arrived, had instituted an emergency resuscitative measure.**

At 4:20 P.M., seventy minutes after UPI sent its teletype report of Dr. Perry's press conference, Dr. Carrico drafted his medical report. He also described the throat wound as one of entrance, using the phrase:

. . . [a] small *penetrating* wound of ant. [anterior] neck in lower ⅓ [emphasis added].[8]

Assisting Dr. Carrico was Emergency Room Nurse Margaret Henchliffe. In a Warren Commission deposition she testified: "It was just a little

* For example, *Dallas News* reporter John Geddie reported that in a November 23 interview, Dr. Perry said: "In the lower portion of [Kennedy's] neck, right in front, there was a small puncture."[7]

** A tube (known as an endotracheal tube) was inserted into the President's mouth and down his throat.

hole in the middle of his neck . . . about as big around as the end of my little finger . . . [that looked like] an entrance bullet hole. . . ."[9] When asked by Specter if it could "have been an exit bullet hole," Nurse Henchliffe insisted that she had "never seen an exit bullet hole . . . that looked like that.* . . . it was just a small wound and wasn't jagged like most of the exit bullet wounds that I have seen."[12]

Another factor reinforcing my conviction that Dr. Perry had not been misquoted was his reaction to the news that the shots were all fired from a building located *behind* the motorcade. Faced with that fact, Dr. Perry did not change his opinion about the wound; on the contrary, he simply assumed that President Kennedy was turned toward the rear when the bullet struck. Thus, on Saturday, November 23, he told the *Boston Globe*'s medical editor, Herbert Black:

It may have been that the President was looking up or sideways with his head thrown back when the bullet or bullets struck him.[13]

I was impressed by that statement, made one day after the assassination, which represented Perry's personal effort to reconcile the conflict. By suggesting a posture for the President that would permit a gunman firing from the rear to inflict an entrance wound in the throat, I thought Dr. Perry demonstrated the firmness of his opinion.

Dr. Perry's reaction was characteristic of the Parkland doctors, who could not be certain, until they saw the Zapruder frames published the following week, what direction the President was facing.**

I used to speculate about the sense of bewilderment these men must have experienced later, looking at those pictures published in the news-

---

* Immediately following this exchange, attorney Specter began a series of questions designed to establish that Nurse Henchliffe did not have qualifications to render such an opinion (e.g., "What experience have you had in observing bullet holes, Miss Henchliffe? . . . Have you ever had any formal studies of bullet holes?") Nurse Henchliffe answered that her experience was limited to five years in the emergency room at Parkland Memorial Hospital and, more generally, her twelve years as a registered nurse. "We take care of a lot of bullet wounds down there—I don't know how many a year," she testified.[10] Her opinion was echoed by Dr. Robert N. McClelland, who arrived too late to see the wound in its pristine condition. He told Richard Dudman of the *St. Louis Post-Dispatch:* ". . . we are familiar with bullet wounds. . . . We see them every day—sometimes several a day. This did appear to be an entrance wound."[11]

** Dr. Robert Shaw said the doctors were "a little baffled" by the throat wound. Shaw said: "The assassin was behind him, yet the bullet entered at the front of his neck. Mr. Kennedy must have turned to his left to talk to Mrs. Kennedy or to wave to someone."[14] Dr. Charles McClelland, aware that the wound was located directly at the centerline of the throat and that a mere "turn" to the right or left really was not enough, said: "We postulated that if it was a wound of entry, as we thought it was . . . he would have to have been looking almost completely to the rear."[15]

papers, *Life,* and *Time,* and seeing for themselves that the President was, in fact, facing forward throughout the shooting.

Each of them had to come to terms with himself on this point and, presumably, they all rejected any sinister implications. This meant accepting the fact that the wound in the front of the throat was one of exit, though surely the strangest-looking exit wound they had ever seen—one which looked just like an entrance wound. It also meant they had to bear the responsibility for speaking out of turn, for confusing the public record in a case of monumental historic importance.

Yet the doctors at Parkland Memorial Hospital described only what they *saw;* it was the wound itself that prompted their reaction. That wound was very small, no more than a quarter inch in diameter; described by Dr. Perry as "spherical . . . rather clean-cut"[16]; and by Dr. Carrico as "an even round wound."[17] In his Warren Commission deposition, Dr. Ronald Jones summed it up in one brief sentence: "The hole was very small and relatively clean-cut as you would see in a bullet that is entering rather than exiting from a patient."[18] Conceding that he had not seen the wound before Dr. Perry made his incision, Dr. Robert McClelland, an Assistant Professor of Surgery, nevertheless testified: ". . . if I saw the wound in its state in which Dr. Perry described it to me, I would probably initially think this were an entrance wound. . . ."[19]

Here, then, was the most persuasive reason for believing that Dr. Perry was not misquoted at his initial press conference—whether it *was* one or not, the hole in Kennedy's throat *looked* like an entrance wound.

Nevertheless, by the time Dr. Perry testified before the Warren Commission, his attitude had changed, markedly. Although he was still describing the throat wound, anatomically, as a small pencil-size hole, just a quarter inch in diameter, Perry no longer maintained it was a wound of entry. "It could have been either,"[20] he said. And he apparently subscribed to the theory that he had been misquoted at the news conference. "It was bedlam," he said:

There were microphones, and cameras . . . and during the course of it a lot of these hypothetical situations and questions . . . would often be asked by someone on this side and [the answer] recorded by someone on [that]. . . . There were tape recorders there and there were television cameras with their microphones . . . I don't know . . . [a] considerable [number of] questions were not answered in their entirety and even some . . . that were [answered], I am sure were misunderstood.[21]

The notion that the problem with the neck wound was Dr. Perry's fault, that it was simply a misquote heard round the world, was fostered by former CIA Chief Allen Dulles. During Dr. Perry's appearance, Dulles bemoaned the "false rumors that have been spread on the basis of . . . these appearances before television, radio, and so forth and so on."[22] Like a man scolding a small child, he even seemed to suggest that Dr. Perry might wish to clean up the mess he had made. Dulles suggested that all the news clippings that resulted from Perry's statements could be collected

. . . and possibly, if you are willing, sir, you could send us a letter, send to the Commission a letter, pointing out the various points in these press conferences where you are inaccurately quoted.[23]

What Dulles apparently had in mind would have been a major project for Perry, for he suggested that "each clipping [be] dealt with separately."

. . . obviously, if you have answered one point in one clipping it won't be necessary to answer that point if it is repeated in another clipping.[24]

"Yes, sir," answered an apparently chastised Perry, "I can and will do this."* [25]

But what Dr. Perry told reporters (which, as Dulles knew, was of great legal significance) should have been a matter of simple, determinable fact. If so many reporters with tape recorders were there, weren't his words preserved on magnetic tape? Couldn't they be retrieved, transcribed, and studied?

Here again, the twenty-six volumes presented a strange appearance. Numerous transcripts of news conferences held at Police Headquarters were published, made from audio and videotapes obtained from the three major networks and their Dallas affiliates, but Dr. Perry's news conference was not among them.

During the Warren Commission investigation, Arlen Specter requested the Secret Service to obtain videotapes and transcripts of the Parkland press conference. Secret Service Chief James Rowley reported back that after reviewing the material at all the Dallas radio and TV stations, as well as the records of NBC, ABC, and CBS in New York City, "no video tape or transcript could be found of a television interview with Doctor Malcolm Perry."[26]

But a transcript did exist. A special transcript had been made—a White House transcript, the same kind that was made of every presidential news briefing or news conference. This was done because the Dallas doctors' press conference was organized by the White House press staff, who were with the President in Dallas and stayed at Parkland Memorial Hospital afterward.

I knew nothing about this transcript at the time I wrote the *Ramparts* article, and my first hint that any transcript existed came in June 1967 when CBS broadcast a four-part documentary defending the Warren Report. Walter Cronkite, discussing Dr. Perry's first meeting with reporters, said: "The neck wound, Dr. Perry told the press, looked like an entry wound. . . . In the transcript of that news conference there's no doubt that

---

* This, of course, was never done.

Dr. Perry made it sound as if he had a firm opinion."[27] CBS said Dr. Perry was wrong, and Cronkite read no direct quotations by Dr. Perry.

Cronkite's reference to "the transcript" indicated that CBS had a document which no one else seemed to have—certainly not the Warren Commission at the time of the official investigation. I made a fruitless attempt to obtain the transcript from CBS in 1968. In 1976, I learned that an employee of CBS News had located the document, and knew something about its background. I contacted him and was told CBS had secured its copy from a file at the White House in the course of interviews conducted in preparing the 1967 broadcasts. It was an official White House transcript, and its designation was "1327-C."

Eventually I obtained a copy from the Lyndon Johnson Library in Austin, Texas. It was the first "official" news conference in the records of the Johnson White House.

White House transcript 1327-C makes the debate concerning what Dr. Perry said about the throat wound on November 22 academic. The matter came up three times. Each time, Perry said the throat wound was an entrance. Indeed, reading the transcript, I felt I was returning to Parkland Memorial Hospital on November 22, 1963, to the large classroom where the news conference was held, shortly after 3:00 P.M., about an hour after Kennedy's body left the hospital in a coffin.

Excerpts from Transcript 1327-C

White House staff member Wayne Hawks called the meeting to order. "Let me have your attention, please. You wanted to talk to some of the attending physicians. I have two of them here, Dr. Malcolm Perry, an attending surgeon here at Parkland Memorial Hospital. He will talk to you first, and then Dr. Kemp Clark, the chief neurosurgeon here at the hospital. He will tell you what he knows about it. Dr. Perry." (See Photo 13.)

Dr. Perry said he saw two wounds—one in the neck, the other in the head. The neck wound, said Dr. Perry, was "a bullet hole almost in the midline . . . in the lower portion of the neck, in front . . . below the Adam's apple."

Dr. Clark said the head wound was at "the back of his head . . . principally on the right side, toward the right side."

Dr. Perry was asked whether these two wounds could be caused by one bullet, or did two wounds mean two separate shots?

He replied: "That would be conjecture on my part. There are two wounds . . . one of the neck and one of the head. Whether they are directly related, or related to two bullets, I cannot say."

QUESTION: "Where was the entrance wound?"

DR. PERRY: "There was an entrance wound in the neck."

NEXT QUESTION: "Which way was the bullet coming on the neck wound? At him?"

DR. PERRY: "It appeared to be coming at him."

The reporters kept firing questions. One asked: "Can't we clear this up just a little more? In your estimation, was there one or two [shots]? Just give us something."

Dr. Perry said he couldn't tell. The head and neck wounds might be separate, or they might be caused by one bullet.

A reporter asked: "Doctor, describe the entrance wound. You think from the front in the throat?"

Replied Perry: "The wound appeared to be an entrance wound in the front of the throat; yes, that is correct. . . ."

If I had had transcript 1327-C in 1966, the *Ramparts* article could have been a major news story. But I didn't. And neither did the Commission. Because the Secret Service claimed it could locate no tape or transcript of the Parkland Memorial Hospital press conference, that press conference faded from the record.* From the standpoint of available evidence, what Dr. Perry said was arguable. It was Dr. Perry's assertion that he had merely answered some hypothetical questions, versus a pile of news clippings which said otherwise.

The Warren Report dealt with this situation in a peculiar fashion. Of all the media reports available, it cited only one, that of the *New York Herald Tribune,* dated November 23, 1963, a report that indicated Dr. Perry had stated "merely that it was 'possible' "[29] that the throat wound was one of entrance. Thus, the Warren Commission trivialized this conflict by quoting one of the few versions of the Parkland press conference that reported it incorrectly.**

Though some of the doctors stuck to their initial opinion and prac-

* Although Secret Service Chief James Rowley claimed he could locate no tape or transcript of the Parkland Memorial Hospital press conference, Marvin Garson, a researcher assisting Mark Lane in preparing *Rush to Judgment,* was told by Dallas television executive Joe Long, of radio station KLIF, that the original recordings had been seized by Secret Service agents.[28]

** As the White House transcript shows, the *Herald Tribune*'s report was in error. What Dr. Perry said was "possible" and a matter of conjecture was whether the two wounds he observed were caused by a single bullet—one which went in the front of the throat and out the back of the head. In each instance when Dr. Perry was questioned about the throat wound, he unequivocally referred to it as an entrance wound.

The transcript also contradicts Dr. Perry's Warren Commission testimony. Perry testified that his statements about the throat wound being an entrance were in the context of replies to hypothetical questions. The transcript shows that was not true. On three separate occasions, Dr. Perry said the throat wound was an entrance; in no case was his answer in response to hypothetical questions.

tically argued the point during their Warren Commission interviews, others, including Perry, had become remarkably conciliatory. The adamance was gone. There were no further press interviews about the throat wound. Nor did any of them quibble with the findings of the FBI, leaked in December 1963, that Lee Harvey Oswald was the lone assassin, and that all shots had been fired from behind. The most obvious change in the Parkland doctors' attitude can be traced to mid-December 1963; and it came to light solely through the efforts of journalist Richard Dudman of the *St. Louis Post-Dispatch*.

The Dudman Story of December 18, 1963

Dudman was with the White House press in Dallas and doggedly followed the story of the wound at the front of the throat. On December 1, 1963, nine days after the assassination, the *St. Louis Post-Dispatch* published, on page one, his report that the Dallas doctors persisted in describing the throat wound as an entrance wound. UNCERTAINTIES REMAIN DESPITE POLICE VIEW OF KENNEDY DEATH, was the headline, and the subhead read: POSITION OF WOUND IS PUZZLING—DID ASSAILANT HAVE AN ACCOMPLICE?

"The exact circumstances of President John F. Kennedy's assassination may never be explained, despite the several investigations into the case," was Dudman's prophetic lead. He called the location of the front throat wound, and what the Dallas doctors were saying about it, "the strangest circumstance of the shooting, in this reporter's opinion." Noting that the car was already past the building, and that movie films showed Kennedy facing forward, Dudman rather dryly observed: ". . . the question that suggests itself is: How could the President have been shot in the front, from the back?" He emphasized how sure the doctors were that the wound was one of entry:

Dr. Perry described the bullet hole as an entrance wound. Dr. McClelland told the *Post-Dispatch:* "It certainly did look like an entrance wound." He explained that a bullet from a low velocity rifle, like the one thought to have been used, characteristically makes a small entrance wound, sets up shock waves inside the body, and tears a big opening when it passes out the other side.[30]

Dudman's story continued:

Dr. McClelland conceded that it was possible that the throat wound marked the exit of a bullet fired into the back of the President's neck . . . "but we are familiar with wounds," he said. "We see them every day—sometimes several a day. This did appear to be an entrance wound."[31]

During the next week, there was a series of official news leaks that the FBI, in its report to President Johnson, had concluded that Lee Harvey

Oswald was the lone assassin. On December 10, in another front-page story, Dudman raised the throat-wound question again, pointing out that despite the FBI's conclusion, "a check with the [Parkland] hospital last night disclosed that the [Dallas] surgeons have not been questioned by the FBI or any other investigating agency."[32]

Within a day or two of that story, the situation was apparently rectified, as Dudman reported in the final article of his series, published on December 18. SECRET SERVICE GETS REVISION ON KENNEDY WOUND was the headline, and the subhead read: AFTER VISIT BY AGENTS, DOCTORS SAY SHOT WAS FROM REAR.

Dudman reported: "Two Secret Service agents called last week on Dallas surgeons who attended President John F. Kennedy and obtained a reversal of their original view that the bullet in his neck entered from the front.[33]

"The investigators did so by showing the surgeons a document described as an autopsy report from the United States Naval Hospital at Bethesda. The surgeons changed their original view to conform with the report they were shown."[34]

" 'There was no coercion at all,' Dr. Robert N. McClelland told the *Post-Dispatch*. 'They didn't say anything like "This is what you think, isn't it?" ' [35]

"The surgeons' earlier description of a wound in the front of the President's throat as an entry wound had cast doubt on the official belief that Lee Harvey Oswald was the only assassin. . . . The surgeons now support the official view that both bullets that struck the President were from behind. . . . They now believe that the bullet in the neck entered from the back . . . and passed out through the hole in front, about two inches below the Adam's apple."[36]

Why had the doctors been so persuaded? McClelland, reported Dudman, said that the Bethesda autopsy report shown the Dallas doctors "told of an entry wound which the Dallas doctors had *not* seen in the *back of the neck*" [emphasis added], and it described the throat wound as the corresponding exit. Dudman reported why they had failed to see the rear entrance wound: "Dr. McClelland pointed out that the Dallas doctors were with the President's body only about twenty-two minutes and were working to save his life, not to determine the course of the bullets. 'He was lying on his back on the stretcher,' the surgeon said. 'It was not necessary or possible to examine him in the back. My first impression [that the throat wound was one of entry] was the purest kind of supposition.' . . . That conclusion was on the basis of 'no complete history and no complete examination,' he said. By history, he said, he meant the circumstances of where the bullets had come from."[37]

From Dudman's account, it seemed clear that what persuaded the Dallas doctors was the official autopsy report's description of a rear entry wound they had not seen. "Dr. McClelland," reported Dudman, "said that he and Dr. Perry fully accept the Navy Hospital's explanation of the course of the bullets. . . . 'I am fully satisfied that the two bullets that hit him were from behind,' [McClelland] said. 'As far as I am concerned, there is no reason to suspect that any shots came from the front.' "[38]

The Dudman dispatches cast the testimony of the Parkland doctors in an entirely different light and, when read in conjunction with several other *New York Times* stories, revealed a distinctly evolutionary quality in the official position regarding the wound at the front of the throat. For although the Parkland doctors, on about December 10, 1963, were shown a Bethesda autopsy report calling the throat wound one of exit, only five days earlier, on December 5, 1963, the FBI, presumably in possession of the same autopsy, was—according to the *New York Times*—staging a reconstruction in Dallas on the assumption that the throat wound was an entry wound. The *Times* reported a "competent source" as explaining— as Dr. Perry had previously—that "the President had turned to his right to wave, and was struck [in the front of the throat] at that moment."[39]

Similarly, on November 26, four days after the autopsy was performed, an "informed source" explained the front entry by stating that the first shot had been fired when the President's automobile was on Houston Street, approaching the Depository:

. . . [Oswald] started shooting as the President's car was coming toward him, swung his rifle in an arc of almost 180 degrees, and fired at least twice more.[40]

So, judging either by the "competent source" (which had the car on the right street, but the President facing the wrong way) or the "informed source" (which had the car on the wrong street, but the President facing the right way), these stories fueled suspicions that officialdom was acting on the basis of authoritative information—at least as late as December 5, 1963—that the wound at the front of the neck was one of entry. And, in fact, the December 5 *New York Times* dispatch reporting the FBI reconstruction gave further credence to this idea: "The best authority presumabl[y] on the exact angle of entry is the man who conducted the autopsy. He is Dr. J. J. Humes of the Naval Medical Center, Bethesda, Md." The *Times* contacted Commander Humes for some comment about the situation and, in the next sentence, reported to its readers: "Dr. Humes said he has been forbidden to talk."[41]

Thus, when files of news clippings were analyzed in chronological order, they told this bizarre story: On November 22, Dr. Perry said that the throat wound was one of entrance;[42] later that same weekend, he repeated that statement;[43] then, he proceeded to reconcile the rearward location of the Depository with the entrance wound by having the President facing the rear when he was shot.[44] Meanwhile, a November 26 *New York Times* dispatch also had the President facing the Depository by placing his car on Houston Street when the first shot struck.[45] At this point, publication of the Zapruder frames established that when the shots were fired, the car was on Elm Street, had passed the Depository, and that Kennedy was always facing forward. On December 1, the Dudman story asked: "How could the President be shot in the front, from the back?"[46] Five days later, a *New York Times* dispatch reported that the FBI was reenacting the crime in Dallas on the assumption that—the Zapruder film notwithstanding —the throat wound was an entry and Kennedy, having passed the Depository, was hit while turned to the rear;[47] the same story reported that Commander Humes, the autopsy expert on the "exact angle of entry," had been "forbidden to talk."[48] Finally, almost four weeks after the assassination, with all other possibilities apparently unsuccessfully explored, the culminating report appeared with its curiously suggestive headline: SECRET SERVICE GETS REVISION ON KENNEDY WOUND.[49]

It took a person of unusual faith in government pronouncements to believe this entire sequence was innocent, and I was no longer such a person. It seemed to me that many of those stories could be explained by postulating that Dr. Perry had been correct and that the authorities had in their possession official information, perhaps an autopsy report, which said the throat wound was one of entry; and they were desperately trying to reconcile that fact with the rearward location of the alleged assassin.

Furthermore, when considered in conjunction with the "head-snap" issue, the stories showing the "evolution" of the neck wound shattered any remaining faith I had in the autopsy findings published in the Warren Report. All official accounts seemed to agree that the President had been struck twice—non-fatally in the neck, and fatally in the head. Yet on the question of the *direction* of both shots, both so clearly visible on film (the swoop of his hands to his throat, and then, about five seconds later, the violent backward snap of the head), there were strange and suspicious occurrences. If the Zapruder film was to be accepted in its gross implications, the head shot had been fired from the front; and if the initial opinion of the Parkland doctors was correct, then the neck shot also came from the front. As far as I was concerned, belief in the findings of the Commission required, in the one instance, a violation of the laws of physics, and in the other, a universal mistake by Parkland medical personnel followed by a sequence of extraordinary, but nevertheless innocent, events. Neither seemed possible to me.

The questioning of the Dallas doctors by Warren Commission attorney Arlen Specter reinforced my impression that the Commission was attempting to justify its own predetermined conclusion. I could not understand how a proper investigation could, on the one hand, fail to ask the autopsy doctor why he burned notes, and then interrogate the Dallas doctors in a manner that seemed designed to wring a statement from each of them that would support the Commission's position on the throat wound.

To accomplish this, Specter asked each doctor a long hypothetical question, beginning with the phrase, "Permit me to add some facts which I shall ask you to assume as being true," as if he were preparing a special legal brew, and facts could be "added" the way ingredients are in making soup. The cumulative effect of the "added facts," of course, was to force the doctor to provide the answer Specter was seeking; i.e., that the throat wound was one of exit. Typical was the question asked of Dr. Carrico, which began: "Permit me to add some facts which I shall ask you to assume as being true for purposes of having you express an opinion. First of all, assume that the President was struck . . . when [he] was approximately 160 to 250 feet from the weapon [Oswald's range] . . . being struck from the rear at a downward angle . . . on the upper right posterior thorax [the Bethesda entry wound]. . . . Assume further that the missile passed through the body of the President striking no bones, traversing the neck and sliding between the large muscles [the Bethesda autopsy trajectory] . . . then exiting precisely at the point where you observe[d] the puncture wound to exist [the Bethesda exit wound, at the location the Dallas doctors thought there was a wound of entry]. Now based on those facts was the appearance of the wound in your opinion consistent with being an exit wound?"[50]

I found this questioning ludicrous, outrageous. Among other things, one of the facts Specter was asking the doctor to "assume as being true" was that the bullet had exited where they originally said it had entered! No wonder, then, that Specter was able to elicit the testimony he wanted. Lawyers might call this leading questioning, but in "The Case for Three Assassins," we called it "yanked-from-the-mouth testimony."

For example, Dr. Carrico replied: "With those facts and the fact as I understand it no other bullet was found, this would be . . . I believe . . . an exit wound."[51]

Dr. Perry replied: ". . . with the facts which you have made available and with these assumptions, I believe that it was an exit wound."[52]

Nevertheless, some of the Parkland doctors argued with Specter. Dr. Baxter, for example, noted that such a wound would be "unusual . . . ordinarily there would have been a rather large wound of exit."[53] The answer of Dr. Ronald Jones did more to damage Specter's line of inquiry than any other. It was Arlen Specter's hypothesis—later to become a Warren Commission conclusion—that the bullet which exited the front of the President's throat had gone on to strike Governor Connally. This combined trajectory (to be discussed in detail in the next chapter) was known as the "single-bullet theory." For the single-bullet theory to work, the throat wound not only had to be one of exit, but one caused by a missile exiting at eight hundred feet per second (over twelve hundred miles per hour). Otherwise, it would not have the energy necessary to cause all of Connally's wounds. Dr. Jones explained that at that speed, much faster than sound, the missile has a shock wave and, passing through Kennedy's neck, it might wobble, and therefore it would cause a larger wound of exit than the small pencil-size hole the Dallas doctors had seen. Dr. Jones explained that Specter could have his tiny exit wound, or his high-velocity missile, but not both.[54] Specter seemed to resist:

SPECTER: Would it [the Parkland wound] be consistent, then, with an exit wound but of low velocity, as you put it?

JONES: Yes; of very low velocity to the point that you might think that this bullet barely made it through the soft tissues and [had] just enough [velocity] to drop out of the skin on the opposite side.[55]

Of course, such a missile posed no threat to the welfare of Governor Connally, and Dr. Jones' testimony was not discussed in the Warren Report.

Reviewing all the evidence about the throat wound, I thought the strongest point in favor of the Commission's finding was that the Dallas doctors, by their own admission, had not turned the President over, so they had not seen the rear entry wound. But even that was not definitive because even if they had, who can say how that might have affected their opinion that day? It might not have changed Dr. Perry's opinion at all. The throat wound did, after all, *look* like an entrance wound. Dr. Perry and the others might have concluded that the President was shot from *both* directions, and then stepped before the microphones and cameras and said exactly that. It was impossible to know what might have happened. What seemed clear was that the Dallas doctors, faced afterward with the fact that they had missed a rear entry wound, appeared embarrassed at having spoken out of turn and on the basis of incomplete information, and were unwilling to buck the entire United States government.

In the spring of 1966, then, the issue of the throat wound devolved to a matter of simple credibility, and, at that time, I just did not believe Commander Humes. He was a military doctor—a man reporting to military superiors. He had illustrated his testimony with an artist's drawing, in circumstances where any court would have routinely demanded the production of autopsy photographs and X-rays, and he had inexplicably burned papers, an act which had not been properly investigated by the Commission which was utilizing his testimony as the basis for its major findings about the direction of the shots. Furthermore, his autopsy conclusions seemed the culmination of a whole string of half-baked ideas, and of a process of trial and error much of which, incredibly enough, seemed to have been reported in the newspapers.

Yet in the final analysis, I had to make a frustrating admission: The evidence I had assembled did not prove that the throat wound was one of entrance. Legally, an autopsy report has much greater weight than the clinical opinions of doctors.

The initial medical opinion of the Dallas doctors was smoke, but not fire. It was evidence indicating something was wrong. It was one more piece of the puzzle—and it took its place, as such, in "The Case for Three Assassins."

CHAPTER 4

The Zapruder Film and the Timing Problem

THE KENNEDY ASSASSINATION resembles a gigantic puzzle. The twenty-six volumes and the National Archives contain a wide variety of data, so it was necessary to have a flexible scheme for sorting facts. The working hypothesis I proposed in 1966 was the "three-assassin model," not because I believed Kennedy was murdered by a conspiracy of exactly three shooters, but because that model provided the simplest way of explaining a variety of medical, ballistic, and eyewitness data about the shooting.

Why the necessity for a "third assassin"? Why not just two—one up front, inferred from the "grassy-knoll" evidence, and one to the rear, at the "sniper's nest"? Because additional data, unrelated to the grassy knoll, indicated two gunmen were shooting from behind.

The critical problem was the timing of two shots which, according to the Commission, struck from the rear in less time than it takes to fire the sniper's rifle twice.

The back-to-front trajectory through Kennedy's neck was a conclusion of the Kennedy autopsy. The back-to-front trajectory through Connally resulted from the combined testimony and medical reports of the Dallas doctors who treated his wounds. The timing conflict arose because the Commission had in its evidence the home movie taken by bystander Abraham Zapruder, which was tantamount to a clock—one that told time in eighteenths of a second. FBI Lab tests determined that 18.3 frames of film passed through the camera each second.[1] Each produced a photograph of the car as it proceeded down the street; indeed, each frame corresponded to a specific location of the car on Elm Street. Since the frames were separated by eighteenths of a second, the time between any two events could be obtained by simply counting the number of frames between them.

The time squeeze developed because the alleged murder weapon was a bolt-action rifle and there was an upper limit, imposed by its mechanism, to the rapidity with which it could be fired. When the rifle was tested by the FBI Lab to determine the time required to operate the bolt and then reload, it was found to have a minimum firing time of 2.3 seconds, or forty-two frames on the Zapruder film.*[2] The Commission's own analysis, however, revealed that there was a "time-window" only thirty frames wide (between frames 210 and 240) during which both men had to be hit—if the shots were fired from the sniper's nest at the sixth floor of the Texas School Book Depository.[3] (See Fig. 2.)

Thus, the FBI Lab data established that only *one* shot could have been fired during a time span when, according to the Commission, *both* men had been hit. For example, if the first shot was squeezed off at frame 210, then another could not have been fired until frame 252; but the Commission's analysis established that Connally had been hit by frame 240.[4]

I could easily visualize what this meant in terms of the Commission's attempt to reconstruct the crime. Its case against Oswald centered upon the alleged murder weapon, the rather difficult-to-operate 1938 bolt-action rifle. According to the medical data, both men, who were seated one in front of the other, were struck from the rear. According to the timing data, both were struck in less than the minimum time necessary to fire successive shots. The alternatives: either one bullet passed through both men, or there was a second gunman firing from behind.

In one of its most controversial findings, the Commission concluded that a single bullet passed back-to-front through Kennedy's neck, and went on to produce all five of the Governor's wounds—entering at the extreme right side of his back, traveling through his right chest in a downward and forward direction, exiting from beneath his right nipple, passing through his right wrist, and then wounding his left thigh. This is known as the "single-bullet theory." As Warren Commission attorney Norman Redlich succinctly put it, "To say that they were hit by separate bullets is synonymous with saying that there were two assassins."[5]

No one claimed that a high-powered rifle bullet could not make this journey through two men—only that, in this particular case, it did not happen that way. Considered together, the objections to the single-bullet theory comprised the case for the "third assassin."

Those objections fell into four main categories.

1. The Zapruder Film Showed the Two Hits Were Separate. Students of the Zapruder film argued that the film showed the event just didn't happen that way, that for at least ten film frames after the President was visibly

* That did not include any time to aim the rifle.

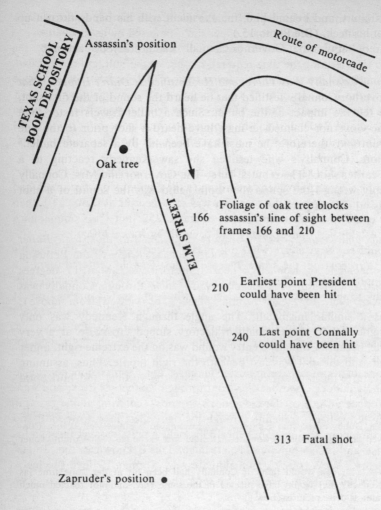

Figure 2.
Elm Street map, with Zapruder film frame numbers

reacting—frames 223–233, approximately—the Governor showed no sign of having been hit. Only after frame 233 did he react.

This argument was so persuasive that *Life* magazine, which owned the film, devoted a cover story to it in November 1966. Large white letters on an all-black cover asked: DID OSWALD ACT ALONE? A MATTER OF REASONABLE DOUBT. On the cover was frame 230, showing Governor Connally, apparently unhurt, and behind him, the President with his hands thrown up in front of his neck. (See Photo 15.)

The rebuttal was that Governor Connally had a delayed reaction.*

2. Governor Connally Was There, and He Testified It Didn't Happen That Way. Governor Connally testified that he heard the sound of the first shot, and *then* felt the impact of the bullet. Since a bullet travels faster than sound, the Governor claimed he must have heard a shot prior to the one that hit him and, therefore, he must have been hit by a separate bullet.[8] Furthermore, Connally's wife testified she saw Kennedy reacting to a separate, earlier shot.[9] The rebuttal here: The Governor and Mrs. Connally were simply wrong—the sound they both heard was the sound of a shot which missed the car entirely.

3. Connally and Kennedy Were Not Properly Aligned for the Single-Bullet Trajectory. (See Photo 16.) Critics noted that, according to the Bethesda autopsy, the angle of Kennedy's neck trajectory was about 17 degrees (to the horizontal), whereas the downward angle through Connally was almost twice that. In the horizontal plane (i.e., viewed from above), there was a similar mismatch: The angle through Kennedy was only slightly right to left; the Connally trajectory sloped crosswise at a very steep angle, because Connally's entry wound was on the extreme right, under the armpit, and the exit was just beneath the right nipple. Thus, assuming normal posture, the medical diagrams in *both* the vertical and horizontal

---

* When the Zapruder film was screened by the Warren Commission, Commissioner Allen Dulles noted that Kennedy was reacting to a bullet well before Connally showed any sign of being wounded. He had this exchange with Commissioner John McCloy:

> DULLES: . . . you would think if Connally had been hit at the same time [as Kennedy, he] would have reacted in the same way, and not reacted much later as these pictures show.
>
> MCCLOY: That is right.
>
> DULLES: Because the wounds would have been inflicted.
>
> MCCLOY: That is what puzzles me.
>
> DULLES: That is what puzzles me.[6]

Despite the fact that the shot which struck Connally—assuming he was hit only once—shattered ten centimeters of his rib, fractured his right wrist into several pieces, and pierced his left thigh, the Commission argued that Connally had a delayed reaction. On this point, the testimony of Dr. Robert Shaw, the Parkland surgeon who treated the Governor's chest wounds, is illuminating:

> MCCLOY: But there could be a delay in any appreciable reaction between the time of the impact of the bullet and the occurrence?
>
> SHAW: Yes; but in the case of a wound which strikes a bony substance such as a rib, usually the reaction is quite prompt.[7]

planes failed to match; in addition, no frame of the Zapruder film showed the two men in the alignment necessary for the combined trajectory.

The rebuttal: Kennedy and Connally were probably hit by the "single bullet" when both were obscured by the sign and, therefore, not visible on the film.*

4. No Bullet Ever Transited Kennedy's Neck on a Downward-Sloping Trajectory. The Warren Commission concluded, based on the Bethesda autopsy, that the first shot to strike Kennedy, the non-fatal shot, "entered at the back of his neck and exited through the lower front portion of his neck,"[13] nicking Kennedy's necktie knot as it exited. This conclusion that a bullet *transited* Kennedy's neck was critical. Obviously, Governor Connally could not have been struck by the same bullet which hit Kennedy *unless* that missile first passed completely through Kennedy's body. Thus, a transiting neck trajectory was the medico-legal foundation for the single-bullet theory and, had the Bethesda autopsy report contained some *other* conclusion, the one-bullet/two-victim theory could never have been posited in the first place.

Consequently, all medical evidence that contradicted that transiting conclusion impugned the single-bullet theory as well. These arguments could be viewed as attacks on the integrity of the autopsy report and represented an implicit accusation that the Bethesda autopsy findings were

---

* During the Commission's investigation, Arlen Specter attempted to elicit testimony from the FBI firearms expert, Robert Frazier, that both Kennedy and Connally were properly aligned to be struck by a single bullet. Frazier was asked to give his expert opinion on the basis of a set of highly questionable assumptions:

SPECTER: . . . Mr. Frazier, assuming the factors which I have asked you to accept as true . . . as to the flight of the bullet and the straight-line penetration through the President's body . . . do you have an opinion as to what probably happened during the interval between frames 207 and 225 as to whether the bullet which passed through the neck of the President entered the Governor's back?

FRAZIER: There are a lot of probables in that. First, we have to assume there is absolutely no deflection in the bullet from the time it left the barrel until the time it exited from the Governor's body. . . . I feel that physically this would have been possible. . . . However, I myself don't have any technical evidence . . . which would support it as far as my rendering an opinion as an expert. I would certainly say it was possible but I don't say that it probably occurred because I don't have the evidence on which to base a statement like that.[10]

Frazier elaborated: "We are dealing with a hypothetical situation here. . . . So when you say would it probably have occurred, then you are asking me for an opinion, to base my opinion on a whole series of hypothetical facts which I can't substantiate."[11]

Despite this, the Warren Report stated: ". . . Frazier testified that it probably struck Governor Connally."[12]

deliberately fudged to accommodate the single-bullet theory. There were three general arguments: (1) that the throat wound was one of entrance; (2) that the back wound was lower than the throat wound; and (3) that there was no path through the body.

The throat wound was one of entrance, not exit.

As previously noted, the initial opinion of the Dallas doctors was that the throat wound was an entrance. I believed that it was and this belief affected my interpretation of Kennedy's movements on the Zapruder film, my conception of how the shooting took place, and my opinion, at the time, of the honesty of the autopsy examination.

If the throat wound was an entrance, it meant that when President Kennedy appeared on the Zapruder film emerging from behind the highway sign and raising his hands toward his throat, he was reacting to a bullet which had just been fired by an assassin hiding somewhere toward the front. Furthermore, an entry wound in the throat rendered irrelevant all arguments over whether Kennedy's and Connally's reactions were separated by too great a time period for both to have been hit by a single bullet fired from behind. Obviously, both men weren't hit by the same bullet if Kennedy was struck from the front.

My view of the throat wound allied me with the more radical critics, for it implied the autopsy was not just incorrect, but deliberately false. It meant there was a bullet somewhere in the President's body which hadn't been reported by the autopsy doctors. That's what I believed at that time. The bullet must have remained inside the body because the only other wound of exit was in the head.*

What, then, became of the bullet? Where did it lodge? I had no specific theory, but in preparing the *Ramparts* article, we quoted a *New York Times* dispatch filed four days after the assassination:

Dallas, Nov. 26 . . . Dr. Kemp Clark, who pronounced Mr. Kennedy dead, said one [bullet] struck him at about the necktie knot. "It ranged downward in his chest and did not exit," the surgeon said.[14]

The back wound was lower than the front throat wound; hence, even if the throat wound was an exit, the trajectory sloped upward, not downward.

The timing problem and the height of the back wound were closely related. Only if the rear entry was high enough could the bullet be said to have transited on a downward-sloping trajectory. Only if the wound was high enough could the single-bullet theory be true.

When Humes testified, he brought with him three artist's drawings

---

* The back wound was definitely not an exit wound. The head wound couldn't be the exit, because the Zapruder film established it was caused by another shot fired more than five seconds after Kennedy reacted to his throat wound.

depicting Kennedy's wounds which were accepted in evidence by the Commission in lieu of the X-rays and photographs. One of these—Warren Commission Exhibit 385—showed a large arrow passing through the neck from back to front, tilted downward at an angle of about 17 degrees to the horizontal. The front portion of the arrow, labeled "out," passed through the site of Dr. Perry's tracheotomy incision; the rear portion, labeled "in," entered the President's body through a wound at the back of the neck, just about where the bottom of the neck joins the top of the right shoulder. In accordance with this drawing, the Warren Report referred to the rear entry wound as being located "at the back of his neck,"[15] and "near the base of the back of President Kennedy's neck, slightly to the right of his spine."[16] (See Photo 16A.)

Discussing the exact trajectory angle, the Warren Report gave the impression of great precision, solemnly stating: "The probable angle through the President's body was calculated at 17° 43′ 30″."[17] That conjured up a standard of accuracy normally associated with a scientific laboratory—or an astronomical observatory. It was akin to reporting the time of the assassination down to the thousandth of a second.

The numbers came from an elaborate re-enactment of the assassination the Commission staged in Dallas.*

Given this preoccupation with precision and the fact that the trajectory through Kennedy's neck and, consequently, the entire single-bullet trajectory, would have been dramatically affected if the rear entry was not exactly where it was supposed to be, it aroused considerable suspicion to find so much evidence in the twenty-six volumes contradicting Humes' artist's drawing, and indicating that the rear wound was not in the back of President Kennedy's neck at all, but a good deal lower. Indeed, about a half foot lower, about six inches below the top of the right shoulder, in the President's *back*.

If that was so, then the single-bullet theory was clearly a construct, based on a false Bethesda autopsy conclusion.

The Clothing Holes. (See Photos 17 and 18.) FBI ballistics expert Robert A. Frazier testified to the Commission that the back of the President's coat and shirt contained matching holes located five and three-eighth

---

* A car similar to the Presidential limousine was used, two FBI agents acted as models for Kennedy and Connally, and the clothing of each was marked with chalk where the bullet allegedly entered. In addition, a camera rigged to take a picture through the telescopic sight of the rifle provided a view from the sniper's nest. The Report stated that to determine the exact angle of the neck trajectory, the limousine was placed at the spot on Elm Street where that shot supposedly struck, and "A surveyor . . . placed his sighting equipment at the precise point of entry on the back of the President's neck . . . and measured the angle to the end of the muzzle of the rifle. . . ."[18] After correcting for the slope of Elm Street, the Report came up with its monument to accuracy: 17 degrees, 43 minutes, 30 seconds.

inches and five and three-quarter inches, respectively, from the top of the collars of those two garments.[19] It is obvious that a hole located nearly a half-foot down from the top of the collar does not correspond to a wound described as being "in the rear of the neck."

Possibly, Arlen Specter and Commander Humes had discussed the matter of the "low" clothing holes sometime before his testimony. This could be inferred from the glib manner in which the two addressed the point. The Commission explanation was that when the President waved to the crowd, his clothing rode up on his back.*

The Commission presented no evidence to support this theory, and a photograph taken at the time did not show the President's coat climbing up his neck.**

Secret Service Testimony. Secret Service Agent Glenn Bennett, riding in the right rear seat of the follow-up car behind the President when the shots were fired, stated, "I looked at the back of the President. I heard another firecracker noise and saw the shot hit the President about *four inches down from the right shoulder* [emphasis added]."[21] The Commission accorded "substantial weight" to Bennett's observations, adding: "His notes indicated that he recorded what he saw and heard at 5:30 P.M., November 22, 1963, on the airplane en route back to Washington, prior to the autopsy, when it was not yet known that the President had been hit in the back."***[22]

Significantly, Bennett's observations as to where the shot struck were consistent with the clothing holes as well as the location given by those at the autopsy who actually saw the wound on the body.

The most explicit testimony on this subject to be found anywhere in the twenty-six volumes was that of Secret Service Agent Clinton Hill. Hill was brought to the morgue by Agent Roy Kellerman, after midnight, for the

---

* SPECTER: As to the muscular status of the President, what was it?

HUMES: The President was extremely well developed, an extremely well-developed, muscular young man with a very well-developed set of muscles in his thoraco and shoulder girdle.

SPECTER: What effect would that have on the positioning of the shirt and coat with respect to the position of the [President's] neck in and about the seam?

HUMES: I believe this would have a tendency to push the portions of the coat which show the defects here somewhat higher on the back of the President than on a man of less muscular development.[20]

** Furthermore, while the coat could conceivably crease, it appeared physically impossible for a closed shirt collar to be lifted four to six inches when the President raised his right hand to wave, yet that was what it had to do to comport with the "high" position shown in Commission Exhibit 385, the artist's drawing used to show the trajectory through the President's neck.

*** The Commission, ignoring the "low" hit described by Bennett, used his testimony to support its claim that Kennedy's non-fatal wounds were caused by a bullet fired from behind.

specific purpose of viewing the wounds. When Arlen Specter asked Kellerman why he had done so, Kellerman replied: "More witnesses, Mr. Specter; I think more to view the unfortunate happenings it would be a little better [*sic*]."[23] Hill was questioned by Congressman Hale Boggs:

BOGGS: Did you see any other wound other than the head wound?

HILL: Yes, sir; I saw an opening in the back, about six inches below the neckline to the right-hand side of the spinal column.[24]

The testimony of Secret Service Agent Hill was corroborated by that of both Roy Kellerman and William Greer, who were both present throughout the autopsy. Greer described the rear wound as being "in the soft part of that shoulder."[25] Kellerman described it as "the hole that was in his shoulder."[26] Neither man described it as a neck wound.

The Autopsy Diagram. (See Fig. 3.) The 26 volumes contained a set of standard autopsy body charts—one a rear view of the body, the other a

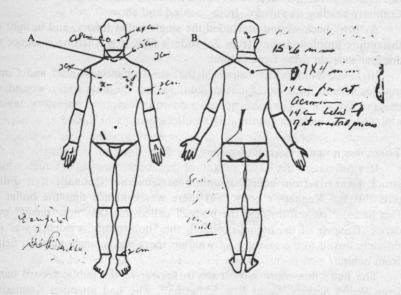

Figure 3.
Autopsy diagram annotated at the time of the postmortem
Note that the rear wound is marked as a back or shoulder wound (see "B" on rear view at right) and not as a neck wound, as shown on navy artist's drawing prepared in March 1964 under Humes' supervision and used during Warren Commission testimony. (See Photo 16A.) Also note that on this diagram, the rear wound is depicted as lower than the wound at the front of the throat (marked by "A").

front view—annotated by the doctors during the autopsy. On the front diagram, the location of the tracheotomy wound is clearly shown, and it is barely below the collar line.[27] On the companion (rear-view) diagram, the rear entry is depicted by a dot.[28] That dot is much further below the collar line—at a location consistent with the clothing holes, and the testimony of Secret Service Agent Clint Hill. During his testimony, no one asked Dr. Humes to explain the discrepancy.

All this evidence—the testimony of the Secret Service agents who saw the wound, the placement of the dot on the pathologist's diagram, and the holes in the President's clothing—suggested that the rear wound was "low," about six inches below the top of the collar, and hence below the frontal throat wound which pierced the knot in the President's necktie. Any bullet entering at that "low" location and traveling downward would have exited—if it exited at all—below the breast line, even if it traveled downward only at the relatively shallow angle of 17 degrees. If the bullet was somehow deflected and traveled upward, passing out through the wound at the front of the neck, then it would have flown harmlessly over the Governor's head. Clearly, such a bullet could not have been the one which struck Connally heading downward, from "behind and above."

A "low" back wound precluded the single-bullet theory, and in light of the timing problem arising from Zapruder's film, it was strong evidence of another assassin firing from behind.

In 1966, many critics suspected that the Commission staff and Commander Humes had modified the data, raising the rear entry wound so that the two wounds were aligned on a downward-sloping trajectory, laying a plausible foundation for the single-bullet theory.

There was no path through the body.

Regardless of the exact height of the back wound, a bullet which struck Kennedy from behind couldn't hit Governor Connally if it didn't pass through Kennedy's body. Yet there was evidence that the bullet in fact had not passed through the body. I called this the "non-transit" evidence. Because of the timing problem, the "non-transit" evidence was intimately linked to the question of whether there was a single assassin firing from behind.

The first "non-transit" evidence to appear in the public record came from Secret Service Agent Roy Kellerman, who had attended Kennedy's autopsy. When the twenty-six volumes were released, critics focused on the following snippet of his testimony. Kellerman testified:

There were three gentlemen who were performing this autopsy. A Colonel Finck —during the examination of the President, from the hole that was in his shoulder, and with a probe, and we were standing right alongside of him, he is probing inside the shoulder with his instrument and I said, "Colonel, where did it go?" He said, "There are no lanes for an outlet of this entry in this man's shoulder."[29]

If Kellerman's description could be credited, the wound went nowhere —it was a shallow hole which simply terminated. The bullet which caused it, therefore, could not have struck Connally.

Kellerman's testimony was corroborated by Secret Service Agent William Greer, also present at the autopsy:

SPECTER: Was anything said about any channel being present in the body for the bullet to have gone on through the back?

GREER: No, sir; I hadn't heard anything like that, any trace of it going on through.[30]

In 1969, at the Shaw trial, Colonel Finck testified the wound's depth was "the first fraction of an inch."[31]

The Warren Report and Evidence the Autopsy Was Changed

Since the Warren Commission's reconstruction of the crime was based on an autopsy with a "high" back wound and a transiting neck trajectory, the critics fastened on contrary data in the public record and used it to formulate a theory the autopsy had been changed.

Evidence for that theory came from early news reports, and the Warren Report itself.

On December 18, 1963, the *Washington Post* and the *New York Times* published stories quoting "official" sources familiar with the autopsy. The autopsy findings, the *Post* reported, disclosed that a bullet, fired from the rear, "was found deep in his shoulder," adding that it "hit the President in the back shoulder five to seven inches below the collar line."[32] The *Times* said "the first bullet made what was described as a small, neat wound in the back and penetrated *two or three inches* [emphasis added]."[33] In January, the *Times* reported that the first bullet "hit the President in the back of his right shoulder, several inches below the collar line. That bullet lodged in his shoulder."[34]

Under normal circumstances, the autopsy report itself—not news stories about its reported conclusions—should be the most reliable source of information about the autopsy findings. But the Bethesda autopsy report was not made public until ten months after the assassination, when it first appeared as Appendix IX of the Warren Report. Given the reputation of the *Washington Post* and the *New York Times*, it was reasonable to believe that both papers based their accounts on sources who had access to official documents.

Several odd passages in a section of the Warren Report titled "The President's Neck Wounds" suggested there was something to news reports of "non-transit" as well as to Kellerman's testimony, and that the autopsy had in fact been changed. Two paragraphs, which had a rather defensive ring, were devoted to describing events which occurred during a time period referred to as "the early stages of the autopsy." The Report conceded that during these "earlier stages," the Bethesda doctors had been "unable to find a path."[35]

According to the Report, the doctors "at that time . . . did not know that there had been a bullet hole in the front of the President's neck when he arrived at Parkland Memorial Hospital because the tracheotomy incision had completely eliminated that evidence."[36]

I found this explanation hard to swallow. The implication was that Humes didn't find a path because he didn't even suspect the bullet exited—all this because he thought the hole at the front of the throat was simply a tracheotomy, and was unaware the tracheotomy was done over a bullet wound. But on November 22, 1963, news of that wound was on both wire services, and hence on all major radio and TV networks.

Another factor, implied the Report, created confusion: "While the autopsy was being performed, surgeons learned that a whole bullet had been found at Parkland Memorial Hospital on a stretcher which, at that time, was thought to be the stretcher occupied by the President. This led to speculation that the bullet might have penetrated a short distance into the back of the neck and then dropped out onto the stretcher as a result of the external heart massage."[37]

The Warren Report was careful to assert that Commander Humes had never actually concluded that the bullet failed to transit, claiming that the "theory" that the bullet only penetrated a short distance was rejected "during the autopsy."[38]

As Commander Humes continued his examinations, said the Report, he found that the bullet *had* transited the President's neck: "the surgeons determined that the bullet had passed between two large strap muscles and bruised them without leaving any channel."[39]

Thus, the Report implied there was a passage through the body, but no clear evidence of a path.

By the next morning, said the Report, when Humes telephoned Dr. Perry, he had already concluded that a bullet passed back to front through the neck and exited at the site of Dr. Perry's tracheotomy incision. Humes then received confirmation for this when Perry informed him he had performed his tracheotomy over a bullet wound.

Legally, it was an important distinction that Humes' call to Perry merely "confirmed" a conclusion he had already reached.* Otherwise, if

---

* From page 89 of the Warren Report: "Commander Humes, who believed that a tracheotomy had been performed from his observations at the autopsy, talked by telephone with Dr. Perry early on the morning of November 23, and learned that

Humes changed the autopsy after speaking with Perry and learning for the first time from *him* about another bullet wound, then the autopsy, as evidence, would be considerably weakened. For the critical "transit" conclusion, so essential to the single-bullet theory, would be only a *deduction* made after the autopsy, and not the result of direct examination of the body.

Humes himself testified the doctors had never actually found a continuous track: "Attempts to probe in the vicinity of this wound were unsuccessful without fear of making a false passage. . . . We were unable . . . to take probes and have them satisfactorily fall through any definite path. . . ."[40] When McCloy said, "I am not clear what induced you to come to that conclusion [that the bullet transited] if you couldn't find the actual exit wound by reason of the tracheotomy," the autopsy surgeon replied: "The report which we have submitted, sir, represents our thinking within the 24–48 hours of the death of the President, all facts taken into account of the situation."[41] What other "facts" played a role in the formulation of his autopsy conclusions?

Many critics thought the fine distinctions made by Humes and the Commission about when he learned of the throat wound, and when he formulated his "transit" conclusion, masked something sinister: an autopsy conclusion changed at the behest of the Warren Commission. A coverup had occurred: First the Commission had discovered the timing problem; then Humes was induced to make the change from non-transit to transit to lay the foundation for the single-bullet theory.*

---

his assumption was correct and that Dr. Perry had used the missile wound in the neck as the point to make the incision. This confirmed the Bethesda surgeons' conclusion that the bullet had exited from the front part of the neck."

* And, according to this theory, Commander Humes, by claiming that Dr. Perry's tracheotomy incision caused him to be ignorant of the throat wound, was deliberately inserting into his own testimony a justification for accounts emanating from the autopsy room that the bullet had not transited. By saying there had been "confusion" at Bethesda, accounts such as Kellerman's, contrary to the final conclusion, could be explained away.

On this point, Vincent Salandria's original article in the March 1965 issue of *Liberation* set the tone. After quoting the Report's claim that Humes did not know about the bullet wound at the front of the throat, Salandria wrote:

"In the above dissertation, the Warren Report asks of the reader that he swallow the idea that the tracheotomy incision had 'completely eliminated' the evidence of a bullet hole in the front of the neck. The Report begs the reader to believe that Commander Humes did not know what the Parkland Hospital doctors were telling the world on the 22nd of November, i.e., that President Kennedy had suffered a wound in the front of the neck through which a tracheotomy was performed. They ask us to believe that the government pathologists at Bethesda undertook an autopsy on the evening of November 22nd, 1963, on the President without consulting with any doctor at Parkland Hospital in Dallas. We are asked to believe that Commander

Despite these suspicions, it was impossible to prove such chicanery. Kellerman's testimony, standing alone, certainly didn't overturn the Commission's finding that a bullet transited the President's neck. And the mismatch between the "low" clothing holes and the "high" neck wound, while suspicious, didn't prove the autopsy had been changed.

Nevertheless, I viewed the "transit" autopsy conclusion skeptically. Like most critics, I thought the December 1963 news stories, Kellerman's testimony, and the "low" clothing holes were evidence the autopsy report published in the Warren Report was not the original.

What no one suspected, however, was that stored at the National Archives, in the unpublished files of the Commission, was documentary evidence indicating the existence of such an "earlier autopsy report"— evidence far stronger than anything yet in the public record.

The FBI Summary Reports and the Transit/Non-Transit Conflict

Early in 1966, the National Archives released the FBI Summary Report on the Assassination—a four-volume work summarizing the FBI's findings as of early December 1963. Also released was the FBI Supplemental Report, dated January 13, 1964.

The December 9, 1963, report stated:

Medical examination of the President's body revealed that one of the bullets had entered just below his shoulder to the right of the spinal column at an angle of 45 to 60 degrees downward, that there was *no point of exit, and that the bullet was not in the body* [emphasis added].[42]

The January 13, 1964, report repeated the non-transit assertion:

Medical examination of the President's body had revealed that the bullet which entered his back had penetrated to *a distance of less than a finger length* [emphasis added].[43]

Humes talked with Dr. Perry of Parkland Hospital for the first time on November 23, 1963. Such an idea seems to fly in the face of common sense."

Later, Salandria continued his theme that the transiting trajectory was a construct employed to account for the shooting in terms of three shots:

"No small wonder it was that the idea did not immediately occur to the pathologists that this hit down in the President's back emerged high up in the front portion of his neck. Such unusual insights germinate in the human mind only after considerable time is devoted to the consideration of the possible existence of more plausible alternatives. In this case, apparently, there were no other alternatives available. That accursed shortage of ammunition which restricted the Commission to but three shots interposed itself again."

Besides being unequivocal on the question of transit, both reports gave a "low" description of the rear wound, consistent with the clothing holes. The December 9 report said it was located "just below his shoulder"; the January 13, 1964, report said it was in the "back."[44]

The FBI documents stated the information being reported came from "medical examination of the President's body." That implied there had been an earlier, different version of the Bethesda autopsy. What else could be meant by "medical examination" other than the Bethesda autopsy? It seemed reasonable the FBI would have had a copy since the Bureau had been charged by President Johnson with investigating the assassination. The FBI, it seemed, had gone to press with the earlier version.

That, essentially, was the view put forth in Edward Epstein's *Inquest*, published in May 1966, and the first book to make use of the FBI Summary and Supplemental Reports, documents the author acquired about eight months before they were released at the National Archives. And how had Epstein, a graduate student at Cornell, obtained copies? From none other than Wesley J. Liebeler.

Liebeler had a farm in Newfane, Vermont, and on June 30, 1965, about three months before I met Liebeler at UCLA, Epstein interviewed him there for his master's thesis.[45]

On his farm, Liebeler had a small personal archive from his days on the Commission, a collection that journalist Fletcher Knebel, who wrote an article about Epstein's book, described as "a treasure trove of documents that indicated fights within the Commission and possible substantive errors by the Commission." Liebeler permitted Epstein access to some of that evidence. When Epstein saw the FBI Summary Report with the "non-transit" autopsy conclusion, he was convinced he had found evidence the Warren Commission had changed the Kennedy autopsy findings. Knebel said Epstein's research then became "freighted with excitement as he followed the tracks of what seemed to be a big story."[46]

Liebeler, at a public meeting in New York in September 1966 claimed that Epstein's access to the documents was accidental.* However it hap-

---

* Wesley Liebeler was a panelist at a discussion of the Warren Report at the *Theatre of Ideas* in New York City on September 30, 1966.

Conceding that much of Epstein's book was based on "my own personal files that I let him look at," Liebeler explained: "He came up to my farm in Vermont and advised me that he had been given access to the files in the Archives. So I said 'Fine, in that case, you can look at mine. I'm too busy to talk to you right now.' He looked at my files [and] it later turned out that he hadn't in fact been given access to the Commission's files, and so when his book came out about a year later, I discovered that I had in effect written a book for Mr. Epstein, or a very large part of it, or made substantial contributions to it. So I think, in a sense, I'm perhaps closer to the underpinnings of Epstein's book than anybody else, [with the] possible exception of Mr. Epstein himself, who unfortunately isn't here tonight. He's in England, selling his book."[47]

pened, Epstein emerged from Liebeler's barn with Warren Commission documents which were, at the time, still withheld by the FBI.

The FBI's Summary and Supplemental Reports were large spiral-bound documents with big print and wide margins. They appeared superficial. Indeed, compared with the Warren Report, the FBI assassination report read like a child's picture book. Yet had the Commission not been created, this might have constituted the Government's official report on Kennedy's murder.

Earl Warren and his colleagues were not particularly impressed. Publicly, in December 1963, they praised the FBI, muting their criticism, noting that the report was "skeletal," and announcing they had requested the Bureau supply the individual FBI agents' reports, on which the Summary Report was based. Behind closed doors, the Commissioners were disquieted by the FBI's product.*

Commissioner McCloy was puzzled: "Let's find out about these wounds, it is just as confusing now as could be. It left my mind muddy as to what really did happen. . . . Why did the FBI report come out with something which isn't consistent with the autopsy when we finally see the autopsy?"[50]

Critics asked the same question. The FBI information comprised only a few sentences in a five-volume work; yet Epstein structured his entire book around those sentences. Similarly, Mark Lane, whose *Rush to Judgment* was just going to press, quickly amended his chapter dealing with the medical evidence.

Both authors set the stage by juxtaposing these two facts:

—a transiting trajectory like the one in the navy autopsy was essential to the Commission's single-bullet theory;

—the FBI Summary Reports stated that the bullet did not transit.

Which was true: the autopsy conclusion reported by the FBI or by the Warren Commission? Epstein commented: "One of these documents changed a central fact of the assassination."[51]

---

* The conversations quoted here are from transcripts of the Commission's Executive Sessions, which weren't declassified until the spring of 1968.

Commissioner Allen Dulles complained: ". . . I think they [the FBI] ought to assume the responsibility of writing them so we can read them." Commissioner John McCloy defended the Bureau: "I think that you've got to bear in mind that they were under pressure to get this to us, and this only purports to be a summary. The grammar is bad and you can see they did not polish it all up. It does leave you some loopholes in this thing but I think you have to realize they put this thing together very fast."[48] When the conversation turned to one of the more glaring loopholes, here was the Commissioners' perplexed reaction:

BOGGS: There's nothing in there about Governor Connally.
WARREN: No.
COOPER: And whether or not they found any bullets in him.
MCCLOY: This bullet business leaves me confused.
WARREN: It's totally inconclusive.[49]

Epstein said the change took place sometime after January 13, 1964, the date of the FBI Supplemental Report, and clearly implied that it happened after January 27, when the Commission screened the Zapruder film and discovered the timing problem. Lane said essentially the same thing—the "original" autopsy report had been "withdrawn and modified."

But the two men, whose books dominated the 1966–67 debate, parted ways as to what this meant.

Lane, believing Oswald to be innocent, suggested in *Rush to Judgment* that the "original" autopsy report had been changed to support the Commission's preconception that Lee Harvey Oswald was the lone assassin.[52] In public lectures, Lane was less polite: He practically came right out and said the Warren Commission had framed Lee Harvey Oswald.

Epstein took a different tack. He, too, accused the Commission of deliberately lying. But, believing Oswald to be guilty, he implied the Commission was justified.

Epstein argued that the Commission had a dual purpose: to ascertain facts, but also to dispel rumors. Everything was fine as long as the two coincided, as when its investigative machinery could be put to work exposing false and malicious gossip. But suppose a particular "conspiracy" allegation appeared, on closer inspection, to have substance? That's when the Commission displayed its split personality—if not a double standard—in evaluating evidence. For example, when confronted with the allegation that Oswald was a government informant, J. Lee Rankin said: "We do have a dirty rumor . . . and it must be wiped out insofar as it is possible to do so by this Commission."[53] Epstein described the Commission's behavior in looking for innocent explanations as a quest after "political truth."

I first read *Inquest* in June 1966. I thought Epstein was wading in very deep waters when he extended his "political truth" concept to the deliberate falsification of the Kennedy autopsy. It was one thing for lawyers to ignore ugly alternatives, but falsifying an autopsy meant changing a written record, and that would be a complex and most deliberate act. It would involve more than erasing a line or two in a section marked "Conclusions." The report was handwritten by Humes, who gave sworn testimony confirming it. Changing it would require that the original handwritten document be destroyed and redrafted; that the original typewritten copy be retyped (and all previous copies retrieved); and that all the autopsy doctors agree to give false testimony.

It seemed to me absurd to believe that Arlen Specter could arrange this himself. Redlich, J. Lee Rankin—perhaps even one of the Commissioners—also would have to be involved. And Commander Humes would have to be recruited—he certainly did not take orders from a presidential commission.

Epstein ignored all such details, and managed to have it both ways. The Commission had deliberately falsified the autopsy report—presumably with the help of Humes—but its motive was benign. The Warren Report was not really a lie, just a white lie—something like telling children the stork brought them.

Epstein arrived at the major conclusion of *Inquest* in a paragraph that did much to shape the debate in 1966:

> If the FBI reports are accurate, as all the evidence indicates they are, then a central aspect of the autopsy was changed more than two months after the autopsy examination, and the autopsy report published in the Warren Report is not the original one. If this is in fact the case, the significance of this alteration of facts goes far beyond merely indicating that it was not physically possible for a lone assassin to have accomplished the assassination. It indicates that the conclusions of the Warren Report must be viewed as expressions of political truth.[54]

"Political truth" was jargon, a substitute for "lie." Yet through the use of that phrase, Edward Jay Epstein managed to eat the cake of conspiracy, yet remain very "respectable" by hardly appearing to take a bite.

However one chose to characterize the conflicting information, the FBI Summary Reports suggested two medical "facts" had been changed:

1. The autopsy conclusion itself was changed from non-transit to transit;
2. The rear wound was misreported at a higher location so the trajectory would slope downward.*

I remember my first impression very clearly. If the National Archives had FBI reports which contradicted the Bethesda autopsy, what else might be in there? Was the Archives a convenient rug under which disagreeable data had been swept; the "secret compartment" of the Kennedy assassination investigation?

One critic, upon first reading the FBI Summary and Supplemental Reports, commented: "Among the most devastating critics of the Warren Report, is the FBI."**[56]

Superbullet

To those who found it difficult to believe that Kennedy and Connally were struck by one bullet, what elevated the improbable to the impossible was the condition of the bullet that allegedly scored the double hit. The Warren Report gave little hint that this bullet—designated Exhibit 399—

---

* One Warren Report critic, years later, called this "verbal plastic surgery."[55]

** Salandria's reasoning reflected the thinking of most critics at that time. He wrote: "Since the FBI must have at least partly based its findings of no exit from the President's back wound on the original autopsy report, and since the present autopsy report describes a missile as exiting from 'the anterior surface of the neck', the burning of 'preliminary draft notes relating to the Naval Medical School Autopsy Report' may be a euphemism for an original autopsy report which was burned."[57]

was in near-perfect condition (see Photo 19). No picture of it was published in the Report, which simply described it as a "nearly whole bullet" found on a stretcher at Parkland Memorial Hospital. Nor did the Report mention that when the bullet first arrived at the FBI Lab on the evening of November 22, 1963, its surface bore no visible trace of blood or tissue; or that several of the doctors, when shown the bullet, immediately commented upon its pristine condition, and voiced their objection to the Commission's theory. None of this information was included in the Warren Report, but all of it could be found in the twenty-six volumes, released ten weeks later. What appeared to be a sequence of deliberate misrepresentations and evasions relating to bullet 399 increased the impression that the single-bullet theory was a contrivance, and the Report a fraud.

But this reaction took time to develop. At first, the Report appeared to be firmly based upon scientific evidence. Any doubt that the rifle in evidence was the murder weapon seemed indefensible in the face of assertions that the FBI Laboratory had established unequivocally that the assassination bullets had been fired from that gun. The procedure seemed foolproof; the tests, definitive.

As in fingerprint identification, a match, if it exists, is unique, and the examiner can testify that the bullet was fired from the weapon "to the exclusion of all others."*

When the twenty-six volumes were released, it became evident that the FBI ballistics tests could be valid, yet prove nothing. It was a shock to turn to page 49 of volume 17 and see, for the first time, a picture of the bullet which had made the bone-shattering journey.

"Nearly whole?"

The bullet looked intact! It seemed indistinguishable from either of the two FBI test bullets whose picture was published as Warren Commission Exhibit 572. The critics and the Commission parted ways when it came to what this meant. The Commission, viewing the match through the FBI's ballistic microscope, confidently concluded that 399 constituted evidence tying Oswald's rifle to the crime. But to me, a more significant match was the one visible to the naked eye: the unmutilated condition of 399 suggested that, like the test bullet it resembled, it was probably another bullet

---

* When a bullet is fired, it spirals as it passes through the barrel. As a result, rifling marks peculiar to that gun barrel are engraved on the surface—often called the "jacket"—of the bullet. In a murder investigation, it is a relatively simple matter to determine whether a particular bullet was fired from a particular rifle. First, a test bullet is fired from the suspect weapon into a large tank of water. Because it is decelerated relatively slowly, its surface is undamaged and a clear imprint of the rifling of the barrel through which it passed is obtained. To test whether a recovered bullet was fired from a particular weapon, that bullet and a test bullet are examined, side by side, in the comparison microscope. If both bullets were fired from the same rifle, the comparison microscope will reveal that fact, because they will display identical rifling marks—i.e., there will be a "ballistic match."

fired into a tank of water, or some cotton, and then planted on a stretcher at the hospital, to inculpate Oswald as the assassin.

Ray Marcus wrote a monograph assembling all the evidence on the question of 399 arguing its illegitimacy as evidence. The title: *The Bastard Bullet*.

An examination of the record quickly produced a list of references establishing that, whether or not it was physically possible for a bullet to follow that particular trajectory and come out in so undamaged a state, the Commission had overstated the case.

FBI ballistics expert Robert A. Frazier testified that bullet 399 was "clean" and had no trace of blood or tissue on its surface.*

Bullet 399 weighed 158.6 grains. Frazier weighed five bullets, picked at random, and found that bullet 399 was "underweight" by such a miniscule amount—3 grains (1/180 of an ounce)—that the difference could well be accounted for by normal variations in the manufacturing process: "there did not necessarily have to be any weight loss to the bullet."[59] In 1969, at the New Orleans trial of Clay Shaw, he testified that 399 was, except for a slight flattening at the base, "in practically original condition."[60]

But a bullet doesn't lose weight the way a person on a diet does. It suffers a weight "loss" because pieces of it are knocked off in a collision. The nub of the matter was that whatever struck Connally's wrist (the radial bone), smashed it into several pieces. A number of the doctors testified 399 could not have done such damage yet emerged intact, particularly since, as far as they could tell, there was more metal in the wrist than the minuscule amount "missing" from 399—at most, about three grains from its base.

Specter showed 399 to Commander Humes: ". . . Now looking at that bullet, Exhibit 399, Dr. Humes . . . could that missile have made the wound on Governor Connally's right wrist?" Humes replied: "I think that is most unlikely. . . . The reason I believe it most unlikely that this missile could have inflicted either of these wounds [referring also to the President's head wound] is that this missile is basically intact; its jacket appears to me to be intact, and I do not understand how it could possibly have left fragments in either of these locations."**[61]

---

* EISENBERG: Did you prepare the bullet in any way for examination? That is, did you clean it or in any way alter it?

FRAZIER: No, sir; it was not necessary. The bullet was clean and it was not necessary to change it in any way.

EISENBERG: There was no blood or similar material on the bullet when you received it?

FRAZIER: Not any which would interfere with the examination; no sir.[58]

** Similarly, Humes declined to associate 399 with the wound in the Governor's thigh, because Parkland Memorial Hospital X-rays reportedly showed that the thigh bone contained metal fragments. "I can't conceive of where they came from this missile," testified Humes.[62]

Similar reactions came from Colonel Finck, the forensic pathologist at the autopsy, and Dr. Shaw, who attended Connally at Parkland Hospital.*

Indeed, the Governor's wrist was a major problem. And the Commission, in conducting tests, simply developed more evidence which went against its own thesis. Through the facilities of Edgewood Arsenal, wound ballistics tests were conducted. Bullets were fired at the wrists of cadavers— and a picture of such a bullet, badly smashed up, with its nose considerably flattened, was published as Warren Commission Exhibit 856. It made a striking contrast with Exhibit 399. (See Photos 19 and 20.)

Despite the metal fragments reportedly in Connally's body, the undeformed and bloodless state of the bullet, and the testimony of the doctors that 399 could not have caused the wrist wound, the Warren Report concluded: "*All the evidence* indicated that the bullet found on the governor's stretcher could have caused all his wounds [emphasis added]."[65]

This was one of the few statements bordering on an outright lie published in the Warren Report.**

Was Bullet 399 a Plant?

At about 1:00 P.M., Parkland Memorial Hospital engineer Darrell Tomlinson was operating the elevator between the ground-floor level, where the emergency rooms were located, and the operating suites on the upper floors. Near the elevators on the ground floor were two four-wheel

* When Specter asked ". . . Could [399] have been the bullet which inflicted the wound on Governor Connally's right wrist?" Finck replied: "No, for the reason that there are too many fragments described in that wrist."[63]

Dr. Shaw testified: ". . . As far as the wounds of the chest are concerned, I feel that this bullet could have inflicted those wounds. But the examination of the wrist both by X-ray and at the time of surgery showed some fragments of metal that make it difficult to believe that the same missile could have caused these two wounds. There seems to be more than three grains of metal [the maximum amount missing from 399] . . . in the [Governor's] wrist . . . [and] I feel that there would be some difficulty in explaining all of the wounds as being inflicted by bullet Exhibit 399 without causing more in the way of loss of substance to the bullet or deformation of the bullet."[64]

** Another distortion of the record was interesting. It was a common presumption that Governor Connally was hit by only one bullet, but when Dr. Shaw, in his appearance before the Commission, was asked whether one bullet did in fact cause all Connally's wounds, he replied: "I have no firm opinion."[66] Nevertheless, the Report said: "In their testimony, the three doctors who attended Governor Connally at Parkland Hospital expressed independently their opinion that a single bullet had passed through his chest; tumbled through his wrist . . . punctured his left thigh . . . and had fallen out of the thigh wound."[67]

hospital stretchers, pushed up against a wall. One of them had been put there by Tomlinson earlier when he wheeled it from the elevator and placed it alongside another stretcher. Then, "an intern or a doctor"—Tomlinson was not sure which—came to use the men's room in the elevator lobby. Tomlinson described what happened next:

He pushed the stretcher out from the wall to get in, and then when he came out he just walked off and didn't push the stretcher back up against the wall, so I pushed it out of the way where we would have [a] clear area in front of the elevator. . . . I pushed it back up against the wall . . . bumped the wall and a spent cartridge or bullet rolled out that apparently had been lodged under the edge of the mat.[68]

Although the condition of the bullet and the doctors' objections ought to have raised suspicions about the bullet, Arlen Specter's major concern seemed to be which stretcher the bullet came from, not how it got there. For the single-bullet theory to work, the bullet had to come from the Governor's stretcher, since he was the second victim along the trajectory. And one of those two stretchers—the one Tomlinson had removed from the elevator—was probably the Governor's. The other stretcher was not connected with either victim.*

Specter, when he took Tomlinson's testimony, apparently wanted him to say that he had found the bullet on the "elevator" stretcher, since that implied the bullet had been found on Connally's stretcher. But Tomlinson would not oblige. He said he found the bullet on the "other" stretcher. If true, that would definitely make 399 a plant. How else could an assassination bullet end up on a stretcher not connected with the treatment of either victim? When Tomlinson picked the "wrong" stretcher, Specter promptly displayed his lawyerlike skills and, in a rare case of cross-examination in the twenty-six volumes, attempted to shake the witness's testimony.**

Specter's questioning irritated Tomlinson, who interrupted with an outburst that ended: ". . . I'm not going to tell you something I can't lay down and sleep at night with either."[71]

About a week later, Specter was back in Washington assuring Commissioner Allen Dulles about where 399 was found: "May I say, Mr. Dulles, on that subject, I took several depositions . . . in the Dallas hospital and I think we have a reasonably conclusive answer . . . in fact, it came from the stretcher of Governor Connally. . . ."[72]

---

* Kennedy's body remained on its stretcher until the coffin arrived.

** SPECTER: Now, Mr. Tomlinson, are you sure that it was stretcher "A" that you took out of the elevator and not stretcher "B"?

TOMLINSON: Well, really, I can't be positive, just to be perfectly honest about it. . . .[69]

SPECTER: You say you can't really take an oath today to be sure whether it was stretcher "A" or stretcher "B" that you took off the elevator?[70]

What About the Two Fragments?

There were several problems with the planted-bullet hypothesis that I deliberately omitted in drafting "The Case for Three Assassins." To write about them would have required departing from the hard evidence and entering the area of conjecture. They raised questions for which, in 1966, there seemed no satisfactory answers.

Bullet 399 was not the only ballistic evidence connecting Oswald's rifle with the crime. Two large bullet fragments—one the nose portion of a bullet, the other the tail portion—found in the President's automobile (Commission Exhibits 567 and 569, respectively) also had been identified by the FBI Lab as coming from the rifle found in the Depository, "to the exclusion of all other weapons."* (See Fig. 4 and Photo 21.)

Faced with the fact that *three* pieces of ammunition tied Oswald's rifle to the crime, critics who believed 399 was a plant proceeded to analyze the situation in a manner I found most peculiar. Preoccupied with the nearly intact state of 399 (because that was the basis for arguing it had been planted), they viewed the *damaged* state of Exhibits 567 and 569 as evidence of authenticity—i.e., as proof that the Carcano rifle had been fired at Kennedy. Certainly, the damaged condition of those two fragments made them more plausible as "expended ammunition," but being scrunched up did not prove they had been fired during the assassination. It only meant that they had been fired into something hard.

This prompted a question about 399 and its alleged role in a plot to frame Oswald: Why would anyone plant a bullet in such pristine condition? I had no satisfactory answer. But it was clear that my approach to the question of fake ballistics differed from the other critics. I entertained the possibility that the entire sniper's nest found at the Depository—the piled-up cartons, the three spent shells by the window, the rifle, etc.—was nothing more than a setup; a false crime scene. That meant that in considering the possibility of fake ballistics, my starting point was not the "found" ammunition, but the "found" rifle.

I asked: Was the rifle found at the Texas School Book Depository fired at Kennedy during the assassination? If not, then all three pieces of ammunition had to be fake. But if the gun had been fired at the President, there was no need to plant any ammunition. To my way of thinking, it was "triple or nothing"—all the ammunition was planted, or all of it was authentic.

Many critics entertained a hybrid hypothesis: that Oswald's rifle had

---

* To those not acquainted with ballistics, it might seem that a bullet has to be in the near-perfect shape of 399 for there to be a conclusive ballistic match. Not true; as long as enough surface area remains to display the rifling characteristics, a definitive match can be made. The two fragments found in the limousine met this requirement.

The Puzzle

Three pieces of found ammunition in JFK case (large enough to make a ballistic match).

Description	*Location where found*	*Time*
1 whole bullet	On a stretcher at Parkland Memorial Hospital, Dallas, Texas	Between 1:00 P.M. and 2:00 P.M.

2 fragments
  1 nose portion
  1 tail portion
	In the presidential limousine:
	  Near front right seat
	  On floor near front right seat
		About 10:00 P.M. on Friday evening

Pertinent facts:

— all three pieces of ammunition ballistically matched Oswald's rifle "to the exclusion of all other weapons";

— these three pieces of ammunition were the only recovered ammunition large enough to be ballistically matched to any weapon;

— the only metal recovered from Kennedy was two tiny slivers from the brain;

— the only metal recovered from Connally was tiny fragments from the wrist;

— the only other metal found in the car was tiny scrapings taken from the windshield and from the carpet.

Figure 4.
Table presenting ballistic data

been used to inculpate him in the shooting (accounting for the two large fragments in the car), and then, as an insurance policy on the ballistic evidence, an undamaged bullet had been planted on the hospital stretcher, just in case "real" bullets fired by Oswald's rifle failed to turn up. To me, that scheme seemed the riskiest of all. What could prove more disastrous to any conspiracy to frame Oswald than for an "extra" bullet to be found, its illegitimacy established by the simple fact that it was superfluous? The Commission could argue, however implausibly, that 399 had been the bullet which passed through two men, causing seven wounds. Suppose there had been no role for it at all?

There was another factor at work. Planting a perfectly clean assassination bullet on a hospital stretcher had the air of a prank; it was outlandish; outrageous. But planting two bullet fragments in the President's limousine was quite different. That involved planning, imagination, and access to the limousine. It implied that someone had literally assembled a "false ammunition kit" to be used in connection with the Kennedy assassination to complement the "false crime scene" at the Depository. If anyone went to such lengths to plant two battered, but ballistically identifiable, bullet fragments in the automobile, then how could he have been so stupid as to place a bullet "in practically original condition" on a stretcher at the hospital? That question haunted any planted-bullet theory.

Also, if all three pieces of ammunition were fake, then what had be-

93

come of the authentic ammunition? In 1966, there seemed no ready answer to that question. I wondered whether that might be the reason why the autopsy X-rays and photos were not shown to the Commission.

Another significant difference between the stretcher bullet and the two "limousine fragments" concerned *where* they were found. Parkland Memorial Hospital was relatively unguarded. But the limousine was under the constant guard of the U.S. Secret Service. The fragments were not discovered until about 10:00 P.M. on November 22 while the car was in the White House garage. If the fragments were planted, it didn't seem likely that could have been accomplished by an outsider. To some, the information that the automobile was in Secret Service custody proved the fragments had to be authentic. To me, it raised the possibility that a plot had penetrated that agency.

Thus, all theories postulating "planted" ammunition, while interesting food for thought, raised very serious problems for which there seemed no sensible answers in the spring of 1966.

In assembling "The Case for Three Assassins," we sidestepped these issues by concentrating on the evidence indicating 399 could not have struck both men and suggesting it had been planted. We did not theorize about the wider implications, but concluded:

> Whatever else is true, bullet 399, contrary to the Commission's findings, was not a superbullet. It did not cause Governor Connally's wounds. It did not travel through the bodies of both men. It did not defy the laws of probability, the laws of physics, and the laws of forensic pathology.
> What it did do was appear mysteriously in Parkland Hospital.[73]

The single-bullet theory provided an excellent example of what, for me, was one of the most disturbing aspects of the Kennedy assassination back in 1965: the extent to which judgments about physical evidence inevitably led to judgments of a political nature. When I began my research, I found it difficult to believe the authorities would lie, and my initial interest stemmed more from being intrigued with the event as an unsolved crime, and my somewhat naive and abstract interest in seeing that "justice" was done, than from any political or ideological motivation. Yet my research inevitably affected my political beliefs. Judgments about the head snap, for example, or whether the condition of bullet 399 precluded the single-bullet theory, ultimately led to judgments about the Commission, and the government in general. Years before, I wouldn't have presumed to pass such judgments; I would have deferred to established authority. The equalizer was the availability of the Commission's own evidence. The twenty-six volumes eliminated the notion that the authorities had some secret knowledge, or rationale, behind their verdict. It came down to simple judgments about facts, and the pervasive question was: If I could see something was wrong, why couldn't the Warren Commission?

Ramparts Magazine and "The Case for Three Assassins"

By the time I finished writing "The Case for Three Assassins," I was overcome with a sense of acute frustration. By then I was quite familiar with the twenty-six volumes, and it was becoming evident that, despite the massive amount of data available in those large blue-bound books, there was little chance of finding any meaningful "solution" to the crime. All one could do was utilize the existing evidence to offer an alternate reconstruction of the shooting—i.e., to offer a multiple-assassin theory, such as the three-assassin model I had constructed. There seemed no way to go beyond that point—to find out, for example, who the "other shooters" were, much less identify the intellectual authors of the crime.

I found this difficult to accept. My entire training in science and engineering consisted of learning theories and procedures to use in solving complex problems, and I knew it was usually the application of a simple and elegant procedure which lay behind the solution of a complex problem. The method was not mysterious, but much work might be required to crank out the answer.

The problem with the Kennedy case was that no solution seemed possible, nor was any procedure for finding one apparent.

On a more mundane level, I was frustrated because, despite all the work, it seemed highly unlikely that *Ramparts* magazine would ever publish "The Case for Three Assassins." Warren Hinckle kept referring to the manuscript, which ran about thirty thousand words, as a "damn legal brief." To him, the details about wounds, shots, and trajectories—all that was unimportant, a lamentable obsession with minutiae. That attitude was echoed by Congressman Carl Albert. Opposing a new investigation, he told the *New York Times*: "I never have managed to get very excited about minor inconsistencies such as an extra bullet."[74]

The University of California only has so much patience with students who do not follow the prescribed schedule. Because of my extracurricular activity, I had now accumulated four "incompletes" in my course work. So I cleared my desk, stored my set of the twenty-six volumes, and resolved to do nothing but schoolwork. For thirteen months, I had thoroughly indulged my curiosity—studying those volumes, blowing up photographs, and telephoning witnesses. That research was more meaningful than anything I had ever done in school, but the problem seemed insoluble. The time had come to get on with my life. I would always be an interested bystander, but I resolved to put the assassination behind me, to return to school and for the rest of the summer do nothing but attend to my studies.

There was one exception. In mid-July, San Francisco radio personality

Joe Dolan arranged a telephone hookup to my apartment in Los Angeles and I spent about two hours on the air, as his "studio guest," explaining all the intricacies of the case. It was the first time I had been on a radio program, and I was flattered to be introduced as "a man I regard as an expert."

The assassination controversy was heating up that summer. In May, *Inquest* had been published, and *Rush to Judgment* would appear in mid-August. The week I was on the air, history professor Jacob Cohen's article, "The Vital Documents," appeared in *Nation*.[75] Cohen, who accepted the Commission's findings, stressed the seriousness of the Commission's failure to examine the autopsy X-rays and photographs. No one even knew their exact whereabouts, although it was widely assumed the Kennedys had legal title to them. Cohen suggested they be placed in the National Archives and examined by a panel of scholars. "Sinister accusations have been made," he wrote, "and the longer these X-rays and photos are hidden, the more credible these accusations will appear. If there is something sinister afoot, let us expose it. If there is not, let us silence these accusations and also inhibit what promises to be decades of dreary fantasizing."[76]

Certainly, I was one of those who believed something sinister was afoot, and that the production of authentic X-rays and photographs would surely overturn the findings of the Warren Commission. If the Zapruder film were any indication, the X-rays and photographs would unequivocally establish that the head shot came from the front.

In my apartment during the broadcast was Oxford-trained physicist Jim Riddle, the UCLA physics professor who was willing to be publicly quoted on Newton's laws. He was going to be the on-the-air expert on the head snap and explain to the radio audience, just as he had in the draft of "The Case for Three Assassins," why the President's head ought to go forward, not backward, if struck from behind.

That was the issue which had started me down the road of intense involvement, and to me, as with Jim Riddle, it was a very simple one. Sounding professorial and very British, Riddle earnestly explained that "when you go to a shooting gallery and shoot at the little ducks, they fall away from you, not toward you."*

---

* Over the years, other physicists jumped into the fray, justifying the motion seen on the Zapruder film by arguing that if the head fragmented and some of the fragments flew forward fast enough, the rest of the head would go backward. I never found this purely hypothetical argument very convincing, especially since the record contained persuasive evidence (e.g., the testimony of Charles Brehm and others) that a fragment was blown off the President's head toward the rear.

CHAPTER 5

The Sibert and O'Neill Report and the Emerging Controversy

THE FALL OF 1966 began with a personal trauma because of the four "incompletes" I had piled up at UCLA. I had promised the Dean they would be completed by the beginning of the fall term, but the *Ramparts* offer had proved irresistible.

So in late September 1966 I found myself sitting in the office of Dean Robert S. Elliott explaining why I hadn't fulfilled my promise. But Dean Elliott would hear none of it. We had made a deal. With considerable disgust, he asked: "How long are we going to futz around with you?" Dean Elliott was a proper man. Whatever he was thinking, he said "futz."

Slowly, he read out loud a letter he had written to the Dean of the University recommending—in effect, ordering—my dismissal. One line I remember vividly said that I had "gone off on a tangent on the Kennedy assassination."

At some point during the meeting, deciding I had nothing to lose, I argued back. Did it really matter whether or not I took an extra six months, even a year, to get my master's degree? What was the purpose of a university anyway? Wasn't it a place where students were taught to believe that the truth will out?

I tried to explain to Dean Elliott that there was obviously something wrong with the Warren Report. It seemed possible that through dint of sheer hard work with the available data, the truth could be ferreted out.

But it was no use. I was dismissed.

It was a stunning blow. Until that moment, the Kennedy research had been only an avocation, but now it had cost me a career goal. Ironically I was being dismissed from a technical curriculum; yet the catalyst for my interest in the assassination had been the head snap, something I never would have thought so important had I not taken my technical training so seriously in the first place.

I was angry and bitter.

In the summer and fall of 1966, the media began covering subjects which, a few months before, were the shop talk only of assassination researchers. Matters I had spent months studying in great detail were suddenly the subject of stories in *U.S. News & World Report, Look,* and *Newsweek. Inquest* was published in May and Lane's *Rush to Judgment* in August. It had become legitimate to doubt.

Inquest provided the first inside look at how the Warren Commission investigation had proceeded, from inception to conclusion. The work had been divided into six areas, each assigned to a two-man team whose job it was to review the investigation already conducted (by the FBI), perform further investigation as required, and then write up that area as a chapter of the Warren Report. Two areas were of principal importance to me. Chapter 3, primarily devoted to the number and direction of the shots, had been investigated and written by Arlen Specter, working alone.* Chapter 4, setting forth the case that Oswald was the assassin, was investigated by Joseph Ball and David Belin.

The teams worked under General Counsel J. Lee Rankin, with major roles played by Norman Redlich, Howard Willens, and Alfred Goldberg. Epstein reported that Goldberg and Redlich wrote and rewrote the chapters of the Report so many times that "although more than thirty persons had had a hand in writing [the Report], it was written mainly by two men: Norman Redlich and Alfred Goldberg."[1]

What I found most interesting was the contribution made by Wesley Liebeler, the man I had come to know so well.

Liebeler's partner on the Commission was Albert Jenner. The two of them were responsible for a complete biography of Lee Harvey Oswald, which was to become Chapter 7 of the Warren Report: "Lee Harvey Oswald: Background and Possible Motives."** There had been considerable overlap, however, and Liebeler had contributed to areas other than his own. Consequently, he had become something of a generalist. Epstein painted him as an in-house devil's advocate, but Liebeler's devil's advocacy seemed to be more than an academic exercise, for it extended well beyond the end of the investigation. It was clear that Epstein would not have been able to propound the "changed autopsy" theory in *Inquest* if Liebeler had

---

* Although the Report mentioned nothing about it, Francis Adams, Specter's senior partner, made a *de facto* resignation from the Commission.

** Chapter 7, forty-eight pages long, was supplemented by the sixty-eight-page Appendix XIII, "Biography of Lee Harvey Oswald," also written by the Jenner/Liebeler team.

not given him the FBI Summary Reports, but there was more to it than that. Even a cursory examination of Epstein's rather thin book—only 156 pages of text—revealed that Liebeler had been a major source of quotes and anecdotes critical of the Commission:

Item. Liebeler thought one lawyer should get an overall view by reading all incoming FBI reports (which totaled approximately twenty thousand pages). Rankin rejected this suggestion, saying it could be done only "if time permitted."[2]

Item. Liebeler said that despite the FBI's extensive investigation that effort "was less thorough than it appeared to be."[3]

Item. Liebeler said the staff did the work, not the members of the Commission. Asked what the Commission did, he replied, "In one word, 'nothing.'"[4] The staff had no direct access to the illustrious Commissioners —everything was funneled through J. Lee Rankin.

Item. Liebeler painted a picture of a staff more eager to investigate than the Chief Justice; he said Rankin was "too responsive" to Warren, and didn't "stand up" to the Commission.[5]

Item. "To protect the rights of witnesses," the staff was prohibited from challenging them. As a result of these constraints, some of the attorneys felt "they were reduced to deposition takers."* [6]

Item. Liebeler provided background concerning the apparently unreliable testimony of Marina Oswald, the wife of the accused and one of the Commission's most important witnesses. Mrs. Oswald's recollections were primary source material in numerous areas. Yet her story kept changing. Liebeler said she was "approximating the truth," anticipating what she thought the Commission wanted to hear and adjusting her responses accordingly.[8] Liebeler provided Epstein with a memorandum written by Norman Redlich expressing sentiments probably felt by most of the staff:

Marina Oswald has lied to the Secret Service, the FBI, and this Commission repeatedly on matters which are of vital concern to the people of this country and the world.[9]

When the staff wanted to subject Marina to a much stiffer interrogation, Rankin refused, saying the Chief Justice considered himself "a judge of human beings" and that he and his fellow Commissioners fully believed Marina's testimony.[10] At a staff meeting, several counsels protested—one threatened resignation, several others came close to walking out. Liebeler asked why Warren objected; Rankin replied only: "The Chief [Justice] doesn't want it." At this point, wrote Epstein, "Rankin lost control of the meeting."[11] Liebeler said that because of the Commission's eagerness to

---

* When Burt Griffin—investigating how Ruby got into the basement of Dallas Police Headquarters—challenged the testimony of Dallas Police Sergeant P. T. Dean, Griffin was severely reprimanded by Warren for doing so.[7]

believe Marina's story through all its twists and turns, some of the staff began referring to Marina and her questioners as "Snow White and the Seven Dwarfs."[12]

Item. At the first meeting with the staff, Warren cautioned that their work might involve national security matters; at their last meeting, he said they should view their relationship with the government as one between lawyer and client; and that any knowledge they had of the Commission was to be considered privileged.[13] Warren did not want to publish the twenty-six volumes.[14]

Then there was the Liebeler memorandum of September 6, 1964, drafted just as the most critical chapter of the Warren Report, number four, titled "The Assassin," was sent to the printer. Originally drafted by the team of Joseph Ball and David Belin, this chapter set forth the evidence that pointed to Oswald as the assassin.

Liebeler's memo attacked as dishonest the way this chapter reported the evidence and arrived at its conclusions. When Liebeler saw the galley proofs, he immediately recognized its major deficiency: "It read like a brief for the prosecution," he said, and drafted his twenty-six-page critique which warned: "To put it bluntly, this sort of selection from the record could seriously affect the integrity and credibility of the entire report."[15]

At first, Rankin refused to accept Liebeler's memorandum: "No more memorandums! The Report has to be published!"[16] And the memorandum embroiled Liebeler in a controversy with Redlich, who had rewritten the chapter from the Ball/Belin draft. Finally, the memo was accepted and Redlich was called to Washington, where he explained that he had written the chapter exactly as the Warren Commissioners had wanted it done.

One point at issue was the chapter's reliance upon the testimony of Helen Markham in its version of the Tippit murder. There were many sound reasons for disbelieving Mrs. Markham.* But when Liebeler told Redlich he thought her testimony was "worthless," Redlich shot back: "The Commission wants to believe Mrs. Markham and that's all there is to it."[18] And Redlich's version of the chapter relied heavily on her testimony.

A similar conflict arose over Redlich's description of Oswald's marksmanship. Liebeler believed the chapter misused and quoted evidence out of context, creating the illusion that the shots were "easy" and that Oswald was a proficient rifleman. The phrase "easy shots" came from the testimony of Marine Corps officers unaware of the timing problem. "I do not see how someone can conclude that a shot is easy or hard," wrote Liebeler, "unless he knows something about how long the firer has to shoot. . . ."[19] He

---

* She gave conflicting accounts of the Tippit killer, and was so agitated at the time that she somehow managed to leave her shoes on the roof of a police car.[17]

termed the treatment of this question "simply dishonest," noting that it failed "to set forth material in the record tending to indicate that Oswald was not a good shot."*[20]

Liebeler concluded his memo: "These conclusions [that Oswald was a good shot and that the shots were "easy"] will never be accepted by critical persons anyway."[21] As he had in the Markham case, Redlich responded to Liebeler's criticisms by propounding the virtues of being a team player: "The Commission judged it an easy shot, and *I* work for the Commission."[22]

Epstein's book gave my perception of Liebeler new dimensions. I was most anxious to see him when he returned to UCLA, curious to know what he'd say about the book, how it might affect his public stance on the assassination, and whether he might let me have a look at that famous twenty-six-page memorandum.

The Sibert and O'Neill FBI Report

Meanwhile, Paul L. Hoch, a graduate student in physics at Berkeley, turned up another piece of the puzzle. Hoch had noted that Secret Service agents Kellerman and Greer, who attended the President's autopsy, testified that two FBI men had also been present—James Sibert and Francis O'Neill. Greer described how thoroughly the two FBI agents covered the autopsy, making it clear that the FBI stuck to the event like glue.

Despite the obviously important roles assigned to agents Sibert and O'Neill, they were mentioned nowhere in the Warren Report. Had the two FBI agents made a report? Did the Commission have it? It wasn't in the twenty-six volumes—indeed, the only mention of Sibert and O'Neill was the several references made by Kellerman and Greer. That's where the matter stood until June 1966, when Hoch journeyed to the National Archives in Washington. One of the items on his agenda was to determine whether such a report—an FBI agent's account of the navy autopsy—actually existed, and obtain a copy if it did.

Hoch couldn't find it, but before departing Washington, he left a request suggesting the archivist—then in the process of declassifying the Warren Commission's records—search for the document by scanning FBI name indices at the back of the huge FBI reports (often eight hundred pages apiece) under the names "Humes," "Boswell," and "Finck." Awaiting him when he got home was an envelope from the Archives containing

---

* Of principal importance was the testimony of Nelson Delgado, a Marine Corps buddy of Oswald's who actually witnessed Oswald firing on the range. Delgado testified that Oswald often missed the target completely, an event he vividly recalled since a red flag, called "Maggie's drawers," was waved each time it happened.[23]

the five-page, single-spaced report of agents Sibert and O'Neill: "Autopsy of Body of President John Fitzgerald Kennedy."*[24]

The document was incredibly detailed, listing those present, including many names not mentioned in the doctors' testimony, recording the entry and exit of people from the room, even noting the time of the first incision (8:15 P.M.). Much of it was written as a running narrative, and in the midst of that narrative was some of the most persuasive evidence against the single-bullet theory that would ever be found: Sibert and O'Neill stated that the autopsy doctors had concluded the bullet did *not* transit. Hoch immediately sent copies of the document to many researchers.

When I received my copy, one of the first things I did was check what the doctors said that night about the head trajectory. To my surprise, the Sibert and O'Neill report said that Humes concluded Kennedy was struck in the head from the rear.[25] It was one thing for the critics to suspect Humes perjured himself months later when he gave his Warren Commission testimony. Yet here was a document which said Humes came to that conclusion on Friday night. I didn't know what to make of that.

But on the neck trajectory and the single-bullet theory the Sibert and O'Neill report immediately redirected my thinking. The two FBI agents could now be added to the list of those who saw the doctors—Humes, in this instance—fruitlessly probing the back wound. Furthermore, they referred to it as a "low" back wound, not a "high" neck wound.** Sibert and O'Neill described in detail what they had observed:

During the latter stages of this autopsy, Dr. Humes located an opening which appeared to be a bullet hole which was *below the shoulders* [emphasis added] and two inches to the right of the middle line of the spinal column.

This opening was probed by Dr. Humes with the finger, at which time it was determined that the trajectory of the missile entering at this point had entered at a downward position of 45 to 60 degrees. Further probing determined that *the distance traveled by this missile was a short distance inasmuch as the end of the opening could be felt with the finger* [emphasis added].[26]

There was nothing about the bullet transiting, or about the doctors connecting the back wound to the wound in the throat (referred to, incidentally, as a tracheotomy). The only connection made was between the hole in the back and the bullet found on a Dallas stretcher.

That happened when the Bethesda doctors discovered that ". . . no complete bullet of any size could be located in the back or any other area of the body as determined by total body X-rays and inspection revealing

* This FBI report appears as pages 281–287 of the FBI's Dallas Field Office report of 10 December 1963. That Dallas Field Office report, approximately eight hundred pages long, was designated Commission Document 7.

** This "low"/"high" nomenclature, used to describe conflicting evidence on the back wound, was introduced in the previous chapter (see pp. 75–79).

102

there was no point of exit. . . ."[27] At this juncture the two FBI men made a telephone call to the FBI Laboratory and were informed "that the [FBI] Laboratory had received through Secret Service Agent Richard Johnsen a bullet which had reportedly been found on a stretcher in the emergency room of Parkland Memorial Hospital, Dallas, Texas. . . . Agent Johnsen had advised the Laboratory that it had not been ascertained whether or not this was the stretcher which had been used to transport the body of President Kennedy."[28]

FBI agents Sibert and O'Neill immediately informed Commander Humes about this bullet, and his response was to associate this Dallas stretcher bullet with the shallow wound: "Immediately following receipt of this information," wrote Sibert and O'Neill,

. . . this was made available to Dr. Humes who advised that in his opinion this accounted for no bullet being located which had entered the back region and that since external cardiac massage had been performed at Parkland Hospital [during which Kennedy, lying on his back, was soundly thumped on the chest by Dr. Malcolm Perry] it was entirely possible that through such movement the bullet had worked its way back out of the point of entry and had fallen on the stretcher.[29]

Later that evening, according to the two FBI agents, Dr. Humes reiterated this "non-transit" finding as an official autopsy conclusion: "Dr. Humes stated that the pattern was clear that one bullet had entered the President's back and worked its way out of the body during external cardiac massage and that a second . . . bullet had entered the rear of the skull. . . ."[30]

From this it seemed clear that Dr. Humes did *not* believe the rear wound was the entry for a bullet which traveled through the body—at least he didn't the night he performed the autopsy.

The Sibert and O'Neill report, then, represented a direct challenge to the single-bullet theory, since that theory depended on a transiting neck trajectory, and a "high" neck wound. Like most critics, I initially assumed that the vivid non-transit evidence in this report was the reason it had not been published. In short, I believed the Commission had changed the autopsy to permit a double hit and thereby resolve the time squeeze posed by the Zapruder film. Then, to cover their tracks, the FBI's eyewitness description of the autopsy, with its no-transit, "low" wound testimony, was squirreled away at the National Archives.

I soon became aware, however, that while the Sibert and O'Neill report *did* support the theory that the Bethesda autopsy report in evidence was not the original, it seriously undercut the hypothesis that the Warren Commission had made the change.*

* This may seem contradictory, but the confusion disappears if one keeps in mind that the issues of *whether* the autopsy was changed and when (and by whom) it was changed, were different. To be sure, the Sibert and O'Neill FBI report—

The critics based their case for an earlier autopsy report on the no-transit statement in the FBI Summary Report, reasoning that the FBI officials who drafted it used as their source a copy of the original Bethesda autopsy report. But it now seemed that the FBI summaries were based instead on this newly discovered narrative written by two FBI agents who attended the autopsy.*

With the appearance of the Sibert and O'Neill FBI report, it was apparent that we critics were wrong, and that *Inquest,* which set forth our argument, contained a major error.

I first learned of this from a letter published in October 1966 in the *New York Review of Books,* which stated that it was "obvious" that information from the Sibert and O'Neill report "formed the basis for the FBI reports of December 9th and January 13th."[31] Checking this claim, I was surprised to find that the sentences about the autopsy in the FBI Summary Reports were a direct paraphrase—almost word for word, in some instances—of statements made on pages 4–5 of the Sibert and O'Neill report. (See Fig. 5.)

Thus, in one fell swoop, the critics' major evidence for the existence of an earlier Bethesda autopsy report, revised by the Warren Commission for political purposes, simply disappeared. What emerged instead was rather strange—something that defied classification and which I initially found most confusing: two separate and conflicting sources of information about the Kennedy autopsy—the FBI's Sibert and O'Neill report, and the navy's Bethesda autopsy report.

The existence of two distinct sources exposed the fallacy of theorizing —as if the government were one vast monolith—that simply because the FBI Summary Report of December 9, 1963, had a sentence saying "no-transit," that the Bethesda autopsy report, as of December 9, 1963, said

---

describing the doctors' behavior at the time of the examination—*was* evidence of an earlier version of the autopsy diagnostics. But that was quite different from the claim that, months later, a written autopsy report was changed by the Commission in the service of "political truth" (as propounded by Epstein in *Inquest*).

* The difference was crucial. If, as *Inquest* argued, the autopsy conclusions mentioned in the FBI Summary Reports came from a navy autopsy report, the FBI Summary Reports would be evidence that the autopsy report, published in the Warren Report, was not the original. But if the FBI Summary Reports were based merely on the individual report of two FBI agents attending the autopsy—i.e., if it was simply the case of one FBI report (the Summary) being based upon another (the Sibert and O'Neill report)—then differences between the FBI Summary Reports and the navy autopsy report proved no such thing. An alternative explanation for why the FBI Summary Report contradicted the Bethesda autopsy report might be that the report of the two FBI agents was wrong. Obviously, determining the exact source of the non-transit statements in the FBI Summary Report was of considerable importance. At stake was whether or not the Warren Commission published the autopsy report it received.

The Puzzle

BEST

From the Sibert and O'Neill FBI report	*From FBI Summary Reports*
	December 9, 1963, Report:
During the latter stages of this autopsy, Dr. Humes located an opening which appeared to be a bullet hole which was *below* the *shoulders* and two inches *to the right of* the middle line *of the spinal column.*	Medical examination of the President's body revealed that one of the bullets had entered just *below* his *shoulder to the right of the spinal column at an angle of 45 to 50 degrees downward,* that there was no point of exit, and that the bullet was not in the body.
	January 13, 1964, Supplemental Report:
This opening was probed by Dr. Humes with the finger, at which time it was determined that the trajectory of the missile entering at this point was that of *a downward position of 45 to 60 degrees.* Further probing determined that the distance traveled by this missile was a short distance inasmuch as the end of the opening could be felt with the finger.	Medical examination of the President's body had revealed that the bullet which entered his back had penetrated to a distance of less than a finger length.

Figure 5.

Comparison of Sibert and O'Neill report and FBI Summary Reports

Note that in the case of the December 9, 1963, Report (right), the paraphrasing links the two reports not only fact by fact, but, as the italics show, almost word for word. In the January 13, 1964, Supplemental report, the statement that the bullet had "penetrated to a distance of less than a finger length" is obviously a reference to the incident in which Dr. Humes probed the wound with his finger. Had the information come from an autopsy report, a measurement would have been given for the depth of the wound. It is unlikely that any autopsy document would describe the depth of a wound using the rather imprecise (and highly unprofessional) yardstick: "less than a finger length."

"no-transit." Or: Simply because the January 13, 1964, FBI Supplemental Report reflected a "non-transit" finding that that proved the Bethesda autopsy, as of that date, said "no-transit." Yet Epstein's *Inquest* contained exactly such oversimplified reasoning: "If the FBI's [Summary Report] statements are accurate, it would appear that the [navy] autopsy findings were revised some time subsequent to January 13, 1964."*[32]

---

* I now understood why Epstein was able to build such a convincing case that the Warren Commission had changed the Bethesda autopsy. The time frame for any purported change was critical in identifying who did it. If the autopsy findings had been revised *after* January 13, 1964, the date of the FBI Supplemental Report, then the Warren Commission *would* be a prime suspect, for it was in late January that the staff lawyers, analyzing the Zapruder film, discovered the Kennedy/Connally time squeeze, and it was the alleged change from non-transit to transit which permitted the double hit and surmounted that problem.

Differing sources of autopsy information explained the variation between the FBI reconstruction of the crime and the Warren Commission's. For while both investigations relied on the sniper's nest with its three spent shells, suggesting three shots fired, and on the three pieces of recovered ammunition, which the FBI Lab ballistically matched to the rifle found at the Depository, their starting points were different. For the Warren Commission it was the navy autopsy report with its transiting neck trajectory that permitted a double hit; but for the FBI it was the Sibert and O'Neill account of the autopsy, with its non-transiting trajectory that did not. Thus, the FBI reconstructed the assassination as three shots/three hits: the Warren Commission, three shots/two hits, with one bullet striking two victims. (See Fig. 6.)

This contradiction, of course, is what caused many critics to think the Warren Commission had changed the autopsy report. In Epstein's case this mistake resulted from his relying on documents in Wesley Liebeler's barn while overlooking one at the National Archives. Unfortunately for Epstein, the Sibert and O'Neill report never made it to the barn.*

There was a final twist to the *Inquest* saga. When Paul Hoch distributed the Sibert and O'Neill report, Epstein made it an appendix to his paperback edition, omitting mention that the document seriously undercut the book's central thesis.**

I bought a copy of the new edition—it was a convenient way to purchase both the Sibert and O'Neill report and the text of the FBI Summary Report for just over a dollar.

When I first perused the FBI Summary Report, I became aware of some weird deficiencies in the FBI investigation. The December 9, 1963, Summary Report was the FBI's answer to Lyndon Johnson's November 22 call for a complete and thorough investigation to uncover the truth about the crime of the century. Yet the report was so superficial it made no mention of the timing problem posed by the Zapruder film—the critical circumstantial evidence that more than one assassin might have been firing. Even worse, it made no mention of the wound at the front of Kennedy's throat! As the report also omitted any mention of Governor Connally's wounding, John McCloy's observation that ". . . it does leave you some loopholes . . ."[33] seemed a monumental understatement.

* Liebeler once explained his limited document collection, which filled only one steamer trunk, squatting on the floor beneath a table in his UCLA Law School office, by the fact that when he left the Commission in the fall of 1964, he only owned a Volkswagen.

** "New Medical Documents," ran a flyer on the cover. A more accurate banner would have read: "Newly released documents prove the major thesis advanced by this book is wrong. Read all about it in the Appendix."

FBI (three shots — three hits)

Shot Sequence	Recovered Ammunition
1. Kennedy (in a shallow back wound, then out on the stretcher)	Bullet 399 (Kennedy's stretcher)
2. Connally (all his wounds)	Indefinite
3. Kennedy (fatal shot)	Two large bullet fragments in car

Warren Commission (three shots — two hits, one miss)

Shot Sequence	Recovered Ammunition
1. Kennedy/Connally (single-bullet trajectory) (bullet found on Connally's stretcher, having fallen from Connally's left thigh wound)	Bullet 399 (Connally's stretcher)
2. Kennedy (fatal shot)	Two large bullet fragments in car
3. Missed shot (can be either first, second, or third shot fired; Report draws no conclusion)	

Figure 6.

Two reconstructions: the FBI versus the Warren Commission

Note that bullet 399 must be found on Kennedy's stretcher in the FBI reconstruction, whereas it is found on Connally's stretcher in the Warren Commission reconstruction.

But both the FBI Summary and the Warren reports took the sniper's-nest evidence at face value, and both concluded that Oswald was the lone assassin. So it was no surprise that shortly after *Inquest* was published an FBI spokesman brushed aside the autopsy conflict and told *Look* magazine: "It is completely contrary to the facts to indicate that the FBI and the Commission are in opposition on the findings of the Commission."[34]

Nevertheless, the question persisted: Why did this report by two men present at the Bethesda autopsy contradict the navy autopsy results published in the Warren Report? How was one to reconcile the "transit" conclusion of that autopsy report with the "no-transit" information furnished by Sibert and O'Neill? In short, I still wondered whether, the critics' error notwithstanding, the Commission had really published the autopsy it received. And if they did, was that autopsy changed somehow before it reached them?

The Commission's handling of the matter only intensified my suspicions. If Sibert and O'Neill were innocently in error, why hadn't they been called to give sworn testimony? And why hadn't their report been published in the twenty-six volumes, along with an explanation of the error? Why was all this only coming to light in 1966?

To my mind, the most suspicious factor was the plethora of evidence suggesting the rear wound was "low" in the back, not "high" in the neck. These two issues—the exact location of the rear wound and whether the bullet transited—apparently were entwined. Those who watched the autopsy on November 22, and saw the wound itself, were the source of information on both points: that the bullet did *not* transit and that the wound was "low." Only the navy autopsy report said the missile transited, and placed the rear entry wound high enough (in the neck) for it to do that.

I came to appreciate how much more suspicious the situation was with both factors present by imagining the same non-transit/transit conflict but with the rear entry wound located unambiguously in the base of the neck, *above* the shoulder blade, exactly where the Warren Report said it was. In that case, the Dallas tracheotomy incision might have caused some temporary confusion, but no dispute over basic facts. A change in the autopsy from non-transit to transit could have been understandable, especially if done to rectify an innocent error resulting from the Dallas tracheotomy having obliterated a frontally located bullet exit hole.

But here the issue was not so simple. Experts might disagree over whether there was a path through the President's body, but any lay observer, it seemed to me, was competent to judge whether the hole he saw was in the *neck* or in the *back*. It was the shifting location of the back wound that made the Warren Commission's conclusion that a bullet transited the neck seem so contrived.

When *Inquest* was published, *Look* assigned Fletcher Knebel to do a story about it. He interviewed several Commission attorneys, one of the autopsy doctors, and an FBI spokesman. All strongly denied there had been any change in the autopsy. Of course, had there been collusion between the Warren Commission and the autopsy doctors, parties to such an affair would surely not confess merely because they were questioned by a journalist. But the denials were vehement. Were all these men bluffing?*

---

* Dr. Boswell, the Chief of Pathology at Bethesda and one of the three autopsy doctors, said: "Our autopsy report went downtown to Admiral Burkley [the President's physician] at the White House on November 25, after the three of us [Humes, Finck, and Boswell] had signed it on [Sunday] November 24th. It appeared in the Warren Commission Report exactly as it was written November 24th, and it was never changed or altered in any way."[35]

Arlen Specter said: "It is ridiculous to indicate that the autopsy findings were changed after November 24, when Commander Humes finished the report. I saw both the longhand and the typewritten reports when I came to work for the Commission in mid-January. They were identical, and neither was changed from the original in any way at any time."[36]

Redlich also denied there had been any change, pointing out that he came to work a month before Specter, on December 20, 1963.[37]

And if the Warren Commission didn't change the autopsy, who did? And why? Only the Warren Commission seemed to have a motive for such a conspiracy—i.e., to pacify the public and quell doubts.

September 30, 1966: Liebeler and the Critics

The first news I had of Wesley Liebeler in the fall of 1966 concerned his participation, along with fellow attorney Burt Griffin, in a panel discussion at the Theatre of Ideas in New York City. Also on the panel were Warren Report critics Sylvia Meagher, Dr. Richard Popkin—a major proponent of the planted-bullet theory—and Leo Sauvage, a French journalist for *Le Figaro*.*

The discussion was recorded by Pacifica Radio, and I heard a tape of it over a year later. It was a dramatic head-on confrontation between the critics and the Warren Commission attorneys over what was shaping up as a major issue but one not clearly recognized as such at the time: the problem of "missing" bullets. The early discussion was dominated by the question of who was right in the non-transit/transit conflict, the FBI or the navy. Griffin said: "I think what we're dealing with here . . . is possibilities . . . what is really the likely possibility: that these three physicians were mistaken, or that the FBI agents who overheard some conversations of autopsy surgeons were mistaken."[38]

Liebeler emphasized that when it came to the issue of who was correct, the FBI agents or the autopsy doctors ". . . the statement of an FBI agent who was present at the autopsy comes pretty low on the totem pole, a good deal below the weight to be given to the report of the autopsy surgeon itself."[39]

Liebeler demeaned the importance of the FBI statements and stressed the cursory glance he had given the FBI Summary Report while on the Commission: ". . . I read through it once . . . put it aside, never looked at it again . . . I know that's what the other lawyers did too." He characterized their Report as "a very poor job" and "pretty sloppy work." He said: "It never occurred to me when I gave Epstein this material that this alleged contradiction was in there."[40]

Burt Griffin said that if the FBI was correct about the wound being shallow and the bullet not transiting, then "all three of them [the autopsy surgeons] would have to be involved in some kind of conspiracy to falsify this [autopsy] report. That's what it comes down to . . . all of you are [really] suggesting that Humes and his two other colleagues lied."[41]

The discussion then turned to allegations that the bullet found on the

* Sauvage had covered the assassination and his book *The Oswald Affair* was published in the United States in the summer of 1966.

stretcher at Parkland Memorial Hospital had been planted. Liebeler criticized Sauvage for his emphasis on 399: "That's not a proper way to approach the problem because as you well know, Mr. Sauvage, there were two other fragments that were found in the car that were also fired from Oswald's rifle—not just 399. Now, Mr. Sauvage, we find two pieces of lead in the car. And we find that the President has been hit [in the head] by a bullet that has shattered. . . . These two pieces of lead were fired from Oswald's rifle to the exclusion of all other rifles. Now, if these two [fragments] didn't come from the bullet that hit the President, then where did they come from? And where *is* the bullet that hit the President?[42]

"This ['planting' hypothesis] is absolutely absurd, it seems to me. All the lead that was found came from Oswald's rifle.* There isn't another piece of lead in sight. And you're sitting there and telling me that it apparently was just a coincidence that Oswald's bullets were in [the President's] car?"[43]

Somewhat testily, Mr. Sauvage replied: "But Mr. Liebeler, you forget one thing. *You* are the prosecutor. *You* have to establish the proof. Not *I*. *I* am a newspaperman. . . . You have no right to ask me questions. *I* have the right to ask you questions."[44]

Burt Griffin chimed in: "It seems to me the proof that you're grasping for, Mr. Sauvage, would have to be a bullet actually in the President's body. Once the bullet gets through the body [of the three pieces of ammunition in the Kennedy case, two were in the car and one on the stretcher], how can you *prove incontrovertibly* that the bullet hit the President. You've got to rely on circumstantial evidence, and I submit that this is pretty good circumstantial evidence."[45]

The argument continued. "If 399 didn't hit them, then what did . . . ?" asked Liebeler. "That was for you to find out," replied Sylvia Meagher. Griffin observed: ". . . it seems to me, if you think separate bullets hit the President and the Governor, you've got two bullets that you've got to explain, 'Where'd they go?' "

SAUVAGE: No. *You* have to explain it.

GRIFFIN: No, no, no, no. No.

SAUVAGE: What do you mean?

GRIFFIN: Where did the bullets go? I mean, we're reasonable men. What happened to them?

SAUVAGE: You're in 1966, Mr. Griffin.

GRIFFIN: [Cutting in again] Did they evaporate?

---

* In using this expression, Liebeler undoubtedly meant "all the [ballistically identifiable] lead." There were tiny lead particles recovered from Kennedy's brain at autopsy, but they were far too small to offer any surface area large enough for the purposes of ballistic matching. Similarly, small lead particles were recovered from the windshield and rugs of the car, and from Governor Connally's wrist.

SAUVAGE: [Continuing] About three or four hundred years ago, when someone was accused of something, he had to prove he wasn't a murderer. This has changed, you know.[46]

This dramatic exchange demonstrated the chasm separating the critics and the attorneys. The critics felt the Commission's reconstruction was missing "extra" assassins; the attorneys clearly felt the critics' theories had a corresponding deficiency: "missing" bullets.

When the critics continued to press this line of attack, Griffin, commenting on the planted-bullet theory, erupted: "Now what did the conspirator do? Shoot it out with Oswald's rifle, recover it somewhere, put it in his pocket, wait for the time that the Governor's stretcher would be there in the hospital, and run up and put it in?"[47]

Liebeler noted the prescient nature of any plot which could foresee the numerous other facts in the case with which the bogus bullet would have to conform (such as the fact that authentic bullets did not turn up, so there would be a plausible role for the planted bullet). Excitedly, he cut in, shouting: "And foresaw all this! Foresaw it was going to be necessary! . . ."[48] Griffin commented: "We could never have uncovered a conspiracy of that character. That guy was a mastermind. He was better than [Conan] Doyle."[49]

Liebeler made another observation: ". . . [if] somebody was going around planting bullets and pieces of lead, pieces of bullets that had been fired from a rifle that belonged to Oswald, [then] presumably, Oswald was not involved in this at all . . . I mean, that's the only [conclusion] you can arrive at from that line of argument."[50]

Liebeler gave his views on such a conspiracy, a conspiracy in which the entire "crime scene"—i.e., the sniper's nest—was false: ". . . there's nothing that we can say here tonight that can preclude the possibility that those bullets [were] planted. There's no question about it. And [that] there wasn't some great, huge conspiracy involved here, in putting the rifle up there, and planting the bullets. . . . But if there *was* such a conspiracy, it would have involved, it seems to me, a good number of people. And it's impossible for me to believe that *some* evidence wouldn't have been found of it."[51]

Griffin agreed. And with regard to any theory that the FBI, the chief investigative arm of the Commission, had been involved in any chicanery, he said: "I submit that until we have *some* indication that the FBI deliberately deceived us, or something like that, we just have to accept the fact that they may have picked up the evidence and brought it to us."[52]

But suppose the conspiracy operated on a more fundamental level, suppose the plotters actually fabricated evidence—the bullet and two fragments, for example—to deceive the FBI. Griffin stressed the difficulty connected with any theory positing that the incoming evidence itself was fake: "None of us could have any basis for making any conclusions," he said.[53]

No one realized the profound issues that lay dormant in this discussion: Suppose all three pieces of ammunition *were* planted; suppose the crime scene *was* false; suppose the Commission was dealing with appearance, not reality—how could you prove it?

The discussion moved on. What seemed to concern the attorneys were procedural mistakes which detracted from the credibility of the Report. Liebeler deplored the Commission's failure to examine the autopsy X-rays and photographs. It was poor procedure. "If it had been my decision to look at the pictures or not, I haven't the faintest question as to what I would have done: I would have looked at them. And the Commission should have looked at them, but they didn't."[54]

Yet despite his support for the Commission, there was a certain defensiveness on Liebeler's part. ". . . maybe when some of the facts come out as to the way the Commission operated," he said, "you can better appreciate the position that the staff was in in this circumstance; and ask yourself what you, sir, would have done in the same or similar circumstances. I'm not asking to be absolved of any responsibility for anything that I had anything to do with—I'm not asking it now, and I'm not going to ask for it. I'm just going to ask you to consider the evidence on both sides of the question fairly and then make up your own mind as to whether the basic conclusions of the Report are correct or not."[55]

I next met Liebeler on October 7, 1966. I was on the campus that day and found, to my surprise, that Lane was there and I had just missed a lecture he gave. The school newspaper reported that afterward both Lane and Liebeler would debate in a student lounge. I ran to that room, crammed with about two hundred people, and found the two of them squared off against one another, and on the brink of a heated confrontation.

It was a sorry affair and the spectacle saddened me. Liebeler blew his stack. I had never seen him behave that way before. His personal dislike for Lane was obvious; clearly he regarded him as a demagogue. And Lane attacked the Commission's conclusions in the manner of one who was exposing a *moral* crime, a hoax, and a fraud.

After this steamy confrontation, I went over to the UCLA Law School. Professor Liebeler was in the lobby, amid a throng of law students and faculty. As I stood nearby, he recognized me and motioned me to follow him up to his office.

I hadn't seen Liebeler since the previous spring. His whole demeanor had changed significantly. There was an intensity about him. The stakes were higher. The question was no longer what might happen when the books and articles were written and the public discovered that buried in the twenty-six volumes was a "case for the defense." The public was now finding this out, and Liebeler watched, aghast, as the first perceptions formed—fueled by Lane and Epstein—that there had been a deliberate coverup of immense proportions.

A more detached observer might have reflected that Mark Lane was a historic inevitability once the Commission oversimplified the issues, structured its investigation around certain preconceptions, glossed over conflicting evidence, and then wrote a one-sided Report—one which could be proven one-sided by the simple act of studying the Commission's own published evidence. But Wesley Liebeler seemed to take Lane's criticisms very personally, perhaps because, in Lane's often sarcastic portrayal of how the Commission had behaved, Liebeler could hear the faint echo of some of the complaints he himself had registered while on the staff.

Lane, of course, argued that the Commission had deliberately coaxed a false pattern from the evidence, and framed an innocent man for the crime. It was this accusation—involving his own personal integrity—that stuck in Liebeler's craw.

All had not been sweetness and light between Wesley Liebeler and the Warren Commission. But despite all the problems, serving on a Presidential Commission was an honor and a privilege, was it not?

Now Mark Lane was telling applauding audiences in packed auditoriums that the Warren Commission investigation had been tantamount to an organized conspiracy; and that having served on that Commission would be a shame they would bear for the rest of their lives; that they would forever be held responsible for a great miscarriage of justice.

Most disturbing of all to Liebeler in the fall of 1966 were the people flocking to buy Lane's book. Within weeks of publication, *Rush to Judgment* soared to the top of the best-seller list. The book seemed to be everywhere. Displays of it appeared in all the bookstores, the same stores which, just two years earlier, had been straining to keep pace with the public's seemingly insatiable demand for the Warren Report. To Wesley Liebeler all this was an outrage.

In his UCLA office that day, Liebeler told me his plans. He was going to write a book analyzing the critics' charges. If the Commission had made mistakes, he would own up to them. "I have no intention of writing a servile defense of the Warren Report," he said.[56] But on the other hand, if the Commission was right, he would say so, and vehemently. Furthermore, in his book there would be a clear distinction between essential and nonessential criticism; for example, between charges arising from the onesided manner in which the Report was written and the issue of whether, in the final analysis and despite numerous deficiencies which Liebeler viewed as inconsequential, the Commission had in fact come up with the right answer. If the conclusions were correct, did it really matter whether the Commission had failed to find the cause of the smoke on the grassy knoll, or failed to call every witness in Dealey Plaza, or even failed to acknowledge that its conclusions might, to some persons, appear improbable?

Liebeler had retained the prominent New York literary agent, Sterling Lord, and gotten a book contract with a major New York publishing house, W. W. Norton. The need for a book such as his, he thought, was clear. It was needed to end the rampant confusion as to what theory of the assassination was truly supported by an impartial appraisal of all the evidence accumulated in the twenty-six volumes.

As a result of all the charges and countercharges, Liebeler felt that one conclusion was painfully evident. And he emphasized to me that day what he told the *New York Times* two weeks later: "What is needed at this point is one piece of work which sets forth both sides objectively."[57]

From the plan Liebeler outlined, it was clear he was under no illusions about the difficulty of researching the Commission's voluminous records. Published without an index, it was anybody's guess what might be in there. Once, the year before, he had referred to the twenty-six volumes as a "legal Frankenstein." So he had mounted a substantial research effort at the UCLA Law School. He received a grant of about ten thousand dollars from the University of California, and hired three research assistants. Their primary job was to examine Mark Lane's book with a fine tooth comb and prepare detailed memoranda on Lane's footnotes, one by one, checking the substantiation of Lane's many charges.

Liebeler intended to augment the time and effort he could devote to his book project by teaching a course on the Warren Commission. Formally titled "Legal Problems in Areas of National Security," the course would be in the form of a seminar, and about twenty-five students would participate. Each student would select an area of the Commission's investigation and have the responsibility of submitting a research report analyzing published criticism to determine whether the Commission's conclusions were supported by the evidence. Liebeler expected a synergistic interplay between the book project and the course. The research papers submitted in the course might be the basis for sections of his book.

At the meeting on October 7, Liebeler made me a proposition. First, he invited me to attend the course and play devil's advocate. He wanted to do everything possible, he said, to make sure his students were exposed to what the critics were saying. He obviously did not want a bunch of toadies agreeing with their professor just to get a good grade. If I agreed, the class would be given my home telephone number, and told to call if they needed any help finding their way around the documents in the twenty-six volumes, or in understanding the criticisms being raised on any particular point.

Second, to insure that he properly understood the critics' charges, Liebeler wanted to extend this "devil's advocate" role to our personal relationship. He suggested we meet as often as necessary for detailed discussions. To facilitate our own communications, while preventing any misunderstanding about his position on the Report, he suggested that we tape record our telephone conversations—a suggestion which surprised me and for which I was unprepared, as I owned no tape recorder at the time and had never recorded a telephone conversation in my life.

I was skeptical of Liebeler's offer, and tried to test his intentions. I suspected that the picture showing Oswald holding his rifle, published on the cover of *Life* magazine, was a fake—but I had not done the type of careful research necessary to demonstrate that. I said to him: "Suppose I convince you that this picture is a phony? What will you do with it?"

"Then I will treat it as a phony," Liebeler replied.[58]

But more important, on the question of the number of shooters—an area in which I considered myself a specialist—Liebeler conveyed the impression that his book might accept the possibility of multiple assassins, if there were real grounds for doing so.

There was an element of challenge in Liebeler's offer. He held out the inducement that if I could demonstrate that the Warren Report was wrong in any major way, he would say so in his book. The idea of persuading a Warren Commission attorney to take the side of the critics—perhaps even ask for a new investigation—attracted me powerfully. He could generate enormous pressure for a new investigation. And Liebeler implied he *was* persuadable.

The events in my own life during the previous two weeks influenced me. My academic career had just come to an end. I was bitter about that and beginning to question certain attitudes I had cherished for years. I had begun college with a contempt for lawyers and a high regard for scientists. Now, the same week I was dismissed from graduate school because of a failure to comply with regulations, a law professor extended this extraordinary invitation. It was an offer too inviting to refuse.

From the way he was organizing both his book and class, it was clear that Wesley Liebeler intended to devote at least a year of his life, if not more, to completing what he thought of as certain unfinished business. Liebeler asked the library to order several extra sets of the twenty-six volumes. He arranged for *Life* magazine to ship the 4-by-5-inch transparencies made from the individual frames of the original Zapruder film to California. There, at the Beverly Hills offices of Time-Life, those attending his seminar could examine these crucial primary source materials.

Consistent with his self-image as an insider, Liebeler wrote FBI Director J. Edgar Hoover, informing him of his project and asking for help in a few areas. A similar request went to the National Archives. Hoover, who had opposed the creation of the Warren Commission in the first place, and viewed their investigation in an adversary light, going so far as to use FBI files to search for derogatory information about the

Warren Commission staff, acknowledged Liebeler's letter with a reply no different from that he would have sent any critic of the Warren Report: "[As] you are no doubt aware . . . the Warren Commission, upon termination of its activities [deposited its records with] the National Archives and Records Service."*[59] From the Archives, Liebeler learned that only a small portion of the Commission's voluminous records had been processed and, to his chagrin, learned that he would not even be able to examine his own office files! Liebeler's steamer trunk—which I viewed as "Archives-West"—might be most helpful; as would other materials which, he joked, were stored in his barn in Vermont.

When word of Liebeler's course first got out, the reaction was mixed. Among the former Warren Commission attorneys, the course was viewed skeptically. There were some snickers, and a lot of kibitzing. Fellow attorney Sam Stern referred to this new investigation as "Cecil B. DeLiebeler and his cast of thousands." Public reaction was less cynical. Quite a few citizens perceived Liebeler as a crusader, and wrote letters of encouragement—with one or two, as I recollect, even enclosing small checks so they might receive a copy of the "Liebeler Report." But on the subject of money, what really irked Liebeler was the behavior of the publishing industry. Despite his former official position, and his use of a well-known New York literary agent, Liebeler's advance had been modest. Now, as a result of some publicity, publishers who wouldn't speak with him before were deluging him with telexes, telegrams, and letters and offering him many times the money specified in the contract he had signed just weeks before.

That hurt. I do not believe Liebeler was writing the book primarily to make money, but no one—and especially Wesley Liebeler, a man with a deep interest in economics (his specialty at UCLA was antitrust law)— likes to sell a product just weeks before it doubles or triples in price.

Within a day of Liebeler's offer to me, I telephoned Sylvia Meagher with the news, and was astonished by her reaction. What I viewed as a great opportunity, Mrs. Meagher viewed as a danger. The conversation

---

* FBI documents released in 1978 tell the story of what happened when Liebeler's letter was received at FBI headquarters. A five-page memo was drafted by Inspector Malley, who had been the FBI liaison with the Commission, to Assistant Director Cartha DeLoach: "During the existence of the Warren Commission," read the memo, "Wesley Liebeler was the most obnoxious attorney on the staff. . . ."[60] The problem, it seemed, was that when Liebeler wanted something done, he had a habit of picking up the phone and asking the FBI to do it, instead of writing the required letter. The memo said: "Based on our experience with Liebeler we certainly could not expect favorable treatment in any book he would write." The memo recommended: ". . . it is not felt we should render any assistance whatever to Liebeler."[61] The file shows that the Los Angeles Field Office was so instructed and told to notify headquarters if Liebeler called.[62]

was filled with stern warnings about being co-opted, which quickly escalated into advice not to attend Liebeler's course. She even suggested I unlist my telephone number to insure that neither Liebeler nor his students could contact me. A few days later a letter arrived, expressing sentiments which marked the beginning of a lot of trouble between me and some of the critics:

> I want to urge you again, this time in writing, to consider with the greatest care the implication of further "collaboration" with L. It is clear that you have absolutely nothing to gain . . . the prospects of converting a person who is so committed to a particular point of view—and indeed, to self protection—is really illusory.[63]

Mrs. Meagher then made clear that she considered that it would be a breach of faith to discuss with Liebeler the work being done by the critics, including the contents of her still-unpublished manuscript. She warned against funneling any material, verbal or written, obtained from her or anyone else "to our adversaries" whose purpose was "to find a way of . . . destroying it."[64]

I had vouched for what I accepted as Liebeler's honest intentions, but Mrs. Meagher insisted that by associating with him I risked "the appearance of having sold out. . . ."[65]

I didn't see it that way at all.* This would be my chance to pin Liebeler down on any number of issues.

I was irritated by Meagher's letter, as well as by the hostility and suspicion encountered when word spread that I would attend Liebeler's class. On Monday, October 10, I encountered Mark Lane at an autograph party at a Los Angeles bookstore. When I introduced myself, he looked at me sharply and said: "I hear you are working with Liebeler." Lane's remarks were mild. Some of the other critics said they didn't want to have any further contact with me, and, clear across the country, Harold Weisberg somehow got it into his head that the entire purpose of my relationship with Liebeler was to research the criticisms raised in his privately published tome, *Whitewash*. For the first time, I sensed that the critics behaved as a cult, and that unquestioned loyalty to the group was a high priority. The penalty for deviation: ostracism.

I found myself cut off from my peers and I was surprised and hurt.

During this period Liebeler was preoccupied with the idea that if the Commission didn't respond to the critics, a completely false revisionist

---

* Replying to Mrs. Meagher, I wrote that I viewed Liebeler as an intellectual adversary. "I have no intention of collaborating on a defense brief, nor will I end up doing so, being tricked into doing so, or doing so without having intended to do so, under any guise whatsoever." And I added: "I would like to know why I do damage by talking to him about published arguments in a hallway or in an office when he has faced the same published arguments from others (including yourself) on a podium."[66]

history of the event would emerge and prevail. Public opinion about both the assassination and the Commission's investigation would be reshaped along the lines set forth in *Rush to Judgment*.

While Lane was addressing the UCLA student body on October 7, Liebeler held a televised press conference, charging that Lane was touring the country "lying to sell books." When Lane threatened to sue Liebeler for libel, Liebeler publicly dared him to do so.[67] No suit was ever filed. Liebeler often distinguished between legitimate and illegitimate criticism, and reserved his favorite epithet for Lane. It was the one he used to characterize anyone who did not discuss matters of evidence with the civility, decorum, and rationality he thought appropriate, anyone he thought excessively wild-eyed in the pursuit of truth. To Wesley Liebeler, Mark Lane was "that madman."

I found myself in a most peculiar position when arguing with Liebeler about Mark Lane. Often I would agree with some point Lane had made about the Warren Report but disagree with his tactics or style of presentation. I didn't think it was necessary to present only one side of the record to prove the Report wrong, and with Lane, that was Liebeler's pet peeve.

Despite Liebeler's objections to Lane, there was no one more effective at tearing apart a Commission conclusion than Wesley Liebeler. Indeed, one time Liebeler came right out, scoffed at the puerile nature of Lane's book, and practically bragged that he could have written a far better critique of the Report. Liebeler's view was that Lane's whole book was a hodgepodge of minutiae, with no central theme and no definitive evidence which overturned the Commission's conclusions—that Mark Lane was, in effect, attempting to nibble the Commission to death. Liebeler loved to quote Yale Law Professor Alexander Bickel: "Great trial lawyers . . . have an instinct for the jugular. Mister Lane has an instinct for the capillaries."[68]

Yet I sometimes thought Liebeler would have enjoyed exchanging places with Lane, out there on the lecture circuit expounding his beliefs and bringing the truth to the "people," with all the attendant public adulation. But that was all so unseemly. It wasn't his style. He was too much of an elitist.

But it was Liebeler's fundamental beliefs, not his style, that concerned me. Was he interested in the truth? This was important to me because I was trying to ascertain just how serious he was about giving the critics' case a fair hearing in his book. On the day he invited me to attend his class, we had an argument. In view of his professed intent to write a fair and balanced book, I questioned his unequivocal public stance defending the Report. He looked up at me and said: "Are you saying that's a bit intellectually dishonest? . . . Go on and say it, it is." But I had a different interpretation and I told it to him. I said, "You're like a bull, and every time Mark Lane waves his flag, you come out charging." Liebeler agreed. "It would be best if I kept my trap shut."[69]

The Puzzle

This aspect of Liebeler, the public versus the private man, both fascinated and upset me. On the one hand, he seemed genuinely interested in whether anything had slipped by the Warren Commission. On the other, his anger at Lane seemed to be transmuted into a public pose that there was nothing wrong with the Warren Report.

I cannot blame anyone who followed the public debate back in those days for failing to recognize the Liebeler I got to know in private. That Liebeler emerged in one-on-one situations. If we were alone, having a conversation in his office, for example, he was open, friendly, curious, and very funny. And he seemed, at the very least, skeptical, and often irreverent, toward the Commission's most fundamental conclusions. But let a single person enter, especially one of his students, and Liebeler transformed. The change of tone was abrupt. Suddenly he became sarcastic, even mean and snickering, thereby explaining my presence by suggesting that he was only humoring me.

My relationship with Liebeler was, and would remain, ambiguous.

CHAPTER 6

Redefining the Problem:
The Autopsy as "Best Evidence"

WHEN I WAS ABOUT TEN YEARS OLD I read Edward Bellamy's Utopian socialist novel *Looking Backwards: 2000–1887*. Originally published in 1887, it is narrated from the standpoint of a man who wakes up in the year 2000 in a world more idealistic and just.

Certain passages made a vivid impression on me, and set the tone for ideas about law and lawyers I carried for many years to come, reinforcing an early belief that science was a higher, more moral pursuit than law.

"We have no such things as law schools," said the main character in Bellamy's futuristic world. "The law as a special science is obsolete. It was a system of casuistry which the elaborate artificiality of the old order of society absolutely required to interpret it, but only a few of the plainest and simple legal maxims have any application to the existing state of the world. Everything touching the relations of men to one another is now simpler, beyond any comparison, than in your day [so] we . . . have no sort of use for the hair-splitting experts who presided and argued in your courts."[1]

And then, in a passage which stuck in my mind through my years at college, Bellamy described his view of that "old order" of society, and why it needed so many laws: "Formerly, society was a pyramid poised on its apex. All the gravitations of human nature were constantly tending to topple it over, and it could be maintained upright, or rather upwrong (if you will pardon the feeble witticism) by an elaborate system of constantly renewed props and buttresses and guy ropes in the form of laws. . . . Now society rests on its base, and is in as little need of artificial supports as the everlasting hills."[2]

Those passages did not transform me into a socialist, but they did convince me I should not become a lawyer. Now, ironically, I found myself looking forward to my first real contact with that world which Bellamy viewed with such disdain.

I was confident I could convince Liebeler's students that their professor was wrong and that the Commission's version of the shooting was demonstrably incorrect. But the first order of business was to convince Liebeler himself. The private meetings he had requested quickly turned into an intense debate. Our initial meetings took place during the two-week period beginning Monday, October 10, 1966. We met at the Beverly Hills offices of Liebeler's friend and fellow Warren Commission attorney, Joseph Ball.

We focused on whether or not there were assassins firing at Kennedy from the grassy knoll. And since we were starting from scratch, I began again with the head snap.

I tried to impart to Liebeler a sense of the physics involved; what it meant to have something like the Zapruder camera, which chopped up time into eighteenths of a second; what it meant to have that much information about a collision: eighteen photographs per second. I explained the inviolate nature of Newton's laws, and what it meant to say momentum was "conserved" in a collision; that the momentum "before" had to equal the momentum "after," that one could write an equation to that effect, and that the momentum in this case was that of a rifle bullet coming in at a velocity of about two thousand feet per second, or about fifteen hundred miles per hour. That momentum would be transferred along the line of flight, to the object struck—the President's head.

"In that first second after impact, which way do you think *your* head would move," I asked, "if it suffered a collision with an object going at fifteen hundred miles per hour?" I explained to Liebeler that, because of the law of momentum conservation, one could simply look at the film and, by measuring the momentum of the President's head after the collision, compute the speed and direction of the bullet with which it had collided. I emphasized that precise computations notwithstanding, the very direction of the motion—the head moved backward—proved that a force had been applied from the front.

Of course, there were several possible alternate explanations, and they all came up in the course of our discussion.

First, was it possible that the President was thrown backward by a sudden acceleration of the automobile? I argued that could be ruled out, and cited evidence that the car did not accelerate until more than three seconds after the fatal shot.*

---

* Secret Service Agent Clint Hill said it did not accelerate until after he put one foot on the left rear step of the auto. FBI photo expert Shaneyfelt testified that Hill placed one foot on the bumper of the car at frame 368, fifty-five frames (more than three seconds) after the fatal shot,[3] and that he didn't have both feet on the bumper until frame 381, 3.7 seconds after frame 313.[4] Had the car accelerated at

Second, could a neuromuscular reaction have caused the head snap? In drafting "The Case for Three Assassins," I had visited the UCLA Brain Research Institute and discussed that possibility with a number of doctors and researchers. A neurosurgeon emphasized to me the speculative nature of this explanation. If the motor areas of the brain were severely damaged, or if the neural pathways from the brain to all the muscles were severed—and a right rear skull injury described by the Dallas doctors implied just such damage—the President's body would either go limp or undergo a violent momentary spasm, in which his extremities would splay outward stiffly. But aside from the head snap, Kennedy's body simply sagged after the fatal shot, evidence he had not undergone a neuromuscular spasm. Consequently, any motion would be governed by the forces of the collision itself.*

I explained all this to Liebeler. A neuromuscular reaction couldn't be disproved, but it was of low enough probability to be safely ignored. I waited for his reaction, curious to see whether he would seize upon the impossible-to-disprove explanation and play a lawyer's game with me. But he accepted what I had to say, and waved me on.

Despite my concern that he not play a lawyer's game with me, I played a lawyer's game with him. I deliberately withheld the small forward motion of the head between frame 312 and frame 313, first shown to me by Dr. Richard Feynman at Caltech. I knew Liebeler well enough to realize that if I told him about the forward 312–313 motion, he would pounce on it as proof that the shot struck from behind, and then subscribe to any of the "alternate explanations" for the subsequent backward motion.

Our entire relationship would degenerate into a technical debate over whether the President had a neuromuscular reaction, or whether "Jackie pushed him," or any number of alternate explanations one could dream up to account for that backward motion.** But I didn't want to engage in a nit-picking debate. I wanted to change Liebeler's outlook, to make him

---

frame 313, it was unlikely that Hill could have overtaken it. He testified that when the car did accelerate, ". . . the initial surge was quite violent, because it almost jerked me off the rear stepboard."[5] Hill's testimony was corroborated by that of Governor and Mrs. Connally, both of whom testified that the car did not accelerate until after the head shot.[6]

In addition, Dr. Riddle noted in his own study that had the car accelerated, Jacqueline Kennedy ought to have been thrown to the rear, but she did not move relative to the car, and the film shows the same was true for Governor and Mrs. Connally.

* After doing some library research, I learned of the stiffening called "decerebrate rigidity," but that takes several minutes to take effect. The backward motion started within an eighteenth of a second—fifty-five milliseconds—of the impact.

** That particular explanation was impossible to disprove because her hands were not visible.

take the possibility of conspiracy seriously. The evidence on the side of the critics was so substantial, I felt, that if he would just acquaint himself with the details, he would do something about it. So I withheld that item.

My strategy seemed to work. The head snap seemed to disturb Liebeler, and we proceeded to discuss in detail the entire range of evidence pertaining to the grassy knoll.

I brought my photo blowups to Joe Ball's law offices. We pored over them. I admitted that attempting to "see" what was in those pictures required an act of photo interpretation; it was the head snap that was of paramount importance. That was how I reasoned: The head snap justified belief that an assassin had fired from the front; the photos were simply a means for locating the assassin.

But Liebeler reasoned along different lines. To him, the autopsy report provided evidence that the shots came from the rear, while the sniper's-nest evidence—particularly the rifle, mail-ordered to Oswald's post office box—justified the belief that Oswald was the assassin. We were on different wavelengths. Sometimes it seemed that our debate was not about the Kennedy assassination, but about the proper way to arrive at the truth, to determine what Liebeler often referred to as "the reality of the event." The assassination was merely an illustrative example of a more profound difference. At heart, our conflict was epistemological.

But Liebeler was interested in my approach. He looked at the photographs most carefully. We discussed why, if other shooters were there, they weren't seen.

I said that most of the critics I knew believed that if assassins were not seen, that was because no one had noticed them. Why? "Because everybody was looking at the President" was the standard answer—one I found unreasonable and foolish.

I said I thought it absurd that plotters who had given any thought to the problem in advance would send some hired guns to Dealey Plaza and then depend on their speedy legs, an accident of mass psychology, and some pot luck not to be seen. Especially if remaining unseen was integral to a plan to make it appear that all shots had come from the easy-to-find sniper's nest. More had to be involved. Remaining unseen could not be left to chance. If there were grassy-knoll assassins, then somehow they had been concealed.

Liebeler followed this argument with interest. He seemed aware that *if* there were shots from the front, then *something* must have been concealed, both from bystanders at Dealey Plaza on November 22 and from the Commission itself.

But although Liebeler heard me out, in the end he rejected the case for a grassy-knoll assassin—the head snap, the witnesses, the photo blowups. Everything.

Why?

As far as I could tell, he had just one reason. Sitting in Joe Ball's law offices, my photo blowups spread out before him, Liebeler's response to my argument about the primacy of Newton's laws was to return to the Kennedy autopsy report. That was the final defense, his ultimate reason for refusing to believe that any shots struck from the front, or that there were assassins on the grassy knoll. But he did more than just cite the report and dismiss me. He threw out a challenge, and posed a question.

If my argument about the physics was correct, how did I explain the autopsy testimony, that the fatal shot struck from behind—i.e., that the entry wound was at the rear of the head? Liebeler emphasized that Commander Humes' testimony was paramount. He kept saying that Humes' testimony was far better evidence than the Zapruder film, far better than anything I had come up with—it was the "best evidence," he said. He could not ignore it simply because I claimed that Humes' conclusion conflicted with Newton's laws.

I didn't understand Liebeler's reasoning, or even his use of language. Why was Humes' testimony more reliable than Newton's laws? Why did he call it the "best" evidence? I didn't know, but Liebeler's line of argument shifted the burden to me to establish that Commander Humes was not telling the truth.

I couldn't do that. I could only respond that I didn't know how to account for Commander Humes, but that really wasn't my responsibility. Humes couldn't possibly be telling the truth, I said, if my analysis of the physics was correct. I didn't care what the man said—either in his written report or when he testified under oath before the Commission. As far as I was concerned, the backward motion on the Zapruder film made Humes' testimony irrelevant.

Besides, Humes was a navy officer, and Bethesda was a navy hospital. So wasn't the Warren Commission relying on the military, specifically the United States Navy, to tell it from where, on Elm Street, the shots came? I found the impressions of the assassination eyewitnesses far more reliable. And they were buttressed not only by the film, but by the testimony of the Dallas doctors, most of whom said a bullet exited the rear of the President's head. And besides, I said, throwing the ball back in Liebeler's court, how could he, as an attorney, rely on that navy autopsy report when the doctor who wrote it burned his first report? And could Liebeler please explain to me how his fellow attorney, Arlen Specter, had permitted Humes to testify about that without asking him to explain why?

Liebeler simply said he did not know. And anyway, Liebeler pointed out, the fact that Humes burned some notes was not evidence that the report he submitted was false. As far as Liebeler was concerned, I had to prove the doctor had deliberately lied. Did I really believe that? he wanted to know. Furthermore, if a shot struck from the front, where was the bullet? I had no satisfactory answer for any of these questions.

The Puzzle

Our entire debate, it seemed, was narrowing down to belief in the integrity of a single navy officer's examination of the body—the examination itself, the report he wrote, and the testimony he gave to a presidential commission.

The arguments Liebeler and I had at Ball's law offices ran parallel to the discussions which took place in his law class, and any idea that I was going to win large numbers of converts—indeed, even a single convert—soon went glimmering.

Liebeler's class was a painful and frustrating experience. I was a minority of one. The students all disagreed with me, and most thought my way of viewing the evidence was rather strange, even foolish. Planted bullets? A false autopsy report? Shooters concealed in Dealey Plaza? Prove it.

There was much talk of "hard" evidence in Liebeler's class. They all took the sniper's-nest evidence seriously—that was "hard" evidence. What about the head snap on the Zapruder film? Didn't that prove the rifle had not fired the fatal shot?

No.

Like Liebeler, the class relied on the autopsy report. The autopsy report was the "hard" evidence, the "best" evidence, the evidence which told them how Kennedy had been shot, how the assassination had occurred—two shots, from behind.

Other "hard" evidence included the rifle, the stretcher bullet, the two large bullet pieces found in the automobile. The "hard" evidence was assembled just as in the Warren Report. The autopsy report established the shots came from behind. The ammunition proved the rifle was the murder weapon. The step from the Carcano rifle as the murder weapon to Lee Harvey Oswald as the assassin began with the fact that the rifle had, after all, been mail-ordered to Oswald's Dallas post office box from Klein's Sporting Goods in Chicago. The documents proving that was so were also "hard" evidence.

The rest followed the same lines as the Warren Report. Oswald carried a package to work that day. Oswald's palmprint was on the rifle. Fibers from Oswald's shirt were found in the rifle. Oswald was last seen on one of the upper floors, shortly before noon. A witness identified Oswald as the person seen shooting from that window.

Every one of these propositions tying Oswald to the sniper's nest could be disputed, but to Liebeler's class, the pattern was persuasive. The idea of an elaborate frameup? Sheer fantasy.

Arguing with the students and listening to them deliberate, I soon realized an investigation did not have to be an organized conspiracy to start with the Warren Commission's evidence and come to its conclusions. All that was needed were lawyers.

Among my peers in 1966, this was a radical notion. The first-generation Warren Report critics not only believed the Warren Report was wrong, but that the Commission's legal staff had perpetrated a deliberate coverup.

But what I saw in Liebeler's class made me understand that no coverup was necessary. Liebeler's class was like a miniature Warren Commission, and week after week, I was more upset as I watched the process unfold.

What was it about lawyers? An excessive respect for authority? An innate conservatism? An unwillingness to believe that evidence could be planted or faked? Why the tendency to take the sniper's nest at face value? And why the uniformity? Why did they all follow so closely in the footsteps of the Commission? The behavior of the class seemed to reassure Professor Liebeler that the Commission had been right all along, and I began to see all hope of persuading him otherwise going down the drain.

It would be easy to say that Liebeler's students were bucking for a grade, or that law students were politically conservative—but I was convinced that was not the explanation. There was something about their training which made them reason as the Warren Commission had, particularly when it came to reconstructing the shooting. I became intrigued, for I realized that understanding the students' thinking provided the key to understanding how the Commission lawyers had functioned.

I was at loggerheads with other Warren Report critics about this. Once I tried to explain to Marcus what I saw taking place in the law class. Marcus thought he understood from his analysis of the Zapruder film frames published in volume 18 exactly when and from what direction Kennedy was struck. He had a theory of crossfire. "You don't understand," I would say. "They don't care about the Zapruder film. To them, it's not really evidence. All they care about is the autopsy report." Marcus replied I was being brainwashed by Liebeler. I insisted that what I was witnessing in that class involved the way lawyers were trained to think.

I cannot overstate how upsetting I found that class. I often went home with a splitting headache. My standard for perceiving reality was different. Many of my views were based on interpretations of the Zapruder frames. Liebeler's students simply disagreed. But there was more to it than that. A fundamental difference in approach, a difference intimately connected with vocabulary. Liebeler and his students talked like ordinary laymen, but their words often had special meanings.

My first confrontation was with the rather innocuous word "fact." "Fact" had a significantly different meaning for Liebeler's students than for me. To me it was a "fact" that two plus two equals four, that a rectangle has four sides, and that the sum of the angles in a triangle is 180 degrees. But in law, facts were not the immutable truths established by science—facts were merely the opinions of a jury. After hearing both sides present evidence, this group of twelve reasonable men (another expression bandied about quite a bit in Liebeler's class—the "reasonable man," the ideal juror) determined what the facts were, and rendered a verdict.

Some of this was new. Of course I knew that juries reached verdicts and determined whether someone was innocent or guilty—but I had not understood that meant the jury found the facts. This view of the jury as a "fact-finder" had certain ramifications: It meant that a "fact" was just about anything that group of twelve people could be persuaded to believe, by whatever means. Under these circumstances, quite a gap could develop between the "facts" and the truth, between what a jury could be persuaded to believe and what had actually happened.

My exposure to this view of facts, fact-finding, and the lawyer's way of determining truth affected my own outlook. I began to gauge the strength of an argument by its ability to persuade a jury. By that standard, reality acquired a rather malleable and pliant quality. I began to see how Liebeler's students perceived the assassination, why they seemed to view everything through that prism of "hard evidence."

Consider the case being made against the Warren Report by the critics. In terms of persuading a jury, what could actually be proved? Suppose, for example, I had to persuade a jury that the backward motion on the Zapruder film was the result of a shot from the front. Presumably, I would find a physicist to so testify. But there might be another scientist who would testify differently. Who would determine which of these two was correct? The jury, of course. Thus, the legal process reduced the head snap to an argument among experts.

I remember one of Liebeler's students taking me to task on this very point. He knew little about physics, nor did he seem concerned that the backward motion of the President's head was a physical event which demanded an explanation, and for which there was only one correct explanation. But he was at pains to explain to me, since I was always carping on the head snap, that what I or anyone else said really didn't matter. Experts *always* disagreed. The student's message was that the behavior of a twelve-man jury was the ultimate test as to what was or was not a fact. And because a jury would probably divide, upon hearing two experts argue, the backward motion of the head lost its force as a fact.

I was getting a vivid education about how lawyers perceive reality and how codified their procedures are in determining what evidence is credible. The potential pitfalls of the legal mind were not unknown to the man running the investigation. At the first staff meeting, J. Lee Rankin, the General Counsel, cautioned those assembled not to accept the FBI conclusion that Oswald was the assassin, but to gather the facts in an objective manner. "Truth," he told them, "is your only client."[7]

Watching Liebeler's class, I found it difficult to believe that a lawyer's way of viewing reality could be offset by that directive. Instructing a lawyer his client was "truth" would not transform him into a detective. Liebeler's class abounded with valuable clues as to how the Warren Commission's legal staff had approached the job of analyzing the evidence and investigating the Kennedy assassination.

Indeed, their attitude reminded me of an incident which occurred when I first met Liebeler. On November 30, 1965, at our third meeting, I rattled off my own reconstruction of the shooting. The head snap, I said, precluded Oswald's being the person who fired the fatal shot, because that shot came from the front. The wound at the front of the throat, described by the Dallas doctors as an entry wound, precluded that shot's having been fired by Oswald, since the President was facing forward and Oswald was allegedly located behind the motorcade. So (ignoring Governor Connally for the moment) all that was left was the rear entry wound for the non-fatal shot, the one described by the autopsy witnesses as being "low" in the back. That shot, I told Liebeler, might have been fired by someone at Oswald's alleged location, but that's all there was, I said.

Retorted Liebeler: ". . . and three spent shells."[8]

That remark, "three spent shells," did not prove that Oswald had fired the fatal shot, but it did epitomize the mentality of the Warren Commission attorneys, always arguing to that hypothetical jury. In a section subtitled "Number of Shots," the Warren Report stated:

The most convincing evidence relating to the number of shots was provided by the presence on the sixth floor of three spent cartridges which were demonstrated to have been fired by the same rifle that fired the bullets which caused the wounds.[9]

That statement could have been drafted by any of Liebeler's students, all of whom took the sniper's-nest evidence at face value, regarding the sixth floor of the Depository as a temple of "hard" evidence, "hard" facts. The grassy knoll, down the street, was treated with derision and scorn—the source, perhaps, of some extraneous noises. Echoes.

Sometimes I felt like screaming: Don't you people realize that something is terribly wrong here? There is too much improbability at large in the official version. A head could not go backward when hit from behind. A bullet which traveled through two men, shattering a rib and breaking a wrist, shouldn't come out practically undamaged, and with nary a trace of blood. But, like iron filings to a magnet, Liebeler's students were attracted to the "hard evidence." And the considerations I raised were seen as just "loose ends."

That was another law school favorite—every case had loose ends. Didn't I know that? Like a legal spare tire, they would trot out that category to deal with any number of inconsistencies or implausibilities I employed to punch holes in the official version.

I found my dissent dissected, analyzed, categorized, and finally discarded.

Sitting in that class, I could never quite decide whether the legal approach was an exercise in critical thinking, or an escape from reality. One strong impression was that lawyers played a game with evidence, one with its own special rules, habits of mind, and vocabulary. They restructured reality for juries. To Liebeler and his students, we were all participants in moot court; the assassination had been denuded of an objective reality. All that was left were arguments that could be made to that hypothetical jury. Most disturbing, however, was the implicit justification, an attitude that the objective truth in the Kennedy assassination was unknowable—and so the legal truth was as good an approximation as any.

My attitude differed markedly. I felt the truth, at least about the mechanics of the shooting, was knowable. The assassination was a collision between bullets and bodies, lots of data were available, and it was possible to determine how it had happened. In this regard, I found the behavior of the Warren Commission in setting forth the single-bullet theory almost comical.

Although the Commissioners all subscribed to the lone-assassin conclusion, some were most reluctant to sign a report stating one bullet struck both men.[10] Senator Russell, for example, flatly refused.[11] What ensued, according to John McCloy, was "the battle of the adjectives."[12] On this critical issue, where the alternatives were clear, where the Commissioners had to choose between the theory of a double hit or the conclusion of a second assassin, the Commissioners, all lawyers, behaved as if they were drafting a piece of legislation. They searched for compromise language. Finally, like good negotiators, they split the difference. The evidence was "persuasive," they concluded, that a single bullet had "probably" hit both men.[13]

The legal approach gave me the creeps. Sometimes I thought that if lawyers had invaded the field of mathematics, two-plus-two-equals-four would have been a compromise, worked out after a jury had heard both sides—one arguing the sum was three, the other that it was five.

On Thursday, October 20, 1966, an incident occurred which marked a turning point in my understanding of the workings of Wesley Liebeler's mind. It was also the key to how lawyers assess evidence. At noon, Liebeler gave a one-hour talk at the UCLA Law School, much of which was devoted to a defense of the single-bullet theory. I took a seat toward the back of the lecture hall and watched him use the autopsy report to make a devastating attack on Epstein's book. I was astonished to learn something new—a fact in full public view, but ignored by most of the Warren Report critics, and whose significance I, certainly, had failed to appreciate.

In *Inquest*, Epstein cited the clothing holes, the dot on the autopsy diagram, and verbal descriptions by FBI and Secret Service agents of the wound location as evidence that the wound in question was a "low" back wound, not a "high" neck wound.*[14]

Liebeler decimated this line of attack. He skillfully noted that Epstein had ignored a crucial piece of evidence: the *measured* location of the wound reported by Humes in the text of the autopsy report.

As Liebeler's talk unfolded, I grew increasingly embarrassed. Epstein wasn't the only person who had ignored the measured location. In writing "The Case for Three Assassins," so had I. I had just assumed that the centimeter measurement cited in the autopsy report corresponded to the "low" location suggested by the clothing holes and the diagram dot.

Well, it didn't, as Liebeler, who took little for granted, soon discovered. The autopsy report said the wound was located "14cm [5½ inches] below the tip of the right mastoid process [the bony protuberance behind the ear]."[15] Liebeler had gone to the trouble of having someone perform this measurement on him. Triumphantly he announced the result. The spot cited in the autopsy report wasn't as low as the one suggested by the clothing holes (nearly a half-foot from the top of the collar), nor as high as the one shown in the artist's drawing (above the shoulder blade in the base of the neck). It was somewhere in between. Furthermore, according to the measured location, the rear wound was indeed above the wound at the front of the throat.

Ridiculing Epstein for having ignored such crucial evidence, Liebeler said his own analysis showed the clothing had to ride up only about two and a half inches for the clothing holes to match the wound location. Thus, a downward-sloping neck trajectory and, concomitantly, the single-bullet, was possible after all.

I was astonished. I had no idea that the 14cm location for the wound designated a spot significantly higher than the clothing holes. And it was a complete surprise that that spot was higher than the wound at the front of the neck. By relying on the Bethesda autopsy report, Liebeler had come up with a piece of data which supported the single-bullet theory.

But just a minute. Something still seemed odd. Why were there all these different locations for the back wound? Why did the data sort into three groupings: "low," "medium," and "high," as if the object of discussion was not a wound location, but a thermostat setting? And what was Liebeler's justification for choosing the "medium" position cited in the autopsy report? Simply because it was consistent with the single-bullet theory?

Immediately after his talk, I bounded up the stairs to his office and asked him all these questions: Why, of all the evidence, was he placing so

* This "high" location was depicted in the navy artist's drawing utilized by Commander Humes to illustrate his testimony.

much reliance on that "14cm" location? I was not arguing, just inquiring about his methodology. When it came to selecting evidence, why did he pick and choose as he did?

Liebeler was a nice man, a courteous man. He kept his voice down. A perfect gentleman, really. And he was a very funny man. But dealing with him on these matters had been absolutely infuriating. I felt like a pincushion. In the beginning, I could not figure out what the problem was. I had concluded that Liebeler and I just viewed reality differently, and our debate acquired overtones of just whose methodology was superior. This was a perfect example. Once again, Wesley J. Liebeler had reached into the grab bag of the twenty-six volumes and come up with a piece of data to defend the Commission's conclusions. But since there were three separate indicia as to the wound's location, what justified his selecting the one he did? What was his criterion?

Liebeler looked at me with a certain amount of perplexity and contempt and answered my questions by asking a series of his own.

LIEBELER: He [Humes] used a ruler to measure that?
LIFTON: Yes.
LIEBELER: He can read his ruler?
LIFTON: Yes.
LIEBELER: He can write down what he measured?*

Liebeler's reply caught me completely off guard. He employed the language of science, a measurement made with a ruler, to justify what I had viewed as most improbable: a downward-slanting trajectory through Kennedy's neck. I felt co-opted. How can one rebut a measurement?

Furthermore, Liebeler noted something else. The 14cm measurement was not just typewritten in the autopsy report—it was handwritten in the margin of the diagram filled out in the autopsy room, the same diagram which the critics were carping on because it showed the dot as "low." (See Fig. 3, p. 78.)

The dot had simply been misplaced, said Liebeler. What was more important, the spot on the diagram where an autopsy doctor happened to touch the paper with his pen or the number handwritten in the margin? What was significant, argued Liebeler, was the number written in the margin. Liebeler's reasoning seemed sound: Humes could measure, couldn't he?

I found Liebeler's reliance on that marginalia and his willingness to dismiss all contrary evidence fascinating. But still, my basic beliefs did not change. There was just too much evidence indicating the wound was "low."

And what made him believe in the primacy of the notation? At first, I thought he viewed it as just common sense. But later I realized that, for

---

* This dialogue was recorded in a letter I wrote that night.

Wesley Liebeler, more was at stake. I was witnessing a specific instance of a broad legal concept which he repeatedly invoked in our ongoing debate—the concept of "best evidence."

Liebeler always cited the Kennedy autopsy findings as "best evidence." When I first heard Liebeler use the phrase, I did not understand what it meant, or why he felt his evidence was "better" than mine. "Good," "better," and "best" were all ordinary English words, and I had no idea that I was encountering the secret vocabulary of lawyers. I came by this knowledge only after months of arguing with Liebeler and his students, and studying books on evidence.

The "best-evidence" concept, impressed on all law students, is that when you seek to determine a fact from conflicting data, you must arrange the data according to a hierarchy of reliability. All data are not equal. Some evidence (e.g., physical evidence, or a scientific report) is more inherently error-free, and hence more reliable, than other evidence (e.g., an eye-witness account). The "best" evidence rules the conclusion, whatever volume of contrary evidence there may be in the lower categories.

The best-evidence concept was not just something Liebeler used in his professional life. It seemed to permeate his entire psychology, his approach to existence. Liebeler seemed to believe that people who didn't perceive reality in terms of "best evidence" had not perceived reality at all—that is, they had glimpsed the appearance, but not, to use one of his favorite terms, "the reality of the event." In a letter I wrote the evening Liebeler lectured me on Humes and his ruler, I described Liebeler's rationale for dismissing contrary evidence about that wound location:*

Liebeler's position about the hole on the President's back is quite simple. It is *exactly* where it is specifically measured to be as officially stated in the Government's autopsy report: 14cm down from the right mastoid process. Acknowledging the fact that others "saw" it elsewhere and that Humes' drawing shows it higher, [Liebeler] simply argued that the only precise and legally validated location of this wound is the [one given] in the official report. Who are we to believe, he argued, some artist? Or some Secret Service agent?[17]

With the word "saw" in quotation marks I captured something important about the psychology of this particular Warren Commission attorney. Liebeler knew that the wound was only in one place, and his message was clear: The "best evidence" of where the wound was located was where Humes measured it, and the "best evidence" of where Humes measured it was the notation made in the margin of the autopsy diagram. To Wesley Liebeler, all contrary observations were misperceptions.

---

* For example, Secret Service Agent Hill's report stating the wound was "6 inches down from the neckline"[16]; or, at the other extreme, the artist's drawing depicting the wound considerably above the top of the shoulder blade—i.e., above the location cited in the autopsy report.

The Puzzle

That dialogue was responsible, I believe, for advancing my thinking on the subject one more notch. I had never had that mental image before— Humes, ruler in hand, standing at the autopsy table, having just measured the location of a small hole on the President's body.

It led to a valuable insight. From the standpoint of a lawyer like Liebeler, the story of Dealey Plaza—the basic geometry of the crime—was derived from measurements and evaluations of wounds made in the Bethesda autopsy room. The incident drove home, once again, the utter dependence of the Warren Commission on the autopsy doctors for their reconstruction of the assassination.

Liebeler's response to the grassy-knoll witnesses provided another example of his use of the "best evidence" concept. Commander Humes examined the President's body and testified that no shots struck from the front. But a veritable crowd of people on Dealey Plaza—at least sixty-four witnesses—disagreed. Liebeler, like the Commission, rejected those accounts and relied instead on the autopsy conclusion. As the Warren Report said, there was no "credible evidence that the shots were fired . . . from any other location."[18]

Why weren't the grassy-knoll witnesses "credible"? The Report never spelled out the Commission's reasoning. Originally, I thought the label was capricious, a semantic device. But Wesley Liebeler explained to an audience at Stanford University on October 17, 1966: "I think the best way to think about this problem," he said,

at least the way I try to think about it—and I think the way the Commission analyzed it too—[is that] there were witnesses all over the place who saw all kinds of things happening. There were shots coming from behind the grassy knoll . . . there were shots coming from the School Book Depository . . . there were six shots, ten shots—you know, all kinds of things.

The *best evidence* [emphasis added] of where the shots came from, it seems to me, is the autopsy report itself, which indicates perfectly clearly, based on a scientific examination of the body of the President . . . [that] the shots were . . . fired from behind and above. Now when you compare the scientific evidence of an autopsy report with eyewitness and earwitness testimony of a group of people at a time like that . . . I think it's perfectly clear that you've got to favor the scientific autopsy evidence.[19]

For Liebeler, the grassy knoll problem was almost metaphysical—a question of how a legal investigation should proceed to separate appearance from reality. To hear Liebeler tell it, people in Dealey Plaza had witnessed the appearance, but by basing its conclusion on "best evidence," the Warren Commission had determined the reality.

Now there's no question [that] lots of people testified the shots came from [the knoll]. But . . . the autopsy report indicates that the shots came from behind and weren't fired from there. . . . [So] you just have to conclude that [the shots] didn't come from there, even though people thought they [did]. No doubt they're sincere about it, but I just think they're mistaken.[20]

When I finally came to understand this line of reasoning, I was amazed —not because I disagreed with it in principle, but because I disagreed with the application of it in this case.

I was astonished that Liebeler, his class, the Warren Commission, or anyone else would place such trust in the Bethesda autopsy, given the circumstances. Besides the unexplained burning of autopsy documents, there was the head snap on the film, and conflicting information and opinion from the Dallas doctors. The fact that the autopsy was done at a military hospital seemed suspicious to me.

But willy-nilly, Liebeler applied the "best-evidence" concept. He labeled the Bethesda autopsy "best evidence" and based his view of the shooting on that. Liebeler shifted the burden of proof to me, and obstinately maintained that the autopsy findings must be the starting point—unless I could impeach Humes as a witness, and thus impeach his autopsy conclusions as evidence. My evidence is better than your evidence, my witness is better than your witness—that's what Liebeler was saying. Only one witness counted—James J. Humes, the autopsy surgeon, the man who examined the President's body.

I had gained a vital insight, although I'm not sure I fully appreciated it at the time: Any conspiracy which could result in a false Kennedy autopsy report could mislead an entire legal investigation as to the number and direction of the shots. No "coverup" was necessary—at least not in the sense the critics were using that term. If there were grassy-knoll shooters, it hardly mattered whether their concealment was perfect, whether their activities created smoke which was seen, or sounds which were heard. None of that mattered. From the standpoint of a subsequent legal inquiry, those assassins would be rendered invisible as long as the autopsy said the shots came from behind. No plot or "coverup" was necessary because the Warren Commission staff had all gone to law school. They all followed the same orthodox and thoroughly predictable procedures for fact-finding. They sought, and based their conclusions upon, the "best evidence."

I found the situation painfully frustrating. I couldn't prove the Bethesda autopsy report was false, or that anyone had lied. My "proof" was the head snap shown on the Zapruder film. My attitude—mostly unspoken— was: "Well of course the doctors lied. They must have lied. How else explain all that grassy-knoll evidence?" But to Liebeler and his class I was just another person with an arguable opinion about the head snap and an unsupported theory about the doctors.

Furthermore, Liebeler had something else to throw at me whenever I argued that shots struck from the knoll. Besides invoking the autopsy as "best evidence" and haranguing me about Humes and the ruler, he demanded to know: "Where's the bullet?"

The scorn in Liebeler's voice, whenever he asked this question, always nettled me. I had no ready answer, other than to make an *ad hominem* attack on Commander Humes. Liebeler's argument was based on geometry, anatomy, and the obvious fact that a bullet, once it enters the body, must go somewhere.

If a shot struck Kennedy's head or neck from the front, either it passed all the way through, or it lodged inside the body. If the bullet remained in the body, it would be visible on X-rays. Commander Humes, however, testified that there were no bullets or fragments of any consequence inside the body. If the bullet passed all the way through, it would, upon exiting, punch out an exit wound whose edges would gape, a wound easily distinguishable from the small puncture created by a bullet's entry. But Humes testified the President's body showed only two entry wounds, both on the rear surface, one at the base of the neck, the other at the base of the skull.*

Was Humes lying about the wounds and the absence of bullets inside the President's body? That seemed to be the bottom-line question. Indeed, my argument that the President was struck from the front was tantamount to an accusation that the autopsy results were deliberately false. Of course, I wasn't trying to argue that specific proposition—I was merely trying to argue conspiracy in terms of a grassy-knoll shooter on Dealey Plaza. But in rebutting my argument, Liebeler's strategy seemed to force me to bear the greater burden of calling all three autopsy doctors liars, a burden I could not carry.

Nevertheless, Liebeler's claim that the autopsy conclusions were "best evidence" overlooked an irregularity in the Commission's procedures intimately linked with the credibility of the autopsy testimony. And Liebeler's discomfiture on the subject was apparent.

Despite all the talk of "best evidence," the Warren Commission had not followed that concept. For the "best evidence" of the President's wounds wasn't what the doctors said, but the sixty-five X-rays and photographs of President Kennedy's body that the Warren Commission had failed to examine.

Instead, the Commission followed a peculiar procedure in which Humes was permitted to illustrate his testimony with three artist's drawings made under his supervision. As Humes explained: ". . . we did not know whether or not the photographs which we had made would be available to the Commission.** So to assist in making our testimony more understandable to the Commission members, we decided to have made drawings, schematic

---

* An easy way to visualize the Bethesda autopsy conclusions was to think of Kennedy's wounds as coming in two matched pairs: For each of the rear entries, there was an exit. Whatever had entered from the rear had exited heading toward the front. Thus Humes' testimony not only reported an *absence* of any wounds (or bullets) indicating the President had been shot from the front, but the presence of wounds indicating he had been shot from the rear.

** The twenty-six volumes gave no hint who was responsible for determining whether, as Humes put it, the X-rays and photographs "would be available."

drawings, of the situation as we saw it, as we recorded it, and as we recall it."*[21] (See Photos 16*A*, 23, and 24.)

The three large drawings, Warren Commission Exhibits 385, 386, and 388, were then placed on easels while Humes testified. Exhibit 385 was a side view of the President, showing a downward-sloping arrow passing through the President's neck wounds. Exhibit 388 was another side view of the President showing an arrow passing back to front through the President's head wounds. Exhibit 386 was a rear view, and showed the two rear entry wounds, one at the back of the neck, the other at the base of the skull. A rather tame substitute for the X-rays and photographs, the three drawings illustrated how the Warren Commission said Kennedy had been shot.

Specter questioned Humes about the accuracy of the drawings and their use in lieu of medical photographs. Humes' responses seemed carefully qualified; indeed, his testimony contained remarks, almost apologies, implying their inadequacy. "I must state these drawings are in part schematic," he said. "The artist had but a brief period of some two days to prepare these. He had no photographs from which to work, and had to work under our description, verbal description, of what we had observed."[23] Specter asked Humes whether it would be "helpful" in "redefining the drawings if that should become necessary" to have the photographs. Humes answered in the affirmative: "If it were necessary to have them absolutely true to scale. I think it would be virtually impossible for him to do this without the photographs."[24] Later in the testimony, Humes said the drawings were only "schematic representations,"[25] "the photographs would be more accurate"[26]; they would be "far superior" to his "humble verbal description."[27]

To those familiar with the accuracy and precision with which a skilled medical artist can work, Humes' tone seemed extremely deferential and oddly defensive, and his self-deprecating remark about his "humble verbal description" always made me think of the good doctor as Uriah Humes.

The upshot was clear: The Warren Commission had followed irregular procedure with no explanation. Furthermore, there was no indication what had become of the X-rays and photographs. Secret Service Agent Kellerman testified that when the autopsy was over, he brought the materials back to the White House and turned them over to Robert Bouck of the Protective Research Section of the U.S. Secret Service. As far as the twenty-six volumes revealed, the trail ended there.

---

* Dr. Humes testified that the drawings, Warren Commission Exhibits 385, 386, and 388, had been "made under my supervision and that of Dr. Boswell" by Mr. H. A. Rydberg, a navy medical illustrator, and that he and Boswell "supervised directly Mr. Rydberg in making these drawings," i.e., they had told Rydberg exactly what to draw.[22]

Like many of the first-generation Warren Report critics, I responded to this state of affairs with intense skepticism. When I first purchased the twenty-six volumes in 1965, I believed the Commission had failed to examine the X-rays and photographs as part of a plan to falsify autopsy testimony by creating conditions in which Commander Humes' testimony would not be subject to verification. The fact that the drawings were created by the same doctor who had inexplicably burned "certain preliminary draft notes" fueled my suspicions. In those early days many critics suspected that the grassy-knoll problem had been eliminated through misleading autopsy testimony, and the Commission had conveniently tailored its procedures to avoid discovering it had been lied to.

I tried to avoid saying these things to Liebeler because he became quite annoyed at the extent of my suspicions. And, on this particular issue, he was at pains to assure me that the only reason the Commission hadn't examined the X-rays and photographs was that they had acceded to the wishes of the Kennedy family. The Commission, he said several times, had been "excessively deferential" to the Kennedys. Gradually, I came to accept this explanation, especially since Liebeler himself seemed genuinely irritated at this state of affairs. Nonetheless, whatever its motives, the Commission's investigation contained a loophole. Had someone taken advantage of it?

Over the summer of 1966, the controversy escalated. The publication of *Inquest* and *Rush to Judgment* led to public calls for the production of the X-rays and photos. It was becoming painfully apparent that all multiple-assassin theories postulated by the Warren Report critics could be demolished if the X-rays and photographs verified the autopsy findings. "Failure to publish or preserve such evidence cannot be construed in any light favorable to the Commission," wrote Lane.[28]

In his July 1966 article in the *Nation*, historian Jacob Cohen described his own fruitless attempts to locate the X-rays and photographs, which included a search at the National Archives and inquiries directed to the Treasury Department (which oversees the Secret Service), Commander Humes, Admiral Burkley (the White House doctor), and even Robert Kennedy. The X-rays and photographs were nowhere to be found. "Sometimes it all seems like a weird joke," wrote Cohen, ". . . the one set of documents which could disarm the speculations of [the Commission's] most serious critics had seemingly disappeared."[29]

Cohen reported that he had interviewed Arlen Specter on June 13, 1966, and that Specter told him "he had not seen any of these documents, and that when he asked Justice Warren for them Warren said that the Commission had decided 'not to press the matter.' "[30] The implication, of course, was that the Kennedys had the materials and would not relinquish them to the Commission, or at least that was what Arlen Specter was told.

In July 1966 Paul Hoch went to Secret Service Headquarters in Washington, D.C. to make inquiries. He was handed a terse, one-page statement, which read in part:

The X-ray films were used for the briefing of the Warren Commission's staff on the autopsy procedure and results.[31]

A briefing? When? Who did the briefing, and for whom? This statement flatly contradicted everything Liebeler had told me. I began to wonder whether Liebeler had told me the truth, or whether Specter was perhaps hiding things from Liebeler.

At about that time, Specter was interviewed by Philadelphia journalist Gaeton Fonzi. Specter said that he had wanted very much to see the X-rays and photographs, but had been overruled. It was the Warren Commissioners themselves who decided it "was not necessary" to examine them, a decision made "out of considerations of taste and respect for the dead President."[32] Had the decision been his, implied Specter, it would have gone the other way, but the matter was not in his hands: "The President of the United States didn't want Arlen Specter to do the investigation of the assassination of President Kennedy. The President of the United States appointed the Commission to do that job."[33]

Then, on October 10, 1966, *U.S. News & World Report* published a cover story defending the Warren Report, and featuring an interview with Specter. Included was the following exchange; its significance was apparent when one recalled that the validity of the single-bullet theory was dependent upon the exact location of the back wound:

Q. Could we get to this matter of the pictures of the President's body? Have you seen the pictures?

A. The complete set of pictures taken at the autopsy was not made available to me or to the Commission. *I was shown one picture of the back of a body* [emphasis added] which was represented to be the back of the President, although it was not technically authenticated. It showed a hole in the position identified in the autopsy report. To the best of my knowledge, the Commission did not see any photographs or X-rays.[34]

Specter's answer was startling. Previously, except for the Secret Service statement, which seemed puzzling and possibly in error, we had no evidence that the Warren Commission had any contact whatsoever with any of this material. Now we knew better. There had been at least one "exception." And the scene conjured up was bizarre: the father of the single-bullet theory, fully cognizant of conflicting evidence as to the location of the back wound, being shown a single picture "of the back of a body which was represented to be the back of the President. . . ."[35] Where had this strange scene taken place? And why? Had there been an "off-the-record" confrontation in which a skeptical Specter had insisted on being shown such evidence so he could be sure he was not being lied to?

The Secret Service statement about a briefing and Specter's strange comment suggested that during the official investigation the U.S. Secret Service had in its custody a set of autopsy X-rays and photographs which purportedly confirmed the Bethesda autopsy report. What had become of them?

Nobody seemed to know for sure. By mid-October 1966 disbelief in the Warren Report mounted. *Rush to Judgment* was on the best-seller list, Lane was touring the country alleging conspiracy, and *Life* was preparing a cover story using frames from the Zapruder film to attack the single-bullet theory. The Warren Commission attorneys were in the awkward position of defending the Report but having to concede that they hadn't seen the "best evidence."

Then things began to change. News items appeared saying that the X-rays and photographs were at the Justice Department, or that the Kennedys had them, or that they might be given to the Archives, or that they were already at the Archives. Something was afoot. In his October 17, 1966, address at Stanford, Liebeler said the collection was at the Justice Department, and then, like a man about to play a trump card, he continued: ". . . and I'm going to stand here right now and make a prediction that they *will* be made available under appropriate circumstances."[36]

Liebeler's speech made the wire services, and the reaction of many of the Warren Report critics to this changing situation was revealing, psychologically. For almost two years, they had combed the twenty-six volumes for evidence to prove that shots had been fired from the front, or that the back wound wasn't high enough to support the single-bullet theory, out of a deep belief that the Warren Report was a fraud.

Now, with indications that the X-rays and photographs were about to be produced, many of them backed off.

It was a trap, they reasoned. Neither the Kennedy family nor the government of the United States was about to make available evidence which would overturn the findings of a presidential commission. One had to be incredibly naive to believe that, and the critics were anything but naive. Indeed, the time had long since passed when the autopsy X-rays and photographs could be utilized with any credibility. During the actual investigation, the government had resorted to the outrageous subterfuge of using drawings; now, three years after the assassination, better evidence was about to materialize. There could be only one reason. It must have been forged.

I remember a number of Southern California critics scrambling to "warn" Mark Lane, then promoting his book, not to put so many eggs in one basket, not to invest his credibility and that of the critics in the X-rays and photographs.*

In my discussions with Liebeler, I found myself in a predicament. I could not really believe that the X-rays and photographs would support the Warren Report, yet I was very well aware that it was logically fallacious to begin with the assumption that if they did so, then they must be fake.

The question remained whether it was technically possible to falsify X-rays and photographs to make them conform with a false autopsy report. The critics who talked of faking such materials did so in a rather glib manner, giving scant consideration to the technical obstacles involved. The attitude was widespread that any government which could cover up the truth about a presidential assassination was certainly capable of manufacturing such evidence, if necessary. One line of argument was that it was difficult to tell the X-rays of one body from another. The autopsy photographs would be closeups of the wounds; could we be sure that the body was that of John Kennedy?

But the President died of head wounds, and he also sustained a wound in the front of the neck. The facile assumption that the pictures of the wounds would all be closeups and would not include natural identifying marks was unfounded. Many of the photographs would have to show President Kennedy's face, possibly from several perspectives. Commander Humes had testified that there were from fifteen to twenty pictures of the wounds.

Similar considerations prevailed with respect to the X-rays. X-rays of the head might show Kennedy's dental work. X-rays of his lower back would show his spinal fusion.

Casual talk of using "another body" was gross oversimplification.

The films might have been faked by photo-retouching, but that too was a complex operation. It would have required beginning with the originals, altering them by artwork, rephotographing the altered original, and then substituting the forgeries back in the collection. This would have had to be done for both the X-rays and the photographs, the objective being to bring the collection into agreement with Humes' testimony—two matched pairs of wounds, no bullets in the body, etc. Although technically possible, it would have been immensely difficult.

Furthermore, such a plot appeared to require at least the tacit approval of the medical photographer and the radiologist, since both would be

* For two years, Lane had featured the grassy knoll in his lecture appearances, and charged that the Warren Commission had "transformed" the throat wound from one of entry to one of exit. But now, suppose the X-rays and photographs supported the findings of the Commission?

called upon to authenticate the evidence when it was finally produced. Also, they would have to remain silent when the Warren Report was published containing an autopsy report describing medical "facts" they knew to be false.

These were rather formidable problems. The conspiracy seemed to get bigger and bigger. I could see why Liebeler and Specter, despite some uneasiness about the Commission's not having examined the X-rays and photos, nevertheless could not believe the doctors had lied. "I think it would have been absolutely impossible for the autopsy surgeons to perjure themselves," Specter told *U.S. News & World Report*. "They would have to be in league with numerous other people who were present in the room where the autopsy was conducted, including Secret Service agents and FBI agents and a whole host of people."[37]

Specter pointed to another factor. "At the time the autopsy surgeons testified in March of 1964," he told *U.S. News*, "they had no way of knowing whether the photographs and X-rays would later be available to the Commission to corroborate or impeach their testimony. As a matter of fact, Chief Justice Warren directed a question to Dr. Humes as to whether he would change any of his testimony if the photographs were available— and the record of hearings would speak on that—and Dr. Humes said that he would not."[*][38]

To believe that Humes' testimony was false, one had to believe that a navy commander would deliberately lie, risk criminal charges, and bluff the Chief Justice of the United States.

If Humes testified truthfully, then his testimony would be verified by the X-rays and photographs. In that case, the shooting happened exactly as stated in the Bethesda autopsy report: ". . . the deceased died . . . of two perforating gunshot wounds . . . fired from a point behind and somewhat above the level of the deceased. . . ."[39]

But if Humes testified falsely, then there seemed to be two possibilities:

1. *The X-rays and photos were authentic.* In this case, they would expose a conspiracy on the part of the autopsy doctors to mislead the Warren Commission about the details of the shooting and would become the basis for an accurate reconstruction of the assassination.

2. *False X-rays and photos were prepared to corroborate that testimony.* Here, they would agree with, and appear to verify, Humes' testimony.

---

* Specter was referring to the following interchange:

WARREN: . . . may I ask you this, Commander: If we had the pictures here and you could look them over again and restate your opinion, would it cause you to change any of the testimony you have given here?

HUMES: To the best of my recollection, Mr. Chief Justice, it would not.[40]

This option presupposed some sophisticated, but not impossible, faking of pictures and X-rays. Such a conspiracy would require the tacit approval of the photographer and radiologist.

Liebeler knew he had not been involved in any chicanery and he was certain Specter had not either. What they had done was follow the "best-evidence" concept, rely on the autopsy report, and out of respect for the Kennedys not demand the X-rays and photos be admitted in evidence. In my discussion with Liebeler, I hammered away at the theme that, the attorneys' honesty notwithstanding, the head snap proved Humes couldn't be telling the truth. I thought my argument was having some effect on Liebeler, forcing him to entertain the possibility that maybe Humes had something up his sleeve.

Liebeler was not a man to entertain a complex hypothesis when a simple one would do. When not propounding the virtues of "best evidence," he was lecturing me about another of his favorite analytical tools—"Occam's Razor," the principle that "the simplest explanation is the best explanation." Liebeler often pointed out how easy it was to theorize about a conspiracy, yet how difficult it was, in practice, to conceive of a workable plot. Conspiracies involved too many people. They became unwieldy. They violated "Occam's Razor."

Because of Liebeler's commitment to that principle, I think he automatically rejected any technologically sophisticated conspiracy to falsify photos and X-rays. Liebeler's concerns were simpler. Suppose Humes had simply lied, and all that talk about the "sensitivity" of the Kennedy family was nothing but a cock-and-bull story so that the Commission wouldn't look at the authentic X-rays and photos?

This was Wesley Liebeler's nightmare. Suppose the authentic pictures and X-rays arrived at the National Archives and, lo and behold, they simply did not support the navy autopsy report? Suppose the discrepancies were gross? Suppose they proved shots had been fired from the front? Or showed bullets from "other guns"?

This was a remote possibility, but Liebeler was a cautious fellow. It would be a professional debacle, and they would only have themselves to blame. By failing to adhere to the "best-evidence" concept, they had laid themselves wide open. Revenge might be sweet, but sending Commander Humes to jail for lying to the Warren Commission was not Liebeler's idea of justice.

Liebeler seemed somewhat defensive on the subject of the X-rays and photos, even in public. This was evident in his reaction to the wire service account of his October 17, 1966, Stanford speech. UPI misquoted him, claiming he said the autopsy X-rays proved the shots came from behind. Liebeler immediately called the UPI office in San Francisco demanding a retraction, and then wrote a strongly worded letter: ". . . your story indicates that I said that autopsy X-rays of assassinated President John F.

Kennedy showed 'all shots' fired at him were 'from behind and above.' As I have advised . . . I did not state that this was shown by the X-rays, but rather that it was shown by the autopsy itself. This is clearly reflected in the testimony of Commander Humes. . . ."[41]

Liebeler insisted on a distinction between two types of evidence—the autopsy X-rays and photographs on the one hand, and the autopsy report by Commander Humes on the other. Liebeler's distinction might at first appear picayune, but it was not. Liebeler wanted no misunderstanding. He had believed Commander Humes. He had not been part of any coverup. "I did not make and could not have made the statement about the X-rays," wrote Liebeler, "because I have never seen the X-rays. . . ."[42] Liebeler told UPI that if there was any question about what he had said, they could check a tape recording which had been made of his talk. He sent copies of his letter to several Warren Commission attorneys, and even to Mark Lane.

Liebeler wasn't the only one defensive about the situation. All the Warren Commission attorneys were in the paradoxical position of having to profess confidence in Humes, and at the same time acknowledge that the Commission's procedure had been unorthodox. Their arguments were laced with appeals to faith. Arlen Specter reminded *U.S. News* that the critics' multiple-assassin theories implied "that the autopsy surgeons were perjurers, because the autopsy surgeons placed their hands on the Bible and swore to the truth of an official report. . . ."[43] Warren Commission Attorney Joe Ball said the doctors were "honorable men," and "I don't think they would dare testify contrary to the X-ray findings or to the colored pictures which they took. . . ."[44] And Burt Griffin, maintaining that Humes testified truthfully, nevertheless told the Theatre of Ideas audience: "I did not say that those [the X-rays and photos] were not important."[45] Liebeler told one TV interviewer that the situation "does disturb me as a lawyer."[46]

Off camera, Liebeler saw the Commission's predicament in somewhat comical terms. He once told me that if he were to cartoon the affair, he would show Humes standing before the Commission, having just completed his testimony, clutching the X-rays and photographs tightly behind his back. One of the Commissioners would be saying: "That's very nice, Commander; but now may we please see the pretty pictures?"

By the fourth week of October 1966 I was beginning to rethink the problem. Formerly, my attention was fixed on Dealey Plaza at the moment of the President's death. Now it moved to the autopsy at Bethesda. This shift stemmed in large part from my exchanges with Liebeler, although I'm certain he was not trying to bring it about.

But on October 20, when he flared at me, "[Humes] can read his ruler. . . . He can write down what he measured?" I realized for the first time, months before I fully appreciated the "best-evidence" concept, the extent to which the story of Dealey Plaza came from the autopsy table at Bethesda, the extent to which the Commission had relied upon the autopsy report. That report had been a starting point for the Commission's investigation, telling the lawyers how the shooting occurred.

Many critics didn't realize this. They actually believed the Commission first decided Oswald was the lone assassin, then sat down and colluded with Humes to concoct a report explaining the shooting in terms of a lone assassin. When I communicated such suspicions to Liebeler, his outbursts of laughter were enough to persuade me those notions were without merit. Just from the way Liebeler was behaving, I began to realize the full importance of the autopsy findings as evidence, and this realization caused a significant change in my perspective.

I had always been suspicious of the navy autopsy because it was performed at a military hospital by military doctors. One of my favorite themes was largely intuitive: that by relying on that autopsy, the Warren Commission allowed the U.S. Navy to instruct it from where on Elm Street the shots came.

Now I began to think of Commander Humes as a central figure. Exactly how had Humes been selected to do the autopsy, I wondered. And when was it decided the autopsy would be performed at a navy hospital? The Humes/Specter relationship also seemed crucial—the nexus between the Bethesda morgue and the Warren Commission; between the "best evidence" and the lawyers who wrote the official history of the President's assassination.

Arlen Specter said he had no reason to doubt the integrity of Commander Humes, with whom he spent time working on the single-bullet theory. "I went to see him at Bethesda," Specter told Gaeton Fonzi in July 1966, "and you should see his whole demeanor, his whole approach to the problem. You just wouldn't think for a minute that the guy's fudging anything. You wouldn't think for a minute."[47] The admiration was mutual, as Fonzi learned when he interviewed Humes. "I was very impressed with Specter," said Humes. "He was a very intelligent young man."[48] The young Warren Commission attorney and the career navy officer—was the relationship as it appeared, or had someone gotten conned?

If shots had struck from the front, then it did not seem possible that Humes could have testified truthfully. The conclusion was inescapable that if there was a grassy-knoll assassin, the navy autopsy findings must have been deliberately falsified. But in that case, all three doctors must have lied when they signed the autopsy report, and again in March 1964 when they testified before the Commission. And false X-rays and photographs must have been created—otherwise a conspiracy in which the doctors lied would be easily exposed.

Anything was possible. But I knew it was wrong, methodologically, to enlarge the conspiracy to correct for deficiencies in the original hypothesis. Something was wrong with the original theory. I could not identify the problem, but the symptoms were clear. The conspiracy seemed implausible. There were numerous accessories after the fact, any one of whom could expose the plot. It violated Occam's Razor.

Yet I could conceive of no other way to reconcile the evidence of crossfire with the navy autopsy findings, no other way to falsify the "best evidence."

Until the evening of October 22, 1966.

PART II

A New Hypothesis

CHAPTER 7

Breakthrough

ON SATURDAY EVENING, October 22, 1966, I went to the Hollywood home of a friend of mine, Yoram Kahana, an Israeli photojournalist, who had offered to make some photographs for me. I needed the photographs that night because the next day I was to appear on a local television program opposite Wesley Liebeler.

While Yoram worked in the darkroom, I sat and read his copy of the latest *Saturday Review* which contained an article titled: "JFK in Dallas: the Warren Report and Its Critics," written by Arnold Fein, a civil court judge in New York and a former special counsel to the Kefauver Committee.[1] Judge Fein's article was a review of *Rush to Judgment, Inquest,* and four other recently published books. Much of it was devoted to a discussion of the Bethesda autopsy, and although Fein supported the Warren Report, his article was one of the most thoughtful and interesting I had read. I studied it intently, scribbling notes in the margin. It was filled with insights about the evidence and the psychology of the Warren Report critics.

What really seized my attention was Judge Fein's rebuttal of the theory subscribed to by many critics: that the autopsy published in the Warren Report was not the original, and that the Commission had changed the trajectory of the non-fatal shot from non-transit to transit to support the single-bullet theory.

It was beguilingly easy to subscribe to this idea. All that was necessary was to arrange the data as in Figure 7. What emerged was a pattern incriminating to the Commission. (See Fig. 7.)

Viewing the evidence as outlined in the chart, many critics believed that sometime after late January, when the film was screened and the

Date	Source of Autopsy Information	Conclusion (re non-fatal shot)
Nov. 22	FBI report of agents Sibert and O'Neill	Non-transit[2]
Dec. 9	FBI Summary Report	Non-transit[3]
Dec. 18 (approx.)	Assorted news leaks of autopsy results	Non-transit[4]
Jan. 13	FBI Supplemental Report	Non-transit[5]
Jan. 27 (approx.)	Warren Commission discovers the timing problem[6]	
Mar. 24	Commander Humes testifies; undated autopsy report admitted into evidence	Transit[7] (both Bethesda autopsy report and Humes' testimony state bullet entered neck from the rear and passed all the way through, exiting at the front of the throat)

Figure 7.
The change from non-transit to transit—as viewed by critics

This chart shows why many Warren Report critics—e.g., Epstein—believed the change from non-transit to transit in the neck trajectory occurred *after* the Warren Commission discovered the timing problem in late January, 1964.

Prior to that discovery the three FBI reports all said the bullet did not transit. So did the autopsy results leaked in mid-December. Then, in late January the Commission screened the Zapruder film, discovered the timing problem, and confronted the fact that the assassination could have been accomplished by a single assassin firing the bolt-action rifle only if Kennedy and Connally were struck by the same bullet. In March, Commander Humes testified, and an undated autopsy report was accepted in evidence. That report, contradicting all previous information from the FBI and the December news leaks, stated that the non-fatal shot entered the back of Kennedy's neck, passed all the way through his body and exited at the throat.

timing problem discovered, the Commission changed the autopsy conclusion for political reasons.

Judge Fein attacked this view as misguided. He noted that when it came to the FBI, the critics employed a double standard. On the question of Oswald's guilt, the FBI—which concluded so quickly that Oswald was the lone assassin—was their favorite whipping boy. Yet they cited the FBI non-transiting conclusion in mounting their attack on Commander Humes and the single-bullet theory.

To the critics, the FBI was "pro-conspiracy" on that issue. But on the question of shots from the front, the FBI account of the autopsy agreed with Commander Humes: none from the front; two from the rear.

I found the situation confusing. Why were the FBI and Humes in agreement on the direction of the shots? Was it simply the case that no shots struck from the front?

Judge Fein observed that Humes incurred the wrath of the critics because his testimony undercut their theories of a grassy-knoll assassin. This made me realize my own thinking was inconsistent. If I was going to accept the FBI report on the issue of non-transit, wasn't I obliged to accept the FBI version of the autopsy with regard to the grassy knoll? Either a source was reliable or it was not.*

Contributing to the confusion were the three sources of medical information—the Dallas doctors, the FBI, and the navy—no two of which were in agreement. Surely there had to be a pattern to the disagreement. Searching for it, I created another table, associating the facts provided with the agency of origin. That didn't help. It simply illustrated the confusion. (See Fig. 8.)

Why were there so many conflicting reports? Judge Fein's analysis put me on the trail to the answer. His articles opened my eyes to the importance of a careful chronological analysis, and of a date that I, and most critics, simply ignored: November 24, 1963.

Sunday, November 24, 1963—two days after the assassination, the day Lee Harvey Oswald was murdered by Jack Ruby in the basement of Dallas Police Headquarters, the day before Kennedy's funeral. Commander Humes told the Warren Commission that on that day he finished and signed the Bethesda autopsy report. Most critics simply did not believe Commander Humes, and referred to the autopsy report as "undated." Judge Fein argued that "undated" was an unfair characterization since there was no place on the navy autopsy form for a date. He noted that transmittal documents which *were* dated had accompanied the autopsy submission: Humes filed a certificate stating the autopsy was turned in by 5:00 P.M. that Sunday, and the Commanding Officer at Bethesda, Adm. Calvin Galloway, signed a memorandum sending the autopsy to Adm. George Burkley at the White House on Monday.[8] If the navy autopsy report published in the Warren Report were really drafted months later, after the Commission decided on the single-bullet theory, all those docu-

* A similar anomaly cropped up regarding the credibility of the autopsy doctors. If they were lying about shots striking from the front, why would they tell the truth about bullet 399? Finck and Humes were the critics' star witnesses on that subject. Both testified when shown the bullet that it couldn't have been the missile that caused the Governor's wrist wound. If they were lying to hide an assassin firing from the front, why would they testify against the single-bullet theory? As demonstrated by the "three-assassin" model, that testimony, in effect, placed a second assassin to the rear.

Type of Information Authority	Column 1 Throat Wound	Column 2 Neck Trajectory
Parkland (initial medical opinion)	Entry	✕
FBI	No mention	Non-transit
Navy	Exit	Transit

Figure 8.

Table showing statements of Parkland doctors, FBI, and navy autopsy concerning neck trajectory

Column 1 shows that only Parkland doctors supported the grassy knoll theory; FBI did not mention wound; navy referred to wound as exit.

Column 2 shows that, on the question of transit, Parkland does not apply (since Parkland said throat wound was entry); FBI said no transit; navy said transit.

ments were false. That was no minor matter. Those documents plus Humes' sworn testimony afforded plenty of legal exposure to anyone taking part in such a scheme.

Never before had I taken November 24, 1963, seriously as the date the navy autopsy was submitted. Now I studied Fein's argument carefully. It was a revelation. His point was that if certain chronological sequences were understood, it would be clear that the FBI reports on non-transit were simply erroneous, that Humes told the truth, and that the Warren Commission had published the autopsy it received.

To follow Judge Fein's analysis, I found I had to diagram the flow of information from the autopsy room. Drawing such a diagram—called a "flow chart"—was something I was accustomed to doing when programming a computer. It had never occurred to me to approach the Kennedy assassination that way, and I was surprised at the insight the method afforded. The importance of the two separate sources of autopsy information became startlingly clear.

It was as if there were twin transmission lines emanating from the autopsy room: a navy transmission line, and an FBI transmission line. (See Fig. 9.)

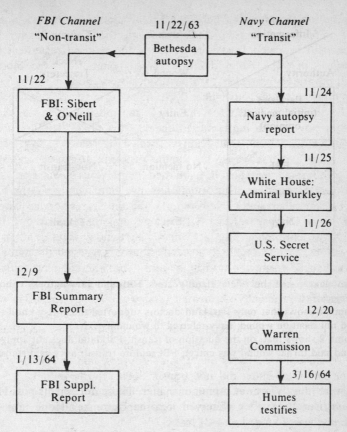

Figure 9.
Flow of information from Bethesda autopsy room

At left: FBI channel disseminates "non-transit" autopsy conclusion based on Friday night information incorporated in Sibert and O'Neill report, written by two agents who attended autopsy.

At right: Navy channel disseminates "transit" autopsy conclusion as recorded in navy autopsy report, submitted by Humes on Sunday, November 24.

The FBI transmission line began with the Sibert and O'Neill report dated November 22,* the source document, followed by the December 9 Summary Report, and the January 13 Supplemental Report. What was significant about the sequence of reports, when viewed as a transmission

---

* The date referred to here appears in the lower left-hand corner of the report, and refers to the date the FBI obtained the information. The report wasn't dictated and typed until November 26, as indicated by two other dates on the document.

line, was that they were all based on Friday night information, *regardless of the date of publication*. Thus, although the FBI Summary Report happened to be dated December 9, 1963, the medical statement in that document—that the bullet did *not* transit—came from the Sibert and O'Neill report, which was in turn based on observations made by two FBI agents on Friday night, November 22, 1963.

The source document for the navy transmission line was the navy autopsy report, which represented Sunday, November 24, 1963, information. It was irrelevant that Humes testified in March 1964, after the Commission had discovered the timing problem, because his testimony only corroborated the report he submitted the previous November.

By tracing the flow of information to two bureaucracies—the FBI (in receipt of the Sibert and O'Neill report) and the Secret Service (in receipt of the navy autopsy report)—it became apparent that the FBI/navy conflict was, chronologically, a Friday-night/Sunday-night conflict. Those two versions, each traceable to a specific source, suggested the autopsy was indeed changed from non-transit to transit, but the change occurred not months later, but between Friday and Sunday, between the time the examination was actually performed (and witnessed by the FBI) and the time Humes turned in his report.

One of Judge Fein's best insights concerned the mid-December 1963 news stories purporting to provide the results of the Bethesda autopsy. Many of those stories, based on "official" sources, said the autopsy showed that the non-fatal bullet did not transit. Such reports initially led me to think that the Warren Commission had not published the autopsy it received. But Judge Fein observed that the December 1963 news stories "were obviously founded on FBI leaks."[9]

That had never occurred to me before. But obviously numerous FBI, Justice Department, and White House officials had access to the December 9 Summary Report, and on one page, that document said the autopsy concluded that the bullet which struck the President's back produced a shallow wound, did not transit, and was probably the one found on the Dallas stretcher.[10] Any reporter who employed an FBI source during this period would be told some or all of these "facts"—all of which derived, ultimately, from the Sibert and O'Neill report. In the twin-transmission-line model, those "non-transit" news stories published in mid-December 1963 were just another example of "Friday-night information" surfacing weeks later.

A prime example was the December 18, 1963, account published in the *Washington Post*, written by Nate Haseltine, the *Post*'s science writer, who characterized his information as "the findings of the as yet unofficial [autopsy] report."[11] Haseltine said the non-fatal shot struck the President "5 to 7 inches below the collar line" and was found embedded in

Kennedy's shoulder. The throat wound, he said, was caused by a fragment from the fatal shot.*

Haseltine's account tripped off a spate of followup stories which showed an even stronger connection to the December 9 FBI Summary Report. Peculiar to that FBI report was its almost explicit statement that the shallow back wound was caused by a bullet found on Kennedy's stretcher in Dallas. The AP followup to the Haseltine story, citing "a source fully acquainted with [the] results of a postmortem examination," said the bullet which had caused the shallow back wound "was said to have been the one that was removed from the stretcher on which Mr. Kennedy was carried into the hospital."[12] That was strictly "Friday-night information" and came from the report of FBI agents Sibert and O'Neill, who witnessed the doctors making just such a connection in the autopsy room.

Studying Judge Fein's article, I was struck by the semantic error being made—possibly by reporters who wrote the "non-transit" stories, certainly by critics who were reading them. When a journalist claimed to report the "autopsy results," that did not necessarily mean his source had access to the navy autopsy report. The same language was used to describe the "autopsy results" described in the December 9 FBI Summary Report. The reporters themselves were probably unaware of the distinction—unaware that the "autopsy results" they obtained from an FBI or Justice Department source differed from the conclusions reported in the official navy autopsy report then at Secret Service Headquarters.

Reading Fein's article, I wrote in the margin: "Here is where the critics go wrong. They don't realize the parallelism in time of two stories."**

* Locating the wound by reference to Kennedy's clothing ("below the collar line"), rather than his body, suggested the source was the FBI. The FBI Laboratory had the President's shirt and jacket, which showed holes about 5½ inches below the top of the collar. Haseltine's account diverged from the Sibert and O'Neill report in that he said the bullet was recovered. In February 1965, responding to a letter from Paul Hoch requesting more detailed information about his source, Haseltine said it was "highly reliable," but was not a doctor. The story, he said, was the result of his own "digging." "Since I went to considerable efforts to get the true version," he wrote Hoch, "I do not believe I was the victim of a plant, or was taken in." He noted: "Apparently my source misunderstood part of the autopsy report he had access to." Haseltine died in 1970.

** This error was widespread. In *Inquest*, Epstein wrote: "These newspaper accounts . . . raise a question as to whether the autopsy report published in the Warren Report was in fact the *original* one."[13] Writing in *Accessories After the Fact*, Sylvia Meagher said: ". . . the evidence that the autopsy report was completed on November 24 fails to account for the leaking of different autopsy findings on December 17 and December 18."[14]

Distinguishing the FBI and Navy Versions

The navy autopsy said the non-fatal rear entry wound was "just above . . . the scapula [the shoulder blade]"[15]—in other words, located high enough so a bullet could pass on through the neck and exit at the front of the throat along a downward-slanting trajectory. But FBI Agents Sibert and O'Neill described it as a "back" wound, and located it "below the shoulders."[16]

Certain other facts now came into focus. In December 1963 there were isolated instances of news stories which *did* report the navy autopsy conclusions correctly—notably, a story in the December 12, 1963, *Dallas Times-Herald,* by Bill Burrus, and in the December 18, 1963, *St. Louis Post-Dispatch,* by Richard Dudman. Burrus' story was datelined "Bethesda, Maryland," and was based on the autopsy report purportedly shown to him by one of the Bethesda pathologists.* Burrus said the bullet transited the President's neck, exiting at the front of the throat, and described the rear wound as being "above President Kennedy's right scapula—commonly called the shoulder blade."[18]

Similar information was contained in Dudman's December 18, 1963, *Post-Dispatch* story about the visit of Secret Service agents who brought a navy autopsy report to Parkland Memorial Hospital the previous week. Dudman, who obtained a partial description of the navy findings from Dr. McClelland, reported the bullet transited the neck, exiting at the throat wound. Dudman referred to the rear point of entry as a neck wound, not a back wound. It was located, he said, "where the right shoulder meets the neck."[19]

Clearly, both versions of the neck trajectory were available in December 1963—and depending upon the reporter's source, he would get either the "transit" and "high" neck wound reported in the navy autopsy report, or the "non-transit" and "low" back wound conclusion in the FBI report.

By conceiving the twin-transmission-line model, I had learned how information was propagated through the bureaucracy—from the navy autopsy room to either the FBI or the Secret Service, and then on to the Warren Commission, with various press leaks along the way.

This knowledge excited me. Suddenly the mystery evaporated from numerous conflicting reports, reducing that problem to manageable dimensions, subject to rational analysis. My previous thinking now seemed too suspicious. Implicit in the strictly linear arrangement of information in Figure 7 was the notion that the United States government was an all-

* In 1978 I learned that Burrus' information indeed came from the navy autopsy report, but was not given to him by a Bethesda pathologist.[17]

knowing monolith which, on any given date, had specific autopsy conclusions to offer; further, that changes were made over a four-month period following the assassination, and that the Warren Commission had engineered an elaborate coverup. I now saw this whole view was incorrect. There was no monolith, only a series of interlocking bureaucracies with two distinct documentary sources of autopsy information wending their way through the system.

Statements of Numerous Officials Reconciled

If, as I now believed, the change was made within the first forty-eight hours, then the apparent contradictions evaporated from various public statements by the FBI, the autopsy doctors, and the Warren Commission attorneys. Having harbored suspicions that numerous officials had lied, it was refreshing to realize they could all be telling the truth, yet the autopsy could have been changed nevertheless.

The FBI could have told the truth when they told the *Washington Post* their reports were correct, for they were based on "medical information at the time."[20] The qualifier, "at the time," so inconsequential before, now jumped to life. This was obviously the FBI's way of vouching for the accuracy of its agents' Friday-night report, while conceding the doctors might have changed their conclusions afterward.

Commander Boswell could have told the truth when he said there was no difference between the autopsy he signed on Sunday, November 24 and the autopsy published in the Warren Report.[21] Even though the implication was misleading, Boswell was correct. The change could have already been made. That meant Specter and Redlich could have been truthful in claiming the autopsy in evidence was the one they found when they reported for work on the Commission.

Yet a change had been made. Who was responsible? *When* it occurred seemed to be the key. Any change within forty-eight hours could only have been made by the doctors themselves.

I now remembered Commander Humes' testimony about burning an earlier autopsy report:

In [the] privacy of my own home, early on the morning of Sunday, November 24th, I made a draft of this report which I later revised, and of which this represents the revision. That draft I personally burned in the fireplace of my recreation room.[22]

This brought a striking insight: After all the rigmarole of tracing the information flow, drawing diagrams, and finally concluding that the change must have occurred over the weekend, I now realized that Humes had almost certainly burned a draft of the autopsy report reflecting the "Friday-night" non-transit conclusion.*

This unsettled me. For over eighteen months I had stubbornly clung to the belief that Humes' original autopsy said the fatal shot struck from the front, that he had burned *that* autopsy and that act had eradicated the grassy knoll from the medical evidence.

But I was wrong. The burned report was probably the non-transit variant of "two shots from the rear."

What did that mean? Was I wrong about shots striking from the front? I put that question aside, and tried to figure out why Humes would make the change from non-transit to transit.**

Ironically, the explanation was in full public view. Humes had mentioned it; the FBI had alluded to it; Arlen Specter had talked of it—but I, convinced that the Warren Commission had made the change because of the timing problem, believed none of them.

Now I put those suspicions aside, and studied Judge Fein's narration again. Humes' story, bizarre as it seemed, was that during the autopsy, he had overlooked a bullet wound.

Humes' Perspective on November 22

When the President's body was brought to Humes, he reported seeing only one wound other than the head wound—that was the hole described by the FBI as "below the shoulders" and by Secret Service Agent Clint Hill as "six inches below the neckline."[25] (See Fig. 10.)

Situated on the front of the neck was another hole, but Humes testified he did not recognize it as a bullet wound; he thought it nothing more than a tracheotomy incision.[26] The accounts of others in the room at the time supported Humes' story. FBI agents Sibert and O'Neill referred to that

---

* But, unlike the Sibert and O'Neill report, this burned report would have had to account for the throat wound that Humes was told about on Saturday. It probably did so by attributing that wound to a fragment of the head shot.

** Critics who believed that the autopsy report was changed months later by the Warren Commission had the problem of accounting for the evidence that it was completed by November 24, and the destruction of an earlier draft had already taken place by that date. That evidence included the "certificate" filed by Humes—stating that he burned "certain preliminary draft notes"[23]—which was dated November 24, 1963, and Humes' Warren Commission testimony that he burned an earlier draft on November 24, 1963.[24]

They dealt with this anomaly in their theory by claiming that Humes' testimony was false, and that his "certificate" was backdated. That view, which I found absurd, implied Humes not only colluded with the Commission, months later, to falsify evidence, but then accommodated them by shifting suspicion away from the Commission and onto himself by backdating a document and testifying falsely that the documents were destroyed on November 24, 1963.

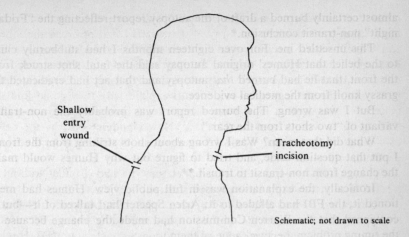

Shallow
entry
wound

Tracheotomy
incision

Schematic; not drawn to scale

Figure 10.

Humes' perspective on November 22

On Friday night, Humes saw this pattern of injury to the President's body, aside from the head wounding.

On the back was a shallow wound, "below the shoulders," according to FBI agents. At the front of the throat was another hole, which Humes thought was a tracheotomy incision.

In front of the FBI, Humes probed the rear entry with his finger. X-rays showed no bullet in the body. Hearing about a bullet found on a Dallas stretcher, Humes concluded this rear entry was made by the stretcher bullet, which had worked its way out of the wound during external heart massage at Parkland Hospital.

hole as a "tracheotomy."[27] They never described it as a bullet wound. Years later when the report of Dr. George Burkley, the White House physician, became available, it also was silent about that wound.[28] So the "bystander" evidence certainly supported Humes' story.

The two FBI men reported that Humes stuck his finger in the rear entry wound and found it went in only "a short distance . . . the end of the opening could be felt with the finger."*[29] The doctors had a wound, but no bullet. Then one of the FBI agents made a telephone call to headquarters and returned with the message that the FBI Lab had just received a bullet from the Secret Service, a bullet found on a stretcher at Parkland Memorial Hospital that may have been Kennedy's. Humes' immediate reaction was to connect the stretcher bullet with the shallow wound.[31]

Narrating this sequence, Judge Fein quoted from the Sibert and O'Neill report. The autopsy doctors, said Fein, "were at a loss to explain why they

* Years later, Dr. Finck testified its depth was "the first fraction of an inch."[30]

159

could find no bullets," and "no complete bullet could be located in the body either by probing or by X-ray."[32] I realized I had not read the Sibert and O'Neill report carefully and had missed the powerful language the FBI agents had employed to describe the degree of puzzlement they witnessed as the autopsy doctors examined Kennedy's body: "The individuals performing the autopsy were at a loss to explain why they could find no bullets."[33] The doctors must have seemed truly confounded to cause the FBI agents to write a sentence like that. Now I understood why the news of a bullet on a stretcher would be snapped up by Humes—it solved his problem.

Humes had a wound without a bullet; now he had a bullet without a wound. The match must have seemed natural.

Humes was apparently so sure about this link between bullet and shallow wound that at the end of the autopsy, according to the FBI agents, he reiterated the connection as an official autopsy conclusion: "Dr. Humes stated that the pattern was clear that one bullet had entered the President's back and worked its way out of the body during external cardiac massage and that a second . . . bullet had entered the rear of the skull. . . ."[34]

But these conclusions would have to be changed.

Commander Humes' "pattern" failed to take into account one of the most publicized bullet wounds in history—the one at the front of Kennedy's throat, a wound designated by Dr. Perry in his Dallas press conference earlier that afternoon as an entrance wound.

On Saturday morning matters came to a head. Humes telephoned Perry in Dallas. He was informed during that call that the hole in the front of the neck was no mere tracheotomy incision, but a tracheotomy *over* a bullet wound.[35] Arlen Specter, in his 1966 *U.S. News* interview, said, "that [call] was when he [Humes] found out that there had been a bullet hole on the front of the neck. . . ."[36]

After talking to Perry, Humes must have realized the extent of his predicament. He had left himself open to criticism that he botched the autopsy. Whatever he wrote from then on would be a deduction, an extrapolation from data gathered the previous evening, but not based on direct examination of the body, which was no longer available—it was in the East Room of the White House. Furthermore, in front of two FBI agents Humes had stated autopsy conclusions that were wrong, that subsequently failed to account for one of the bullet wounds. As Arlen Specter so laconically put it: After that phone call to Perry, Humes "formulated a different [autopsy] conclusion."*[37]

---

* In his July 1966 *Look* magazine article, journalist Fletcher Knebel described it more subtly. After interviewing Commander Boswell and three Warren Commission attorneys, Knebel wrote that the autopsy doctors, following the Humes-Perry telephone call, "then reconstructed and reanalyzed their autopsy work."[38]

From the autopsy report Humes submitted on Sunday, it was reasonable to infer that Humes' re-analysis of his data proceeded along these lines: There was an entrance bullet hole on the rear surface of the body, another bullet wound in the front of the neck, and no bullet inside the body. Humes connected the two wounds along one gunshot trajectory, his logic apparently being that whatever came in the back must have gone out the front. From Humes' standpoint, the Dallas tracheotomy incision had obscured a small bullet *exit* wound.

As I read Judge Fein, I realized that the critics' refusal to believe that Humes could have missed a bullet wound was a serious error. That error prevented a proper understanding of Humes' situation that weekend, of the confused circumstances surrounding the formulation of his final autopsy conclusions. The missed bullet wound explained why the FBI left the autopsy room with one version of the conclusions on Friday night, and why Humes wrote something different on Sunday. The refusal to believe that Humes missed a bullet wound stemmed from a naive idea: that because the November 22 Dallas news reports of the front throat wound loomed large years later, particularly in the clipping files of the critics, those stories necessarily loomed large at the time. But they did not.* Reading Fein's article, I finally began to believe that Dr. Perry's alteration of the throat wound could easily account for Humes' not knowing it was there.

Still, a serious loose end remained. What about Humes' superiors? Surely they must have known about Dr. Perry's news conference. How could they permit him to begin the autopsy without first calling the Dallas doctors to learn what marks and incisions had been added as a result of the Dallas clinical procedures? It was not just a matter of whether James Humes, the individual, happened to listen to newscasts from Dallas. At issue was a suspicious lack of official liaison between Dallas and Bethesda, an irregularity in the Bethesda protocol that remained unexplained.

The Bethesda Snafu and the Warren Report

Once I understood the Bethesda snafu, I could see why so much misunderstanding surrounded the subject.

There were two possible reasons for the change—the "doctor's motive" and the "Commission's motive." The doctor's motive was to account for

---

* Critics, including me, had asked the same question raised by Salandria in his 1965 *Liberation* article: How could Humes not know about a bullet wound that millions of Americans knew about through the news reports of Dr. Perry's press conference?[39] The answer was that Humes had not relied on news reports for his information; he had looked at the body. And Humes testified the Dallas tracheotomy had so disfigured the wound that it was "no longer at all obvious as a missile wound."[40]

a missed bullet wound; the Warren Commission's, to "solve" the timing problem. The former appeared legitimate; the latter was unquestionably illegitimate—changing the autopsy to support a contrived reconstruction of the crime.

Since the change from non-transit to transit accomplished both those ends, it was easy to misunderstand the motive, and to make an error as to when the change was made and who was responsible. In short, it was easy to blame the Warren Commission for a change made by the autopsy doctors.

I began to understand something else; the need to separate problems in the evidence itself from problems pertaining to the Commission's handling of the evidence, to keep my suspicions about the Commission and my rejection of its conclusions from spilling over into other areas.

I now realized that I initially rejected Humes' explanation not because his testimony and autopsy report were improbable, but because the Warren Report's handling of that issue was so shifty.

The Report hid the Bethesda foulup. And, if my assumption was correct, the Commission staff structured its investigation and the published record so the Sibert and O'Neill report would never come to light. Sibert and O'Neill were not called as witnesses, and all FBI reporting of the autopsy—the agents' report, the December 9 Summary Report, and the January 13 Supplemental Report—were omitted from the twenty-six volumes and routed to the National Archives. The Report alluded to the "non-transit" conclusion as mere "speculation" which occurred "in the earlier stages of the autopsy," and as a theory which the doctors rejected *before* they completed their examination.[41] The Warren Report never let on that what it called the "earlier stages" was the autopsy as witnessed and reported by the FBI.*

Having disposed of contrary evidence in this fashion, Redlich, Specter, and Rankin were then able to deal with the touchy situation of the botched autopsy in a few carefully fashioned paragraphs which hewed to the version supplied, under oath, by Humes.

In testimony full of hair-splitting distinctions, Humes claimed that he suspected the bullet passed all the way through Kennedy's body before he learned of the exit wound. Humes testified he inferred this from certain internal injuries—bruising of the neck muscles, and a bruise atop the right lung. But even Humes didn't go so far as to say he concluded the bullet transited before calling Dr. Perry—only that, on Friday night, he considered it a "possible explanation."[42] The Warren Report, however, went

---

* A charitable explanation was that Humes and the Commission were trying to hide what they viewed as an innocent foulup—the missed bullet wound. But the result was to fuel suspicions that the Commission had colluded with Humes to change the autopsy from non-transit to transit.

further. In a critical sentence which had no basis in Humes' testimony, the Report asserted that when Humes telephoned Perry on Saturday morning and learned that the tracheotomy had been made over a bullet wound, that information "confirmed the Bethesda surgeons' conclusion that the bullet had exited from the front part of the neck."[43]

The Warren Commission paid a high price for this sleight of hand. When the FBI reporting of the autopsy surfaced in 1966, the result was predictable: A spate of articles and books interpreted the conflict, incorrectly, to mean the Commission had changed the autopsy. As I studied Judge Fein's article, I was finally persuaded the Commission had done no such thing—what it had done was conceal the fact that the doctors had changed the autopsy. But regardless of when the change was made, and who made it, the question remained: Was it legitimate?

Non-Transit to Transit—A Question of Legitimacy

The change from non-transit to transit should not affect the location of any other wounds observed on Friday night. If legitimate, the change should consist of nothing more than extending an already existing trajectory through a wound the doctors had missed and which, they now concluded, was an exit aperture.

Therein lay the rub. It appeared that another change had occurred between Friday and Sunday. The back wound had moved upward and become a neck wound. The difference was only a few inches, but it was crucial. It gave the neck trajectory a downward slant and permitted the doctors to conclude the wound at the front of the throat was caused by a shot from "behind and above." The old "low"/"high" conflict.

The "Low"/"High" Conflict Revisited

According to FBI agents Sibert and O'Neill, who watched Humes probe the wound with his finger, it was a "back" wound located "below the shoulders."[44] According to Secret Service Agent Clinton Hill, called to the morgue at 2:45 A.M. for the specific purpose of viewing the wounds, it was "6 inches below the neckline."[45] Secret Service agents Greer and Kellerman referred to it as a "shoulder" wound.[46] Except for the autopsy doctors, not a single eyewitness called it a neck wound or placed it *above* the shoulder blade. The location seen by the witnesses was corroborated by the physical evidence of the clothing holes—both the shirt and jacket had holes nearly six inches below the top of the collar.[47] The autopsy diagram itself was marked with a dot below the shoulders.[48]

Nevertheless, the autopsy report submitted by Humes on Sunday, November 24, 1963, described the rear wound as "situated . . . just above the upper border of the scapula [the shoulder blade]."[49] In the artist's drawing Humes had prepared months later to illustrate his Warren Commission testimony, the wound is clearly in the neck.[50] The Bethesda report said it was high enough so that as the bullet traveled downward and forward it "traversed . . . the base of the right side of the neck," exiting at the front of the throat.[51]

I was convinced the change from "low" back wound to "high" neck wound, part and parcel of the change from non-transit to transit, was illegitimate, but now the object of my suspicions was Commander Humes, not the Warren Commission.

Why would Humes raise the wound? Why would he perform "verbal plastic surgery" to connect the back wound and the front wound along a single downward-slanting trajectory? I knew little of Humes' chain of command. Giving him the benefit of the doubt, I simply assumed that he had been pressured. Humes had missed a bullet wound. That must have been embarrassing. Perhaps it made him vulnerable.

This was purely a hypothesis, but enough irregularities surrounded the Bethesda protocol to indicate Humes had been subject to pressures. Papers which Humes described as "certain preliminary draft notes" had been inexplicably burned.[52] Unexplained cross-outs appeared on the handwritten draft.[53] His "clinical summary" of the autopsy read like a prologue for the Warren Report. It asserted that "three shots were *heard* [emphasis added]," and it contained a curious reference to a news report in the November 23 *Washington Post*—the eyewitness account of *Dallas Times-Herald* photographer Robert Jackson that supported the shots-from-behind theory. Humes wrote that Jackson "said he looked around as he heard the shots and saw a rifle barrel disappearing into a window on an upper floor of the nearby Texas School Book Depository Building."[54] Why was such non-medical data included in the clinical summary? I found it easy to believe that Humes had been pressured to raise the rear entry wound so that shots fired from "behind and somewhat above," as the autopsy phrased it, would account for all the wounds on the body. (See Fig. 11.)

In the margin of Judge Fein's article, I scribbled a few notes summarizing my view of Humes' behavior beginning the night of the autopsy when he was "at a loss to explain" why he could find no bullets: "Humes observes. Is confused. Relates to FBI. FBI disseminates, [yielding] Dec. 9 and Jan. 13 with bullet falling out back wound. Humes is pressured; burns; rewrites. Hands over Report." I also made this note:

FBI = Humes before pressure.

That equation was my shorthand for the idea that the Sibert and O'Neill report represented Humes' behavior on Friday night—his honest

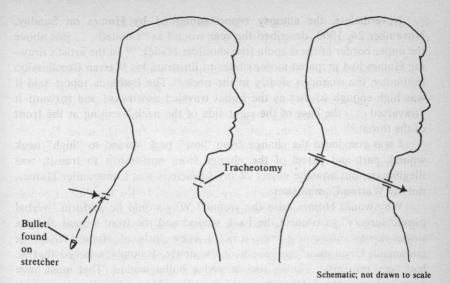

Tracheotomy

Bullet
found
on
stretcher

Schematic; not drawn to scale

Figure 11.
The change from non-transit to transit.
At left: Humes' perspective on Friday night. It includes the low back wound, said to be caused by the bullet found on the stretcher, and the hole at the front of the throat, thought to be a tracheotomy incision.
At right: Neck trajectory in autopsy report submitted on Sunday. The change from non-transit to transit appears to involve the transformation of a "low" back wound to a higher neck wound.

opinion at the time, before "pressure" was applied to produce the Sunday autopsy conclusion.

As I finished reading Judge Fein, my pulse quickened. I had the feeling of closing in on my quarry. The problem was not the Warren Commission, but the events surrounding the formulation of the autopsy conclusions. My preoccupation with the foibles and inadequacies of the Warren Report had actually served as a decoy which prevented me from seeing the real issue.

An autopsy report signed on Sunday, November 24, had gone from Bethesda Naval Hospital to the White House the next day. That report had a rear point of entry which did not conform to much of the evidence and a transiting neck trajectory which depended for its legitimacy on that rear point of entry. And months later, that trajectory would become a vital segment of the one-bullet/two-victim theory.

Illegitimate changes it seemed had taken place within 48 hours of the assassination which would profoundly affect the conclusions of all future investigations. How did this happen? Was there a guiding hand?

Refining the Flow Chart: The Secret Service, the Dallas Doctors, and the FBI

I continued to diagram the flow of information. I now realized that what I called the navy transmission line was a misnomer. While I didn't know who delivered the autopsy report to the White House,* I did know that once there Admiral Burkley sent it to the Secret Service; that on Tuesday, November 26, the day after Kennedy's funeral, Secret Service Chief James Rowley was in possession of it, and that the Secret Service handled all subsequent dissemination.

What happened then?

In the margin of Judge Fein's article, I began to list the dates I could think of in connection with the autopsy. I knew that at some point the Secret Service had shown the autopsy to the Dallas doctors and obtained a reversal of their opinion that the throat wound was an entrance. When did that happen? The page-one story by Richard Dudman in the December 18 *St. Louis Post-Dispatch,* headlined SECRET SERVICE GETS REVISION OF KENNEDY WOUND, indicated that Secret Service visit to Parkland occurred about December 11, 1963.

Now I juxtaposed some dates. December 23 was the day the FBI received the autopsy from the Secret Service. December 11 was the day the Secret Service showed the autopsy to the Dallas doctors.

I added these events to my flow chart. (See Fig. 12.)

The sequence looked peculiar. Why did the Secret Service show the Dallas doctors the Bethesda report two weeks before sending it to J. Edgar Hoover? The Dallas doctors were just witnesses. J. Edgar Hoover was running the investigation.

I reviewed the details of the Dudman story. I had previously kept my attention on the doctors' behavior. Now I noticed that the active participants in the matter were agents of the Secret Service.

Apparently the Secret Service had little trouble persuading the Dallas doctors, one reason being that the Bethesda autopsy report included a rear point of entry they had not seen. Dr. McClelland told Dudman that the throat wound was an exit for a bullet that had entered at that point. They had not seen that rear wound, Dr. McClelland explained to Dudman, because Kennedy was lying on his back. During the twenty-two minutes of emergency treatment they had never turned him over.[56]

I returned to the behavior of the Secret Service in failing to send the autopsy report to FBI Director Hoover for an entire month. During that time the two transmission lines didn't cross. The FBI and the Secret Service

---

* In 1977 Humes told the House Assassinations Committee: "I personally hand-carried the written document to the office of the White House physician about six on Sunday evening."[55] It was apparently the *typewritten* version that was delivered the next day, November 25, 1963.

A New Hypothesis

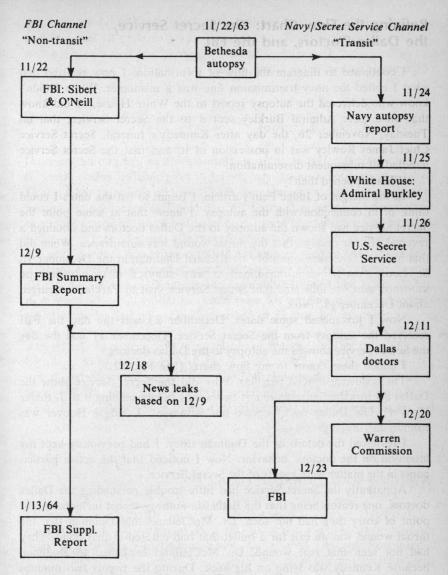

Figure 12.
Twin transmission line showing visit to Dallas doctors, December news leaks, and Secret Service transmission of autopsy report to FBI

had different autopsy information until December 23, 1963. Hoover finally received the Bethesda report two weeks *after* the FBI had delivered its "authoritative" December 9 Summary Report, which made no mention of the throat wound, to the White House.

A New Picture of Humes

Analyzing the flow of autopsy information was like putting the event under a microscope. One by one, several of my cherished beliefs dissolved in the face of evidence that was now readily visible. No longer did I believe the Warren Commission changed the autopsy; I now realized the change occurred within forty-eight hours. No longer did I see the Secret Service as mere couriers of the autopsy report. Apparently they played a more active role, as revealed by their visiting the Dallas doctors and showing them the autopsy report during the same period it was being withheld from the FBI. But the most surprising development concerned Commander Humes. He emerged as a man who, for the most part, was telling the truth, but was in a vulnerable position, subject to pressure, because he had missed a bullet wound.

The other critics, I knew, would laugh at this picture of Dr. Humes, but sitting in Yoram's living room I began to give it credence; I started thinking of the man many regarded as a perjurer, as the truthteller. It was a complete reversal. The villain might be the good guy after all. Why not? I decided to see how this view of Humes applied to my analysis of the head trajectory.

Wrestling with a Contradiction

It quickly became apparent that there was a direct clash between the proposition that Humes was telling the truth in stating the shot came from behind, and Newton's laws, which, when applied to the head snap, indicated it came from the front.

Yet it was not just a matter of Humes' opinion. As Judge Fein pointed out, both the navy autopsy and the FBI report of the autopsy—i.e., both transmission lines—were in agreement: The head shot came from behind. Only the Dallas doctors offered any support for the theory that there were shots from the front by saying that the throat wound was an entry and that a bullet exited from the rear of the President's head. But it was the Zapruder film head snap that I found most convincing.

In a table displaying the data, the facts looked like this:

November 22	Zapruder film (and opinion of most Dallas doctors)	Head shot from front
November 22	FBI at autopsy	Head shot from rear
November 24	Navy autopsy report	Head shot from rear

A similar chart, in the case of the neck trajectory, had proven quite valuable:

| November 22 | FBI | Non-transit |
| November 24 | Navy autopsy report | Transit |

It demonstrated that a change took place between November 22 and November 24.

What did my new chart mean? Unlike the neck trajectory, the breach between "from the front" and "from the rear" did not occur over the weekend. The breach lay between a movie film made in Dallas and the autopsy performed in Bethesda.

I wasn't sure how to proceed. I was looking for some chronological factor I had missed before, something which would reconcile the backward head snap on the Zapruder film with the proposition that Humes had told the truth.

But they seemed irreconcilable. The critical entries in the table were all dated the same: November 22. There seemed to be no time lapse, no opportunity for anything to change.

Had I modified my chart and actually put in the time of day for the November 22 entries, it would have looked like this:

November 22 12:30 P.M. (CST)	Zapruder film	Head shot from front (based on backward motion)
November 22 12:40 P.M. (CST)	Dallas doctors	Head shot from front (based on opinion of most Dallas doctors that exit wound was at rear of head)
November 22 8:00 P.M. (EST)	Navy autopsy Bethesda, Md.	Head shot from rear (Humes' autopsy report and testimony)

The chart showed the divergence of information flows—i.e., that "from the front" changed to "from the rear" between Dallas and Bethesda sometime after 12:30 P.M. (CST) and before 8:00 P.M. (EST).

What did that mean? What had changed?

169

Repeatedly, I tried to reconcile the film with the autopsy. It was maddening. I had been wrestling with the issue for some time. The month before, I was invited to talk at San Francisco State College. To illustrate the conflict between the autopsy report and the Zapruder film I prepared several slides. One illustrated the backward head snap; another showed the navy drawing employed by Humes to depict the back-to-front head trajectory. Still another combined them: on the left was a sequence of Zapruder frames showing the head being thrust toward the rear; on the right, the navy medical drawing illustrating the opposite—that the shot struck from behind. Flashing that slide on the screen, I turned to the audience: "Thus we have a contradiction in evidence."

No sooner had I uttered the words than the thought flashed through my mind: "Contradictions don't exist."

The statement was significant to me because, years before, I had read Ayn Rand's *Atlas Shrugged* which, on one level, was a philosophical mystery. A major theme was that, in logic at least, contradictions do not exist. If one checks the premises of an argument he will always find a hidden premise which if exposed and resolved causes the contradictions to dissolve. Ever since my San Francisco State talk, I had been turning the puzzle over and over in my head. Here was a "contradiction," by God; had I not found an exception to the rule, or was I enmeshed in some trick of semantics?

I made an effort to "check the premises." Which one was wrong? Where was the "hidden premise"? Newton's laws were just Newton's laws. I had faith in my analysis that the backward motion indicated the shot struck from the front. So I shifted to the other part of the apparent paradox. What about Commander Humes? What was the basis for Humes' testimony? Every time I asked that question the reply came back: "the autopsy."

I was trapped inside a labyrinth. I would say to myself: "Humes is telling the truth. The bullet entered from the rear." But the head snap on the Zapruder film, I was certain, showed the fatal shot struck from the front. I was missing something, but I couldn't figure out what it was. I had to relax and go through the steps methodically, logically.

I rephrased the problem slightly. "Assume Humes was telling the truth," I said to myself. "What would have to be true for Humes to have told the truth, yet for that to be reconciled with the motion on the Zapruder film?"

In this attempt to reconcile Commander Humes' testimony with the evidence of the film—in effect, to find some model of conspiracy in which the autopsy doctor did not have to be a participant—I was gripped with intense excitement. There was a way! There was some kind of fraud in the event itself—something associated with the autopsy, a fraud that would deceive even Humes!

More than a decade later, it is difficult to capture the experience as it happened, to put it into words. An idea loomed up, a giant shape seen dimly in a fogbank, an idea that I found impossible to articulate—it simply did not have a name.

On a subconscious level, I knew I had found something. I knew that the two propositions—that Humes was telling the truth and that the shot impacted from the front—were *not* irreconcilable after all, and that reconciling them was the key to the mystery.

I packed up my things, gathered together the pictures Yoram had made for me, bade them goodnight, and, my mind racing, I drove back to my apartment in West Los Angeles. I remember thinking: "My God, we don't even know where the coffin was." I knew the document I wanted to see—the one chronological narrative of the autopsy—the report of FBI agents Sibert and O'Neill.

Searching for a Lost Fact

I entered my apartment and went straight to the bookshelf. I took Epstein's book, opened to the back, and began to read the Sibert and O'Neill report, word by word. The two agents wrote that they had received an instruction from FBI Headquarters to meet the presidential jet and "to stay with the body and to obtain bullets reportedly in the President's body." They had driven out to Andrews Air Force Base.

Air Force One landed—forty minutes late.* The two agents drove in the motorcade following the ambulance that contained Jacqueline Kennedy, Robert Kennedy, and the coffin to the National Naval Medical Center, Bethesda, Maryland. They helped take the coffin into the autopsy room of Bethesda Naval Hospital.[58]

The report was packed with details I had never read. I felt I was actually entering the Bethesda morgue on November 22, 1963. For the first time, I saw the autopsy as a real event. I saw the coffin, the body, the autopsy table. I read slowly, checking for anything irregular, any clue.

I came to page three of the report. The coffin was about to be opened. The autopsy was about to begin. Sibert and O'Neill described the scene.

"The President's body was removed from the casket in which it had been transported and was placed on the autopsy table, at which time the complete body was wrapped in a sheet and the head area contained an additional wrapping which was saturated with blood."[59]

The agents continued: "Following the removal of the wrapping, it was ascertained that the President's clothing had been removed and it was

_____

* Sibert and O'Neill reported they were originally told the plane would arrive at 5:25 P.M., but were subsequently advised it would arrive at 6:05 P.M.[57]

also apparent that a tracheotomy had been performed. . . ."[60] My heart started to pound as I read what came next.

". . . it was also apparent that a tracheotomy had been performed *as well as surgery of the head area, namely, in the top of the skull* [emphasis added]."[61]

". . . surgery of the head area . . ."?!

". . . in the top of the skull . . ."?!

I knew exactly what that meant—*this* was the missing piece of the puzzle.

The Dallas doctors had operated only on the throat. No one had touched the President's head—certainly not with a surgical instrument.

Yet those words, if true, meant that some time after the President was pronounced dead in Dallas, but before the coffin arrived in the Bethesda autopsy room, somebody had performed "surgery" on President Kennedy's corpse.

I was exhilarated, terrified. I wanted to vomit.

This was the answer to the head-snap problem—a logically possible alternative, yet a possibility no one had dreamed of: The President's head had been physically altered. If someone had altered the head, the configuration of the wounds at Dallas was not the same as at Bethesda. The head was thrust backward by the impact of a bullet from the front, yet the autopsy performed at Bethesda showed an impact from behind. Someone had altered the head!

My instinct had been correct. There was no contradiction. I had found the hidden premise, a premise taken for granted by everyone: that the condition of the President's body at Bethesda, Maryland, was the same as it had been at Dallas, Texas. That premise was definitely incorrect if the words in the Sibert and O'Neill report were true. There had been "surgery of the head area, namely, in the top of the skull" somewhere between Dallas and Bethesda. Somewhere between Dallas and Bethesda the President's body had been altered.

I could hardly believe what I had found. I had approached the Kennedy assassination from a scientific standpoint. In the midst of attempting to solve what I viewed as an abstract technical problem, almost a logical problem, I had stumbled into a house of horrors.

The scene conjured up was unbelievable—the lid of a coffin raised at some secret location, unknown hands on the body, tools brought to bear, cutting into the corpse of John F. Kennedy, who had been, just hours before, the most powerful man in the world.

New Questions and Insights

Questions flooded my mind. By whom, when, and where was the "surgery" done? Exactly what did it consist of? What changes were made?

A New Hypothesis

The FBI agents recorded nothing else about surgery, only that one specific, incongruous statement that when the body arrived, it contained "an additional wrapping" on the head, a wrapping "saturated with blood," that when that wrapping was removed, it was "apparent" there had been "surgery of the head area, namely, in the top of the skull."[62] If surgery had been performed, why did the navy autopsy go forward as if nothing were amiss?

I reached for volume 2 and began to reread the approximately thirty pages of autopsy testimony given by Commander Humes. Mostly, it was a detailed description of all damage to Kennedy's body as it lay on the Bethesda autopsy table between 8:00 and 11:00 P.M. on the night of November 22. It was chilling to realize the subtlety and the power of the deception that could be perpetrated if the body was altered. Humes could have told the truth, yet be describing a body which did not reflect the shooting.

There was no way to tell whether the wounds Humes described were on the body in Dallas. That was implicit, but Humes never said so. He never prefaced his answers to Arlen Specter's questions by saying: "At the time *I* examined the body, these were the wounds I saw. . . ." Humes simply described what he observed at Bethesda that night, and the Warren Commission accepted that testimony as an accurate description of wounds inflicted earlier that afternoon.

The entire Warren Report was structured on Humes' description of President Kennedy's body, graphically illustrated by the artist's drawings he brought to the Commission's hearing room, drawings that depicted two back-to-front trajectories.

I visualized the scene. Humes, pointer in hand, stood before Chief Justice Earl Warren, explaining his autopsy conclusions, providing information that was incorrect, but that agreed with what he saw on the autopsy table.

The interchange between Chief Justice Warren and Commander Humes, repeatedly cited by defenders of the Report as evidence the Commission could not have been deceived, rang in my ears:

> WARREN: . . . may I ask you this, Commander: If we had the pictures here and you could look them over again and restate your opinion, would it cause you to change any of the testimony you have given here?
>
> HUMES: To the best of my recollection, Mr. Chief Justice, it would not.[63]

This was the Commission's protection, their insurance policy against perjury, against fraud in the autopsy findings. And so they did not subpoena the X-rays and photographs. Legally, they had taken a calculated risk. The conclusions of one of the greatest murder investigations in the history of the world rested on one man's word of what another man's body looked like.

But the protection was illusory. The problem was not Humes. It was the body.

Now I was intensely interested in the President's body—as evidence. Exactly what did it look like at Bethesda? Exactly what did "surgery of the head area, namely, in the top of the skull" mean? Was Humes aware of such surgery? Humes' testimony, I now realized, was the best looking glass available.

I turned to page 357 of volume 2, where Humes described the condition of the President's head and brain. There were sentences—indeed, whole paragraphs—written in anatomic terminology that was Greek to me. My old suspicions about Humes began to resurface. I wondered whether he was using a highly technical vocabulary to describe "head surgery" to Specter, to avoid saying what he saw in plain English. Words I didn't understand included: parasagittal, occipital lobe, cerebral peduncles, corpus callosum. To understand what Humes was saying, I was going to have to get a medical dictionary and an atlas of anatomy and look up each word. The process would be similar to learning a foreign language.

I noted that Humes did take the trouble to define many of the terms he used. Using these definitions I attempted to visualize what he was describing. He described certain very specific damage to the brain—a deep gash which ran the entire length of the brain, a gash whose depth was approximately five or six centimeters. That was more than two inches!

Humes called it a "parasagittal laceration," and I knew that wasn't discussed anywhere in the Warren Report. I fastened on the word "laceration." Was this a euphemism describing a surgical cut in the brain?

Another point. Humes testified that when he touched the President's head, large pieces of bone fell to the autopsy table. In Dallas the entire body was subject to a considerable amount of motion because Dr. Perry was pounding on the President's chest giving external heart massage. Despite this activity, no one reported pieces of President Kennedy's skull falling to the emergency room cart. I did not understand why pieces of the President's skull should fall to the table in Bethesda if they were not dislodged by the activity in Dallas—unless something had happened to the head between Dallas and Bethesda. Moreover, Sibert and O'Neill reported that the President's body was not only wrapped in a sheet supplied (according to Humes) by Parkland Memorial Hospital, but the head had "an additional wrapping which was saturated with blood."[64] Neither Humes nor the Dallas medical reports in the twenty-six volumes talked of any second wrapping on the head.

Missing Bullets?

I tried to understand Humes' testimony in the context of the Sibert and O'Neill FBI report. The two agents reported that the doctors were puzzled they could find no bullets. Was it possible that they couldn't find bullets because "surgery" had been performed to remove them?

I focused on Sibert and O'Neill's brief description of the doctors' fruitless efforts to find bullets or sizeable fragments in the President's body:

Inasmuch as no complete bullet of any size could be located in the brain area and likewise no bullet could be located in the back or any other area of the body as determined by total body X-rays and inspection [of the hole in the back] revealing there was no point of exit, the individuals performing the autopsy were at a loss to explain why they could find no bullets.[65]

". . . at a loss to explain . . ."?

That indicated a substantial degree of puzzlement; yet before the Warren Commission, Humes' explanation for the bulletless condition of the President's body was straightforward. There were no bullets inside the body, he said, because the President's wounds came in two matched pairs, and each bullet that entered, exited. But if so, then why wasn't that immediately apparent? Were they aware of something strange about the condition of the body at the time they performed the autopsy?

The doctors' behavior suggested they were honest. If Humes was part of a conspiracy to cover up the facts, would he have betrayed such puzzlement in front of the FBI?

I also realized that any pre-autopsy surgery to remove bullets held the answer to Liebeler's repeated taunt: If there's another assassin, then where's the bullet? If the President's body was tampered with prior to the autopsy, other bullets weren't found because they had been removed.

I was amazed at the simplicity of the concept. Previously, I had no satisfactory answer why "other bullets" weren't found, other than to postulate a large conspiracy starting with the autopsy surgeons. Now I saw how many different officials and investigative agencies, ranging from the autopsy doctors to the FBI Laboratory, could be fooled. The secret removal of bullets before the body reached the autopsy room would have severed the ballistic connection between the shooting and the guns of other assassins—before the investigation began. The entire investigative apparatus of the U.S. government could have been misled.

The Entry Wound in the Head: Not Seen at Dallas

I now suspected that the camouflage extended to the small entry wound in the head reported in the navy autopsy. That wound was the medical basis for the Warren Commission's conclusion that the fatal shot struck from behind. Each of the eight Dallas doctors had been asked about that wound. None had seen it. The Commission concluded it wasn't seen because the President was lying on his back, or because the wound was obscured. Were these reasons sufficient? Although the President was lying on his back, the rear of his head was visible. Almost all the doctors observed the large wound at the right rear. Some described it in detail. The entry wound was ¼ by ⅜ inch, and was within an inch or two of the larger wound.[66] Could they all have missed it?

One of those who saw this wound at Bethesda was Secret Service Agent Roy Kellerman. He said it was a little hole, about the size of a pinky finger, beneath the large hole. He said it was low in the back of the head, "in the hairline."[67] I could not understand why Kellerman could see the wound at Bethesda while eight doctors had not seen it in Dallas. Unless it was not seen in Dallas because it wasn't there.

I was now sharply aware of a logical error I had been making. Following the thinking of Salandria and Lane, I had assumed that because the wound wasn't seen in Dallas, Humes was lying about its existence at Bethesda. In *Rush to Judgment,* for example, Lane wrote that "each [of the Dallas doctors] testified that he did not see a bullet hole which the Commission said was there."[68] He chastised the Commission because it "apparently felt constrained to insist on the existence of such an entry wound to support its conclusion."[69] In private conversations, the critics were less elliptic. The belief was widespread that Humes was simply a liar.

But that was the ultimate irony: Humes could have testified truthfully; it was the body that could have lied.

Humes and Allen Dulles: A Strange Interchange

Another passage in Humes' testimony fueled my suspicions that he was aware there was something strange about the condition of the President's head. Former CIA Chief Allen Dulles posed this question regarding the head wound:

DULLES: Just one other question. Am I correct in assuming from what you have said that this wound is entirely inconsistent with a wound that might have been administered if the shot were fired from in front or the side of the President: it had to be fired from behind the President?[70]

Humes' answer, I thought, was rather peculiar: "Scientifically, sir, it is impossible for it to have been fired from other than behind. Or to have exited from other than behind."[71]

Taken literally, Humes seemed to be saying that "scientifically" the shot both entered *and* exited from the rear of the skull, as if the bullet had made a U-turn inside the President's head. Of course, that was not the major import of Humes' testimony, or the drawings he submitted, but I thought this interchange indicated either confusion on Humes' part, or an awareness that the rear of the President's head contained paradoxical information as to the source of the shot.

I could understand why Humes might be confused by what he saw. On the one hand, many of the Dallas doctors reported an exit wound at the right rear of the President's head. But, as Humes testified, there was a smaller hole—unquestionably an entry wound—beneath the larger wound. If my theory was correct, the rear of the President's head might have contained evidence of both entry and exit, and Humes' answer might be a way of sidestepping that issue.

Was my interpretation of Humes' interchange with Allen Dulles correct? Or was it simply a matter of some stilted syntax? Later I would find a number of other double-entendres in Humes' testimony, indicating to me that there was something wrong with the President's body at the time of the autopsy and that when Humes stumbled across such matters, he took refuge in riddles.

The Ambience at Bethesda: Some Initial Speculations

These problems were subtle compared with a number of others that now came to the fore. One was: How did two FBI agents who had no medical training determine there had been "surgery of the head area"? Another: If the FBI statement were true, why didn't Humes tell the Warren Commission about it?

I could only conjecture that Sibert and O'Neill, as FBI agents, were empowered to ask questions. And that somehow they had obtained such information from an authoritative source.

This led to another problem. Why did they present their information so routinely? Altering the President's body would be a crime. Any surgery performed prior to autopsy must have been the dark secret of a conspiracy. Yet, as written in the Sibert and O'Neill report, the statement appeared almost as an afterthought. Had Sibert and O'Neill been on the witness stand, it would be the equivalent of their volunteering, before stepping down: "Oh, yes; one other thing; when the body was removed from the coffin, it was apparent there was surgery of the head area, namely, in the top of the skull."

Why this routine quality? I could only conjecture. Possibly the agents were under a misunderstanding, and thought "head surgery" was part of the medical procedure performed at Dallas.

Then, there was the problem of Commander Humes. The FBI said head surgery was "apparent."[72] If so, I was certain the autopsy doctors themselves must have known of it. Yet Commander Humes made no mention of any such pre-autopsy head surgery either in the autopsy report or in his Warren Commission testimony. There seemed to be three possibilities, three roles Humes could be playing in this affair.

At one extreme, Humes could be part of the conspiracy. I rejected this. If the doctors were part of the plot, why take the trouble to alter the body? Why not just lie?

At the other extreme, Humes might have been unwitting, and have had no idea anything was wrong with the body. In this case, he simply performed the autopsy in routine fashion, wrote up a report, and was honestly surprised to learn that his autopsy conclusions were at odds with so much "Dallas evidence"—the eyewitnesses, the Zapruder film head snap, the opinion of the Dallas doctors, etc.

I took the middle ground. Humes found himself in an impossible situation, I thought. The coffin was opened. The body was unwrapped. Humes saw that surgery had already been performed. He was in a room surrounded by his military superiors—many of them were doctors from the medical department of the U.S. Navy. Adm. George Burkley, Physician to the President, was standing right there. No one said anything. Humes was faced with an ambiguous, possibly sinister situation. What could he do—call the Maryland State Police?

Combining the Hypotheses

One of the last things I did that Saturday night was to combine my newly found evidence for pre-autopsy head surgery with what I had learned earlier that evening about the change in the neck trajectory from non-transit to transit.

According to my theory, still in a primitive stage, here is what had occurred. First, conspirators had secretly altered the condition of President Kennedy's head between Dallas and Bethesda. That alteration, I suspected, reversed the apparent direction of the fatal shot. The altered body then arrived at the Bethesda morgue. Somehow the FBI learned of the head surgery. Nevertheless, the autopsy proceeded. In front of the FBI, Humes drew certain autopsy conclusions. According to agents Sibert and O'Neill, Humes said the "pattern was clear": two shots, both striking from behind.[73] One struck the President in the head and exited through the top of his skull; the other struck "below the shoulders," produced a shallow wound, and fell back out onto a hospital stretcher.[74] Nothing was said about a bullet wound in the front of the throat—that hole was referred to as a tracheotomy incision.[75] (See Fig. 13.)

The next morning, Humes learned he had missed the wound at the

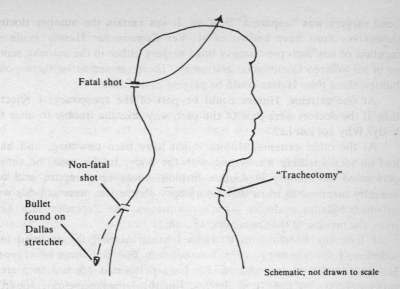

Fatal shot

Non-fatal shot

"Tracheotomy"

Bullet found on Dallas stretcher

Schematic; not drawn to scale

Figure 13.
Friday night autopsy conclusions (according to Sibert and O'Neill)
Non-fatal shot: produces a shallow wound "below the shoulders." Bullet found on Dallas stretcher.
Fatal shot: enters from the rear, exits through the top of the skull.
Hole in front of throat: tracheotomy incision.

site of the tracheotomy. He then modified one of his Friday-night conclusions. In the autopsy submitted Sunday, Humes said the non-fatal shot passed all the way through, exiting at the throat.

A Personal Turning Point

October 22, 1966, marked a turning point for me. By that time, I had spent almost a year and a half studying the twenty-six volumes of the Warren Commission, blowing up the backgrounds of photographs, interviewing witnesses, pursuing the idea that more than one man shot the President, that there had been a conspiracy, that the Warren Commission was wrong.

My discovery of the statement in the Sibert and O'Neill report exposed for the first time a piece of evidence that pointed to a plot within the United States government. If it were true that surgery had been performed before the autopsy, then government officials had to be involved, because the President's body was always in official custody. From the moment of death at Parkland Memorial Hospital until the time of autopsy at Bethesda, the body (and the coffin containing the body) was accompanied by Secret Service agents. No outsider could have had access to the body. A deranged individual, taking advantage of a target of opportunity, could take a shot at the President and possibly put a bullet in his body, but only the highest authority could secretly take one out.

Postmortem pre-autopsy surgery performed on President Kennedy's body seemed to be the connecting link between a grassy-knoll assassin and a government plot. One hand had pulled the trigger that sent a bullet into the President's head; another had secretly extracted the bullet and changed the configuration of the wounds to reverse the apparent direction of the shot. I was mystified how conspirators could plan all this in advance. I hesitated to believe what I had found. It was the model of a ghoulish conspiracy.

My attitudes were in a state of flux that night. Until then, researching the Kennedy assassination was like touring an allegedly haunted house. Those on the tour assume the house is safe. Some of the tourists may get excited, and even scream and shriek a bit, but one suspects they are just pretending. Any danger is illusory. But that evening, when I found that FBI statement, it was as if I had wandered down a previously unexplored corridor, saw something I thought was blood coming from under a door, opened it, and found a real body.

I would have been relieved that night to be told that this discovery, however horrible, was known by those in authority, and that something had been done about it, if only behind the scenes. I would have been relieved to be told that yes, Earl Warren lied; this is what the government of the United States was hiding from the American people—the secret too awful to know. But what I suspected was even more frightening: This is what a conspiracy had hidden from the government of the United States. I was certain I was looking at something new and previously unknown, the mechanism by which a high-level plot had covered its tracks.

I felt isolated and, for the first time, saw the other Warren Report critics as mere tourists engaged in an academic exercise. I had found something fundamental—I had glimpsed the possibility of treason.

CHAPTER 8

Emergence of a New Hypothesis

I AROSE ON SUNDAY MORNING convinced I had discovered the darkest secret of the crime of the century.

I was still incredulous that readily available in the corner drugstore was the Bantam edition of Epstein's book containing the FBI 302 report that surgery had been performed on President Kennedy's body prior to the autopsy. Furthermore, I now realized that the same FBI report was published in an Avon paperback, *The Second Oswald*. The two books had been out about a month. I was certain that other critics would find the statement within days, and the focus of debate would shift from the question of a "second assassin" to the gruesome issue: Who altered the President's body?

As soon as possible, I wanted to speak to Liebeler about that FBI statement. In a few hours we would be on the same TV program, but I decided to say nothing about it on the air. I would confront him privately. The year before when I had asked Liebeler what I should do if I found a witness who saw someone shooting at the President from the knoll, he had said: "Try bringing him to me." What I had found was even more dramatic. How would he react? What would he say? What would he do?

I understood Liebeler's position better now than I had before. He really believed the medical evidence was reliable. My approach had been different. Relying on the Zapruder film head snap, I concluded Humes had lied. We were both wrong. Liebeler was wrong in thinking the medical evidence was reliable; I was wrong in thinking Humes lied. The body itself had been made to lie.

In the short time before the TV program was to begin, I attempted to break new ground, to carry my investigation further. What was the next question I should ask? What should I look for next in that storehouse of information, the twenty-six volumes? Initially, I was confused. It was as if a thousand handles protruded from the subject, and I didn't know which one to grasp first.

One was the Warren Commission. It was an article of faith among those who rejected the Warren Report that the government was deliberately hiding something. Was it pre-autopsy surgery? Was that the horrible secret known, but covered up, by the Commission? I rejected that. I didn't think Liebeler, the other attorneys, or anyone else on the Commission knew about any such surgery. My hunch was that even the FBI, as an organization, didn't know about it, although I supposed agents Sibert and O'Neill might be able to explain why they wrote that statement. I thought that any pre-autopsy surgery was an integral part of the assassination plot, was intended to remain secret forever, and that the FBI statement was a fluke, a piece of information that slipped, unnoticed, through the system.

My attention riveted on the statement itself. It was so bald, so preposterous and, if true, so incredible. It raised all the obvious questions any newsman would ask: What? When? Where? How? Why? I began with "what." Exactly what alterations were made? Were they confined to the head, or was that simply the single part of the body mentioned in this particular statement? I suspected that "surgery of the head area" was merely the tip of an iceberg.

Determining exactly what alterations were made was critical; only then would it be possible to know exactly how the shooting took place: the number of shooters, their exact locations, etc. On that Sunday morning in 1966, such details seemed of paramount importance. More than one shooter, after all, meant a conspiracy. I did not realize, then, that a "conspiracy" of shooters was far less important than a conspiracy to alter the body. But I knew that these alterations would affect the location of the gunmen in my "three-assassin" model and so I began by posing this question: If the autopsy conclusions were false because of surgery performed on the body, how did that affect my previous analysis?

It quickly became apparent that questions of validity regarding the autopsy findings were entangled, in a way I didn't yet understand, with the ballistic evidence linking Oswald's gun to the crime. There was no better example than the relationship between the alleged "head surgery" and the two large bullet fragments found in the automobile.

According to the Warren Commission, those two fragments—the nose and tail portions of a bullet, each of which ballistically matched the rifle found at the Depository—were the remains of the shot that struck Kennedy in the head from behind.[1]

But now the real meaning of those fragments had to be reassessed. There seemed no reason for such surgery other than to change the configuration of the wounds and to remove bullets. If that was the case, what about the fragments found in the car? Were they planted as substitutes?

I now realized that that possibility, which derived from a purely logical argument based upon the premise of head surgery and whether such surgery did in fact change the apparent direction of the fatal shot, turned on the authenticity of the rear entry wound. The issue was elementary.

For Kennedy to have been struck in the head by a bullet from Oswald's rifle, he must have been struck from behind. Consequently, if the rear entry wound, found at autopsy, was created after death, then he was not struck from behind, and could not have been struck by a bullet from that rifle. In that case, the two bullet fragments found in the car could not have inflicted the fatal wound.

Thus there was a logical connection between the authenticity of the rear entry in the head and the legitimacy of the two bullet fragments found in the car.

But those two battered fragments were the epitome of legitimacy compared to the nearly unblemished stretcher bullet which was the remaining link in the ballistic evidence. The stretcher bullet, in the words of an FBI expert, was "in practically original condition"[2] and contained nary a trace of blood or tissue.

If all three pieces of ammunition were planted, the entire ballistic link between the gun and the crime dissolved. That not only meant Oswald's rifle wasn't the murder weapon, it suggested the gun was planted.

This approach was new. I was not basing the inauthenticity of the ammunition solely on the condition of bullet 399, but on the inauthenticity of the two rear entry wounds.

I was surprised at the extent to which the Commission's tapestry of evidence suddenly unraveled if a single autopsy trajectory was false. That hypothesis started a chain reaction. False medical evidence led to false ballistic evidence; false ballistic evidence led to a planted murder weapon. If the body was altered, facts which previously had a clear and natural relationship to one another suddenly went out of focus. Not only were the facts bogus; the relationships were bogus. The falseness was contagious. It was like discovering that an entire deck of cards consisted of nothing but jokers.

My excitement mounted. Amid the confusion, a new definition of the problem was emerging—at least on a technical level. How many shooters there were, and exactly where they were located on Dealey Plaza were questions that could not be answered until it was first determined what was real, and not real, in the evidence. And that depended upon what was genuine and false on the body at the time of autopsy.

Viewed that way, the Kennedy assassination became an extremely interesting technical problem. Was it possible to separate fact from artifact? Appearance from reality? If I could work out a valid method of analysis, I felt certain the right answers would emerge. How to proceed?

I began with the body. The shooting happened only one way. Immediately afterward the body was in one, and only one, condition. Certain authentic ammunition lay in the wake of the crime.

The first step was to establish what the body looked like immediately after the shooting. That would determine how the shooting really occurred.

The Dallas doctors' testimony was my starting point. Only they saw the President's body immediately after the shooting. The Bethesda information applied to the body as of 8:00 P.M. The way to proceed, it seemed, was to compare the Dallas doctors' testimony with the Bethesda autopsy and search for differences—not differences of *opinion* about the direction of the shots, but different descriptions of anatomy—as if one were studying "before" and "after" photographs from the files of a plastic surgeon.

Dallas versus Bethesda. Anatomic differences. That was the question I would have to address to the twenty-six volumes. Like most Warren Report critics, I had thought the issue was the trustworthiness of the observer. The question was: whom to believe—the civilian Dallas doctors or the military Bethesda doctors? But suppose both sets of doctors were telling the truth—the Dallas doctors, when they said the President was shot from the front, and the Bethesda doctors, when they said the President was shot from behind? Suppose opinions differed because the condition of the President's body was changed?

I began my list of Dallas/Bethesda differences with the familiar fact that the rear entry for the head trajectory, observed at Bethesda, was seen by none of the Dallas doctors. Then I recalled that still another wound, observed at Bethesda, was seen by no one at Dallas: the rear entry for the neck trajectory. The possible significance of that now dawned on me. Considered together, this pair of "non-observations" was striking: The two entry wounds on the rear surface of the President's body were not seen at Dallas, yet those two wounds were the foundation for the Bethesda doctors' conclusion that Kennedy was struck twice, and only from behind.

Why didn't anybody at Parkland Memorial Hospital observe the rear entry wound for the neck trajectory? Although the Report never discussed this question, simply referring all mention of the wound to the Bethesda observations, I was aware that news accounts explained that Kennedy was lying on his back. I had never questioned this before. Now, nothing could be taken for granted. All circumstances surrounding any wound observed at Bethesda, but not seen in Dallas, deserved the closest scrutiny.

But I hardly had time to pursue the matter. Soon I was due at television station KTTV, to be one of several guests appearing opposite Wesley Liebeler on a show hosted by Louis Lomax. I collected my pictures of bullets, which I had now mounted on a large display board, some other photos I wanted to use, and headed for the TV studio in Hollywood.

The Lomax Show

A long line of people waited to get inside KTTV's studios. Many of those who showed up were part of an active Los Angeles subculture who viewed Wesley Liebeler as the personification of the government coverup.

Lomax began the program by citing a recent poll. "Mr. Liebeler," he began, "how do you account for the fact that . . . today the American public looks at you and it says, 'I don't believe you'?"[3]

"I can't explain it satisfactorily, even to myself," he said, "but . . . there are a large number of people in this country, myself included, that don't believe everything that the government hands out in its press releases. . . . Now [the critics] have a situation here where, if they can do it, they can show that the government is lying to them. They've got twenty-six volumes of material that the Warren Commission issued in support of [its] Report. It's a finite universe. It's just twenty-six books. . . . And if . . . they can demonstrate that the government has *deceived* them and *lied* to them, they've got an opportunity to take out all of the pent-up frustrations and hostilities toward the government, generally." Now Liebeler started to stutter, and angrily spurted out his own conclusion: "And it's gonna come out on the Warren Commission!"

He ridiculed the idea that any lawyers on the staff attempted to suppress evidence or cover up a conspiracy. All of them, he said, understood the personal implications. "Just take myself . . . I'm a bit vainglorious, I suppose, like every other human being. If I'd been able to find [such] evidence, I would have gone down in history as the discoverer of the greatest conspiracy in the history of mankind."

"So," said Lomax, "you're saying there was no conspiracy?"

"What I'm saying is that I certainly looked very hard for it," replied Liebeler.

As I listened, I wondered how Liebeler would react when I showed him the statement reporting surgery.

Lomax turned to his prepared list of questions: "First, who killed President Kennedy?"

"It's perfectly clear that Lee Harvey Oswald killed President Kennedy," replied Liebeler. Giggles and laughter erupted from the audience.

"Is there *any* question in your mind about that?" asked Lomax.

"There's no question in my mind about that whatsoever," said Liebeler.

Several people in the audience groaned loudly. Someone yelled out in exasperation: "Oh, come on!"

By way of answering the heckler, Liebeler continued: "And I think there can be no reasonable question about that in anybody's mind, if they'll look at the record of what the Commission did, and honestly evaluate the criticism that's been made of that work."

What then, asked Lomax, was there for Liebeler's students to investigate? Liebeler replied that one purpose was to examine the criticism leveled against the Report. A book he was writing would deal with these criticisms, and also explain how the Commission conducted its investigation. Lomax asked a final question before turning to the guests. "Basically, in terms of what it says, its fundamental thrust, do you, without reservation, support the Warren Commission Report on the death of President Kennedy?"

Replied Liebeler: "Well, I'll answer that question this way: Any doubts at all that I have about this whole thing could easily be resolved, and I suggest that it very likely *will* be resolved by the issuance of the autopsy pictures and the X-rays. . . . Because I think this is the best evidence of the location of the wounds in the President's body and I think it's absolutely essential that this evidence be made available. Now I have no doubt about the [Commission's] conclusions, on the basis of the evidence that's in the Report, but I would be happier if these materials were available. . . ."

Lomax commented: "You said 'whatever doubts *you* have' . . . What's in these pictures? What is there *possibly* about these pictures that raises doubt in the mind of an attorney like you who worked for the Commission?"

"It's not anything in the pictures that raises any doubt about it," replied Liebeler. "[But] every lawyer, and every person who has been to law school knows that there are certain gradations of evidence—the so-called best-evidence rule."

I knew exactly what was coming next. It was the same speech I had heard in our private talks, in front of his class, and in numerous hallway conversations at the law school.

"Now it's perfectly clear that the 'best evidence' as to where the location of the wounds in the President's body are, which is a matter that is crucial to the whole evaluation and analysis of the Report, are the pictures that were taken of his body. There's no question about that. Now until that evidence has been presented, I think that every lawyer has the right to reserve a certain amount of judgment until he sees the best evidence available—and that's essentially what I'm saying."

As I listened, I wondered what value the pictures would have if the President's body—the object seen by the camera's eye—had been altered. The same was true of the X-rays. If bullet fragments had been removed, they wouldn't be there when Humes examined the body, nor would they show up on X-rays. If alterations in the body fooled the autopsy surgeon, could the X-ray beam or the eye of the camera have been more discerning?

The dialogue continued.

LOMAX: Is there any question in your mind what these pictures will show?

LIEBELER: None whatever. No.

LOMAX: Have you seen them?

LIEBELER: No, sir, I haven't. But I've seen the autopsy report, and I've read the testimony of the autopsy surgeons that conducted the autopsy of the President, and they were specifically asked if their testimony about the location of the wounds and what happened—how the bullets hit the President—would be any different if the pictures and X-rays were available before them at the time they testified. And they categorically testified that it would not be any different. And that's fine—I accept that testimony, but at the same time, I reserve the right in my own mind to look at the "best evidence" involved, and I haven't seen that yet.

As I listened, I realized that my analysis had gone beyond Liebeler's. Despite his legal training, despite all the high-powered legal jargon about "best evidence," my analysis was in fact more sophisticated. For instance, I now understood why any corroboration between the autopsy testimony and the photos and X-rays might well be meaningless. I was certain that during the past thirty-six hours, I had opened a door that Liebeler never dreamed existed—not because he wasn't smart enough, but because the idea was just unthinkable. Liebeler was too much a gentleman. Even murder has its rules.

Lomax turned to the first guest, a young woman who was boiling mad, angry that a government commission could conclude the shots came from behind, and disregard all the witnesses who thought the shots came from the front. As she went on and on, Liebeler grew angry. To Wesley Liebeler, the problem wasn't the Warren Report, but people like this woman, people not trained to think critically, who didn't understand how to separate appearance from reality.

Liebeler recovered the floor. ". . . I want to respond to that because I am a lawyer, and one thing a lawyer is supposed to do is to be able to analyze conflicting evidence, and compare it and make judgments that are relevant and valued ['Pardon me,' he said, as she tried to interrupt and make several more points] and then to draw the inference of fact that is most logical and most permissible and most apparent from conflicting fact. That's what lawyers are trained to do. That's what judges do every day of the week."

But even Lomax didn't understand what Liebeler was driving at.

"All right," said Lomax, "[but] now we're talking about the grassy knoll."

"I know it," said Liebeler, "I'm trying to explain what kind of judgments you have to make about the value of evidence. And the fact is nobody saw any shots fired from the grassy knoll, nobody saw anybody there with a rifle, nobody found any shell casings, nobody saw anything over there. Some people ran over there. There was a puff of smoke, and people thought the *sounds* came from there. Now the *best* evidence as to where the shots came from, it seems to me, is the scientific analysis of the President's *body* that was made after the event, and it's perfectly clear from examining the nature of these wounds that *all* of the shots came from *behind* and from *above*—there is not a shred of evidence to indicate that *any* of the shots came from anywhere else."

Liebeler pursued the matter further; reading from volume 2, page 360, he went directly to the condition of the President's head, as described by Humes. "The question is by Mr. [Allen] Dulles:

Am I correct in assuming [from] what you have said that this wound in the President's head is entirely inconsistent with a wound that might have been administered if the shot were fired from the front or the side of the President? It had to be fired from behind the President?

Oh, oh, I thought to myself, here comes that weird ambiguous response by Humes.

Liebeler began reading Humes' reply: "Scientifically, sir, it is impossible for it to have been fired from other than behind." Then he stopped. For an instant, I saw him do a double take. He was looking at the words: "Or to have exited from other than behind." He did not read the rest of Humes' answer. Liebeler looked up at the camera and, having barely paused, said: "Now *that's* evidence." And that's a quick-thinking lawyer, I thought.

My turn to debate with Liebeler came. I launched into a discussion of Commission Exhibit 399, the Dallas stretcher bullet. The events of the past twenty-four hours were having their effect on me and I was no longer interested in arguing about the single-bullet theory. The real question was appearance versus reality in the evidence. I said that my interest was "whether the Commission's fact-finding process was good enough to determine whether or not the evidence [it received] was real or whether it was planted. . . ."

Somewhat to my surprise, Liebeler conceded that bullet 399 was considered, a priori, legitimate, and he proceeded to tie 399 to the bullet fragments that were found in the car: "And *they* would have to be planted, too, Mr. Lifton, if this [bullet 399] was a plant. . . ."

It was an extension of our private debate. Liebeler argued that anybody who held that the ammunition that reached the FBI Laboratory was all fake must explain what had happened to the ammunition that had actually inflicted the injuries.

I held my tongue, but "missing bullets" was no longer a mystery. In theory at least, the answer was simple: The metal had been secretly extracted from Kennedy's body.

My presentation concluded with a picture of the grassy knoll possibly showing smoke.* As it flashed on the TV screen, I narrated: "Up near the corner of the wall is smoke—apparently seen by others, [which] appears in color in that picture." (See Photo 6.)

Liebeler retorted: ". . . it's perfectly clear that there was a puff of smoke or steam up there. . . . Now you know, of course, that there is a steam pipe that runs through the area back up there?"

"I don't," I interjected, refusing to be Liebeler's straight man.

"You don't know that? Well, I know that," said Liebeler, somewhat testily. Liebeler said all the grassy-knoll witnesses weren't questioned because those who were "saw nothing up there." And he again cited the autopsy results as "the 'best evidence' . . . and the reason we didn't go into this any further. . . ." He said, "The nature of the wounds and the holes in his clothing indicated scientifically beyond any doubt that the shots could *not* have come from there. . . ."

Exasperated, Liebeler practically shouted: "Now what do you want us to do—go over there [to the knoll] and look for fairies? Or a goblin?"

A goblin?! "No, Professor Liebeler," I wanted to answer, "I want you to find out who altered the President's head before the autopsy, because that's why, on the autopsy table, it showed no sign of a shot from the grassy knoll."

I said no such thing. The audience would have found such an allegation preposterous. They would have thought I was crazy. A typical Southern California nut.

The camera zoomed in on the alleged puff of smoke, and Lomax asked: "Mr. Liebeler, do you concede that that is a puff of smoke?"

"Yes, and I want Mr. Lifton to tell me if he thinks it came from a rifle or not!"

Liebeler knew the answer I would give to that one. In private, I had told him I didn't think the smoke could have come from a gun. Modern guns don't smoke—not that much. But I couldn't accept the steampipe as the source. The steampipe running through the railroad yard was much further back, and no one I knew who had visited Dallas ever saw it giving off puffs of smoke. I thought the notion that that pipe belched smoke just

* In 1979, the House Assassinations Committee reported that its photo experts could find "no evidence" of smoke visible on the Nix film in the area of the retaining wall near the pergola. But the report failed to address the question of smoke seen at the location being discussed here—at the opposite, or southwest, end of the retaining wall.[4]

as the President's car passed by was laughable. I replied that I didn't know what caused the smoke, but I wasn't about to ignore it, either.

Lomax turned to Liebeler and asked: "Well, do *you* know where it came from?"

"Well, I don't know absolutely where it came from," said Liebeler, "but I know that it hasn't got any relevance to this assassination, because of the fact that it couldn't possibly have come from a rifle."

Within minutes of that exchange, the program was over. As the technicians put away the equipment, and the studio audience was leaving, I walked over to Liebeler. "Jim,* there's something really important that I've found. And I must speak to you about it as soon as possible." I told him it would take several hours. Liebeler didn't even ask me what it was about. He suggested we meet the next afternoon at Joe Ball's law offices in Beverly Hills.

When I came back from the TV studio, I didn't know where to begin. I had just a little less than twenty-four hours to prepare for my meeting. There were the twenty-six volumes. I wanted to read them all again from my new perspective.

My girl friend, a premedical student at UCLA, joined me. I began with Commander Humes' testimony in volume 2, and returned to the hypothesis that if "surgery" had been performed on John Kennedy's body, Commander Humes suspected it, and conveyed his suspicions to the Warren Commission by disguising them in technical language.

With Judy at my side, I began to reread page after page of testimony I had never read closely before. The passage packed with anatomic terminology began on page 355. I focused on the parasagittal laceration in the brain. It was important that I understand every term—that I attain some minimal fluency, so I could succinctly explain to Liebeler just what Humes was describing. I began to read aloud.

"There was a longitudinal laceration of the right hemisphere which was parasagittal in position."

The sagittal plane, testified Humes, was a vertical plane through the midline, which would divide the brain into right and left halves. "*Para*-sagittal," Judy explained, was a plane parallel to the sagittal plane, but just off center. Viewed from above, a "parasagittal laceration" would appear as a line running back to front and parallel to what I, as a layman, might call the back-to-front "centerline" of the head.

Humes' testimony seemed so peculiar. He appeared to conceal nothing, and carefully defined each technical term used.

That "parasagittal laceration," said Humes, ran "from the tip of the occipital lobe . . ."[5]

* Wesley J. Liebeler was known as "Jim."

"Where's the occipital lobe?" I asked.

Judy pointed to the lower area of the back of her head.

I put my left index finger at the back of my head, just right of center, where Humes seemed to describe the "tip of the occipital lobe."

That laceration "extended . . . to the tip of the frontal lobe."[6]

"Where's the tip of the frontal lobe?" I asked. Judy pointed to her forehead, above the eyes.

I put my right index finger on the front of my forehead.

Poised this way, I tried to imagine a laceration almost three inches deep that went clear across the brain.

Could this be the "surgery"?

"David," Judy exclaimed, "that sounds like an exploratory incision."

Suddenly, numerous insights fused. Judy's words gave the surgery a purpose: It was exploratory. Her words conjured up the image of someone with a scalpel, searching for metal in the brain. This created a cut which Humes described in technical language in the context of gunshot wounding. In the margin of my volume 2, I wrote: "exploratory incision!"

Was I nuts? Was this information in every public library in the country?

I had to check this out with a doctor. I counted on my neurosurgeon friend to give me an opinion.

Liebeler was fond of saying that this or that had been considered and rejected by the Commission. I knew for certain that no one on the Commission had considered this issue. The Warren Report contained no explanation for what appeared to be a back-to-front slice through the brain—any more than it contained an explanation for the words "surgery of the head area" in the Sibert and O'Neill report.

Later that evening, I turned to the other major question—the rear point of entry for the neck trajectory, the wound no one saw in Dallas because, according to press reports, Kennedy was lying on his back. Now, I took a much closer look at that explanation: Was it likely that, because of Kennedy's posture on the emergency cart, no one at Parkland Hospital knew about that wound?

I rummaged through the twenty-six volumes, examining the testimony of the Dallas doctors, and the reports of the nurses and orderlies who had washed the body. I found not a single mention of that wound.

Did I have the right to conclude, based on such "negative evidence," that the wound wasn't there? I examined the argument closely.

Whether or not that wound would be seen depended, to some extent, upon its location. According to Humes, the wound was above the shoulder blade ("situated just above the upper border of the scapula"). If the wound was that high, it seemed to me the Dallas doctors might have been able to see it, if it was there. The doctors had as much as twenty-two minutes with the President. Several of them described the awful wound they saw at the right rear of the head. Could they have missed a wound which was located just where the right shoulder meets the base of the neck?*

My skepticism about the wound's visibility was tempered by this factor: I didn't believe the wound was where Humes said it was. I believed it was "beneath the shoulders," the location given by FBI agents Sibert and O'Neill, and corroborated by the placement of the dot on the autopsy diagram and the clothing holes. If the wound was that low, it was more likely the medical people in Dallas didn't see it.

Still, at least one doctor and several nurses and orderlies could have been aware of the wound regardless of where it was located. I recalled that Dr. Carrico, already present in the emergency room when Kennedy arrived, said that one of the first things he did was to perform a manual examination of the President's back.

"Without taking the time to roll him over and look or to wash off the blood and debris," Dr. Carrico testified, "and while his coat and shirt were still on his arms—I just placed my hands at about his beltline or a little above and by slowly moving my hands upward detected that there was no large violation of the pleural cavity."[7]

Would Dr. Carrico have missed the wound? Although Carrico testified that he didn't think his manual examination would have detected "a small bullet entrance,"[8] I doubted that. The hole was big enough for Dr. Humes to insert his finger in it, and Clint Hill described it as an "opening in the back."**[9]

Another point excited my suspicions. Shortly after Kennedy arrived at Parkland, both his shirt and jacket were removed. This must have occurred within minutes. As the tracheotomy was performed, doctors inserted tubes in the front of the President's chest, just below his nipples, yet the President's shirt exhibited no holes corresponding to those tubes. The Parkland Memorial Hospital report of Nurse Diana Bowron provided details: "Miss Henchliffe and myself removed the President's clothes and they were placed in a shelf in a corner of the room."[10] Would these two nurses have failed to see any rear entry wound? Even if the wound was below the shoulders, it was hard to believe they could miss it while removing the clothing. What if it was above the shoulder blade, at the base of the neck, where Humes reported it?

After Kennedy was pronounced dead, the same two nurses had another

---

* If so, then they had missed two entry holes on the rear of the body—the rear entry wound for the head, just beneath the large hole on the head, as well as the rear entry wound for the neck trajectory.

** But Carrico, like all the Dallas doctors, was in the embarrassing position of having failed to notice two bullet entrance wounds on the rear surface of the body. That was why I believed he assured Specter that he didn't think his manual examination would "detect a small bullet entrance."

opportunity to see the President's back. Nurse Bowron wrote: "Miss Henchliffe and myself prepared the body by removing the remaining clothes . . . we then washed the blood from the President's face *and body* [emphasis added] and covered him with a sheet. During this time, we were assisted by David Sanders, the orderly. . . ."[11] Other reports indicate that Nurse Pat Hutton and Nursing Supervisor Doris Nelson were also in the room, and assisted.[12] Thus, at least two, and possibly five persons—Nurses Bowron, Henchliffe, Hutton, Nelson, and Orderly Sanders—had an opportunity to observe the President's back on that occasion. Yet the Warren Report noted that the Dallas doctors "were never aware of the hole in the back of his neck until they were notified of it later."[13]

I had never questioned this before; now I became deeply skeptical that such a wound, regardless of its exact location, would have gone unobserved by the people who removed the clothing and washed the body. And if any of the nurses and orderlies had seen the wound, I thought news of that fact would quickly have spread through Parkland Hospital.*

Was the back wound really there in Dallas?

The notion of a false back wound was bizarre. How could such a wound have been created? According to the FBI, the wound was so shallow Humes felt the end when he probed it with his finger.[14] It seemed obvious that if that wound was false, it could not have been made with a gun. A bullet would have penetrated more than a quarter of an inch; yet Humes could find no damage to the underlying muscle.

I now spotted a flaw in my thinking. An entry wound was just a hole and Humes' reference to it as a "missile" wound, however suggestive, did not constitute evidence it had been made by a bullet. If false, the back wound must have been made with some kind of an instrument. In notes made the next day, preparing to speak with Liebeler, I referred to it as the "punched-out" wound.

Humes testified that the back wound was "sharply delineated"[15] and seemed to go out of his way to volunteer that both rear entry wounds had identical contours. The rear entry for the neck trajectory, he said, was "similar in all respects when viewed with the naked eye to the [entry] wound in the skull."[16] Gruesome as it seemed, Humes' language conjured up the mental image of the mold on the end of a cookie cutter. I tended to view both rear entries as a pair. The idea that one of them might have

---

* Another factor would insure that it did. Presumably, the Parkland staff was reading the newspaper and magazine accounts detailing attempts to save the President's life. Those reports said the Dallas doctors observed two wounds—a large wound at the back of the head, and a small hole at the front of the neck. It seemed to me that any nurse or orderly who knew of an additional wound would have realized that doctors with whom they worked every day were making a serious error in their statements to the press.

been made with a tool caused me to reconsider, and subsequently reject, my initial assumption that the other rear entry, the one in the head, was created by a gun.

Also, I wondered why, if two successive shots, allegedly inflicted during the assassination, produced such similar contours upon entry, one blasted a large hole through the relatively sturdy bone of the skull, while the other produced only a small, shallow wound in the flesh.

Another factor raised doubts about the legitimacy of the back wound. The original handwritten draft of the autopsy contained certain changes and addenda which in the context of body alteration were suggestive.* The rear point of entry was described as a 7 x 4 mm "oval puncture wound."[17] The word "puncture" was crossed out,[18] and the edited description, carried over to the typewritten version, described it as simply a 7 x 4 mm "oval wound."[19] What prompted that change?

In a section titled "missile wounds," Humes referred to the back wound as a "wound of entry."[20] Then he inserted the word "presumably" before the words "of entry."[21] The amended phrase read: "presumably of entry."[22]

Why *presumably* of entry?

It was obviously not an exit wound. The adjective seemed redundant, unless Humes sought to qualify not his conclusion about the direction from which the instrument of injury broke the surface of the skin, but his certainty concerning the cause of the injury—i.e., whether it was an entry caused by the impact of a bullet, or a puncture created by some other means.

Taken together, these changes suggested a strange state of mind. Was Humes compelled in some way to write an autopsy report on a body he suspected had been altered?

Next I confronted the question of motive. Why put a false entry wound on the President's body?

I was confused. That little hole on Kennedy's body represented evidence of a shot fired on Dealey Plaza. But, I asked, why would anyone want to create additional punctures on the body? Wasn't that the equivalent of creating additional shots fired?

Then I saw that the issue was not one of arithmetic—i.e., the number of shots—but one of geometry, the direction of the shots. How did the pattern of wounds affect Humes' conclusions on that score? Did a false back wound persuade him that the wound in the throat was an exit?

---

* The word "original" in this context refers to the holograph draft of the autopsy admitted into evidence when Humes testified before the Warren Commission, and published as Warren Commission Exhibit 397. This is to be distinguished from a (possibly) earlier draft of the autopsy that Humes testified he burned in his recreation room fireplace on Sunday, November 24, 1963.

That was my tentative hypothesis, but I did not understand why a false rear entry wound could by itself fool the autopsy surgeon. If the throat wound was an entry, the bullet ought to have been in the body. What became of that bullet? Did Humes lie? I didn't want to believe that. It was central to my new hypothesis that Humes told the truth. I had no answer to that puzzle.

I remember another puzzle. Supposedly the doctors didn't even know about the wound at the front of the throat; they thought that hole was a tracheotomy incision. So why put a puncture at the rear to deceive Humes about a wound at the front, if Humes didn't even know about that wound anyway?

But the gravest deficiency of my theory was this: If someone attempted to deceive Humes by creating a false rear entry wound, he ought to have placed it *above* the wound at the front. Otherwise, there could be no appropriate relationship between the false wound and the hole at the front. The two wounds would not line up along a downward-slanting trajectory. Yet according to the evidence I found credible,* the rear entry wound was *below* the shoulders.

Here was a plot so powerful it obtained secret access to the body, so ingenious it altered the body to deceive Commander Humes, but so stupid that it inflicted a false rear entry wound in the wrong place—too "low" to be the point of entry for the wound at the front!

I couldn't figure it out. All I knew was that nobody saw a rear point of entry at Dallas, that it appeared for the first time at Bethesda, and that its location, according to the "Friday-night evidence," was below the wound at the front. I also knew that by the time the autopsy was written on Sunday, that wound was being reported as above the shoulder blade, at a position which was roughly lined up with the wound at the front, along a downward-slanting trajectory.

What did all this mean? Everything seemed on the brink of making sense, but a satisfactory solution escaped me.

The fact was that on October 23, 1966, my analysis was very primitive. I was still coming to grips with a radical idea: that discrepancies between Dallas and Bethesda represented anatomic changes made on the body, not mere errors of observation. But I was still several steps away from enough information, and enough insights, to discern the true strategy behind the changes.

When I understood that the back wound might be false, I saw that the mid-December visit to Parkland Memorial Hospital by Secret Service agents

---

* The FBI witnesses at the autopsy, Clint Hill's testimony, the "low" clothing holes, and the "low" placement of the dot on the autopsy diagram.

carrying the autopsy report was pregnant with implications. Previously, I had viewed the Secret Service agents as aggressive bureaucrats doing some not-so-subtle arm twisting, as they tried to get the Dallas doctors to change their opinion to conform with an official report—epitomized by Dudman's *St. Louis Post-Dispatch* headline: SECRET SERVICE GETS REVISION OF KENNEDY WOUND.[23] But the entire neck trajectory was a fabrication if the back wound was false. Now I was struck by the fact that the same agency which had possession of the body on November 22 showed the autopsy to the only doctors who had seen the body before alteration. It seemed there might have been another dimension to the interaction between the agents and the doctors, something more subtle, and more ominous.

The Bethesda autopsy was then a secret document. Showing the Dallas doctors the autopsy report, the Secret Service agents showed them authoritative evidence of a rear entry they had failed to observe. The existence of such a wound might have made them think they had been mistaken about the wound in the throat. It might have done more. It might have destroyed their confidence in their own observations.*

The navy autopsy report was an authoritative document. Unless a Dallas doctor was prepared to believe he was being shown a fraudulent report by federal agents—a very unreasonable stance to take at the time—he had to assume that report accurately described the wounds on the body at the Bethesda autopsy. Confronted with such unimpeachable evidence, the doctors must have believed that because of their failure to observe the rear point of entry, they had seriously erred both in their initial medical reports, and in their statements to the press. Because of those statements much of the world thought there was an assassin firing from the front. The doctors must have been acutely embarrassed. (See Fig. 14.)

In the twenty-six volumes I found reverberations from the December Secret Service visit when the Dallas doctors testified. Commissioner Gerald Ford asked Dr. Carrico if he had "read and analyzed" the Bethesda report.[26] Carrico, who had seen it only during that brief December visit, replied: "I have not read it carefully. I have seen it."[27] Ford then asked if there was "anything in it that you have read that would be in conflict with your observations."

"Nothing at all in conflict," replied Dr. Carrico. Then, the first doctor at Kennedy's side, and the man who felt no wound in Kennedy's back

---

* Dr. McClelland described to Dudman how the Secret Service agents "showed them the long autopsy report and pointed out the place where it described the course of the bullet in the President's neck."[24]

"There was no coercion at all," he said, explaining that he now agreed with the government's position about the throat wound. "They didn't say anything like, 'This is what you think, isn't it?' "[25]

But it seemed to me that it all came down to what you meant by coercion.

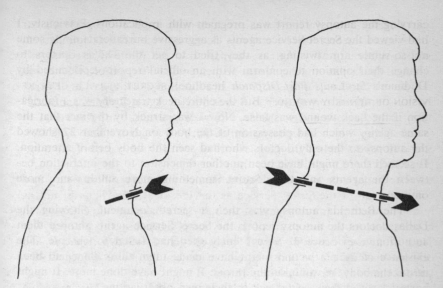

Figure 14.
Before and after the Secret Service visit to Dallas
Left: Diagram illustrates Dr. Perry's initial view that the throat wound was an entry wound.
Right: Diagram illustrates trajectory shown Dr. Perry in navy autopsy report.
Dr. McClelland told reporter Dudman that the Dallas doctors had failed to observe the rear entry wound because they had not turned the President over.

when he performed his own manual examination, said: "It certainly *adds* to the observations that we made [emphasis added]."[28]

I began to wonder. What was the real purpose of that Secret Service interview with the Parkland staff? Was it to investigate? To record the doctors' publicly expressed opinion that the throat wound was an entrance? Or was it to persuade them they were wrong—and that a wound at the rear, a wound they had not seen, was really there?

My attention moved to the "matching" clothing holes in the back of the President's shirt and jacket. If the wound itself was made after death, those holes were too. Who could have done that? Who had possession of the garments? I had barely raised these questions when I realized that the same organization that had custody of the body also had the clothes: the U.S. Secret Service.

This triggered the realization of yet another connection between vital evidence and the Secret Service. The Secret Service produced the three pieces of ballistically identifiable ammunition that connected Oswald's rifle to the crime. The two large bullet pieces came from the President's car which was in Secret Service custody. Secret Service officials found them on Friday evening while the car was parked in the White House garage.[29]

And the Dallas stretcher bullet also entered the stream of evidence via the Secret Service. Found at Parkland Memorial Hospital by Darrell Tomlinson, it was turned over to Secret Service Agent Richard Johnsen.[30] The result: Sometime after the doctors were "puzzled" and "at a loss to explain" why they could find no bullets in the President's body, the U.S. Secret Service supplied the FBI Laboratory with three pieces of ammunition that linked Oswald's rifle to the crime.[31]

The major role played by Secret Service and navy officials surprised me. I thought of the Secret Service as the President's bodyguards, not as investigators of the murder; and of the navy as a bureaucratic entity which happened to enter the chain of events simply because the autopsy was done at a navy hospital. Now I realized that these two agencies had original custody of the most crucial evidence, the basic evidence—the bullets, the body, the autopsy report.

My focus shifted dramatically. No longer did I see the primary issue as whether Arlen Specter had argued the single-bullet theory honestly, or whether the Commission attorneys had colluded in a coverup. The real question was the legitimacy of the evidence before them.

Going through this tentative analysis was a strange experience. Few of the facts were new to me—what was new was my perspective. I became conscious of chronology, the significance of the sources of evidence, and the way certain evidence depended upon other evidence for legitimacy. The case of the back wound and the clothing holes was an example. I had questioned the location of the back wound given in the Bethesda autopsy report, but I had never doubted that a legitimate bullet wound existed. Now I saw that the basic data could have been falsified.

I felt like a child at a puppet show who thinks the puppets are people, and then, for the first time, sees the strings leading to the puppeteer.

Here the problem was not distinguishing between puppets and people, but between facts and artifacts.

The idea that the entire machinery of the investigation could be derailed by causing it to ingest artifacts, in place of facts, was radical.

Calling Home

Sometime on Sunday I telephoned my parents in New York. Eleven years later, they remembered that phone call vividly. I was told I sounded "breathless," "scared," and absolutely in mortal terror of the knowledge I had acquired. My parents wondered how much of what I was saying was imagination, and how much was reality. To my conservative family, some of the charges I had been making over the past year or so sounded bizarre —that more than one man shot the President, that photographic enlargements revealed others on the grassy knoll. But anything I said previously seemed tame by comparison. "This," they recalled, "was the last straw."

"Do you know that they altered the body?" I kept repeating incredulously.

"Can you believe it? Can you believe it?"

My mother responded as any mother might: "How could you find out something like that? How could you know that, and nobody else know it?"

"It's right there in the documents!" I said. "It's in an FBI report. All they had to do was look. There is even testimony about it. The information has been there all the time! Nobody has seen it! Nobody is looking at the evidence the right way!"

The statement sounded strange. My parents thought this was the final hurdle from reality to fantasy. Years later they told me: "It sounded as if you had to say it out loud. That if you didn't say it out loud, it wouldn't have reality."

My hypothesis satisfied the analyst in me. But it brought me head-on with painful emotions. I was coming to grips with mortality. John Kennedy's body was an emblem of horror, fact or artifact. It traveled from the autopsy table to a flag-draped coffin and the earth of Arlington. I talked easily of entry and exit wounds, but those were abstractions. When I thought of the President's body, I thought of the majesty of the funeral—the horses, the muffled drums, the band playing "Hail to the Chief." My discovery represented the solution to a mechanical puzzle, but emotionally I was horrified. It was evidence of a desecration, a profanation of the body of the Chief of State.

That night was the first of many when I slept with the lights on, or did not go to sleep until after sunrise. I had nightmares.

Call to Neurosurgeon

One of the first things I did after waking on Monday morning, October 24, was to call my friend, the neurosurgeon. At my meeting with Liebeler, I hoped to avoid making statements about Kennedy's brain based on "common sense" or "my girl friend, who is a premed." Not that I mistrusted either, but I knew Liebeler was a man who respected authorities.

My phone bill shows a one-minute call just after 10:00 A.M.—the doctor was probably not in—and then an eighteen-minute call about a half-hour later. I remember that call vividly.

I told the doctor I had an unusual request. I wanted to read him a description of the damage to Kennedy's brain, because I had found it puzzling. I then read Humes' testimony regarding the "parasagittal laceration." The doctor replied that he could see why I was puzzled, because I was not describing a gunshot injury; my confusion probably stemmed, he said, from the fact that I was reading from a description of the brain after it was sectioned. His exact words were: "That brain's been sectioned."

"What do you mean, 'sectioned'?" I asked. I had never heard the expression before.

"Cut into; to section," he replied, and explained that as part of the standard autopsy procedure, cuts are made in the brain to expose the interior, and facilitate inspection. "You're probably reading from a report describing the brain after it was sectioned."

I assured the doctor that was not so, that what I read to him was the way the brain was at the time of autopsy.

He asked me to read some of it over again, and I did.

No, he assured me, the brain must have been sectioned. What I was reading to him did not sound like the damage made by a bullet.

I read him some more—portions of the testimony I hadn't completely understood about the "corpus callosum" having been practically severed.

"Where's the corpus callosum?" I asked, wondering if he would place it where Humes did. The corpus callosum, he assured me, was right where Humes said it was, in the center of the brain, toward the bottom. He said it seemed most unlikely that it would be severed right along the midline. That did not sound like a gunshot injury to him.

"Where were the entrance and exit wounds on the skull?" he inquired, and I explained as best I could. Then he wanted to know where the bullet had been found. I told him the bullet was not found inside the head, but in the automobile, in two large pieces. I explained that only two tiny fragments, each about the size of a broken pencil point, were found inside the brain.

Meanwhile, wanting to prepare myself for the type of question Liebeler might pose, I asked: "So what's the exact reason why that damage couldn't come from a bullet?"

"Just use common sense," he replied. I thought it was odd for a neurosurgeon to be appealing to my "common sense" in a matter I assumed could only be analyzed by experts. "How could a bullet create that kind of damage?" he asked. "You're telling me that something entered at the skull at the rear, and then exited somewhere on the right-hand side. And none of it stayed inside the head. How could a missile which travels a path so that it exits on the right-hand side still create the practically straight-line damage you're describing to me, which goes all the way to the front of the head?"

He cautioned me that he didn't draw any conclusions from what I had read to him. I was probably just making an error, and whether I realized it or not, was reading from a description of the brain after it had been sectioned by the autopsy surgeon.

The conversation turned to another anatomic term: the left cerebral peduncle. Humes said there was a tear through the left cerebral peduncle.

"The left cerebral peduncle was torn?" said the doctor, his voice again tinged with incredulity.

"Yeah, the left cerebral peduncle," I replied.

My doctor friend said emphatically that the damage sounded like it had been made with a knife. I tried to get him to explain to me just where my cerebral peduncles are located. They are on the underside of the brain —which, very roughly, means that they are located just above the roof of the mouth.

Learning anatomy over the telephone was almost impossible. The doctor urged me to come by his office and bring with me Humes' drawings of the wounds. He would answer any questions I had. "I'll draw in the brain damage for you, on his drawings; you can see for yourself why it was probably not caused by a bullet."

And he again cautioned me to check, because he felt sure I was reading from a source describing the brain after sectioning.

I asked the doctor one more question. "If you were a witness in court, what evidence would you want to back up the opinion you're giving me here? I mean, are the words I've read you themselves sufficient, or would you want something more?" I was groping for further information for my meeting with Liebeler. I was really asking: "Is this just your opinion, and if so, is there some way of getting proof?"

I half expected him to say he'd want the autopsy photographs of the brain. I was completely unprepared for his answer: "I'd want to see the brain."

The President's brain?

Sensing my confusion, he explained that when he talked of cuts made in the brain at autopsy, that sort of thing wasn't done while the brain was still in the head. He explained that at an autopsy, the brain of the deceased is removed, like any organ, and a standard procedure followed. It is usually put in a jar or tray, and a special solution called a "fixative" added, so as to harden the tissue, to make it more gelatinous. Then, at a later time, the brain is examined. In any event, he said, the brain is not buried with the body; it becomes a laboratory specimen.

He explained why he'd want to see it. The verbal description I was reading from simply did not contain as much information as a photograph, and a photograph would not contain as much as the brain itself. "I'd want to look at it myself, and actually see the damage," he said, explaining that otherwise, his opinion would be based on some other doctor's verbal description.

"Where's the brain today?" he asked. I told him I hadn't the foggiest idea. That question had just never come up. On that note, we said good-bye.

Getting off the phone, I tried to absorb what I had learned.

The President's brain was evidence. That was such a peculiar idea, such a totally unexpected, shocking idea. More shocking was the true significance of the brain as evidence—not evidence of a second assassin, but critical evidence to show whether someone altered the body, whether there had been "surgery of the head area" on the body of the President of the United States—prior to the autopsy at Bethesda Naval Hospital.

I had only a few hours left before my scheduled meeting with Liebeler. I sat down at the typewriter and made notes on what I had learned in the past thirty-six hours. My head was bursting with information I didn't want to forget: excerpts from the testimony, ideas, insights. It was as if I had discovered a city hidden beneath the desert, and had barely begun to excavate. I needed a crude inventory of what I had unearthed. It took four pages.

Page one was devoted to quotes from the Sibert and O'Neill report. As I typed the heading, "FBI Report—Sibert and O'Neill" at the top of the page, and the date, I noted that the date on the Sibert and O'Neill report was November 26, 1963.*

November 26? That was the Tuesday after the assassination. Did the FBI agents wait until the first business day after Kennedy's funeral to dictate and type up their report of the autopsy? That seemed peculiar.

As quickly as possible, I typed up excerpts, putting in capital letters the statement about head surgery on page three, and the paragraph on page four stating that "the individuals performing the autopsy were at a loss to explain why they could find no bullets."[32]

Next, I wrote a page and a half dealing with the entry wound at the back of the head. Armed with my new hypothesis, all my previous doubts about the existence of that wound at Bethesda dissolved. I was now sure it was on the body at the time Humes performed the autopsy. I studied his testimony with interest. Now I was really interested in what a bullet wound in the head must look like.

Humes said the wound was in the right rear of the head, "2.5 centimeters [1 inch] to the right, and slightly above" the external occipital protuberance (the bony bump at the center of the back of the head, toward the bottom).[33] To better understand Humes' testimony, I substituted the ordinary English word "hole" for "defect," the technical term Humes always employed:

* There are three dates on each FBI report: the date the interview was conducted, the date the report was dictated, and the date the report was typed up. In the case of the Sibert and O'Neill report, the date "11/22/63" appears in the lower left, indicating that was the date the information was received. But the date dictated and date typed are both listed as November 26.

This wound . . . was in a portion of [the] scalp which had remained intact . . . [and] when one reflected the scalp away from the skull in this region, there was a corresponding [hole] through both tables of the skull in this area . . . there was a through and through [hole] corresponding with the wound in the scalp.[34]

In considerable detail, Humes described how it was possible to determine, with absolute certainty, from the way the bone broke, that the hole in the skull was made by something that went "from without . . . to within."[35]

In my notes, I wrote: "Humes describes precisely and exactly why the wound in the rear of the head was an entrance wound."

I wrote this because it was sobering to realize that a small hole on the rear of the President's head had such significance as evidence—that it was like a vector, pointing toward the Texas School Book Depository as the source of the shot. Until that weekend, I had not looked at damage on the body that way—as legal evidence. But each puncture on John Kennedy's body was evidence of a shot which struck, evidence which defined, for any subsequent investigation, the way the shooting had occurred.

I made some notes on the other rear entry wound not seen at Dallas—the one for the neck trajectory. Contemplating Humes' fruitless attempts to probe it with his finger, I wrote: "The strongest indication that it is not a rifle bullet is that it didn't go in any further." I reconsidered the conflict between the "high" location given by Humes, and the "low" location suggested by the holes in the back of the President's coat and shirt. I toyed with a novel interpretation of that conflict. Suppose Humes was correct, and the rear entry wound was above the shoulder blade, in the base of the neck? If so, then the mismatch between "low" clothing holes and "high" body hole was subject to an entirely unexpected explanation. Might the mismatch be the result of the clothing holes having been created independently of the body hole, that is, when the clothes were off the body?

I turned to another subject: the interaction between Commander Humes and his chief interrogator, Commission Attorney Arlen Specter. It was my theory that Humes was an honest man in an impossible situation, and trying to communicate crucial information to Specter, in technical language. Rereading the transcript of Humes' testimony, I had the sinking feeling that however honest Humes' intentions, his message had no chance of getting through, because Arlen Specter seemed unable to understand basic anatomic terminology. In the midst of Humes' testimony about the rear entry wound in the skull was this interchange:

SPECTER: You are referring there, Doctor, to the wound on the lower part of the neck?

HUMES: No, sir; I am speaking of the wound in the occiput.[36]

In my notes, I wrote: "Excellent example here of how Specter just couldn't follow." I wondered how Specter, if he got confused over which rear entry Humes was talking about, could possibly understand any of the more complex anatomic descriptions of damage to the brain.

Another point. As I re-examined the autopsy report and the related medical testimony, I was struck by the existence of information that was subject to re-interpretation if the body was altered. That hypothesis provided an entirely different backdrop against which to evaluate the evidence. What surprised me was that important data seemed to be lying in plain view, but its significance was only apparent in the context of body alteration.

One example was Humes' use of the phrase "presumably of entrance" and "presumably of exit" when characterizing some of the wounds. I felt that phrase was justified only in the case of the throat wound—Humes hadn't seen that wound in its pristine condition because of the Dallas tracheotomy. But why was "presumably of" modifying Humes' reference to the rear entry wound for the non-fatal shot? And why did Humes again employ that phrase in connection with the wound of exit in the head?

I thought Humes must have suspected that some of the damage was made after death. Had this theory come up during the Warren Commission investigation, Humes could have been subjected to some pretty stiff cross-examination on his subtle use of the English language.

Another example of previously "invisible" data which now commanded attention came up during the testimony of Secret Service Agent Roy Kellerman, who attended the Bethesda autopsy. Kellerman's testimony contained a passage I had never noticed before, but which now jumped off the page. Referring to the large wound in the President's head, which the Bethesda doctors designated an exit, Kellerman testified: "This was removed."[37]

"Removed?" That, I thought, was an odd way of referring to a hole supposedly created by a bullet. Kellerman's language aroused Specter's curiosity:

SPECTER: When you say "This was removed," what do you mean by this?

KELLERMAN: The skull part was removed.

SPECTER: All right . . . [but] when you say "removed," by that do you mean that it was absent when you saw him, or taken off by the doctor?

KELLERMAN: It was absent when I saw him.[38]

And that's where the matter rested.

When and Where?

Concluding my notes, I turned to a question that had perplexed me since the wee hours of the morning when I discovered the FBI statement about head surgery: When and where was it done?

It was one thing to postulate that the body had been altered, and that government officials were involved. It was quite another to establish that there was a time and place when it could have happened, when anyone had the means and the opportunity. Indeed, to all outward appearances, it seemed impossible.

On November 22 Kennedy's coffin was at the center of attention. It bobbed in and out of public view, as reporters and TV cameramen tracked its every move on the journey from Dallas to Bethesda.

In the time that remained before my meeting with Liebeler, I reviewed what I knew about the whereabouts of the coffin—from accounts I had read in newspapers and magazines, and from what I had gleaned from the twenty-six volumes.

As far as I could tell, the casket made its first appearance on the scene when a hearse from a local Dallas undertaker arrived at the emergency entrance of Parkland Memorial Hospital. The arrival of the hearse and pictures of the coffin being taken inside the hospital were broadcast on national TV. Shortly thereafter, TV cameras recorded the hurried egress of the coffin from Parkland, with Jacqueline Kennedy running alongside. The coffin was loaded aboard the hearse, Jacqueline got inside, and the vehicle drove away, bound for Love Field—the Dallas airport. There, the coffin was put aboard *Air Force One*.

The next public appearance of the coffin was several hours later, at Andrews Air Force Base outside Washington, D.C. On national TV, millions of Americans witnessed the arrival of *Air Force One*, carrying President Johnson and the body of his slain predecessor. The scene was unforgettable.

The big jet rolled to a halt. A large military cargo lift approached the side door to unload the coffin. The hatch was opened. There, glinting an ugly yellow in the moonlight, was the Dallas coffin, mute testimony to what had occurred earlier that afternoon. Slowly, the coffin was lowered from the plane. Jacqueline Kennedy stood beside it, in her blood-stained dress, her hand tightly clutching that of Attorney General Robert Kennedy, who had rushed on board, via a front entrance, when the plane rolled to a halt.

The coffin was carried to a waiting navy ambulance. Both Jacqueline and Robert Kennedy got inside, and the ambulance pulled away. Both drove with the body all the way from Andrews Air Force Base to the doorstep of Bethesda Naval Hospital.

Seated in the third car behind the ambulance were FBI agents Sibert and O'Neill—I knew that from their report.[39] FBI headquarters had sent the two agents to Andrews Air Force Base to meet the plane, and they were under instructions "to stay with the body and to obtain bullets reportedly in the body. . . ."[40] Upon arrival at Bethesda, they accompanied the body to the autopsy room.

On the surface, then, any alteration of the body seemed impossible. From Parkland Memorial Hospital in Dallas to the Bethesda autopsy room, there was no time or place when it could have been done.

Yet, if my hypothesis was correct, it *did* happen. Sometime, somewhere, somehow, while the nation was reeling from what appeared to be a senseless murder, conspirators had obtained secret access to the President's body and altered its appearance before it reached the autopsy table. If my theory was correct, there was method lurking behind the madness of that day.

I found that juxtaposition chilling to contemplate—that secret and grotesque machinations had taken place behind a facade of senseless tragedy. It meant that the account of the shooting disseminated by the major media on November 22, 1963—the Dallas Police version that Kennedy died at the hands of a lone gunman then under arrest—was false. It meant the presidency of the United States had changed hands under false circumstances. The implications were almost too frightening to contemplate.

The meeting with Liebeler was rapidly approaching. I skimmed through the testimony and reports of those who had been with the coffin, and filled two pages with notes. The question "where?" was looming up as a major mystery. I began to form a preliminary hypothesis.

Then I jotted down a brief list of "things to research":

—all attempts by anyone to feel the back of the President;
—did the President have to be turned over to see even [a] back wound?
—Where is the brain today?
—Re-interview Humes today!

I gathered my typed notes, my copy of volume 2, containing Humes' testimony, and Epstein's paperback, which contained the Sibert and O'Neill report, and went to the offices of Ball, Hunt, and Hart in Beverly Hills.

CHAPTER 9

October 24, 1966—A Confrontation with Liebeler

I DROVE TO JOE BALL's law offices in Beverly Hills. I was horrified by what I had found, and wanted to act. But I was painfully aware that as a twenty-seven-year-old ex-graduate student, I had no credentials—no one would give a hoot about what I had to say. But if I convinced Liebeler, he might do something. And people would listen.

The receptionist at Ball, Hunt, and Hart recognized me, and asked me to wait in one of the outer offices. I looked over my notes. I was beginning to feel something like camaraderie for Liebeler. I understood better now why he thought the critics were nit-pickers.

The critics presented antitheses to the Commission's theses. If the Commission had a paper bag in evidence that was thirty-five inches long, the critics found witnesses who said it was twenty-five inches long. If the Commission cited an autopsy report that said the shots came from behind, the critics tabulated a list of eyewitnesses who said the shots came from the front. There was practically nothing of importance in the Report that wasn't disputed. Liebeler thought it was all part and parcel of an uncritical skepticism: "These people just don't believe anything the government says," was the way he put it.

But raising questions was quite different from proposing the solution to the mystery. What I had might lead to the solution. I had found that most valuable tool for a scientist confronting a complex problem: a working hypothesis.

In a laboratory one tests the hypothesis by setting up experiments and collecting data. In this case data had been gathered by the Warren Commission—which meant, in effect, the results of all previous investigations conducted by the Dallas Police, the Secret Service, the FBI, and so forth.

The trouble was, much of it was inherently contradictory. Now I had a hypothesis which explained contradictions.

I realized that an altered body provided the basis for reconciling (1) the conflicting opinions of the two groups of doctors, and (2) the Bethesda autopsy report with the Zapruder film head snap and the accounts of many Dealey Plaza witnesses who thought the shots came from the front. Those witnesses were not mistaken. If the body was altered, it was the autopsy report that was disqualified as evidence. The smoke was real, the sounds were real, and the fresh footprints in the mud behind the fence on the knoll probably were made by assassins. There really were shooters up there. And the images I saw in the photographs probably were real. If the body was altered, then the relative status of all the evidence changed dramatically.

I was beginning to understand something else—that I approached conflicting evidence differently than lawyers did. Watching Liebeler and his students, and studying the Warren Report, I saw that lawyers, presented with a conflict in evidence, behaved as if they were obliged to choose: Do I believe Smith or Jones? This eyewitness or that autopsy report? It was as if their minds were offended by the contradictory data, and so were quick to brand one source or another as either in error or deliberately false. My attitude was different. I tried to account for all the evidence, to reconcile all the data.

Finally, the door opened and Liebeler walked in. We exchanged greetings, and went to the conference room we had used the week before. Liebeler enjoyed Ball's law offices, which were palatial compared to his boxlike office at the UCLA Law School. Here, he could work without being bothered by stray phone calls, or by students knocking on his door to chat or pass the time.

Liebeler settled into a chair behind a desk in the corner of the room, and leaned back. He had a look on his face which translated to: "Okay, I'm here. Now what's this all about?"

I did not blurt out "Well, sir, I think they altered the President's body before the autopsy." I knew that if I simply pointed to the statement in the Sibert and O'Neill report, he would dismiss it out of hand—just another FBI statement. So what? What could it really mean?

Sensing the problem, I sensed the solution. I must start by getting Liebeler to understand and accept my methodology, the form of chronological analysis I was employing, what I called "time-line analysis."

I would start with the neck trajectory, and apply the method to the non-transit/transit conflict. That was a conflict between the report of two FBI agents, who attended the autopsy, and the autopsy report submitted by Commander Humes. The FBI reported the bullet did not transit; Humes said it did. On a time line, that suggested only that the doctors changed their minds between Friday, when the two agents witnessed Humes performing the autopsy, and Sunday, when Humes submitted his own report. It was that simple.

Resolving the conflict, on a time line, had sent me down my own path of discovery, persuading me that Humes told the truth, and had not, months later, changed the autopsy at the behest of the Warren Commission. Now, I saw that it offered a useful analogy.

I knew that if I could get Liebeler to see the FBI/navy conflict on a Friday/Sunday time line, that would be the first step toward getting him to view Dallas/Bethesda conflicts on a Friday-noon/Friday-evening timeline. The principle was the same. Common to both was the idea that something changed, in time, and that change cropped up in the Warren Commission's evidence in the form of conflicting medical information. But whereas the change from non-transit to transit represented a change in the opinion of Dr. Humes (who said one thing in front of the FBI on Friday night, but wrote something different on Sunday), any change between Dallas and Bethesda concerning the direction of the fatal shot signified a change made on the President's body.

I was certain Liebeler would be interested in the time-line analysis as it pertained to the changed neck trajectory. It was the perfect rebuttal to Epstein's book.* Liebeler knew the Warren Commission had not changed the autopsy, as Epstein suggested. Yet he knew the Sibert and O'Neill report, as well as the two FBI Summary Reports, all contradicted the autopsy. Publicly, he had argued that the FBI was simply wrong.**

I began by explaining my twin-transmission-line model. On a blackboard in Ball's conference room, I drew diagrams that illustrated the two transmission lines—connoting information flow—leaving the autopsy room, one corresponding to the FBI report of the autopsy ("Friday-night information"), the other to the navy autopsy report ("Sunday information"). I explained my theory that the time factor supplied the answer to the charge that the Commission changed the autopsy. The change, I explained, took place *before* the Commission was even formed, over that first weekend—between the time the two FBI agents witnessed the examination and the time the doctors submitted their report.

I had barely begun when Liebeler asked if he could take notes. I had

---

* It was Epstein's misunderstanding of *when* the non-transit/transit change took place that led him to believe the Commission faked the autopsy in order to construct the single-bullet theory.

** On September 30, at the Theatre of Ideas in New York, he had said: ". . . what is really the likely possibility: that these three physicians were mistaken, or that the FBI agents who overheard some conversations of autopsy surgeons were mistaken . . . ?" He answered his own question: ". . . the statement of an FBI agent who was present at the autopsy comes pretty low on the totem pole, a good deal below the weight to be given the report of the autopsy surgeon itself."

no objection and was, in fact, flattered. Liebeler took out a yellow pad and a pencil and, as I talked, he occasionally wrote questions.*

One of the first things I discussed was the date the FBI received the autopsy report. Recent accounts in *Look* and *U.S. News,* I explained, said that the FBI did not obtain a copy until December 23, 1963. That date was provided to rebut Epstein's accusation that the FBI "non-transit" statements were based on an "earlier" Bethesda autopsy. These accounts claimed that the "earlier" autopsy report came from the two FBI agents who were there. I believed that, I said, and accepted December 23 as the date the FBI first received the autopsy. Why didn't the Secret Service send over a copy immediately? Was it really true that the FBI investigation went forward for a full month following the shooting without an official autopsy report?

Liebeler wrote:

1. When did the FBI get the autopsy report?

Next, I reviewed the episode of the missed bullet wound, and the circumstances under which Humes changed the autopsy from non-transit to transit. The missed bullet wound gave the doctors a legitimate reason for changing the autopsy conclusion. Yet when examined closely, the change appeared illegitimate because the location of the rear point of entry also changed between Friday and Sunday. Somehow, it moved up several inches, and was transformed from a "low" back wound to a "high" neck wound. This relocation gave the trajectory the downward tilt essential to the theory that both the throat wound and the rear point of entry were caused by a single shot fired from "behind and above."

I told Liebeler I didn't think that Humes, a mere commander in the U.S. Navy, would dare, on his own authority, to misreport the location of a wound. He must have been subjected to some kind of pressure. But it was impossible to find out who was really responsible.

"That's simple," said Liebeler. "Get Humes under oath, and ask him."

Liebeler wasn't kidding; his whole tone was that of a man who still had the power of subpoena at his disposal.

Liebeler wrote:

2. What conversations did Humes have with SS, FBI, or anyone else from 11/22—[until] he submitted the autopsy report?

Then I described the circumstances of the delayed transmission of the autopsy from the Secret Service to the FBI. Although the FBI hadn't been given the autopsy until December 23, 1963, Richard Dudman's account in the *St. Louis Post-Dispatch* made clear that the Secret Service had shown

---

* I have them in my possession as I write this account. Combined with the four pages of typewritten notes I brought along that day, they permit me to reconstruct the conversation.

the autopsy to the Dallas doctors about December 11, and used that document to get them to change their opinion about the throat wound.

I asked Liebeler the same question I asked when first reading Judge Fein: Why did the Secret Service show the autopsy report to the Dallas doctors before sending it to FBI Director J. Edgar Hoover?

Exactly what had happened during those interviews? Why had the doctors changed their opinion?

I stated my hypothesis. Each group of doctors was subject to some kind of pressure. Humes hadn't even known about the wound at the front of the throat. He could be persuaded that what had gone in the back must have come out the front. The Dallas doctors didn't know about the wound in the back. Shown the autopsy report, they could be persuaded that by missing that wound, they had made erroneous public statements, statements causing unjustified rumors about an assassin firing from the front and suggesting a conspiracy.

Each group of doctors had missed the wound seen by the other group. Each group underwent a change of opinion after being told about the observations of the other group.

Defenders of the Report might say that such changes were to be expected—each group had seen only half of a puzzle. What I found odd was that each group changed their opinion about the piece of the puzzle they had personally observed, based upon information supposedly found at the other end of the line.

The chief operators of this carousel of changing facts and opinions seemed to be the U.S. Secret Service.

Liebeler said this was the first he had ever heard of Dudman's story, or of the Secret Service visit to Dallas. He wrote two more questions:

3) What agents showed the autopsy report to the drs. in Dallas as reported in December 18, *St. Louis Post-Dispatch*—where are the [agents'] reports?
4) Why wasn't the FBI given the autopsy right away—or at least told of its results?

Now I discussed how the events during the forty-eight hours following the autopsy affected the Warren Commission's reconstruction of the crime, months later. The change from non-transit to transit made it possible for the Commission to conclude that one bullet passed through two men.

I reviewed what happened in late December 1963 and January 1964, immediately after the Warren Commission was formed, when the staff reported for work and began to analyze the incoming evidence. From the FBI, the Commission received a report stating the bullet did not transit, a report which said the shallow back wound was probably caused by the bullet found on the Dallas stretcher. From the Secret Service, the Commission received the navy autopsy report, with the transiting neck trajectory. The Zapruder film was to reveal that Kennedy and Connally were struck in less time than it takes to fire successive shots from the alleged murder weapon.

I told Liebeler I still thought that bullet 399, because of its un-damaged and bloodless condition, must have been planted; and that in view of the distinctly separate reactions of Kennedy and Connally, the double-hit trajectory seemed unlikely. But what I now wanted to know was how the marriage of this queer bullet with this improbable trajectory had come about. The question was whether the single-bullet hypothesis was Arlen Specter's brainchild, as most critics suspected, or whether Specter had been presented with the component parts of the double-hit and then, somehow, been led to assemble them.

One of these components was the stretcher bullet. On whose stretcher was it found: Kennedy's or Connally's? It seemed suspicious to me that the FBI, which reported a non-transiting trajectory, said it was on Kennedy's stretcher. This fitted neatly with its theory that the bullet had fallen out of a shallow back wound. The Warren Commission, which said the bullet passed through Kennedy's neck to strike Connally, was able to conclude the bullet was found on Connally's stretcher.

Why was it, I asked, that two investigations—the FBI's and the Warren Commission's—could each conclude the bullet was found on the stretcher which could accommodate its reconstruction of the crime?

I explained I was toying with a new question: Assuming 399 was planted, could we distinguish between its intended role on November 22, and the role assigned to it by the Commission? I conjectured that in coming up with the single-bullet theory, the Warren Commission staff had assembled the pieces of a construct in a way not originally planned by those who planted the bullet, but under compulsion by an unforeseen development—the Zapruder film and the wounding of Connally. What had been intended originally? I did not know, but I felt certain no con-spiracy would plant a bullet in mint condition with the intention of claiming it made a bone-crushing journey through two men.

Liebeler responded with the argument he always used whenever I charged that 399 was a plant. If 399 was a plant, he said, then the two fragments in the car must also be planted. Liebeler's logic, with which I agreed, was that if the rifle had been used, there would be no need to plant a bullet on a stretcher. Authentic fragments would serve to link the rifle to the crime. But the discoveries I had made over the weekend—specifically, the possibility that both rear entries were false wounds—gave me good reasons to suspect that the rifle hadn't been used at all.

Now, Liebeler asked: If both 399 and the fragments in the car were planted, then what became of the bullets actually fired at Kennedy? Was it my claim that all the assassination bullets had disappeared?

I simply replied that the Secret Service, which seemed to be involved in the delay in transmission of the autopsy report to the FBI, also found the fragments in the car. Furthermore, I added, it seemed to me that I had read, somewhere in the twenty-six volumes, that those two fragments were found by an Assistant Secret Service Chief.

Was Liebeler aware of that? No, he replied. I said that the circumstances of the discovery of those two fragments seemed odd to me, since the automobile itself was evidence, and it was the FBI that searched the car. Why was it the Secret Service, and not the FBI, that came up with the two bullet fragments linking Oswald's rifle to the crime? I did not know who the Secret Service official was, but I promised to try to find out.

On his pad, Liebeler wrote:

5) Who found the fragments in the car?

We went back to bullet 399 and the origins of the single-bullet theory. I argued that if there was anything contrived about Humes changing the autopsy conclusion, then it was entirely possible that contrivance spread to the Warren Commission's investigation too. I now fully accepted, I said, that the Commission had not changed the Kennedy autopsy report. What I had in mind was something more subtle: the Commission's being "fed" the hypothesis, along with the changed autopsy report.

Exactly how did the single-bullet theory first come up? I asked. In *Inquest,* Epstein reported Specter as saying it was Humes who first suggested it. Specter made a similar statement during Humes' testimony.

I suspected Specter had been lobbied. I said that if others in the government had spotted the timing problem before the autopsy was sent to the Commission, then it was possible the staff's analysis of the film had been monitored, so that if they discovered the "problem," they could be fed the "answer"—i.e., the double-hit theory—which they could then assemble the way a child builds a structure from an Erector set.

I admitted that this was conjectural, but it was the final leg of the journey of information from autopsy room to the pages of the Warren Report, during which time the trajectory seemed to sprout like the beanstalk in the fairy tale—first, non-transit to transit, and then onward to include Governor Connally.

Liebeler wrote:

6) Ask Arlen just when time constraint became apparent—and who thought of the 1 bullet theory first.

Liebeler had a contented expression. I had brought him useful ammunition to rebut the critics. Explaining the FBI/navy autopsy conflict, I had undercut a major charge against the Commission—that it had changed the Kennedy autopsy report. Now I proceeded into deeper waters.

I wanted to bring Liebeler back to our position the previous week when, discussing the head snap, he kept taunting me that a bullet ought to be in the head if Kennedy was shot from the front.

To provoke him I made a deliberately illogical jump. From talk of information flow and time lines, which must have sounded more like a discussion in systems analysis than an argument about the Warren Report, I suddenly shifted gears. Almost absent-mindedly, as if nothing Liebeler said previously about missing bullets had made any impact whatsoever, I said: "Well, Jim, then someone fired from the grassy knoll, and that's why Kennedy's head snaps to the rear on the Zapruder film."

My change was abrupt. In discussing the neck trajectory, I had been careful to distinguish between theory and fact. Now, my manner was slipshod and flippant.

Liebeler, obviously disappointed to see me go off my "good" behavior, reacted immediately. He looked at me, disgusted, as if to say, "Haven't we been through this before?" Then, he took the bait. Annoyed at having to explain it still another time, he said: "But there's only one problem, David. If he was shot from the front, then where's the bullet?"

"Oh, that's simple, Jim." I got up, walked around the desk, and took up a position directly behind him, as if I were his barber.

"Oh, that's simple, Jim," I repeated. "You see, the answer to that is . . ."

Now I took my right index finger and put it firmly atop Liebeler's forehead, just to the right of center, and drew it from front to back across his scalp, tracing out the parasagittal laceration in the brain described by Humes.

As I did so, I continued, calmly: ". . . they simply sliced into Kennedy's head, and took the bullet out."

I mimed the motions of reaching into Liebeler's skull. Holding the putative bullet in my hand, I returned to my chair on the opposite side of the desk.

I was shaking with excitement. I had just made a perfectly logical, yet utterly outlandish statement, and hadn't presented a shred of evidence for it.

As I walked back to my chair, Liebeler stared at me in silence, quizzically yet warily, as if to say: "You don't think you can get away with that—do you?"

I picked up my notes, focused on the passage which I had typed in red, and, trying to control my voice, continued: "And that's why, when the body arrived at Bethesda, it was reported that there was, quote, 'surgery of the head area, namely, in the top of the skull.'"

Liebeler burst out at me instantly, in utter disbelief—as if he knew that I wasn't kidding, but still hoped this was just my idea of some kind of bad joke.

"*Where* does it say that?!" he demanded.

"Right there, in the Sibert and O'Neill report," I shouted back. I tossed my paperback copy of Epstein's book across the desk at him.

Liebeler snatched up the book and stared at the passage which I had underlined. His hands were trembling slightly.

I wanted to proceed, to get on with a complex presentation, correlating the anatomic information provided by Humes with that FBI statement about surgery. But Liebeler called a halt. He got up and began pacing back and forth across the room. He was obviously shaken.

"David," he said, "do you *realize* what you've found?"

He put it in the form of a question. He must have sensed that I didn't fully understand the significance of my own discovery—not the *legal* significance, anyway.

Then he answered himself: "You've found new evidence!"

Pacing up and down the length of Joe Ball's conference room, Liebeler repeated that statement several times, as if he were making a pronouncement that I had just done the impossible.

Liebeler's response elated me. The unvarying reaction of the Warren Commission and its staff to whatever the critics turned up was to maintain they had found no "new evidence." To which the critics, infuriated, retorted, "What's wrong with the old evidence?" That a Warren Commission attorney was telling me that I had found "new evidence" made me feel I had hit the jackpot. Furthermore, I knew very well that the phrase "new evidence" was normally used by an attorney to characterize information he felt sufficient to reverse a conviction and reopen a case.*

Seeing Liebeler's reaction, I could hardly control myself. I had so much other information bottled up. Now I tried to relate everything I had found in the last thirty-six hours at once. It is difficult to reconstruct the rest of that day's meeting, but I remember the highlights.

I told Liebeler that a perusal of Humes' testimony had revealed certain passages which were Greek to me, but I had learned they represented a linear damage pattern in the brain, and when I read them to a neurosurgeon, he assured me it sounded like the damage was made with a knife.

I read the passage about the parasagittal laceration aloud to Liebeler, and showed him where it was located, on page 356 of volume 2. I also showed him where Humes testified that the corpus callosum, a structure connecting the right and left hemispheres of the brain, and located deep within the head, had apparently been bisected. Then I turned to the other testimony which had aroused my suspicion—Humes' statement that as he examined the head, and pushed the scalp about a bit, substantial pieces of skull bone fell to the autopsy table.

* Liebeler's response was also in marked contrast to what he said on September 30 at the Theatre of Ideas when he dismissed the Sibert and O'Neill report and characterized it as ". . . pretty low on the totem pole" of evidence.

What the hell was going on? I asked. I told Liebeler I doubted that such large bone pieces (Humes testified they were up to four inches across) could have been loose at Dallas, or they would have fallen to the table when Dr. Perry was pounding on the President's chest, administering cardiac massage.

I wrapped up my briefing on the head wounds by noting that the rear entry was not seen at Dallas. If secret alterations were made on the head, I said, then it was reasonable to conclude that a wound which wasn't seen in Dallas simply was not there. I threw Liebeler's own words back at him, the words he had spoken just the day before on the Lomax show:

That's what a lawyer's job is, Mr. Lomax. You've got to draw inferences. You've got to draw inferences from the facts that you have.

What facts did we have in this case, I asked. Simply these: In Dallas, no doctor saw the rear entry head wound, despite the fact that many of them looked directly at the wounded area and described the large wound at the right rear, a wound located within an inch of where the entry was supposedly located. Yet at Bethesda, all three autopsy doctors observed the rear entry wound, and even Roy Kellerman, a layman, saw it. I invoked the Zapruder film head snap as evidence the shot struck from the front; hence, the Dallas "non-observations" of a rear point of entry were all the more significant. Finally, I appealed to common sense: If the Sibert and O'Neill statement was true, if there had been "surgery of the head area" prior to autopsy, what reason could there be other than to alter the autopsy findings in order to falsify the direction of the head shot and obliterate evidence of a grassy-knoll shooter?

The rear entry wound in the President's head, I argued, was a false wound.

Liebeler asked me how I thought such a wound had been made. I replied with a hypothesis I would, within weeks, reject: That bizarre as it sounded, a pistol must have been used. That, I said, might also explain why the head was in such a shattered condition at Bethesda. I stressed that this was pure speculation. The legal record that that wound was not reported by anyone in Dallas was undeniable.

To believe surgery had not occurred, I said, one had to dismiss two separate sources of data: the FBI's report of "surgery of the head area"; and my neurosurgeon friend's interpretation of Humes' description of the brain damage.

I argued that Humes had to know there had been surgery. How could he have provided a verbal description that conveyed the image of a cut, yet not have realized what it was he had seen?

Liebeler wanted to verify what I was saying. The existence of the FBI statement could not be denied. But my assertions about Humes' testimony fell into a different category—they were based on opinions from others. I was not a doctor. Liebeler could see that I was so impressed with what I had been told that I was treating those opinions as facts.

Liebeler said he knew a competent pathologist in Los Angeles, a friend who worked at a nearby hospital, in whom he had confidence. "Do you mind if I call him up?" he asked, a slight trace of challenge in his voice. "Not at all," I replied.

Liebeler reached for the phone. I was nervous. Suppose Liebeler's friend gave him a different opinion? I would look foolish. Two days before, I knew nothing about the anatomy of the brain. Now here I was glibly tossing about the terminology of neuroanatomy, in this bizarre context, as if I were a specialist. I told Liebeler that my friend was a neurosurgeon, and had given me his best opinion, and that I was confident he ought to be able to distinguish a description of a knife cut from damage normally created by a bullet.

Soon Liebeler had his friend on the telephone. I could only hear one side of the conversation.

"Hi, Joe—Jim Liebeler here. Listen Joe, I want to read to you a description of a brain, and I'd like you to give me your opinion as to the cause of death."

That was fair enough, I thought. Liebeler was attempting to objectify the situation. He had mentioned nothing about gunshot wounding, or about Kennedy.

Now, with volume 2 opened before him, Liebeler began to read from the passages in Humes' testimony which I had underlined.

When he finished reading, there was a long pause, as he awaited his friend's answer. But Liebeler's description had apparently aroused his friend's curiosity. Instead of answering, he responded with a question of his own. Slightly irritated, Liebeler barked into the phone: "What does it matter *whose* brain it is? It could be Sadie Garfunkel's brain! I just wanted to know the cause of death."

As Liebeler got his answer, his face flushed red. He put his hand over the mouthpiece, turned to me, and whispered: "He says it sounds like he was hit by an axe."

An axe?

Liebeler thanked his friend for his opinion, and hung up.

Liebeler looked up; our eyes met. With this new confirmation of my hypothesis, the fear and queasiness I had first felt on Saturday night started again.

"What are we going to do?" I asked, softly.

"Well," he replied, poker-faced, with the confident tone of a man who knew exactly what the situation required, "I guess we'll just have to get the FBI to jimmy up some evidence that Oswald ordered an axe!"

I described what I had learned from my neurosurgeon friend—that the brain was evidence, that the best way to determine if there had been pre-autopsy surgery on the brain was to examine the brain itself, that this was far superior to interpreting Humes' testimony. I asked Liebeler if he knew the whereabouts of the brain. He hadn't the faintest idea.

I wanted to get on with our briefing, but Liebeler's mind was off somewhere else. He wanted to know if I'd like a drink. The entire tone of our meeting was changing. I got a feeling of complete concession on his part—as if the scales had just tipped, decisively. I had discovered the key to the mystery, and Liebeler had thrown in the towel. He was willing to listen to anything else I had to say about this—he wanted to hear it all—but let's relax. Let's calm down. Let's take our time. Life is short.

Liebeler mixed us some drinks. I proceeded with the rest of the notes I had made.

I explained the general approach I thought was necessary if the body was altered. To know where the guns which fired at Kennedy were located, I said, it was necessary to determine what was false and real on the body at the time of autopsy, and the only way to learn that was to compare the Dallas and Bethesda descriptions of the body—only the Dallas doctors saw the President immediately after the shooting.

In comparing the Dallas and Bethesda testimony, I said, it was essential to realize that both groups of doctors could have told the truth. Conflicts between the two groups—whether it was in the wounds observed or opinions about the direction of the shots—could be the result of alterations having been made on the body.

I reviewed the evidence concerning the other rear entry wound nobody saw at Dallas, the rear entry for the non-fatal shot. According to the autopsy report, that wound was located above the shoulder blade in the base of the neck. I explained why I thought that wound, if it was there, ought to have been observed in Dallas—either by the doctors and nurses during the twenty-two minutes of emergency treatment, or by the nurses and orderlies who washed the body and put it in the coffin.

The authenticity of those two rear entry wounds, neither of which was observed at Dallas, was fundamental, I said, and was intertwined with the authenticity of the three pieces of recovered ammunition which ballistically matched Oswald's rifle. Bullets from Oswald's gun could not have inflicted the President's wounds if the President was not struck from behind.

I reviewed the strange terminology in Humes' autopsy report—his use of "presumably of" in description of the rear entry in the neck—and observed that if the rear entry was false, it must have been made with a tool, not a gun, because it was shallow. I noted that the mismatch between the "low" clothing holes and the "high" body hole was subject to new interpretation if that wound was false: That mismatch might be an error made by the conspirators, the result of their creating the wound when the clothing was not on the body.

At some point in our discussion, Liebeler popped the question that had been bothering me for the past thirty-six hours: "If you're right about all this, then where could it have been done?"

I hesitated to answer. There wasn't that much information in the twenty-six volumes. What I had found, in my hasty reading, had led me to a conclusion that seemed preposterous.

I hemmed and hawed a bit. "This is really speculative," I told Liebeler, searching for an acceptable way to proceed into the unbelievable.

Liebeler had little patience. What had I found? Where did I think the body had been altered? He was interested, he assured me.

"Okay, okay," I said, and I blurted out: "I think it was done on the airplane."

Liebeler winced.

"The airplane?! What the hell makes you say that?"

I replied that it was a process of elimination. The problem boiled down to tracing the President's coffin through the events of the day. From what I could see, there were just three time periods:

1. Dallas: from Parkland Memorial Hospital until the coffin was put aboard *Air Force One* at Love Field;
2. Airborne: en route from Dallas to Maryland;
3. Maryland: from Andrews Air Force Base to the autopsy room at Bethesda.

I began with Dallas. How could anything have occurred in Dallas? I asked. The car raced to the hospital. Then, with Jacqueline running beside him, the President was rushed into the emergency room. He was surrounded by doctors and nurses. People who I would call "Kennedy loyalists" were everywhere. At 1:00 P.M., the President was pronounced dead. A sheet was drawn over his head. Silently, the doctors and nurses left the room. Obviously, nothing happened between the time of the shooting and the pronouncement of death.

During the next hour, a coffin arrived at the hospital. People came and went from the emergency room. At one point, Jacqueline entered the room, and put her ring on the President's finger. A priest entered, and anointed the President with holy oil, and said prayers. Again, Kennedy loyalists were everywhere. Based on the presence of Jacqueline, the presence of loyalists, and the nurses and orderlies who washed the body and prepared it for the coffin, it was insane to think that anything could have occurred between the pronouncement of death and the time the body was put in the coffin.

Then the coffin was wheeled from the hospital to the undertaker's hearse. I told Liebeler what I knew about the argument that developed— the fact that certain people in authority (e.g., the Secret Service) did not want a Dallas autopsy. On the surface, the argument appeared to be a procedural matter, but it might mean something else: Maybe certain officials did not want a Dallas autopsy because the body alterations had not yet been done.

Following that dispute, the coffin was put in the hearse. Jacqueline got inside, and rode with the coffin to the airport. The coffin was put aboard *Air Force One*.

So much, then, for Dallas. I just didn't see how such clandestine activity could have taken place there.

I turned to Bethesda. *Air Force One* landed at Andrews Air Force Base. Again, Jacqueline stayed with the coffin. I recalled the scene of her standing on the cargo lift as the coffin was lowered from the airplane to the ground. The coffin was put into a gray navy ambulance. Then Jacqueline, with Robert Kennedy, entered the navy ambulance and drove to the doorstep of Bethesda Naval Hospital. Obviously, nothing happened during the period when the President's widow and the Attorney General were with the coffin.

Jacqueline and Robert Kennedy left the ambulance at the main entrance of Bethesda. Only one leg of the journey remained—from the front of the hospital to the autopsy room. For that time period, I turned to the testimony of Secret Service Agent Roy Kellerman.

I had a number of reasons for believing Kellerman was a truthful witness. He argued with the Commission about the number of shots fired —the only government witness to do so: ". . . there have got to be more than three shots, gentlemen,"[1] he said, basing his opinion on the fact that Kennedy had four wounds, Governor Connally had five, and the windshield was damaged.

Because of this argument with the Commission, Kellerman was a hero to the Warren Report critics. He was an honest layman among the high-falutin' lawyers. He tried. Vincent Salandria dedicated his 1965 *Liberation* article to Kellerman.

My good feelings toward Kellerman were reinforced by a telephone conversation I had with him several weeks before about some other matters connected with the assassination. So I turned to Roy Kellerman, whom I trusted, for information about the body at Bethesda. Kellerman had accompanied the body from *Air Force One* to the morgue. I was particularly concerned with the last leg of the journey, for which the documentation in the twenty-six volumes seemed sparse: from the front of the hospital, where Jacqueline and Robert Kennedy left the ambulance, to the autopsy room.

Kellerman testified:

Let's come back to the period of our arrival at Andrews Air Force Base, which was 5:58 P.M. at night. By the time it took us to take the body from the plane into the ambulance, and a couple of carloads of staff people who followed us, we may have spent 15 minutes there. And in driving from Andrews to the U.S. Naval Hospital, I would judge, a good 45 minutes. So there is 7 o'clock.

We went immediately over, without too much delay on the outside of the hospital, into the morgue. The Navy people had their staff in readiness right then. There wasn't anybody to call. They were all there.[2]

To my mind, Kellerman's testimony demonstrated that nothing could have occurred between the time *Air Force One* landed and the start of the Bethesda autopsy. And exactly what time was that? A quick reading of the Sibert and O'Neill report provided pertinent information. The two agents wrote: ". . . the first incision was made at 8:15 P.M."[3]

In the notes I prepared for the meeting with Liebeler, I had typed:

Comment: Body arrives at 7
FBI report (S and O) says "first incision made at 8:15"
Therefore, all we have to do is rule out that anything happened between 7 and 8:15 and we have *proved* that it took place before that.

That was my approach on October 24, 1966. It couldn't have happened at Dallas; and it couldn't have happened at Bethesda. Therefore, it must have happened aboard the airplane.

Lending an additional touch of suspicion to the "airborne" time period was a statement in the Sibert and O'Neill report that the plane arrived one-half hour late. Sibert and O'Neill reported that after they arrived at Andrews Air Force Base, they were informed by Air Force authorities the plane would land at 5:25. "Subsequently" wrote the two agents, an Air Force Colonel "advised that the plane would arrive at 6:05 P.M."[4]

Was something on board taking longer than anticipated? That's what I suspected.

The notes Liebeler made during this part of our discussion reflect my emphasis on the airplane. His questions 1 through 6 all concerned the neck trajectory, and represented his response to the introductory phase of my presentation. Now he wrote four additional questions:

7. Why was the plane ½ hour late?
8. Sibert and O'Neill said surgery had been performed on the President's head—If so—who did it? & when?
9. When were the clothes removed [from the President's body]?
10. Who was on the airplane?*

As the conversation proceeded, the discussion shifted from "how" and "where" to who was responsible. I said it seemed to me that if the body was altered, then Secret Service officials had to be involved. How else could someone get access to the coffin? This brought us back to the Secret Service visit to Dallas, with the Bethesda autopsy report, in mid-December 1963.

I went over the visit in detail—the facts suggested the Secret Service

* These handwritten notes were left in my copy of volume 2 of the Warren Commission hearings which I left behind that day in Joe Ball's law office and retrieved several days later.

agents might have shown the Dallas doctors an autopsy describing a back wound that had not yet existed in Dallas, and used the document to get the doctors to reverse their opinion about the wound at the front of the throat.

It is difficult, years later, to re-create the atmosphere of that afternoon. Liebeler's response to my ideas was acceptance, fear, and incredulity. The assassination was not yet far enough removed to be a historical event. We were still in the political shadow of an enormous transfer of power. Lyndon Johnson, who took office on *Air Force One* in Dallas, was now President of the United States. Neither of us explicitly articulated the question that ran like a theme behind our discussion: Was the government of the United States legitimate?

The statement about surgery appeared in an FBI report just recently published, a report that might come to general public attention within days. November 22, 1966, the third anniversary of the assassination, was just a month away. Debate about the Warren Report's conclusions was beginning in the press. Mark Lane's *Rush to Judgment* had been published in August, and was now a best-seller. *Life* magazine was about to distribute a special edition, much of it to be devoted to an analysis of the single-bullet theory, with color photographs from the Zapruder film which *Life* owned. The cover would read: DID OSWALD ACT ALONE? A MATTER OF REASONABLE DOUBT. The *Life* headline epitomized the gulf that separated the ideas being discussed by Liebeler and me from the media's conception of "conspiracy."

The media seemed to view the major issue as a "second shooter" who had, somehow, escaped official detection. "Conspiracy" was viewed as something like a human interest story, one centered on the identity of that second shooter. For example, Robert Donovan, the Washington Bureau Chief of the *Los Angeles Times,* wrote: "The possibility that Oswald had an accomplice staggers the imagination at this late date. Who could such a person be? If he exists where is he? What is he doing? Is he still a potential menace? Such a question has a fantastic ring to it."*[5]

Donovan found a second shooter "fantastic"; yet here we were talking about a plot involving high officials of the United States government. And we were doing it in the law offices of Joseph Ball, the senior Warren Commission attorney who, along with David Belin, wrote chapter 4 of the

---

* To many in the media, the issue was a joke. The critics were nit-pickers and the Commission was being victimized. I recall one cartoon which showed a congressman being warned about a constituent: "Be careful; this man has a set of the twenty-six volumes."

Conrad published a cartoon showing all the members of the Commission crouched down inside a presidential limousine, as it passed in front of the Depository. Bullets were flying in from every direction. One Commissioner popped his head up to take a look, and said: "Well, I say this is some kind of conspiracy . . . !"

Warren Report. That chapter, primarily based on the sniper's-nest evidence found at the Texas School Book Depository, concluded that Oswald was the lone assassin. It was an ironic setting for that extraordinary discussion.

When I finished presenting my case, Liebeler began a series of phone calls. The first person he called was Susan Wittenberg, a brilliant UCLA law student whose judgment he respected. Susan was versed in the details of the case and aware of my debates with Liebeler. Several weeks later, she told me that when she picked up the telephone, Liebeler announced: "Lifton's found surgery." He asked her to come to Ball's office as soon as possible.

As we waited, our discussion continued.

I turned to Humes' state of mind. Did Humes have a conscious awareness of surgery, or was he fooled? Because of the two medical opinions—the one from my neurosurgeon, the other from Liebeler's pathologist—the mood of the moment was that Humes did know, that he understood what he had seen, that it was no accident that his testimony read as it did. But at that point, Liebeler and I parted ways.

I tended to view Humes as a hero to history, as a man in an incredibly tight spot, trying to communicate to a presidential Commission information he apparently felt he could not deal with via his own military chain of command. Liebeler did not share this view.

I prattled about what a hero Humes was, and how Specter had made an understandable error. Liebeler leaned back in his chair and growled: "Whom do we burn? Humes or Specter?"

The words about surgery were plain English in an FBI report. Specter had failed to follow it up. He had not done his job—that seemed to be Liebeler's attitude.

I pointed out that Specter had failed to follow through other things. For instance, he had never asked Humes why he burned his notes. Liebeler thereupon reduced the matter to one of carelessness. He was certain nothing sinister was involved where Specter was concerned. "Arlen," he said, "paints with a broad brush."

We returned to Humes. It was essential to ask Humes certain questions. I said I had some extra money in the bank. I would be glad to join Liebeler on an airplane east, to speak with Humes personally. Liebeler apparently had something else in mind.

He picked up the phone and called Joseph Ball. Ball was at the Long Beach office of the firm, about thirty miles away. When Ball came on the line, Liebeler mentioned nothing about surgery. But he asked if he had any tape-recording equipment which could be hooked up to the phone, because he was thinking of calling up some of the people with whom the Commission had dealt—notably, the autopsy surgeon, Dr. Humes. I only heard one side of the conversation, and it was mostly small talk. Ball, apparently, argued it wasn't necessary. Then, I was startled to hear Liebeler say, in a very serious tone: "Joe, did you ever get the feeling we were being led down the garden path?"

What a question! I would never forget it. The public image of these men was so different. They paraded about in the vestments of established authority, saying that nothing was wrong with the Warren Report. Now I was getting a look at their private world. These were the lawyers who wrote the official history of the great event. I had just heard the man who wrote Oswald's biography, chapter 7 of the Report, asking the man who wrote chapter 4, which presented the case against Oswald as the lone assassin, whether they all had been deceived.

Liebeler wanted to make another call, but he would not let me listen, perhaps because he noticed how I perked up when he made that remark to Ball. This call was to Arlen Specter in Philadelphia. Specter had vouched for Humes in an interview with journalist Gaeton Fonzi, saying that he visited Humes at Bethesda and spoke with him at some length: "You just wouldn't think for a minute that the guy's fudging anything. You wouldn't think for a minute."[6] And it was Specter who, in an interview published just two weeks before in *U.S. News,* defended the Bethesda autopsy as "comprehensive, thorough, [and] professional"; who rationalized Humes' burning documents because "he did not quite have the perspective of a historian," and "had never performed an autopsy on a President. . . ."[7]

Now Liebeler disappeared into an office and talked to Specter for about ten minutes, informing him about the statement in the Sibert and O'Neill report that there was surgery on the President's body prior to autopsy. When Liebeler returned, I asked: "What did he say?" Liebeler avoided answering. So I asked again. Liebeler shook his head from side to side, parrying my query. I persisted. Indeed, I pestered Liebeler quite a bit, asking again and again and again. Somewhat exasperated, Liebeler finally blurted out his impression of Specter's motivation: "Arlen hopes he gets through this with his balls intact."

A topic of conversation to which we kept returning that day was my suspicions about the Secret Service. The Secret Service had the body, distributed the autopsy report, had the automobile, had the clothing, sent the three pieces of ammunition to the FBI Laboratory. The Secret Service, in short, was the original custodian of all the suspect evidence, not to mention the fact that the Secret Service had major responsibility in planning the trip to Dallas.

I remember I said to Liebeler: "You know, if we forget about the number of shooters, and just look at all the evidence from the standpoint of whether the body was altered, this theory explains a lot." Liebeler responded: "It explains everything."

I was exhilarated. I had puzzled and puzzled over the contradictions for eighteen months. It was so satisfying to know that everyone had told the truth, the part of the truth he had witnessed—whether he was a bystander at Dealey Plaza, an emergency-room doctor in Dallas, or an autopsy doctor at Bethesda. These accounts were all part of one integrated reality once we understood that the body had been altered.

Before this insight, the twenty-six volumes had been like a multivolume mystery story which made no sense. Now the reason was obvious. Offstage, in this historic drama, was a scene nobody saw. No wonder the visible part of the drama was confusing—this secret, bloody thing had happened behind closed doors.

Mixed with the elation was fear. I had felt it in a personal way. Liebeler, I thought, experienced it in a wider, social context. Wesley Liebeler was a political conservative. That afternoon, in Joe Ball's law office, I sensed him struggling with information which, if true, could threaten the fabric of our society. It was the same issue many critics speculated Earl Warren had wrestled with—truth versus social stability.

Critics had been openly speculating that Earl Warren knew some secret truth about what really happened on November 22, a truth so horrible it couldn't be made public because to do so would be to create political and social chaos. In the name of social stability, Earl Warren had willingly participated in a coverup, falsely inculpating Oswald as the lone assassin. Much of this sentiment stemmed from a statement made by Warren in February 1964 when a reporter asked whether all the testimony would be made public: "Yes, there will come a time. But it might not be in your lifetime," said the Chief Justice.[8] What was it? Stop treating us like children. We want to know; we have a right to know! This was the attitude of many critics I knew.

Now, I had discovered evidence which, if true, fitted the description of something that awful, and I could see Liebeler wrestling with the very problem that the critics had attributed to Warren.

From what he said and did, it was clear that Liebeler feared the prospect of the more bellicose Warren Report critics publicly charging that the government had altered John Kennedy's body as part of an assassination plot. He saw the potential for social unrest, particularly in view of the strong feelings of the American people toward President Kennedy and the highly charged atmosphere surrounding the assassination controversy. How would the public react? Would they believe the Warren Commission hadn't known about this? The Commission could claim innocence only at the price of admitting incompetence. The evidence was in the Commission's own files.

Liebeler leaned back in his chair and asked, rather solemnly, what I intended to do with my discovery. What I had found was a very serious matter, he said. It ought to be investigated properly. And he personally would like to see that it was followed through. Would I be willing to keep it to myself, at least for the time being? Liebeler said the next step was somehow to get those X-rays and photos made available for inspection, to see what they showed. He didn't think anyone's interest would be served if, on the basis of incomplete information, wild charges and countercharges were hurled back and forth. So would I agree to remain silent?

Liebeler knew that I had a tie to *Ramparts* magazine, and that I was co-author of an article on the medical evidence which hadn't yet gone to press.

I agreed to his request at once. Liebeler was in a position to do something. The previous year, he had gone directly to J. Lee Rankin on the matter of the unexplained splice in the Zapruder film, and that was less serious than this. I expected he would be true to his word.

Was I being co-opted? At the time I certainly didn't think so. It was a simple trade. Liebeler would see what he could do—he would make his best effort—but he had no intention of being associated with me if my strategy was to make a public argument out of such a ghoulish matter.

I told Liebeler I did want to speak to one critic—Sylvia Meagher. She was serious-minded. I was certain that when she heard my hypothesis she would keep my confidence and would change her own views about the Commission.

I was overcome with the feeling: "This is bigger than all of us." I was sure that if only the right Warren Commission attorneys would join with the right critics, there could be an effective, united front. We could agree that there were things wrong with the Warren Report. Most important, we could agree that we had all been deceived. We could begin again.

I wanted to make this call alone. Liebeler obliged, and suggested I use the phone in one of the inner offices. I entered, closing a heavy oak door behind me, and dialed Mrs. Meagher's number in New York City.

The conversation started innocently enough. I raised Wesley Liebeler's name guardedly. Only two weeks earlier, Mrs. Meagher had told me what a dangerous person he was, that I should disconnect my phone number and not attend his class. Yet I knew it was my acquaintance with Liebeler that had made my discovery possible.*

I had barely mentioned Liebeler when there was an explosion on the other end of the line. The screaming and screeching which poured forth from the phone was so intense that I had to take the earpiece and hold it

---

* The critics' conclusion that the Commission "covered up" had created blind spots in their research effort. My friendship with Liebeler caused me to put aside my suspicions and realize that a person could, in good faith, hold the Commission's position. That prompted me to discard the "coverup" hypothesis and forced me to examine the evidence itself for an explanation of the contradictory data.

about a foot and a half away. Still, at that distance, Mrs. Meagher was clearly audible.

Didn't I understand what a terrible person Liebeler was? Didn't I understand what a despicable, deliberately fraudulent investigation had been conducted? Whose side was I on, anyway? Was I a traitor?

I wanted to reply, but I found it physically painful to put the earpiece near my head. During brief pauses, I held the telephone upside down, and tried to get in such pacifying expressions as: "Yes, Sylvia . . ."; "Yes, but . . ."; "Please, Sylvia . . ."

These efforts were of little use. Eventually, Mrs. Meagher subsided, leaving me with an indelible impression of the animus she bore toward the attorneys. I managed to get off the phone and, flabbergasted, opened the door to rejoin Liebeler.

I pushed open the heavy door. Liebeler sat on a large couch in the outer office, a pained expression on his face. "David, do you know that I could hear her screaming at you through that oak door?"

That episode banished some of my naiveté. The assassination was not a technical problem. It was a political problem. The participants in the debate had vested interests. Where you stood and what you believed depended on how you viewed yourself and your relation to the society.

The critics had a vested interest in the charge that the Commission had deliberately covered up the truth. The Commission had a vested interest in the charge that Lee Harvey Oswald assassinated the President.

When Susan Wittenberg arrived, the atmosphere became cheery, even a bit manic. Liebeler asked me to state my ideas again, and I did so. I said I had begun with the proposition that Humes had told the truth, and had attempted to reconcile the Zapruder film head snap with the Bethesda autopsy report. That had led me to take a closer look at the autopsy proceeding itself. I told how, examining the Sibert and O'Neill report on a line-by-line basis, I had found the statement about head surgery.

I described the technical passages in Humes' testimony, discussed nowhere in the Warren Report, and told of my doctor friend's reaction, and Liebeler's friend's reaction. We talked about Humes. Susan exclaimed: "Can you imagine his position in all this, if he knows?" Liebeler said: "Lifton here asked whether Specter knew anything about forensic pathology—I think that's a pretty damn good question, don't you?"

When the subject of "where was it done?" came up, I added a bizarre twist I hadn't mentioned previously. I noted that in discussing the movements of the coffin, we were making an assumption—that by following the coffin, were keeping track of the body. Was that assumption justified? I asked. The meeting acquired a giddy quality; I couldn't resist a stroke of humor.

"Ah, yes," I said, adopting an exaggerated Germanic accent, and the manner of a professor at a lecture, "philosophy has the mind-body problem; physics, the three-body problem. This brings us to the coffin-body problem." A grin spread over Liebeler's face.

Briefly, I stated the coffin-body problem. Two other Air Force planes flew back from Dallas—one designated *Air Force Two,* which usually carried the Vice-President, and another, a cargo jet, which carried the automobile back to Washington. The "coffin-body" problem was this: Was it possible that John Kennedy was not in the coffin put aboard *Air Force One?*

I said that a quick run through the documents, particularly the reports of the nurses at Parkland Memorial Hospital, convinced me this was not the case. The President's body must have left Parkland in that Dallas coffin—there was, after all, no "second coffin." Nevertheless, the possibility we were considering presupposed real villains and a major subterfuge somewhere along the line. So a question such as this had to be posed—if only to be ruled out.

That afternoon, Liebeler accorded the concept of postmortem surgery complete credibility—it was not a question of "that's a nice theory, but . . ." Liebeler treated it as fact, an amazing discovery.

The assassination was more than a homicide to Wesley Liebeler—it raised a metaphysical question: how to determine truth, what Liebeler called "the reality of an event." Liebeler and I lived by different systems. In this argument, Liebeler's system had failed him; mine came through. I think Liebeler was astonished that my concern for a simple matter of physics had led me not only to a unique theory, but to documentary evidence that none of the lawyers on the Commission even suspected was in the files. At one point Liebeler said to Susan: "Do you realize we are in the presence of someone who has a superior contact with reality?"

Later that afternoon, Liebeler himself couldn't resist a bit of clowning. I remember Susan and I seated, with Liebeler standing before us mimicking what it would be like, and the attention that would follow, when the time was right and he, Liebeler, called a press conference to announce this new development to the world. Susan was looking up at him, as if he were standing on a pedestal. Not imagining the subject would become my major preoccupation over the next fifteen years, I said: "Don't forget to give me my footnote, Jim, because I discovered this."

Susan retorted good-naturedly, "You?!! David, do you realize how famous he's going to be?" All three of us joined in this pantomime of the future. Wesley J. Liebeler, Esq., announcing to the world at large that the Warren Commission had been the victim of a gigantic deception. That there was evidence previously ignored in the Commission's files—"new evidence," if you will—that the President's body had been altered before the autopsy.

But was it really going to be that easy? Was the happy ending just around the corner? The first indication I got to the contrary occurred during one of the last phone calls Liebeler made—to fellow Warren Commission attorney Burt Griffin, in Cleveland.

Burt Griffin was the first person to rain on my parade.

Burt Griffin was a good friend of Liebeler's, from his days on the Commission. Griffin had been the junior lawyer on the two-man team of Griffin and Leon Hubert, responsible for the Ruby area. Was there a conspiracy in Ruby's shooting of Oswald? How did Ruby get into the basement of Dallas Police Headquarters at the exact moment Oswald was being transferred from the city to the county jail? What were Ruby's connections with underworld figures? These were the questions with which the team of Hubert and Griffin grappled during the investigation. Over the years, researchers have made distinctions between those on the staff who were reasonable, and those who were not; those who understood the complexity of a problem, and those who oversimplified. The Warren Commission had its true believers. Burt Griffin was not one of them.

Liebeler called Griffin and spoke with him alone for about five minutes. Then he emerged from one of the inner offices, and told me to pick up an extension phone.

"Burt," he said, "I want to introduce you to David Lifton. He's a critic here in Los Angeles."

Although the details are vague, I cannot forget the essential drift of the conversation.

"Hello, Mr. Griffin," I said respectfully. "What do you think of that statement in the Sibert and O'Neill report that when the body arrived, there had been 'surgery of the head area, namely, in the top of the skull'?"

"Well, what do you think it means?" he said, as if we had both glimpsed the same clouds, and were about to argue whether that meant it was going to rain. "And why would anybody want to do that?"

Liebeler had grasped the implications instantly. Griffin either did not, or was pretending not to. But before I could answer, he asked another question: "How do you know it wasn't done at Parkland Memorial Hospital?"

This was foolishness.

"At Parkland?" I exclaimed. "Look, Mr. Griffin, there was no surgery of any kind done at Parkland."

"Well, how do you know that?" he asked.

"How do I know? Because I've read the medical testimony in the twenty-six volumes. Nobody did anything like that at Parkland. All they did there was some life-saving surgery, making little cuts in the right and left extremities for intravenous feeding, and an incision in the neck for a tracheotomy."

Well then, said Griffin, how did I know that "surgery of the head area" might not refer to the tracheotomy, since the neck could be construed as part of the head. I reminded Griffin that the full quote was: ". . . it was apparent that a tracheotomy had been performed *as well as* [emphasis added] surgery of the head area. . . ." And, I added, the next words were most specific: ". . . namely, in the top of the skull."

Griffin persisted. Okay, suppose there was "head surgery." "How do you know it wasn't a life-saving measure?"

I was a little annoyed. "Mr. Griffin," I said, "Humes describes a back-to-front slice in the brain. Even if you do surgery on the head, you don't practically cut the brain in half. That's absurd."

It was a disjointed conversation, with some strange pauses. I found myself having to explain everything. With Liebeler, it was different. It was as if we had been communicating in shorthand. Perhaps Griffin was preoccupied with something else. Perhaps he really didn't understand. In any event, the idea that anyone would touch the President's body before the autopsy seemed beyond his comprehension. There was no shock whatsoever. He seemed bemused, querulous. At one point he said: "Besides, how do you know what these words are based on? Humes never told us anything like that."

"But he did! He did!" I exclaimed. "That's what his testimony was all about. He was describing it!"

Even I had to admit that sounded convoluted.

I had joined a theory about Humes' state of mind with another about the President's body. Was that justifiable? Perhaps, but then, perhaps not. Maybe I was caught in a self-reinforcing maze of my own making.

When I got off the phone, I felt distinctly uneasy. Presented with the same information, Griffin and Liebeler had responded entirely differently. Why? Why was it that Liebeler had seemed to accept it, while to Burt Griffin it was just another statement in an FBI report?

"My God," I thought, "is this, too, going to have to be debated?" The valuable thing I learned from my conversation with Burt Griffin was exactly that—it was <u>not going to be easy</u>. The process of thrust and parry was starting all over again.

<u>Surgery of the head area? Prior to the autops</u>y?
<u>Prove it.</u>

About five hours had passed since I had walked into Ball's law offices. The office had closed, and the three of us were sitting alone. There was a sudden "clankety-clank" sound coming from the hallway.

What's that?" asked Liebeler, sharply, looking worried.

A New Hypothesis

I stepped out in the hallway and encountered a kindly looking janitor, pushing a cart with a broom. As he entered the room, wishing the three of us a good evening, I quipped, "Oh, that's just a CIA agent disguised as a janitor."

Several hours later, I went to Ship's, a restaurant/coffee-shop near the UCLA campus, for dinner. There weren't many customers inside, and sitting alone at the counter was Jim Liebeler. He seemed deep in thought. A partly eaten hamburger was on the plate in front of him. Sensing his mood, I felt it inappropriate to join him. As I walked past him at the counter, I paused and said softly: "Hi, Jim." He was so startled his hamburger almost fell off the counter.

That's the last incident I remember from October 24, 1966—Jim Liebeler at the counter of Ship's coffee shop, his hamburger teetering dangerously, on the brink of falling into his lap.

A Search for New Evidence

A Search for New Evidence

Photo 1. Aerial photo of Dealey Plaza

County Criminal Courts Building

County Records Building

UNION TERMINAL NORTH TOWER   TEXAS SCHOOL BOOK DEPOSITORY   Alleged assassin's window

STEMMONS FREEWAY
To Parkland Memorial Hospital

HERTZ RENT A CAR

UNDERPASS

Monument

Wooden fence   GRASSY KNOLL   Sign

ELM ST.

Curb chipped during shooting

DEALEY PLAZA

HOUSTON ST.

COMMERCE ST

Motorcade route

Old Court House

1. Steve Wilson
2. S.M. Holland, Austin Miller, Frank Reilly, James Simmons, Clemmon Johnson, Luke Winborn
3. Charles Brehm and son
4. James Tague
5. Jean Hill and Mary Moorman
6. Abraham Zapruder
7. Emmett Hudson
8. Lee Bowers
9. Mr. and Mrs. William Newman

10. Mr. and Mrs. John Chism
11. Orville Nix
12. Mary Muchmore
13. Philip Willis
14. Mrs. Donald Baker
15. Billy Lovelady, Roy Truly, et al.
16. Victoria Adams
17. Howard Brennan
18. Charles Bronson
19. Location of many deputy sheriffs

Photo 2. Zapruder film—head shot sequence
Top, President Kennedy just before impact (frame 312). *Middle,* At impact (frame 313).
Bottom, After impact (frame 321). Copyright © 1967, LMH Co. All rights reserved.

Photo 3. Willis slide 6—bystanders run toward grassy knoll after shooting. Just beneath the Fort Worth sign can be seen motorcycle officer Clyde Haygood, who has parked his cycle and is beginning to run up the knoll. The Newmans can be seen crouched on lawn behind station wagon. Copyright © 1964, Phil Willis.

Photo 4. Moorman photograph—corresponds to Zapruder frames 313-315.

Photo 5. The sniper's nest, as reported on November 22, 1963

A, Wire service photo shows trajectory from window to street. *B,* View from sniper's nest.

A   B

Photo 6. Frame from Nix film shows Clint Hill climbing aboard car. The dark area in front of upper left-hand corner of the wall was widely interpreted as smoke by critics in 1966.

Photos 7-9. The Dallas police investigation as it was reported the weekend of November 22, 1963

7. Police converge on Depository.

8. The hiding place of the sniper, according to police.

9. Lt. Carl Day, head of the Dallas Police Department Crime Lab Unit, displays the rifle found on the sixth floor to reporters on Friday night at police headquarters.

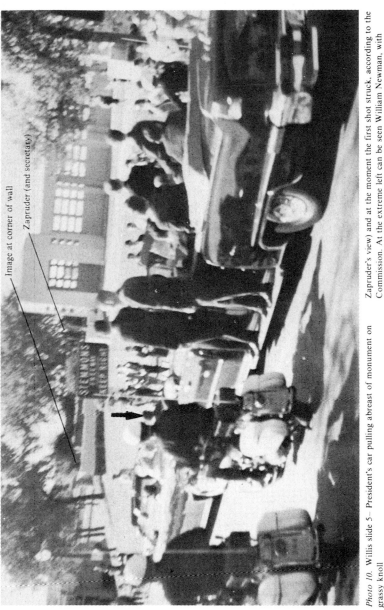

Image at corner of wall

Zapruder (and secretary)

Photo 10. Willis slide 5— President's car pulling abreast of monument on grassy knoll

Black arrow points at Kennedy; the car in foreground contains eight Secret Service agents and two White House aides. Note Abraham Zapruder, filming the motorcade (to the right of Stemmons Freeway sign). This picture was taken as the car disappeared behind the Stemmons sign (in Zapruder's view) and at the moment the first shot struck, according to the Commission. At the extreme left can be seen William Newman, with children. Standing behind Stemmons sign are the Chisms. At edge of wall, atop knoll, appears a black, manlike blob—gone by the time Willis took his next picture (Willis slide 6, see Photo 3). Copyright © 1964, Phil Willis.

Photo 11. Bronson slide, discovered during the 1978 congressional investigation, shows the President's car at about frame 230 of Zapruder film, and offers a comprehensive view of the Dealey Plaza eyewitnesses at the time of the shooting. Copyright © 1978, Charles Bronson.

Photo 12. Frame from Muchmore film

President's car has moved directly in front of the wall on the knoll. To Kennedy's right are Mr. and Mrs. William Newman and their two children. The Newmans said shots came from directly behind them. To Kennedy's left was Charles Brehm and his son. Brehm told Dallas papers on November 22, 1963, that from the way the President jolted backward, he thought the shot struck from the front. The woman behind Brehm, whose identity is unknown, is filming the shooting.

Labels on image:
Zapruder's position
Newmans
Emmett Hudson
Mary Moorman (right)
Jean Hill (left)
Brehm and son
Kennedy's location at fatal shot

Photo 13. Bond slide 4—reaction of bystanders to shooting

In the lower left are Brehm and son. Brehm told *Dallas Times Herald* he thought Kennedy was hit from the front. Jean Hill thought shots came from across the street, "just people shooting from the knoll." Mary Moorman took a Polaroid photo before being pulled to the ground by Hill. Right of center, above the curb, are the Newmans and children (crouched on lawn). Mr. and Mrs. Newman, interviewed immediately afterward, said shots came from directly behind them, not from the Depository building up the street. On the stairs, Emmett Hudson thought shots came from directly over his head. Several of the motorcycle patrolmen raced up the grassy knoll immediately after this picture was taken.

Photo 14. Parkland doctors' press conference
   Drs. Kemp Clark (left) and Malcolm Perry (right) answer reporters' questions at news conference arranged by White House staff member Wayne Hawkes (center, in bowtie). White House stenographer "Chick" Reynolds (in front of Clark) takes a transcript. Watch on Perry's left hand indicates 2:18 P.M

Photo 15. Frame 230 of Zapruder film shows Kennedy reacting to throat wound while Connally appears unhurt.

Photo 16. Juxtaposition of Kennedy and Connally medical diagrams showing non-alignment of trajectory in vertical plane
   A, Warren Commission Exhibit 385—Navy drawing of trajectory through Kennedy's neck
   B, Secret Service diagram of trajectory through Connally

A   B

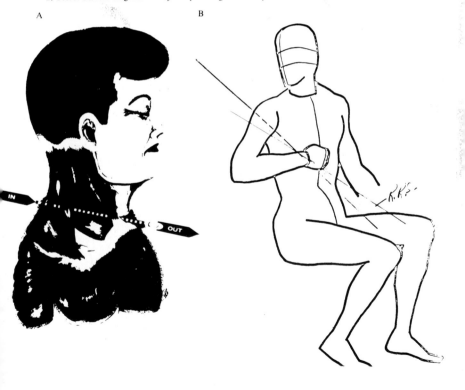

Photo 17. FBI Exhibit 59—FBI lab photograph showing back of President Kennedy's suit coat with bullet entrance hole, which was measured at 5⅜ inches below top of collar

Photo 18. FBI Exhibit 60—FBI lab photographs showing damage to President Kennedy's shirt and tie. *Top,* View of back of President Kennedy's shirt with close-up of bullet entrance hole measured at 5¼ inches below top of collar. *Lower left,* Nick in tie; *Lower right,* Slits in front of shirt.

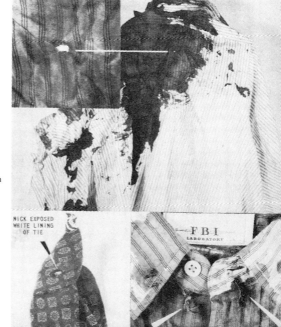

Photo 19 (left). Bullet 399—found on Dallas stretcher
Photo 20 (right). Bullet 856—fired through wrist of a cadaver

Photo 21. Two bullet fragments found in limousine—Warren Commission Exhibits 567 and 569

Photo 22. Base of bullet 399, showing minor distortion and area where some metal was missing

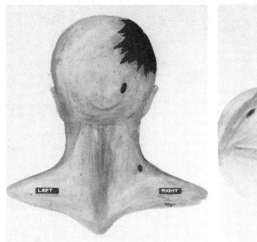

Photo 23 (left). Warren Commission Exhibit 386—Navy medical drawing showing rear view of Kennedy's wounds

Photo 24 (right). Warren Commission Exhibit 388—Navy medical drawing showing trajectory through Kennedy's head

Photo 25. Wesley J. Liebeler, while on the Warren Commission

A

B

Photo 26. At Andrews Air Force Base, the coffin is unloaded from *Air Force One* and put aboard a Navy ambulance.

A, Dave Powers (at left) and Larry O'Brien (at right) take hold of coffin and begin to remove it from lift. Godfrey McHugh (in uniform) is visible just behind Powers.

B, Secret Service agents Kellerman and Greer (in front of Jacqueline and Robert Kennedy) take coffin off lift. Sailor with back to camera is Hubert Clark of Military District of Washington (MDW) casket team. McHugh and Powers can be seen immediately to his left.

C, Agents put casket into the rear of the Navy ambulance as Jacqueline and Robert Kennedy look on. Uniformed serviceman leaning over to assist is USAF Sgt. Richard Gaudreau of MDW casket team. Visible to the left of Jacqueline is her secretary, Mary Gallagher; to the right is President Kennedy's secretary, Evelyn Lincoln, and White House assistant Kenneth O'Donnell.

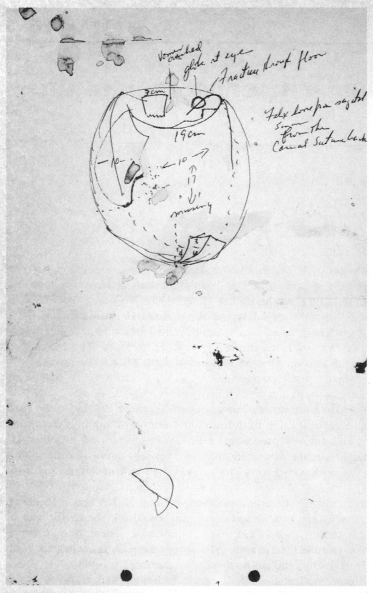

Photo 21. Boswell diagram of skull

This sketch, made at autopsy, is a top view of Kennedy's skull. Note the 10 by 17 area marked "missing"; measurements at the rear apparently pertaining to bone fragments; and the following marginalia: "vomer crushed"; "globe rt eye—Fracture through floor"; "Falx loose from sagital sinus from the coronal suture back." The record contains no amplification of the area on the forward left side of the skull marked "3 cm." The half-moon-shaped figure at the bottom may be an attempt to sketch in the partial circumference of the bullet entry wound. Color photographs of this diagram (available from the Archives) establish that the gray blotches seen here are bloodstains.

CHAPTER 10

The Liebeler Memorandum

DOMINATING THE SOUTH END of the UCLA campus was the Center for the Health Sciences, one of the world's largest medical centers, a huge complex of buildings housing the UCLA Hospital, the Medical School, a cluster of research institutes including the Brain Research Institute, and thousands of square feet devoted to classrooms and laboratory facilities for undergraduate and graduate courses in the life sciences. The building was a beehive of activity. One focal point was the UCLA Biomedical Library, twelve floors high, containing six hundred thousand volumes and an enormous collection of medical periodicals.

The day after my confrontation with Liebeler, I went to the library. I needed to educate myself, to learn the elements of anatomy, forensic pathology, and autopsy procedure. I had to be able to tell whether Humes' technical language described ordinary missile wounds or concealed something extraordinary. I would try to learn the fundamentals on my own.

The UCLA Medical Center was a fabulous resource. It was full of readily accessible medical specialists, because UCLA was a teaching hospital. If you didn't know something, you could ask somebody who did—a medical student, a resident, even a professor. There were many useful exhibits. Outside the anatomy laboratories large glass enclosures contained human skeletons, and cut-away exhibits showing the brain.

How complicated could forensic pathology and anatomy really be? The doctors who examined Kennedy's body were once premed students. Premed courses were no more difficult than the math and physics I had once studied. An autopsy in a gunshot case didn't deal with complex matters of science—it was merely an examination of mechanical damage, an inventory of holes outside the body, and damage inside the body, and a determination that a missile entered here, bruised this organ, and exited there. Taking apart a body was an act of medical carpentry.

I collected an assortment of texts. For the basic anatomy of the head, I used *Grant's Atlas of Anatomy;* for the brain, the famous CIBA brain drawings. I found many texts about forensic pathology, with chapter after chapter of case histories of the strange and awful deaths encountered by autopsy surgeons. It was real-life Agatha Christie.

But it was slow going. When I referred one of Humes' words to the medical dictionaries, the definition usually contained additional words I didn't understand. Soon I had long lists of words to look up. Each mention of a bone sent me to *Grant's Atlas*. It was a rather narrow education, but I must have looked important. At one point a student came up to me, and said with deference: "Sir, I don't want to disturb you—I'm just a premed. But in what year do we get that course?"

I began with the Bethesda autopsy report. Under the section "General Description of the Body," Humes wrote: "The body is that of a muscular, well-developed and well-nourished adult Caucasian male. . . ." Kennedy's weight and height, and a description of the surgical cuts made on the body in Dallas, were given. Then, under "Missile Wounds," the following description of the major head wound appeared:

There is a large irregular defect of the scalp and skull on the right involving chiefly the parietal bone, but extending somewhat into the temporal and occipital regions.[1]

I looked up each word. "Defect," I soon learned, meant "hole." The large diagrams in *Grant's Atlas* made clear the locations of the parietal, temporal, and occipital bones.

Humes wrote that the defect involved "chiefly the parietal bone" but extended "somewhat" into "the temporal and occipital regions." He gave its maximum dimension as 13cm (5⅛ inches).[2] I studied the diagrams in *Grant's Atlas* carefully.

The large head wound extended from the rear of the head (Humes said it extended "somewhat" into the occipital area) almost one-half foot toward the front of the head. I tried to visualize what this large hole in the skull must have looked like. Humes wrote: "In this region there is an actual absence of scalp and bone. . . ."[3] Testifying before the Warren Commission, Humes said the defect was in an "area [which] was *devoid* of *any* [emphasis added] scalp or skull"; but, he noted, "the scalp was intact completely past this defect."[4]

The diagram drawn at the autopsy by Dr. Boswell showed an even larger hole. It was a view of the skull from above (see Photo 27) and showed a 10 by 17cm area marked "missing."[5] Had Humes understated the true dimensions?

Forensic pathology texts stressed that in analyzing a gunshot case, brain damage had to be distinguished from skull damage. I now turned to the brain damage, to the parasagittal "laceration" described by Humes. It ran the complete length of the brain, from the "tip" of the occipital lobe to the "tip" of the frontal lobe. I also reviewed the back-to-front laceration through the corpus callosum. The symmetry of these cuts was remarkable. By definition, the parasagittal laceration was parallel to the centerline, known as the sagittal plane. Would a bullet cause such symmetric damage? The fact that the scalp was entirely missing over the skull hole suggested to me that some of this damage might have been caused by human design.

How could I settle the matter?

I might consult forensic pathology texts with their many illustrated examples of gunshot injuries of the head. But what if it turned out that such damage patterns were not found in typical wounds? That would not prove these particular lacerations could not be inflicted by gunshot.

In frustration, I turned to the President's neck wound.

The neck wound posed a real puzzle. The Dallas doctors said it was an entrance. The Bethesda doctors said it was an exit. I accepted the statements of the Dallas doctors, but this presented a problem. If a bullet entered the front of the neck, where did it go? Commander Humes testified that X-rays taken at the autopsy revealed no metal inside the President's neck or chest.

I carried my inquiry one step further. If a bullet entered from the front, where might it have lodged? Could it have been extracted? Through what orifice?

There didn't seem to be any. The only hole on the body through which one might reach such a bullet was the one through which the bullet, under this assumption, had entered—the wound at the front of the neck. That wound, of course, had been enlarged slightly by Dr. Malcolm Perry, during the tracheotomy.

I turned to Dr. Humes' testimony and read the section about the tracheotomy incision. Humes testified that it was "some 7 or 8cm in length."[6]

Seven to eight centimeters? Could it really have been that large? I could hear Liebeler's taunt: "Humes can measure, can't he?"

I turned to Dr. Perry's medical report and testimony. He made no mention of the length of the tracheotomy incision. And why should he? It was minutia—the length of a routine incision made every day in emergency rooms.

Yet I needed that detail. It bore directly on the question of whether a bullet had been extracted. Why not telephone Perry and ask about the incision length?

At first I was reluctant to do so, but if I didn't ask, how was I going to find out?

My curiosity finally overcame my inhibitions. But I needed a cover story. Liebeler had said I could, if I wished, turn in a research paper. I built my story around that idea.

It was October 27, 1966. Alone in the quiet of my apartment in West Los Angeles, I placed the call. When Dr. Perry came on the line, I went through my whole pitch. The student wrestling with a research paper. The meticulous professor with a penchant for detail. He even wanted the size of the tracheotomy incision.

Dr. Perry was friendly and sympathetic.

I asked, "So do you recall, perhaps, how large the incision was?"

Dr. Perry didn't hesitate a moment.

"Two to three centimeters," he replied.

As I talked to Dr. Perry, I had opened volume 3 of the twenty-six volumes, containing his Warren Commission testimony. As Perry replied, I scrawled "2–3cm" in the margin.

Trying to remain calm, I asked, "Dr. Perry, might it be possible that the incision you made was three and a half centimeters?" Yes, he replied, it could have been. I paused, then went for the next increment. Could it have been four centimeters? Perry hesitated a bit, then said yes. He explained that it was not good to make an incision larger than necessary. That was a basic tenet of surgery, he said. As innocently as possible, I asked Perry if his incision could have been 4½ centimeters. He said he really doubted it was that large. It just wasn't necessary. Perry sounded distinctly uneasy.

I pressed the matter no further. The conversation established to my satisfaction that Dr. Perry remembered a tracheotomy incision much shorter than the one that Humes described in his sworn Warren Commission testimony. For the first time, I had reason to suspect that unauthorized surgery had been performed not only on the head, but on the neck as well. I had the beginnings of an explanation for the absence of bullets.

But I had a queasy feeling about the call. However convincing I found Dr. Perry's responses, the call itself had a fragile quality. The only evidence I had of what Perry told me was my memory of it, and the marginalia, "2–3cm," made as he spoke. Nothing could prevent Dr. Perry from changing his story—indeed, there was precedent for believing that he would do so. On November 22, 1963, Dr. Perry said the throat wound was an entrance. After the Secret Service visited him with the Bethesda autopsy in mid-December, he changed his opinion to conform with that report. Many Warren Report critics were furious with Perry, believing he had copped out on a crucial issue. On the phone with me, Perry was at pains to explain that under certain conditions, a bullet exit wound can give a misleading appearance.

What would happen when Perry found out that in volume 2 of the Warren Commission Humes testified that the tracheotomy incision was 7–8cm? Would Perry stand fast at the 2–3cm he told me? There was only one "first time" when he could be asked the question. A conversation like that ought to be tape recorded.

The next day, I acquired a recorder, along with an attachment for recording phone calls.

I decided to call as many of the Dallas doctors as quickly as I could. I hoped to get to them in one or two evenings, before they had a chance to talk to one another.

The telephone call to Dr. Perry drove home the fact that I was dealing with the tip of an iceberg. In just five days, I had found evidence pertaining to alterations in *two* separate areas of the body. The Perry call concerned the throat wound. The Sibert and O'Neill FBI report talked of "surgery of the head area." Then there were the two rear entry wounds—neither of which was observed in Dallas.

It struck me that I was not just pursuing a new conspiracy theory. This was an entirely different way to address the Warren Commission's records.

Wesley Liebeler had repeatedly stressed that in basing its findings on the autopsy, the Warren Commission had relied upon the "best evidence." Now I saw the body as the central piece of evidence—indeed, it was the body that was the "best evidence," and I had to collect all data that might indicate anatomic alteration.

I would have to follow two separate trails of evidence: one pertaining to the neck trajectory, and one pertaining to the head trajectory. Different documents were involved, different questions, and, more important, different events on the Zapruder film. The film showed two events clearly: first, Kennedy reached for his throat. Then, about six seconds later, his head exploded and his entire head and upper torso were thrust backward. If the body was altered, the motions shown on the film would have to be re-evaluated too.

I was anxious to get on with the work, for I was aware that I had barely scratched the surface. But an obstacle loomed—my status as a graduate student. Intending to file an appeal of my dismissal, I went up to UCLA and spoke to several officials. A professor gave me advice. If I was so fired up about the Kennedy assassination, why not devote full time to it, and get it out of my system?

I began thinking about doing that.

During this period, I spoke with Wesley Liebeler several times, and one afternoon I joined him for drinks at a restaurant near UCLA.

Only eight days had passed since our dramatic meeting at Ball's law office, but Wesley Liebeler was undergoing a transformation.

Liebeler wore two hats. First, there was Wesley Liebeler, ex-Warren

Commission attorney, who had quasi-official status. Then there was Wesley Liebeler, private citizen, the law professor who was writing a book, who implied that if I could prove the Commission wrong, he would say so.

On October 24, at the meeting at Ball's office, Liebeler had been stunned by the FBI statement about head surgery. His behavior then made me hope that he would do something. Perhaps he would call a news conference, or incorporate my discovery in his book. In that case, the hypothesis of post-mortem surgery would surface under prestigious auspices. I expected Liebeler's book would be a major pronouncement.

But the Liebeler of November 1 was changed. Gone was the talk of news conferences, or airplane trips east, of calling Humes or Boswell to record their responses to hard questions.

Now when I said I was thinking of a full-time commitment to investigate the surgery hypothesis, Liebeler cautioned me against it. When I spoke of my academic problems, and said I found engineering boring, he said I should consider law school, that he might help me get into UCLA.

In the JFK matter, he insisted the next logical step was securing the release of the X-rays and photographs. That was the evidence that could resolve all the questions I had raised.

I had different ideas about the X-rays and photographs. I thought they might provide evidence that the body had been altered. I wondered how revealing the pictures were. Would a knife cut show up? Would it be distinguishable from a bullet's damage? All this was conjecture, because the photographs and X-rays were not available.

What was available was the Sibert and O'Neill statement about "surgery of the head area." But about that, Liebeler's enthusiasm had cooled. He never said it was not important. He now said it was not sufficient. Wesley Liebeler wasn't going to put his career on the line on the strength of a statement in a single FBI report.

That night I made the decision to devote full time to the case. Somebody had to follow up this hypothesis, to analyze the medical data from this new viewpoint. Somebody had to question the Dallas doctors. Liebeler certainly wasn't going to. I decided I would. My goal would be to write a technically oriented monograph marshaling the evidence that President Kennedy's body was altered prior to autopsy. I thought the project would take about six months. I never dreamed I was embarking on something that would preoccupy me for the next fifteen years.

On Wednesday morning, November 2, 1966, I read in the *Los Angeles Times* that the Kennedy family had just donated the photographs and X-rays to the National Archives. I telephoned Liebeler at the UCLA Law School. I had set up the tape recorder to call the Dallas doctors. From that day forward, I tape recorded all my conversations with him, too.

Liebeler hadn't heard about the story. I read it to him, along with the essential details: that the family had turned over to the government about sixty-five X-rays and photographs; that under conditions laid down by the President's widow, the records would be available only to official federal agencies. "Unofficial investigators," the story said, could see the material only with the consent of the Kennedy family's legal representative, Burke Marshall, who had served as Assistant Attorney General during the Kennedy administration. Such consent would be exceptional during the first five years of the agreement.

I told Liebeler I had rejected his friendly advice of the day before, not to pursue the matter full time. "This thing is too important to me," I said. "I want it written up correctly, and as accurately and as rapidly as possible. And it's worth it to me. I don't care if I lose a few weeks."

"Well, what's it worth to you at this point, if these X-rays and pictures are available?" said Liebeler. "Supposing we can look at them?"[7]

"I think that would be wonderful," I replied.

"But that won't solve your problem, you don't think?"

I told Liebeler that qualified pathologists would soon see the evidence, and what bothered me was that they might conduct their examination oblivious to the possibility that wounds they were looking at were man-made. I suggested that a "critical paper . . . should be whipped up as soon as possible" so that any potential examiner of the material could read the paper, and then examine the evidence with due regard for that possibility. Otherwise, I said, any pathologist might provide a meaningless "verification" of the wounds described in the Bethesda autopsy report.

Liebeler agreed, and then asked me to prepare a list of questions to be addressed to the autopsy pictures and X-rays. "I've been requested to do that. . . . I'd like you to do it. . . . Then, we can get together . . . go through it, and prepare a memorandum on it."

Liebeler told me that the request came from Howard Willens, a Justice Department lawyer who was one of Rankin's two special assistants during the life of the Commission.

Then Liebeler told me that, just before I called, he had received a phone call from Senator Richard Russell.

"Did you tell him about any of the surgery?" I asked.

"I told him about this FBI report, yeah," said Liebeler.

"In other words, he knows about that now."

"He knows about it now. Yeah. And his first response was, 'Well, were they medical men?' "

Liebeler remarked that Russell raised "the first, most obvious question, which is how were they [Sibert and O'Neill] able to make a judgment like that? Russell said: 'You know, they shot the whole top of his head off. It's pretty hard to tell very much about anything.' "

Added Liebeler: ". . . which is what I expected his reaction to be."

The conversation turned to Humes. News reports said that Humes and

Boswell had gone into the Archives the day before and "authenticated" the pictures.

"So what?" I said. "You see, Jim, all he's going to do . . . [is] authenticate [them] the same way he did before the Warren Commission."

The problem, I said, was that everything now turned on interpretation of Humes' testimony. Everything he describes was really there—on the body that night, and then in the photos of the body. I called this the "double-entendre" problem with Humes' testimony.

Liebeler replied, "That loses a little of its force now, doesn't it?"

"No," I replied. "It's on the record," and I reminded Liebeler that his own friend had said that it sounded as if Kennedy's brain had been hit with an axe.

Liebeler diminished the importance of that. In any event, he went on, the problem at hand was what questions to address to the pictures. He outlined his plan. "I propose that a group of several people go and look at these pictures and that these questions be answered." He said he didn't know who would be in the group.

I said that any re-examination by Humes seemed to me to be meaningless. "He can authenticate and say yes, that is what I described in my testimony. And it will be a perfectly true, literal statement."

Liebeler answered that the first order of business was to get a memorandum prepared. It would be a memo that dealt with everything— wound locations, all questions that had been raised in the critical literature, and this new question I was raising, the Sibert and O'Neill statement about surgery.

Liebeler said that with such a memorandum at hand, "I think that [Burke] Marshall is not going to be able to refuse permission to the staff to observe these pictures."

What pathologists would examine the material? "How do you deal with the problem of bias?" I asked. "Don't you think it's possible for pathologists to have bias?"

"Oh sure, sure; of course I do. . . . I suppose that the initial inclination of the Justice Department would be to get the kind of pathologist that they think would agree with Humes, and Boswell and Finck. I mean, let's not pull punches about that."

I returned to Commander Humes' testimony, and reminded Liebeler how his pathologist friend had reacted to Humes' description of the parasagittal laceration. "That has to be dealt with," I said. "Well," replied Liebeler, "that's why I've been asked to prepare this memorandum."

I persisted, pointing out that resolving it required more than having a pathologist merely confirm that such a laceration appeared in photographs of the brain.

"We'll ask him what he *meant* by it. How's that, for Christ sake?"

Liebeler was angry. "[We'll] put it in the memorandum and ask him what he meant by it; ask him to respond."

"Exactly. You mean Humes?"

"Yeah, Humes."

"Very good." I felt relieved.

Liebeler continued: "We'll put in the memorandum that we've been asked to submit on this question, that Commander Humes should be asked what he meant by the testimony and set it forth. These are questions that should be addressed to the pictures, in a sense, but also to Humes. . . . He can also be asked to look at the pictures and indicate what he was talking about when he gave this testimony."

Liebeler's voice was now rising again, as he shouted into the phone: ". . . and *what he meant* by that testimony. What was he talking about? Was he talking about a wound that was inflicted by the bullet, or in *some other way*?"

I was relieved. Liebeler was back to his old style again. I told him: "I made a decision last night. I'm writing this whole thing up."

"All right. [But] write up, at this point, if you will, just a series of questions that can be answered by looking at the pictures. Never mind writing some goddamn historical monumental analysis of conspiracy. Let's just look at the questions that can be answered by the pictures. Let's focus on that now. Okay?"

That was fine with me, I said.

I hung up, my mind racing. What was going on? At first, Liebeler seemed stunned by the Sibert and O'Neill report and my hypothesis, then he beat a careful retreat, insisting that nothing could be done until the X-rays and photographs became available. Now, suddenly, they had been made available, and Liebeler admitted he had close liaison with the Justice Department.

Events were moving quickly. Somebody might soon question Humes. There could be only one "first time." I wanted to be the first questioner.

I telephoned information in Bethesda, and obtained the home phone number of Commander Humes. I placed the call.

When Commander Humes came on the line, I said that I was attending Wesley Liebeler's seminar at the UCLA Law School. "Yes, I've heard of that," he said.[8] I said I wanted to ask a few questions, that I realized he might not be able to answer (I assumed the navy did not want him to grant interviews), but perhaps he could help me. Humes replied that he didn't know what he could tell me. ". . . Our position with regard to this whole situation is that we testified before the Warren Commission, we gave a report, and we expressed our interpretation of the facts as we saw them, and we haven't changed anything—from then till now."

I replied that the *Los Angeles Times* had reported that he had authenticated the pictures. "That's correct," said Humes. "They're the same pictures that you took?" I asked. "Correct," he replied.

I said I thought I had made a research discovery about his testimony. I quoted the passages describing what I thought were anomalies: the parasagittal laceration, the laceration through the corpus callosum, and the way the bone fell off the head without any work being done with a surgical saw. Then I added that I had discovered additional evidence. I didn't say it was an FBI report. I said it was a document written by a witness to the autopsy which said surgery had been performed on the head, and said so in lay language.

I told Humes what I thought had happened—in essence, that he and the Warren Commission had not communicated properly, not because of any deliberate desire, on his part, to mislead, but because of the context in which his testimony was presented. He had described accurately everything he saw, but it was all being taken in the context of gunshot wounding, because of the method of presentation—chiefly, because of the three navy drawings Humes used, drawings which showed the wounds, but which, because of the arrows indicating the path of the bullets, cast everything in the context of gunshot injury.

"And my own personal opinion, Dr. Humes, was that you were trying to say something. And that the man at the other end of the line, the lawyer involved, Specter, simply because he didn't have the training in forensic pathology, did not understand what you were saying."

There was a pause, and Humes, stuttering, replied: "You've lost me here somewhere, young fellow. I don't know what you—I . . . I . . . I missed the point."

Suddenly, a burst of static came on the line. I couldn't hear. I yelled "Hello? Hello?" Then I heard a click, and the line was dead.

I flashed for the operator and asked her to re-establish the connection. Within seconds, a female voice came on the line. It was Humes' daughter. Her father was not there. Then another female voice—Humes' wife. Mrs. Humes said her husband had gone to a meeting and she suggested I call him at his office at Bethesda Naval Hospital. I was reluctant to call Humes there, because I was aware he was under military orders not to talk. I said I would try him at home again, later.

The call to Humes excited me. Important officials could be reached by telephone. I decided to try Sibert and O'Neill. FBI agents aren't doctors. How did they know "surgery of the head area" had been performed?

I could not locate Francis O'Neill, but there was a James W. Sibert listed in Carrolton, Maryland, and after placing a person-to-person call and having it rerouted, I located him in Quitman, Georgia.

When Agent Sibert came to the phone, I identified myself, told him I was attending a class at the University of California, Los Angeles (UCLA)

Law School, conducted by Professor Liebeler, and that I needed information for a paper I was writing.

Sibert first refused to speak with me. "I'm in no position to answer any questions on this. I have to clear it with our Headquarters," he said.[9]

I was more than willing, I said, to have him clear this entire matter with Headquarters, but perhaps he might find my question "so insignificant that there's nothing wrong with answering it." If, after hearing my question, he felt he still wanted to clear it with Headquarters, that was fine, too. "Okay," he replied. He would listen.

I pointed out that his report on the autopsy had just been published in the appendices to two separate paperback books: *Inquest,* by Edward Epstein, and *The Second Oswald,* by Dr. Richard Popkin. In that report, I said, he and Francis O'Neill made the statement that following the removal of the wrapping on the President's head, it was apparent that a "tracheotomy" had been performed. Neither he nor O'Neill was a doctor, I said.

At the word "tracheotomy," Sibert cut me off. "Well, I'll tell you, before you waste any more time, I'm not going to be able to answer any of your questions on this." He repeated that I would have to "clear it" through his Headquarters. How would that be done? "Well," he said, "you'd have to write to our Headquarters, in Washington, D.C." Fine, I said, but could I please say a few words to him. "Go right ahead," he said. "I'm going to read you a statement which I think is important in your report," I said. "I want to question you about [the statement] because I'm a very concerned citizen." I then read aloud, slowly, to Agent Sibert, the statement in his report that when the President's body was removed from the coffin and the wrapping taken off, it was "apparent" that there had been "surgery of the head area, namely, in the top of the skull."

Sibert replied, "Well, I'll tell you, as I told you [before] . . . there's no use your wasting your time, really I can't—I hope you understand my position, but . . . I can't answer any of your questions." Then he added: "The record speaks for itself." He emphasized, however, that he could answer no questions about it.

Well, then, could he tell me who actually wrote the report—he or O'Neill? "It was pointed out in there both were present," replied Sibert.

I agreed to write FBI Headquarters. But I wanted it to be a matter of record that I had personally called Agent Sibert and inquired about this specific sentence in his report. I wanted Sibert to know exactly what question I would be asking in the letter he was advising me to write. I explained all this.

Sibert seemed a bit edgy. "Let me get your name, here, now what did you say your name was?"

I spelled my name for him. He repeated the letters, apparently as he wrote it down. I repeated my question. I wanted to know, I said, what it was he had witnessed that permitted him to write the statement about surgery in his report. He repeated that I must write directly to the FBI, "because you understand my position, I mean anything will have to be cleared on this. In the first place," he said, "I mean, I don't even know who I'm talking to, even though you tell me [who you are]."

He added:

. . . but the report stands for itself, I think . . . so if you have any further question, I'd just suggest that you write to the Bureau Headquarters.

I pointed out that, given the nature of my inquiry, FBI Headquarters would presumably have to ask the question of either him or O'Neill, because they were there, they had written the report, and they were the only people who could explain the statement about surgery.

I thanked Sibert for speaking with me. His last words were: "Okay, Mr. Lifton. That's L-I-F-T-O-N, right?"

November 2, 1966, had been extraordinary. The press announced the X-rays and photographs had been turned over to the Archives. I had been asked by a Warren Commission attorney to help draft a memorandum that would govern what questions would be addressed to that evidence. I had interviewed FBI Agent James Sibert and Commander James J. Humes. All things seemed possible.

The next morning, Thursday, November 3, I resolved to call Dr. Humes again, but I began the day with a call to Liebeler. I said that now I better appreciated his position, that I understood that he wasn't "ready to walk out on the end of the gangplank unless every board is absolutely filled with evidence."

"But of course I'm not," he replied.[10] "Because if I do that, I destroy my effectiveness in trying to get these [autopsy] pictures out."

I also said, without mentioning that my source was a conversation with Humes the day before, that I believed that Humes would insist no pre-autopsy surgery took place. Suppose that happened? I asked.

I didn't like his reply. "Yeah, but my God, if the pictures are there, and we look at the pictures, and we get our own independent pathologists to look at the pictures; and we put in the memorandum that we submit . . . that we want Humes to explain the significance of this testimony—what the hell more can you do?"

If that was the outcome, I said, I would still feel obligated to press the question publicly.

"Go ahead. Go ahead," said Liebeler. ". . . you can do anything you want to; I'm not going to tell you what to do, but at that point, I'd have to say that you're behaving in an irresponsible manner."

I didn't believe I was behaving irresponsibly. I had no intention of letting the issue be raised, and quelled, behind closed doors, without public hint that such a serious matter had been considered. I had seen too many cases in which the so-called "experts" were wrong.

Liebeler disagreed. "Because if an independent autopsy surgeon looks at the pictures . . . and he is asked: 'Is there any indication from examining these pictures if there's surgery to the top of the President's head?' And he says, 'None whatever.' And if you want to go ahead and make an argument that there *is*—God, there's nothing I can do to keep you from doing it."

This reinforced my determination to get back to Humes, and made me aware that Liebeler and I were probably going to end up on opposite sides.

We returned to the immediate issue. "I think the first thing to do," said Liebeler, "is get a very precise and well-thought-out memorandum. . . . What I want from you now is all the questions that you think should be asked of these pictures. Let's put them in the memorandum; let's ask them. If they [officials] don't answer them, then you're not going to be the one who's going to be screaming about it—I'm going to scream about it in my book. And I'll put it to Marshall just as bluntly as that. 'Look, either you *do* this, or I'm going to put it in my book, and you can accept the consequences of it.' And he won't dare refuse at that point. I can't believe he will. If he does, then the hell with him. Screw him."

Liebeler argued: "But if you want to go out and write some article in some extremist magazine *before* we raise the question with Marshall [Liebeler seemed to be concerned about my relationship with *Ramparts*], I think that you destroy your effectiveness, and, in a sense, you destroy mine. Because if we can show this to Marshall and say: 'Look, this question *hasn't* been raised yet, but it's *gonna* be raised if you don't *do* something about it. So let's do something about it.' "

Liebeler tried to assuage my fears that he would evade the issue. "You know, I'm not going to try and duck out from under this thing with some propaganda public statement by Humes, or Specter. That's the last thing I want." And, his voice rising in exasperation, he said: "These guys have messed these things up from start to finish . . . and the only way this can be stopped, and put to rest, if it can be put to rest, is to do it right for a change. . . . If this doesn't work, you go and write anything you want to any place you want to. I wouldn't even ask you not to. What I do want to ask you to do is do the memorandum first. Let's submit it to Marshall. Let's get the reaction from Marshall."

That was fine with me, but something else was now on my mind: the role played by a bone fragment that was brought to the morgue during the latter stages of the autopsy.

The Late-Arriving Bone Fragment

I had become increasingly intrigued by Humes' enigmatic answer to Commissioner Allen Dulles' question whether the fatal shot *must* have struck from behind: "Scientifically, sir, it is impossible for it to have been fired from other than behind." And then he added: "Or to have exited from other than behind."[11]

Was that just scrambled syntax, or was Humes confronted with "scientific" evidence of both entry and exit from the rear of the head?

Study by now acquainted me with forensic pathologists' normal procedure for distinguishing entrance from exit wounds in the skull. It was a matter of scientific facts, observed directly.

When a missile enters the skull, it leaves one damage pattern on the outside—i.e., the side of impact—and another, entirely different pattern on the inside surface. As it enters the skull, the bullet produces a small hole, about the size of the missile, on the outer surface. As the bullet breaks through to the skull's interior, a larger, beveled-out hole is produced on the inside surface. This larger hole is shaped roughly like a cone, and the effect is called "coning." ("Beveling" and "shelving" are also terms used.) The reverse is observed when a bullet emerges from within the skull, producing an exit wound. In that case, the smaller hole will occur on the skull's inside surface (the impact side, for an exiting missile), and the larger, beveled-out hole will be produced on the outside surface. (See Fig. 15.) Thus, when looking at a bullet hole in the skull, it is easy to determine the bullet's direction, because the base of the cone (the larger hole) points in the direction the missile is traveling, and the tip of the cone (the smaller hole) points back toward the source.[12]

Texts on forensic pathology stress the reliability of this method in distinguishing entrance from exit wounds, even if only a portion of the wound is available.

Commander Humes testified that when he examined the skull, he found two holes: a small hole at the rear, and a larger one, situated above it. The small hole contained evidence of entry—i.e., it exhibited coning on the inside surface. But, in examining the large hole, Humes could find no evidence of exit. He was explicit: "A careful examination of the margins of the large bone defect [hole] . . . however, failed to disclose a portion of the skull bearing . . . a wound of—a point of impact on the skull [i.e., impact on the inside surface of the skull by an exiting missile]."[13]

In this state of affairs, Humes testified that the large wound "would represent" an exit wound.[14] Humes' determination was not a conclusion based on direct observation, but a deduction based on two other facts. One was that the only other hole in the head, the small wound at the rear, exhibited "coning," and was definitely an entry. The other concerned bone

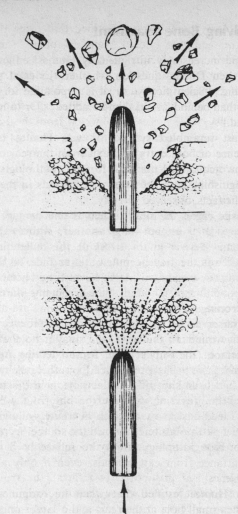

Figure 15.
Beveling

Diagram illustrates that a missile striking a surface of the skull—whether entering or exiting—creates a small hole on the side of impact and a larger, beveled-out hole as it emerges from that surface. This "beveling" effect permits a distinction to be made between bullet entrance and exit wounds of the skull, since the larger, beveled-out hole will be on the side opposite the point of impact. Thus, if the exterior surface of the skull exhibits beveling, the wound is an exit; if the interior surface does, it is an entrance.

brought to the autopsy room. Humes testified that three pieces of skull-bone were brought, and that one of them exhibited "shelving" on the outside surface. That was evidence of exit, and was the basis for the statement, in the autopsy report, that what he was handed was "a portion of the perimeter of a roughly circular wound presumably of exit. . . ."[15]

What I came to realize was that despite Humes' testimony that as he performed the autopsy, large pieces of bone fell from the President's head to the autopsy table, the actual medico-legal evidence of exit was contained in a piece of bone *not* on the President's head at the time of autopsy.

Two questions demanded to be asked. One was: Where was the bone found? The second: What was the bone's anatomic origin—where on the head did it come from?

The record was vague. Humes testified that someone presented him with the three pieces of bone, but he wasn't sure who this was, or where the bone was found—"either in the street or in the automobile, I don't recall specifically," was the way he put it.[16] Nor did Humes ever specify where on the head they originated. At one point, he testified that because of the shattered condition of the skull, "the fragments were so difficult to replace in their precise anatomic location. . . ."[17]

I found this failure to be specific somewhat suspicious, and explained why. The only bone fragment available on Friday night that I knew about came from the rear of Kennedy's head. Secret Service Agent Clint Hill testified that when he ran to the President's limousine, the right rear of the President's head had been shot off, and was lying in the rear seat of the car.[18] This implied the President was shot from the front. FBI agents Sibert and O'Neill reported, based on an interview the following week with Gerald Behn, Chief of the White House Detail of the Secret Service, that the bone fragment brought to the autopsy room had been recovered from the limousine.[19]

It seemed Humes had juxtaposed two facts: the rear entry wound and a fragment of an exit wound whose anatomic origin was the rear of the head. If so, the autopsy conclusion about the fatal shot stood on shaky ground. Was that the reason why Humes replied, to Dulles' question, "Scientifically, sir, it is impossible for it to have been fired from other than behind. Or to have exited from other than behind"?[20]

Liebeler disagreed, and attacked my reliance on Clint Hill. "Hill doesn't know what the hell is included in the back of the head or the front of the head. He found it in the car. It's bone. What the hell does he know about that?"[21]

The two of of us then became embroiled in a debate as to exactly where the large wound "presumably of exit" was located. The more we argued, the more I realized I had work to do. Relying on different witnesses, Liebeler and I came up with different locations for the fatal wound. On one thing we both agreed: the autopsy photographs would probably settle the question of the bone fragment's origin by showing the fragment itself, and the hole from which it came. These questions would be covered, in detail, in the memo.

I told Liebeler I'd work on questions for the memorandum, but that first, I wanted to see my friend, the neurosurgeon. He had promised to help me analyze the autopsy report.

Dr. Morris Abrams* was about forty-five, and held an appointment at the UCLA Medical School. He graciously consented to meet me that day to continue the anatomy lesson we had begun the previous week by telephone. He asked that I bring all the autopsy documents.

We got right down to business. Dr. Abrams had persisted in the belief that I had misread a medical report describing the brain after it had been sectioned during the autopsy. Now he could see that was not the case. The autopsy report and testimony convinced him that Humes described the brain as he found it.

He looked at Humes' drawings of the wounds, and his descriptions of the brain. His brow furrowed as he studied the material. He said if this was all gunshot wounding, then it was the strangest wounding he had heard of. Dr. Abrams could not understand how a bullet entering and exiting where Humes said it did—both these wounds were on the right—and leaving only two tiny fragments on the forward right-hand side of the head, could have made the three lacerations Humes described. It seemed there must have been cutting prior to the autopsy.

As Dr. Abrams went on, it became apparent that I did not understand how deep these cuts were inside the head. (See Fig. 16.) Dr. Abrams took the drawing Humes had made depicting the skull wounds, and sketched in the brain lacerations. The problem was, said Dr. Abrams, that because the cuts were so deep, and because of their general location—one, for example, was far to the left—there was no plausible relationship between the lacerations in the brain, the wounds in the skull, and the found metal.

Abrams went through each of the three lacerations described by Humes.

The Laceration Through the Left Cerebral Penduncle. That laceration was on the left side of the brain, on the underside.[22] (See Figs. 17 and 18.) On the head, it was just above the roof of the mouth. What caused it? It was nowhere near a line connecting the "in" and "out" skull wounds Humes described, so it could not have been made by the part of the bullet alleged to have passed through. Furthermore, the only fragments in the brain were on the forward right side. What caused this laceration on the left underside? Abrams suggested that someone probably had to get at the underside of the brain to remove some metal there—that was his thought.

* Not his real name.

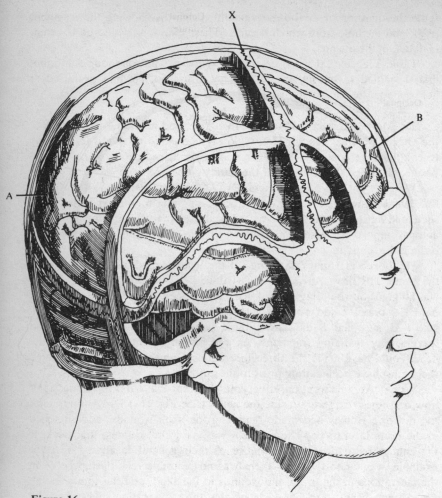

Figure 16.
Cut-away view showing the brain inside the head

Points A and B represent opposite ends of a parasagittal laceration running from the "tip of the occipital lobe . . . to the tip of the frontal lobe . . ."—which is the way Humes found the brain at autopsy. Point X marks the coronal suture, the forward border of the parietal bone. According to Humes' description, the fatal skull wound extended no farther forward than this, comprising "chiefly the parietal bone but extending somewhat into the temporal and occipital regions." Questions raised: Why does the laceration in the brain extend all the way to the "tip" of the frontal lobe, and where is the instrument of injury that caused this back-to-front slice?

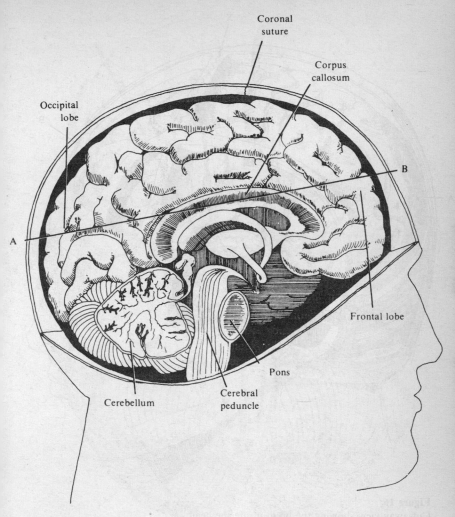

Figure 17.

Cut-away view of head and brain

The corpus callosum is a fibrous mass of tissue connecting the two hemispheres of the brain. It lies at the bottom of the great cerebral fissure (the crevice between the two cerebral hemispheres). Commander Humes reported a back-to-front laceration through the corpus callosum.

In addition, Humes reported a parasaggital laceration that ran the entire length of the brain. (Note: In a top view, the parasaggital laceration, depicted here by line A-B, would be to the right of the corpus callosum.) Finally, Humes reported a laceration through the left cerebral peduncle.

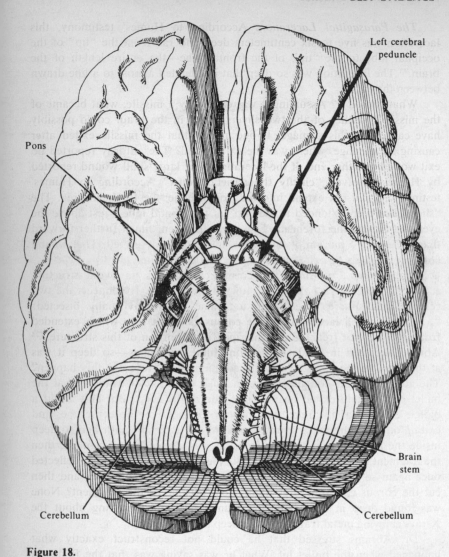

Figure 18.

The brain viewed from below—the left peduncle cut

Arrow points to location on the brain's underside where Humes found the left cerebral peduncle severed.

The Parasagittal Laceration. According to Humes' testimony, this laceration was five to six centimeters deep and ran from the "tip" of the occipital lobe to the "tip" of the frontal lobe—the entire length of the brain.[23] The laceration was so deep that it extended almost to a line drawn between the ears.

What caused it? Assuming it was caused by a missile, what became of the missile? Neither of the two slivers found in the brain could possibly have caused all this damage. If one argued that the missile exited after causing the damage, where was the exit wound? The autopsy reported no exit wound at either end of the laceration. The large skull wound reported by Humes involved "chiefly the parietal bone." According to Humes' testimony, it did not extend into the frontal bone, the forehead area. The "slice," however, extended to the "tip" of the frontal lobe—just above the eyes and behind the forehead. Thus, the slice went much further forward than the forward margin of the exit wound Humes described. That wound could not provide an exit for such a hypothetical missile.

The Corpus Callosum. The corpus callosum is an ovoid structure exactly at the center of the brain, toward the bottom. It connects the two cerebral hemispheres. According to Humes, it was virtually bisected: ". . . there was a laceration of the corpus callosum . . . which extended from the posterior [rear] to the anterior [front] portion of this structure."[24] Abrams sketched in the laceration on Humes' drawings—so deep it was at the level of the ears. Again, the question was: How did this happen? The autopsy report concluded, on the basis of the skull wounds, that the bullet entered and exited on the right side of the head. But how could a bullet, entering at the rear, one inch to the right of the centerline, and exiting on the right, cut a structure well to the left of its path and so deep inside the head? If one hypothesized this was caused by a fragment, then the fragment must have detached itself, veered off to the left, then deflected once again so that it was traveling along the brain's centerline, and then cut the corpus callosum. But what, then, became of the fragment? None was found deep in the brain, and Humes mentioned nothing about the X-rays showing metal fragments that deep inside the head.

Dr. Abrams stressed that he could not reconstruct exactly what happened when the bullet hit. What he was saying was that the Bethesda autopsy explanation—attributing everything to the passage of a bullet—was not very plausible.

Toward the end of our meeting, Dr. Abrams and I discussed how a blue-ribbon panel might proceed. Abrams emphasized that the autopsy photographs were not enough. He would want the brain.

Dr. Abrams noted several other things. First, the page in the autopsy report describing Kennedy's brain was actually a supplementary autopsy report dated December 6, 1963, and referred to an examination made that day. Second, Humes had written: "In the interest of preserving the specimen coronal sections are not made."[25] That was most unusual, explained Abrams. The brain is normally sectioned in autopsies where death results from a head injury. Why wasn't that done here? Why was there an "interest" in preserving the specimen, and where was it now? Questions, but no answers. But this was certain: As of December 6, 1963, Kennedy's brain was in a formaldehyde-filled bottle at Bethesda Naval Hospital.

As I left Dr. Abrams' office, he loaned me his personal copies of *Grant's Atlas* and the CIBA brain drawings. The human body, I now realized, was evidence, and it was nice having my own set of blueprints.

Calling Dr. Humes

I left Abrams' office convinced that the brain lacerations were irreconcilable with gunshot injury. And if Dr. Abrams could see that, from reading Humes' descriptions, then surely, I thought, Humes must know. He had examined the body. He must have had second thoughts.

Returning to my apartment, I telephoned Humes person-to-person at Bethesda Naval Hospital. After a delay of about five minutes, he took the call. The conversation lasted about twenty-five minutes, and was one of the most extraordinary experiences I had in my research.

I began where we had left off, pointing out to Humes that his own testimony, when read to other doctors, elicited the opinion there had been cutting in the brain. Humes' initial response to this was: "I think you're whistling in the dark, my friend. I mean, I'd just read the testimony for what it was, and that's all there is to it."[26] He also said: "I think that you should confine yourself—if you're interested in the Warren Report, read our testimony . . . and take it as the observation of a person qualified to judge what he sees."

I then asked him if the three drawings he submitted in lieu of X-rays and photographs—the ones showing the wounds, and containing little arrows to indicate the path of the bullet—accurately defined the context in which all damage described in his testimony was to be understood: the result of gunshot wounding. "Precisely," said Humes. "And any of these things you're describing are damage as a result of the bullet, going through?" "Precisely," he repeated. "And there is nothing to any other interpretation?" I asked. "Precisely," he replied a third time. "And, in particular, there's nothing to any interpretation that there was surgery done before the body reached your hands?" "Absolutely," he said.

I then asked if he had ever heard of FBI agents Sibert and O'Neill. "No," he responded. I told him what the two agents had written, quoting directly from the report. Humes denied any responsibility; his exact words: "I'm not responsible for their reports."

I told Humes there was a serious conflict between what he testified to and what the FBI reported. I said that Professor Wesley Liebeler, at the UCLA Law School, was drafting a memorandum on the subject; that the memorandum would very likely go to others in the government, and that he, Humes, would probably be questioned about it in the future. As far as Liebeler was concerned, I said, "All he'll want is for you to say just what you've said to me; that there is nothing to this, but that it's in the context of a missile wound. And these lacerations that you are describing," I concluded a bit sarcastically, "couldn't possibly be surgical cuts."

For a moment, Humes said nothing.

I added: "And I mean, if that's the way it is, that's the way it is."

"That's certainly our interpretation," said Humes. For the first time his voice faltered.

In terms of the hard information transmitted, Humes' denials were unequivocal. But some of his responses led me to believe that Humes was aware that something was wrong, but couldn't come to terms with it.

That, at least, is what I came to believe as I pushed harder and harder, trying to get him to betray his state of awareness.

I said: ". . . and people who've seen these descriptions say: 'Well, it could be a missile wound, possibly. But it could also be something else.' "

"But *why*," responded Humes, almost petulantly, "would it be anything else, I ask you?"

I said nothing. Humes cleared his throat.

"*Why*, for God's sake?" His tone sounded urgent.

"Why?" I asked.

"Yeah," said Humes.

I said nothing. For several seconds there was silence. I could hear Humes breathing.

Was it possible Humes didn't understand the implications of bullets being removed, or of *anything* being done to the body before it was examined? I replied: "Well, you see, that would cause me to speculate. And I would rather not."

"Well, I think you're speculating too much already," he said, almost scolding me. "I think you could probably spend your time in a lot more fruitful ways, my boy," he said, sounding almost fatherly, "in my opinion, really, than to try and twist things around from the way they're stated."

"Well, I think they're stated very clearly," I replied. I assured Humes that I would not quote his testimony out of context, but I again reminded him of how other doctors had responded to the descriptions he provided, and referred to the possibility of a new investigation, one focused on the new information about head surgery in the FBI report. Somewhat ingenuously, I said that if he was questioned on this in the future, "and you're going to say it isn't so, well that's it, right?" This elicited no response. I added: "I mean, that's the end of it."

"Well . . . uh . . . uh . . . I don't know what I'm gonna say." Now Humes sounded rattled. "I appeared before the Warren Commission, I gave sworn testimony, and that is the end of it."

Finally, after much dueling and fencing, I made the following statement: "As far as 'Why?', I don't know. But certainly if an operation or if any kind of surgery was done to extract a bullet, or to do anything in the head before the body reached you, that doesn't mean there's anything sinister about it, but it does mean it certainly never came to the attention of the Warren Commission, and it ought to have."

I paused. Humes said nothing. I continued: "I mean, that's probably a minimum statement you could make if such a thing had happened."

Very softly, Humes interjected: "I certainly think it ought to have."

"What's that?!" I said, my voice rising.

"I say," he repeated, "I would certainly *think* it ought to have come to their attention."

Humes' entire tone had changed.

"I know," I replied. "And I'm—" Abruptly, I stopped. Humes was continuing to speak.

". . . like to know who! By *whom* it was done!"

Humes paused.

"And *when*!"

Again, a pause.

"And *where*!"

"Right," I said, assenting.

I waited for more. Humes expelled a deep breath. It was clearly audible.

"Right, right," I continued, hoping he'd say more, something more explicit. "And certainly, if *you* thought it had been done, wouldn't *you* have mentioned it to the Warren Commission?"

"I would certainly hope I would," said Humes.

I was flushed with excitement. This was the same Commander Humes I knew from volume 2 of the Warren Commission—enigmatic, speaking in riddles. Of course Humes told them! But it was all so subtle; that's why his testimony read the way it did. The damage in the brain had more than one interpretation—and Humes was perfectly well aware of that.

Now I was at a loss for words. I should have pushed forward, but I didn't. I retreated.

"Well, that's what I thought. So the whole affair just puzzles me."

"Well, I don't; I think you better take some other area of it to be puzzled by than *that,* my friend. I don't think you . . . I mean, I just think it's . . ."

Commander Humes paused. Then he said one word: "Ridiculous."

I started to reply, but Humes interrupted. As if he wanted not to hurt my feelings, he added, "I'm sorry. I don't mean to ridicule your interest.

But I think in this particular area . . . I . . . I just . . . uh . . ." he paused again, choosing another word. "It's fan*tas*tic, let's put it that way."

The conversation ended. I played the tape back—again, and again, and again—studying it as closely as any document I have ever studied on this case, searching for Humes' psychology among the nuances of the responses, the changes in tone. Soon, I could recite portions of it by heart.

But what to make of it? I can only report the role it played in my life that day. It was an important catalyst. Humes' responses encouraged me to continue my investigation. I was left with the impression that Humes was aware that something had been done to the body before it reached him.

Most important, the personal contact with Humes convinced me he was not part of any plot. Humes might be uneasy about the autopsy report, but the mystery revolved around the body. As a source of data, I believed Humes could be trusted.

Later that evening, I called Liebeler. I did not say I had spoken to Humes. I told him I had spent the afternoon with my neurosurgeon friend, who said that if he had to judge allegations about pre-autopsy surgery of the head, he would demand to see the brain—that without the brain, there would be fruitless debate over what the photos showed, whether a particular pattern of damage was a line on the photograph or a cut on the cadaver. "Well, that depends on how jagged the cut is," responded Liebeler. But he agreed the brain was crucial. "If it's available, we can raise that question."[27]

The conversation turned to Humes. "I'm sure Humes is just going to deny this whole thing," I said.

"I'm sure he is, too," said Liebeler.

"Is there any value in a denial?" I asked. "Is a denial more valuable than a 'no comment'?"

"Oh, I would think so," said Liebeler, "because I think you have to make a judgment as to what Humes is up to at this point; if he's making an ingenuous denial . . ."

"Suppose he makes a righteously indignant denial—'You're taking this out of context! You're twisting my words around. I never meant that.' "

In a somewhat exaggerated fashion, I mimicked Humes.

"All right," said Liebeler, "then I think you can't go any further than that. If the brain is gone, *I* can't. I have to take Humes' word for it. That's the end of it, as far as I'm concerned."

"What do you mean, 'That's the end of it'?"

"I accept it. There's no more I can do."

"You mean, then you have simply raised the unanswered question?"

"That's right."

"And find it's a moot point?"

"Well, one that can't be answered."

"What happens, then, to the validity of the autopsy report conclusions?"

"Well, that's for every citizen to make up his own mind about."

I asked Liebeler if he could still write a book defending the Warren Report, if Humes denied surgery, but if the matter was unresolved. "It depends on what I believe," he replied. "If Humes denies there is anything to this, I'd be inclined to believe him."

Liebeler made clear the purpose of the memorandum was to force the Kennedys to make the X-rays and photos available for an independent inspection. I asked who the memo would go to. "To Burke Marshall, and to Howard Willens, and to Arlen Specter, and to Burt Griffin, and to all the Commissioners," said Liebeler. In a macho tone, he explained his tactics: "In other words, buddy, 'Here's the knife. See it?'"

"Yeah," I replied.

"All right. It's your move." He laughed. "I'm not a very nice guy, you know, David."

But I was puzzled. How could all this remain behind the scenes? The mere fact that a Commission attorney wrote such a memo would create a public stir if it became known. Did he intend to make the memo public? I asked. "Well, I'm not going to make it public until I get a decision on it," he replied, "but I'm going to let it be known that if they don't make a decision on it, that it's going to be made public. . . . You know, that's the name of the game, buddy: 'Monkey on the Back.' You got to put the monkey on the back, and then they'll do something. And the memorandum is going to put the monkey on their back, isn't it?"

I told Liebeler that regardless of what the memo precipitated, I intended to publish a piece on the subject of pre-autopsy head surgery. How long did he feel I should wait? "I think we have to give Marshall a reasonable period of time in which to respond to this memorandum," he said. "Like a month—something like that. And at that point, I'd be perfectly happy for you to go ahead." Liebeler said the connection between the memorandum and anything I published would be obvious, but it didn't bother him. "The people who are involved will be perfectly well aware of the fact—some of them are now—that you and I know each other, and that we are talking to each other, [so] they'll know what's going on."

The conversation came back to the whereabouts of the President's brain. "I don't know where the brain is, or *if* it is," said Liebeler.

"Well, I think Humes would know that, maybe," I said.

"Well, all right, we'll try to find out," said Liebeler. The question would go into the memorandum. But he was skeptical of getting meaningful answers: "I think that the breach between our view of this, and the view of the Justice Department, is so vast that it's really going to take an awful lot of pushing and hauling to get any kind of cooperation out of them."

I asked what he meant. "I think the Justice Department doesn't really have a serious idea of what the hell is involved here . . . their view is that they all want it to go away, and they haven't got the guts to take a stand, and they haven't got the guts to go back to Humes; and they don't want to look like they are opening it up again. And they are going to play their cards just too close to their chest. . . . It will finally blow up. But I'm not going to be involved. I'm not going to be caught in it."

We talked about Humes again. What value might it have, I asked, if I contacted Humes personally? Not much, said Liebeler. "You have to go about it in such a way that the question is raised with him officially."

But wouldn't a personal approach be useful, merely from the standpoint of determining what Humes would say when and if he was approached officially?

"If your theory is right," said Liebeler, "he isn't going to tell *you* about it."

"No, he'd deny it," I replied.

"Of course."

"Indignantly," I said.

"Of course. And that puts him in the box even further. . . . We're even less likely to get the truth out of him if your theory is correct."

I agreed, but there was always the outside chance the improbable might happen. I told Liebeler that earlier that evening, I had gone to a liquor store to buy a bottle of wine. As I was leaving, I glanced in the direction of a rack of newspapers. A banner headline was partially obscured by a parked automobile, and all I could see was a portion on the right-hand side. Big black letters spelled out: . . . SURGERY.

"My God," I thought, "Humes has cracked. The story has broken!" I ran to the newsstand only to find that the complete headline read: LBJ TO UNDERGO SURGERY. President Johnson was going to Bethesda Naval Hospital for surgery on his throat and abdomen, undoubtedly a safer and more medically approved operation than "surgery of the head area."

Liebeler laughed. "And you dropped your wine bottle?"

Liebeler and I discussed credit. I said I had no objection to providing information, to helping, but it was clear now that the concept was original, that I had discovered the evidence, interpreted it, and brought it to his attention, and that I would appreciate it if, in the memorandum, he gave me at least a footnote.

Liebeler resisted. He said it would be politically unwise to have my name on the memo. Then he said, "I'm perfectly willing to indicate to you that the memorandum is the result of conversations with you and me, and that you helped draft it." Later, he softened. "I was just trying to think what the Chief Justice's reaction would be if he saw that . . . he wouldn't know who you were, and it would immediately arouse suspicion in his mind," mused Liebeler. Finally, he decided a footnote "probably wouldn't hurt." "We could put the footnote at the end," he joked, "and maybe nobody would notice it."[28] That was settled on Friday, November 4. The meeting to draft the memo was set for 10:30 Saturday morning, at Joe Ball's law offices in Beverly Hills.

The drafting session lasted almost all day. Besides Liebeler and me, three UCLA law students were present, paid research assistants whose salaries came from a ten-thousand-dollar grant Liebeler had obtained for his UCLA course. All three knew about the surgery matter, but Liebeler assured me they would "keep their mouths shut."

I came prepared with lists of topics. On each, I gave a short talk, Liebeler and his students made notes, and a lively discussion ensued. Twice, Liebeler brought up issues that were new to me.

1. Skullbone Brought to the Autopsy Room. The agreed facts were that Commander Humes could not find any evidence of exit on the skull itself; but he did find it on a bone fragment brought to the room later in the autopsy. Humes testified three pieces of bone were brought to him and one showed "beveling."

Now Liebeler made a discovery. He noted that on page 4 of their report, FBI agents Sibert and O'Neill devoted a brief paragraph to the bone-fragment incident, and their account differed from Humes'.

First, the FBI said that one bone fragment, not three, was brought to the room. It was a rather large section of the skull—the FBI reported it measured 10 by 6.5cm (4 by 2½ inches). The agents wrote that when this fragment was presented to Humes, he "was instructed that this had been removed from the President's skull."[29]

When Liebeler first read that statement, a look of perplexity crossed his face. Humes was "instructed"? By whom was he "instructed"? And why the word "removed"? Humes told the Commission he wasn't sure who brought the bone or where it came from, but it was probably found either on the street in Dallas or in the automobile. But why would anyone delivering bone found in either place "instruct" the autopsy doctor it had "been removed from the President's skull"?

The FBI statement jibed with the testimony of another autopsy eyewitness, Secret Service Agent Roy Kellerman. He used the same word in referring to the large head wound. "This was removed," Kellerman testified. Specter asked what he meant. Kellerman pointed to his own head, to where the large wound was located on the President's skull, and simply repeated: "The skull part was removed." Specter pressed further: "All right, ... [but] when you say 'removed,' by that do you mean that it was absent when you saw him, or taken off by the doctor?" Replied Kellerman: "It was absent when I saw him."[30] Specter dropped the matter.

What concerned me, and I think Liebeler, too, was not just where the bone was found, but what this FBI statement implied about Humes' knowledge on November 22. If Humes was "instructed" something had been "removed," then, on Friday night, he may have been under the impression that some kind of (presumably) legitimate surgery had been performed prior to the autopsy.

Now I was quite interested in where the bone was supposed to have come from. Initially, Humes testified the three fragments were brought from Dallas by FBI agents. Specter, apparently aware that the FBI did *not* report flying any bone from Dallas to Washington, asked, "Might that have been a Secret Service agent?"

HUMES: It could be, sir; these things—

SPECTER: At any rate, someone presented these three pieces of bone to you?

HUMES: Someone presented these three pieces of bone to me, I do not recall specifically their statement as to where they had been recovered. It seems to me they felt it had been recovered either in the street or in the automobile, I don't recall specifically.[31]

Humes' "I don't recall" was in stark contrast to the FBI's statement that Humes was "instructed" a single fragment had been "removed."

I told Liebeler the emerging picture was rather bizarre. Some time after it was noted that no evidence of exit could be found on the skull itself, an unidentified person enters the autopsy room and hands the doctor a portion of an exit wound. According to the FBI, the doctor is "instructed" this bone had "been removed." The Secret Service, however, maintains the bone came from the limousine. The doctor can't "recall" who brought it or where it came from, but it does contain the crucial evidence of exit. Whatever was needed seemed to be readily supplied, which prompted me to wonder whether there was a "spare parts" room out behind the morgue.

2. The Exit Wound in the Throat. The second matter Liebeler raised concerned how Humes arrived at the conclusion that the non-fatal shot passed back to front through Kennedy's neck. Liebeler uncovered an interesting anomaly.

Testifying before the Warren Commission, Humes said he found the following data:

1. An entry wound on the back of the neck.
2. A bruise atop the right lung and some bruising on the neck muscles.
3. A hole on the front of the neck.

Humes joined these three findings—he "connected the dots," so to speak—and concluded that a bullet passed all the way through Kennedy's body.

But according to FBI agents Sibert and O'Neill, Humes did not come to this conclusion on Friday night, at the time he examined the body. That evening, Humes associated the rear entry wound with the bullet found on a Dallas stretcher, and characterized the throat wound as simply a tracheotomy incision.[32] Yet Humes testified that at the time of the autopsy, because of the bruise atop the lung, he was "able to ascertain with absolute certainty" that the bullet had passed the apical portion of the right lung.[33]

Liebeler posed this question: If on Friday night Humes determined the bullet got as far as the top of the right lung, how could he fail to realize that the hole in the front of the throat was a bullet wound? Humes couldn't have it both ways—he couldn't maintain that on Friday night he knew "with absolute certainty" what caused the lung bruise, yet not know that the throat hole was a bullet wound until Saturday morning. In the intervening hours, before he called Perry, what did he think had become of the bullet?*

Liebeler had no answer. But such unresolved anomalies indicated the atuopsy conclusions did not flow directly from the body.

Liebeler still wanted an answer to the second question he had scribbled the previous week during our long meeting at Ball's office: "What conversations did Humes have with SS, FBI, or anyone else from 11/22—[until] he submitted the autopsy report?"

At the end of the day, Liebeler left for home with a thick folder of notes. He said he was going to spend most of the rest of the weekend drafting the memo. I should call him on Monday.

On Monday morning, he invited me to come up and see what he'd written about pre-autopsy surgery.

I was impressed. The memo proposed a legal proceeding to verify the autopsy report. Liebeler suggested that all former members of the Commission, the three autopsy doctors, FBI agents Sibert and O'Neill, the three Secret Service agents who attended the autopsy, three independent experts in forensic pathology, any former lawyers from the Commission who desired to attend, and a representative of the critics should be present at the proceeding.

"The meeting should consider the questions set forth below and any other relevant questions that might be propounded by the Commissioners or by counsel selected for this purpose."[34]

Liebeler quoted the paragraph in the Sibert and O'Neill report about head surgery and quoted the passages from Humes' testimony about brain lacerations. The memo proposed that the autopsy doctors be asked what they meant by their testimony. The memo asked: Was the President's brain preserved? If so, where was it now?

True to his word, Liebeler gave me a footnote—the memo said that

---

* Alternatively, if on Friday night Humes did not believe the bullet passed all the way through, then what did he think caused the bruise atop the lung?

the statement in the Sibert and O'Neill report had been brought to his attention by David Lifton of Los Angeles.

The rest of the memo dealt with other questions: the fragments brought to the room, precise inventories of the X-rays and photographs, and exactly how Humes arrived at the conclusion that a bullet transited the neck.*

Liebeler proposed publication of a full report of the proceedings. He said a qualified medical illustrator should be given access to the X-rays and photographs "with instructions to prepare such drawings, based on these photographs and X-rays, as may be necessary to reflect accurately the nature and extent of wounds inflicted upon the President." He proposed the drawings should "be made available to the public" and that "immediate release of the X-rays should also be considered."[37]

It seemed to me that if such a proceeding took place, and such questions asked, it would be tantamount to re-opening the investigation. An entirely new record would be created once Humes and Boswell and Finck were back under oath. The questions about pre-autopsy surgery would now be asked.

I returned to my apartment proud of the role I had played. In my mailbox was a letter from Sylvia Meagher. Anyone unacquainted with the mentality of the Warren Report critics would have thought the letter strange. For sharing my information with Liebeler, I was accused of a double cross, of an "indisputable breach of faith." It was clear from the letter I had joined her list of "accessories after the fact."

Sylvia Meagher represented the view that the Commission and its staff were conscious concealers of the truth—deliberate, criminally culpable liars.

I could no longer subscribe to that view, for it failed to take into account falsified evidence. Many critics didn't allow for that possibility. In their world, events had occurred in two stages: First, there was the murder of John F. Kennedy. Then, the Warren Commission came along and "covered it up." But if Kennedy's body was altered, then events had occurred in three, not two, stages: first, the murder; then, the erection of a disguise; and finally, the deception of the official investigation.

---

* Regarding the lung bruise, Liebeler called for a "specific examination of color photographs which were made of the contusion . . . to verify the cause of that contusion."[35] A section was devoted to Humes' Friday-night opinion. Liebeler proposed that the autopsy doctors should be asked if they ever held the opinion attributed to them by the FBI that the bullet did not transit. Liebeler noted Humes' Warren Commission testimony that he had been able to determine with "absolute certainty" that the bullet bruised the right lung. Humes should be asked "why the entrance wound in the base of the neck and the contusion . . . did not imply to him the existence of an exit wound in the anterior neck, before he spoke with Dr. Perry."[36]

* * *

Within a day of the time I first saw the draft of the memorandum, Liebeler invited me, with one or two of his research assistants, to lunch with Dr. W. Jann Brown, a UCLA pathologist. Liebeler had given Brown the autopsy report and testimony—the same materials I had given Dr. Abrams. Brown was a respected pathologist who later became chairman of the department. I expected Liebeler would get another opinion that something about the brain lacerations was strange.

We met at the cafeteria at the Medical Center and, as lunch proceeded, I became alarmed. Dr. Brown believed Lee Harvey Oswald, acting alone, assassinated the President. He didn't hide his view. He said the idea of a second assassin was "inconceivable." Brown simply brushed aside Humes' autopsy testimony about the brain laceration. "Somehow," the bullet had done all that—he wasn't specific.

At first, I said nothing. I just sat there with growing irritation. If Dr. Brown found a second assassin "inconceivable," how could he be objective as a pathologist? And I didn't think Liebeler was being fair about it. He was catering to Brown's biases—in effect assuring him that there was of course nothing wrong with the autopsy, but this minor point had arisen, and he, Liebeler, just wanted to make sure there was nothing to it.

As Brown talked, I made notes. I have them today. The bullet, said Brown, could have "roamed around in the head" and created all the lacerations described by Humes. I retorted: "But Dr. Brown, the bullet didn't 'roam around.'" I reminded him of the skull wounds. The bullet exited, I said.

Brown then made the argument that the cuts in the brain could have been caused by the fragments found in the brain. I reminded Brown that only two tiny fragments were found, the largest not more than a quarter inch long. Brown replied with what Liebeler and I came to refer to as the "spinning-fragment" argument—that if the fragment spun, like a propeller, it would present more of its cross-section, and cut a wider swath, than if it simply traveled across the brain, presenting its point. I couldn't buy that. The lacerations were much bigger than either of the two fragments, no matter what orientation one postulated as they traveled through the brain.

Finally, I said: "Dr. Brown, suppose this wasn't Wesley Liebeler. Suppose you didn't know he was with the Warren Commission. Suppose you didn't know this was the autopsy of President Kennedy. Suppose you were just given this autopsy to read. What would you think?" Brown responded it read as if the President's head were cut up by an eggbeater. At this point, one of Liebeler's students suggested that perhaps there had been some sort of legitimate life-saving surgery at Parkland Memorial Hospital that caused the long parasagittal laceration. That was too much even for Dr. Brown. A worried look crossed his face. Ridiculous, he said. Such a back-to-front cut wouldn't have any legitimacy as a life-saving procedure. Anybody who would make such a cut in the brain, while someone was alive, ought to be put in an insane asylum. Fine, I said. "But would you know whether the damage to the brain was caused by a gun, a knife, or both?"

Liebeler's behavior galled me. A typical lawyer. I had an expert who said one thing, so Liebeler had found himself an expert who said something else. That was the way to neutralize an argument before a jury, but was it the way to find the truth?

I knew I hadn't heard the last of Dr. Jann Brown.

A day or so later, Liebeler telephoned. He'd be leaving for New York with the memorandum the following day. Did I have a copy of the Sibert and O'Neill report? Yes, I did. Fine, he said, then would I mind bringing it to his office as soon as possible? He wanted to make it an attachment to the memorandum. "I think it would be more appropriate if we made a copy of the actual FBI report rather than the back of Epstein's book," he said, and burst out laughing.[38]

It was a private joke. The barn door was wide open, and the horse gone, but Liebeler wanted to avoid focusing on the futility of the situation: that such an important FBI statement completely escaped the Commission's notice, but was now available, in paperback, in every supermarket and drugstore in America. Wesley Liebeler couldn't turn back the clock, but he could adopt the format of the past: the staff memorandum. As though it was January 1964 and the report had just come in from J. Edgar Hoover, Wesley Liebeler was pointing out to the Chief Justice, Rankin, and the others, that the Sibert and O'Neill FBI report ("see attached") contained an important allegation deserving further investigation.

Then Liebeler told me something else. "I changed the memorandum a little bit," he began. "I took out the reference to the Humes testimony," he said, referring to the three brain lacerations. I stiffened. So that was the result of the Jann Brown meeting, I thought. Then, in the same breath, Liebeler threw me a bone. He had decided to put considerably more emphasis on the FBI statement, and I was no longer a footnote. Liebeler read the complete passage. It was point 5:

"The photographs and x-rays should be used to determine the validity of the following statement set forth in the Sibert and O'Neal [*sic*] Report:

Following the removal of the wrapping (from the President's body), it was ascertained that the President's clothing had been removed and it was also apparent that a tracheotomy had been performed, *as well as surgery of the head area, namely, in the top of the skull* [emphasis added].

"In this connection, it should be noted that no surgery was performed at Parkland Hospital in the area of the President's head.

"Attention was first drawn to the above statement by Mr. David Lifton of Los Angeles. Mr. Lifton is quite familiar with the Report and the underlying evidence. He has agreed not to focus public attention on this matter until an attempt has been made to effect a responsible analysis of the autopsy photographs and x-rays to determine whether or not the Sibert and O'Neal [sic] report is accurate. In assessing the probable public reaction to the statement concerning surgery in the President's head area, it should be noted that neither the Sibert and O'Neal [sic] report nor the comment about head surgery is set forth or discussed anywhere in the Report or the twenty-six volumes of underlying evidence."[39]

I was surprised by Liebeler's statement that I had "agreed not to focus public attention" on the issue. He seemed to be using our informal agreement to pressure others to act.

Liebeler's emphasis also surprised me. The memo didn't say: If the body was altered, our findings are based on an invalid autopsy. It stressed the "probable public reaction" when the public learned of this FBI statement, as if my discovery had created a public relations problem, not raised a serious question of faked evidence.

Liebeler asked if I could come by his office. "I want you to look at the memorandum before I leave, and I want to tell you what I plan to do. I want to make sure that you're happy, and still, and quiet, for the period that I'm gone, so that I can get a chance to work this thing out with Marshall and the Commission. We both know the importance of this thing being kept quiet . . . because once it gets out then we lose all our thrust, all the chance we've got to get access to the pictures."[40]

I knew what worried Liebeler—my connection with *Ramparts*. It was *Ramparts'* heyday. Each month's issue featured a muckraking article, heralded by a barrage of publicity which made it page one news. Liebeler was impressed. He knew I had spent the previous summer writing an article on the medical evidence, which had not yet appeared. Now he worried that with a single phone call to Warren Hinckle, *Ramparts* would be making national headlines with a story that Kennedy's body was altered.

To prod Liebeler into acting, I deliberately fostered these fears. But it was all a bluff. The irony was that Wesley Liebeler had given me a far more sympathetic hearing than the so-called "radicals" running *Ramparts*. Warren Hinckle and Robert Scheer simply did not take the assassination seriously as an issue. And since Hinckle worried about publishing an article alleging that three persons shot at Kennedy, in my wildest dreams I couldn't imagine sitting down with him and saying: It's actually more complex than that, Warren. They altered the body." Hinckle would have thrown me out of the office. In November 1966 the idea was just plain unbelievable. But not to Wesley Liebeler. Liebeler understood the possibilities, and the implications. And he was going on record with the Chief Justice.

Liebeler said when I came by his office, would I please bring with me a large aerial photograph for him, so he could illustrate the location of the knoll on a TV program in New York. He also told me he was going to stop by Dallas, en route, to look at the knoll. "I never really gave it much thought," he said. Now he wanted to walk around there, walk into the railroad yards, get the smell of the place. But he was worried that the press would see him down there. WARREN COMMISSION FINALLY GOES TO DALLAS, he laughed. What a headline. He also said that while in New York, he would speak with John McCloy.

Before getting off the phone, Liebeler reminded me I had promised to do him a favor. I was supposed to buy him an attachment for his recorder, so he could tape the conversations we were having. "Get a good one," he said.

At Liebeler's office, I saw the memo for the first time. The page with Humes' descriptions of the brain lacerations had a big "X" across it. What a pity. The problem with the FBI statement, standing alone, was that it wasn't clear what "surgery of the head area" meant. The combination of the FBI statement and Humes' testimony about the brain lacerations was much more powerful.

I tried to see it from Liebeler's point of view. The statements about the lacerations were subject to interpretation. It was one expert versus another. The Sibert and O'Neill report was in plain English. The words were there—in black and white. So in a way, Liebeler had made the memo less vulnerable.

I wondered what the other Commissioners and the Kennedys would think when they saw the memo. And I still wondered whether it wasn't necessary to spell out the implications—how head surgery could reconcile the head snap, the grassy knoll, the conflict between Dallas and Bethesda "for those too dumb to add," as I had said to Liebeler on the phone. "That's in the memorandum, I think," he said. "I talk about the Zapruder film." Yes, he did, but it wasn't explicit, and that bothered me. Nowhere did Liebeler bluntly say: "A body is evidence. John Kennedy's body is evidence. If someone altered that body, our entire investigation was structured on false evidence."

Something else had vanished. Gone was Liebeler's explicit question: Where is the brain today? Instead, without specifying the context, Liebeler asked: "Has any other physical evidence developed in connection with the examination conducted by the autopsy surgeons been preserved? If so, where is it located?" Why was Liebeler being so coy?

Something else. Despite Liebeler's surprised reaction at the drafting session to the FBI statement that Humes was "instructed" bone had "been removed," he completely omitted that from the memo.

But this wasn't a time to argue. The memo was just a start. If a legal proceeding was convened, there would be plenty of time to lobby, to see that the right questions were asked. This was merely a foot in the door. Could the door be pushed open?

Liebeler left for Dallas and New York, and I plunged ahead with my own research. Next on my list was a letter to FBI Headquarters following up my phone call to FBI Agent Sibert. I addressed it to J. Edgar Hoover.

"Dear Sir," it began, "Last week, I contacted FBI Agent James W. Sibert, Jr., by phone where he was vacationing in Georgia." Sibert, I noted, was one of two FBI agents at the autopsy, and he and Agent Francis O'Neill made a report. I quoted the passage that when the coffin was opened, it was "apparent" there had been a tracheotomy "as well as surgery of the head area, namely, in the top of the skull." I underlined the statement, as Liebeler had in the memo. "My question was," I continued, "precisely what did these two agents . . . witness which enabled them to make this statement? . . . Did one of the autopsy doctors present . . . point out that head surgery had been done on the President? . . . If the agents . . . did not rely on any doctor's statement . . . what direct observations or other criteria enabled them to make this statement?"[41]

I said Agent Sibert stated that he could not discuss the matter with me, and suggested I write to FBI Headquarters. I deliberately omitted Sibert's comment, "the report stands." I had heard of Hoover's wrath, and knew that if I indicated Sibert had made any response whatsoever, it could lead to disciplinary action. FBI Agent James Hosty, in charge of the Oswald file at the Dallas office, was reprimanded and given a disciplinary transfer for talking out of turn to the Dallas Police. Liebeler often joked that Sibert and O'Neill would soon be joining Hosty—"somewhere in Alaska."*

I concluded my letter by noting that Sibert and O'Neill presumably knew the basis for the statement about surgery, and suggested they be questioned in formulating a reply.

I dated my letter November 9, 1966, posted it, and then turned to the next piece of unfinished business: interviewing the remaining Dallas doctors about the length of the tracheotomy incision.

---

* Hosty was transferred to Kansas City.

CHAPTER 11

The Tracheotomy Incision: Dallas vs. Bethesda

DR. PERRY'S STATEMENT to the press on November 22 that the hole in the front of Kennedy's throat was an entry wound was the most widely publicized evidence of a grassy-knoll shooter.

It was easy to visualize such a shooter trying to hide his existence by running away afterward. But I now realized that the simple act of widening the bullet hole on the body and extracting the bullet could permanently banish such a shooter from the most important historical record of the event—the President's body.

Once that happened, it wouldn't matter what Dr. Perry said. The body itself would be cited as evidence that no such shooter existed, that Perry was wrong.

My call to Dr. Perry had provided me with the first concrete evidence that someone enlarged the incision he had made before the body reached the autopsy table. Perry had said "2–3cm," which contrasted with Humes' "7–8cm." What would the other doctors say?

The first person to see President Kennedy was Dr. Charles Carrico. Although it was Dr. Perry's tracheotomy incision which made headlines around the world, it was Dr. Carrico, then completing his residency in surgery, who first attempted resuscitation, inserting an endotracheal tube directly into the mouth and down the throat, then withdrawing the tube later as Perry performed the tracheotomy. Carrico, I thought, must have had a clear view of the entire tracheotomy operation.

On November 8, 1966, I telephoned him, introducing myself as a UCLA graduate student attending a legal seminar held by "Professor Wesley Liebeler, who was on the Warren Commission." I told him I was doing a paper on the tracheotomy operation.

"Dr. Perry testified that he made this incision in the neck . . . you were there when this happened. Correct?"

"Right."

"Could you tell me approximately the length of the tracheotomy incision that was made?"

"Gee. It's been a while. Probably—it would just be a guess—between two and three centimeters, which is close to an inch."

"Between two and three centimeters?"

"Yes."

I asked: "Do you think the incision that Dr. Perry made might have been, let's say, four centimeters?"

Replied Carrico: "Oh, I really don't know. But it, that would probably be the upper limit. I doubt if it was that large."

As with Perry, the confident tone of Dr. Carrico carried the message that he did not need more than an inch to insert a tracheotomy tube.

The next doctor was Charles Baxter, who assisted Perry with the tracheotomy.

I posed the question:

LIFTON: Now, about what was the length of the incision?

BAXTER: Oh, it's roughly an inch and a half.

LIFTON: . . . you could see the incision before they placed the tracheotomy tube into the incision?

BAXTER: Oh, yes. Yes.

LIFTON: So at that time you remember it as being an inch and a half [3.8cm]?

BAXTER: Yeah, roughly.[1]

The assassination, I commented, was three years before. How sure was he of the details? "It's pretty vivid," replied Baxter, adding: "It's such a common operation that it's just standard. I think he probably had the most standard of standard operations . . . you do exactly what you're trained to do . . . if it wasn't standard, I don't know what it would have been."

Besides asking each doctor about the incision length, I also sought his reaction to an 8cm (3.2in) incision.

I asked Jenkins: "Do you think the incision could have been three and a quarter inches?" "No, I don't think so," he replied.[2]

Dr. Carrico responded: "Jiminy Christmas. How big is eight centimeters?" "Three and a quarter inches," I replied (actually it is 3.2 inches). Replied Carrico: "It would be certainly the exception. It would have to be an unusual circumstance."[3]

Carrico asked me if the autopsy report gave the incision length, but I dodged the question.

I asked Baxter if he ever made tracheotomy incisions that were three inches long: "No, we seldom do. You don't need that much."[4]

Dr. Peters told me of his most vivid recollection. The incision had been made when he walked into the room, and Dr. Perry had one, possibly two, fingers in it. Quantifying his recollection of length was difficult. Dr. Peters estimated: "With two fingers, there's about, well, an inch and three quarters . . . at most, it was two inches."[5]

In the course of my inquiries about length, I developed some contrary data, and evidence that doctors at Parkland were discussing my calls.

The problem first arose with McClelland. I had trouble reaching him, and had to leave my name. When I did reach him, I had the feeling he was anticipating what I was going to ask. When I came to the question of incision length, his reply agreed exactly with Dr. Humes' testimony: "In centimeters, that would be something like eight centimeters, seven or eight centimeters."[6] I asked McClelland whether he thought that was the usual length of a tracheotomy. McClelland, a professor of surgery at Parkland Memorial Hospital, replied: "That's about the usual length, uh huh."[7] McClelland then admitted he had heard about Liebeler and his course. Curious to see just how far McClelland would go to allay my suspicions, I asked: "Would you say that if eight [centimeters] is the normal size, would you say they sometimes run up to, let's say, ten to twelve centimeters?" (Twelve centimeters is 4.8 inches.)

"Oh, they might. They might," replied Professor McClelland. "You just make whatever's necessary to get into the neck. And it's conceivable that in certain people with rather short stocky necks, that you might have to make an incision that large a size."[8]

Try as I might, I found it difficult to imagine having to make a tracheotomy incision nearly five inches long to get into someone's neck. I concluded that Dr. McClelland, whose statements about the throat wound being an entry had received such widespread publicity, did not wish to become further embroiled in the assassination controversy.

Dr. Jones was the only other doctor who gave me an answer that agreed with Humes' testimony: "Probably two and a half or three inches, somewhere along in there. . . ."[9] He also told me that Dr. McClelland had told him I had called and asked about the length of the incision.

During these interviews, another criterion for estimating the incision length arose. Dr. Carrico explained that a tracheotomy tube had a flange— a piece of material perpendicular to the tube, that permits the tube to "sit" on the patient's neck. To keep the tube in place, straps from the flange are often tied around the neck. Carrico suggested that I determine what kind of tracheotomy tube was used and measure the flange. If the incision didn't extend beyond the flange, that would provide at least an upper limit. Dr. Carrico said he had no recollection of whether this particular incision extended beyond the flanges, but that normally it didn't. I decided to ask this question of the remaining doctors on my list.

Dr. Baxter said he didn't think the incision could be seen beyond the flange, whose width he estimated at 1¼ inches, at most.[10] Jenkins didn't know.[11] McClelland said the incision did extend from the flange.[12] Jones, who had talked with McClelland, said the same thing.[13] Dr. Akin, who had given me a 2½-inch incision estimate, was nevertheless emphatic that the incision would not show beyond the flange. "Tracheotomy tubes are far too wide for an incision to be showing beyond that, unless an unreasonably large incision has been made."[14]

What, then, was the flange size on the tracheotomy tube used on President Kennedy? The tube was not saved, but Dr. Baxter told me it was definitely a plastic one, and it was either a number seven, eight, or nine. I checked a medical catalog and found the maximum width was 4cm.*

My flange-length research corroborated the estimates I received from Drs. Perry and Carrico that the tracheotomy incision was "2–3cm" long.

As I continued studying the autopsy data, I discovered two facts.

I had assumed that Humes' statements about incision length, under oath before the Commission, were the same as those he made in the autopsy report. Now I found a difference. The incision, Humes testified, was "some 7 or 8cm in length," but Humes wrote in the autopsy report that the length was 6.5cm.[15] Was that significant?

Then I made a second discovery. The relevant sentence read: "Situated in the low anterior neck at approximately the level of the third and fourth tracheal rings is a 6.5cm long transverse wound with widely gaping irregular edges."[16]

". . . widely gaping irregular edges?"

A tracheotomy incision, made with a scalpel, should be a slit. Its edges might gape, but they certainly ought not to be "widely gaping." As for "irregular," I wasn't sure what Humes meant by that word. If he meant "serrated," the word could not refer to the incision Perry made. Perry used a scalpel, not a saw. "Widely gaping irregular edges" didn't conjure up the image of a slit.

My data regarding length was fragile. It depended upon the recollections of the Dallas doctors. The information regarding edges depended only on whether the scalpel used by Perry could leave the edges described by Humes. I was tempted to call Perry and the others I had interviewed to ask about the incision edges, but I couldn't bring myself to do it. My questioning regarding incision length probably seemed strange enough; if

---

* In 1973, Parkland Memorial Hospital was renovating the emergency room area, and offered to sell the National Archives implements used in the emergency room—not *the* implements used on November 22, 1963. One item provided was a plastic tracheotomy tube. At my request, the Archivist measured the flange length. It was 1¼ inches long (1¼ inches is 3.1 centimeters).

I now called back and asked for more details, it would only increase suspicion. But I did have three interviews left.

Dr. McClelland goaded me into asking the question with his talk of a 7–8cm incision as being "usual." I asked him about the edges:

LIFTON: . . . Could you tell me, if you were going to describe the edges of the incision, do you have any idea . . . were they smooth edges? Was it a smooth incision?

MCCLELLAND: Well . . . as I say, when I got there, the incision had been made; and according to Dr. Perry's statement to me as I walked in the room, the first thing he said to me was that there was a wound in the neck, through which he had made the incision. Just as an extension of this wound . . . So I actually did not see the edges of the tracheotomy where it had extended it. *And it was smooth*, uh, since it was made, of course, with a knife [emphasis added].[17]

A few days later, I talked with Dr. Peters:

LIFTON: In what words would you best describe the edges of that incision?

PETERS: Oh, I guess "sharp."

LIFTON: Sharp?

PETERS: Yeah.

LIFTON: In other words, because it was made with a knife by a surgeon?

PETERS: That's right. It was a fairly neat incision, pretty close to the midline.[18]

Dr. Jones used the same word: "sharp."[19]

Now I had information indicating that two characteristics of that wound—length and condition of the edges—changed between Dallas and Bethesda. The two factors were mutually reinforcing, and the implication was clear. If that wound was altered, someone had tampered with evidence of a grassy-knoll shooter, and the proof was engraved on President Kennedy's body.

I went over the argument step by step, looking for loopholes.

Dr. Carrico testified the throat wound was "5–8mm in size."[20] Dr. Perry testified it was "roughly 5mm in size or so."[21] When Humes spoke with Perry by telephone on Saturday morning, he made notes. The throat wound, according to those notes, was "only a few mm. in size 3–5mm."*[22] Dr. Baxter estimated its size as "4–5mm in widest diameter."[24] So, "roughly 5mm"—about ¼ inch—was part of the record, and nobody challenged

* Apparently referring to his conversation with Humes, Dr. Perry testified to the same numbers again; but the printed transcript erroneously shows "cm." (centimeters) instead of "mm." (millimeters). As published, Perry's testimony reads: "I recall describing it initially as being between 3 and 5cm in size and roughly spherical in shape . . ."[23] A wound 5cm across would be 2 inches wide.

that number. Even while concluding the small hole was an exit, the Warren Commission never disputed the Dallas doctors' size estimates.

Another factor. Dr. Perry, upon seeing Kennedy, immediately noticed that at exactly the spot where one normally does a tracheotomy was a small hole in the neck. He testified: "I asked Dr. Carrico if this was a wound in his neck or had he begun the tracheotomy. . . ."[25] That Perry even entertained the idea that a 5mm wound (5mm is ½cm) might be a tracheotomy incision seemed an indication of how small an incision he normally made. Perry continued: ". . . and he [Dr. Carrico] said it was a wound and I, at that point, asked someone to get me a tracheotomy tray, and put on some gloves and initiated the procedure."[26] Perry testified: "I then began the tracheotomy [by] making a transverse incision right through the wound in the neck."[27] Perry then pushed aside strands of muscle and fat, exposing the trachea itself; he then incised the trachea's forward surface and inserted the tube.

Supposedly, Humes received the body in just this condition—at the front of the throat was a small hole, cut across by a horizontal, 2–3mm incision. Yet Humes reported the wound was 6.5cm long, with "widely gaping irregular edges."

Could these two descriptions be reconciled?

I could think of only one explanation: that the edges of the bullet wound were the source of the "widely gaping irregular edges" described by Humes. I analyzed the Dallas doctors' descriptions closely. Dr. Carrico: "fairly round, had no jagged edges";[28] Dr. Perry: "rather clean cut";[29] Dr. Baxter: "did not appear to be a jagged wound";[30] Dr. Jones: "relatively smooth edges,"[31] "a very small, smooth wound";[32] Dr. McClelland: "minimal tissue damage surrounding it on the skin."[33]

Moreover, the bullet wound itself was only 5mm across. Consequently, only 5mm of the transverse wound Humes described—i.e., bullet wound plus tracheotomy incision—could have any raggedness. The rest, supposedly, was made with Perry's scalpel. Since five millimeters is only half a centimeter, a very small portion of the transverse wound—considerably less than 10 percent—included the original bullet wound, and so might show some raggedness.* I found it difficult to believe that Commander Humes would describe a 6.5cm horizontal slit, containing a small irregularity at the center, as a 6.5cm wound with "widely gaping irregular edges,"[34] and testify that it was "no longer at all obvious as a missile wound."**[35]

---

* For example, if the wound was 5mm—taking Dr. Perry's maximum figure—and the transverse wound was 6.5cm (Dr. Humes' minimum number), then the wound would show some raggedness along only 7.7 percent of its length.

** Another difference between Dallas and Bethesda observations concerned the exact location of the cut. Dr. Baxter testified: "Our tracheotomy incision was made

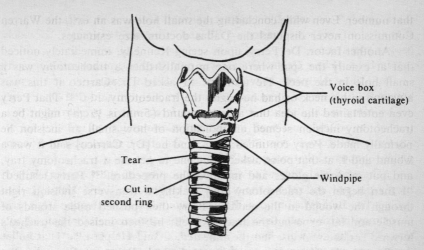

**Voice box
(thyroid cartilage)**

Windpipe

Tear

**Cut in
second ring**

Figure 19.
Diagram of President Kennedy's neck after tracheotomy

Similar considerations applied to the insertion and retrieval of a tracheotomy tube, which was little more than 1cm wide. Doctors told me no skin tearing or tissue loss occurred by its insertion and retrieval, and the edges of the incision could simply be pushed back against one another after the tube was withdrawn. But that would be rather difficult if the incision was in the condition described by Humes.

---

in the second tracheal ring."[36] The autopsy report described a defect "at approximately the level of the third and fourth tracheal rings."[37] (See Fig. 19.)

This difference in descriptions was related, in turn, to how much of the trachea was damaged by the bullet, how much was removed by Dr. Perry, and whether additional cutting took place before the body was seen by Humes.

Dr. Perry testified there was an injury to the right lateral wall of the trachea.[38] Dr. Baxter testified that the tracheotomy tube "was placed into the trachea . . . below this tear in the trachea."[39] With regard to the damaged area of the trachea, he further stated: "We did not dissect [it] out."[40]

If so, and if the tracheotomy tube was inserted below the original tracheal injury, there should have been two separate tracheal defects at the time of autopsy. One would be where the tracheotomy had been incised to receive the tube; the other, the site of the original tracheal injury.

At Bethesda, Dr. Humes reported but one defect in the trachea. He testified: ". . . I am unable to say how much of the defect in the trachea was made by the knife of the surgeon, and how much of the defect was made by the missile wound."[41] Humes' testimony was inconsistent with Baxter's testimony: "We did not dissect [it] out."[42]

Humes' testimony suggested to me that in the course of widening the wound, the two defects in the trachea became one.

I couldn't get over the contrast between Dallas and Bethesda: ". . . sharp . . . a fairly neat incision . . ."[43] and "smooth,"[44] versus ". . . widely gaping irregular edges."[45]

In 1968, *Where Death Delights* was published, an authorized biography of Dr. Milton Helpern, New York City Medical Examiner and a man known as the father of forensic medicine. Dr. Helpern said that Dr. Perry's tracheotomy incision should not have interfered with a proper determination of the wound, and took the Warren Commission to task for implying the bullet wound "was obliterated,"[46] that the tracheotomy had "completely eliminated that evidence."[47]

"The staff members who wrote that portion of the [Warren] Report simply did not understand their medical procedures," said Helpern, who quoted the Bethesda autopsy that the wound was "extended as a tracheostomy incision and thus its character is distorted at the time of autopsy."[48] "The key word here is '*extended*,'" said Helpern.[49] "That bullet wound was not 'eliminated' or 'obliterated' at all. What Dr. Perry did was to take his scalpel and cut a clean slit away from the wound. He didn't excise it, or cut away any huge amount or tissue, as the [Warren] Report writer would have you believe."[50]

Dr. Helpern's opinion was based on what a tracheotomy normally consists of, and on what the Bethesda doctors ought to have found. Helpern explained that by pushing the incision edges against one another, the original outline of the wound would have been revealed. "It should have been studied, and finally photographed," he said, obviously annoyed that three pathologists—one a forensic pathologist—hadn't done such a simple thing.[51]

In 1969, at the Shaw trial, Dr. Pierre Finck was asked why the autopsy surgeons had not "reconstructed" the wound. "I examined this surgical wound," replied Finck, "and I did not see the small wound described by the Dallas surgeons along that surgical incision. I did not see it."[52] He said: "I examined both edges of the surgeon's surgical incision. . . . a very close gross examination. . . . I did not see that wound in the front . . . I don't know why it is not there."[53]

Dr. Finck's testimony suggested to me that additional cutting may have taken place after the Dallas tracheotomy.

Dr. Humes' description raised still another question: How could two pathologists call something a "surgical incision" which had "widely gaping irregular edges?"

Certainly Perry created no such thing. But if Perry didn't, who did?

The original impetus for my inquiries into the size and shape of the tracheotomy incision was: If a bullet entered from the front, where did it go, and why wasn't it present at the autopsy?

Only the Bethesda doctors examined the interior of the body. Now I asked: What parts were within reach of that wound, and was there evidence that a bullet had lodged inside?

In November 1966, when I first asked this question, I was amazed to realize the potential significance of Commander Humes' detailed exposition about a bruise atop the right lung. It was another fact in public view I had hardly noticed before.

The autopsy report stated: "A 5cm diameter area of purplish red discoloration and increased firmness to palpation is situated in the apical portion of the right upper lobe."[54] Humes testified: "The area of discoloration . . . was wedge shaped in configuration, with its base toward the top of the chest and its apex down toward the substance of the lung."[*55]

I re-examined the Dallas doctors' testimony about their attempts to resuscitate the President. Those accounts provided evidence that a bullet had entered the chest—indeed, it was clear that that was where a number of doctors thought a bullet had lodged.

Dr. Carrico, using a laryngoscope, closely examined the President's windpipe. He reported that on the right side of the trachea was a ragged tear. Carrico inserted a tube into the windpipe, via the mouth. At the end of the tube was an inflatable cuff, which, Carrico testified: "should prevent leakage of air around the tube, thus insuring an adequate airway."[57] Carrico positioned the cuff below the tracheal injury, and inflated it.

Had the only wound to Kennedy's respiratory system been this hole in the trachea, then Carrico's procedure would have been sufficient. It wasn't. Carrico testified: "After the endotracheal tube was inserted and connected, I listened briefly to his chest, respirations were better but still inadequate." He said: "Breath sounds were diminished, especially on the right."[58] It appeared that there was another hole somewhere in the President's respiratory system.

At this point, Dr. Perry arrived, and decided a tracheotomy was in order. Performing this operation, Perry observed signs that the President's right lung might be punctured.

One symptom was a deviated trachea. Dr. Perry testified: "The trachea was noted to be deviated slightly to the left."[59] A deviated trachea could be a sign of a collapsed lung. Another indicator was frothing blood—blood with air bubbles—associated with the wound. Dr. Peters described a "bubbling" sensation in the chest.[60] Dr. Jones said that as Perry did the tracheotomy, there was a "gush of air."[61] And Dr. Marion Jenkins talked of "the obvious physical characteristics of a pneumothorax."[62]

Dr. Perry testified he noticed "both . . . free blood and air in the right

---

* It is somewhat out of sequence to mention this here, but Humes testified: "Once again Kodachrome photographs were made of this area in the interior of the President's chest."[56] No such photographs are in the official collection at the National Archives.

superior mediastinum. That is the space that is located between the lungs and the heart at that level." He continued: "I did not see any underlying injury of the pleura, the coverings of the lungs, or of the lungs themselves. But in the presence of this large amount of blood in this area, one would be unable to detect small injuries to the underlying structures. The air was indicated by the fact that there was some frothing of this blood present, bubbling which could have been due to the tracheal injury or an underlying injury to the lung."[63] To relieve this condition, Perry asked that chest tubes be inserted.*

For all these reasons, then—the torn, deviated trachea, the inadequate respirations, especially on the right, and the free blood and air in the chest cavity—several Dallas doctors believed there was chest damage.

The Dallas doctors' record made clear that some of them thought a bullet from the front lodged in the chest. The *New York Times* quoted Dr. Clark as saying the shot struck at the level of the necktie knot, and that it "ranged downward in his chest and did not exit."**[66] Dr. Marion Jenkins testified that although he now believed the wound of the neck was an exit, he had changed his original opinion. "The first day I had thought because of his pneumothorax, that . . . one bullet must have traversed his pleura, must have gotten into his lung cavity, his chest cavity, I mean, and from what you say now [speaking to Specter, who told Jenkins of the autopsy findings] I know it did not go that way. I thought it did."[68]

The Dallas opinions were based upon observations of the President in his agonal moments, and made a suggestive contrast with the Bethesda data about the lung bruise. Nothing proved the bruise must have been made by a bullet which lodged there and had been removed. The bruise was simply one item in a pattern of circumstantial evidence.

* Dr. Clark testified: "It was the assumption, based on the previously described deviation of the trachea and the presence of blood in the strap muscles of the neck, that a wound or missile wound might have entered the President's chest."[64]

  SPECTER: Well, what was there, Dr. Clark, in the deviation of the trachea and the presence of blood in the strap muscles of the neck which so indicated?
  CLARK: Assuming that a missile had entered the pleural space, if there had been bleeding into the pleural space, the trachea would have been deviated or had there been leakage of air into the pleural space, the trachea would have been deviated, as it is the main conduit of air to the two lungs. Collapse of a lung would have produced, or will produce deviation of the trachea. There being a wound in the throat, there being blood in the strap muscles and there being deviation of the trachea . . . Dr. Perry assumed that the findings in the neck were due to penetration of the missile into the chest. For this reason, he requested chest tubes to be placed.[65]

** Clark denied this quote before the Warren Commission, but he did testify that, initially, Dr. Perry "felt that the missile had entered the President's chest."[67]

280

Humes didn't ignore the lung bruise. He simply interpreted it differently. To Humes, the bruise was evidence a bullet passed through the body; it was an internal injury "connecting" the rear entry with the wound at the front. But I now realized that same bruise, combined with evidence the throat wound was enlarged, could also mean a bullet fired from the front had lodged there and been removed. That, in turn, would explain why the small, smooth tracheotomy incision metamorphized into a large hole with "widely gaping irregular edges."

And the bruise also provided the answer to yet another puzzle.

The rear point of entry was not observed at Parkland Memorial Hospital, and I had postulated it was man-made. Maybe that was why it was so shallow—Finck testified its depth was "the first fraction of an inch"[69] —why the clothing holes didn't match the body hole, and why Humes referred to it as "presumably of entry." Initially, I assumed the purpose of any such man-made puncture was to deceive the autopsy surgeon about the nature of the wound at the front. But there was a problem with this theory. A frontal entry would leave a bullet inside the body, a bullet the autopsy doctor would easily see on an X-ray. Consequently, the creation of a false rear entry seemed insufficient to fool the autopsy doctor about the nature of the throat wound.

Now that problem disappeared. If, in conjunction with the creation of a false rear entry, the throat wound was enlarged and a bullet extracted, the result would be a "matching" pair of wounds and no bullet inside the body. This "pairing," and the absence of a bullet inside the body, would create the appearance that whatever went in the back must have gone out the front. The direction of the shot would have been reversed.

It was just a theory, but my conversations with the Dallas doctors started me thinking along these lines. The wounds must be viewed as pairs. On a cadaver, two wounds determine a gunshot trajectory just as, in geometry, two points determine a straight line.

Humes' drawings showed Kennedy's body pierced by two arrows— one trajectory through the head; another through the neck. President Kennedy had two *pairs* of wounds.

Looking at the wounds in pairs provided a meaningful way of correlating alterations made at the front with the sudden appearance at Bethesda of an entrance wound at the rear. By altering the wounds in pairs, an entire trajectory could be fabricated before the autopsy even began.

Another point: If a frontal entry was enlarged in order to remove a bullet, the act of removing the bullet was tantamount to the creation of circumstantial evidence that the frontal wound *must* have been an exit. The logic of paired wounds was simple: Bullets don't disappear. If there was an entry at the rear, and no bullet inside, the bullet must have passed all the way through and come out the front.

How this logic worked during the autopsy on Kennedy's body, which contained no bullets, was vividly illustrated in the Shaw trial testimony of Colonel Finck. Finck described the situation on Friday night, when the available data included a rear point of entry, and before the doctors learned that the tracheotomy incision had been made over a bullet wound: "I have to base my interpretation on all the facts available and not on one fact only. When you have a wound of entry in the back of the neck and no wound of exit at the time of autopsy, [and] when the X-rays I requested showed no bullets in the cadaver of the President, you need some other information to know where the bullet went . . . that bullet has to be somewhere. . . ."[70]

Dr. Finck explained that the information received from Dallas that there was another bullet wound caused all the facts to fall into place: ". . . I was puzzled by having a definite entry in the back, a bruise in the pleural region, that is the region of the cavity of the chest . . . and the three of us . . . we saw that bruise, and the following day knowing that a small wound had been seen in the front of the neck, that made very much sense to me: an entry in the back, a wound in the front and a bruise in between due to the passage of the bullet."[71]

This episode taught me a lesson: At an autopsy, individual facts are not interpreted out of context, but are affected by the presence of other facts. The lung bruise, the wounds, the absence of bullets—all these were medical "facts" on the body of John F. Kennedy. And their medical interpretation was determined by the pattern they *appeared* to create when considered in relationship to one another.

In his memorandum, Wesley Liebeler raised an important question about the lung bruise. Since on Friday night the doctors observed the rear entry wound as well as the lung bruise, why didn't those two pieces of information, by themselves, imply the existence of a bullet wound at the site of what they were calling a tracheotomy incision? How could the doctors claim they didn't know a bullet exited from the front until Saturday morning, when they were told there was a bullet wound at the front of the neck?

At the Shaw trial, Colonel Finck testified he was "puzzled" at the combination of a "definite entry" in the back, a bruise in the lung, but no corresponding exit. Finck's account may be an understatement; the FBI reported that the doctors were "at a loss to explain why they could find no bullets."[72]

Surely Finck's puzzlement increased upon learning that underneath the so-called tracheotomy incision was a bullet wound. Although that solved one problem, it raised another: Why wasn't the wound seen? Dr. Finck testified about the matter as if disappearing wounds were just one of those unusual occurrences that sometimes plague an autopsy: "I don't know why it is not there." In his Warren Commission testimony, Humes was almost apologetic about it.*

The question inevitably arises—it certainly preoccupied me—as to what the autopsy doctors thought as they examined the body and encountered such anomalies.

I realized their exact state of mind might never be known, but the issue would not go away. It came up again when I began analyzing the possibility that the back-to-front neck trajectory might have been artificially created. If so, the rear point of entry had to have been fabricated.

No one at Parkland Memorial Hospital reported seeing a back wound. This included the doctors (who never turned the body over) as well as those who washed the body and placed it in the coffin. At first, the fact that no one there mentioned a back wound was my main, though admittedly thin, evidence it was fabricated afterward. Then, after interviewing the Dallas doctors, I found the following passage in Dr. Perry's testimony about the two telephone calls he received from Commander Humes on Saturday morning, November 23: ". . . he asked me at that time if we had made any wounds in the back."[74]

The record went no further. Dr. Humes did not explain his question. Like the FBI statement about surgery, his query lay unnoticed in the public record.

Humes' question to Perry caused me to review in detail the basis in the evidence for the commonly accepted conclusion that President Kennedy was struck from behind, that a back wound really existed in Dallas. The major physical evidence, aside from the wound, were the holes in the shirt and jacket. I had no way of proving those clothing holes were false. All I could do was draw the obvious inference. If the back wound was false, then someone must have made those holes before the clothes reached the FBI Laboratory.**

---

* MCCLOY: May I ask this: In spite of the incision made by the tracheotomy, was there any evidence left of the exit aperture?
HUMES: Unfortunately not that we could ascertain, sir.
MCCLOY: I see.[73]

** The first detailed information about the size of those holes was published in 1979, in the House Assassinations Committee report, based on measurements made by the Committee's own panel of experts. The jacket hole, described as elliptical, was measured at 1.5cm by 1cm.[75] The shirt hole, also elliptical, was measured at 1.2cm by 0.8cm.[76]

The Carcano bullet was 6.5mm in diameter. Translating these dimensions to areas (using the formula for an ellipse), the jacket hole was 117.75 sq. mm, and the shirt hole was 75.36 sq. mm. The bullet's cross-section was 33.17 sq. mm. Thus, the

The Secret Service had the clothing. The Secret Service and navy officials had the body.

Going through the evidence one item at a time, I now realized I had forgotten something important: One Dallas eyewitness did mention the back wound—Secret Service Agent Glenn Bennett. In his report, Bennett claimed he saw the bullet strike.

Bennett was seated in the right rear of the followup car, directly behind Kennedy aide Dave Powers, and he pinpointed the impact point with precision: "about four inches down from the right shoulder."[78] It was a quote I knew by heart, because in constructing the case against the downward-slanting neck trajectory required by the single-bullet theory, Bennett was one of the critics' favorites: a witness who placed the wound "low," corroborating the clothing holes, not "high" in the neck, as stated in the navy autopsy. But my concern was different—not whether the wound was several inches one way or another, but whether it was there at all!

I took a closer look at Bennett's statement: ". . . I heard what sounded like a firecracker. I immediately looked from the right . . . and looked toward the President who was seated in the right rear seat. . . . At the moment I looked at the back of the President I heard another firecracker noise and saw the shot hit the President about four inches down from the right shoulder."[79]

Bennett stressed the fact that he was looking at the President, right "at the back" when the shot struck. Bennett's statement was corroboration for the autopsy. I had never viewed it in that light.

I began to wonder. Could a person see a bullet strike dark clothing at about fifty feet? Was that plausible? Was Bennett's view obstructed by Dave Powers, seated in front of him? And by Agent Emory Roberts, sitting in front of Powers? How had Bennett managed to see something no one else saw? Which way were they all facing?

Mentally, I ran through the pictures which might show Bennett. Two came to mind. One was Willis slide 5, taken from the rear, and corresponding to Zapruder frame 202, within one second of when the non-fatal shot struck. Another was the Altgens picture, taken from the front, about three seconds later, after the shot, and corresponding to Zapruder frame 255.

---

coat hole was 3.55 times as large as the bullet's cross-section, and the shirt hole was 2.25 times as large. No investigation has addressed these large discrepancies.

Still another point. Dr. Finck reported, in notes transmitted to higher authority on February 1, 1965: "I was denied the opportunity to examine the clothing of Kennedy. One officer who outranked me told me that my request was only of academic interest."[77]

The superior officer was not identified.

From my collection of 35mm slides, I retrieved Willis slide 5. Lacking a projector, I studied it under a magnifier.

Clearly visible were six of the agents in the followup car. With one exception, they were facing forward, or toward the front. The exception was Glenn Bennett. His entire body—head, shoulders, upper torso—was turned to the right. He seemed to be looking at the bystanders on the sidewalk, or off toward the monument on the grassy knoll. He was certainly not looking at President Kennedy. (See Photo 10.)

Now I studied the Altgens photograph, taken after the shot struck. There was Glenn Bennett—still looking to the right.

Bennett couldn't see a bullet strike "4 inches down from the right shoulder" if he was looking in another direction. As evidence, his statement lost its force; and the Bethesda autopsy, some of its corroboration.

But this question remained: If Bennett didn't see the shot strike, then why did he say he did? Why did he stress he was looking at Kennedy, when the photographs seemed to show otherwise?

My first reaction was that it was an innocent error. Besides, a close look at Glenn Bennett's handwritten report raised other questions about his powers of observation and recollection. To navigate Dealey Plaza and pass in front of the Depository, the President's car made a "dog-leg" turn—first a 90-degree turn to the right; then a hairpin turn to the left. Wrote Bennett: ". . . we made a left-hand turn and then a quick right."[80] After the shooting, a number of witnesses reported the sounds of the shots to the right rear, the direction of the Depository. Wrote Bennett: "I drew my revolver and looked to the rear and to the left, high left." And he added: "But was unable to see any one person that could have rendered this terrible tragedy."[81]

Gradually, my initial belief that Bennett's report was an error gave way to a different interpretation. Bennett's account was corroboration for the autopsy. Could that have been its purpose? I resisted that idea because it seemed too subtle. Who would ever think of Glenn Bennett's report as "corroboration?"

Then I came across a letter from Secret Service Chief Rowley, in the twenty-six volumes, transmitting Bennett's handwritten notes to the Warren Commission, and calling attention to their significance: "There is forwarded herewith a copy of the original notes made by Special Agent Bennett. . . . The significance of the attached notes is that they were prepared by SA Bennett on the President's plane during its return flight to Washington on November 22, before the details of President Kennedy's wounds became general knowledge."[82]

Chief Rowley's letter made the issue of corroboration nearly explicit, and that taught me a valuable lesson. In analyzing the assassination evidence, a legal perspective was essential. My approach was more naive. I tended to view the witnesses as random observers. Maybe that was legitimate when it came to the ordinary passersby, but I was dropping my guard when I extended that supposition to government agents. My own theory about the body being altered implied (1) the existence of a disguise, and (2) a profound legal insight on the part of anyone behind this affair. Any plan ingenious enough to identify the body as the central piece of evidence would surely provide the appropriate corroboration to support alterations that were made. Not to do so would be as foolish as to create a false back wound, but neglect to punch holes in the clothing.

As Rowley noted, the significance of Secret Service Agent Bennett's report was that it was "prepared . . . before the details of President Kennedy's wounds became general knowledge."[83] The other side to that coin was that if the wound was false, the tables turned. And Bennett's report transformed from evidence corroborating the autopsy to evidence impeaching Glenn Bennett.

A similar issue was raised by an account provided by Secret Service Agent Roy Kellerman, who was sitting in the front right seat of the Presidential limousine. He told the FBI that when the shots rang out, he turned toward the rear and "observed President Kennedy with his left hand in back of him appearing to be reaching to a point on his right shoulder."*[84]

For someone to cock his left elbow sharply and extend his left hand behind his head "reaching" for "a point on his right shoulder" is a rather striking, if not contorted, posture.

And if the Zapruder film didn't exist, I could easily imagine the Commission placing great weight on Kellerman's observation, just as they did on Glenn Bennett's claim that he saw the bullet strike "four inches down from the right shoulder." But the Zapruder film does exist, and it shows no such motion. President Kennedy, upon being struck, raised both hands sharply toward his throat. What Kellerman said he saw never happened.

Both Kellerman's and Bennett's accounts raised the same question: whether Secret Service agents in the motorcade were mistaken in what they saw, or whether they made false eyewitness reports so that the alleged movements of the President during the last moments of life would comport with the trajectories on the body at the time of autopsy.

I recalled once again the visit of the Secret Service to Dallas, as reported by Richard Dudman in the December 18, 1963, *St. Louis Post-Dispatch*: SECRET SERVICE GETS REVISION OF KENNEDY WOUND. The "revision" concerned the Dallas doctors' opinion of the throat wound.

---

* Kellerman was interviewed by FBI Agents Sibert and O'Neill on November 27, 1963, at the White House. Their FBI report was routinely forwarded to the Warren Commission, but was not published. I obtained it from the Archives in 1969.

Now that "visit" was beginning to make better sense: Was the body altered not only to eradicate evidence of frontal entry, but actually to "reverse" the direction of the shot? Did the Secret Service visit the one group of doctors who had seen the body before it was altered to "sell" them the autopsy report, to persuade them that a bullet exited at the spot they thought it entered?

The Warren Commission had failed to investigate any of this. Glenn Bennett was never called as a witness. Kellerman was never questioned about the statement he made to Sibert and O'Neill. The Secret Service agents who visited the Dallas doctors were never identified. And Humes was never asked about this query to Perry: ". . . he asked me at that time [November 23] if we had made any wounds in the back."[85]

Liebeler returned from New York a few days after I interviewed the Dallas doctors. The third anniversary of the Kennedy assassination was just days away, and several major journalistic pieces were being prepared. *Life* was about to publish numerous frames from the Zapruder film, and to make a significant dent in American public opinion with its story: DID OSWALD ACT ALONE? A MATTER OF REASONABLE DOUBT.

On Monday, November 14, UPI ran a story about *Esquire*'s publication of a frame from the Nix film. The Nix film was taken from the opposite side of the street. It was valuable because the background showed the grassy knoll. Critics had examined the film purchased by UPI. Now, as evidence of conspiracy, *Esquire* was publishing a photo blowup purportedly showing a grassy-knoll assassin.

I was interested, yet detached. My entire perspective was changing. The body was the Rosetta Stone to Dealey Plaza. We could debate till doomsday what we thought was in the background of a photograph. Lacking truly definitive images, it was very subjective—like a Rorschach test. Believers in conspiracy tended to perceive the optical data differently, and this would always be so.

What now impressed me was the simple logic linking the grassy knoll and the body. Assassins from the front could not have shot the President unless his body was altered prior to autopsy—it was that simple. There were no entry holes on the front of the body. And there were no bullets inside the body. And according to Humes, at least, there were no exits to the rear. So unless one postulated Humes lied about basic facts, there couldn't be a grassy-knoll assassin.

Moreover, because of my discovery regarding Agent Glenn Bennett, the problem seemed more complex. Not only did I believe shots from the front had been "erased"; I now had serious doubts whether any shots struck Kennedy from the rear. The rifle found at the Depository no longer impressed me. The gun could be a prop. Whether it was or not depended on the authenticity of the ballistic evidence; but that, in turn, depended on the validity of the rear entry wounds. Everything depended on the body.

On November 17, 1966, I telephoned Liebeler to see how his trip had gone. I didn't tell him about the Dallas interviews I had conducted.

Liebeler said he had given five copies of the memorandum to Burt Griffin. Griffin was to give one copy to Ed Gwirtzman, a friend of Robert Kennedy. Liebeler didn't know what Griffin would do with the rest. He said he was now in the process of drafting a cover letter to Rankin, and he was going to send copies of the memo, and that letter, to all former Commissioners, and to many members of the staff. Liebeler said that on the trip to New York he hadn't talked to Burke Marshall, "because Ball had talked to him in the meantime, and advised that there wasn't any use in talking to him at this point." He also said: "I think it's going to take longer than we had originally thought. And so, when push comes to shove, you're just going to have to go ahead and do whatever you think you have to do." As to the surgery quote in the Sibert and O'Neill report, Liebeler said: "There is nothing we can do about it. If it comes out, it comes out. But I'm not talking."

Liebeler told me about his Dallas trip, and his impressions of Dealey Plaza. He had spent three or four hours walking through the area, and even got someone to let him up in the railroad tower. "It's much smaller than you have any idea," he said, "and you get up in that railroad tower, and you can see the area behind that picket fence, you see *everything* over there—it's not more than 200 feet away, I would think. There just isn't anything behind that picket fence that couldn't be seen from that railroad tower."

I agreed. I knew that was a problem. To answer it, I had proposed the idea of camouflage, and tried to analyze the photographs from that standpoint. But it was hopelessly subjective. Yet that's why camouflage works—there is a blending. I had proposed that perhaps the shooters were up in the treeline. I thought I saw images up there. Liebeler wouldn't hear of it: "Nah, nah, nah—those trees, that's just fantasy. Those are scrawny little trees."

Liebeler told me more about his trip to Dallas. He had gone to Parkland Memorial Hospital to investigate further the question of the stretcher bullet: Specifically, which stretcher was it found on? For the single-bullet theory to be correct, it had to come from Connally's stretcher, because Connally was the second victim on the trajectory. But the issue was clouded because the original FBI position was that the bullet came from Kennedy's stretcher. I had the feeling that the Commission had concluded it came from Connally's stretcher not because of any hard evidence, but because that was a requirement of the single-bullet theory.

But now Liebeler found a new fact which tipped the balance.

Darrell Tomlinson found the bullet on one of two stretchers standing opposite a bank of elevators on the ground floor of the hospital. In his testimony, one was designated stretcher A, the other, stretcher B. The issue was whether Tomlinson could remember which stretcher he had found the bullet on, because he had removed one of the stretchers from the elevator earlier, and it was that stretcher—the elevator stretcher—which was Connally's.

Liebeler told me he went to Parkland Memorial Hospital and questioned Doris Nelson, the nursing supervisor. Doris Nelson told him that Kennedy's stretcher remained in the emergency area well after Kennedy's body left the hospital in a coffin. But that happened shortly after 2:00 P.M., and Tomlinson found the bullet well before. So that meant that no matter which stretcher Tomlinson found the bullet on, it couldn't have been Kennedy's, if Doris Nelson was correct. "And I cross-examined her on that carefully," said Liebeler.

I was impressed with this new line of argument. It eliminated Kennedy's stretcher entirely. It also raised the planting issue: A legitimate assassination bullet was unlikely to be on a stretcher not connected with either victim. As Liebeler put it: "Either it came from Connally's stretcher or it was planted."

Simply because of its condition, I still believed it was planted. Only now there was a new twist to the problem: Why would anybody want to plant a bullet on Connally's stretcher? Surely, no one could have seen the necessity for the single-bullet theory that early.

Another puzzle. What Doris Nelson told Liebeler, it seemed to me, was something the FBI could have ascertained on November 22. Probably numerous hospital personnel knew that Kennedy's stretcher had remained in the emergency room area. Why, then, had the FBI not availed themselves of that information? Why had they come to the conclusion it was on Kennedy's stretcher? Something strange went on, but I couldn't put my finger on it.

These aspects of my conversation with Liebeler were stimulating, but a negative side was emerging. A rift was developing. I had hoped Liebeler would team up with me, but he was beating a hasty retreat, constructing a mosaic of "innocent explanations" to counter the case for conspiracy. In hallway conversations, encounters in his office, Liebeler was turning against the surgery hypothesis. Matters came to a head during a phone call we had about a week after his return from New York, on November 25, 1966.

I had watched Dr. Brown, the way he said he was "repulsed" by the idea of a second assassin, and I was wondering how Liebeler proposed to convene a group of objective experts, experts who wouldn't be "repulsed."

"What do you want, then," retorted Liebeler, "a group that's attracted to the idea? That is what you want, of course."

Liebeler insisted: ". . . you're going to have to rely on the judgment of a group of pathologists here, and I don't know how you can avoid that. There's no way in which you *can* avoid that."

He added: "Nobody said there wasn't going to be any cross-examination."

"Who's going to do it?" I asked.

Liebeler said he didn't know, but pointed out that the memorandum suggested that counsel be appointed. "I would hope that . . . I would be appointed one of the counsel. Now I have no control over that, obviously. But I certainly would hope that would happen."

I didn't think Liebeler could be objective. He had already told me that if Humes denied there was anything to the hypothesis, he would believe him. When I pointed this out, he got mad. "You're apparently unable to comprehend," he said angrily, "the basic fact here of a professional operation. That's one of your problems, and this is one of the problems all you people have with the Warren Report. I don't give a goddamn what my position is on this . . . a lawyer can make an argument. It doesn't make a difference what he personally believes."

I said I didn't think anybody was deliberately going to conduct a whitewash. "I think," I said, "that people have a psychological commitment to a certain point of view that operates almost subliminally."

Liebeler just said: "Yaaacchhh!" as if he had bitten into a sour plum.

I returned again to Dr. Brown, my "Exhibit A" of a man who could be thought to have a disabling bias, someone who was "repulsed" at the idea of a second assassin. Liebeler said he was sure any group of experts would be objective. But then, his voice rising to a shout, he said: "You couldn't find a goddamn pathologist in the country who wouldn't be repulsed at the idea that you've set forth! Not a one!"

"That's not my fault," I reminded him.

"Well, all right," he said, "you are describing a condition of reality."

Liebeler said that if I was concerned about the way things were going, I should prepare a detailed list of questions that should be asked at such a proceeding, and give it to him, and he would see they were asked.

I told Liebeler that I hoped the Warren Report critics would have an opportunity to supply "their" pathologist. "If you've got a forensic pathologist that you want in there," he said, "why, I'd like to talk to him. You talk about this guy Abrams. I don't know. He's been talking to you for God knows how long. I don't know what his problem is."

Liebeler then angered me further by demeaning the importance of the head snap—"this so-called 'head snap,' " was the way he put it.

"That is *so* inconsequential to me that I wouldn't even ask anybody about that in this proceeding," he said.

"What??!" I practically yelled. "So inconsequential, eh? That proves the bullet came from the front, and your entrance wound is at the rear, and surgery is the hypothesis at stake. There are no bullets in that body, the FBI sent two agents down there to get the bullets from the body, and they found there were no bullets, and that surgery was performed. They say so in their report. This is the absolutely crucial issue—"

"The crucial issue here," said Liebeler, "it seems to me, is what the autopsy report shows."

"Under *investigation* is the autopsy," I retorted.

"All right, fine," he said. "But I think that's the first step. If the autopsy report is inconclusive, *then* the other stuff becomes relevant. If the autopsy report is conclusive, and everybody agrees that it is . . ."

Liebeler's hierarchy was strict, and he adhered to it rigidly.

Liebeler then went on: "I'm telling you there isn't anything we can do that will satisfy you about this. That's becoming more and more clear to me as time goes on. You've got a commitment to this that goes way beyond rationality, and you're never going to change your mind, no matter *what* happens. I can't help that. I'm sorry about it."

I was surprised at his harshness of tone. "In other words," I said, "you really feel that Oswald assassinated the President alone, that all the shots came from the back, that there was no smoke on the knoll, that if there was, people were mistaken; that there was no surgery on the body."

Liebeler cut me off. "Look, the question isn't what *I* think. The question is what it's going to take to satisfy a reasonable person about these issues. And I don't think there's anything that can satisfy you."

I said that all this was quite a change from how he had reacted when first shown the statement about surgery in the FBI report just weeks earlier. "I reacted to the *presence* of that statement in the FBI report," he said, in a very sharp tone, clearly making a distinction between the "presence" of the statement and whether it was true. "If you make any representations that I *ever* thought, or ever suggested, that there was anything to the notion that there was surgery in the President's head, you're just absolutely misrepresenting the position that I took. I reacted to the presence of that statement in the FBI report, in terms of the effect that that would have on the whole event. Now if there was surgery on the President's head, then I presume that Humes and Finck and Boswell were smart enough to see it, don't you?"

"Do I think they were smart enough to see it? Yes," I replied.

"All right then. . . . All we can do then is ask them about it; and let's look at the pictures and the X-rays."

A vital factor was the President's brain. "I think it may very well be that the brain isn't available," said Liebeler, "and it's going to be difficult to do much with that, but we can certainly try. There isn't a helluva lot more we can do, is there?"

It wasn't clear where Liebeler was getting his information that the brain wasn't available, but this was about the third time he had mentioned it in the space of a month.

I was aghast at Liebeler's attitude. There was plenty that could be done. But a man disinclined to believe anything had happened if Humes denied it wasn't going to get to the bottom of this affair.

I reminded him of the way he had edited the memorandum. "What about the statement of the three incisions, which you didn't put in the memorandum . . . the three incisions which Dr. Abrams, who is a board qualified pathologist, said were obviously caused by someone cutting into the skull?"

"Oh, 'obviously,' " retorted Liebeler. "I don't know. I left them out because Dr. Brown, who is also a board qualified pathologist, didn't say anything of the kind."

The conversation then turned to how a pathologist ought to be questioned about the matter, and I cited my approach to Dr. Brown—urging him to forget this was the Kennedy assassination, that it was supposed to have happened in a certain way, according to the Warren Report. He had to just focus on the brain lacerations—completely out of context, and determine their cause. That, I said, was the way to "objectify" the situation.

"No, you don't try to 'objectify' the situation," argued Liebeler. "You try to isolate a few events from the whole goddamn picture!"

"But your 'whole picture,' " I retorted, "includes Oswald firing from behind, alone. Don't you realize that?"

"But there's evidence that there's somebody firing from behind," replied Liebeler. "There's external evidence. And there's the physical evidence. There's the pathology."

By "pathology," Liebeler meant the two rear entry wounds. But I thought that was circular reasoning—using the "psysical evidence" (the sniper's nest: rifle, shells, etc.) to argue the shots were fired from the rear, thus validating the autopsy; or using the rear entry wounds to prove that internal damage must have been caused by bullets going forward. In both cases, the autopsy, having been thus validated, was then invoked to prove that all shots came from the rear. It was tantamount to saying that Kennedy was struck from behind because a rifle was found behind the motorcade, or because there were two little holes on the rear of the body—reasonable inferences, perhaps, in any ordinary murder case, but not, I was convinced, in this one.

"Jim," I said, "anybody that wants to get at the truth here has to isolate the picture."

"Just a minute," he said. "No pathologist deals with a situation that way. He tries to get as much of the facts as he can. Now if it turns out that the autopsy doesn't show evidence of people firing from behind, then that would be very interesting. The only problem I have with that is that the autopsy that's already been conducted . . . . *did* show that. Now if this fact is verified by the additional investigation, as far as I'm concerned, that is the end of it."

Liebeler's "additional investigation" would be meaningless. It amounted to nothing more than verifying that the autopsy photographs showed the two rear entry wounds. But of course they would. Those two wounds were on the rear of the body; and therefore they would be in the photographs of the body. The issue was whether they were there in Dallas.

I told Liebeler what was now obvious to me: "You're . . . a lawyer defending a client. And the client is the Warren Report. I brought you this important discovery, and now you're going to defend the Warren Report against that discovery."

"How can you say that?" he asked. "What am I trying to defend, in the context of this proceeding?"

"Well, it hasn't taken place yet," I said, "but I obviously view you as an adversary on this issue, and you view me that way, too. And that's all right. That's why there should be an adversary proceeding over this issue. How can you have people with an adversary position conduct an objective proceeding when there's no adversary representation?"

"Nobody said there wasn't going to be any adversary representation," said Liebeler.

"Who's going to provide it?" I asked. "The paper memorandum?"

"You've got the idea," Liebeler said angrily, "that in order for somebody to provide an adversary position, they've got to believe in it. That's the notion that you've got."

"No, I don't," I said. "I have seen you play the devil's advocate. But the question is: Who's going to do it here? Is there someone who's going to say 'I am the devil's advocate,' and that is his position?"

"I expect that I'll have a sign on my back when I walk in," cracked Liebeler. " 'D.A.' It can stand for either 'District Attorney' or 'Devil's Advocate,' can't it?"

I asked if he really thought there was going to be such a proceeding. "I don't know. I know that some people are interested in it. That's all I know." Liebeler said the *New York Times* was obviously going to be a factor: "They've got reporters going all around the country talking to everybody on the staff and the goddamn Commission." Earlier that week, Liebeler told me that when he was in New York, he had shown the memorandum to Harrison Salisbury, then an editor running a Kennedy investigation, who had skimmed the first three or four pages, but hadn't read the part about the Sibert and O'Neill report.

Meanwhile, I came back to a major factor that continued to bother me: Liebeler's apparently changed beliefs on the question. I reminded him of the way he had behaved on Monday afternoon, October 24, in Ball's office, when I drew my finger across his scalp and demonstrated the simplicity of a plot which could change basic facts about Dealey Plaza by simply removing bullets from the body. The FBI statement about surgery had hit him like a ton of bricks. I asked him to please explain how his attitude had changed so much in just a few short weeks.

"It hit me like a ton of bricks because with that in the FBI report, there's really no explaining, there's nothing in the record that specifically deals with that. It would have a very adverse impact on the whole thing. It would be enough, as I told you then, I think [there] would be a very strong push for a new investigation. Now I'd like to clarify it, that's what I want to do. . . . You think I'm taking the position, or that I could take the position, even emotionally or psychologically, that if there was surgery in the President's head, that I don't want to know about it? . . . Jesus Christ, if it's there, I certainly would like to know about it, wouldn't I? Those arguments are all spelled out. If there's surgery in the President's head, I'd like to know about it. Blow the whole thing up. I don't give a goddamn about the Johnson administration, or Earl Warren, or the Establishment. I owe them no allegiance, for Christ sake! They're so unalterably opposed to me at this point—I mean, my God, how simple-minded can you be?"

Liebeler returned to his favorite theme—Dealey Plaza was a small place. Police ran up the grassy knoll and into the railroad yards afterward and didn't find anyone. "Is there a holy ghost up there, shooting invisible guns?" I chided Liebeler for circular reasoning—using the absence of living, breathing assassins on the grassy knoll as "evidence" that shots didn't strike from the front.

"No, no. We're not using that evidence to reason circularly. But the findings of the autopsy are the bottom on which this whole thing rests, and that destroys the circularity of the argument. Because if that is a correct report, and accurately reflects the condition of the body, then that's the end of the discussion."

I couldn't have agreed more.

"Suppose I have one more ace card on surgery?" I asked. "Suppose I make more surgical discoveries?"

"If you have, fine," he replied, "I'd be interested to know what they are." Liebeler's voice betrayed a mixture of nervousness and curiosity.

"Well, I'm working on some more stuff," I replied, and we said our good-byes.

My relationship with Liebeler had turned a corner. I no longer felt free about sharing my research with him and decided not to tell him about my interviews with the Dallas doctors. I intended to stay in touch, but I would pursue the hypothesis of postmortem surgery on my own.

CHAPTER 12

An Oral Utterance

As the third anniversary of the Kennedy assassination approached, I anxiously awaited a reply from the FBI to my November 9 letter inquiring about the basis for the head surgery statement in the Sibert and O'Neill report. To gain attention, I had deliberately begun the letter with the bald statement that I recently had spoken to FBI Agent James Sibert. I knew how sensitive the FBI was about its agents speaking to anyone outside the Bureau about official business. Then, I focused on the statement about head surgery, underlining the words "surgery of the head area, namely, in the top of the skull."

I knew the FBI answered inquiries from citizens. The year before, I had written a detailed letter pointing out that two frames of the Zapruder film were reversed, as printed in volume 18.* The FBI promptly responded with a letter signed by Director J. Edgar Hoover, saying that I was correct, attributing the reversal to a printing error.[1] This "printing error" was no small matter, because the reversal of those two frames obscured the otherwise clear backward motion of the head immediately following the fatal shot. Hoover's letter added that the FBI had checked with the National Archives, and the slides were labeled correctly there.

Had the FBI hierarchy noticed that the Sibert and O'Neill report contained information about head surgery?

Testifying before the Warren Commission, Director J. Edgar Hoover said: "All the reports that come in from the field are, of course, reviewed at Washington by the supervisor in charge of the case, and then in turn by

* I had arranged for a friend to sign that letter because, at the time, I was working at North American Aviation and was concerned it might jeopardize my security clearance. By 1966, I realized that such worries were misplaced.

the assistant director of the division, and then in turn by Mr. Belmont, who is the Assistant to the Director. Reports in which there is a controversial issue or where statements have been made of the existence of some particular thing that we have never heard of before, I myself, go over these to see that we haven't missed anything or haven't had any gap in the investigation so it can be tied down."[2]

Head surgery was controversial, and certainly fell into the category of "some particular thing that we have never heard of before." Yet as far as I knew, it had never been investigated. On the other hand, no attempt had been made to hide it. Could it have been overlooked?

If one held to the popular image of the FBI, that might seem preposterous, but the records of the Warren Commission revealed the FBI had all the problems of any large organization burdened with paperwork. The agents gave the statement no particular emphasis. The two sentences matter-of-factly reporting surgery were virtually hidden in a five-page, single-spaced report. Moreover, the criminal procedure implied by the information was not apparent: that surgery performed on the body of a dead man could, by changing the gunshot trajectories, falsely structure, in advance, the findings of the autopsy. I knew of no work of fact or fiction that described such a modus operandi.

On Monday, November 21, 1966, I opened my mailbox to find the FBI reply—indeed, a letter signed by J. Edgar Hoover, acknowledging my November 9 inquiry, and informing me that the FBI had turned over all its work to the Warren Commission, and the Commission had turned its records over to the National Archives, and suggesting that "answers to any questions you may have concerning the work performed by . . . the FBI would be available through review at the National Archives."[3]

Was this a form letter? I was disappointed, perplexed, and suspicious.

Five days later, on Saturday morning, November 26, it was front-page news that FBI Director J. Edgar Hoover had issued a statement on the assassination controversy—his first in three years. Most of it concerned the Kennedy autopsy, and a verbatim copy was in the *New York Times*.

One paragraph caught my eye. Said Hoover: "The FBI reports record oral statements made by autopsy physicians while the examination was being conducted and before all facts were known. The autopsy report records the final findings of the examination."[4]

This appeared to mean that the information that there was "surgery of the head area, namely, in the top of the skull" came from the mouth of an autopsy doctor. That strengthened my hypothesis.

The only doctors present at the time the body was removed from the coffin were Humes and Boswell.

Hoover's statement, although primarily devoted to the autopsy, was ostensibly in response to the issue raised by the Warren Report critics that the FBI report of the autopsy contradicted the navy autopsy report, published in the Warren Report. The FBI said the non-fatal bullet made only a shallow penetration and then fell back out. The autopsy report said it passed all the way through the body. Hoover explained the conflict by describing the flow of information from the autopsy room, and his explanation, I was pleased to note, coincided with my "twin-transmission-line" theory—that there were two distinct sources of information; that the FBI report applied to what was seen and heard on Friday night; the autopsy report represented the "final findings." On Friday night, the navy doctors didn't conclude the bullet passed all the way through, because they didn't know about the wound at the front of the throat, supposedly "obliterated" as a result of the Dallas tracheotomy. I had different ideas about the so-called "tracheotomy" incision, but I understood what Hoover was saying, and I could agree with his conclusion: "While there is a difference in the information reported by the FBI and the information contained in the autopsy report concerning the wounds, there is no conflict."[5]

The FBI's statement that the bullet made only a shallow penetration and then fell back out came from page 5 of the Sibert and O'Neill report. The statement that it was "apparent" that there was "surgery of the head area" was on page 3. Both items were medical information, and I saw no reason to believe that Hoover's statement applied to one, but not the other. The FBI men did not themselves evaluate wounds, distinguish entrance from exit, and differentiate gunshot injuries from surgery. The FBI agents were note-takers. In short, I viewed Hoover's statement as an official explanation of how the two agents obtained the medical information incorporated in their five-page report, and that it applied throughout.

This was a crucial assumption. If it was correct, either Humes or Boswell recognized there had been surgery. This was the second indication that Humes might have known something was wrong with the body—the first being his question to Dr. Perry as to whether Perry "had made any wounds in the back."[6]

But if either Humes or Boswell recognized head surgery had been performed, why wasn't that reported to the Warren Commission?

Another detail. The FBI agents reported two wrappings: ". . . the complete body was wrapped in a sheet and the head area contained an additional wrapping which was saturated with blood."[7] Humes testified that he and Boswell opened the casket and that "the President's body . . . was wrapped in a sheet labeled by the Parkland Memorial Hospital, but . . . was unclothed once the sheet was removed from his body."[8] Commander Humes made no mention of any additional blood-soaked wrapping on the head.

What about others at the autopsy?

Documents show that twenty-three people were present.[9] Of primary interest to me were high-ranking officers with medical training—for example, Adm. George Burkley, the President's doctor. But Burkley wasn't the only high-ranking navy doctor there. Present also were four officers representing the chain of command above Commander Humes: Adm. Edward Kenney, Surgeon General of the Navy; Adm. Calvin Galloway, Commanding Officer of the National Naval Medical Center at Bethesda; Capt. Robert Canada, Commanding Officer of Bethesda Naval Hospital; Capt. John Stover, Commanding Officer of the United States Navy Medical School. All were navy doctors. None reported the existence of any post-mortem surgery. If the FBI report was correct, then they, too, ought to have heard the doctor's statement, or noticed the "apparent" surgery. None was called to testify, but they presumably agreed with the conclusions of the autopsy, which was performed under their command, and in their presence.

The way the record stood, it was as if two FBI agents, men with no medical training, left the room with information nobody else possessed. In light of Hoover's statement, I was beginning to wonder whether, at the outset of the autopsy, someone said something he wasn't supposed to, and then said no more.

The FBI statement about head surgery was a needle in the haystack, but except for the fact that it required some sophistication to understand, I believed it was the closest thing to a "smoking gun" in the Kennedy case. I knew of no other explicit evidence pointing to an internal government plot. I was confident the Warren Commission hadn't noticed it. Now I was beginning to wonder whether my call to Sibert and letter to FBI Headquarters had an effect, whether there was a connection between my questions and Hoover's carefully worded statement that the FBI report recorded "oral statements made by the autopsy doctors."

There were a number of other channels, besides my letter and phone call, by which the information about the surgery statement could have reached the FBI's higher echelons. On November 16, Liebeler's memorandum, which devoted an entire page to the statement, went to the Justice Department, and to all former Warren Commissioners. Liebeler told me he had personally spoken to one of the Commissioners about the memo—Gerald Ford.

One of Liebeler's three assistants told me that one Warren Commissioner had gone to the LBJ ranch, where Johnson was recuperating from his abdominal surgery, and had shown the memo to the President. I asked Liebeler if this was so, and got a terse "no comment," with the sharp question, "Who told you that?" I received the impression that it was true. I checked the *New York Times*, and later the Austin, Texas papers, and found that not one but *three* former Warren Commissioners had gone to the ranch during this period: McCloy, Ford, and Boggs.

Was it possible that Hoover's statement was unrelated to the fact that an FBI report contained this crucial piece of information?

In his memorandum, Liebeler had talked of the "probable public reaction" when the statement became known. Was the image-conscious FBI staking out a position that would minimize its responsibility?

On November 27, 1966, the day after the statement was published, I telephoned Liebeler.

Liebeler didn't know I had written the FBI. He chided me for applying Hoover's statement to the head surgery quote in the Sibert and O'Neill report. Liebeler said it applied only to the issue of whether or not the bullet transited the body. "That's Hoover trying to deal with the fact that the Sibert and O'Neill report seems to contradict the autopsy report, and focusing on the alleged contradiction, and not being aware, or focusing on, the surgery point. Now what you're trying to make out of that, of course, is that Hoover, by making that statement, says that the autopsy surgeons said there was surgery in the head. Now you can make that argument, certainly, but clearly that's not what Hoover had in mind at all."[10]

Liebeler didn't explain how he knew exactly what "Hoover had in mind," but he obviously understood the implications of Hoover's statement applied throughout the Sibert and O'Neill report: Establishing that a doctor made the statement about surgery not only strengthened the inference that head surgery was recognized by someone competent to judge, but implicated the doctors by their subsequent silence. Clearly annoyed by the public record that was being created, Liebeler continued: "And that's the problem with this whole goddamn piecemeal approach—everybody gets into the act, shoots off their mouth, looking at a particularly narrow point, and nobody ever sees the whole picture." Liebeler's "whole picture" apparently no longer included surgery.

Now I told him I had written the FBI a letter several weeks before about the point.

"Saying what?" Liebeler asked.

"About surgery," I said.

"Oh, about surgery?" His tone changed.

"Yeah," I said.

"Oh, really," he said. There was a pause. He added: "What did you do *that* for?"

He was obviously very annoyed.

I was glad. "Well, I'm carrying on my research, you know," I replied.

Then Liebeler observed that if, in response to a specific question, Hoover replied that the information came from a doctor's oral statement, that would be "a stronger statement, because you focused his attention on that particular thing." I didn't tell Liebeler the reply Hoover had actually made. I implied it said the same thing as the *New York Times* statement. At which point Liebeler took a new tack—that it didn't matter what the

FBI said now, or in response to any letter I had written earlier. "Who do you suppose wrote the answer?" asked Liebeler. He said he didn't know, but that it was probably some underling who answered the mail. And certainly my correspondence was unrelated to the *New York Times* statement.

Later, Liebeler made another point: Just because Hoover said the FBI statements recorded oral statements of the doctors did not preclude their having recorded other information—like the personal observations of the agents.

I took another look at the Sibert and O'Neill report. Not all the information came from utterances made by an autopsy doctor. For example, Sibert and O'Neill methodically listed the names of twenty-one people in the room. Similarly, they reported: "The first incision was made at 8:15 P.M."

But when it came to medical information, I believed Hoover's statement applied throughout the report.* As I envisioned the scene, as the wrapping was removed, the doctors made comments and the FBI agents made notes, which became two sentences in their report.

None of this meant that the FBI agents had to understand the significance of what they were reporting. The body had been received from another hospital. The agents might well suppose the doctors' comment referred to life-saving surgery performed at Parkland.

I now knew that, at Dallas, there was no "surgery" of the head.

To nail this point down, I asked additional questions when I interviewed the Dallas doctors about the tracheotomy incision. It was a touchy point because it made my phone call seem all the more strange. But I asked anyway, of Drs. Clark and McClelland.

LIFTON: You were the person that did sign the death certificate?
CLARK: That's right.

---

* I examined the two sentences carefully. They set forth *five* separate statements of fact. I was willing to grant that three could fall into the category of direct observaiton, but the two critical ones did not:

1. When the body was removed from the casket, it contained an "additional wrapping." Presumably, the doctor didn't have to narrate to the FBI agents that there were two wrappings on the body—they could see that for themselves.
2. The additional wrapping was "saturated with blood." That too could be directly observed.
3. Following the "removal of the wrapping . . ."—that seemed to indicate that the agents were actually present when the wrapping was removed.
4. ". . . it was apparent that there had been surgery of the head area . . ."
5. ". . . namely, in the top of the skull."

The last two seemed to me to be medical judgments. I didn't see how the FBI agents could make either of these two assessments on their own, but they made sense in terms of Hoover's statement that medical information came from the autopsy doctors.

LIFTON: Could you tell me what type of work was done, besides just sopping up blood, on the head?

There was a pause. Clark said nothing. "Did they just place some bandages there?" I asked. Clark answered: "No, no bandages were placed."

"No bandages were placed?" I repeated.

"No," said Clark.

"Did they do any—did they—" I couldn't bring myself to ask it the way I wanted to. Instead, I blurted: "Nobody touched the head, did they, with a cutting instrument?"

"No," replied Clark, firmly.[11]

I had a similar exchange with Dr. McClelland:

LIFTON: You were there during the whole time until he was pronounced dead—weren't you?

MCCLELLAND: That's right, yeah.

LIFTON: I see . . . did they do anything to the head other than to try to get the blood, sop up the blood?

MCCLELLAND: No. No. No. The only attempts that were being made were actual resuscitative ones . . . the two medical emergencies are airway and blood loss. And his chief one was of course when he came in—was airway. And blood loss was being taken care of by other people who were putting in intravenous shut-down tubes, running in fluids and blood. At the same time, we were giving the tracheotomy.[12]

My calls to McClelland and Clark only corroborated the existing 1963 record—there was no "surgery of the head area" performed in Dallas. But that didn't mean the FBI agents knew that. They could have recorded remarks about head surgery at Bethesda without the slightest inkling as to their significance.

The question that continued to intrigue me was what actually happened inside the FBI as a result of my phone call and letter. In 1966 I had little hope of ever seeing that question resolved, but the Freedom of Information Act changed everything. So it is necessary to pick up this aspect of the story twelve years later, because what was a locked government file in 1966 became publicly available in January 1978.

In January 1978, under the Freedom of Information Act, the FBI declassified nearly one hundred thousand pages of its records concerning the Kennedy assassination.

I asked researchers in the Washington, D.C. area to go to the files for November 1966 to try to locate the correspondence. I was elated to learn it was there—that there were documents with my name on them; internal FBI memos; and an AIRTEL from Baltimore to Washington regarding the phone call I made to Sibert.

The documents show that on November 4, 1966, two days after my phone call, Sibert telephoned Headquarters and spoke with Supervisor Kenneth M. Raupach. Apparently, Raupach told Sibert to put it in writing. The next day, November 5, 1966, the same day Liebeler and I and his students were meeting to discuss the memorandum, Sibert sent an AIRTEL —an internal FBI communication—to Headquarters. It was addressed: "Director, FBI," and signed by the Agent in Charge of the Baltimore office.

AT 6:25 P.M. ON NOVEMBER 2, 1966, began the AIRTEL, MR. DAVID LIFTON, GRADUATE STUDENT, UNIVERSITY OF CALIFORNIA, TELEPHONICALLY CONTACTED SA [SPECIAL AGENT] JAMES W. SIBERT, WHILE ON ANNUAL LEAVE. . . . LIFTON STATED HE WANTED TO ASK SOME QUESTIONS REGARDING THIS AUTOPSY. LIFTON WAS ADVISED THAT NONE OF HIS QUESTIONS COULD BE ANSWERED. HE THEN ASKED WHERE HE SHOULD DIRECT AN INQUIRY, AND STATED HIS QUESTION RELATED TO THE STATEMENT MADE IN THE AGENTS' ACCOUNT THAT "IT WAS APPARENT THAT A TRACHEOTOMY HAD BEEN PERFORMED, AS WELL AS SURGERY OF THE HEAD AREA." LIFTON STATED HE DESIRED TO KNOW WHICH PERSON AMONG THE MEDICAL PERSONNEL HAD MADE THIS STATEMENT.[13]

I have compared the Baltimore AIRTEL, drafted by Agent Sibert, with my own tape recording of the conversation. The AIRTEL is accurate. But whereas, in the recorded conversation, Sibert then made the first of his two comments that "the report stands," the AIRTEL continued: SA SIBERT AGAIN INFORMED LIFTON THAT NO COMMENT COULD BE MADE CONCERNING THE AUTOPSY; AND IF HE DESIRED TO WRITE A LETTER REGARDING SUCH INFORMATION, IT SHOULD BE ADDRESSED TO THE DIRECTOR, FEDERAL BUREAU OF INVESTIGATION, WASHINGTON, D.C. HE ADVISED THAT HE INTENDED TO WRITE SUCH A LETTER AS SOON AS POSSIBLE.[14]

The AIRTEL concluded with an accurate statement of what I said at the end of the call to Sibert: LIFTON ADVISED THAT HE WAS DISAPPOINTED THAT THE AGENT COULD NOT ANSWER HIS QUESTION, SINCE HE CONSIDERED THIS QUESTION TO BE OF PARAMOUNT IMPORTANCE.[15]

Sibert's AIRTEL was routed to supervisors Raupach and Shroder in the General Investigative Division.

Markings on the document also show that a check was run on me in FBI files: "NR [apparently, "no record"] re Lifton, BuFile," read a notation attributed to "Mr. Toler, Service Unit, 11/8/66."

On November 14 my letter arrived. Copies were sent to high officials in the FBI, including Associate Director Clyde Tolson, Assistant Director Alan Belmont, and Assistant Director Cartha DeLoach. The letter was stamped: EXP PROC.—apparently, "expedite process."[16] Both my letter and the AIRTEL from Sibert went to the desk of Alex Rosen, Assistant FBI Director in charge of the General Investigative Division. Rosen's division —"Division 6"—handled the assassination investigation. The released documents made it clear that Rosen played a major role in the day-to-day supervision of the investigation.

On November 17 Rosen sent a memorandum to FBI Assistant Director Cartha DeLoach, who handled Crime Records, the FBI's public relations division.* It began: "Purpose: To advise a citizen's letter has been received asking questions relating to observations of our Agents who attended the autopsy of President Kennedy. Acknowledgement letter attached."

"Background:" began the next section, which described my call to Sibert, and said I wanted to question him about the autopsy and the FBI report he co-authored. Rosen's memo continued: "Mr. Lifton referred to an FBI report indicating that the report said the President's body was removed from the casket and was placed on the autopsy table. He then quoted the following information contained in the report . . ."

Verbatim, Rosen then quoted the statement concerning "apparent . . . surgery of the head area." In his memorandum to DeLoach, Rosen underlined the passage, just as I did in my letter.

Rosen continued: "Briefly, Mr. Lifton wants to know what our Agents witnessed which formed the basis for their comments regarding the head surgery performed on the President, and in substance, requested an elaboration regarding the autopsy."[17]

Rosen wrote: "Mr. Lifton is referring to the FD-302 [the FBI's formal designation for a 302 form] submitted by Sibert and O'Neill dated 11/26/63, which sets forth information *orally furnished to them by the autopsy physician* [emphasis added]."[18]

Obviously, Liebeler had been wrong when he charged that Hoover's statement quoted in the *New York Times* applied only to the non-transit issue and not to the statement about head surgery.

Rosen's memo concluded with a brief review of my prior phone contact with Agent Sibert (as noted in the AIRTEL from Baltimore). Then he wrote: "Mr. Lifton's letter is one of several letters that have been received asking for information, and although his letter is being acknowledged, he will be referred to information made available to the National Archives."[19]

After noting that "Mr. Lifton was not identified in Bureau files," the memo concluded with "ACTION": "Attached for approval is a letter to Mr. David S. Lifton."[20]

There, in black and white, was the explanation of how I had been fobbed off with what appeared to be a form letter, while the highest echelons of the FBI were put on notice about the issue I had raised.

---

* Initials on the memo indicate it was drafted by Kenneth Raupach, a supervisor at FBI headquarters.

Copies of Rosen's memo went to the Domestic Intelligence Division, and five officials in the FBI chain of command, including Inspector Malley, who was the number one man in Rosen's division, and had been the liaison with the Warren Commission. On page 2, where the proposed letter of reply was noted, several of them scrawled their initials: the FBI supervisors, Malley, DeLoach. And in a handwriting I now knew well, "Ok H"—the imprimatur of the Director, J. Edgar Hoover.

There was an intriguing footnote to the story of Rosen's memorandum. He said my letter inquired about "the basis for [our Agents'] comments regarding *the* [emphasis added] head surgery performed on the President."[21] Rosen's wording surprised me. He could have referred to it as "alleged head surgery" or in some manner that left open the possibility that the FBI agents were in error. But he didn't. To Alex Rosen, I had inquired about "the head surgery performed on the President." Was this just poor wording? Or was Rosen under the impression, as I suspected Sibert and O'Neill were, that some type of legitimate surgery had preceded the Bethesda autopsy? To this day, I don't know.

Other documents in the 1978 FBI release painted a vivid picture of the way FBI Headquarters' officials viewed the Sibert and O'Neill report. The matter came up repeatedly in 1966, when the first wave of assassination books was published, because press reports seeking to explain the difference between the FBI version of the autopsy and the Navy's official autopsy report alleged that the FBI account was simply inaccurate, or that the FBI agents were not always present in the room, or that their information was unreliable hearsay.

According to top FBI officials, none of this was true. "Our Agents obtained their information from the head pathologist and remained in the autopsy room until the physical examination was completed,"[22] wrote Alex Rosen in one memo to Cartha DeLoach. In a series of memos between June 1966 and October 1966, the FBI autopsy data were referred to as: ". . . oral information furnished on 11/22/63, by the doctor performing the autopsy . . .";[23] ". . . the initial findings of the doctors performing the autopsy . . . verbally made to two of our Agents who observed the autopsy . . .";[24] ". . . the doctors' statement to our agents . . .";[25] ". . . the autopsy report, as furnished orally to our Agents . . .";[26] ". . . the oral autopsy report . . ."[27]

On June 2, 1966, Supervisor Shroder called Sibert about the press allegations. Wrote Shroder: "SA Sibert stated today that all of the information set forth in their FD-302 dated 11/26/63 concerning the autopsy was obtained from Commander James J. Humes, Chief Pathologist, Bethesda Naval Hospital. None of the information obtained was hearsay."[28]

Yet the FBI didn't want to spell out its position publicly. In one memo, Rosen wrote: "We do not have to explain to anyone our reporting procedures . . . nor offer excuses as to why we reported the matter in the manner in which we did. The reports speak for themselves."[29]

Moreover, the FBI's position was that even though the navy autopsy findings were different, ". . . no need has arisen to make any retraction as we accurately furnished all information received to the Commission. . . ."[30] In one memo, Rosen was blunt as to why the FBI reports diverged from the navy autopsy report: "The confusion comes about as a result of the examining physicians changing their original theory as furnished to our Agents on 11-22-63. . . ."[31] Director Hoover personally wrote in the margin of that memo: "The confusion which has developed would never have occurred, if we had obtained the autopsy report originally. . . ."[32]

The foregoing all came from documents at FBI Headquarters, what the Bureau called "SOG": Seat of Government. In the fall of 1978, I obtained additional information by filing a Freedom of Information Act request for documents written by Sibert and O'Neill in 1966, on file at the FBI's Baltimore Field Office.*

That file contained additional memos, written in June 1966, when the agents received several phone calls from Headquarters, and apparently had to defend their report. In one, they wrote: ". . . the agents submitted no conclusions of their own . . . all information furnished in the FD-302 was obtained from the Pathologists who were in attendance at the autopsy."[33] They also replied to a Headquarters official who asked whether the measurements of the bullet fragments and the bone fragment cited in the report "had actually been measurements furnished by the Pathologist or had been . . . conclusions reached by the Agents. He was informed that all figures set forth in such FD-302 had been obtained from the Pathologist performing the autopsy."[34]

In another memo, Agent Sibert wrote that their report was based on "autopsy findings as stated by Dr. Hume[s]."[35]

The position of Sibert and O'Neill was unequivocal, and the care with which they reported on each phone call received in 1966 only strengthened the impression that they were meticulous in their work.

One other "loose end" of the 1966 story re-emerged in 1975, when former FBI Assistant Director Cartha DeLoach testified before the Senate Select Committee on Intelligence (the Church Committee). DeLoach was close to Johnson. Shortly after the assassination, Johnson requested that DeLoach be his FBI liaison, and ordered a special White House telephone installed in DeLoach's bedroom. In his definitive work, *FBI*, journalist Sanford Ungar described DeLoach as being "as close to Johnson as any FBI man below the rank of Director ever became to any President in the Bureau's history. Perhaps closer."[36]

---

* Sibert and O'Neill worked out of the Hyattsville, Maryland, Resident Agency, which was a subunit of the Baltimore Field Office.

In early November 1966, Johnson requested, via DeLoach, background memoranda on eight Warren Report critics whose books and articles had dominated the controversy.* And apparently his interest did not end there.

DeLoach's 1975 testimony raised the question of a possible connection between Liebeler's memorandum which, I am certain, was brought to the LBJ ranch in early November, and the Hoover statement issued on November 25.†

> SEN. SCHWEIKER: You testified that the FBI was asked to put out a statement saying Lee Harvey Oswald acted in a singular capacity —without any plot involved. Is that correct?
>
> MR. DE LOACH: That's absolutely correct, sir, and it should be a matter of record in the FBI files.
>
> SEN. SCHWEIKER: The White House was asking the FBI to put out this statement. Is that not correct?
>
> MR. DE LOACH: That's correct, Senator.**[37]

The fact that "A" (Liebeler's memo) is followed by "B" (White House request to FBI re Oswald) doesn't prove that "A" caused "B," but I have often wondered what President Johnson thought when he was brought a memorandum written by a former Warren Commission attorney concerning evidence in the public record about unexplained surgery on his predecessor's body.***

---

* The critics were: Edward Epstein, Sylvan Fox, Joachim Joesten, Penn Jones, Mark Lane, Richard Popkin, Leo Sauvage, and Harold Weisberg. The information was provided by Hoover to Marvin Watson on November 8, 1966.

** Under the Freedom of Information Act, I filed a request with FBI Headquarters for the documents DeLoach referred to. The FBI claims they cannot be found.

*** Within days of its receipt at the Justice Department, David Slawson, former Warren Commission attorney then working in the Office of Legal Counsel, wrote a memo to Ramsey Clark, then Acting Attorney General. "Subject: Warren Commission, autopsy photographs and X-rays—Letter from Wesley J. Liebeler to J. Lee Rankin dated November 16, 1966."[38]

Regarding Liebeler, Slawson assured Clark: ". . . I know him well. He is honest and responsible but has a tendency to get overly excited on occasion." Then, for almost three pages, Slawson went on and on, not once mentioning any of the substantive issues raised by the memo, but treating the entire affair as a public relations problem. He reported that Liebeler was in touch with Harrison Salisbury at the *New York Times*, that Salisbury wanted the *Times* to call for a new investigation, and that public opinion was building for a new inquiry. "There is still a reasonable chance of spiking this thing by a re-investigation limited to aspects of the autopsy, but if public opinion continues to develop as it has over the past few months we may soon be faced with a politically unstoppable demand for a free-wheeling re-investigation of *all* aspects. . . . The lunatic fringe already allege, or broadly hint, the involvement of the highest echelons of the Government in the assassination."

Slawson never once mentioned the page in the memo devoted to the FBI report

* * *

The FBI explanation confirmed my belief that the statement about surgery recorded an oral utterance made by an autopsy physician. That put the onus on whichever doctor made the statement, and others present. If one of the examining physicians said there had been surgery, and said so in the presence of his military superiors and perhaps the White House physician, Admiral Burkley, why did the autopsy go forward? The body was evidence; the autopsy was conducted to determine the details of the shooting. Why didn't the existence of unexplained pre-autopsy surgery become a focus of attention and concern? Why would Humes perform an autopsy on an altered body?

And if some explanation was provided, what was it?

The Sibert and O'Neill report had widespread implications.

But even as I realized the value of this FBI report, I also realized its limitations. It was not anatomic evidence. It didn't reveal what "surgery of the head area" consisted of.

Consequently, in November and December of 1966, I took the next step.

___

of head surgery—presumably it was just another detail which got Liebeler "overly excited."[39]

I learned of Slawson's response to Liebeler's memo in April 1980. At my request, it was declassified and released under the Freedom of Information Act.

CHAPTER 13

The Head Wound: Dallas vs. Bethesda

MY INVESTIGATION OF THE throat wound showed me the importance of meticulous "before and after" research. It was necessary to compare the Dallas and Bethesda observations for changes in size and shape. I had not done that in the case of the head wounds. The only Dallas/Bethesda difference I knew of was the Bethesda doctors' report of a small bullet entry hole beneath the larger, fatal wound. No one in Dallas saw that smaller wound, and I suspected it was man-made. But I paid no attention to the size and shape of the fatal wound because I thought "surgery of the head area" meant surgery performed on the brain, to remove metal, and I had rather hastily concluded that the only anatomic evidence that such a procedure would create would be brain lacerations. Now I realized that I had failed to explore the implications of my own theory: If someone removed metal from inside the brain, how did he get through the skull? I had been taking for granted a crucial proposition: that the fatal wound was the same at Dallas and Bethesda. But would not the procedure to gain access to the brain necessarily alter the size and shape of the skull wound, just as the probing for metal in the neck had apparently changed the tracheotomy incision?

I took a closer look at the testimony and soon became aware that when the Dallas doctors described the fatal wound, they used the phrase "occipitoparietal." It was in the testimony of Drs. Perry, Carrico, Peters, Baxter, McClelland, Akin, Jones—just about all the Dallas doctors, it seemed. "Occipitoparietal" indicated the right rear of the skull, toward the bottom.

But when Commander Humes described the wound, he called it "chiefly parietal,"[1] which placed it farther right and higher.

My suspicions had also been aroused by my conversation with Dr.

Paul Peters. I had called Dr. Peters about the tracheotomy incision. Of all the Dallas doctors, he was the friendliest, and we talked for nearly an hour on Sunday morning, November 12, 1966. Peters told me of his shock upon entering Trauma Room One: "I can remember seeing the look on his face, so to speak, which was something that I will always remember. His face was just as familiar to me as my next door neighbor's—I had seen it so many times. And I, of course, wasn't aware of how badly he had been injured. I had just wandered in there to help, because I thought he had been shot through the arm, or shoulder, or something, and I might get to meet him, you know, and visit with him. And hell, there he was lying up on that trauma cart—obviously mortally wounded. That was my first thought—that he's probably dead."[2]

Dr. Peters said he took up a position near the head of the table on the left side. He emphasized that the head wound was situated directly at the back, that it was actually necessary to get to the back of the head to get a good view of it.

But that was not the impression I had from Humes' testimony, or the FBI report. Agents Sibert and O'Neill reported that Humes said the bullet exited "through the top of the skull."[3]

I realized these differences could be important, and decided to look more closely at the head-wound descriptions. I wanted data on the dimensions, size, shape, how the scalp looked—anything that might provide criteria for comparing Dallas observations with those recorded at Bethesda.

I began by making a list of all persons at Dallas who might have seen the fatal wound and where each person's account could be found. For most, the source was the twenty-six volumes of the Warren Commission. But news accounts were also important. A statement made to a news reporter—assuming it was quoted accurately—provided a fresher account than one made four months later to the Warren Commission. The oath was not as important as the date the information was given.

My first pass was merely exploratory—I wanted to see if there were any differences at all. One discovery followed another. Soon my head was bursting with citations, as I went from the Dallas descriptions to *Grant's Atlas of Anatomy,* to be sure I understood what the Dallas doctors were saying, then back to the Bethesda autopsy report. It was back and forth, back and forth, a pell-mell rush through the records as, a piece at a time, I unearthed a dramatic schism between the Dallas and Bethesda descriptions of President Kennedy's fatal wound.

The Bethesda description was already familiar. There was a huge hole about six inches across in the top of the head. The hole extended all the way from the rear of the skull, in the occipital area, nearly six inches toward the front, and was completely uncovered. Humes said its largest dimension was "approximately 13cm"—5⅛ inches.[4] The wound may have been larger than that. At the autopsy, Commander Boswell made a drawing of the skull which depicted the wound as a roughly rectangular area with measurements of 10 by 17cm (3.9 by 6.7 inches). Inside that area, Boswell had written "missing."[5] (See Photo 27.) Whatever its exact dimensions, the hole was huge. Secret Service Agent William Greer told me in an interview years later that President Kennedy's head, at Bethesda, looked "like a hardboiled egg with the top sliced off."[6] At the rear of the head, just beneath the large hole, one inch to the right of the centerline, Commander Humes reported the existence of a small rectangular entry wound—15 by 6mm (¼ by ⅝ inch) in size.[7]

That is not the way the President's head appeared earlier that afternoon, at Parkland Memorial Hospital. None of the Dallas doctors saw the small entry wound subsequently reported by Commander Humes. More important, the only major wound noted by the Parkland doctors (approxi-

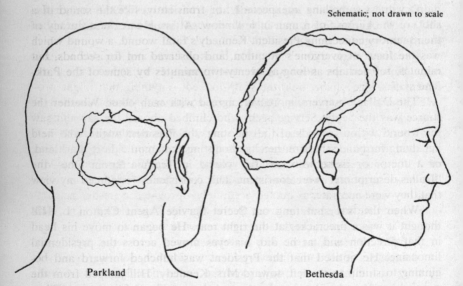

Schematic; not drawn to scale

Parkland   Bethesda

Figure 20.

The Parkland/Bethesda conflict concerning the President's head wound

Left: Drawing illustrating the hole seen at Parkland Hospital, as described by doctors in medical reports and Warren Commission testimony. Dr. Carrico estimated the size as 5 by 7 cm (2 by 2¾ inches). Parkland doctors located this wound in the right occipitoparietal area.

Right: Large irregular hole, 13 cm across (5⅛ inches), described in Bethesda autopsy, extending from rear (occipital area) and involving chiefly the parietal bone but extending also into the temporal area.

mately 2½ inches in diameter) was located in the right rear portion of the head. The bones were sprung outward, and a flap of scalp was associated with the wound. The *top* of the President's head was in place—it was not "missing." (See Fig. 20.)

I had discovered an important conflict in the record. Two groups of doctors saw the President, and in every way that words could be used to describe the wound—size, location, condition of the scalp—their descriptions differed.

But this "conflict in the record" was an abstraction, significant only if the Dallas observations were accurate. If they were, the "conflict" represented anatomic changes made on the wound itself.

Could the Dallas descriptions be relied upon? Often, I had seen Liebeler and his students ridicule the grassy-knoll witnesses by arguing, as a general proposition, that eyewitnesses were unreliable, an argument invoked so frequently it seemed like a legal cliché. But I was not persuaded. These were medical eyewitnesses—in most cases, trained physicians. They didn't witness something unexpectedly, or transiently, like the sound of a shot, or the glimpse of a man in a window. At issue was the accuracy of their memory concerning President Kennedy's fatal wound, a wound which was the focus of everyone's attention, and observed not for seconds, but minutes, for perhaps as long as twenty-two minutes by some of the Parkland staff.

The Dallas observers, moreover, agreed with each other. Whether the source was the Secret Service agent who climbed aboard the car and saw the wound within seconds of the shooting, the President's wife who held her dying husband's head in her hands during that mad ride to Parkland, or a doctor or nurse who saw the wound in Trauma Room One—the "Dallas descriptions" were consistent. This consistency reinforced my view that they were accurate.

When the first shot rang out Secret Service Agent Clinton L. Hill thought it was a firecracker at the right rear. He began to move his head in that direction and, as he did, his eyes moved across the presidential limousine. He noticed that the President was hunched forward and beginning to slump to the left, toward Mrs. Kennedy. Hill jumped from the running board and began running toward presidential limousine. Films show that Hill's outstretched hand touched the handle on the left rear of the car about one second after the fatal shot struck.

As Hill scrambled aboard the turtleback of the limousine, he recalled Mrs. Kennedy shouting, "They've shot his head off."[8] She had risen out of her seat and was reaching, Hill said, "to her right rear toward the back of the car for something that had blown out."[9] Hill forced her back into the rear seat and, as the car sped away, got his first good look at what had happened. "As I lay over the top of the back seat," he wrote in his report,

I noticed a portion of the President's head on the right rear side was missing and he was bleeding profusely. Part of his brain was gone. I saw a part of his skull with hair on it lying in the seat.[10]

Testifying before the Commission in March 1964, Hill said:

The right rear portion of his head was missing. It was lying in the rear seat of the car. His brain was exposed.[11]

Seated beside the President, Jacqueline Kennedy was the closest witness to the event. The twenty-six volumes of the Warren Commission heightened the mystery of what she had seen, because the Commission censored her description from the published transcript. The cryptic statement, "Reference to wounds deleted," appeared on page 180 of volume 5. Mrs. Kennedy's words remained classified until 1971.

"I was just down and holding him," Mrs. Kennedy testified of the moment when the car sped away. She added:

But from the front there was nothing. I suppose there must have been. But from the back you could see, you know, you were trying to hold his hair on, and his skull on.[12]

When Mrs. Kennedy testified "from the front there was nothing," I thought she meant that no wound was visible when the President's head was viewed from the front. Secret Service Agent Roy Kellerman testified that at Parkland the President's face was "clear"—that it appeared unwounded.[13] Mrs. Kennedy's next statement, "I suppose there must have been," was evidently her way of indicating that she simply must have been mistaken on this point. After all, according to the autopsy, a substantial portion of the top of her husband's head was gone, and that should have been easily visible as she held the President in her arms. Mrs. Kennedy's final statement, "But from the back you could see, you know, you were trying to hold his hair on, and his skull on," was obviously a reference to the damage visible at the rear of the head.

Accompanied by a motorcycle escort, the President's automobile sped to Parkland Hospital. In an interview with Theodore White on November 29, 1963, published fifteen years later in his memoir, *In Search of History,* Mrs. Kennedy described what she did to keep the exposed brain from falling out of the wound: "All the ride to the hospital . . . I kept holding the top of his head down, trying to keep the brain in." By pointing the head downward, a wound at the right rear would be pointed upward, preventing the escape of additional tissue. "Maybe I could keep it in," said Mrs. Kennedy, "but I knew he was dead."[14]

When the limousine lurched to a halt at the emergency entrance, the first persons to reach the car were nurses Pat Hutton and Diana Bowron, pushing four-wheel stretcher carts. In her report covering that day's events, Nurse Hutton wrote:

Mr. Kennedy was bleeding profusely from a wound on the back of his head.[15]

Similarly, in her Warren Commission deposition, Nurse Bowron testified she observed "one large hole" in "the back of the head."[16]

The first physician to see the dying President in Trauma Room One was Dr. Charles Carrico, who testified in March 1964 that the wound was in the "right occipitoparietal area"—which is where the occipital bone joins the rearmost portion of the right parietal bone:

SPECTER: Would you describe as precisely for me as possible the nature of the head wound which you observed on the President?

CARRICO: The wound that I saw was a large gaping wound, located in the right occipitoparietal area. I would estimate [it] to be about 5 to 7cm [2 to 2¾ inches] in size, more or less circular.[17]

* * *

SPECTER: Was any other wound observed on the head in addition to this large opening where the skull was absent?

CARRICO: No other wound on the head.[18]

Dr. Carrico was not alone with the President for long. Other doctors and nurses began streaming into the room.

Among the first were Dr. Ronald Jones, the senior surgical resident, and Dr. Malcolm Perry. Dr. Jones testified the head wound was "a large wound in the right posterior . . . a large defect in the back side of the head."[19]

Dr. Perry began the tracheotomy. In a medical report written that afternoon, he said the President's head wound was located in the "right posterior cranium [skull]."[20] In his Warren Commission deposition, he testified it was in "the right occipitoparietal area."[21]

Dr. Akin corroborated this description: "The back of the right occipitalparietal portion of his head was shattered with brain substance extruding."[22]

Gradually, when I coupled them with data about size, I grew to appreciate the precise nature of the Parkland descriptions employing words such as "occipital," "parietal," and "occipitoparietal," and the incompatibility of such descriptions with the Bethesda description of a top head wound. But it took repeated reference to the diagrams in *Grant's Atlas,* and careful attention to medical terminology. Locations on the head are identified by corresponding locations on the skull. The human skull is composed of many separate bones which join each other along lines whose edges are serrated. The seams by which one bone is connected to another are called "sutures."

The occipital bone is located at the bottom of the back of the skull.

It is shaped roughly like a triangle standing on its base. The two sides of the triangle, the right and left lambdoid sutures, join the occipital bone with the right and left parietal bones. The two parietal bones extend, in wrap-around fashion, to the major bone at the front of the skull—the frontal bone. (See Fig. 21.) The two parietal bones also wrap around

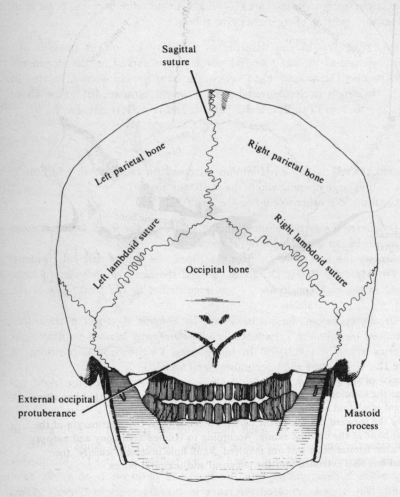

Figure 21.

Rear view of skull

Note how the occipital bone joins the left and right parietal bones along the left and right lambdoid sutures, respectively. The right lambdoid suture marks the right occipitoparietal area, where the wound was seen at Parkland Hospital.

Note external occipital protuberance. Cerebellum is below this point on the skull and rests against inward-curving portion of the occipital bone.

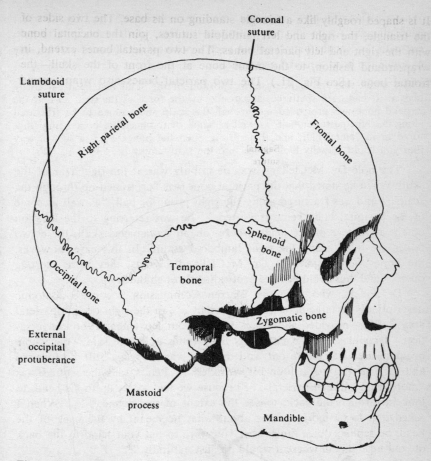

Figure 22.
Side view of skull

Note the location where the right parietal bone joins the occipital bone along the right lambdoid suture. This is the right occipitoparietal area.

Note the forward margin of the parietal bone. It joins the rear margin of the frontal bone at the coronal suture. According to Humes' testimony and autopsy report, the frontal bone was not involved. Skull hole involved "chiefly" the parietal but also extended into the temporal and occipital bones.

toward the top of the skull, where they join each other along the sagittal suture. That suture divides the left and right sides of the skull, and extends from the top of the occipital bone, at the rear, to the rear of the frontal bone. (See Fig. 22 for side view.)

The most graphic description of the President's fatal wound in the

Warren Commission's evidence was that provided by Dr. Robert McClelland. "As I took the position at the head of the table . . . to help out with the tracheotomy, I was in such a position that I could very closely examine the head wound," he testified,

and I noted that the right posterior portion of the skull had been extremely blasted. It had been shattered, apparently by the force of the shot, so that the parietal bone was protruded up through the scalp and seemed to be fractured along its right posterior half, as well as some of the occipital bone being fractured in its lateral half, and this sprung open the bones . . . in such a way that you could actually look down into the skull cavity. . . .[23]

The hole Dr. McClelland was describing was at the right rear of the skull. When he stated that the parietal bone was "protruded up through the scalp"[24] and was fractured along the right posterior half, "as well as some of the occipital bone being fractured,"[25] he was referring to the location on the right rear of the head, where, on an undamaged skull, these two bones are fused along the right lambdoid suture. In this case, however, the bones were visible. In Dr. McClelland's words, they were "sprung open"[26] and thus could be seen protruding through the scalp.

Dr. Peters, who gave the Warren Commission a concise anatomic description—"a large defect in the occiput . . . in the right occipitoparietal area . . ."[27]—provided additional detail in our November 1966 conversation. "I could see the back of his head quite well," he said, "the whole occipital area was blown out, and the skin was shoved a little bit forward and his parietal was a little bit wrinkled."[28] Peters said the wound was "more occipital than parietal . . . because we had to get up to his head, to look in through the back, to see the extent of the wound. . . ." When I asked him to be more specific about what he meant by the back of the head, he replied: ". . . much as if you were to put your hand to the back of your head, about where it would go, just naturally."[29]

Dr. Carrico, who said the wound was 5 to 7cm across, was the only Dallas doctor to give the Warren Commission a numerical estimate of size, but during our November 1966 phone call, Dr. Peters volunteered one: "about 7cm across" [2¾ inches].[30]

Some skull bone was missing where the Parkland doctors saw the hole in the head. That may have been what passed over the right rear of the car after the fatal shot struck and what Secret Service Agent Hill saw Mrs. Kennedy reaching for. Bystander Charles Brehm said that he, too, saw something he thought moved toward the rear.[31] On Saturday afternoon, November 23, William Harper, a Dallas medical student, found a large bone fragment on the grass adjacent to the south side of Elm Street (to Kennedy's left). Harper took the bone to Methodist Hospital, where it was examined by Dr. Cairns, the Chief Pathologist. According to an FBI interview, "Dr. Cairns stated the bone specimen looked like it came from the occipital region of the skull."[32]

According to Cairns' identification, the fragment found by William Harper came from the same anatomic location where Dr. McClelland, and many other Dallas observers, saw the wound in the President's head. That such a fragment should end up in the street was not surprising. Like almost all the other doctors at Parkland, Dr. McClelland originally believed, before he learned anything about the Dallas Police Department's version of the crime, that the wound he observed at the right rear of the President's head was an exit wound.[33]

Indeed, six Dallas doctors testified the wound in the rear of the head was an exit wound; and a seventh, Dr. Kemp Clark, said it *could* be an exit wound, but it was also possible the wound was "tangential";*[34] Dr. Jones testified it "appeared to be an exit wound in the posterior portion of the skull";**[35] Dr. Perry referred to it as "avulsive";[37] Dr. Jenkins, referring to the region as "exploded," said, "I would interpret it being a wound of exit";[38] and Dr. Akin said: "I assume that the right occipito-parietal region was the exit."[39]

Like McClelland, several postulated a trajectory which proved to be incorrect, but which illustrated their thinking about the nature of the head wound. As Dr. Peters explained to me: "I was trying to think how he could have had a hole in his neck and a hole in the occiput, and the only answer we could think [of] was perhaps the bullet had gone in through the front, hit the bony spinal column, and exited through the back of the head, since a wound of exit is always bigger than a wound of entry."***[40]

Dr. Perry didn't hesitate to give his opinion about the head wound in interviews he gave on Saturday, November 23, to John Geddie of the *Dallas Morning News,* and Herbert Black, Medical Editor of the *Boston Globe*. Accounts of both interviews were published in Sunday's newspapers. Geddie reported: "The head wound, he [Perry] added, appeared to be 'an exit wound' caused when the bullet passed out."[41] To Black, Perry acknowledged it was peculiar that "rather than entering" from behind, the bullet exited "despite the fact the assassin shot from above down on to the President." But he assured Black that the wound he saw on the head was an exit: "We know that the big damage is at the point of exit." He offered this explanation: "It may have been that the President

---

* A tangential strike occurs when a bullet doesn't enter and leave the body at two distinct locations, but practically travels a tangent to the wounded area. Clark's theory offered a medical explanation of how it was possible that the President had what appeared to be an exit wound on the rear of the head, yet was nevertheless shot from behind.

** In November 1966 Dr. Jones told me: "The whole back side of his head was blown off, and there were fragments of skull hanging out . . . it appeared to be more on the right side than on the left side . . ."[36]

*** See Chapter 2 where Peters' statement to the Warren Commission on this point is quoted.

was looking up or sideways with his head thrown back when the bullet or bullets struck him."[42]

The man who pronounced Kennedy dead, and the senior physician present in Trauma Room One, was Dr. Kemp Clark, Associate Professor and Chairman of Neurosurgery at Southwestern Medical School. While holding out the possibility that the fatal wound was perhaps not an exit, Dr. Clark was in agreement with the others as to where it was located. Shortly after 2:00 P.M., Dr. Clark appeared with Dr. Perry at a news conference at the hospital. According to the transcript, Dr. Clark described the head wound as "a large, gaping loss of tissue" located at the "back of his head . . . principally on his right side, towards the right side."[43] Clark used similar language in his medical report, time-dated 4:55 P.M. on November 22, and in his Warren Commission deposition given in March 1964. On both occasions, he described the wound as being in the "back" of the head. His medical report called it "a large wound in the right occipitoparietal region, from which profuse bleeding was occurring."[44]

I came to realize that one factor which worked to obscure the differences between Dallas and Bethesda was the use of the same adjective—"large"—by both groups of doctors to describe a wound of different size and shape. But Humes, unlike the Dallas doctors, seemed startled by the amount of skull missing: "massive," "huge," and "so great" are words he used.[45]

While Dr. McClelland succinctly described the wound in a few sentences, Humes stated in his report that "the complexity of the fractures tax satisfactorily verbal description."[46] The photographs, he told the Commission, were "far superior" to his "humble verbal description."[47] He testified: "This was so large, that localization of it in a descriptive way is somewhat difficult . . . its greatest dimension was approximately 13cm [5⅛ inches]."[48]

Where was this wound whose maximum dimension—5⅛ inches—was nearly twice that reported in Dallas, and whose area was almost four times as large?*

---

* A precise comparison between the areas of the Parkland and Bethesda skull wounds is not possible because the exact shapes are not known. To compute area, some assumptions about shape must be made. Dr. Carrico testified that the Parkland wound was "more or less circular."[49] At the beginning of his Warren Commission deposition, when he first specified the size of the wound, he gave but a single dimension ("4 to 5cm"), referring to it, nevertheless, as an "area." Later in his deposition, and then again in testimony before the entire Commission, he testified it was "5 to 7cm in size" and "5 by 7cm."[50] For the purpose of computation, I estimated the Dallas wound to be rectangular, 35 square centimeters (5 x 7cm) in size.

At Bethesda, Dr. Humes called the wound "irregular" and gave its greatest

In the autopsy report, Humes used economy of words in describing the wound:

There is a large irregular defect . . . involving chiefly the parietal bone but extending somewhat into the temporal and occipital regions. In this region there is an actual absence of scalp and bone producing a defect which measures approximately 13cm in greatest diameter.[51]

Again the anatomy diagrams were needed to decipher Humes' description. The parietal bone (see Figs. 21 and 22), where Humes said the wound was "chiefly" located, extends from the occipital area at the back to the frontal bone. In addition, Humes noted that the wound extended into both "the temporal and occipital regions."[52] Both these bones adjoin the parietal, but are located in entirely different areas of the skull. The occipital is at the back; the temporal is just above the ear. At Bethesda, then, one huge hole began at the back of the head, extended "approximately 13cm" toward the front, and went so far down on the right side that it also extended into the temporal region.

If the basic question is whether the record indicates there was any change at all in the size of the wound between Dallas and Bethesda, it is immaterial whether that change is 380 percent or 500 percent. But I was fascinated by the fact that the Boswell diagram gave dimensions considerably larger than Humes' 13cm "greatest" dimension, and led to a size increase of nearly that magnitude—500 percent. Boswell's diagram was a top view—the perspective, looking down from above—and I believed that the 10 by 17cm measurements cited were better evidence of the wound's size than the "approximately 13cm" cited by Humes.[53] In a 1967 interview with CBS newsman Dan Rather, Humes said the measurements on the autopsy diagram were "precise."[54] Boswell told me, in July 1979, that he personally made the 10 by 17cm measurements using a centimeter

---

dimension as 13cm but Dr. Boswell's skull diagram showed a roughly rectangular wound with dimensions of 10 by 17cm. If one assumes the Bethesda wound was rectangular, and, to be conservative, uses the dimensions 10 by 13cm (using the 10cm width from the Boswell diagram, and the 13cm "greatest dimension" given in Humes' testimony and autopsy report), then the Bethesda wound area is 130 sq. cm (10 x 13cm), and the ratio of Bethesda to Dallas is 130/35, or 3.7. The result is not very much different if one assumes the Bethesda wound was roughly circular, and uses Humes' 13cm "greatest dimension" as its diameter. In that case, the Bethesda wound would be 132.7 sq. cm (Area = $\pi D^2/4$), and the ratio of Bethesda to Dallas is 132.7/35, or 3.8.

A substantial increase occurs, however, if both measurements listed by Boswell are correct. Then the Bethesda wound area climbs to 170 sq. cm (10 x 17cm), and the Bethesda-to-Dallas ratio increases accordingly, becoming 170/35, or 4.9. Thus, if the Boswell diagram is accurate, the Bethesda wound was nearly five times the size of the Dallas wound.

scale.[55] Exactly why Humes, with Boswell's measurements before him, cited a smaller number in the autopsy report, was peripheral to the major issue, but one I found intriguing.*

Another striking difference between Dallas and Bethesda was whether the two groups of doctors perceived the top of the President's head to be present, or gone. A reasonable reading of the Dallas evidence, if only by the absence of testimony to the contrary, was that the top of the head was substantially intact. It was present. But Commander Humes was explicit that he was describing a "defect"—a hole "devoid of . . . skull." And on the autopsy diagram, Commander Boswell inscribed one word inside the 10 by 17cm (3.9 by 6.7 inches) area: "missing."[57] According to Boswell's diagram, 170 sq. cm (26.35 sq. inches) of the top of the President's head was simply gone at the start of the autopsy.

---

* After telling CBS that the measurements were "precise," Humes added: "They are used as an aide-memoir, if you will, to the pathologist as he later writes his report."[56] But Humes did not cite the head-wound measurements made by Boswell in the autopsy report, and the situation is anomalous. I realized this from my on-going debate with Liebeler about the exact location of the back wound. In that case, Liebeler continually cited the autopsy measurement as "best evidence." When I cited the recollections of autopsy eyewitnesses who said the wound was lower, Liebeler replied: "Humes can measure, can't he?" The autopsy report was the final authority, not just because Humes was a doctor, but because the quantitative data cited was based on measurements made with a ruler.

From that debate, I learned two things. First, the body itself was evidence—indeed, "best evidence." Second, when it came to obtaining information from the body, a measurement made at the autopsy table was, legally, superior to a location specified on the basis of someone's recollection. Those were the rules of the game, at least from a legal standpoint.

Yet in the case of the head wound, there was an unexplained departure from that procedure: "Precise" measurements were made, the diagram containing them was incorporated in the official working papers of the autopsy, yet Humes cited a considerably smaller number in the autopsy report, modifying the cited dimension with the word "approximately."

Was Humes deliberately understating the damage he saw and employing "approximately" as a fudge factor? The innocent explanation was that Humes didn't realize that Boswell had diagrammed the skull, because the diagram was drawn on the back side of the autopsy face sheet. Consequently, Humes, in writing the report, cited an approximation based on his own recollection when more precise information was available—ironically, on the reverse side of the same piece of paper which contained the back-wound measurements.

Whatever the explanation, the 4cm difference was no minor matter, because for a given shape, the area varies as the square of the linear dimension. This becomes important in comparing Dallas and Bethesda. As described elsewhere (see previous footnote), when Humes' "13cm" largest dimension is used as the basis for computing the size of the Bethesda wound, Bethesda exceeds Dallas by a factor of 3.7 or 3.8. When the measurements made by Boswell are used, the area of the Bethesda wound climbs substantially, and Bethesda exceeds Dallas by a factor of nearly five.

The Scalp

Commander Humes testified that the large hole he described was not only devoid of bone, but of scalp too. He was most specific on the congruence of the scalp and skull holes: "This defect involved *both* [emphasis added] the scalp and the underlying skull."[58] He told the Warren Commission the skull hole was in an "area [which] was devoid of any scalp or skull," language I always thought a bit odd. Humes struck me as a man who says the hole in the bagel was at a place in the bagel where there was no bagel. In plain English, Humes' testimony meant that the enormous hole he observed at Bethesda was entirely uncovered.

That was not the way the fatal head wound appeared at Dallas. Dr. McClelland described the right-rear "Parkland wound" as being formed by underlying bones which were "protruding up through the scalp."[59] Writer Jimmy Breslin, who interviewed some of the Parkland doctors for an account published on Sunday, November 24, reported the existence of a "huge flap" in the "occipito-parietal, which is a part of the back of the head."[60] According to the doctors Breslin interviewed, this damage had been created by a projectile exiting toward the rear. And Dr. Peters told me that whereas the wound was centered in the occiput, the *scalp,* in the parietal area, was "wrinkled."[61]

If the condition of the President's head was the same at Parkland as at Bethesda, not only did the Parkland doctors miss a 13cm hole in the top of the skull, they missed one which would have been obvious even upon cursory examination, since the scalp was gone too.

The difference in size, location of the wound, and in the condition of the scalp were persuasive evidence that something happened to the President's head between Dallas and Bethesda. Then I learned about another way of looking at the problem, and it provided still another index of change: the type and amount of exposed brain tissue observed by both groups of doctors.

What Was Visible Through the Skull?

Both the Dallas and Bethesda doctors described the part of the President's brain they could see through the hole in the skull. I compared those descriptions of exposed brain. They confirmed the Dallas doctors' description of the location of the skull wound. Most important, the comparison revealed that a much greater portion of the brain was visible at Bethesda than at Dallas, and this provided more evidence that the two groups of doctors were looking at the brain through holes of different sizes.

In Dallas, Dr. Marion Jenkins noted exactly what part of the brain was visible: "The cerebellum protruded from the wound," wrote Jenkins in his report drafted at 4:45 P.M., on November 22.[62] Jenkins repeated this to the Warren Commission: "Part of the brain was herniated; I really think part of the cerebellum, as I recognized it, was herniated from the wound."[63]

To locate the cerebellum and study its position inside the head, I consulted the CIBA brain drawings. The cerebellum is a roughly spherical mass of tissue at the bottom of the back of the brain; when the brain is inside the head, the cerebellum is located just in front of the occipital bone. (See Fig. 23.)

Dr. Jenkins' statement that the cerebellum "protruded" through the skull corroborated an occipitoparietal skull wound location. The cerebellum could hardly be described as "protruding" through a huge wound at the top of the skull.

Observations about the cerebellum, considered in conjunction with the size of the wound, tended to localize the wound at the rear of the head. A wound two and three quarter inches across, the dimension to which Dr. Carrico testified (and corroborated by Dr. Peters), could not both expose cerebellar tissue and extend far forward on the head.

Moreover, from texts I studied, and conversations with doctors at the UCLA Brain Research Institute, I learned that cerebellar tissue is easily distinguished from other brain tissue by its color and texture.

Regarding cerebral versus cerebellar tissue, Dr. Kemp Clark, the neurosurgeon, had expertise. At a news conference with Dr. Perry about fifteen minutes after Kennedy's body had been removed from Parkland, Clark said the head wound was at the right rear.[64] In his report filed that afternoon, Dr. Clark observed that in addition to cerebral tissue, ". . . a smaller amount of cerebellar tissue [was] present also."[65] In his summary submitted to Rear Admiral Burkley the next day, he wrote: "Both cerebral and cerebellar tissue were extruding from the wound."[66] And to the Warren Commission, he testified that "cerebral and cerebellar tissue [was] damaged and exposed."[67] Clark testified that it was the loss of the "right occipital" lobe of the brain—tissue at the back of the brain—which would have most impaired Kennedy's competence had he survived the wound.[68]

Several other doctors provided corroboration.

Dr. Baxter, whose medical report stated that the "occipital" bone was "missing," testified that "the cerebellum was present—a large quantity of brain was present on the cart. . . ."[69]

Dr. Carrico noted the presence of "shredded macerated cerebral and cerebellar tissues both in the wounds and on the fragments of the skull attached to the dura [the membrane covering the brain]."[70]

Dr. Charles McClelland, whose description of the "right posterior" skull wound was the most detailed of all the Dallas doctors, noted that when one looked down into the cavity created by the bones "sprung open"

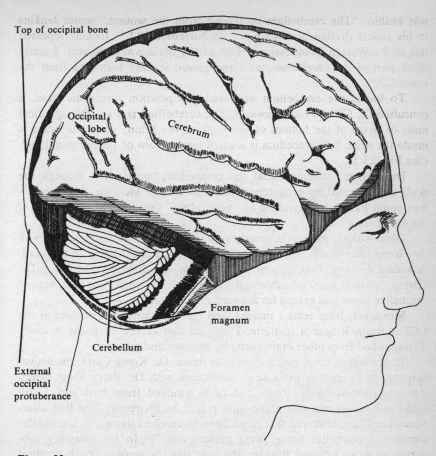

Figure 23.

Relationship of cerebellum to skull

The cerebellum is beneath the upper lobes of the brain, and this drawing shows how deep within the skull it is located. It rests against the bottom of the occipital bone. The occipital bone curves inward at the external protuberance (EOP). The EOP is the bony prominence that can be felt at the bottom and back of the head. Almost the entire cerebellum is below that point.

Note the location of the foramen magnum—the hole in the skull through which the spinal cord enters. The foramen magnum is located in the occipital bone, which forms much of the base of the skull. Dr. Peters said that when he looked at the wound, he thought he could see the occipital lobes of the brain resting against the foramen magnum, because the cerebellum had been damaged or blasted out.

at the right rear, "you actually [could] look down into the skull cavity itself

and see that probably a third or so, at least, of the brain tissue, posterior cerebral tissue and some of the cerebellar tissue had been blasted out. . . .

The cause of death, I would say, would be massive head injuries with loss of large amounts of cerebral and cerebellar tissues. . . .[71]

Dr. Peters gave me a most vivid description, but he employed unfamiliar terminology: the "foramen magnum." It is the hole in the base of the skull through which the spinal cord enters, and connects to the brainstem. The foramen magnum is located in the bottom portion of the occipital bone, a bone which curves back down behind and under the skull, forming a substantial portion of the skull's base. Situated directly above and behind the foramen magnum, resting on part of the occipital bone, is the cerebellum. Above the cerebellum are the occipital lobes of the brain. (See Fig. 23, and Fig. 17, page 253.)

Trying to impress upon me the location of the wound he saw, Dr. Peters said: "I'd be willing to swear that the wound was in the occiput, you know. I could see the occipital lobes clearly, and so I know it was that far back, on the skull. I could look inside the skull, and I thought it looked like the cerebellum was injured, or missing, because the occipital lobes seemed to rest almost on the foramen magnum. Now I didn't put my hand inside his head and lift up the occipital lobes, because I wasn't about to do that under the circumstances . . . [but it] looked like the occipital lobes were resting on the foramen magnum. It was as if something underneath them, that usually kept them up from that a little ways, namely, the cerebellum and brainstem, might have been injured, or missing."[72]

There could be no doubt about what part of the head Dr. Peters looked at; or how far down the back of the head the fatal wound he saw was located. Dr. Peters' statement that he saw the occipital lobes resting on the foramen magnum was not the description of a casual observer.

Dr. Peters corroborated five Dallas doctors' testimony in the Warren Commission records that cerebellar tissue was visible in the skull wound.* These observations clearly indicated where the Dallas wound was located. Another index was size.

There was a sharp difference between Dallas and Bethesda concerning the amount of exposed brain visible—and, by implication, the size of the skull "window" through which these two groups of doctors were looking at the brain.

---

* Still another Dallas doctor noticed the cerebellum was partially visible through the skull wound. In a January 1978 staff interview with the House Assassinations Committee, Dr. Malcolm Perry said that after Kennedy died, he briefly inspected the head wound: ". . . there was visible brain tissue . . . and some cerebellum seen. . . ."[73]

Humes said: "Clearly visible in the above described large skull defect and exuding from it is lacerated brain tissue which on close inspection proves to represent the major portion of the right cerebral hemisphere."[74]

In Dallas, Dr. Peters said he could see the occipital lobes "resting against the foramen magnum," and Dr. Jenkins reported the cerebellum "protruded" from the wound.[75]

In other words, in Dallas, the hole was small enough so that the cerebellum "protruded" through it, but at Bethesda it was large enough for the right cerebral hemisphere to be "clearly visible."

The Dallas doctors' descriptions raised the question: Was there room on the back of the head for both the wound they saw and the "little hole" beneath the "big hole" reported by the autopsy surgeons? I wondered what Peters thought when Specter questioned him:

PETERS: . . . I noticed that there was a large defect in the occiput.
SPECTER: What did you notice in the occiput?
PETERS: It seemed to me that in the right occipitoparietal area that there was a large defect. There appeared to be bone loss and brain loss in the area.
SPECTER: Did you notice any holes below the occiput, say, in this area below here?
PETER: No, I did not . . .[76]

I asked Peters what he thought Specter meant by that question, by a hole "below the occiput." "It was my impression," Peters told me, "he was referring to the wound at the back of the neck. . . . And I didn't see any wound back there."[77]

I asked: "In other words, the wound you saw in the occiput was low enough that if he [Specter] went any lower, he'd already be down in the neck?" "Yeah, that's right," replied Peters. I should have known this from studying *Grant's Atlas of Anatomy,* but I first understood it completely during my call to Peters. To eliminate any misunderstanding, I rephrased my question. "Picture a wound located two and a half centimeters to the right of the external occipital protuberance"—this was Humes' location for the entrance wound, 2.5cm to the right, and then "slightly above"— "where would that be in relation to where you saw Kennedy's [wound]?"

"That would be about the center of it, maybe," said Peters. "The center of the wound I saw would be, yes, an inch or two to the right of the external occipital protuberance. I'd say that. Of course, you see, I wasn't down there making any measurements. He had his hair on his head, and all that. But I know it was in [the] occipital area, on the right side." I asked the question once again. Peters replied, again, that the spot I was designating would be "pretty close" to the center of the wound he saw—

that the wound he saw "might have gone just a little bit higher, but it would be pretty close to the center of it, yeah."

The conversation continued:

> LIFTON: So when he [Specter] said to you: "Did you notice any holes below the occiput, say, in this area below there," you were already thinking in terms of below that location, back in the neck somewhere?
>
> PETERS: Yeah.[78]

I wondered whether Arlen Specter knew where the occipital bone was located. If he did, how could he possibly ask a group of doctors whether they saw a wound "below the occiput," and still be referring to a location somewhere on the back of the head?

I also wondered how many other Dallas doctors were confused as Dr. Peters was by Specter's questioning. How many of them understood Specter to have asked whether they saw a wound in the back of the President's neck?

Finally, I realized that the rear Bethesda entry wound in the head was so far down on the back of the skull that the autopsy report's description that it was "slightly above" the external occipital protuberance was imprecise at best. Even assuming the large Bethesda wound was the "large" Dallas wound extended toward the front, the "little hole" beneath the "big hole" had to be where the skullbone still existed. No hole could appear inside another hole. Or was Humes lying about its existence? I didn't believe that.

How far back, then, did the "big hole" at Bethesda extend? "Somewhat" into the occipital area, said the autopsy.[79] How high up on the back of the head, above the external occipital protuberance, was the Bethesda "little hole"? "Slightly above," said the Bethesda autopsy report.[80] Was all this imprecision deliberate? The fact was that the relationship between the rearmost portion of the big hole, at Bethesda, and the little hole just beneath it, depended upon what Humes meant by "somewhat" and "slightly."

For the first time, I appreciated the layman's description of Secret Service Agent Roy Kellerman, who saw the body at Bethesda, and said that the little hole "was in the hairline." Specter, apparently surprised, replied, "In his hairline?" "Yes, sir," replied Kellerman.[81]

A wound of entry, so far down on the back of the head that it was "in the hairline," made sense to me. If the rear Bethesda entry was that low, all the descriptions could be reconciled. The Dallas doctors could see a wound at the right rear. The wound could have been enlarged by the time the body reached Bethesda, and there would still be room on the bottom of the back of the head—"in the hairline," as Kellerman said—for a small entry wound.

Recapitulating, the conflict between the Parkland and Bethesda doctors concerned two wounds: the little entry wound at the rear and the "large" fatal wound. The small entry wound was not observed by anyone at Dallas. With regard to the "large" wound, the conflict between Dallas and Bethesda consisted of these four elements:

1. *Size.* At Dallas, the hole was described as 2¾ inches across; the Bethesda autopsy said it was 5⅛ inches across, and a diagram gave a largest dimension of 17cm (6.7 inches);
2. *Location.* The Dallas wound was described by most of the doctors as "occipital" or "occipitoparietal." The Bethesda doctors said the hole was "chiefly parietal," but extended "somewhat" into the occipital region;
3. *Scalp.* The Bethesda wound was entirely uncovered. Humes said it was devoid of scalp. At Dallas, the bones sprung outward, protruding up through the scalp;
4. *Brain tissue visible.* At Dallas, the cerebellum "protruded through" the wound. At Bethesda, the "major portion" of the right hemisphere of the cerebrum was "clearly visible."

The Dallas/Bethesda conflict regarding the fatal head wound was built into the records of the Warren Commission. One could debate what it meant, but its existence could not be denied. On November 22, 1963, two groups of doctors saw the President's head, and their descriptions diverged. Only three explanations seemed possible.

1. Parkland Was Right and Bethesda Was Wrong. In that case, the Bethesda autopsy surgeons falsely described a right rear (occipital) wound as a wound at the top of the head ("involving chiefly the parietal"), quadrupled its area, and incorrectly stated that half of the President's brain was "clearly visible" through the hole in his head.

2. Bethesda Was Right and Parkland Was Wrong. In that case, the many witnesses who saw the wound in Dallas somehow mistook a 5⅛-inch hole at the top of the head as a much smaller hole at the right rear.

3. Both Groups of Witnesses Were Correct. Each correctly described the wound as it existed at the time they saw it. Their descriptions conflicted because the size and location of the wound had been altered during the time interval that separated the two groups of observations.

I rejected the first alternative on the grounds that the Bethesda surgeons performed a formal autopsy, made measurements, and exposed photographs and X-rays. It was simply not plausible that their description of the head wound should be so incorrect.

The second alternative required a more qualified judgment. The Dallas doctors' official task was to save the President's life. They did not concentrate primarily on making and recording accurate observations. I concluded, however, that it was not plausible that trained personnel who observed the President for about twenty minutes should (a) fail to notice a half-foot hole in the top of Kennedy's head, a hole which, according to Humes, was completely uncovered, and through which the major portion of the right side of the brain was "clearly visible," and then (b) collectively misreport that wound as being much smaller, and located at the right rear. Even though the President lay on his back, and the rear portion of his head might have been partially obscured, the top was certainly visible. I could not conceive of Dr. Charles Carrico, for example, working within inches of the President's head as he inserted an endotracheal tube, failing to notice that half the top of the President's head was missing. I couldn't conceive of Dr. Peters saying the scalp in the parietal area was "wrinkled" if it was gone. The Dallas descriptions were not only internally consistent, they were corroborated by the testimony of other witnesses, such as Secret Service Agent Clint Hill, who climbed aboard the automobile at the site of the assassination, stared at the wound, and remained with the President throughout the ride to Parkland Hospital.

Finally, the Parkland testimony concerning the skull-wound location was anatomically consistent with the same doctors' observations regarding what part of Kennedy's brain—the cerebellum—was visible in the wound at Dallas; with neurosurgeon Clark's testimony that it would have been damage to the occipital lobes of the brain which would have been most detrimental to Kennedy, had he survived; and with Dr. Peters' statement to me that he could see the occipital lobes clearly, and that they seemed to be resting on the foramen magnum.

Of the three alternatives, only the third was plausible. President Kennedy's fatal wound must have been altered.

The Parkland and Bethesda descriptions differed, but they overlapped. It was evident that the smaller "occipitoparietal" Parkland wound could be part of the much larger "chiefly . . . parietal" Bethesda wound, but not vice versa. The overlap indicated that the smaller wound at the right rear was enlarged by removal of bone and scalp to include the top right side of the head.

In addition, if Humes' description was to be credited, a small puncture wound—15 by 6mm (0.59 by 0.24 inches)—had been added low on the back of the head, just below the rearmost perimeter of the large Bethesda wound.

From my standpoint, these two acts—the enlargement of the fatal wound and the addition of the little puncture—comprised the "surgery of the head area."

According to my research, the FBI report recorded an oral statement made by one of the autopsy doctors—Dr. Humes, according to the Baltimore Field Office memos—at the time the body was first lifted from the coffin and placed on the autopsy table.

But if I was correct, how did Humes know that what he saw was the consequence of surgery? My analysis was based on "before-and-after" research. I could sit in a library and compare the Dallas and Bethesda observations; I could spend an hour on the phone with Dr. Peters. But Commander Humes didn't have that opportunity. According to his testimony, he was simply notified by his superiors that the body was being brought to Bethesda, that he was to perform an autopsy. As far as was known, he had no information whatsoever about the condition of the President's head in Dallas. What, then, caused him to say anything about "surgery"? That remained a mystery.

A primary goal of the Bethesda autopsy was to establish the bullet trajectories. Trajectories are determined by the entire wound pattern—the location of the entry wound and its relationship to the wound exit.

How did the alterations of the head change that pattern?

At Dallas, there was an egg-size hole at the right rear of the President's head. From the way the bones and scalp exploded outward, almost every doctor who saw that wound evaluated it as an exit. The Dallas doctors, therefore, inferred that the President had been shot from the front.

Where, then, was the entry?

I now realized that all my previous information about entry wounds, that is, what I used to view as medical evidence of a "second assassin" to the right or left front, had to be re-evaluated. Its primary significance was not as evidence of a "second assassin" but evidence of what the body looked like in Dallas, before alteration.

On the question of frontal entry, the Dallas medical record was confusing. As previously described in Chapters 2 and 3, it contained information which fell into three categories:

In the throat, out the back of the head (See Chapter 2, pages 41–43)

This trajectory was the result of the Dallas doctors making a false inference on the basis of the two wounds they saw: the throat wound, and the wound at the back of the head. In determining where an entry wound was located in the head, this inferred trajectory was of little use. However, it did demonstrate the strength of the Dallas doctors' belief that a shot exited from the rear.

Left temporal entry (See Chapter 2, pages 45–47)

Legally, the strongest evidence of a frontal entry wound on the head was the handwritten report of Dr. Robert McClelland that President Kennedy died of a "gunshot wound of the left temple."* This report was corroborated by Dr. Marion Jenkins.

---

* Years later I found that Richard Dudman reported in the December 1, 1963, issue of the *St. Louis Post-Dispatch* that one of the physicians who attended Kennedy specified that the left temporal wound was "a small *entry* wound." Dudman did not name the doctor, but it was probably McClelland, who was quoted elsewhere in the same article.

Right temporal entry (See Chapter 2, pages 43–45)

Two Dallas bystanders, William Newman and Marilyn Sitzman, who had a clear view of the right side of the President's head, said the shot struck in the right temporal area. Newman specified the right temple in a TV interview made within an hour of the shooting. Highway Patrolman Hurchel Jacks, who saw the President at Parkland, said the entry wound was located "above the right ear or near the temple."*

The most authoritative report of right temporal entry was indirectly attributed to Adm. George Burkley, the White House physician. It was a UPI dispatch which was then broadcast on NBC TV that afternoon. Years later, I learned from a film and a White House transcript that the source was not Burkley himself but Press Secretary Malcolm Kilduff. At 1:30 P.M., CST, in a classroom at Parkland Memorial Hospital, Kilduff announced the President's death to a stunned White House press group. Then he answered a few questions. The transcript of that news conference contained these exchanges:

Q: How many times was the President shot?

KILDUFF: The President was shot once, in the head. . . . Dr. Burkley told me it is a simple matter . . . of a bullet right through the head. . . .

Q: Can you say where the bullet entered his head, Mac?

KILDUFF: It is my understanding that it entered in the temple, the right temple.**[84]

---

* No Dallas doctor made the flat statement that a bullet entered the right temple. Two did mention damage to the temporal *bone,* which extends rearward to the occipital bone and joins it in the occipito-temporal area (see Fig. 22). In his November 22 medical report, Dr. Charles Baxter wrote that "the rt. temporal & occipital bones were missing. . . ." Dr. Baxter continued: ". . . & the brain was lying on the table . . ." —possibly a reference to the exposed brain touching the emergency room cart through a wound at the right rear. However, Dr. Baxter was inconsistent in his anatomical descriptions. Although his November 22 report mentioned the occipital but not the parietal bone, his later testimony did the opposite: "this wound was in the temporal parietal plate of bone"; "literally the right side of his head had been blown off."[82] On November 22, Dr. Marion Jenkins also noted that "there was a great laceration of the right side of the head (temporal and occipital). . . ." This was consistent with a right rear wound, the "exploded area" where Jenkins testified he thought a bullet exited.[83] In summary, the testimony of these two doctors does not provide strong support for the hypothesis of a right temporal entry (indeed, Jenkins is one of the two "left temporal" witnesses) nor does it invalidate the picture drawn from the testimony of the Dallas observers as a whole, of a wound at the right rear of the head much smaller than the Bethesda wound.

** Kilduff's remarks were apparently the source of the notation in reporter Seth Kantor's notebook (which became a Warren Commission exhibit): "intered [*sic*] right temple."[85]

As Kilduff spoke the last words, he raised his right hand, and pointed with his index finger at his right temple. (See Photo 28.)

The evidence of a right or left temporal wound was spotty, and I found that troublesome. I was never able to come to any final conclusion as to whether the President was struck from the right front or left front. Conceivably, he was struck from both right and left front.

The Dallas record contained evidence to support each of these interpretations and each has its pros and cons:

A right frontal entry, for example, correlated nicely with the Dallas eyewitnesses who believed a shot originated from the grassy knoll. It also correlated with the leftward and backward motion on the Zapruder film. But it failed to account for the left temporal medical evidence. One forensic pathologist with whom I spoke told me he thought it would be odd for a bullet entering the right front to make a right-angle turn and blow out the right rear of the head—it was more plausible for a shot from the left front to blow out the right rear.

A left front entry correlated well with the data from McClelland and Jenkins. It also had the advantage of suggesting a plausible left-front to right-rear bullet trajectory. But it, too, had disadvantages, and they were serious. Why did the Zapruder film show the President being thrust to the left, if the shot came from the left? And where was such an assassin hidden? As mentioned earlier, there was another grassy knoll off to the left. But if that's where the gunman was, why did so many eyewitnesses think the shots came from the right front?

The possibility that both patterns of evidence were correct, that is, that the President was shot twice in the head from the front, opened up another can of worms. Searching the record I found some evidence indicating there might have been two head hits.* But if that was so, why did the Zapruder film show only one impact?

Eventually, I concluded that it was not possible to decipher the head-wound pattern further without a more detailed analysis of the Zapruder

* The principal witness for two head hits is Charles Brehm. Brehm was standing at curbside, to Kennedy's left, and the limousine had just passed Brehm's position when the President was struck in the head. On November 22, 1963, Brehm told reporters the President was hit twice, that he saw two violent reactions.[86] It is usually assumed that the two reactions Brehm described were those seen on the Zapruder film—Kennedy's hands swooping toward his throat, and the head shot. But the "throat swoop"—so obvious on the film—was not obvious to all bystanders.

The film clearly shows that as the President passed him, Brehm was applauding.[87] I realized that Brehm's applauding provided the basis for re-interpreting his account. Brehm would not have applauded if he knew the President had been shot. Therefore, it is likely Brehm did not see the "throat swoop," and that his account of two "violent" reactions—broadcast within an hour of the shooting—referred to two shots which struck after Kennedy passed his location—two separate head shots.

film. I also concluded that if there were two head hits, the film itself must have been altered to conceal that fact.* I grew philosophical about the question: Was it really crucial to determine whether the gunman who shot Kennedy was situated to the right front, or the left front, or whether there were gunmen at each location?

What seemed most important was the evidence indicating the head wounds were altered. Whether the shot struck from the left front or the right front, this central feature of the Dallas evidence remained—almost every Dallas doctor agreed that there was an exit wound at the rear of the head.

But by the time the body reached Commander Humes, the pattern was different. The egg-size exit hole at the right rear of the head became a huge hole at the top of the head. Bone which surrounded the alleged right temporal entry was absent. Humes reported that the huge hole, comprising the "upper right side"[89] of the head, extended "somewhat"[90] into the temporal area.** Just beneath the rearmost circumference of that huge hole was the small puncture, which Kellerman testified was "in the hairline."[91]

To any autopsy doctor, there could be no mistaking the pattern Humes saw at Bethesda the night of the assassination: two holes—one big hole, one little hole; essentially, a back-to-front trajectory through the head.

The Warren Commission, apparently unaware of the conflict between the Dallas witnesses and the Bethesda autopsy report, cited the navy autopsy findings as the medical basis for its conclusion about trajectory, and drew no distinction between Dallas and Bethesda, simply noting that

---

* The Zapruder film seemed to indicate only one impact to the head from the front. But in 1976, there was a new development. Scientists at the Itek Corporation analyzed the Zapruder film for CBS News, one goal being to explain why the head snapped backward even though the assassin supposedly fired from behind. Although much of the report was devoted to establishing the theory that this was the result of Jacqueline Kennedy pushing the President backward, Itek's report was nevertheless a source of much valuable technical data. Buried in the report was Itek's statement that according to its measurements, the President's head "appears to receive a second impulse backward between 315 and 316."[88] If one discards the specious hypothesis of Jacqueline Kennedy as the cause of the President's rapid movement to the rear, this second rearward acceleration increases the probability that Kennedy might have been shot more than once from the front. The matter is fertile for further study.

Another point. The probability argument previously given (See Chapter 2, page 51) about the unlikelihood of two head hits applied to shots striking within one eighteenth of a second. Those probabilities don't apply here because the Itek study would space the two shots about three eighteenths of a second apart (assuming an unaltered film). If the film was altered (if frames were deleted), the shots might have been even further apart.

** If Humes had seen a bullet entry wound in the left front of the head, that would raise fundamental questions about the accuracy and the truthfulness of his description of the head.

"the large opening on the right side of [Kennedy's] head was the wound of exit."[92]

Arlen Specter seemed insensible to the conflict. Sometimes, when questioning the Dallas doctors, he substituted the Bethesda description for the Dallas description he had just been given under oath. For example, when Dr. Clark testified that he examined the wound "in the back of the head . . . in the right posterior . . ." Specter said: "Now, you have just described the large hole in the top of the head."[93]

Years later, Specter remained unaware of the difference. In a 1966 taped interview with journalist Gaeton Fonzi, Specter reminisced about the confusion of the Dallas doctors, chuckling as he recalled their view that a bullet entered at the throat, hit the spinal column, and then "bounced up through the top of the skull." "Weird? But conceivable," he commented, apparently unaware that he had combined the Bethesda description of the head wound with the initial Dallas opinion about trajectory.[94]

By December 1966 I had grasped the essential fact that there were two anatomically conflicting descriptions of the head wound, both in the public record, and I was beset by feelings that what I had discovered was too fantastic to believe. Meanwhile, *Ramparts* did a sudden turnaround, "The Case for Three Assassins" was scheduled for publication, and I had to make final revisions.* I was faced with a peculiar problem.

In the approximately six months since I had drafted it, my entire perspective had changed. I was no longer as interested in the conspiracy to shoot the President as I was in the conspiracy to alter his body, and my problem was how to deal honestly with a variety of Dallas/Bethesda conflicts in the context of a "multiple-shooter" conspiracy, without revealing what I now believed to be their root cause—an altered body. I was now

---

* Although dealing with the subject of the secret alteration of Kennedy's body was deadly serious, and on a personal level, sometimes frightening, my relationship with *Ramparts* magazine offered unintentional comic relief. Irritated that *Ramparts* would not publish "The Case for Three Assassins" when it was written, the previous June, I had given my copy of the manuscript to a friend who was editor-in-chief of the UCLA student newspaper. They were about to go to press on November 22, 1966, when Hinckle heard of it, and that apparently caused its value to zoom. Hinckle had *Ramparts'* attorneys threaten a lawsuit. Then he proposed a deal. If they would just hold off for about six weeks, until after the January 1967 *Ramparts,* containing the article, was on the stands, the *UCLA Bruin* could reprint it with permission. Hinckle then had the article printed separately on a rush basis, and bound into the January issue, at the last minute, as a second feature.

Years later, Hinckle wrote a memoir, "If You Have a Lemon, Make Lemonade," and spent about ten pages on his relations with the Kennedy critics. In the book, I am described as a "pushy UCLA engineering student," and Hinckle was still angry at the memory of my manuscript—so much so that he apparently forgot he published it.[95]

painfully aware that what many of the critics called evidence of a "second assassin" was actually a manifestation of—or circumstantial evidence of—body alteration. There appeared to be a "second assassin," and Kennedy appeared to have been caught in a crossfire, because the records of the Warren Commission contained two anatomically conflicting versions of the wounds.

Briefly, I toyed with the idea of approaching Warren Hinckle and Robert Scheer, attempting to explain all this, and suggesting a change in the article's focus from "multiple assassins" to body alteration. But I couldn't do that. It was clear that the senior management at *Ramparts* was ill-prepared to grasp a theory as sophisticated as the one I was proposing.

It didn't matter whether the hypothesis was logical. The barrier was psychological. Conspiracy was a ladder that had to be climbed step by step. It was unreasonable to expect someone to shift overnight from acceptance of the official version to complete disbelief. To believe the body was altered, you had to go through an intellectual initiation process—first, grappling with the medical contradictions and the grassy-knoll testimony; then, positing a "second assassin" which the government was "covering up" by failing to take into account all the evidence; finally, taking a closer look, realizing how unlikely it was that Humes lied about basic facts, and that the only plausible explanation for the Dallas/Bethesda conflicts was that the body had been altered. The idea was simple, but its plausibility depended on formulating the problem differently, on realizing that the body was the central piece of evidence—in legal terms, that the body was the "best evidence"—and that the conclusions of a legal investigation could be completely falsified by altering the "best evidence."

Another factor: I still had no firm idea where the alterations had been made. The simplest and most logical rebuttal to my medical analysis was: When and where could it have been done? I was anxious to tackle that problem, and knew one thing for certain: If I published an article, based purely on the medical evidence, I would be widely ridiculed, and that would hinder my ability to question any witnesses about the movements of the President's coffin.

All things considered, I decided the conservative approach was, for now, the proper one. In the *Ramparts* article, I cited the Dallas descriptions of the head wound as part of the case that an assassin had fired from the front. As to Bethesda, I raised the usual questions about why Humes burned his notes, why artist's drawings had been used instead of X-rays and photographs, but nowhere did I mention what I now realized was crucial: The Dallas and Bethesda wounds were anatomically different.

With one exception, the Warren Report critics seemed to be unaware of that anatomic distinction. The exception was Haverford philosophy professor Josiah Thompson, whose book, *Six Seconds in Dallas,* was published in November 1967. A feature of Thompson's analysis was the "double motion" shown on the film.* Thompson focused on this double motion, believing it indicated shots to the head from both directions—first from the back, then from the front. Thompson's detailed examination of the medical evidence appeared to support his theory and his analysis received widespread publicity.

Thompson recounted the Dallas descriptions of the head wound in detail, and published an excellent sketch of the egg-size wound at the right rear of the head. He set forth the Bethesda description. Then he wrote:

The pattern that emerges from this study of medical evidence is a dual one. From the Parkland doctors we get the picture of a bullet that struck the right front of the President's head . . . ranged backward causing massive damage to the right brain hemisphere, sprung open the occipital and parietal bones, and exploded out over the rear of the limousine. From the Bethesda surgeons we get the picture of a bullet entering the rear of the President's head and driving forward. . . . Putting the two pictures together we discern outlines of the double impact. First, a bullet from behind exploding forward, and in that same split second another bullet driving . . . [the] skull in the opposite direction. . . .[96]

This was the essence of the cross-fire theory to the head, but it was based on an analytic error. "Putting the two pictures together" was incorrect. Both pertained to the same body, but to different times. Six hours separated those two observations.

By joining the pictures, instead of contrasting them, a weird hybrid was created: a cross-fire theory that was supported neither by the autopsy report, which contained no evidence of shots from the front, nor by the Dallas observations, which gave no support to shots from the rear.

The essence of my emerging theory was that on November 22, the President's body was a target, the autopsy at Bethesda was the official examination of the target, and the outcome of the investigation had been changed by altering the target before that examination.

But cataloging the evidence concerning the four Bethesda wounds, I was aware that the strength of the evidence indicating fakery was not the same in all four cases. For example, I considered the two Bethesda rear entries. The essence of the case that they were fake, that they had been added to the body, was that no one saw them at Dallas.** But taken out of context in that fashion, the idea was bizarre. I respected the probabilities. The more implausible a hypothesis, the more evidence is required to support it. The evidence that made fake rear entries plausible was provided

---

* This forward motion is discussed in Chapter 2.

** That inference, based on the unlikelihood that two wounds really there had gone unobserved, was supported by certain related circumstances, such as Humes asking Perry whether he (Perry) made the back wound himself.

by the total picture that emerged from analyzing all the testimony, primarily the testimony about the other two wounds, the one in the throat and the fatal one in the head.

There the situation was entirely different. It wasn't necessary to evaluate what witnesses failed to see. One simply had to compare the descriptions of two wounds which were, in fact, observed by both groups of doctors.

Indeed, I came to believe that the case for body alteration rested on those two wounds, and the strongest evidence concerned the fatal wound.

First, of the four Bethesda wounds, the fatal wound was the only one whose alteration was explicitly alleged in an FBI report. And the evidence indicated that Sibert and O'Neill's statement that there had been "surgery of the head area" was an oral utterance by one of the doctors made at the outset of the autopsy.

Second, altering the head wound left a broad trail of evidence in the form of conflicting descriptions because so many Dallas doctors saw the wound, and described it in detail, and because getting inside the head was immensely disruptive. It involved cutting away scalp and removing bone. It meant making a little hole into a much bigger hole. That change was gross, and because the fatal wound was the focus of attention both at Dallas and Bethesda, a gross change could be documented with a high degree of reliability. My "before-and-after" research did exactly that, demonstrating that gauged by four separate criteria—size and shape, anatomic location, condition of the scalp, and the amount of brain visible—the fatal wound changed markedly from Dallas to Bethesda.

Indeed three separate sources of evidence—the FBI statement, the Dallas observations, and the Bethesda observations—all converged around one central idea: that the fatal wound was altered. To deny that, one had to believe that a great variety of erroneous data all coincidentally and falsely created the appearance that surgery was performed.

In 1966, I looked at the problem just that way—that were I a lawyer presenting information to a jury, I would rest my case for anatomic alteration on the fatal wound. But then I would go one step further. I would argue that if the body had been altered in any way, then all Dallas/Bethesda differences would have to be reinterpreted. Just as a handwriting expert, finding evidence of forgery in two words of a four-word signature, would label the entire signature a forgery, I believed a similar approach was justified here, in the case of Kennedy's cadaver and its four wounds.

The entire cadaver was evidence. Once medical forgery was established in the case of two wounds, it was a gratuitous assumption to believe that the remaining two wounds were legitimate.

On this point the legal principle seemed clear. If the body was altered in any way, then the autopsy was impeached as evidence. Certainly, it was no longer the "best evidence" of what the body looked like immediately after the shooting. What remained were the Dallas observations. Imperfect though they might be, they were the most reliable indicator—in effect, the "best evidence"—of what Kennedy's body looked like immediately after the shooting, and no Dallas doctor or nurse saw either rear entry wound.

The notion that the assassin's target was secretly altered, not just to change wounds which were already there, but to add wounds which weren't, was indeed fantastic. But the abundance of evidence about the fatal wound convinced me. The fantastic was true.

CHAPTER 14

Trajectory Reversal: Blueprint for Deception

I STEPPED BACK and tried to analyze the entire wound pattern.

At Bethesda, there were four wounds: two rear entries, one for the fatal shot, one for the non-fatal shot; and two exit wounds, the large head wound, and the wound at the front of the throat.

I assembled the Dallas/Bethesda data in a table. (See Fig. 24.) There were two parallel patterns, one for the neck, the other for the head.

In neither case was a rear entry observed in Dallas. In both cases, the wounds designated as exits in the Bethesda autopsy report were described as smaller by Dallas observers. The tracheotomy incision got bigger and acquired widely gaping irregular edges. The fatal wound—an egg-size hole at the right rear—was almost four times as large at Bethesda, encompassing much of the right side of the head. In each case, there seemed to be internal injuries consistent with the removal of bullets from inside the body —brain lacerations in the case of the head, lung bruising in the case of the neck.

I realized there were essentially two interpretations of the data—two ways of viewing how the President was actually shot, and what effect pre-autopsy surgery had on the apparent bullet trajectories. Which interpretation was valid depended on whether the two rear entries observed at Bethesda were genuine or false.

If the rear entries were genuine, the President had been shot from both directions, although two of his wounds—the throat wound and the head wound—appeared to have been enlarged to eliminate evidence of frontal entry.

If the rear entries were false, the President had been shot only from the front. In that case, the alteration of the body had two effects: (1) sup-

	Dallas	Bethesda
The Neck		
Back Wound	NOT OBSERVED	Entry above shoulder blade
Throat Wound	Entry	Exit
Trajectory	Front-to-back	Back-to-front
The Head		
Back Wound	NOT OBSERVED	Small hole just below large head wound
Large Head Wound	Size: 2¾″ Character: Exit at rear	Size: 5⅛″ Character: Exit from top right side
Trajectory	Front-to-back	Back-to-front

Figure 24.
Table showing differences between wounds at Dallas and at Bethesda and corresponding differences between trajectories

pressing shots from the front; (2) fabricating shots from the rear. The result: The direction of all shots had been reversed.

I could understand why, if the President was shot from both directions, his body might have been altered to suppress evidence of shots from the front.

But why would anyone reverse the direction of the shots? Lee Harvey Oswald's rifle was found near the sniper's nest behind the motorcade. If it was intended to create the appearance that shots were fired from behind so as to implicate Oswald as the assassin, why not fire the real shots from behind? Shooting from the front compelled the plotters to go to extraordinary lengths to conceal the true situation.

I tried to look at the problem as if I were a plotter whose goal was to murder the President and to inculpate Oswald as the sole assassin by false medical and ballistic evidence. It was necessary that:

1. all bullets (or sizeable bullet fragments) fired by the real assassins be removed from the body before the autopsy;
2. at autopsy, the side of the body that had faced Oswald's position must show entry wounds only; the opposite side, exits only.

In short, at autopsy, the wounds had to form a trajectory pattern which, projected backward, "pointed" toward the sniper's nest "above and behind" the motorcade.

Bullet Removal

Bullets could be easily located by taking an X-ray, but to retrieve them, one could not create holes arbitrarily. At autopsy, every hole would be classified as either an entrance wound or an exit.

One way to proceed would be to start at the wound of entry and use surgical instruments to probe inside the body, attempting to follow the wound track. But that could make it necessary to enlarge the wound. If the entry was on the side of the body facing the sniper's nest, that would present a problem. Entries are small punctures; exits are larger gaping wounds. Enlarging a rear entry could create the appearance of an exit on the rear surface—impermissible, for that would create the appearance of a wound inflicted from the front.

But an entry on the side of the body facing *away* from the sniper's nest would present no such problem. An enlarged hole on that side could be passed off as an exit.

Indeed, what could and could not be done to the body after death stemmed from a simple principle: A little hole could be made into a bigger hole, but a hole could not be made smaller or made to vanish.

Wound Geometry

At autopsy, the side of the body which had been facing the sniper's nest must show entries only; the opposite side must show exits only. An entry wound could be enlarged to mimic an exit wound; the reverse was not possible. This had implications. The side of the body facing a shooter could be viewed as an erasable blackboard— erasable in the sense that any entry on that side could be made to "disappear" by enlarging it, making it appear to be the exit of a shot fired from the opposite side.

Assuming the geometry in Dallas—i.e., at the time he was shot, the President was facing forward and the sniper's nest was behind him—it was clear that, if I were a plotter, this procedure of enlarging entries could be used to "erase" shots from the front.

But there was a condition. For each such entry transformed into an exit, a suitable entry must exist on the rear surface of the body.

If I could somehow arrange to leave that side of the body unmarked, then the required "companion" entries could be created wherever they were needed.* The problem I would face would be how to leave the rear surface unmarked.

---

* If I positioned shooters to the rear and relied on genuine entries, a number of problems would arise. First, there would be no guarantee that such entries would be positioned "above and behind" the holes at the front, yet they must be, since my goal was to fabricate downward-slanting trajectories. Second, if the genuine rear entries

Evidently, I should fire no shots from the rear. That would leave the rear surface clear of entries. But how could I prevent shots fired from the front from bursting through, leaving exit wounds?

The problem of whether a bullet will or will not pass all the way through a person's body is one faced every day by law enforcement. Police officials must constantly worry that an officer's bullet will transit the body of the intended target and hit a bystander. To avoid this, some police departments use hollow-point (i.e., soft-nosed) ammunition.

A hollow-point bullet has a small portion of the nose removed, so that when it strikes, it begins to spread out immediately; that, in turn, causes much greater wounding and it also brings the bullet to a halt rapidly. A hollow-point bullet has far less chance of going all the way through the victim than a bullet with a hard metal jacket.

Consequently, it seemed that if I were a plotter, I could arrange to leave the rear surface free by firing only from the front, using hollow-point ammunition. The body, after the shooting, would have entry wounds on the front and bullets inside. By enlarging the frontal entries, I could retrieve the metal, leaving holes which could pass for exits. Then I could put whatever entries were necessary on the rear surface.

I could get the bullets out as long as I was prepared to reverse the trajectories.

What I found intriguing was the way these two problems—bullet removal and trajectory alteration—were intertwined and the way this particular scheme, which I dubbed "trajectory reversal," solved both at once. (See Fig. 25.) The problems were intertwined because it was impossible to get at bullets inside the body without affecting the wounds on the surface, yet the wounds determined the trajectories. Trajectory reversal solved both problems simultaneously because enlarging a bullet entry hole at the front (1) provided access to a bullet to be extracted, and (2) turned an entry into an exit.

So whether the motive was to retrieve metal or to create exits facing away from the sniper's nest, as part of a plan to fabricate "back-to-front" gunshot trajectories, the result was the same. Pre-autopsy bullet removal and trajectory reversal went hand in hand.

The seemingly paradoxical consequence of this analysis was that to be

---

were made by any weapon other than Oswald's, the problem of bullet removal would again arise. But my analysis demonstrated that recovering a bullet through its wound of entry would probably require the enlargement of that hole, creating the appearance of an exit—impermissible, if the wound was on the rear surface.

Ideally, what I wanted on the rear surface were entry wounds positioned exactly where they were needed, without the problem of having to extract any bullets which caused them. The simple way to accomplish this would be to leave the rear surface clear and create the rear entries, as needed, after the shooting.

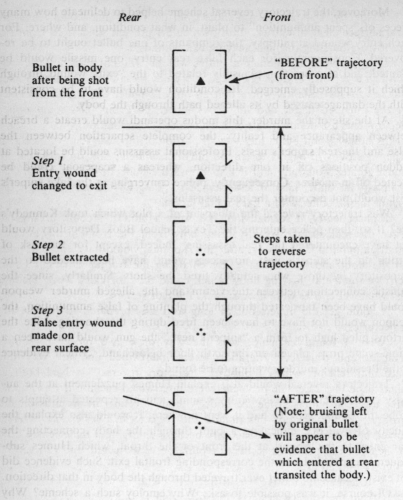

Figure 25.
The mechanics of trajectory reversal

able to shoot the President, retrieve the bullets, and insure that afterward it appeared the shots came from behind, the real bullets had to be fired from the front.

What struck me about trajectory reversal was that in principle, at least, it could be planned in advance. As part of the murder, it could be planned to shoot from the front and then, by altering the body, make it appear that the shots came from behind, from the direction of a pre-arranged sniper's nest.

Moreover, the trajectory reversal scheme helped to delineate how many pieces of "spent ammunition" to plant, in what condition, and where. For each entry wound at autopsy, the remnants of one bullet ought to be recovered. Consequently, for each false rear entry, one missile would be planted, and at a location plausibly related to the "exit" wound through which it supposedly emerged. Its condition would have to be consistent with the damage caused by its alleged path through the body.

At the site of the murder, this modus operandi would create a breach between appearance and reality: the complete separation between the false and the real sniper's nests. Professional assassins could be located at hidden positions off in one direction, whereas a scapegoat could be located off in another. Consequently, police converging at the fake sniper's nest would not encounter the real assassins.

Was trajectory reversal the blueprint of a plot which took Kennedy's life? If so, then police entering the Texas School Book Depository would not have encountered the real assassins. Indeed, except for the task of setting up the sniper's nest, no access would have been needed to the Depository by those who actually fired the shots. Similarly, since the ballistic connection between the victim and the alleged murder weapon would have been fabricated through the planting of false ammunition, the weapon would not have to have been fired during the shooting. Like the cartons piled high to form a "sniper's nest," the gun would have been a crime-scene prop, placed on the sixth floor beforehand, critical evidence in the President's murder, waiting to be found.

Trajectory reversal would also explain Humes' puzzlement at the autopsy over finding a shallow entry wound, and his repeated attempts to probe the wound, only to find it went nowhere. It would also explain the paucity of evidence indicating a path through the body connecting the rear entry to the wound at the front of the throat, which Humes subsequently concluded was the corresponding frontal exit. Such evidence did not exist, because no bullet ever traveled through the body in that direction.

Of course, it was possible to ask: Why employ such a scheme? Why not fire Oswald's rifle from behind? True, that would eliminate the necessity of retrieving bullets from *that* rifle. But the problem, as I believed a plotter would see it, was that more than one assassin would almost certainly be required to accomplish the assassination with precision because of numerous unpredictable factors: the position of bystanders, the President's posture, etc. And once the decision was made to use any gun beside Oswald's the problem of bullet removal would again arise. Solving it would require secret access to the body before autopsy, and alterations made in accordance with the trajectory reversal scheme. But now there would be an additional complication: distinguishing between "non-Oswald" bullets to be extracted from the body, and "Oswald" bullets to be left inside.

Ultimately, I concluded that if the plotters planned to alter the body for any reason, it made no sense to use Oswald's gun at all, when it could so easily be connected to the body afterward, during pre-autopsy surgery.

Although my table of Dallas/Bethesda data suggested the trajectory-reversal hypothesis, there were two discrepancies I noted immediately. First of all, at Dallas there appeared to be an exit wound at the rear of the head. That meant that a bullet or a fragment had passed all the way through. If I was correct, that certainly wasn't the intent of the plotters. Nevertheless, that wound made no difference to those who altered the body, the reason apparently being that the enormous hole created during pre-autopsy surgery subsumed both the original frontal entry and the egg-sized exit at the rear. The result, at Bethesda, was a single enormous hole at "the top." In November 1966, when I first formulated the trajectory-reversal scheme, the Kennedys had just deposited the autopsy X-rays and photographs in the Archives, with the restriction that no one outside the government could see the material for five years. I was most curious to know what the X-rays and photographs would someday reveal about the rear portion of the large head wound, since the evidence indicated it was originally an exit wound in Dallas.

The second discrepancy concerned the location of the rear entry for the neck trajectory. There was evidence that the hole had been created too low to serve as the entry for a bullet which exited from the front of the throat. For several weeks, a satisfactory answer to that problem eluded me, but then I had a series of insights which seemed to provide an explanation.

The evidence that the wound was "low" consisted of:

1. the clothing holes in the shirt and coat—5½ inches below the top of the collar;
2. the placement of the dot—but not the measurement—on the autopsy diagram, indicating the rear entry was below the throat wound;
3. the recollections of autopsy eyewitnesses. Sibert and O'Neill said it was "below the shoulders," and FBI reports referred to it as a back wound.[1] Secret Service Agent Hill said it was "six inches below the neckline."[2]

What struck me was that all this evidence was "Friday night evidence" —the "dot" was placed by Boswell on Friday night; the witnesses who saw the wound were basing their recollections on what they saw on the body at the autopsy on Friday night. And of course the clothing holes which matched the wound were in the clothing as it reached the FBI Laboratory on Saturday morning. I presumed they had been made by Friday night.

These Friday-night data were inconsistent with the subsequent autopsy conclusion that the bullet passed all the way through, but it was *not* inconsistent with what was being said about the bullet on Friday night at the autopsy. At Bethesda, the shallow wound made sense. It was "paired" with the bullet found on the Dallas stretcher. Indeed, upon hearing about the existence of such a bullet, the autopsy doctors immediately made the connection between the wound (which had no bullet) and the Dallas stretcher bullet (which wasn't associated with any particular wound).

Reviewing the facts, I drew the diagram I had drawn so many times before to illustrate Humes' perspective on Friday night—as reported by FBI agents Sibert and O'Neill—a simple line drawing of Kennedy showing a back-to-front head trajectory, a hole thought to be a tracheotomy incision at the front of the throat, and a shallow back wound. Then I drew a dotted line connecting the back wound with a bullet which supposedly fell from that wound and was found on the Dallas stretcher. (See Fig. 13 in Chapter 7.)

Suddenly, it dawned on me that both these entities—both bullet and wound of this bullet/wound pair—were on my list of fake evidence. I had suspected the bullet was planted because of its unmutilated condition, because there was no blood or tissue on it, and because of the strange circumstances under which it was found. I suspected the wound was phony because (1) it wasn't seen in Dallas (nor felt by Dr. Carrico, who did a brief manual examination of the back); (2) photographs showed that the Secret Service agent who said he saw the bullet strike was looking off in another direction; (3) Dr. Perry testified that Humes asked him "if we made any wounds in the back"; and (4) Humes, when referring to that wound, used the phrase, "presumably of entry."

But although I had viewed the back wound as fake and the bullet as planted, I had never looked at them as a pair. Yet this atypical bullet and this atypical wound fit like nut and bolt. Could that be coincidence?

Immediately, I realized that the wound I suspected of being fake might have been deliberately created as a "receptacle" for the bullet I suspected was a plant, and that my diagram illustrated an important possibility: Conspirators who viewed the President's body as evidence were in a position to fabricate a specific false impact situation on the rear surface of the body.

I was startled at the level of detail at which the plotters could fabricate evidence, the verisimilitude such a scheme would afford.

A bogus bullet/wound match offered the perfect excuse for a nearly intact bullet to reach the FBI Laboratory. The cover story was so simple—and it was one that would be promulgated by no less an authority than the autopsy surgeon. The bullet had only gone in a little way, broken no bones, and then "fallen out" of the body. The doctor might honestly believe it! Presented with a wound without a bullet, and a bullet without a wound, what other conclusion could he draw? The result would be that the FBI would receive a pristine bullet, logically related to a trajectory deduced by the autopsy doctor, the perfect specimen for its ballistic microscope, hard evidence linking Oswald's rifle with the President's murder.

Another insight. If the alteration of the body was planned as part of the assassination plot, and if a phony bullet/wound match was part of that body-alteration scheme, then the bullet could be planted well before the autopsy. In short, the concept of a preplanned bullet/wound match held the answer to those whose response to the critics' hypothesis of a planted bullet was to ask: How could anyone plant a bullet so "early"? How could a plotter know, at such an early hour, that other bullets would not be found, or that the autopsy findings would be such that this bullet would fit with other facts of the case?*

Indeed, turning those questions around, it seemed to me that if bullet 399 was a plant, then its early planting was an indication that the plot to alter the body was integral to the plot to shoot the President—i.e., that it was planned, as part of the murder, to secretly falsify the circumstances of death.

A fake bullet/wound pair would certainly explain the "low" back wound. The wound was originally created to match the bullet and for no other reason, so its precise location would not have been critical. I found that explanation appealing. The Friday-night association between stretcher bullet and back wound was recorded in three FBI reports—the Sibert and O'Neill report, and the two FBI Summary Reports, based on the Sibert and O'Neill report. Essentially, my hypothesis implied that those reports—considered highly authoritative at the Justice Department—recorded an appearance which was the original intention of plotters who planted the bullets and altered the body.**

But now a new loose end emerged. If the back wound was created to be paired with the stretcher bullet, then how did the plotters intend to account for the wound at the front of the throat? Immediately, what came to mind were news accounts published in mid-December 1963, supposedly

* Such arguments were made by various defenders of the Warren Report. Lawrence Schiller wrote: ". . . if somebody was going to plant a bullet to frame Oswald, he would have been foolish to plant a near-pristine bullet—which could only increase suspicion."[3] AP reporters Gavzer and Moody wondered: "And what if another bullet had also been found?"[4] Jacob Cohen said the notion of a planted bullet "is absurd . . . the conspirators, in advance, could not have known where to drop the bullet, or how it would fit into the case. . . ."[5] Dr. Lattimer said: "I see no possible way anyone could have fired a bullet into a bale of cotton, let's say ten feet thick, [and] recovered the bullet—you know, it takes you hours to find a bullet like that when you're digging it out. . . ."[6]

** The December 9, 1963 FBI Summary Report stated: "Immediately after President Kennedy and Governor Connally were admitted to Parkland Memorial Hospital, a bullet was found on one of the stretchers. Medical examination of the President's body revealed that one of the bullets had entered just below his shoulder to the right of the spinal column at an angle of 45 to 60 degrees downward, that there was no point of exit, and that the bullet was not in the body. An examination of this bullet by the FBI Laboratory determined that it had been fired from the rifle owned by Oswald."[7]

based on "authorized" leaks of the autopsy conclusions. Those accounts said the throat wound resulted from a fragment of the head shot.*

The throat wound, however, could not have been caused by a fragment of the head shot, because the Zapruder film showed Kennedy reaching for his throat a full five seconds before he was struck in the head. Separate motions; separate bullets. Consequently, if the body had been altered to account for the throat wound as a fragment of the head shot, then the body had been altered "incorrectly." Of course, any body alterations created the groundwork for incorrect (i.e., false) autopsy conclusions, but this particular false conclusion happened to be inconsistent with what the Zapruder film showed were Kennedy's movements during his last moments of life.

Now I began to understand what might have happened. The Zapruder film wasn't processed and screened in Dallas until late Friday afternoon, but the body had been altered by those who didn't take into account what it showed. That was sheer conjecture, but were it not for Zapruder's film, an autopsy report could probably have been written saying the President was shot twice—once by a bullet which struck in the back, created a shallow wound, and then fell back out; and then a second time by a bullet which struck the head, with a fragment of bone or metal emerging from the wound at the front of the throat.**

---

* Some examples. On December 18, 1963, the *Washington Post* reported: "A fragment was deflected and passed out the front of the throat." The same day, the *New York Times*, quoting "a reliable source familiar with the autopsy findings," reported: "The pathologists at Bethesda, the source said, concluded that the throat wound was caused by the emergence of a metal fragment or piece of bone resulting from the fatal shot in the head." The December 27, 1963 issue of *Time* and the December 30, 1963 issue of *Newsweek* carried similar reports. Despite the near unanimity on this particular point, these accounts differed on the question of whether the bullet which caused the shallow back wound was found on the stretcher or inside the body, and the result was a profusion of accounts, none of which seemed to agree with another. The atmosphere is best captured by a *Washington Star* report on December 18, 1963, which begins as if the subject were the latest price of an item on the Commodities Exchange: "Here is the new account of the wounds, as reported by a source fully acquainted with results of a post-mortem examination conducted at the Bethesda Naval Hospital. . . ."

** I later realized that the problem was more complex, and a more fundamental explanation for why the body had been altered "incorrectly" revolved around the plotters' failure to realize the throat wound existed at all! That hole was situated near the usual spot for performing a tracheotomy, and Dr. Perry made his incision through the wound. But the original wound was so small (3–5mm) that it would have appeared as nothing more than a minor raggedness at the center of a tracheotomy incision of "2–3cm"—the length Perry told me was the one he made. Consequently, if conspirators obtained access to the body, and for some reason did not know the tracheotomy had been performed over a bullet wound, they might at first ignore that wound entirely. I guessed that something along these lines had occurred. Moreover,

Was that what Humes had written in the autopsy report he burned on Sunday, November 24? That was a subject for speculation.*

Aside from these two discrepancies—the low back wound and the existence, in Dallas, of an egg-sized exit at the right rear of the head—my table of Dallas/Bethesda comparisons fit the trajectory reversal pattern and explained numerous conflicts of observation in terms of a systematic plan to alter the body. There were twelve entries in the table—six pertaining to the neck; six to the head. One could argue with each individual item in the table (e.g., the rear neck wound was actually present in Dallas, but had been missed by all the doctors; or the Dallas observers were wrong in believing the throat wound was an entrance), but the table accurately reflected the record. Two parallel patterns did exist in the evi-

---

once such an error was made, it could not be corrected if the plotters realized they had missed a bullet wound at the front, widened that wound, and took out metal. A "low" rear entry, once created, would be a permanent fixture on the body.

* I wasn't the only one doing the speculating. Shortly after I explained this whole sequence to Wesley Liebeler in October 1966, Liebeler met with the editors of *Life* and said that he was "certain" Humes burned the original draft because it reflected a finding contrary to the official report. My source for this was Liebeler himself. Josiah Thompson, in his book *Six Seconds in Dallas*, had attributed the statement to a "distinguished member of the Commission's staff," and in a November 1967 conversation, which took place shortly after Liebeler first saw a copy of Thompson's book, which had just been published, Liebeler admitted that Thompson was referring to him. Thompson reported that the *Life* editor with whom Liebeler had met had made a record of what Liebeler said in a memorandum to the files.[8]

Although I believed there had been an earlier draft of the autopsy, I did not subscribe to the notion that that draft ever reached the Warren Commission—indeed, that it ever got out of Humes' possession.

Many critics believed otherwise because when the transcript of the January 27, 1964 Executive Session became available, it showed General Counsel J. Lee Rankin puzzled by the throat wound, stating: "We have an explanation there in the autopsy that probably a fragment came out of the front of the neck. . . ."[9]

I thought Rankin was confused by what the FBI said (or at least implied) about the navy autopsy findings in the January 13, 1964 FBI Supplemental Report, which he and the others were perusing at that meeting. The January 13 report contained photographs showing that there was a hole at the front of the President's shirt near the collar button and, after describing those holes in detail, stated: "The Chief Pathologist at Bethesda Naval Hospital had advised that the projectile which had entered the President's skull region had disintegrated into at least 40 particles of bullet fragments as shown by the number located."[10]

The juxtaposition of these two statements—one about the holes in the front of the shirt, the other about fragments from the head shot—seemed designed to convey the impression that the clothing holes were caused by a fragment of the head shot; ergo, so was the throat wound.

The FBI report writer was probably in a peculiar position. The Sibert and O'Neill report—the primary source—made no mention of the throat wound (because

dence, and yet they pertained to entirely different areas of the President's body.

Could that be coincidence?

I was aware that the evidence for alteration (or outright fabrication) was not equal in the case of all four wounds. Consequently, I drew a distinction between whether the body was altered at all and whether it was altered exactly the way I suspected—i.e., according to the trajectory-reversal scheme. Suppose, for example, I was correct that two of the wounds—the throat wound and the head wound—had been enlarged, but incorrect that the two rear entries were fake. In that case, Kennedy was shot from both directions, and body alteration was performed only to suppress shots from the front.

But because I found the evidence for fake rear entries persuasive, and because, at a simple mechanical level, it seemed impossible for anyone to have distinguished between "Oswald" and "non-Oswald" bullets, I believed that if the body was altered, it must have been altered in accordance with a preplanned scheme such as trajectory reversal. Indeed, I became keenly aware why proving the two rear entries were fake would be of

---

Humes thought it was a tracheotomy on Friday night); yet the FBI Laboratory received the President's shirt, which had holes near the collar button. Unless the report writer was given access to the navy autopsy report (which didn't reach the FBI until December 23, 1963, and which, according to documents released in 1978, was considered a sensitive document and held in a file in an Assistant Director's office), he would be forced to rely on the Sibert and O'Neill document, and practically have to speculate on what caused the hole in the front of the shirt. The result was a peculiar paragraph which conveyed the impression that the autopsy showed the throat wound resulted from a fragment of the head shot. That paragraph, I believed, was the basis for Rankin's statement.

In 1968 I found persuasive evidence that the Warren Commission only received one navy autopsy report, the one it published, in the preliminary report of Warren Commission attorneys Ball and Belin, dated February 26, 1964, available at the National Archives. Ball and Belin noted that "The FBI report on the autopsy of the President . . . does not coincide with the actual pathological examination." They then quoted the Sibert and O'Neill version, which said the bullet did not transit, and repudiated it as ". . . hearsay . . . contradicted by the formal autopsy report which under date of December 20 was sent by Secret Service. . . ."[11]

To believe the Commission received an earlier navy autopsy report, it was necessary to believe either that numerous attorneys were lying or that General Counsel Rankin had hidden the existence of this "earlier" autopsy, which he discussed in an executive session, from staff members such as Ball and Belin. I opted for the explanation that the Commission received only one autopsy report from the Secret Service, the one with which Ball and Belin compared the FBI report, and that Rankin was confused at the January 27, 1964 meeting.

A corollary to this discussion: If my analysis of the January 13, 1964 Supplemental Report was correct, and represented the thinking of the FBI bureaucracy, then such officials were probably the source of the news leaks attributing the throat wound to a fragment of the head shot.

paramount importance, because at stake were significant issues concerning the structure and workings of the plot which may have taken the President's life.

Plot Structure

Fake rear entries would mean that President Kennedy had ridden into a well-engineered ambush: shooters to the front, fake sniper's nest to the rear. Fake rear entries would be circumstantial evidence of a plan in force, at the time of the shooting, to alter the body afterward, because fake rear entries would indicate a high degree of pre-arrangement regarding the location of shooters, as well as a false sniper's nest, with respect to the body. Indeed, one could go a step further. Because the gun at the sniper's nest had been mail-ordered to Oswald's post office box, fake rear entries would mean that the conspirators who murdered the President planned to frame Lee Harvey Oswald for their crime.

Oswald's Behavior and Whereabouts

From my first reading of the twenty-six volumes, I was impressed with Oswald's behavior and alleged whereabouts at the time of the shooting. For example, it was a fact that within ninety seconds of the shooting—at most—Oswald was on the second floor of the Texas School Book Depository. This was established by an encounter he had with Dallas motorcycle officer Marion Baker, who was riding escort in the motorcade. Within seconds of the shooting, Baker jumped off his cycle, dashed into the Depository, asked building manager Roy Truly to show him the way to the upper floors, and followed as Truly ran up a stairway at the rear of the building.* Baker later testified his interest was drawn to the upper floors because he saw pigeons fly off the roof. When Truly was halfway between the second and third floors, he noticed the officer was no longer behind him. Truly returned to the second-floor landing, walked the twenty feet to a vestibule door, opened that door, walked through the vestibule and into a lunchroom, to find Officer Baker, gun drawn, facing Lee Harvey Oswald. The Warren Report noted: "Truly thought that the officer's gun at that time appeared to be almost touching the middle portion of Oswald's

---

* Pauline Saunders, a Depository employee standing in front of the building when the motorcade passed, told the FBI that a police officer in a white helmet ran into the building "within ten seconds of the shooting."[12]

body."[13] I believed Oswald came within a hair's breadth of being shot. Baker asked Truly: "Do you know this man; does he work here?" Truly replied "Yes."[14] The officer let Oswald go. Truly testified that Oswald "didn't seem to be excited or overly afraid or anything. He might have been a bit startled, like I might have been if somebody confronted me."[15] Baker testified that he left the stairwell and ran the twenty feet to the vestibule door and then into the lunchroom because, as he rounded the second-floor landing, he caught a glimpse of someone through the small glass window in the upper part of the door.[16]

Truly testified that after Baker released Oswald, and he and the officer continued their climb up the stairway, Officer Baker said: "Be careful, this man will blow your head off."[17]

The Commission analyzed this encounter from the standpoint of determining "whether Oswald could have descended to the lunchroom from the sixth floor by the time Baker and Truly arrived."[18] Its own reconstruction established the encounter had occurred between seventy-five and ninety seconds of the shooting, and it argued that Oswald could have left the sniper's nest, traversed the sixth floor to the rear, hidden the gun, and come down four flights of stairs in that time.[19]

I was skeptical. At the time, Oswald did not seem out of breath, and there was no witness who recalled anyone running down four flights of stairs in the Depository. Indeed, one witness, Victoria Adams, testified she was on the stairway at that time, and heard no one.[20] The Commission concluded she was wrong as to when she was coming down the stairs.[21]

Then there was the issue of the Coke. The original news accounts said that when Baker first saw Oswald, the latter was drinking a Coke. This seemingly minor fact was crucial, because if Oswald had time to operate the machine, open the bottle, and drink some soda, that would mean he was on the second floor even earlier than the Commission's reconstruction allowed. In a signed statement Officer Baker was asked to make in September 1964, at the tail-end of the investigation, he wrote: "I saw a man standing in the lunchroom drinking a coke."[22] A line was drawn through "drinking a coke," and Baker initialed the corrected version.[23] Police Captain Will Fritz, in his report on his interrogation of Oswald, wrote: "I asked Oswald where he was when the police officer stopped him. He said he was on the second floor drinking a Coca Cola when the officer came in."[24]

If I were a juror, I would have believed Oswald already had the Coke in hand, and indeed, had drunk some of it, by the time the officer entered the lunchroom.

After finishing his Coke, Oswald left the building and boarded a bus. When the bus bogged down in traffic, he got off and took a cab. Cabdriver William Whaley testified that an elderly lady approached his cab at about the time Oswald did, and Oswald offered her the cab—hardly the behavior of an assassin making a getaway.[25]

Then there were the Oswald denials. As Oswald was being driven to police headquarters after his arrest at 2 P.M., Sergeant Gerald Hill suggested that when they arrived Oswald might wish to hide his face from reporters. "Why should I hide my face?" he replied. I haven't done anything to be ashamed of." Patrolman K.E. Lyon, who was in the car, reported: "Enroute to City Hall, Oswald . . . kept repeating, 'Why am I being arrested?' "[26] Under interrogation, he repeatedly denied he was the assassin ("Oswald frantically denied . . . shooting President John F. Kennedy," reported FBI Agent Hosty),[27] and when he was being led from one place to another, he would shout these denials to reporters in the hallway. On Friday night, he told reporters: "I'm just a patsy."[28] On Saturday, confronted with a barrage of questions about whether and why he shot the President, he yelled: "I don't know what kind of dispatches you people have been given. I have not committed any act of violence."[29]

On Saturday, Oswald was visited in his jail cell by his brother Robert. Robert Oswald testified that when he asked his brother how he could possibly maintain his innocence, Lee Oswald replied: "Do not form any opinion on the so-called evidence."[30]

When Oswald made that statement, he probably had in mind the paraphernalia found at the sniper's nest (the gun and three shells) and the photograph showing him posing with a rifle, a picture he claimed was a composite. But the most important evidence against Lee Harvey Oswald was the President's body.

The President's Body and the Case Against Oswald

Without rear entries, Oswald couldn't be the assassin. Consequently, an autopsy report *with* rear entries could be viewed as evidence "against" Oswald, as inculpatory evidence. An autopsy reporting *no* rear entries would be exculpatory—establishing Oswald's innocence because shots didn't strike from behind.

The notion that the autopsy report, and by implication, the President's body itself, was evidence against Oswald, was not at first obvious. But once that dawned on me, I re-examined the problem. By altering the body, was it possible to fabricate the Oswald case in advance, in conjunction with the shooting?

When the body was viewed from the front, the alterations could be construed as "erasing" a grassy knoll shooter; from the rear, as constructing a case against Oswald. But what did the rest of the case consist of? I broke it down into its component parts.

The evidence fell into three categories:

1. Evidence connecting Oswald to the gun.
2. Evidence connecting Oswald directly to the victim.
3. Evidence connecting the gun to the victim.

I found it convenient to visualize the case as a triangle whose vertices represented Oswald, the rifle, and the victim. The three sides represented the three categories of evidence. (See Fig. 26.)

It was clear that if this triangle could be fabricated, then Oswald could be framed.

(A) The Oswald-Gun Connection. The primary link connecting Oswald to the gun was microfilmed records from Klein's Sporting Goods in Chicago. Those records showed that in March 1963, Klein's received a mail-order coupon for a rifle, and subsequently shipped a rifle—serial number C2766 —to one A. J. Hidell at P.O. Box 2915, Dallas, Texas.[31] P.O. Box 2915 was Oswald's post office box; and A. J. Hidell was an alias he had used in distributing Fair Play for Cuba leaflets the previous summer in New Orleans. FBI handwriting experts testified that the handwriting was Oswald's.[32]

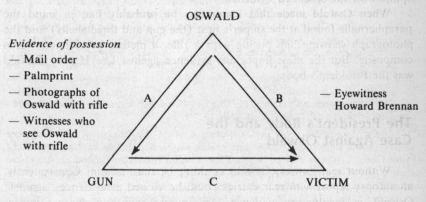

Evidence of possession
— Mail order
— Palmprint
— Photographs of
   Oswald with rifle
— Witnesses who
   see Oswald
   with rifle

OSWALD

A   B

— Eyewitness
   Howard Brennan

GUN   C   VICTIM

— Autopsy trajectories: 2 shots from behind
— Ballistics: 3 pieces of ammunition
   fired from Oswald's rifle—
   1 intact bullet found
   on stretcher; 2 large fragments
   found in car

Figure 26.
Case against Oswald viewed as a triangle
   A. Oswald — Gun
   B. Oswald — Victim
   C. Gun — Victim

Another aspect of the Oswald-gun link was evidence indicating possession. FBI fingerprint expert Sebastian Latona testified that he examined the gun after it was received at the FBI Laboratory on Saturday, November 23, and that ". . . the latent prints which were there were of no value."[33]* However, on November 29, 1963, the FBI Lab received Oswald's palmprint which the Dallas Police Department said had been "lifted" from the underside of the rifle barrel on November 22, 1963, before the rifle was sent to Washington.[36] Because this print arrived so belatedly, many critics questioned its legitimacy. Liebeler, too, had suspicions and liked to tell the story that it was at his insistence that the FBI examined the lift itself, microscopically, to see whether other identifying marks could be developed to prove that the palmprint in fact came from the rifle, and not from some other surface that Oswald touched while in police custody. The FBI Lab found that irregularities in the lift corresponded exactly with imperfections on the rifle barrel, and so, argued Liebeler, there could be little question that Oswald actually handled the rifle.**[37]

---

* The gun was brought to Washington by Dallas FBI Agent Vincent Drain. In 1971, while reviewing tapes of local Dallas radio broadcasts at the National Archives, I found evidence that the Dallas Police couldn't find any prints, either, before they released the rifle to FBI Agent Drain on Friday night. Dallas newsmen Joe Long and Gary DeLaune of radio station KLIF were at police headquarters and in touch with Dallas detectives. On Friday evening, both broadcast reports that the rifle contained no fingerprint evidence. A typical report by DeLaune: "Once again, that late report from police headquarters. No fingerprints found on the weapon which had been located in the building from which the fatal shots were fired. The . . . rifle, turned over to the FBI, is being sent to Washington . . . but this is a big disappointment to those investigating today's assassination."[34]

On Saturday, when Captain Fritz, Chief of Homicide, was asked, "Were Oswald's prints found on the rifle?" he replied, "No, sir."[35]

** On August 28, 1964, in the closing days of the Commission investigation, Liebeler wrote Rankin a memorandum asking why Dallas Police Lt. Carl Day, head of the Crime Lab, who claimed he lifted the print on November 22, had photographed other prints on the rifle which were of no value, but failed to photograph the palmprint. Liebeler's memo, along with a letter he drafted over Rankin's signature, was forwarded to the FBI. "Lt. Day should be questioned concerning his usual practice in photographing prints and in establishing beyond question that a print in fact appeared on a particular object from which it was claimed to have been lifted. If he did not follow his usual practice in instant case, we would like to know why he did not."[38] Liebeler requested that Day make a written statement. FBI Agent Drain interviewed Day, who declined to supply a written statement. Day said that he didn't photograph the palmprint because Chief Curry told him to turn the rifle over to the FBI, that he "literally took him at his word," and he stopped processing it. Day said he didn't protect the palmprint with cellophane—as he did the other less valuable smudges—because the print was on the underside of the barrel, protected by the wooden stock when the rifle was assembled.[39] In 1967 Liebeler said he was satisfied the Oswald palmprint came from the rifle barrel, because of the FBI Laboratory's finding when the lift was examined microscopically. But I found a serious loophole in this analysis. I realized that it might be possible to fabricate the evidence by bringing the rifle to the morgue,

Other evidence establishing possession were the pictures showing Lee Harvey Oswald with the rifle, published in *Life*. A controversy swirled around these pictures because, when they were first shown to Oswald, he said somebody had pasted his head on another man's body.[49]

Could the Oswald-gun link be fabricated? In principle, there was no need for fabrication. I could grant, for the sake of argument, that Oswald in fact ordered and possessed the rifle found at the sixth floor of the Texas School Book Depository, and that if there was a plot to frame Oswald, the problem was simply to get Oswald's rifle.

(B) The Oswald-Victim Link. I reserved this leg of the triangle for eye-witness evidence linking Oswald directly with the shooting. There were six witnesses cited in the Warren Report who made statements that someone appeared to be at the window, or that they glimpsed a gun. Only Howard Brennan made a positive identification.

Brennan's identification was beset with so many problems, however, that even the Warren Commission didn't rely on it. The story of how

---

after Oswald's death, and simply pressing it against his hand. Immediately I checked the record for information regarding the whereabouts of the rifle, and learned that after being examined at the FBI Lab in Washington it was sent back to Dallas on Sunday, November 24.[40]

On Sunday night, Oswald's body was kept at the Miller Funeral Home in Fort Worth. I ordered microfilms of both Fort Worth papers, hoping to find a story about the assassin's body's overnight stay at the morgue. The November 25, 1963 *Fort Worth Press* carried just such a story: BODY OF JFK ASSASSIN IS UNDER GUARD IN FW. The story said the morgue was "a lonely place" and described the round-the-clock guard maintained by the Fort Worth police. It also included this detail: "An FBI team, with a camera and a crime lab kit, spent a long time in the morgue."

The implication was that Oswald was fingerprinted *after* he died. But I could find no FBI reports in the record of any such postmortem fingerprinting at the Miller Funeral Home. There was, however, a fingerprint card dated November 25, 1963, in the 26 volumes. The origin of this card was unclear. It was received by the FBI in Washington on November 29, the same day the palmprint arrived. The Dallas police were listed as "contributor" and Oswald, it said, "refused to sign." When FBI expert Latona was asked the reason for the second post-assassination submission, he could only make the implausible suggestion, "It was made, I believe, in order to advise us formally that the subject, Lee Harvey Oswald, had been killed."[41] In July 1980, I located Jack Moseley, who wrote the *Fort Worth Press* story. Moseley, who was editor-in-chief of the *Fort Smith* [Arkansas] *Southwest Times-Record,* told me he definitely saw federal agents going into the room with a crime lab kit "for extended periods of time . . . someone said they were fingerprinting him, that they were taking prints off the corpse . . . they did something in the preparation room, one or more times. I'm convinced of that."[42]

I spoke to ex-FBI Agent Vincent Drain, who had personal custody of the rifle. Drain said he never brought the rifle to Fort Worth, that he turned it over to the police on Sunday, November 24, 1963, after he returned with it from Washington. Drain said he doubted there had been any postmortem fingerprinting because the FBI already had a fingerprint record of Oswald from the Marines.[43]

I contacted Paul Groody, the funeral director at the Miller Funeral Home, where

Brennan at first failed to identify Oswald in a lineup; of the FBI reports stating that he could not identify him; of how he later changed his mind; of how he said the man was standing at the window (that was impossible because the window was close to the floor and only half open, so anyone there had to be kneeling)—all this became the subject of whole chapters in books criticizing the Warren Report.

The Warren Report alluded apologetically to some of the deficiencies in Brennan's testimony, and then, in what seemed to me to be an attempt to have it both ways, stated: "The Commission, therefore, does not base its conclusion concerning the identity of the assassin on Brennan's subsequent certain identification of Lee Harvey Oswald as the man he saw fire the rifle."[50]

---

the body had been embalmed. I asked if there was any postmortem fingerprinting as reported in Moseley's story. "Oh, yes, yes, I was there. That's exactly what they did." I asked Mr. Groody if he personally witnessed it. He replied: "I was not in the room at the time; but I had to clean up his fingers after they got through fingerprinting him. They put black gook on his fingers, and they can't get it off; so they leave it up to me to clean his fingers off; so they did fingerprint him." I asked Groody if there was ink on the palms. "It was a complete mess of his entire hand, which would lead me to believe that they did take prints of his palms." Groody estimated the embalming was completed by 1:30 A.M. and that the fingerprinting, which took about a half hour, took place sometime between then and 5:00 A.M.[44] Neither Groody nor Moseley saw a rifle or a rifle barrel brought to the embalming room.

I then located Vince Drain's unpublished FBI report of his round trip from Dallas to Washington with the rifle. Drain took possession of the rifle on Friday night at 11:45 P.M.; left Dallas aboard an Air Force plane at 3:10 A.M., November 23; arrived in Washington at 6:30 A.M., and brought the rifle to the lab. The FBI's examiner then found no prints of any value or any evidence that a lift had been made. Drain returned to Dallas with the rifle early on the morning of November 24 and, after a delay when Oswald was shot, transferred the rifle back to the Dallas police on Sunday afternoon at 3:40 P.M.[45] Oswald's body, at that time, was in the morgue at Parkland Hospital, where it remained until about 10:30 P.M., under police guard.[46]

A postmortem palmprint could have been placed on the rifle at the Dallas morgue after 3:40 P.M., or later in Fort Worth.

As the weekend progressed, the statements of Dallas officials appear to indicate a more optimistic attitude with respect to the fingerprint evidence. On Friday night, as previously noted, Captain Fritz, Chief of Homicide, denied any prints were found. Fritz' immediate superior, Deputy Police Chief Stevenson, head of the Criminal Investigation Division, was non-committal. District Attorney Wade parried several fingerprint questions over the weekend, responding shortly after midnight on Friday, "That's part of the evidence that we'll determine a little more definitely later on. The gun has just been sent to Washington."[47] On Sunday evening, during a televised press conference, Wade volunteered: "Let's see. The—his fingerprints were found on the gun. Have I said that?" On the audio tape a reporter, who sounds rather startled, yells: "You *didn't* say that." Wade continued: "Palmprints rather than fingerprints . . . under, on part of the metal, under the gun." "When did you know that?" asked the reporter. "Before sending the gun to Washington?" Replied Wade: "Before. They were found by the Dallas police."[48]

Wesley Liebeler used to stress that the Commission had concluded Oswald was the assassin based on physical evidence at the crime scene, which established that Oswald's gun was the murder weapon, not on Brennan's identification. Brennan's testimony simply established that someone was up there.

Faking the Oswald-victim link would have been easy. Someone had to be up there, but that "someone" did not have to be Oswald. The plotters simply had to have someone stand near the window, roughly of Oswald's height and weight, and appear to fire a gun at the President. By creating that appearance at the sniper's nest, at the time of the shooting, eyewitnesses would be sure to crop up, such as Howard Brennan.*

But had these witnesses glimpsed the appearance or the reality? That would depend on the body.

Indeed, these two legs of the triangle demonstrated something important: It would not be possible to frame a man for a motorcade assassination by erecting a false sniper's nest, placing his gun nearby, and having someone appear to fire it, while shooters hidden elsewhere actually carried out the crime. An honest autopsy would immediately exculpate the accused. The autopsy would show that the bullets came from another direction, and the bullets would fail to match the gun. A ballistic *mis*match would be as conclusive of Oswald's innocence as a ballistic match was of his guilt.

To any plotter wishing to fabricate the gun-Oswald-victim triangle, the problem would be manufacturing the gun-victim leg of the triangle. In short, the problem would be how to falsify the medical and ballistic evidence.

(C) The Gun-Victim Connection. I viewed the gun-victim connection

---

* I also assumed that in setting up this false appearance, the plotters would see to it that three loud noises, corresponding to the three spent shells, would be set off somewhere "above and behind" the motorcade. In 1979, the House Assassinations Committee, after analyzing a tape recording of the shooting created at Dallas police headquarters when a microphone on a police motorcycle in the motorcade was accidentally left open, concluded that four shots were fired, one from the front. If trajectory reversal occurred, the three noises from behind would have to be re-analyzed to determine whether they were gunshots or blanks. Since a shock wave precedes the sound of a supersonic bullet, the presence or absence of such a shock wave could be used for this purpose. But, while simple in theory, detecting a shock wave on the worn Dallas police tape is problematic. The Committee's experts testified that about 25 percent of the time, a signal interpreted to be a shot might be preceded by a shock-wave-like "spike" that was, in fact, nothing more than random noise.[51] The experts noted that whereas the "shot" from the front was preceded by a shock-wave-like spike, such a spike preceded only one of the three "shots" from the rear. The other two lacked a shock wave, explained the experts, because the microphone wasn't positioned correctly with respect to the sniper's nest.[52] The entire matter is ripe for review if the body was altered, especially since the Committee's tests, while detecting four shots, did not rule out the possibility of more.

as consisting of two parallel links—the ballistic evidence, which linked the gun to Kennedy's body, and the gunshot trajectories themselves, which, like arrows protruding from the body, linked the location of the sniper's nest to the location of the President at the moment the shots struck.

To falsify the ballistic evidence and the trajectory information, the plotters must either recruit the investigators themselves, or falsify the evidence. For example, if the FBI Laboratory received the genuine assassination bullets, performed the tests, and found those bullets were not fired from Oswald's gun, to then falsify that report it would be necessary to recruit FBI personnel into a conspiracy to lie about the facts. This could be avoided by falsifying the facts themselves, by sending the FBI Laboratory bullets which *had* been fired from Oswald's gun. The same principle applied to the President's body, the source of trajectory information. It was simpler to make changes on the body before the doctors examined it than to present them with an unaltered body and attempt to persuade them to falsify their reports—for example, to maintain that wounds existed which they didn't see.

Moreover, unlike a ballistics examination, which would be carried out in the privacy of the FBI Laboratory, it was inevitable that the autopsy examination would be conducted in a roomful of witnesses—people who would not only see the body, and could provide an independent account of the wounds, but could provide an account of what conclusions were being drawn as the doctors conducted the examination. As it turned out, the most important such "bystander witnesses" were FBI agents Sibert and O'Neill.

If, to avoid altering the body, the doctors were recruited into a plot, then, to deceive the bystander witnesses, the doctors would also have to sham the autopsy—for example, bend over a body which showed frontal entry and pretend not to see what was really there. Indeed, they would have to make false oral statements, at least for the benefit of the FBI, as they performed the examination.

If the body was unaltered, and the autopsy doctors both shammed the examination and then falsified their report, still another problem would remain: the X-rays and photographs.*

It was easy to say such evidence could be faked, but in practice the technical problems were anything but trivial. X-rays of the head might be tested for authenticity through dental identification, and photographs of

---

* In any homicide investigation, the autopsy X-rays and photographs are an integral part of the autopsy protocol. In this case, Chief Justice Earl Warren declined to make them part of the Warren Commission's evidence, but that was purely his option. He could have decided otherwise. Indeed, one reason the Warren Commission attorneys said they felt confident the autopsy doctors could not have lied was that they could not have known whether the Commission would ultimately demand to see that evidence.

the head wounds would have to be convincingly faked from several angles—a near impossibility.

From a technical standpoint alone, it made no sense to attempt such a feat—in effect, to leave the most important evidence, the body, unaltered, buried in a cemetery, where an exhumation would readily reveal the lie—when to avoid these problems it was only necessary to recognize that the body was evidence and make plans to alter it prior to autopsy.

In both the realms of ballistics and geometry, that would create a firm connection between gun and victim. And, in principle at least, there would be no need to recruit anyone in the FBI, no need to falsify the autopsy photographs or X-rays or recruit any of the personnel who examined the body, and no need to worry about the autopsy eyewitnesses. If the body was altered, the autopsy itself would be reduced to a grotesque charade, and the case incriminating Oswald would be based on a foundation of false facts.

The alteration of the body would mean that the "solution" to the crime —i.e., a false case against Oswald—was constructed in conjunction with the shooting.

The Secret Service and the Bullets

Once I had formulated the trajectory reversal hypothesis, I further explored the implications of where the ammunition was found, and how it was handled.

One facet of my hypothesis was that it demonstrated, in theory at least, that the plotters could know, once they saw the body, how much ammunition was needed, and so could coordinate the planting of bullets with the fabrication of trajectories. Indeed, it would be possible to know, in general terms, where to plant the bullets. Any bullet which supposedly traveled on a forward and downward path would probably end up in the automobile—which, from the standpoint of the trajectory reversal plan, was a mobile crime scene, the container for the body at the time of the murder. The automobile was exactly where two large bullet pieces were found, and the automobile, like the body, was in the possession of the Secret Service.

The car was flown from Dallas to Washington aboard an Air Force jet and driven to the White House garage. Shortly after 10:00 P.M., Deputy Secret Service Chief Paul Paterni, and Floyd Boring, Assistant Special Agent in Charge of the White House detail, began an inspection. In a letter to the Warren Commission, Secret Service Chief Rowley stated: "In running his hands over the front cushion of the automobile, Deputy Chief Paterni found a metallic fragment in the front seat in the area between left and right front seat."[53] A second fragment was found by Thomas Mills, a hospital corpsman assigned to Dr. Burkley's office, who was requested by Paterni and Boring to accompany them on the inspection.[54]

Like the two fragments in the car, the stretcher bullet entered the mainstream of the FBI investigation via the Secret Service. Shortly after it was found by Darrell Tomlinson, it was turned over to Secret Service Agent Richard Johnsen. Agent Johnsen carried it back to Washington, presumably in his pocket, and then turned it over to Secret Service Chief Rowley, in the Executive Office Building, adjacent to the White House, at 7:30 P.M.[55]

I came upon something else. On Friday night, Chief Rowley himself played a role in causing the autopsy surgeon to match that bullet to the back wound.

Secret Service Agent Kellerman testified that the autopsy had been under way for some time, when the doctors raised the body off the table. "Nobody was aware until they lifted him up that there was a hole in his shoulder. That was the first concrete evidence that they knew that the man was hit in the back first."[56] "This Colonel Finck . . . raised him and there was a clean hole."[57]

About this time, Kellerman told how he received a message. "I was informed by navy personnel that I should call Mr. Rowley."[58] Kellerman placed the call from a hallway telephone. "This was my first knowledge that they had found a projectile," he testified.[59]

The record shows Arlen Specter's reaction to Kellerman's receiving a call at Bethesda from the Secret Service Chief.

SPECTER: . . . from whom was the call again?

KELLERMAN: Mr. Rowley, Chief of Secret Service.

SPECTER: You got the phone call from Mr. Rowley?

KELLERMAN: Yes.

SPECTER: Who had called him, if you know?

KELLERMAN: This I don't know.

SPECTER: But at that time Chief Rowley advised of the detection of the bullet on the stretcher and brought you up to date with what information was known at that time?

KELLERMAN: Yes, sir.[60]

When Kellerman returned to the morgue, he apparently passed on the information to the two FBI agents; they reported about a call they initiated to FBI Agent Killion at the Firearms Section of the FBI Laboratory. Killion, they wrote, "advised that the laboratory had received through Secret Service Agent Richard Johnsen a bullet which had reportedly been found on a stretcher in the emergency room of Parkland Hospital. . . ."[61]

Once Humes was informed of this, the connection between bullet and shallow back wound was immediate, and Sibert and O'Neill wrote: "Immediately following receipt of this information, this was made available to

Dr. Humes who advised that in his opinion this accounted for no bullet being located which had entered the back region and that since external cardiac massage had been performed at Parkland Hospital, it was entirely possible that through such movement the bullet had worked its way back out of the point of entry and had fallen on the stretcher."[62]

Was it a coincidence that Chief Rowley happened to call the autopsy room at just the time when the doctors were puzzling over what to do about an inexplicable wound? Rowley was never asked about the call during his Warren Commission testimony, and in a detailed memorandum to his files, dated December 19, 1963, and devoted entirely to how he received bullet 399 from Agent Johnsen and sent it to the FBI, Rowley made no mention of the call to Roy Kellerman at the Bethesda morgue. He simply noted that FBI Agent Elmer Todd "was given the bullet enclosed in an envelope. . . . The time of delivery was approximately 8:50 P.M., Friday, November 22, 1963. The bullet was to assist the FBI Laboratory in ballistic tests of the gun subsequently brought to Washington from Dallas, Texas, as the gun used by the defendant Oswald."[63]

My analysis of the case against Oswald as a gun-victim-Oswald triangle showed the primacy of the gun-victim connection. My analysis of that leg of the triangle showed the major role played by the Secret Service as the custodians of all the suspect evidence.

If that triangle was actually fabricated, then the effect of such chicanery was best seen by examining the FBI investigation. Several U.S. agencies investigated the assassination, but the FBI was the investigative arm of the U.S. Department of Justice, and it was the FBI which was charged, by President Johnson, with making a full and complete investigation, and submitting its conclusions in a formal report.

If the body was altered, this is what it looked like to the FBI. From the Dallas Police, the FBI Laboratory received a rifle. From the U.S. Secret Service, it received three pieces of ammunition. Upon examination, it was immediately established that the weapon fired those bullets. Once the FBI Laboratory reported the gun-bullet match, the rifle was considered the murder weapon. When Sibert and O'Neill returned from Bethesda bringing autopsy conclusions that both shots came from behind, that only corroborated, in the realm of geometry, what was already known from the ballistics tests. The gun-victim link was established. As far as the FBI was concerned, President Kennedy was murdered by Oswald's rifle, and the shots came from the direction of the Texas School Book Depository.

That the FBI made these tests and drew exactly these conclusions within the first twenty-four hours became a matter of record in 1978, when they released, under the Freedom of Information Act, their nearly 100,000-page internal archive.

Those documents show that by noon on Saturday, November 23, the FBI had concluded that Oswald was the assassin based on the fact that the bullets sent by the Secret Service matched the rifle received from Dallas.*

By Sunday, Assistant FBI Director Alan Belmont reported that he was sending two FBI supervisors to Dallas to "prepare a memorandum to the Attorney General . . . to set out the evidence showing that Oswald is responsible for the shooting. . . . that Oswald is the man who killed the President."[66]

That document would become the December 9 FBI Summary Report.

The FBI would spend months investigating Oswald's background—his trip to Russia, his trip to Mexico, his activities in New Orleans the summer before, handing out leaflets for the Fair Play for Cuba Committee—and the State Department and the CIA would contribute to those inquiries; but all that was filigree.

The central fact was that if President Kennedy's body was altered, and false ammunition planted, then *within twenty-four hours* of the murder, the U.S. Department of Justice had been deceived and, on the basis of phony evidence, had arrived at false conclusions about the murder of the President of the United States.

I returned to the question: Was the President's murder and the alteration of his body part of one integrated disguise? Or were they separate acts—a murder followed by an impromptu coverup? In short, was body alteration "before the fact" or "after the fact?"

Whichever was the case, high government officials must have been involved, because only they had access to the body.

"After the Fact"

In this case, in the hours after Kennedy was assassinated, the U.S. Government, presumably with benign intent (i.e., in the interest of political

---

* The initial FBI report to the White House, drafted on November 23 by Supervisor Fletcher Thompson, indicated Oswald was the assassin, and relied heavily on the ballistics tests showing that the three pieces of ammunition—the stretcher bullet, and the two fragments found in the car—came from the rifle found at the sniper's nest.[64]

Another document showing the general attitude of FBI supervisory officials on November 23, 1963, was written by the number-two man at the New Orleans Field Office, and records what he was told by a headquarters supervisor with whom he spoke at 11:20 A.M. that day. "I asked him whether or not there was anything he could tell me concerning the case as all our information was coming via radio and TV . . . and he stated in this case we needed the evidence to tie it in as Oswald was admitting nothing; that the gun, bullets and everything else was in the Laboratory and it looked good."[65]

stability), decided to falsify the facts of Kennedy's death. A covert action was undertaken to obtain access to the body before the autopsy as part of a plan to alter the evidence so that it would appear that only one man shot the President. By 2:00 P.M., the Dallas Police had arrested Oswald for the murder of a police officer. Because he worked in the Texas School Book Depository, where a sniper's nest had been found about an hour before, he was immediately considered a suspect in the President's assassination. Under this hypothesis, the Federal Government, hearing about the arrest, and knowing about Oswald's background—he was a returned defector, had handed out leaflets for the Fair Play for Cuba Committee in New Orleans, had been to the Russian and Cuban embassies in Mexico City the month before—immediately set out to provide an autopsy report and ballistics data which would link Oswald's gun to the crime. The necessary alterations were made to the body and the necessary bullets planted. The result: A navy autopsy report, which said Kennedy was struck twice from behind, and an FBI ballistics report that stated the bullets had been fired from that rifle.

If this is what happened, then the Secret Service must have played a major role, because the Secret Service had custody of the coffin, and all three pieces of ammunition came into the investigation via the Secret Service.

If all this was part of a "benign" after-the-fact coverup, then presumably top Secret Service officials were involved in seeing to it that ammunition from Oswald's rifle was "found" in the car and then sent to the FBI, so that when the rifle arrived from the Dallas Police, there would be a ballistic match, and the gun would appear to be the murder weapon.

There were a number of serious defects in this "after-the-fact" hypothesis. By definition it permitted no preplanning, but how could so much have been done so quickly without it? In addition, it required the convergence of numerous improbable circumstances. For example, from the standpoint of those who altered the body, it had to be a fortuitous circumstance that whoever shot the President just happened to shoot him only from the front, making it easy to alter the body and create the appearance that shots were fired from the rear; and it was also a fortuitous circumstance that Oswald, although he did no shooting, was nevertheless arrested by the Dallas Police; and that his gun turned up at the building at 1:22 P.M., about thirty-five minutes before the arrest.

Then there was bullet 399, the pristine stretcher bullet. It was found so early—possibly by 1:00 P.M., and certainly no later than 2:00 P.M., when the President's body left the hospital. Yet the police didn't have Oswald's gun until 1:22 P.M.,[67] and it wasn't fired, as far as is known, until it reached the FBI Crime Lab in Washington the next day.

Because of its subsequent pairing with the shallow back wound, the mysterious appearance of bullet 399 on a Dallas stretcher—if that bullet was a plant—represented one of the earliest overt acts of conspirators who intended to alter the body. If that conspiracy was hatched "after the fact," one had to believe that the decision to plant 399 was made after Kennedy was shot at 12:30 P.M.; that the gun was then obtained, and fired; the bullet retrieved, taken to Parkland Hospital, and planted there. And all this was accomplished before Kennedy's body left the Dallas hospital at 2:00 P.M., and before Oswald was even arrested, a seemingly impossible feat even if the plot was carried out by a professional intelligence unit.

And certainly any such "benign" after-the-fact conspiracy presupposed the official involvement of people skilled in the techniques of covert operations, e.g., the CIA. Yet in 1966, there was not a shred of evidence to indicate that any of the legitimate intelligence apparatus of the U.S. Government had been used to implement such a plan.

Finally, common sense dictated that no such "benign" alteration of the body had taken place. Even if the new President of the United States knew, on November 22, of some secret, dangerous truth, and was intent on hiding it in the interests of, say, avoiding a war, and so wanted to issue a "political autopsy," the alteration of the body seemed totally unnecessary. He had only to issue direct orders through the military chain of command. If the problem was essentially political, it seemed farfetched to believe that legitimate channels in the government would be involved in such grotesque physical alteration of evidence.

To alter the President's body before the autopsy, before autopsy photographs, before autopsy X-rays, was to destroy an irreplaceable record, the *only* accurate record of the shooting. It was to falsify history—not temporarily, until passions cooled, but forever.

For these reasons, I found the idea that the President's body was altered "after the fact," for benign political reasons, to be a weak hypothesis.

"Before the Fact"

This theory implied that the alteration of the body was an integral part of the plot to take the President's life. In that case, trajectory reversal was the mechanical basis for a disguise. It provided a way of dealing with the President's body in two contexts—as a person to be murdered, and as evidence to be altered.

By altering the body, the conspirators who murdered the President could fabricate a false "solution" to the crime. If this was the case, then as the limousine sped away from Dealey Plaza carrying the mortally wounded President, three general tasks remained to be done:

1. attention had to be called to the sniper's nest on the sixth floor of the Texas School Book Depository, so that the Dallas Police would find the "murder weapon";

2. the real assassins, probably located in the railroad yard, somehow had to make their getaway, unseen by bystanders;
3. the President's body had to be altered before the autopsy, and the appropriate ammunition planted, to correlate with the trajectories.

If these tasks could be accomplished, the conspirators would have committed the perfect crime.

The record contained evidence of all three types of activity.

Calling attention to the sniper's nest.

Why did the Dallas Police Department focus its investigation so quickly at the sixth floor of the Depository? I knew that the Warren Commission had turned up several witnesses who thought they saw someone firing a gun from that location, but most of those accounts didn't become available for quite a while after the shooting. Yet the Police Department converged on the building quickly. I turned to the Dallas Police radio transcripts searching for an explanation.

I was aware that Officer Marion Baker ran into the building within seconds of the shooting, supposedly because he saw pigeons fly off the roof. Examining the radio transcripts, I soon found that other men in Baker's unit played major roles in focusing attention on the Depository. Later, when I obtained a tape of those broadcasts, I could hear their voices as that extraordinary drama unfolded.*

The first transmission was made by motorcycle escort Robert Hargis, between 12:34 and 12:35 P.M. The transcript reads: "A passerby states the shots came from the Texas School Book Depository Building." The dispatcher replied: "Get all the information."**

The next transmission came within the minute, at 12:35, and was made by Officer Clyde Haygood. "I just talked to a guy up here who was standing close to it and the best he could tell it came from the Texas School Book Depository Building here with that Hertz Renting sign on top." The dispatcher replied: "Get his name, address, telephone number there—all the information that you can from him."[69]

Within two minutes, Haygood signaled the dispatcher, was recognized, and transmitted: "Get some men up here to cover this building, this Texas School Book Depository. It is believed the shots came from there. If

---

* I have studied the tape itself and four versions of the transcript—the Dallas Police version (Sawyer Exhibits A and B in the twenty-six volumes), the FBI version (Commission Exhibit 1974), a Secret Service version (CE 705), and one circulated with the police tape itself, and published in the back of Judith Bonner's book: *Investigation of a Homicide*.[68]

There are minor differences. Except where noted, I will quote the FBI version.

** Officer Hargis was #136. Quoted here is his transmission as it appears in Sawyer Exhibit A. This transmission also appears on the tape itself. For some reason, it is omitted from the FBI transcript, CE 1974. Hargis is in Photo 13, standing between two cycles.

you're facing it on Elm Street looking toward the building, it would be the upper-right-hand corner, the second window from the end."[70]

Haygood's transmission, made before 12:37 P.M., specified the exact window.*

Within a minute, Motorcycle Officer Brewer came on the air: "We have a man here who says he saw him pull the weapon back through the window from the southeast corner of that Depository building."** The dispatcher acknowledged: "Ten-four."

What was peculiar about these transmissions is that two came from officers who photographs showed were running up the grassy knoll.*** Thus, it appeared that despite their initial reaction, the officers made transmissions which provided information to the dispatcher which would cause him to focus on the Depository. Indeed, Haygood actually pinpointed the precise window.

In each case, the officer claimed he had a witness, and the dispatcher said, as he did to Haygood: "Get his name, address, telephone number there—all the information that you can from him."

Yet in no case was the witness ever produced.

When the officers were questioned about who provided the information, their responses were not particularly useful.

BELIN: Do you remember anything about the description of the man [who] said that the shot came from the second window from the end in the upper-right-hand corner?

HAYGOOD: No.

BELIN: Do you remember if he was white or Negro?

HAYGOOD: He was a white man. . . .

* Officer Haygood was assigned number "142." Before the Warren Commission, he testified he made both transmissions quoted here.[71] For some reason, the FBI, in transcribing the second transmission, said it was made by number 22, "LL Hill."[72] Both the tape and Haygood's own testimony established that this is incorrect. In the Dallas police transcript (Sawyer Exhibit A), he is identified as the source of both these transmissions, as #142. I quote the actual tape here. The FBI transcript reads: "Get some men up here to cover this school depository building. It's believed the shot came from, as you see it on Elm Street, looking toward the building, it would be upper right hand corner, second window from the end."[73]

** Officer Brewer was assigned number 137.[74] The FBI transcript is quoted here. Listening to the tape, you can hear Brewer specify a floor, but which one is unclear. My transcript of the tape reads: "We have a man here that said he saw him pull the weapon back through the window off the [second or seventh] floor of the southeast corner of that depository building." Sawyer Exhibit A reads: ". . . from the window off the second floor of the. . . ."

*** Willis slide 7 shows Officer Haygood, having dismounted from his cycle, running up the knoll, his gun drawn. A picture taken by Wilma Bond shows Robert Hargis having ascended the knoll near the railroad tracks.

BELIN: Do you remember whether he was young or medium or old?

HAYGOOD: That would be a guess on my part. I don't recall. He was just a medium age.

BELIN: Do you remember if he was dressed in a suit or not a suit?

HAYGOOD: Best I remember, just sports clothes. I mean, it consisted of no tie or coat.[75]

Officer Brewer was asked for a description.

BELIN: Do you remember whether this man that you talked to was a white male or a Negro?

BREWER: He was a white man, the best of my memory.

BELIN: Do you remember anything else about him?

BREWER: No, sir.[76]

Each officer claimed he was stopped by someone.

I was left with a choice. Either the transmissions were contrived—i.e., had no basis in fact—or there was a person walking around Dealey Plaza who systematically approached the police officers, told each he saw the shooting, pointed to the building (in Haygood's case, actually specifying the window), and who then, having played his role, simply walked off the stage of history, never to be heard from again.

Within about two minutes of these transmissions, the Dallas Police dispatcher made a general broadcast on Channel 1, which flooded the area with police, many of whom then entered the building. "Attention all squads. Report to downtown area, code 3 [emergency—red lights and sirens], to Elm and Houston, with caution."[77]

An ancillary mystery was why, since the transcript showed these broadcasts focused attention on the building, and since Haygood actually specified the correct window, it took the police about forty minutes to find the sniper's nest and the three spent shells. I found it difficult not to entertain the suspicion that perhaps the arrangement of the sniper's nest hadn't been completed.

In documents I obtained from the Archives in 1968 was an FBI report which said that a witness at a window on an upper floor of a nearby building had told a Dallas lawyer she saw "some boxes moving" in the window from which the shots allegedly came.[78] Over a decade later, photographs taken within moments of the shooting were analyzed by photogrammetric experts who were consultants for the House Assassinations Committee. Their conclusion, which the House Committee included in its report: "There is an apparent rearranging of boxes within 2 minutes after the last shot was fired at President Kennedy."[79]

Files I studied years later at the Archives reveal that in the final stages of its investigation, the Warren Commission legal staff became aware of this uncomfortable forty-minute lapse between the time of the shooting and the time the sniper's nest was found. Over J. Lee Rankin's signature, a letter drafted by Al Goldberg was sent to the FBI on November 2, 1964, about six weeks after the Warren Report was published, asking for an explanation and suggesting further investigation. On November 12, 1964, Hoover replied, and declined to investigate further. "The significance of this time lapse," he wrote, "is not readily apparent when considered in the light of the scientific examinations and findings of the evidence found." As to the cause of the delay, Hoover wrote: "Traffic congestion from the Presidential motorcade and the subsequent assassination could have contributed to the delay in the arrival of members of the Dallas Police Department Crime Laboratory."*[80]

The President was assassinated at 12:30 P.M. and the transmissions pinpointing the sniper's nest had been made by 12:38. What happened during the next five minutes was even more remarkable. The police dispatcher broadcast Oswald's description, as that of "the suspect."

The source was Inspector Herbert J. Sawyer, who had gone to the front of the Depository and set up a "command post." Sawyer's source, in turn, was another unidentified witness. Questioned by the Warren Commission, Sawyer couldn't provide very much detail: "I remember that he was a white man and that he wasn't young and he wasn't old. He was there."[83]

The police transcript told the story of what happened just prior to 12:45 P.M.

> SAWYER: The type of weapon looked like a 30-30 rifle or some type of Winchester.

* Goldberg would not let the matter drop. On November 18, he sent another letter: "It is appreciated that the members of the Dallas Police Crime Laboratory may have been delayed by traffic in reaching the building, but there is ample evidence that search of the sixth floor had already been undertaken by other law-enforcement officers. It would therefore be desirable to know when, if ever, information was transmitted to the officers engaged in searching the building that the shots had been fired from the sixth floor, or more specifically, from the southeast corner window on the sixth floor. It is appreciated that the failure to communicate this information to the officers in the building might well have been the result of the turmoil and uncertainty that prevailed, but it would still be desirable to have this information on the record and available for future reference and research."[81] Goldberg attached to his letter an article in the *New Republic*, "Warren Report—Case for the Prosecution," one of the earliest critiques, and noted: "Analysis and criticism of the Commission Report in the press (see attached article) has pointed to this significant time lag in the discovery of the carton, cartridges, and rifle. For future reference and research purposes, and to render the investigation more complete, it would be desirable to secure more precise information on these points."[82] That letter, written almost two months *after* the Warren Report was published, is one of the last in the file. Hoover made no reply.

DISPATCHER: It was a rifle?
SAWYER: A rifle, yes.
DISPATCHER: . . . any clothing description?
SAWYER: About 30, 5' 10", 165 pounds.[84]

Having received the height, age, and weight, the dispatcher now re-broadcast the information. Listening to the actual police tape years later, a friend of mine discovered that the police dispatcher had added something:

Attention all squads; the suspect in the shooting at Elm and Houston is supposed to be an unknown white male, approximately 30, 165 pounds, slender build, armed with what is thought to be a 30-30 rifle. Repeat. . . .[85]

Oswald was definitely of "slender build." But the information transmitted from Inspector Sawyer to the dispatcher did not include that. All men who are 5' 10" and 165 pounds are not necessarily of "slender build," and if the dispatcher, in the few seconds between the time he received the information from Sawyer and when he broadcast it, himself drew that inference, that might be a sign of good police work. But the addition of those two words could also be a sign that, like the witness who provided information to the police in Dealey Plaza, someone had provided the fact, "slender build," to the dispatcher of the Dallas Police Department.*

The records of the Dallas Police transmissions revealed that within minutes of the shooting, the police focused on the sniper's nest as the source of the shots, and someone of Oswald's description as the "suspect."

In short, judged by the first fifteen minutes, the Dallas Police investigation appeared to contain the Warren Commission conclusions, in embryonic form.

The grassy knoll within minutes of the shots.

Photographs show a stream of people converging at the grassy knoll after the shooting. So exactly how a group of assassins made their getaway from there was a mystery. One police officer who ran to the knoll was Joe Marshall Smith. Smith testified that as he approached the area, gun drawn, he encountered someone in civilian attire who claimed to be a Secret Service agent.[87] The records show that no Secret Service men were on the grassy knoll—the only Secret Service men were with the motorcade. Smith's encounter with a Secret Service man was one of three such encounters described in the Warren Commission records, and it raised the possibility that the conspirators shielded their escape by having men pose as Secret Service agents.[88]

* This discovery was made by Steven Bailey. The addition "slender build" actually appears in the FBI transcript of the Channel 1 and Channel 2 transmissions,[86] but it is more striking when actually heard on the tape.

Altering the body.

From Dallas to Bethesda, the President's body was in the custody of Secret Service and navy officials. Also in the custody of the Secret Service was the President's clothing and the Presidential limousine.* Both bullet fragments were found in the car.

If the body was altered and false ammunition planted in the car, it was difficult to believe that Secret Service officials were not involved in the plot. To think otherwise, one had to believe that inside the Secret Service responsible officials and agents were themselves the victims of a deception so perfectly executed it never came to their attention.

From the standpoint of research, the problem was separating the good guys from the bad guys. It seemed unreasonable to believe the Secret Service was involved en masse, but seemed just as unlikely that not a single agent or official was involved.

The "getaway," the focusing of the police investigation on the sniper's

---

* The record contains evidence indicating the limousine's windshield may have been switched. At Parkland Memorial Hospital, journalist Richard Dudman reported that he and a companion noted the windshield had a hole in it.[89]

Corroboration of Dudman's contemporary account came from interviews, conducted in 1971 by an assassination researcher, with two Dallas motorcycle officers, Sgt. Stavis Ellis and Patrolman H.R. Freeman. Both were in the escort preceding the President's car, and then went to the hospital. Asked to describe the car at the hospital, Sgt. Ellis volunteered, "There was a hole in the left front windshield." "You sure that was a hole?" asked the interviewer, who suggested it might have been some lesser kind of damage. "It was a hole," replied Ellis. "You could put a pencil through it. . . . You could take a regular standard writing pencil . . . and stick [it] through there." Ellis recalled that at Parkland, when he commented on the hole, "Some Secret Service agent ran up [and] said, 'That's no bullet hole. That's a fragment!' It wasn't a damn fragment. It was a hole." Ellis' account was corroborated by Officer Freeman. He too volunteered that at the hospital he saw a hole in the windshield, and he was emphatic about what he saw: "[I was] right beside it. I could of touched it. . . . It was a bullet hole. You could tell what it was."[90]

The limousine was flown to Washington and driven to the White House garage, where it was examined by a five-man team from the FBI Laboratory. Secret Service agent Charles Taylor, Jr., who witnessed that examination, wrote in his report, "Of particular note was the small hole just left of center in the windshield."[91]

The next week, a windshield was removed from the automobile and stored in the White House garage. In March 1964, the Secret Service sent a windshield to the FBI Laboratory, which determined that it contained no hole, only damage on the outside surface. The inside surface was smooth.[92] I called this the "hole/no-hole" conflict, and the question it raised was whether the windshield on the limousine, on November 22, 1963, was the same windshield sent to the FBI Laboratory in March 1964.

The record is further clouded by a January 6, 1964 letter written by Secret Service Chief Rowley, transmitting Taylor's report to the Warren Commission. Rowley made no mention of the agent's assertion that the windshield had a hole. He did, however, state that Special Officer Davis and Special Agent Geis, neither of whom were mentioned in Taylor's report, were present when the automobile arrived, that both ran their hands over the windshield, and that the outside surface was "smooth and

nest (and on a "suspect" fitting Oswald's description), and the alteration of the body—these were the three principal tasks the conspirators had to accomplish after the shooting. If body alteration was part of the plan, then the overall plot must have appeared like this to someone on the inside:

1. a preselected patsy—someone who would be eliminated afterward— would be maneuvered into position at the location which would become the "crime scene";
2. plans would be made to murder the President as he passed the "crime scene";
3. evidence would be planted at the "crime scene" so that the local authorities would be deceived, and arrive at the conclusion that the preselected patsy was the assassin.

The most important part of such a plot was that the body would be altered, and false ammunition planted, so that the autopsy report, the "best

---

unbroken."[93] Thus, Rowley's letter contradicted, without explanation, a significant allegation in the Secret Service report it transmitted.

Still another twist. On November 27, 1963, shortly before the windshield was removed from the limousine, it was examined by Secret Service Agent Roy Kellerman, who ran his hand over the outside surface and found it to be smooth. The damage, he testified, was on the inside surface. Kellerman believed this indicated a bullet struck the safety glass from the inside. But in fact, according to testimony later given by FBI Lab experts, safety glass breaks in the opposite fashion. If a bullet does not strike with enough force to pierce the windshield, a shot from behind will cause damage to the front surface, and vice versa.[94] The windshield sent to the FBI Laboratory had the damage on the front surface only; the inside (back) surface was smooth.[95] In short, that windshield constituted evidence of a shot from behind.

Testifying before the Commission in March 1964, Kellerman was asked to run his hand over the inside surface, the surface he believed was damaged on November 27, 1963. He commented: ". . . it feels rather smooth today."[96]

In February 1972, assassination researcher Robert P. Smith interviewed Bill Ashby, crew leader of the Arlington Glass Company team that removed the windshield on November 27, 1963. It was Ashby's recollection that the inside surface of the windshield was damaged.[97]

If the witnesses—Dudman, his companion, Sgt. Ellis, Officer Freeman, and Secret Service Agent Taylor—who saw a hole in the windshield on Friday are correct, and if Kellerman and Ashby are correct, that would suggest two windshield switches occurred: First a windshield with a hole was switched for one with no hole, but with damage to the "wrong" side (i.e., "wrong" from the standpoint of a scenario in which all shots were supposed to come from behind); and then—a second switch—a windshield with damage on the rear (inside) surface was replaced by one damaged only on the forward (outside) surface.

The contradiction between the FBI and Secret Service records on the question of windshield damage is epitomized by a clash between the FBI Supplemental Report, dated January 13, 1964, and Secret Service Chief Rowley's letter to the Commission, dated January 6, 1964. FBI Director Hoover reported: ". . . the windshield was cracked. . . ."[98] Chief Rowley wrote: ". . . . there is no hole or crack through the windshield."[99]

evidence," would state the shots came from the direction of the sniper's nest, and the bullets would implicate the "found gun" as the murder weapon.

I called this the "triple-convergence" hypothesis because it involved bringing together in Dallas the shooters, the patsy, and the evidence.

I was under no illusion that I could ever determine the identity of the shooters, and I could only speculate as to how someone like Oswald might have been selected as the patsy and maneuvered into position at the Depository. They were separate areas for investigation—indeed, research projects. What I did know was that if the body was altered, and if I was correct that the direction of the shots was reversed, then this "triple convergence" scenario was the essential structure of the plot that took President Kennedy's life.

The realization that the entire plan revolved around the secret alteration of the body changed my perspective as to what constituted a "solution" to the Kennedy assassination. I was no longer interested in who put the bullets into the President's body, but who took them out.

My view of Oswald also changed.

When Oswald was murdered in the basement of Dallas Police Headquarters on November 24, 1963, many commentators said that we would never know why he shot the President. But if Oswald was the unwitting agent of a plot that altered the body, then what died with him was not the motive for a murder, but who he was, and why he was working at the Texas School Book Depository.

One frustration of my research was that although the public record contained excellent sources of evidence to establish that the body had been altered, I saw no way to adduce direct evidence this was "before the fact." Of necessity, the case was circumstantial. In general, I believed that if I could define the overt acts of the body-alteration conspiracy, then the closer to 12:30 P.M. (the time of the shooting) that any such acts occurred, the more probable it was that body alteration was planned as part of the crime.

For that reason, I thought the "early" planting of bullet 399 was a powerful indicator that body alteration was planned as part of the murder.

The "Early" Planting of Bullet 399

When the hypothesis that 399 was a plant was first published in 1966, defenders of the Warren Report posed this question: How was it possible for anyone to know, so soon after the shooting, that the bullet would fit into the facts of the case, as those facts emerged? Suppose other bullets had been found? Suppose there was no role for that bullet?*

If bullet 399 was intended to be matched to a false back wound planned in advance, those questions were answered.

All these criticisms failed to recognize the possibility of a plot which constructed the "solution" as part of the crime. That failure, I came to believe, resulted from two blind spots which rendered the notion of planted ammunition seemingly impossible. The first was the unwillingness to believe the assassination might have been an inside job; the second, a failure to realize that the body was evidence, and was subject to manipulation and control like any other item of evidence.

My hypothesis demonstrated the flaw in such criticisms. If the conspirators who planted the ammunition also controlled the alteration of the body, bullets could be planted before the autopsy which would appear legitimately related to "trajectories" deduced *during* the autopsy.

Indeed, the early arrival of bullet 399, if it was planted, was powerful evidence that the plan to alter the body was part of the assassination plot.**

The notion that quite soon after the shooting, conspirators might be planning what trajectories to fabricate led me to explore further my hypothesis that the back wound had been placed "low" by mistake.

---

* As to the bullets which would have to be missing if the ones in evidence were planted, Jacob Cohen wrote: "And why on November 22, 1963, would any government agency or local policeman have wanted to conceal any evidence concerning the assassination? At that time it could not have been clear to anyone what role a particular item of evidence would play in the overall case for a single assassin."[100] Cohen ridiculed the notion of any group being able to mastermind such a scheme, referring to their headquarters as "Conspiracy Central."[101]

Two AP investigative reporters, Gavzer and Moody, after a six-month study of the issues raised by the Warren Report critics, wrote that to believe in a bullet planted so early, "it is necessary to conjure a being of superior intelligence, craftiness and prophesy. . . ."[102]

At a public debate with several critics in September 1966, former Warren Commission lawyer Burt Griffin commented: "We could never have uncovered a conspiracy of that character. That guy was a mastermind. He was better than [Conan] Doyle."[103]

** On this score, Dealey Plaza eyewitness Jean Hill reported a conversation she had within an hour or so of the shooting at the Sheriff's Department, with two Secret Service agents. Mrs. Hill testified she said: "Am I a kook or what's wrong with me? . . . They keep saying three shots—three shots . . . I know I heard more. I heard from four to six shots anyway." She said one of the agents replied, "Mrs. Hill . . . we heard more shots also, but we have three wounds and we have three bullets, three shots is all that we are willing to say right now."[104]

At the time of this conversation, two of the three pieces of "found" ammunition—the two fragments in the car—had not yet been discovered.

The "Low" Back-Wound Question Revisited

A fascinating aspect of any plot which could alter the body and plant false ammunition was the dual quality of its power and vulnerability. Its power would come from the ability to falsify history at the source, to fabricate the very evidence on which all future legal investigations would depend. But the plotters would be vulnerable because in playing for such high stakes, decisions would have to be made at a rather early hour, and any mistakes would be almost impossible to eradicate. Once the plotters committed themselves to a particular version of the shooting and sent the evidence on its way, the wheels of bureaucracy would turn, and the result would be notes, reports, etc.—the usual paraphernalia of investigation. Consequently, if some circumstance were not taken into account, and the evidence was altered "incorrectly," it would be too late, or at least extremely difficult, to call back the evidence, and write a postscript to the false history.

A perfect example was the "low" back wound. Pursuing the "mistake" theory, I tried to put myself in the conspirators' position, return to the circumstances that existed during the first hours after the murder, and understand how such a mistake could have been made.

Although the error itself was the "low" placement of the wound, its hallmark—indeed, its cause—seemed to be the failure to account for the throat wound properly. The trajectory-reversal scheme worked on the principle of alterations made within the framework of already-existing wounds, yet it seemed that whoever placed the rear wound "low" was apparently unaware that the hole in the front of the throat was a bullet wound, not just a tracheotomy.*

What I sought was some plausible explanation as to how, in the early hours, it might be possible for someone to make such a mistake, how it might be possible for someone not to know that the President had a throat wound. Some years later, I believed I came up with an explanation.

In 1968, the U.S. National Archives released a document it had just received from the Secret Service, which had not been provided to the Warren Commission—the navy death certificate made out by Admiral

---

* Under this theory, it no longer would have mattered, once the hole was placed "low," whether the plotters realized they had overlooked the throat wound, and proceeded to widen it and retrieve any bullet inside. The rear surface was like an indelible blackboard, and any rear entry created "low" could not be erased. Consequently, the evidence indicating the throat wound was widened and a bullet removed could not be cited to refute the possibility that this kind of error might have been made. The question, in considering this hypothesis, is: What was the conspirators' state of knowledge, and what did they do during the first few minutes after they obtained access to the body?

George Burkley, the White House Physician, on November 23, 1963.[105] Burkley reported the head injury (giving no direction for the shot) and only one other wound: "A second wound occurred in the posterior back at about the level of the third thoracic vertebra."[106]

Dr. Burkley made no mention of the throat wound; indeed, his November 23 report was evidence that he was then unaware of its existence.

I tried to understand why Dr. Burkley, who had been to Dallas with the President—indeed, he had been in Emergency Room One at Parkland Hospital—could be under such a misimpression.

Burkley was in one of the rear cars in the motorcade, and when the shooting occurred, his car was diverted to the Trade Mart, causing a serious delay. For a while, according to his own report in the twenty-six volumes, he "had no knowledge of the whereabouts of the motorcade."[107] Dr. Burkley immediately arranged for a car to take him to the hospital.*

Burkley's entry into Parkland Hospital was observed by UPI reporter Merriman Smith, who was on a hallway phone dictating the story unfolding before his eyes. Years later, a UPI executive in New York made available to me a copy of the original teleprinter output. Since each UPI transmission had a time stamp, the UPI ticker tape is an accurate source of chronological data.

At 12:53 P.M., UPI reported: "A few minutes later [referring to '12:50' mentioned in the previous sentence] Rear Admiral George Burkley, USN, the White House Physician, rushed into the hospital. He headed for the emergency room. . . ."[109]

Thus Burkley arrived at the door of the emergency room about fifteen minutes after Kennedy. Assuming that Dr. Perry had performed the tracheotomy by that time, what Burkley saw when he entered was the President with a wounded head, and a tracheotomy tube rising out of his throat.

When the tube was removed after the pronouncement of death, anyone who arrived late and who had seen it in place, would assume that the hole in the front of the throat had been created by the tracheotomy, and have no reason to believe otherwise unless told by a Dallas doctor that the tracheotomy incision had been made over a bullet wound.

Burkley was apparently under just such a misunderstanding. At the autopsy, despite the fact that Humes was puzzled at the rear entry (for which he could find no exit), Burkley never spoke up and informed Humes that the hole at the front represented a bullet wound, not just a tra-

---

* *Newsweek* reporter Charles Roberts was at the Trade Mart, and later wrote that he "ran, literally" into Burkley as he was about to leave, and "pleaded with him to take me to the hospital." Roberts said that "the doctor, whom I had known for years, slammed his car door in my face. . . ."[108]

cheotomy. The navy death certificate he made out the next day was good evidence he didn't know about the throat wound, and his delayed arrival in the emergency room explained why.*

In short, Dr. Burkley made the same mistake, in his report, as I suspected had been made by those who altered the body. From this, I did not draw the inference that Burkley was involved in a plot, only that his case illustrated how someone might not know, in the hours after the shooting, that Kennedy had a throat wound.

If, as a result of such a misunderstanding, the back wound was made "low," and intended to serve only as a receptacle for the stretcher bullet, the plotters would then have found themselves in the embarrassing position of having to account for the throat wound as the exit of that bullet after they had made the rear entry too low for that purpose. At that point, they might consider creating another, higher entry, but that would add another shot to the assassination. Practically, I concluded they would have no choice but to somehow maintain that the shallow entry, regardless of its "low" position, was in fact higher, and was the entry for a missile which exited at the throat. In other words, the plotters would have had to reposition the wound in the record, even though it was too late to make the change on the body.**

My analysis did indicate that a change from non-transit to transit and an attendant "raising" of the back wound occurred over the weekend of November 22, between the time the autopsy was conducted and the time the report was turned in.***

I assumed Humes had been pressured by the military chain of command. Certainly, he was vulnerable to pressure, because he had missed a bullet wound, the throat wound, at the autopsy. However the change was accomplished, the evidence indicated it did occur. The result: a transiting trajectory through the neck in the autopsy report that Commander Humes brought to the White House on November 24, 1963, the day before the President's funeral.

The Warren Commission structured the single-bullet theory on that "transiting" navy autopsy conclusion. But the original "no-transit" autopsy

---

* Shortly after 2 P.M., Dr. Perry participated in a press conference which could have been another potential source of information, but by that time, Dr. Burkley was en route back to Washington, aboard *Air Force One*.

** Later I changed my view. See Chapter 30.

*** See Chapter 7, "Breakthrough," where I discuss the "twin-transmission line" model of information flow from the autopsy room, and explain how discrepancies between the FBI reporting of the autopsy and the final conclusion in the navy autopsy report indicate a change made over the weekend.

conclusion was recorded in three FBI reports.* Consequently, the record invited the interpretation that the Commission changed the autopsy from non-transit to transit to solve the timing problem.

My trajectory-reversal theory suggested that the change from non-transit to transit was necessitated by an "incorrectly" altered body. In front of FBI agents Sibert and O'Neill, Humes examined the body in that condition—with a "low," shallow back wound—and the autopsy conclusions he drew during that examination became the FBI's record of the body. I viewed those autopsy conclusions as akin to a first draft of the autopsy report. The navy autopsy report was a revised edition.

My analysis distinguished between activities taking place in three time periods: the faking of facts on the body, on November 22; the possible pressuring of Humes to change an autopsy conclusion over the weekend; and the much-criticized "single-bullet" reconstruction of the Warren Commission, months later. My theory also demonstrated that although conspirators who could alter the President's body might play havoc with reality, unforeseen events could have played havoc with their plan. Abraham Zapruder's film was an accident of history. Similarly, it was probably sheer coincidence that Kennedy was shot in the throat at exactly the spot where a surgeon does a tracheotomy. But such circumstances would have had to be reckoned with.

By tracking the changes in a sequence of official reports, I could now see how a bullet originally planted to match a shallow wound became a bullet the Commission pressed into service to account for seven wounds on two men.

A most intellectually satisfying synthesis occurred when I joined my trajectory-reversal theory to my hypothesis that the body had been altered "incorrectly." The result demonstrated that if you understood how the body appeared to each group of observers, it was possible to explain the reports they wrote, the trajectories they posited, and the numerous conflicts among them. I found it convenient to use three line drawings to demonstrate Kennedy's wounds, and the trajectories, in three frames of reference: the Dallas doctors'; the FBI's; and Commander Humes'. (See Fig. 27.)

The combined sequence demonstrated how two groups of changes—one on the body, the other in the Bethesda autopsy conclusions—could create the existing conflicts in the record. Changes on the body would

* The three are the Sibert and O'Neill FBI report; the December 9, 1963 FBI Summary Report; and the January 13, 1964 FBI Supplemental Report. The latter two reports are based on the Sibert and O'Neill report. (See Chapters 5 and 7.)

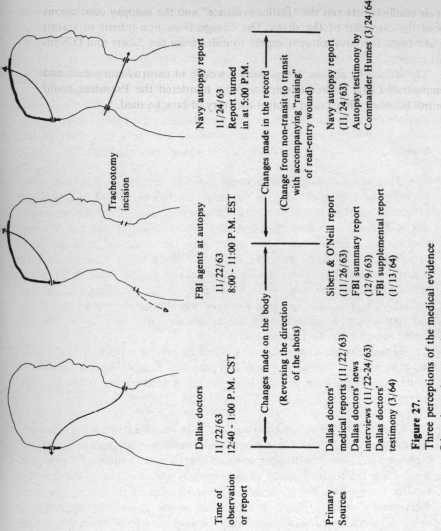

Tracheotomy incision

Dallas doctors	FBI agents at autopsy	Navy autopsy report

Time of observation or report

Dallas doctors
11/22/63
12:40 - 1:00 P.M. CST

FBI agents at autopsy
11/22/63
8:00 - 11:00 P.M. EST

Navy autopsy report
11/24/63
Report turned in at 5:00 P.M.

← Changes made on the body →
(Reversing the direction of the shots)

← Changes made in the record →
(Change from non-transit to transit with accompanying "raising" of rear-entry wound)

Primary Sources

Dallas doctors' medical reports (11/22/63)
Dallas doctors' news interviews (11/22-24/63)
Dallas doctors' testimony (3/64)

Sibert & O'Neill report (11/26/63)
FBI summary report (12/9/63)
FBI supplemental report (1/13/64)

Navy autopsy report (11/24/63)
Autopsy testimony by Commander Humes (3/24/64)

Figure 27.
Three perceptions of the medical evidence
Schematic; not drawn to scale

create conflicts between the "Dallas evidence" and the autopsy conclusions about the direction of the shots. The change from non-transit to transit would cause the navy autopsy report to differ from the Sibert and O'Neill FBI report.

The combined sequence explained a wealth of contradictory data and demonstrated that if the conspirators who murdered the President could control his body, they could control the story of how he died.

CHAPTER 15

Winter, 1966–67

ONCE THE LIEBELER MEMO WENT OUT, I anxiously awaited the outcome. Each time I saw Liebeler, I asked if he had any word. Each time he answered no.

I noticed that at least one or two Warren Commissioners made statements that could be related to the memo. Ford and Boggs talked of the desirability of having the X-rays and photographs examined by a team of experts. But there was no public indication that the information about surgery had any effect whatsoever.

Liebeler considered his memorandum a sensitive document, and he refused to give me a copy. The mere fact that Liebeler had written such a document was significant, but I could produce no proof he had done it.

He did, however, permit me to make detailed notes from a copy of the memo he kept in his office. He also said, as he watched the pace of my own research increase, that if I ever obtained a publisher for the book I used to mention I would someday write, that I should have the publisher contact him if I wanted to publish the memorandum.*

Just before Christmas 1966, Liebeler took a second trip to New York. Before leaving he called to ask if I had prepared a list of additional questions pertaining to the autopsy and the alteration of the body. I politely said I had not. I intended to remain in touch, to attend his class, but it was now clear that eventually we would be adversaries, and I no longer felt obligated to inform him of every piece of data I might dig up.

On January 4, 1967, after his return, we spoke by telephone for over

---

* The Justice Department's copy of Liebeler's memorandum was made available to me under the Freedom of Information Act in September 1979. It is now a public document.

an hour. Liebeler said that while in Washington he had telephoned both Humes and Boswell. Humes refused to speak with him—a reaction I suspected (but didn't tell Liebeler) was the result of my conversation with him on November 3. Liebeler told me: "He just didn't think he was going to talk to anybody about it unless the government did something in an official way about it."

Liebeler said that Boswell did speak with him, but that he didn't bring up the issue of surgery. But, said Liebeler, he was now thinking about giving him a copy of the memorandum and asking him to respond to it.

I expressed my opposition to that, noting that Boswell and Humes probably talked to one another, and that with the prevalence of Xerox machines, "you might as well be giving it to the Department of the Navy."

Liebeler was noncommittal, but years later, I learned that two days after that conversation, Liebeler in fact mailed a copy of the memorandum to Boswell with a covering letter: "I would very much appreciate having your detailed comments on the points discussed in this memorandum," wrote Liebeler. "After I receive your comments, I would hope that it would be possible for us to get together to discuss the matter in even greater detail." Liebeler added: "I have not made this memorandum available to those not connected in some way with the work of the Commission."

On January 11, 1967, within a day or two, presumably, of Boswell's receipt of Liebeler's letter and memorandum, Boswell was interviewed for *Life* magazine by Josiah Thompson, the Haverford philosophy professor who was then a *Life* consultant, writing his book on the medical evidence. Accompany Thompson was *Life* Assistant Editor Ed Kern.

In a telephone conversation ten months later, just before the publication of *Six Seconds in Dallas,* Thompson told me some of the unpublished details of his interview with Dr. Boswell: "Boswell was very evasive . . . really very nervous indeed." Thompson recalled one incident vividly. Informing Dr. Boswell that he wished to question him about certain issues raised by the Sibert and O'Neill FBI report, Thompson reached into his briefcase for a copy of that document. "I think he turned five shades of white. . . . I pulled the report out of the briefcase and showed it to him, and he physically blanched. I handed it to him and said: 'Look, read this paragraph'; and I could see the blood drain from his face."[1] Thompson was baffled by Boswell's reaction inasmuch as all he wanted to question him about was the (by then) well-publicized conflict between the navy autopsy report, which said the bullet transited the body, and the FBI report of the autopsy, which said it did not.

A clear sign that, despite his professed rejection of the surgery hypothesis, Liebeler remained interested in data that might support it occurred early in January 1967. At the time, Los Angeles-based writer-promoter Lawrence Schiller was gathering material for a book on the

Warren Report critics and the controversy they had fomented. Schiller arranged to have someone go to the National Archives and obtain documents as soon as they were declassified. One such document was a memorandum Specter had written after interviewing the autopsy surgeons on March 12, 1964, two weeks before their formal testimony.

Commander Humes, wrote Specter, "explained that they had spent considerable time at the autopsy trying to determine what happened to the bullet because they found no missile in the President's body. According to Commander Humes, the autopsy surgeons hypothesized that the bullet might have been forced out of the back of the President on the application of external heart massage after they were advised that a bullet had been found on a stretcher at Parkland Hospital."[2]

That, of course, was exactly what the FBI had reported, which had led Liebeler to wonder how Humes accounted for the bruise atop the right lung and why the existence of that bruise, as well as bruising in the neck area, didn't imply that the bullet had passed all the way through.

In the autopsy report, Humes described the neck bruising as "considerable ecchymosis of the strap muscles of the right side of the neck and of the fascia about the trachea adjacent to the line of the tracheotomy wound."[3]

Now Liebeler pointed to Specter's paragraph about what Humes and Boswell had said about the cause of that internal bruising: "They noted, at the time of the autopsy, some bruising of the internal parts of the President's body in that area but tended to attribute that to the tracheotomy at that time."[4]

Liebeler noted the significance of that statement: If true it meant that Humes and Boswell initially believed the neck bruising was man-made, and not caused by the passage of a bullet. But that meant that Humes' initial evaluation of the interior bruising supported my contention that the interior of the body had been probed and a bullet extracted.

This information was tucked away in Specter's memorandum. I don't think I would ever have noticed it, or appreciated its significance, had Liebeler not called it to my attention.

In the final autopsy report, the lung bruise as well as the neck bruising was cited as evidence the bullet transited the body. Liebeler had a lively interest in the legitimacy of the non-transit to transit change, and my own "twin-transmission line" theory that showed the change must have occurred over the weekend of November 22. That interest manifested itself in two other incidents. On his November 1966 trip to New York, Liebeler met with *Life* Assistant Editor Richard Billings, and Billings later showed Josiah Thompson a memorandum of their conversation. In that memorandum, Billings wrote that Liebeler believed the reason Humes burned the first report was that it reflected a different autopsy conclusion.

In the same vein, Liebeler wrote Gerald Ford on December 28, 1966, after he had been in Washington and spoken with Boswell. The question posed by Liebeler was: If the facts fell into place the way the doctors eventually claimed, why wasn't a transiting trajectory evident at the time? Why didn't Sibert and O'Neill report that the doctors concluded the bullet passed all the way through?

On this point, Liebeler wrote Ford: "I also talked to Dr. Boswell about the theory I mentioned to you on the sequence involved in the autopsy and the autopsy report. He said that he and the other doctors had considered the theory that the bullet passed through the President's body while they were performing the autopsy, *but that no one articulated that idea*. Make of that what you will." (Emphasis added.)

For me, the big event of that period was a debate between Mark Lane and Wesley Liebeler on January 25, 1967. The Kennedy assassination was a major topic on campus. Lane's book was coming to the end of its sixth month on the *New York Times'* best-seller list. Jack Ruby had just died in Dallas after winning a reversal of his conviction. The Manchester book was in the news. More than five thousand people crowded into the Grand Ballroom of UCLA's Student Union.

That morning I called Mark Lane at his hotel. I was taken with the idea that the Commission had been the victim of a monstrous deception, and was decidedly uncomfortable with the notion that because the Warren Report was written in a one-sided fashion, that meant the investigation was a fraud. "Are you going to argue it's a fraud?" I asked Lane. "It was a fraud from start to finish," he told me. Mark Lane really believed that the Commission lawyers conspired to publish a false report.

Liebeler was going to defend the Warren Report at all costs.

I sat in the audience, a tape recorder on my lap.

"If shots came from the grassy knoll, where are the bullets?" demanded Liebeler. "Where did they go? Please tell us where the bullet that entered the President's throat went?" he demanded of Lane. "Because it didn't exit and it wasn't in the body. And the autopsy surgeons testified to this under oath. And they examined the X-rays at the time they conducted the autopsy."[5]

I don't know what the other students thought, but it was a virtuoso exhibition as far as I was concerned. The fact is that without the insight that the body was altered, the Dallas observations seemed anomalous—what happened to those bullets that entered from the front? Did they disappear?

Liebeler went overboard. He was certain, he said, that all three shots came from the sniper's nest at the TSBD. "When those shots were fired, the entire building shook," said Liebeler, thereby turning the assassination into an event measured on the Richter scale. The audience tittered.

Lane was angered by Liebeler's self-righteousness. He went through much of the grassy-knoll evidence. To Mark Lane, and to most critics, it was obvious that Kennedy had been caught in a crossfire. Toward the end of the debate, he became very emotional. President Kennedy, he said, was a man loved by the country. And who benefited from the act? Lyndon Johnson.

At the first mention of Johnson's name, a few in the audience started to hiss at Lane. "I don't imply for a second that Lyndon Johnson was involved," said Lane. But the Warren Report, he said, was a "false report," and for that Lyndon Johnson bore the "primary responsibility." "We don't buy it anymore," thundered Lane. "And now . . . I say to Lyndon Johnson, let the American people know what happened that day in Dallas . . . Mr. Johnson, let us know who killed your predecessor. We loved him, and we want to know why he died, and how he died. And who did it. And Mr. Johnson, if you do not give us that information, we will remember that in 1968. . . ."[6]

Almost half the audience rose in a standing ovation.

Now Liebeler—who had asked in one of our first meetings: "Did anybody ever think of Lyndon Johnson?"; who had sent his memorandum to Earl Warren to point out that the FBI report said there was surgery on the body; who in that memo had remarked: "In assessing the probable public reaction, it should be noted that this matter is not dealt with anywhere in our Report"—now Liebeler stood up.

He too was concerned with conspiracy. "I appeal to your selfish interest," said Liebeler. "If it would have been possible for any one of us to have found any evidence of a conspiracy . . . and particularly if it had been the kind of conspiracy that Mr. Lane suggests—is it possible for one moment that I, for example, myself, having uncovered evidence of this sort, would have stood there, and kept my mouth shut? If . . . it even had been suggested to me by the Commission that I should do this . . . I myself personally would have walked out in front of the Veterans of Foreign Wars Building in Washington, where we had our office, and held a press conference and announced it, and I would have gone down in history as the man who uncovered the conspiracy to assassinate John F. Kennedy."[7]

He concluded by excoriating Lane for daring to suggest that the man who benefited from this murder was in any way responsible.

It was a very strange experience for me.

A UCLA student wrote a poignant column the next week in the *Daily Bruin,* a reaction to Liebeler's constant prattling that "we were only human." The headline: LIEBELER KILLS FAITH IN "BEING HUMAN."[8] Liebeler clipped it and put it in his files.

I don't know what Liebeler really thought during those weeks. Years later, I saw a column by Joseph Kraft, which I clipped and put in my "Liebeler" file, for it epitomized the way he behaved with me. It was titled: "Henry Kissinger and the Secret Good Guy Technique."[9] It explained that although Kissinger, in public, was quite hawkish, when meeting with peace activists he would behave differently, saying in effect: "Trust me. My public pose is essential for my credibility. I'm really on your side." That's the way Liebeler was—the secret good guy.

What was happening with the memorandum? Sometime in January I found out. Liebeler hadn't admitted it to me, but for a good five weeks he had known the result—he had gotten a stiff rebuff from J. Lee Rankin in a letter dated December 1, 1966. The "copy sent" list was identical to Liebeler's original mailing of his memorandum.

I learned about it one day, walking in the hallway. I remember Liebeler waving the letter at me: "Did you see this? Did you see this?" he asked. I hadn't, but once I did, it seemed to explain Liebeler's behavior.

"Dear Jim," began Rankin. "The Commission was discharged by the President upon presentation of its report and delivery of its files to the National Archives. There is no longer any Commission or staff to act concerning your suggestion in your memorandum of November 8, 1966. In my opinion, the former Commissioners and the former staff of the Commission have no more legal standing to ask that they be allowed to examine the photographs and X-ray pictures made in connection with the autopsy of President Kennedy than any other citizens.

"Thus, if you or any other citizen desires to examine such materials and can persuade the proper authorities to allow you to do it, that is your right. For myself, I am satisfied with the testimony of the autopsy doctors who performed the autopsy and whose statements, in my opinion, were the best evidence of what was seen and heard at the autopsy. In the final analysis, I think our report must stand or fall on the basis of what it contains. Sincerely, J. Lee Rankin."[10]

As far as J. Lee Rankin was concerned, the case was closed. It didn't matter what was in an FBI report, nor did it matter what the FBI might claim the autopsy doctor said at the start of the examination. The autopsy testimony—not the autopsy X-rays and photographs nor anything else— was "the best evidence of what was seen and heard at the autopsy."

For Liebeler, I felt, the reply must have stung. I was sure he took it very personally.

As the winter of 1966–67 passed, I attended Liebeler's class once or twice a week. It was quite an experience. One student gave a paper on bullet 399, and Liebeler said that we had spent more time on the subject in his class than the Warren Commission did.

But there was a definite parting of the ways. Liebeler had backed away from the surgery hypothesis.

At some point in the semester, one of the students gave a paper on the medical and ballistic evidence. The student, of course, was not privy to surgery—only Liebeler's three research assistants knew about it.

Liebeler, as usual, was sitting at the head of the long seminar table. I was at the other end of the table, and the student was going through the evidence—pointing out that the bullets matched that gun; that there was no bullet in the body, so reports of a frontal entry wound had to be false. With great sincerity, the student summed up the case. It had to be that way —it was simple logic; cold hard fact. He didn't see how it would be possible for all those facts to come together like that.

My ears were burning. And while the student was giving this summation, I slowly looked up and glanced in Liebeler's direction, to find that he was staring at me.

In February, New Orleans District Attorney Jim Garrison announced that his office was conducting an investigation of the assassination. Later in 1967, with publicity about Garrison often making headlines, Ray Marcus decided he had to do something. He was impressed with Liebeler's intelligence and, as had I, succumbed to the idea that what this man needed was someone reasonable to talk to—someone like Ray Marcus—and he might change his mind. Ray made an appointment to see him. He told me nothing about this— indeed, just months before, in November, he referred to Liebeler in most uncomplimentary terms, indicating he was not to be trusted. But now he was determined to see if he could change his mind, to persuade him to see the inevitability of a new investigation and how it would accrue to his honor to be the first Warren Commission attorney to call for it.

Years later, in 1974, Ray described the meeting. He went to Liebeler's office with blowups from the Moorman photo, prepared to argue that Kennedy was struck by more than one assassin. It was similar to the presentation I had made to Liebeler back in October 1965. Ray knew nothing of what had been going on between Liebeler and me.

He explained the arguments. Liebeler listened politely, attentively. Then Ray made his pitch. That it was perfectly obvious that the Kennedy case was going to blow up sooner or later, and that in view of his position, Liebeler should consider calling a press conference and saying: "We did the best we could, under the circumstances, but there is now sufficient evidence to warrant a reopening of the case."

Liebeler demurred. "Mr. Marcus," he said, "sometimes we get caught up in things that are bigger than we are."

What, When, and Where?

CHAPTER 16

Chain of Possession:
The Missing Link

Now I TURNED to a different question. When and where could the President's body have been altered? I focused on two time periods: the two-and-a-quarter-hour trip aboard *Air Force One* from Dallas to Washington, and the period between the arrival of the ambulance at the front of Bethesda Naval Hospital and the start of the autopsy.

The former seemed a possibility because in 1966 I was totally unfamiliar with the physical layout of *Air Force One*. The latter seemed a possibility because the ambulance arrived at Bethesda Naval Hospital at 6:55 P.M.,[1] but Commander Humes said he didn't begin the autopsy until 8:00 P.M.,[2] leaving about an hour unaccounted for.

William Manchester was commissioned by the Kennedys to write a definitive history of that weekend. His arrangement with the Kennedys gave Manchester unique access to certain people: the pilot of *Air Force One;* Kennedy's secretary, Evelyn Lincoln; Presidential Assistants Dave Powers and Kenneth O'Donnell; and numerous others. Manchester had assembled a valuable archive, and it was with considerable anticipation that I awaited his book.

The third of a four-part installment of the book appeared in the February 21, 1967 issue of *Look*. It described what took place after Kennedy died at Parkland Hospital, at 1:00 P.M. The body was placed in a coffin, but Dallas officials refused to permit its removal. In the hallway, Earl Rose, the Dallas County Medical Examiner, confronted the Kennedy forces led by Roy Kellerman. Manchester's description of the argument was fascinating.

"Rose . . . turned to leave the nurse's station. Kellerman blocked the way. In his most deliberate drawl, Roy said, 'My friend, this is the body of the President of the United States, and we are going to take it back to Washington.'

" 'No, that's not the way things are.' Rose wagged his finger. 'When there's a homicide, we must have an autopsy.'

" 'He is the President. He is going with us.'

"Rose lashed back, 'The body stays.'

" 'My friend, my name is Roy Kellerman. I am Special Agent in charge of the White House detail of the Secret Service. We are taking President Kennedy back to the capital.'

" 'You are not taking *the body* anywhere. There's a law here. We're going to enforce it.' "

Then Dr. Burkley entered the fray.

" 'Mrs. Kennedy is going to stay exactly where she is until the body is moved. We can't have that.' " Rose wouldn't budge. " 'It's the President of the United States!' Burkley cried.

" 'That doesn't matter,' replied Rose. 'You can't lose the chain of evidence.' "[3]

Eventually, the Kennedy party prevailed, but not before matters got so out of hand that Dr. Kemp Clark, the man who pronounced Kennedy dead, took Parkland Hospital administrator Jack Price aside and told him that he favored using force. "It may come to pinning him down and sitting on him," said Clark, who added, according to Manchester, that "he would be delighted to be among the sitters."[4]

The Kennedy party left for the plane with the nightmarish feeling that the Dallas Police might appear at any moment and try to reclaim the body, or perhaps prevent the plane from taking off. Mrs. Kennedy, Dr. Burkley, and two Secret Service agents rode to the airport in a hearse provided by the Dallas funeral home that supplied the coffin.

The detailed descriptions Manchester provided of the plane, and the flight back, persuaded me that nothing could have been done to the body on *Air Force One*. Jacqueline Kennedy sat next to the coffin in the tail compartment.

At Andrews Air Force Base an army cargo lift was used to remove the casket from the airplane, as the Kennedy party crowded around the tail compartment. The nation saw Jacqueline and Robert Kennedy, Lawrence O'Brien, and Kenneth O'Donnell descending in the lift. A gray navy ambulance pulled up. The casket was placed in the ambulance. Mrs. Kennedy, the Attorney General, and Brigadier General Godfrey McHugh climbed into the back of the ambulance. Secret Service Agent Greer drove. Alongside him were agents Roy Kellerman and Paul Landis. Dr. Burkley entered the ambulance and sat on Landis' lap.[5]

It was a 40-minute drive to Bethesda Naval Hospital. Manchester reported the conversation inside the ambulance. Robert Kennedy slid open the glass partition and spoke to Roy Kellerman. "Roy, did you hear they'd apprehended a fellow in Dallas?" Kellerman hadn't known. "It was one man," said Bobby.[6]

Installment three ended there, with the Kennedy party en route to Bethesda. I looked forward to installment four.

It was a disappointment: Manchester wrote nothing about the arrival of the ambulance at the hospital. The story resumed inside the hospital, on the seventeenth floor, where Mrs. Kennedy spent the night, awaiting the completion of the autopsy so she could accompany her husband's body back to the White House.[7]

Now I awaited the book, hoping it would contain a detailed description of the crucial period omitted from the installments—the arrival of the navy ambulance at the front to Bethesda and the details of how the coffin got to the morgue.

The Warren Report said practically nothing about this time period. A paragraph titled "The Autopsy" said that the trip from Andrews to Bethesda took approximately forty-five minutes, and that the hospital "received the body for autopsy at approximately 7:35 P.M."[8] That was based on Humes' testimony, given in March 1964.[9] No indication was given as to how Humes established the hour.

Secret Service Agent Hill wrote that he stepped out of the ambulance at the front of the hospital at 6:55 P.M.[10]

The Warren Report stated: "X-rays and photographs were taken preliminarily and the pathological examinations began at about 8:00 P.M."[11] Sibert and O'Neill reported: "Upon completion of X-rays and photographs, the first incision was made at 8:15 P.M."[12]

I drew up a preliminary chronology:

6:55   Arrival of the ambulance containing the Kennedys and the casket at the front of the hospital. (Source: Secret Service reports.)[13]

7:35   Body received for autopsy. (Source: Humes' testimony.)[14]

8:00   Pathological examination begins, after photos and X-rays. (Source: Sibert and O'Neill report.)[15]

8:15   First incision made. (Source: Sibert and O'Neill report; Humes' testimony.)[16]

How much time was unaccounted for? The chronology indicated at least forty minutes, sixty-five at most—i.e., 6:55 to 7:35, or 6:55 to 8:00, depending on when the autopsy began.

Then I came across a statement in the Sibert and O'Neill report I hadn't noticed before: "On arrival at the Medical Center, the ambulance stopped in front of the main entrance, at which time Mrs. Jacqueline Kennedy and Attorney General Robert Kennedy embarked from the ambulance and entered the building."[17] The ambulance, at this point, was at the main entrance. Sibert and O'Neill continued: "The ambulance was thereafter driven around to the rear entrance where the President's body was removed and taken into an autopsy room. Bureau Agents assisted in the moving of the casket to the autopsy room. A tight security was immediately placed around the autopsy room by the Naval facility and the U.S. Secret Service. Bureau Agents made contact with Mr. Roy Kellerman, the Assistant Secret Service Agent in Charge of the White House Detail, and advised him of the Bureau's interest in this matter."[18]

By this time, I had developed an eye for what one journalist has called "Bureauspeak."[19] There could be no mistaking what the FBI agents meant when, in one sentence, they wrote that a "tight security" was "immediately" placed around the autopsy room, and then, in the next sentence, that they had to contact senior Secret Service Agent Kellerman, whom they ". . . advised . . . of the Bureau's interest in this matter."[20]

The Secret Service and naval staff had temporarily barred the FBI agents from the autopsy room. Exactly how long this snafu lasted was not clear.

In another document, Adm. George Burkley's nine-page account, "Report of my participation in the activities surrounding the assassination, . . ."[21] I discovered another curious omission. Burkley wrote: "Mrs. Kennedy upon arrival at the hospital went to the 17th floor with the members of the party. The body was taken to the mortuary where I met it and observed its transfer to the table."[22]

Burkley's report gave no hint that between forty and sixty-five minutes elapsed between the Kennedys' arrival and the start of the autopsy.

On March 22, 1967, awaiting the publication of Manchester's book, I typed up six pages of notes: "The record is complete and accurate from motorcade to [Parkland] hospital, from [Parkland] hospital to plane, during the plane trip, and from the plane to Bethesda. Accounts and documents mesh; there are no contradictions, no time lapses. . . . The lapse occurs at Bethesda Naval Hospital . . . [before] the body was delivered to Humes. . . . Not a single witness testified that he was with the body during this time. Not a single document published in the twenty-six volumes accounts for the body during this time. The only document that has any direct and specific bearing as to what happened when the body was unloaded from the ambulance carries a clear interpretation. This is, again, the Sibert and O'Neill report. The body was taken into a room. A tight naval guard was thrown around this room. The two FBI agents assigned to the autopsy were *not* allowed to enter this room. The next thing we know is that Humes gets the body. . . ."

About a week later, *Death of a President* went on sale.

The book was riveting. Manchester was accused of "an almost morbid preoccupation with every last poignant detail of the tragedy."[23] That was exactly what I wanted.

On page 399 of the hardcover edition, there it was: the story of what happened between the front and the back of the hospital, told in just over a paragraph.

Jacqueline and Robert Kennedy had left the ambulance and gone inside the hospital. Manchester wrote:

. . . Godfrey stayed by the coffin; as the honor guard, he meant to remain with the President's body, wherever it went. To his dismay it went nowhere for five full minutes. Everyone seemed to have gone. Even the Mercurys had driven off. McHugh, Greer, and Kellerman and the coffin had been left among the motionless spectators. In the deflected lobby light their eyes shone like cat's eyes. The General started counting them and gave up. He looked down uneasily. He couldn't move the coffin alone. He didn't know what to do. He had been prepared for everything except inactivity.

The muddle was the consequence of a failure in interservice communication. The Army had been as vigilant as the Navy; General Wehle had stationed himself beyond the cornerstone in a staff car, with Lieutenant Bird and his body bearers right behind him in a truck. They had observed Mrs. Kennedy's arrival, but the darkness, the great blocks of silent people, and the many moving vehicles distracted them. It had confused two naval physicians, too. When an ambulance drew away from the curb they called, "That's it—we'll guide you to the morgue." At the morgue Wehle, Bird and the six enlisted men debarked and inspected each other's uniforms while awaiting some movement from the ambulance. It was still as still. The lieutenant crept up and peered inside. It was empty. Even the driver had gone. Panicky, they fled back and saw, among the shining cat's eyes, the uneasy face of Godfrey McHugh. Wehle and Bird colored. The Military District of Washington was meticulous about ceremony; for a casket team to leave a Commander in Chief's casket was an astounding lapse, and after casting about bitterly—and vainly—for the two doctors, they re-formed the tiny escort.

Manchester had thus introduced me to some new characters, the pallbearers, under the command of the U.S. Army, and to a new event, what Manchester called an "astounding lapse"—a mixup between two ambulances.

On November 22, 1963, the Commanding Officer of the Military District of Washington (MDW) was Gen. Philip C. Wehle (pronounced "wheel").* One of MDW's functions was to provide pallbearers and honor guards for funerals held at Arlington National Cemetery, and the headquarters of the unit that supplied them—Company E of the Third Infantry (the "Old Guard")—was at Fort Meyer, Virginia.

When *Air Force One* landed at Andrews, General Wehle and the pallbearers, headed by Lt. Samuel Bird, were at the field with members from the honor guard units of all three services. They were to take the coffin off the plane and escort it to the morgue.[24]

---

* For administrative purposes, as well as for defense, the army divides the country into zones. The area encompassing the nation's capital is known as the Military District of Washington.

Manchester described what happened: Lt. Sam Bird stood atop the motorized lift, his white-gloved hand in salute, as the lift brought him closer to the open hatch on the port side of the airplane, where the Kennedy party was clustered around the coffin. "For the lieutenant," wrote Manchester, "Air Force One's arrival was followed by a chain of small surprises."[25]

First, the Lieutenant didn't understand why Robert Kennedy was in the open doorway, not realizing he had boarded by the front entrance and run the length of the plane in the few seconds since it rolled to a halt. Second, he was disturbed that the coffin was not covered by a flag. But the most important surprise occurred as the lift halted by the hatch opening, and Bird and his men prepared to place the coffin on the lift. He looked up to see Brig. Gen. Godfrey McHugh, a loyal and emotional Kennedy aide, who peremptorily ordered: "Clear the area. We'll take care of the coffin."[26]

Lieutenant Bird and his men returned to ground level. Godfrey McHugh, Secret Service agents, and Kennedy aides placed the coffin atop the lift.[27] Nearby were several MDW helicopters and a gray navy ambulance. As the lift descended, and the nation watched on TV, Robert Kennedy explained the transportation choices to Jacqueline, suggesting she go by helicopter to the White House. "No, no," she said, "I just want to go to Bethesda."[28] Jacqueline spotted the gray navy ambulance and said, "We'll go in that."[29]

Secret Service agents, Kennedy aides, and some of the pallbearers carried the coffin from the lift to the ambulance. (See Photos 26A, B, C.)

Meanwhile, an MDW helicopter pilot who had been assigned to fly the casket to Bethesda was informed there had been a change in plans— the body would be going by car; he would fly the casket team instead.[30] General Wehle, Lieutenant Bird, and six members of the casket team boarded the H-21 helicopter for the ride to Bethesda.*[31] General Wehle, reported Manchester, was irritated. "Having failed to provide a proper military escort here, he was determined to be on hand when the coffin reached Bethesda."[33]

The U.S. Naval Medical Center—of which Bethesda Naval Hospital is just one part—is a complex of low-lying buildings just outside Washington. Rising from the center of the main building is a tower seventeen stories high. The seventeenth floor, the Tower Suite, is reserved for dignitaries. Wings jut out from the main building. At the rear entrance of one wing is a loading dock—a concrete morgue jetty where an ambulance can back in and unload a coffin. A door at the loading dock opens into a

_____

* Army documents I obtained in 1980 indicate that General Wehle was aboard a different helicopter.[32]

basement hallway. Immediately inside, on the left, are the doors to the morgue, emblazoned: RESTRICTED—AUTHORIZED PERSONNEL ONLY.

At the front of the hospital, situated off to the east side of a vast expanse of lawn, is a heliport.

The sprawling grounds at Bethesda were protected by nothing more than a fence, four feet high, made of four horizontal iron bars. As Manchester noted, a child of six could scale it; and when it was announced that *Air Force One* was landing at Andrews, and that the body would be taken to Bethesda, thousands of people gathered on the front lawn. They were a peaceful, respectful crowd.

At about 6:45 P.M., the H-21 carrying Lieutenant Bird and the casket team landed.[34] The Lieutenant and his men took up a position just behind the cornerstone of the hospital in a truck and waited for the ambulance.[35]

Two naval officers now entered the story—Adm. Calvin B. Galloway, the Commanding Officer of the entire Medical Center, and Capt. Robert O. Canada, the Commanding Officer of the hospital itself.

Manchester reported that Captain Canada was concerned about security, and engaged in evasive tactics. "Frantic, he deliberately misled the press." The President's body, he announced, would be taken to the emergency entrance. "Then he mobilized all off-duty corpsmen at the heliport. He expected the worst."[36] But, as Manchester noted, "he couldn't have been wider of the mark. The huge mob was to grow huger, but it was docile. Like the three thousand at Andrews, those here simply gazed."[37]

Shortly before seven o'clock, the ambulance, flanked by a motorcycle escort, came into view in the east on Wisconsin Avenue, trailed by a string of black Mercurys. The third car contained FBI agents Sibert and O'Neill.[38] The procession swung through the main gate, up a long curving roadway, and came to a halt at the main entrance. The time, according to Secret Service Agent Hill, was 6:55 P.M.[39]

With Admiral Galloway standing nearby, Captain Canada opened the door of the ambulance and assisted Mrs. Kennedy.[40] Agents Clint Hill and Paul Landis escorted her through the main door to elevators which would carry them to the seventeenth floor.[41] Godfrey McHugh, with Agents Roy Kellerman and William Greer, remained outside.[42]

I was especially interested in what happened next. Manchester reported a discussion between Admiral Galloway and General McHugh. McHugh told the Admiral the family didn't want an outside undertaker, that Jacqueline wanted everything done by the navy. The Admiral said the hospital didn't have the facilities: "I highly recommend a funeral parlor." McHugh pressed the point, explaining that it was what the family wished. "Isn't it possible?" he asked. "It's not *im*possible," said the Admiral. "It's difficult, though. And it might be unsatisfactory."[43]

Kenneth O'Donnell and Lawrence O'Brien had debarked from one of the limousines and now joined the conversation. Hearing the Admiral's objections, O'Donnell's response was curt: "You've heard the decision from the General."[44] They, too, now headed for the elevators. Admiral Galloway, according to Manchester, left, "perturbed."[45]

It was at this point that the casket team followed an empty ambulance. Manchester did not say how long the "astounding lapse" lasted, or when or where the escort re-formed. In fact, he described the entire episode in a single paragraph. But it was that paragraph I found most intriguing.

At the back of Manchester's book was a list of interviews, with dates. Manchester had interviewed General Wehle on April 29, 1964, and Lieutenant Bird on April 30.[46] He had interviewed Captain Canada on April 14.[47] No other members of the casket team were listed. He had not interviewed Admiral Galloway. There was no way to identify the two naval physicians who, according to Manchester, had started the confusion by saying of the wrong ambulance: "That's it, we'll guide you to the morgue. . . ."

I wanted to know more. It was Wehle and his men who had been misled by the confusion, so I decided to contact Gen. Philip Wehle.

I called the General at his home on Sunday morning, April 7, 1967, three days after I had purchased Manchester's book.

From the first cheery "Hello," I felt I knew Philip Wehle. I told him I was a student doing a paper, that there was a confusing paragraph in Manchester's book, and that I felt I must check the primary sources. General Wehle was direct, forthright, and more than willing to help.

I read him the paragraph. His first response was: "It's fairly accurate, that's right."[48] I was confused, I said, because it wasn't clear from Manchester's account exactly what had happened. When Manchester wrote that McHugh "looked down uneasily. He couldn't move the coffin alone," he made me wonder whether the coffin had been taken out of the ambulance at the front of the hospital. No, said Wehle, it was nothing like that. There were two ambulances. "The second ambulance took off. It was indicated we should follow it, and when we got there [the back of the hospital] we went right over and saw what the problem was, and immediately came back."

I asked Wehle if the second ambulance remained at the rear of the hospital. "I don't know whether it remained there or not, but it drew up there, all right," he said. General Wehle tended to minimize the incident. "The body was not unattended," he said, and he blamed the incident on "the darkness and the instructions we got."

While I had Wehle on the phone, I decided to explore another matter. Manchester had given a detailed description of Wehle's watching the coffin opening. But Wehle told me: "I witnessed no such thing. He's in error there. I was not present when the original casket was opened. I went into the autopsy room after that was done. . . ." I asked General Wehle where he was when the casket was opened. "I was just outside the door," he said.

Wehle did go inside a bit later.

I now understood how Manchester had constructed the book. He had described Wehle witnessing the coffin opening not because General Wehle was there, but because it was reasonable to assume he was. Psychologists have a word for that. When the human eye sees what is only five-sixths of a circle, and the brain misreads the message and assumes the entire circle is present, they call it "closure." Perceptions become a function of one's expectations.

It seemed to me that Manchester must have used the accounts of Lieutenant Bird about the ambulance mixup in a similar fashion. He simply didn't look into it further. Wehle expressed sympathy for Manchester: "The guy is getting taken over the coals. I think he meant well."

About this time I had a discussion with a law professor who taught Evidence. Suppose, I asked him, someone goes to the "Evidence" cabinet in the police department and changes the evidence. What law does that violate?

That discussion taught me something important.

Every item of evidence must have a "chain of possession," a demonstrable record of custody, from crime scene to courtroom. That is why an officer scratches his initials on a bullet before he delivers it to the crime lab; why records are kept of the location of evidence. The rule of law follows common sense. The "chain of possession" requirement is a legal safeguard against the mishandling of evidence, by accident or design.

The same rules apply to the four-hundred-pound coffin containing the body of an assassinated President as to a bullet. The Warren Commission had committed a glaring error—they had failed to establish the chain of possession on John Kennedy's body. The body simply appeared in the autopsy room, the autopsy was performed, and the results showed that the shots came from behind. The Commission had indulged in a presumption of validity. Perhaps that was understandable; perhaps they believed they could assume nobody would touch the President's body.

I asked the professor what happened when no chain of possession existed—what was the legal term? He explained that in court, when a complete chain of possession could not be demonstrated, counsel could ask the court to exclude evidence on the ground it was irrelevant.

"Irrelevant"? Another example of the difference between legal language and plain English. Altered or unaltered, John Kennedy's body was obviously "relevant" as evidence. But lawyers don't view evidence in the abstract; they think (and speak) in terms of prosecuting somebody with it. What the professor meant, applied to the assassination, was that if there was no chain of possession of the body, the Bethesda autopsy results would not have been "relevant" to the prosecution of Lee Harvey Oswald. The autopsy report would simply have been a description of what the body looked like at 8:00 P.M. at Bethesda, but it would be worthless as an indicator of what happened at Dallas. With no chain of possession, the body lost its legal pedigree.

That would have set the stage for dismissal of the entire case against Oswald. The sniper's nest evidence tied the "crime scene" to Oswald, but the medical and ballistic evidence tied the "crime scene" to the President's body.

This conversation changed my perspective. I had approached the problem as a detective—I sought to know what happened to the body at Bethesda. Now I realized I could adopt a more modest goal: finding evidence that would break the chain of possession. I sought to challenge the notion that the ambulance incident at Bethesda had no legal implications, that it was just a minor mixup.

For about six months I did nothing further on the problem. I didn't know how to find witnesses to the ambulance incident or to locate Lieutenant Bird's men. Manchester didn't even identify them.

Then, in November 1967 I had a break. I had ordered the *Dallas Morning News* for November 1963, on microfilm. In it, I came across a wire-service story about the nine men who had carried Kennedy's casket to the grave at the funeral on Monday, November 25. Each man's name was listed, with his home town. The story said: "Seven of them attended the President's body from the time it was brought back from Dallas Friday evening. They served as a security guard at the Bethesda Naval Hospital, where the body was prepared for burial. . . ."[49]

I threw a sheet of paper into my typewriter and copied the list:

1. Army 1st Lt. Samuel R. Bird, the officer-in-charge, Wichita, Kan.
2. Coast Guard YO 2.C. George A. Barnum, Lake City, Minn.
3. Navy SA Hubert Clark, New York City.
4. Marine Lance Cpl. Timothy Cheek, Ocala, Fla.
5. Army Spec. 4 Douglas Mayfield, San Diego, Calif.
6. Army Sgt. James L. Felder, Sumter, S.C.
7. Air Force Sgt. Richard E. Gaudreau, Ashby, Mass.

I decided to interview all the men on the casket team and make a record of exactly what they witnessed that night. It was now four years after the assassination, but recollections that were four years old were better than none at all.

I would say I was doing a paper for a course at the UCLA Law School. The class was studying how government performs small tasks in time of national crisis. My topic: transportation arrangements between *Air Force*

One and the morgue on the night of November 22, 1963. On Sunday, November 19, 1967, I made my first call. It was to Timothy Cheek.

I read him the paragraph in Manchester's book, and asked if he could tell me what happened that night. "This is all vague," he said.[50] He recalled that the men had arrived at Bethesda well ahead of the ambulance, since their helicopter made the trip in about ten minutes. "There was a lot of confusion, because . . . it was supposed to be taken in the front; we got there, and it wasn't there . . . the body wasn't there." He said: "I think we got out of the truck in the front, and then got back in it again, because I remember climbing back in." I asked him how he first realized the body wasn't at the front of the hospital. "We were waiting to move on out," he said. "Lieutenant Bird and, I guess, the General went up with him, and checked on it, and they came back and said it was gone. So then Lieutenant Bird didn't really know what to do, so we went rushing around to the other entrance, to the morgue; and I don't remember if it was there at that time, or what. All I know is that everybody was so disorganized. . . . In fact," remembered Cheek, "Lieutenant Bird wasn't even very well informed. He was trying his hardest to find out something, but everything was such a big mess that they didn't know either. So we just kind of wandered around. But I believe we did follow the wrong one around to the back, and then we did come around again, after we found that it wasn't the right one. All I know is that we finally caught it, and it was at the morgue door. . . ." Cheek summed it up with the standard serviceman's gripe: "See, nobody tells us anything."

I asked Cheek whether two FBI men were present when the ambulance was unloaded. "No," he replied, "there were just the six of us." I asked this because Sibert and O'Neill reported they helped with the casket, but made no mention of a casket team. I suspected that the FBI-assisted casket entry and the casket-team entry might have been separate events.

Cheek told me that while unloading the coffin, he noticed it was damaged. One handle, he said, "was broken completely off . . . it was dented up a lot. I mean, you could see the dent on it." Manchester had mentioned this damage, saying it was caused when the coffin was being loaded from the undertaker's hearse onto the plane at Dallas. Was that correct? I wondered whether the damage might have resulted from some incident that occurred between the front and the back of the hospital.

Cheek also told me that Lieutenant Bird had written a report, and had made a copy for each of his men. The report, I noticed, was listed in Manchester's bibliography. Cheek said he would mail me a copy the next day.

The next person I called—on November 19, 1967—was Brig. Gen. Godfrey McHugh, Kennedy's Air Force aide, and close friend of the family. I learned little from him. McHugh was unaware of any ambulance mixup at Bethesda. He repeatedly stressed that he was with the body at all times. From our conversation, McHugh's personal commitment to stay with the body—emphasized in Manchester's account—was clear. I realized Godfrey McHugh must have been a major obstacle to any plot against the body. He had high rank, and he was close enough to the family to be considered their personal representative.*

Godfrey McHugh seemed to me an eminently decent and trusting man, perhaps naive, and he was at pains to explain that nothing suspicious had happened. McHugh believed the Warren Report was correct, and he questioned my questions. His criticism was always directed at situations, not persons, and he would criticize in hyperboles. "Insane," "idiotic," were words he used. His Scottish brogue came through when he said "idiotic," which he pronounced "idyaaatic."

McHugh clearly remembered the argument in front of Bethesda. He brought it up on the phone, only he, being more polite, didn't call it an argument. But he vividly recalled having to convince some naval officers they should abide by the family's wishes and do the embalming there. How long this discussion lasted wasn't clear. Manchester mentioned it only briefly; and in his conversation with me, McHugh did not indicate how long it lasted.

I asked McHugh about the coffin damage. He said: "The handles were off; the corners were banged up. I don't know how it happened, actually. I don't quite understand. But when you move things from one place to another. . . ."52

"When was the first time you saw that damage, anyway, to the coffin?" I asked.

"When we brought in the casket at Bethesda," replied McHugh.

I thought McHugh's response was significant, because he had been with the casket at Parkland Hospital, when it was put in the Dallas hearse; at Love Field, when it was loaded aboard *Air Force One;* and at Andrews, when it was unloaded from the plane.

My sense that McHugh was naive stemmed from statements he made about what took place in the autopsy room. McHugh described to me in detail the futility of the doctors' search for bullets, despite repeated X-rays. I was so taken by this that I decided to depart from my normal interview procedure. I asked McHugh if it ever occurred to him that somebody had somehow removed bullets before the autopsy. McHugh was totally uncomprehending. He said: "I don't think that taking the bullets out was

* Robert Kennedy put in his hands the responsibility for seeing to it that the embalming was done at Bethesda. Later, the Attorney General asked McHugh to select the casket for the Arlington funeral. McHugh refused because, he said, the military guard of honor never leaves the body. Kenneth O'Donnell and Dave Powers went instead.51

going to help anybody. Let's say there was a bullet in the body, and that [a] high-powered plan very successfully infiltrated . . . the Naval Hospital [and] was able to get the bullet out. What value would it be to pay any man to do that? Or to have it done?"

I pressed the matter no further.

I was certain that if anybody had wanted to get access to the body, he had to deceive Godfrey McHugh. I was left with the impression that that could have occurred.

On Monday, November 20, I called Secret Service Agent Greer. According to Manchester, Greer had been at the front door with McHugh when the admirals argued against embalming at Bethesda. Greer was pleasant. We talked for about thirty minutes, but he was useless as a witness. For reasons I could not understand, he was under the impression that Kennedy's coffin had gone in the front door of the hospital. "I'm . . . a little vague about it, but I am almost sure it went in the front door," he said.[53] Many things were debatable about November 22, but one indisputable fact was that Kennedy's coffin had *not* gone in the front door—the main lobby entrance—at Bethesda. When I told Greer that documents proved his recollection was wrong, he said, "Why would we have stopped and got out at the front if we didn't take it in that way?" It turned out that Greer's recollection was just an impression. In fact, he didn't really know which door the coffin had gone in.

Greer said: "You know, if you can get to Dr. Burkley, he's the guy who will straighten you out on that question. He's a very fine gentleman, the admiral, and he will be very happy, I'm sure, to give you a yes or no answer as to what door it went in. There would be no secret about that."

On that note, the conversation ended.

I said nothing to Greer about it, but the night before, I had talked with Burkley. It was one of the most frustrating conversations I had. Burkley was a stone wall.

I had no sooner identified myself, and said that I was attending a class at the UCLA Law School on the Warren Commission, than Burkley cut in: "Well, I'm sorry. I'm not answering any questions. It's all in the Warren Commission, and you get your information from there."[54] This I found rather ironic, since in Burkley's nine-page report he mentioned nothing whatsoever about the crucial period between the front and the back of the hospital, writing only that he "observed [the] transfer" of the body to the autopsy room.[55]

"I appreciate your calling, but I do not make any comments."[56]

"Can I direct questions to you at the White House then?" I asked.*
"I'm just trying to find out some very simple answers."

"Your questions are all answered in the Warren Commission Report,"

---

* Burkley stayed on as White House physician to President Johnson.

he replied. "That's where you get your information. . . . I will not promise any answer to anything that you ask, because all my answers have come through the Warren Commission. It's nice of you to call, but I'm not going to get involved in your discussion."

I persisted. "I'd like to know one thing. . . ." Burkley interrupted: "You're supposed to ask one thing, and then one thing leads to another."

As for my writing him, he said: "If you want to direct a letter, I don't know who you would address it to."

"Well, I'd want to address it to you."

"Well, you can address a letter, but I can't promise you anything."

I never sent any letter. Dr. Burkley was not giving out any information.

My efforts so far had been unrewarding; I had learned nothing about the ambulance mixup described by Manchester. Then on November 20, after calling Greer, I spoke with James Leroy Felder, in South Carolina.

I read him Manchester's entire paragraph, slowly. When I finished, Sergeant Felder said: "Well, let's put it this way—it's halfway accurate."[57]

"Okay. You tell me how you remember it."

"All right," said Felder, and he began. "There were two ambulances. One was supposed to be the decoy."

"The what?!" I said, rather startled.

"The decoy," replied Felder. "You know, the crowds were there, the crowds all along Wisconsin Avenue out to the hospital . . . and I think it was, use one as a decoy so that we wouldn't have any trouble . . . getting him into the morgue. Now I'm hazy as to what actually happened as far as the brass was concerned . . . we got out of the helicopter and onto the truck. Then the truck took us to the front, and they said, 'No, we'll unload it to the back to get away from the crowd.' Well, they left one out front and they sent another one around back."

"Another what?" I asked.

"Another ambulance," said Felder. "They were using two of them. . . . Purposely. But anyway, when we gathered around back, and the one got there, the one we were looking for really, actually got there, was the correct one and the body was there. I don't know what went on around front with the other ambulance. I know it was there—that was the decoy."

"Can I cut in and ask you some questions, so I get a little cleared up, detail by detail?" I asked. "First, you said they were using two ambulances, and one was a decoy."

"That's right," said Felder.

"Now, first of all, how do you know that? Where did you get that information from?"

"Well . . . we saw the two ambulances. [And] Bird and General Wehle discussed this. . . . It was navy strategy because it was their ambulance that was being used."

Felder continued: "I don't know who made the decision to have them, but we know two were there, and we were told one was used for a decoy, anticipating the crowd, and this sort of thing."

I attempted to take Felder through the story again, step by step. It was difficult. The events had occurred four years before. The first time, Felder said that the first ambulance he saw arrive was the one he thought was the decoy; that it had pulled directly on to the back, and that it was the second ambulance that contained the Kennedys and the casket. Then, he said it was the other way around. I did the best I could, figuring that one scene Felder would never forget was the scene of the Kennedys debarking at the front of the hospital. He said he did see that.

"And while we were watching this, the first ambulance pulls away. And that's when we moved to the rear. Well, that's when people [Felder meant the casket team] began following it. Well, it made a turn and then moved on to the back, and this is where the second ambulance came into the picture."

"Now, which one moves around to the back, the first or the second one?" I asked.

"The first one. The first one. After putting the Kennedys out, then they wheel on around, and folk [were] trailing after them, and so they came on around back. During the meantime, the second ambulance came out of someplace, I don't know where, and moved into the scene. And then everybody's attention was focused on it again. So in the meantime, we were around back removing the body from the ambulance."

I was confused. "But didn't you first follow the wrong ambulance so that—it was simply empty or something?"

"We did. We did. Correct. Now this is, this is the mixed up part." Felder said that the group was in the back of a pickup truck, that they "got lost in the truck," and "it was just mass confusion for a little while. . . . Then, finally we got around back and then we caught the real ambulance; or, the one with the body, then moved in. This was after first driving around the hospital yard, or what have you, you know."

"Yeah," I replied, but I didn't understand. "Let me go through this because I really want to get everything straight so I completely understand. I'm not going to tell you I got it, if I don't. Okay?"

"Uh huh," came the reply.

"Okay," I said. And we began again. "You're at the hospital. You've arrived at the hospital."

"Well, we got there a little ahead of the ambulance," said Felder.

"Right."

"In a helicopter."

"Yeah. And you are parked down there and you're located with Wehle and Bird, and you're all together."

"Right."

"And this ambulance contains the Kennedys," I said.

"That's right."

"And, of course, this ambulance that contained the Kennedys contained the casket too."

"That's right," said Felder.

"Okay. Now, people get out of the ambulance."

"Right."

"Now, the next thing you see—tell me what happens next."

"Next thing, then, it moves off."

"Now this is before any other ambulance arrives?" I asked.

"Before any other . . ."

"Okay. This moves off."

"Right," said Felder.

"Did you follow that ambulance?" I asked.

"We followed that ambulance," replied Felder. Then he added: "At least, we *attempted* to follow that ambulance." (Emphasis as spoken.)

"Now what happened when you attempted to follow that ambulance?"

"We, some—well, we lost it. And we made a couple of turns, and then we got to turn round and come back again."

"Now, one second," I said, trying to maintain my composure. "When you say you followed it, you guys drove a motor vehicle and followed it?"

"That's correct," he replied.

"What vehicle did you drive?"

"Um. The truck."

"Was it a pickup truck?"

"That's right."

"Okay. So you tried to follow this ambulance?"

"Right."

"And you lose it."

"We lose it."

"What do you mean? On the hospital grounds or . . ." My voice trailed off.

"It's a huge complex there," said Felder, matter-of-factly.

"I see." But I still couldn't come to terms with all this. On the tape, I sound like someone just treading water in wonderment. I just didn't know what to say next. "Really," I said. "In other words, you're really kind of following this ambulance, and you lose it."

"That's right," replied Felder.

"Now, when you lost this ambulance, what did you do?"

Felder replied they returned to the front of the hospital where "there was another ambulance." In fact, Felder said that at one point there were two ambulances at the front of the hospital, and it was "confusing" as to which ambulance contained the body.

"What happened next?" I asked.

"We just waited there for a while," he said, "and then finally Bird said: 'Well, I think they're moving the right one back there now.' We got back on the truck and rode around back, and by the time we got there, the ambulance was getting off. And then we removed the body."

I reminded him of Manchester's passage, where they supposedly debarked near an ambulance at the rear, only to find it empty. Felder said he didn't remember that.

"What really happened is you lost the first one while you were in motion?" I asked.

"That's correct," he replied.

I returned to the general theme of the decoy. "At what point did that come up in the conversation where you were told about the navy strategy?"

"That didn't come up until we hit the naval grounds."

"Who informed you people about the strategy?" I asked.

"Lieutenant Bird. Bird said: 'One is being used for a decoy.' " Felder said he wasn't sure exactly when the statement was made.

"But he did say 'One is being used as a decoy'?" I asked.

"Right," replied Felder.

"Now the point is," I said, "that you didn't know there was a second one until you lost the first one."

"That's right," said Felder.

"So this conversation where the explanation is given has to occur after you see two ambulances."

"Apparently it did," said Felder, "because he left us there for a while, and he went to communicate with some of the higher brass, and a couple of other people. And then's when he came back. He said they was using a decoy."

Felder said the conversations between Wehle and Bird occurred on the sidewalk. "Not very far away. We were never separated that far—Wehle and the rest of us." Felder said that Wehle was with an aide, but couldn't remember his name. He stressed that the word "decoy" was used by Bird, but that it had been passed on to Bird from Wehle, "or whoever was with Wehle."

By this time, I had formed a tentative hypothesis—that by this sleight of hand, the ambulance containing the Dallas casket had been able to escape from the casket team's custody, and through the artifice of a "decoy," a deception had been camouflaged as a security measure. Somehow, Godfrey McHugh had been prevented from knowing that any of this took place.

I asked Felder about the coffin damage. He said the same thing McHugh did: He first noticed the damage when they unloaded the casket at the morgue entrance at Bethesda. One of the handles was broken "and it was marred and scratched up some, also. That was the extent of it."

Pursuing my guess that the casket-team entry and the FBI entry might have been separate, I asked Felder if he remembered the FBI helping with the coffin. "Nope, not then," he replied, adding that the only time he remembered the FBI helping with the coffin was at Andrews Air Force Base. Felder said that during the autopsy he had to guard the entrance to the morgue. I asked if at any time he remembered "FBI men trying to get in and you trying to keep them out." Felder said he recalled no such incident. What he did vividly recall were problems with reporters. "I had to throw a couple of them out bodily," he said.

Felder said I should talk to Lieutenant Bird: "He could give you all the details. He was right on top of it." He told me Bird had been wounded in Vietnam, but that I should be able to reach him at John F. Kennedy Memorial Hospital in Memphis, Tennessee.

Toward the end of our conversation, Felder told me that upon leaving the military, he had gone to law school, and was now practicing in South Carolina. He said that when he returned to his office, he would write me a letter and provide me the names and addresses of the remaining members of the casket team.

On November 24, 1967, four days after I had spoken with Felder, Lt. Sam Bird's report arrived in the mail. Timothy Cheek had mailed it from Florida. Dated December 10, 1963, the formal title was: "After Action Report, Joint Casket Team—State Funeral, President John Fitzgerald Kennedy."* I scanned the report quickly, looking for the section covering the events at Bethesda. The morgue entry was described in just a few sentences. Wrote Bird: "After considerable confusion as to where the President's body would be taken the joint casket team removed the casket from the ambulance at the mortuary entrance in the rear of the hospital."[58] Based on my interviews, I thought Bird had telescoped quite a bit of activity into the two words "considerable confusion," but I could understand why he might minimize what had occurred. Most of the report concerned the funeral on Monday. Bird recommended the team be given an army commendation for "performing with flawless military precision, giving dignity and honor to our late Commander-in-Chief during a time of sorrow for all Americans."[59]

One page of Bird's report listed times: from the morgue to the hearse, from the hearse to the White House, from the White House to the caisson, from the caisson to the gravesite. Whenever the casket was moved, Bird noted the time. Of particular interest to me was the first entry: "1. From the ambulance to the morgue (Bethesda) 2000 hours, 22 Nov 63."[60]

"2000 hours" means 8:00 P.M. According to the report of the Joint Casket Bearer Team, the casket was taken inside Bethesda an hour and

---

* The formal title of Sam Bird's unit was Company E, First Battalion, 3rd Infantry, Fort Meyer, Virginia, and, under the Freedom of Information Act, Bird's report is available through the Military District of Washington.

five minutes after the Secret Service reported it had arrived at the front of the hospital. Then I remembered that Commander Humes testified he received the body at 7:35 P.M.[61]—an obvious conflict.

If both Humes and Bird were correct in the times they reported, then the Joint Casket Bearer Team had carried in an empty casket. I added the time to my chronology:

6:45	Helicopter lands at Bethesda. (Source: Bird report.)[62]
6:55	Mrs. Kennedy leaves ambulance. (Source: Secret Service reports.)[63]
Sometime after 6:55	Ambulance chase. (Source: James Leroy Felder.)[64]
Sometime after 6:55	FBI follows an ambulance; kept out of a room. (Source: Sibert and O'Neill FBI report.)[65]
7:35	Humes receives body. (Source: Humes' testimony.)[66]
8:00	Casket team carries in casket. (Source: Bird report.)[67]
8:15	First incision. (Source: Sibert and O'Neill FBI report.)[68]

Felder had urged me to speak to Lt. Samuel Bird, and the next day, November 25, 1967, I telephoned him in Memphis, at the one Veteran's Hospital which bore Kennedy's name.

I introduced myself to Bird and described my project. "I'll help you as much as I can," he said, "but I tell you I had a head injury, and it's affected my memory some. But I'll sure try to tell you as much as I can remember."[69]

I read him the passage in Manchester's book, and asked for his comments.

In a halting voice, he replied: "I'm sorry, but really I don't remember very much. . . . Just let me give you the nurse."

The nurse explained that in Vietnam, Lieutenant Bird sustained a head injury which affected his memory. "Maybe tomorrow, he won't remember you called him tonight," she said.

Lieutenant Bird came back on the line; I wished him the best. Bird said his memory might someday return. But I still had no idea how severe his injuries were. Later, I learned that the man who headed the casket team that buried John F. Kennedy was wounded in January 1967, on his twenty-seventh birthday, in Vietnam, and would be confined to a wheelchair for the rest of his life.[70]

As to his recollections of November 22, 1963, what was left for history was the report he wrote, his statements as recalled by others, and the interview he had given William Manchester in April, 1964.

Several days after speaking with Lieutenant Bird, I received a letter from James Felder containing the addresses of two men I had been unable to locate—Douglas Mayfield in San Diego and Hubert Clark in New York City.

I called Mayfield on December 16, 1967.

Upon hearing the passage in Manchester's book, he said it was generally correct, but when I asked for details, he begged off, saying his recollections were hazy. He said he did remember Lieutenant Bird, perhaps accompanied by Sergeant Felder, going up to the front of the hospital "to find out exactly what was going to take place, and then he came back and said we were going to go around to the back. . . . We went around to the back, and then we waited there, and the ambulance didn't come around right away; and we went back around [to the front]; and by this time, they were just leaving; so then we followed [it] around, and when it stopped in the back, we took it [the coffin] out and took it inside."[71]

I asked Mayfield whether he witnessed the coffin opening; he did not. For a while, Mayfield guarded the door of the autopsy room. When I asked if he remembered any incident where FBI agents were kept out of the room for a while, he replied: "No, not while I was there."*

By now I was persuaded the ambulance mixup was no minor matter, but I needed corroboration for the story Felder had told about a "decoy" ambulance. On December 19, 1967, I called Clark. I was about to read him the passage in Manchester's book when he said: "You want me to correct you when you're off? . . . I haven't forgotten anything."[74] On an impulse, I changed my plan. Did he have an independent recollection that two ambulances were used that night; that one was referred to as the "decoy"? I would never really know if I mentioned it first, so I decided not to. I simply asked Clark to recall whatever he could.

He gave me this account: "From Andrews Air Force Base we boarded a helicopter. We took the helicopter to Bethesda Naval Hospital, where a pickup truck picked us up. Now we followed the ambulance to the front of Bethesda Hospital, where there was a crowd. So rather than go through the crowd, we reversed our course, and went around to the back of the hospital, to the morgue. From [sic] the morgue, we took the casket out of the ambulance. . . ."

I requestioned him step by step, starting from the time the men disembarked from the helicopter and boarded the pickup truck.

"Who drove the pickup truck?" I asked.

"I think it was a navy security guy," said Clark. "I guess he was attached to the hospital."

---

* Mayfield's account differed from all the others in one respect: He insisted the men had been ferried around in an ambulance, not a truck.[72] I concluded that Mayfield was wrong, but Sergeant Felder told me, in a second interview, that at one point the group was split up, and that perhaps Mayfield, somehow, ended up being driven from one spot to another in an ambulance.[73]

"Now . . . you mentioned you followed the ambulance. When did you first make contact with the ambulance?"

"We met the ambulance," said Clark. Then he paused, searching his memory. On the telephone, it was almost a shared experience. He resumed: "As a matter of fact, I think we had to find the ambulance." The words were spoken slowly and carefully. The effort at recall was almost tangible.

"Yeah," I said. "Now could you tell me what you went through to find it?"

"Right," said Clark. "I . . . I can . . . first we went to the front. And it wasn't there, so we went to the back. It seemed like we were running, practically . . ." Again, Clark's voice trailed off. Then it came back to full strength. "Running after a lost coffin," he continued. "This is the way it seemed to me. As a matter [of fact]—this is the way it *was*. That nobody, I mean, you know, there wasn't any preparations made for us, you know, to meet at a specific point. In other words, we were like in the dark as far as where we were supposed to meet the ambulance. And when we finally wound up, it was in the back."

"Okay," I said. "Now . . . I want to go through [this] very carefully. . . ."

The time had come to make a choice. Until now, Clark had mentioned nothing about a decoy, or even anything about a second ambulance. If he couldn't remember, I was going to mention the "decoy ambulance" first and see how he reacted. But I knew that the value of Clark's account would be greater if he came up with it on his own. So I held back and gave it one more try.

"When did you first make contact with the ambulance you knew, well, you thought had the coffin? . . . Do you remember any errors being made? Do you remember following an incorrect ambulance?"

Clark paused. "No, I really don't. Don't recall following the wrong ambulance."

Disappointed, I resigned myself to having to say it first. I began: "Do you remember any talk about . . ."

Suddenly, Clark interrupted. "Hold it, hold it," he said, his voice rising. "Let me see." For a few seconds, neither of us spoke.

Then: "I think there was a decoy," Clark said, "supposedly, to get the people away from the hospital. I think this is the case. It was like a decoy was set up where we were supposed to go one way, and this decoy ambulance, I believe, went another way, to the front. And we went to the back; to the morgue. If, if I'm correct. It's in the back of my mind." He paused. "But I, I think that was the case. That's what happened."

Clark had said it first. Two men—James Felder and Hubert Clark, one in South Carolina, the other in New York—had independently recollected the existence of a "decoy" ambulance at Bethesda on the night of November 22, 1963.

Now I asked Clark to begin at the beginning. Did he remember the arrival of the ambulance containing Jacqueline Kennedy?

"Right, we were there."

"Did you follow the decoy ambulance or go to the back before or after that event?" I asked.

"If I can recall correctly, we had gotten out of the truck . . . in front of Bethesda Naval Hospital, where the big doors are. Then we were told to get back into the truck. And we went around to the back. . . . I remember driving some distance . . . before we actually came in contact with the real casket . . . you know, [the] ambulance with the casket in it . . . This is my recollection."

I asked Clark who first used the words "decoy ambulance." He could not remember exactly who it was, but he commented: "I hate to use that, you know, I don't think it should have been the case."

"What do you mean?" I asked.

"I don't think all the running around was necessary."

I asked Clark to describe exactly what happened after the ambulance with the Kennedys arrived.

"I know we were in front of the hospital when they pulled up," he said. "Because they went in the front way . . . and I think the ambulance took off again, into the crowd."

"Did you follow it?" I asked.

"Yeah. I think that's the one [sic] we, you know, actually went into pursuit of the ambulance. And I remember driving some distance. You know, I don't know whether we were looking for the morgue, or whether this was, ahh, you know, a, a means of decoying, you know, to get away from the crowd." He said: "I remember going some distance in the back of the truck, 'cause we were cold."

Clark's statement that the team had gone "into pursuit of the ambulance" was similar to Felder's recollection that the team "lost" an ambulance while in motion, so I asked: "As you were pursuing it, do you remember losing it and having to return to the front to get your bearings again?"

"I . . . we lost it," he replied.

"Huh?"

"We lost it," said Clark.

"You lost it?" I replied.

"Right, I think we did," said Clark.

"When you say 'We lost it,' " I asked, "is it just a feeling from your memory, or is there something that sticks in your memory that indicates to you you lost it. Any conversation that you lost it, or what?"

"Yes, like conversation," said Clark. "We were saying 'Now where the hell is he? Where did he go? Why is he speeding?' "

"Speeding?" I asked.

"Right. . . . We're talking about the guy, whoever was driving that ambulance," said Clark. "And we were trying to figure out, 'Well, why is he going so fast? We're going to lose him.' I vividly, umm . . . this is what the conversation was."

Clark said it was one of the fellows in the truck who said that, but he didn't remember who.

"Now the ambulance had a flashing red light," I said. "Or they were equipped with it, anyway. Do you remember if the flashing red light was on as it pulled away?"

"It was off," said Clark. "I think it was off . . . I think this was part of the decoy, you know. . . . If the flashing red light was on, it would be an indication that this was the ambulance that [had] the President. . . . But I think that's why they decided to leave it off. . . ."

"So there's definitely no question in your mind that you lost the ambulance you chased?"

"Right," said Clark. "I remember a ride, and it's not from the heliport to the front of the hospital. We were following an ambulance, and we were saying to each other, 'Why is he going so fast? What, is he trying to lose us?' You know, this was what the discussion was: 'What, is he trying to lose us?'"

Clark said that during this time they remained on the Naval grounds. He said he thought the ride lasted "ten to fifteen minutes," and that the truck got up to speeds of "forty-five or fifty." "We followed the ambulance until we lost it," he said. "And then it was like, something about, I would say, another fifteen minutes trying to find, you know, trying to get back to where we started from." It was Clark's recollection that "where we started from" was the front of the hospital. At some point, he said, the men were told to go to the rear, and that the ambulance containing the Dallas casket was already there.

I pointed out that from the front to the back wasn't that great a distance. "Well, we must of went a roundabout way then," he said. "It seems like we went down and around . . . we went someplace, and then that was the wrong place, and if I recall correctly, we came back. You know, like I don't think this guy [referring to the truck driver] knew where he was going."

I asked Clark if he and the team ever had the experience of escorting the ambulance "slowly around from front to back?"

"No, no," he replied.

I asked him more questions—about the coffin damage and the presence of FBI men when the casket was unloaded by the casket team at the rear loading dock. Clark said that he first noticed the coffin damage when they unloaded the casket at the Bethesda rear entrance. This impressed me, because Clark had a good view of the coffin at Andrews. Readily identified by his sailor's uniform, Clark could be seen in photographs taken at the air base, next to the navy ambulance, holding the coffin and assisting in its transfer from the cargo lift to the navy ambulance. As to the presence of FBI men, Clark said he didn't notice any: "No one but us," he said, although two Secret Service men might have been present, and he did mention an incident with McHugh.

"We ran into some difficulty with, uh, McHugh, I think. And he was tough . . . he was pushing one of the pallbearers aside to, you know, get a hand on the casket."

Clark was referring here to what I came to call the "McHugh incident." It was described both in Manchester's book and in Bird's report. General McHugh, apparently quite emotional, wanted to carry his chief's casket into the hospital. This minor irregularity permitted me to identify this particular casket entry.

I was impressed that Clark remembered the McHugh incident, but did not recall the FBI assisting with the casket. Yet Sibert and O'Neill reported: "Bureau agents assisted in the moving of the casket to the autopsy room."[75]

I asked Clark if he recalled an incident in which FBI agents were kept out of the room. He did not. But "someone"—he could not recall who— had an argument with a reporter. That fitted nicely with Felder's recollection. Moreover, since Clark was the only person in a sailor's uniform, it meant that Sibert and O'Neill were probably not referring to the casket team when they indicated that they were prevented from entering the autopsy room by a "tight security" enforced by "the Naval facility and the U.S. Secret Service."

Toward the end of the conversation, Clark said: "I hope you turn up something that, you know, the Warren Commission didn't turn up. I honestly and truthfully believe that, you know, they got the wrong guy."

Hearing this, I began to worry that the story Clark gave me might be colored by his own bias. I asked if he thought there might be something wrong about the decoy ambulance. He replied: "Well, the only thing that I could possibly think . . ." He paused, then continued: "It would have to be, I think, almost impossible that they could have done something. There wasn't enough time. I . . . I don't think." His voice trailed off. Then he added: "But, I admit that, uh, we lost it, we lost the ambulance. I don't know whether this was the ambulance that the body was in, or the decoy ambulance. Like I said, there wasn't any flashing light. If I recall correctly, we had a flashing light."

Clark said "I would go to the end of the world . . . to find out what really happened. . . . Anything that I am saying now, I would repeat. I wouldn't care. . . ."

Clark called McHugh "the only earnest high-ranking officer" and said I should speak to him. I told Clark that I had spoken with McHugh a month before, and that McHugh was under the impression he never left the coffin, which remained at the front of the hospital. "No, no," said Clark, sadly, that simply was not the case.

But I was aware from Manchester's book that McHugh, upon arriving at Bethesda, had been detained at the front, for some unspecified period of time—involved with senior naval officers in a discussion concerning the embalming of the President's body.[76] Manchester devoted only about ten lines to this incident. My own conversation with McHugh provided a much more detailed account.

McHugh told me: "We . . . met a bunch of admirals who told us that . . . 'it was unfortunate,' they told me, and Bobby Kennedy was standing there, that it was impossible to do this—[the] opening of the chest, examination, and all of that. At Bethesda they did *not* do this type of work, and they could not do the embalming there."*[77] McHugh said that Robert Kennedy said: "Look, we don't want to do what the admiral says; we want it done right here." McHugh said: "And Bobby turned to me and said, 'You're in charge, you know what our wishes are. Get going. Let's do it.' "

McHugh continued: "I said, 'All right. Don't worry, it will be done right here.' " Then, said McHugh, Robert Kennedy went into the lobby and on upstairs to the seventeenth floor of the hospital. That part of the conversation, said McHugh, "took five minutes."

"I was left with the ambulance and two Secret Service men and the admirals," said McHugh, who, in his conversation with me, always used the plural, and specifically stated "There were two or three admirals there." McHugh's account continued: "It was very dark. And I told the admirals that the decision was to do all the work at the navy installation. And therefore it was going to be done. And they could always blame an order on the White House, given through me. Then the admiral said: 'Well, you should really think it over a little bit.' I said: 'We can't. Orders have been given to me.' He told me: 'We cannot do a good job of embalming here. Because we do not have the equipment.' I said: 'Look, they must have somewhere a place where they have the equipment. And the navy has enough trucks to go and take the whole damn room there full of equipment and bring it here within the hour.' So he says: 'Sir, they don't do that generally.' I said: 'Okay. They must have some *portable* equipment; but whatever is needed, you can send your trucks . . . and your men.' Then he said: 'Yes, sir. If that's an order, we will do it.' And they did it."

I asked McHugh if, as an Air Force Brigadier General, he could give orders to admirals. He chided me for "talking like a civilian." "The only

---

* This is a verbatim account of what McHugh told me on Sunday morning, November 19, 1967. If his recollection was correct, the admirals not only said they could not embalm Kennedy at Bethesda, but that they could not do an autopsy there either. The latter was obviously not the case. If McHugh was told that, it would make that conversation even more suspicious.

boss I had was the President of the United States," said McHugh, noting that "the White House is higher than Bethesda Hospital."

Examining the transcript, I realized that I had neglected to ask McHugh how long the argument lasted. I filed that on my mental list of unfinished business.

In 1967, I was unable to locate two members of the casket team—Air Force Sergeant Richard Gaudreau and Coast Guard Yeoman George Barnum.

In August 1979, I located both men. Gaudreau had retired from the Air Force after a long service—"twenty-four years, seven months, and two days," his proud mother told me. Gaudreau did not have an independent recollection of there being more than one ambulance, but when I prompted him, he immediately recalled the incident. "I can't really remember the exact details. But I think there was some confusion, and we did go off with another ambulance. . . . I can picture us being led somewhere, and finding something empty; and then being led somewhere else."[78] I asked Gaudreau whether, at the time, he might have written anyone a letter or talked about it. At that point, he said that his wife, Barbara, who was standing by the phone, indicated that she remembered his speaking about it. Gaudreau put Barbara on the phone, and she said that her husband had talked of two aspects of the confusion at the time—that, at Andrews, the Secret Service had insisted on carrying the coffin from the plane to the hearse, and then at Bethesda, "he did mention something about another ambulance."[79]

Next I called Barnum. He said that although he did remember there had been confusion, he could not recall the details.[80] But Barnum didn't have to rely on his memory for information about that night.

He explained that when he reported back for duty after the funeral, his superior at Coast Guard Headquarters directed him to write a report. That officer's interest was purely historical. He knew of someone associated with the Lincoln funeral who, years later, regretted not having created a contemporaneous record. Barnum was surprised to learn that his November 29, 1963 account, which he had saved primarily for his children's benefit, contained details of interest to me.

Here is the portion of that account that deals with the events following the arrival of the casket team, by helicopter, at Bethesda: "We landed just prior to the President's procession. They stopped in front of the hospital, and were immediately swarmed over by people that had come to see the casket. We pushed and shoved our way through the crowd until we were beside the hearse. Immediately we were told to get into a pickup truck that was standing by and go to the rear of the hospital. We were following an ambulance that supposedly had the President's casket in it. Mrs. Kennedy had gotten out of the hearse and gone immediately into the hospital. As we arrived at the rear entrance to the hospital by the morgue, we were informed that the casket had not been driven there. We then jumped back into the pickup and returned to the front of the hospital."[81]

This round trip to the rear, following an ambulance that supposedly had the President's casket, was not to be the end of the confusion. Barnum's account continued: "There were so many people that the instructions were still confusing, and we were told to return again to the rear. We did so and once again we were informed that the casket was not there. We returned again to the front and this time police had cleared a path through the people and the ambulance proceeded to the rear entrance of the morgue. We then proceeded to take the casket into the hospital in an orderly fashion."[82]

By Christmas of 1967, after my telephone calls to the men on the casket team, I faced the fact that I had to collect every bit of information I could find. A single item might be critical. Any witness might have seen something significant, yet be unaware of its meaning. What did each person see? When did he see it? I was convinced that if I could get enough of these pieces, I could assemble the puzzle. I had still to tap another source of information: newspaper stories.

I began making lists of newspapers to order by Interlibrary Loan. It was a hit-and-miss procedure. The assassination was a national news story. Washington reporters from any United States paper might have gone to Bethesda.

What I needed to do was to examine every single United States newspaper for November 23 and November 24, 1963, for all stories about the arrival of the Kennedy party at Bethesda.

I learned that the Micro Photo Company of Cleveland, which routinely microfilms many of America's newspapers, had created a "JFK Memorial Collection"—ten reels of microfilm containing the Kennedy assassination coverage of every major newspaper in the United States, for the period November 22–26, 1963. In the spring of 1968, the bibliographer at the UCLA library agreed to purchase it.

The order would take months to arrive. Impatient, I began to examine newspapers that UCLA had on hand. One day in August 1968, my random search paid off. On page three of the November 23, 1963 *Washington Star* I found a story headlined: MRS. KENNEDY SPENDS NIGHT AT HOSPITAL, by William Grigg.

There was useful information about the ambulance: ". . . hundreds of persons formed a partial circle around the ambulance when it stopped. . . . For at least 12 minutes after Mrs. Kennedy entered the hospital, the ambulance remained in the driveway. Many spectators could see the simple casket within. Military officials, leaning on the open front door of the vehicle, apparently were not sure where the body should be taken. When word finally came, the crowds were pushed back and the ambulance took the President's body to an entrance at the far rear of the hospital."[83]

According to Grigg, the pause in front of the hospital was twelve minutes. Grigg also reported that the time of arrival of the ambulance at Bethesda was 6:53 P.M.,[84] two minutes earlier than the hour in Secret Service Agent Hill's report. Thus, Grigg's account implied the ambulance moved off at 7:05 or 7:07, depending on whether Grigg's 6:53 or the Secret Service's 6:55 was used as the time of arrival.

On page 11 of the *Washington Post* for November 23, 1963, I found another story: OFFICIALS TO VIEW BODY TODAY AT WHITE HOUSE. Several paragraphs dealt in detail with Bethesda, indicating the reporter must have been there.

"More than 3000 persons were crowded onto the Hospital grounds in Bethesda and they surged around the ambulance when it arrived about 7 P.M. . . . The Attorney General escorted the President's widow through the front door and the ambulance containing the coffin sat unattended for several minutes. A Navy cordon finally pushed the crowd back about 15 feet from the vehicle."[85]

Then, in the final paragraph, came this detail: "Adm. Calvin B. Galloway, commandant of the medical center, pushed into the front seat and drove to the rear of the Hospital, where the body was taken inside."[86]

I was stunned. An admiral. Humes' superior. The man in charge of the entire Medical Center. What was he doing driving an ambulance?

Until now, Galloway had been a figure in the background. Two facts sprang to mind: Humes said Galloway was present during the autopsy, and the autopsy report had been signed, and certain changes made, in his office on Sunday morning. Then Galloway's name appeared on the memorandum transmitting the autopsy report from Bethesda to the President's physician, Dr. Burkley.

November 25, 1963

From: Commanding Officer, National Naval Medical Center
To: The White House Physician
Subj: Autopsy protocol in the case of John F. Kennedy,
     Late President of the United States

1. Transmitted herewith by hand is the sole remaining copy (number eight) of the completed protocol in the case of John F. Kennedy. Attached are the work papers used by the Prosector and his assistant.
2. This command holds no additional documents in connection with this case.
3. Please acknowledge receipt.

/s/   C. B. Galloway[87]

A similarly terse memorandum, dated December 6, 1963, transmitted Humes' report on President Kennedy's brain—from Humes' immediate superior, Captain Stover, via Admiral Galloway, to Admiral Burkley.[88]

When the ten-reel newspaper microfilm collection arrived at the UCLA library in the fall of 1968, I read through reel after reel, going through the same four days of November, reported in newspapers from Alabama to Wyoming, but found no new information. Reading so many funeral stories was an emotionally exhausting experience. If my theory was correct, what was lowered into the grave at Arlington was not just the body of John F. Kennedy, but a false diagram of the shooting, a falsified Rosetta Stone to Dealey Plaza. Historical truth was buried at Arlington, and the entire nation had been an unwitting audience to a major fraud.

Later that fall, I marched into Liebeler's office to tell him what I had discovered in the *Washington Post*. In the two years since I had found evidence of surgery, Liebeler had grown reluctant to discuss the subject, and between us there was the quality of a muted duel whenever it arose. Now I brought it up again: "Can you tell me," I demanded, "why an admiral was driving an ambulance?"

Liebeler, whose specialty was anti-trust law, thought about that a moment. Then he looked up from his desk and with a poker face replied: "Maybe the navy was having a union problem."

The *Washington Post* story whetted my appetite for information about the organization and command structure of Bethesda Naval Hospital. I went back to the library to study the U.S. Government *Organization Manual,* the U.S. Navy's *Manual of the Medical Department,* and seven years' back issues of *Military Medicine,* a journal for military physicians.

To me, the navy had meant ships and planes—what the navy calls the "operating forces." Navy Hospitals, I soon learned, were part of the navy's "shore establishment," and were administered by the Bureau of Medicine and Surgery—"BuMed," in navy parlance. The men who ran BuMed and staffed its installations were doctors from the Navy Medical Corps. I was struck by the combination of high rank and medical credentials— admirals who were also doctors, often with their own medical specialties. Here was a subculture of men who had made navy medicine a way of life, and whose duty assignments took them all over the world, from Lake Michigan to the Philippines.

One such "medical admiral" was Dr. Edward M. Kenney. On November 22, 1963, he was the Chief of BuMed and, as such, was also Surgeon General of the Navy.

Kenney's empire was vast. It included twenty-two Naval Hospitals in the United States, hospitals in Guam, Guantanamo Bay, and Japan, over one hundred fifty naval dispensaries, over one thousand medical facilities aboard ships, and naval missions abroad with medical detachments.

Bethesda was a special case. It was more than a Naval Hospital. On navy organization charts, it was formally designated National Naval Medical Center (NNMC), Bethesda. The Medical Center command was the "parent" of five component commands, two of which were the U.S. Navy Medical School, and the U.S. Naval Hospital. The morgue at Bethesda was part of the laboratories affiliated with the Navy Medical School. Commander Humes was Director of Laboratories.

A navy hospital (or medical center) has a Commanding Officer who, according to official literature, "shall exercise complete military jurisdiction within the hospital reservation. . . ." The CO is aided by an Executive Officer, an Administrative Officer, and a number of other assistants. An Officer of the Day "stands the watch." Logs are kept.

The chain of command at Bethesda was as follows: As the Director of Laboratories, Commander Humes reported to Capt. John Stover, the Commanding Officer of the Medical School. On the same level as Stover was Capt. Robert O. Canada, the Commanding Officer of the U.S. Navy Hospital. Both Stover and Canada reported to Admiral Galloway, the Commanding Officer of the Medical Center. Galloway's senior was Admiral Kenney, the Chief of BuMed. As a Bureau Chief, Kenney's senior, on the civilian side, was the Secretary of the Navy. His military superior was the highest ranking officer in the navy, the Chief of Naval Operations, who sits with the Joint Chiefs of Staff.

Admiral Kenney, Admiral Galloway, Admiral Burkley, Captain Canada, Captain Stover—all doctors—attended President Kennedy's autopsy. The chain of command from the autopsy room to the top of the military hierarchy was short. The Navy Surgeon General, who reported directly to the Chief of Naval Operations, was present, as was the naval medical officer who reported to the President of the United States.

Thus surrounded by top officers of the military medical hierarchy, Commander Humes, not qualified in forensic pathology, never having performed an autopsy in a gunshot case,* received the President's body and was told to perform an autopsy, as if nothing were amiss.

In August 1979, I interviewed General Wehle's aide, Richard A. Lipsey. Lipsey's existence was first revealed in the report of the House Select Committee on Assassinations. Looking back on my interview with General Wehle, I noticed he had mentioned, on one occasion, "his Lieutenant," but I had neglected to ask Wehle for the Lieutenant's name. Felder, also, had referred to "Wehle's aide." The House Committee located Lipsey. I interviewed him in August 1979.

I began by stating that I was interested in the circumstances of the

* Dr. Michael Baden, head of the House Select Committee's panel of forensic pathologists, testified before the House Assassinations Committee in September 1978: "Some people assume authority and upon others authority is thrust as happened to Dr. Humes. . . . A well experienced hospital pathologist . . . he had not been exposed to many gunshot wounds and had not performed autopsies in deaths due to shooting previously: neither had the other autopsy pathologists present."[89]

transfer of the body from the front of the hospital to the morgue. I asked that he begin when he arrived at the hospital by helicopter. "All right," he said, but then added, "Let's back up just a little bit, to the airport."[90] Without prompting, Lipsey proceeded to say that there were two ambulances used that night—one at the front of the motorcade, in which Jacqueline Kennedy had ridden, and one much further back. Lipsey said he was told that the body was in the second ambulance, and that Mrs. Kennedy had ridden in an empty ambulance. Lipsey said this was done for security reasons—so the ambulance with the body could go directly to the rear of the hospital, while the crowds congregated at the front of the hospital, around the ambulance that carried Jacqueline Kennedy.

If Lipsey thought the ambulance that pulled up at the front of the hospital contained no casket, I knew he must be wrong. I focused on the "two ambulance" part of his story and questioned him further:

LIFTON: Whose plan was it to have two ambulances?
LIPSEY: You got me—I don't remember.
LIFTON: I mean, was it your plan?
LIPSEY: Not mine.
LIFTON: Was it General Wehle's?
LIPSEY: . . . I doubt it. I think that came from the White House.
LIFTON: Okay. Did you hear the word that night—"decoy ambulance"?
LIPSEY: Absolutely. . . . Yes.
LIFTON: "Absolutely?"
LIPSEY: Yes.
LIFTON: Who did you hear it from?
LIPSEY: I don't remember. We heard that at Andrews Air Force Base . . . we had a little meeting. We were up in a little room, at Andrews, and had a little meeting, before the plane [*Air Force One*] ever landed, and these plans were formulated . . . it was strictly a security measure. . . .

At the end of our interview, I explained to Lipsey that in fact the ambulance that Jacqueline rode in had a casket, and that that ambulance went to the front of Bethesda Hospital. Lipsey's initial response was that that could not have been the case—that if the ambulance that arrived at the front had a casket, then Mrs. Kennedy must have switched ambulances before leaving Andrews Field. When I explained to him that there was no evidence whatsoever that Jacqueline ever switched ambulances, or that she debarked from an empty ambulance, Lipsey conceded that his information was not based on what he saw at Bethesda, but rather on the plan discussed at Andrews.

In September 1979, I located the man who was Chief of the Day at Bethesda—J. S. Layton Ledbetter. Although his recollections of many details were vague, Ledbetter volunteered, when I asked, "Did you witness the arrival of the ambulance?", "Well, I witnessed the arrival of two ambulances. . . . They went to our morgue, one of them did. Actually, I don't know where the other one went."[91]

Ledbetter said that to the best of his recollection, they both came in about the same time, as part of the same motorcade. "There was cars between 'em," he explained, adding that from what he heard the next day—and he stressed this was hearsay whose source he could not pinpoint—"One came in under heavy escort, and all of this," whereas the one carrying the body went to the morgue, and "actually backed in, from what I've heard, even unobserved, and everything."

There was a loose end to my theory. I wanted to know more about Gen. Godfrey McHugh. He was the one witness who believed he had remained with the body. But the accounts I had obtained—the repeated mention of two ambulances and activity apparently accounting for a considerable lapse of time—made me wonder. How could McHugh have been unaware of the casket team's comings and goings?

I supposed, in 1967, that he must have been distracted by the extended discussion he had with the naval officers near the front entrance of the hospital. But I had no specific information as to how long that conversation lasted. In April 1978, I called McHugh again.

It was a strange experience. On the telephone, Godfrey McHugh hadn't aged a bit. His Scottish brogue was unchanged. Without prompting, he brought up the incident at the front of the hospital, repeating what he had told me in 1967, sometimes using identical words and phrases. "I never left his body," said McHugh, and he related what happened at the front door.[92]

"Right at our arrival, they said the embalming could not be done at the hospital," McHugh said. "I had to argue with the hospital, and with the admirals in charge, to admit the President's body. . . ."

McHugh again provided details of the argument, recalling how he told the admirals: "Well, we'll make an exception right now, and you get people from outside, if you don't have your own people, and we will do it that way."

"Did they really put up quite a fuss?" I asked.

"Oh, it took me maybe thirty minutes after we got there," said McHugh. "It's hard to remember how long, but it took a hell of a long time of trying to talk. Everybody was gone, and I was still there discussing how we were going to do it. And I said: 'Now look, we are not going to do it any other way. This is the way they [the Kennedys] want it done, and you are covered, because they can always blame it on me, that [I said] the White House has asked them to do this.' Which was true.

"And they said: 'Well, it could not be done well here, because they [means "we"] don't have the stuff.' And I said: 'Get the stuff. I understand that you don't have it. Get it. You have many trucks. Send two trucks to pick up whatever you have to pick up.' There was no question that it could be done," McHugh said to me, "it was just a matter of making a decision."

"Who were you discussing this with?" I asked.

"With the admirals in charge," said McHugh. "There was quite a bit of brass there, trying to put the pressure on, saying that could not be done, that it was illegal for them to do it. And I said: 'I don't know a thing about it, except that the White House feels, [and] the Secret Service feels that it's safer.' " McHugh explained that a military hospital offered better security.

I asked McHugh where he had this discussion. "Next to the car with the body," he replied. "Next to the car. I was standing there waiting, because everybody else was gone. I was left there . . . arguing the point . . . I saw no reason why we could not obey the instructions."

I commented that that was a "very interesting little anecdote."

McHugh replied: "Well, it just shows they were doing their job properly." And, true to his character, he added: "And I was doing mine, to the best of my ability, which was to follow the orders I had been given."

To Godfrey McHugh, there was nothing sinister about all this; and, indeed, on the surface, there was not. At one point, he reprimanded me: "I don't understand your interest in questions about something that is so totally logical and normal."

The question I now asked was: How could the casket team be chasing an ambulance containing the President's body if Godfrey McHugh was leaning against the ambulance at the front of the hospital, having this argument? Was McHugh's recollection wrong when he believed it took place outside the hospital? Might it have been inside the lobby? Or had McHugh been drawn away momentarily, while a second ambulance glided up to replace the first one?

These details were far from clear. Nevertheless, the discussion McHugh had with navy brass at the front of Bethesda seems to have played a crucial role. It explained how the personal representative of the Kennedy family might have been deceived.

When I began my chain-of-possession research, I was concerned that the anatomic evidence of body alterations would be ignored if I couldn't provide a plausible answer to the question: When and where? But I found it far easier to document that *something* out of the ordinary had happened than to establish the details of that event.

Gradually my attitude changed. I realized that the details were less important than establishing that a significant interruption in the chain of possession of the body had occurred. Legally, that interruption was the basis for impeaching the body as evidence.

Still, my interest in the details persisted, and unanswered questions remained:

1. Where was the body during the time the casket team lost track of the ambulance?
2. Did Sibert and O'Neill enter the autopsy room at the same time as the casket team? What ambulance did they follow "around to the rear entrance,"[93] and whom did they "assist" with the casket?
3. Sibert and O'Neill reported that a "tight security" was "immediately" placed around the autopsy room by the Secret Service and the navy, and that before gaining entry they had to contact a senior Secret Service official and express their "interest in this matter."[94] Was the FBI kept out of the morgue? If so, by whom? And why?
4. Humes testified he received the body at 7:35 P.M.[95] Lieutenant Bird wrote that his team brought the casket into the morgue at 8:00 P.M.[96] Did the casket team carry in an empty casket?
5. Did anyone who came in with the casket team actually witness a coffin opening? Manchester reported that upon seeing the sign on the morgue door, RESTRICTED—AUTHORIZED PERSONNEL ONLY, "Lt. Bird decided that he wasn't an authorized person."[97] Yet James Felder told me that he witnessed the coffin opening.[98] To what extent was I encountering the "closure" phenomenon? Did Felder perhaps accompany the casket to the morgue door, not enter immediately, but later see the body lying on the autopsy table?
6. Was there enough time to make the alterations?

The Warren Commission ignored a whole range of evidence indicating shots were fired from the front. Following orthodox legal procedure, the navy autopsy was considered "best evidence." But it was not. The best evidence was President Kennedy's body.

And my research showed that for perhaps an hour preceding the autopsy, the whereabouts of the best evidence was unknown.

CHAPTER 17

The X-rays and Photographs: 1963–69

Lenses

My analysis demonstrated why the Dallas and Bethesda observations of the President's body could clash, yet both be correct. I thought of the Dallas and Bethesda records as two lenses through which history saw the body of John F. Kennedy.

The Dallas lens indicated shots came from the front—because that is the way the body looked at Parkland Hospital. The Bethesda lens indicated the shots came from the rear, because that is the way the body appeared at 8:00 P.M. EST, when Humes began the autopsy.

The law favored the Bethesda lens, not because Dr. Humes was a better observer than Dr. Perry, but simply because the official autopsy findings were considered better evidence.

There was a third lens—not the metaphoric lens of Dallas or Bethesda, but the lens of the camera that took the autopsy pictures of President Kennedy's body.

The autopsy began with the taking of X-rays and photographs. Immediately following the statement about head surgery, Sibert and O'Neill reported: "All personnel with the exception of medical officers needed in the taking of photographs and X-rays were requested to leave the autopsy room and remain in an adjacent room. Upon completion of X-rays and photographs, the first incision was made at 8:15 P.M."[1]

Before leaving the Bethesda morgue, FBI agents Sibert and O'Neill made an inventory. "The following is a complete listing of photographs and X-rays taken by the medical authorities of the President's body," they wrote. "They were turned over to Mr. Roy Kellerman of the Secret

Service. X-rays were developed by the hospital, however, the photographs were delivered to Secret Service undeveloped:

11 X-rays
22 4 by 5 color photographs
18 4 by 5 black and white photographs
 1 roll of 120 film containing five exposures

Mr. Kellerman stated these items could be made available to the FBI upon request."[2]

Except for a few lines of testimony by Commander Humes to the effect that pictures and X-rays had been taken, and a statement by Roy Kellerman that he brought the undeveloped photographs back to Secret Service headquarters, there was nothing in the Warren Commission Report or the twenty-six volumes about the ultimate disposition of these crucial documents.[3]

No reasonable person expected the Warren Commission to publish such material, but it was one of the surprises of the investigation to learn that the Commission had not even examined the photographs and X-rays.

Instead, the Commission illustrated the autopsy testimony with three drawings, prepared by a navy artist who had never seen the body, working under the supervision of Commander Humes. (See Photos 16A, 23, and 24.)

Executive session transcripts released in 1968 revealed some of what went on behind the scenes. On April 30, 1964, the month after Humes testified, General Counsel Rankin described the Navy drawings as "reconstructions" made by the autopsy doctors, commenting: "And we don't know whether those drawings conform to the pictures of the autopsy or not."[4] The Commission did not know because, according to Rankin, Robert Kennedy had denied that evidence to the Commission: "He said that he didn't think there was a sufficient showing of our need."[5]

The matter had come to a head because Arlen Specter had written a memorandum stating that the X-rays and photographs were "indispensable."[6] Rankin said he thought that Robert Kennedy would now give permission.[7]

McCloy recalled Commander Humes' demeanor: ". . . in connection with the charts that he was representing to us, there was a certain little note of minor inadequacy. . . ."[8]

Humes had testified: "The pictures would . . . perhaps give the Commissioners a better—better is not the best term, but a more graphic picture of the massive defect in 388 [the drawing of the head wounds]."[9]

Warren told Rankin to make arrangements for a Commissioner to view the pictures with a doctor: "I think you can work that out, Lee, to do that, but without putting those pictures in our record. We don't want those in our record. . . . It would make it a morbid thing for all time to come."[10]

The record was silent as to whether such arrangements were made. But in a memoir published posthumously in 1977, the late Chief Justice wrote: "I saw the pictures . . . and they were so horrible that I could not sleep well for nights."[11] Accordingly, wrote Warren, to prevent the pictures from falling into the hands of "sensation mongers," he decided to do without them, and rely instead on the testimony of the autopsy doctors, which he said was "convincing."[12]

This left a record with a strange twist—the Commission's conclusions were structured on the autopsy findings, but the autopsy data came in the form of a written report and sworn testimony, uncorroborated by the autopsy X-rays and photographs.

Numerous columnists speculated about the Commission's failure to examine the X-rays and photographs, and publicly wondered what had become of them. The London *Observer* said: "Nothing in the whole story of the Warren Commission seems in retrospect more remarkable than its failure to demand to see the photographic evidence which would have shown . . . the full details of the wounds on the President's body. . . ."[13]

During this period, the public was unaware that the X-rays and photographs had been turned over to Robert Kennedy about seven months after the issuance of the Warren Report. Until that time, the evidence had remained in the custody of the Secret Service. The transfer took place on April 26, 1965, precipitated by a letter sent from Kennedy to Dr. Burkley, instructing Burkley to make the arrangements: ". . . this material is not to be released to *anyone* without my written permission and approval," wrote Kennedy.[14] A two-page list—subsequently called the "Memorandum of Transfer"—was drawn up enumerating all medical items in the possession of the Secret Service, and the material was brought in a locked chest to the National Archives, and deposited with Evelyn Lincoln, the late President's secretary. Besides the X-rays and photographs, the chest contained copies of the autopsy report, slides of tissue sections, and, according to the inventory, a stainless-steel container which presumably held the brain. Evelyn Lincoln turned the chest over to Robert Kennedy's secretary, Angie Novello.[15]

We learned these details years later. On November 1, 1966, it was announced that the Kennedy family was placing the autopsy X-rays and photographs in the National Archives with special restrictions. No one but the government could look at the material for five years. After that time, Burke Marshall, the Kennedy family attorney, would rule on who could examine the evidence.[16]

The Kennedy announcement was made one week after I discovered the surgery statement in the Sibert and O'Neill FBI report. I was excited. Might the Kennedy family be in possession of photographs and X-rays that could prove surgery?

Within days, my hopes rose higher. The media reported that Humes and Boswell had been called in to see the material, and that they said those were the pictures they took at the morgue on the night of November 22, 1963, that the pictures confirmed their autopsy findings.[17]

The X-rays and photographs had no sooner been placed in the National Archives than many critics changed their tune. In late November 1966, Liebeler and I spoke about this. "Did you see Mark Lane on TV?" he asked incredulously. "Wasn't that priceless? You know, Lane's already taken the position," and now Liebeler lowered his voice to mimic Lane's authoritative delivery, " 'Why, they doctored all the *other* photographs; well, they'll doctor these too!' "

He burst out laughing, but it was an angry laugh. "And everybody applauds," he continued. "Hurray, hurray, the great hero, Mark Lane." Clearly Liebeler didn't like Lane's line of attack, and the credibility such charges were afforded.

"Fine, fine," I said, "but you guys created the investigation which bred this climate."[18] I realized the report could be wrong, and the X-rays and photographs yet be authentic. I wasn't sure that, but for my theory of alteration of the body, I wouldn't harbor the same suspicion about the autopsy photographs and X-rays.

I reasoned that if the body was altered, there was no need to alter the X-rays and photographs. That might have been a primary reason for altering the body—to prepare it to lie to the lens of the camera and X-ray plate, to tell those unblinking witnesses the same false story it told the autopsy doctors.

And that would be their great value. Perhaps the X-rays and photographs would prove surgery. The evidence of organized cutting Humes seemed to describe would be present in the pictures and X-rays. All I needed was the opportunity to examine them from that perspective. I hoped that something would come of Liebeler's memo.

Word of Liebeler's memo had leaked to the press. Without attribution, *Newsweek* mentioned it in connection with the five-year restriction. Paying homage to the "doubters," to whom five years seemed an eternity, *Newsweek* wrote: "Even some cooler heads thought an independent check was in order; one Commission staffer, indeed, suggested showing the pictures to an ad hoc blue-ribbon panel."

"But," continued *Newsweek*, "there were some powerful countervailing voices. Lyndon Baines Johnson, for one, thought it was enough that the evidence was available to any official body." Next came the statement made by Johnson at a White House news conference that week: "I think that every American can understand the reasons why we wouldn't want to have . . . everything paraded out in every sewing circle in the country to be exploited and used without serving any good or official purpose. . . ."[19]

During the ensuing months, I was intensely curious about what had become of Liebeler's suggestion.

For two years, nothing happened, although there were indications that Liebeler was still pushing his proposal behind the scenes. Then, on January 16, 1969, four days before the end of the Johnson Administration, the Justice Department released what came to be known as the Clark Panel report. WARREN FINDINGS ON KENNEDY BACKED BY AUTOPSY PHOTO STUDY, was the page-one headline in the *Los Angeles Times.* "The only outsiders to review the secret autopsy photographs have confirmed the Warren Commission findings that President John F. Kennedy was struck by two bullets fired from above and behind him . . . the Justice Department disclosed. . . . Atty. Gen. Ramsey Clark, with the approval of a representative of the Kennedy family, released the report of a four-man panel of doctors he appointed to study the photographs, X-rays and clothing sealed in the U.S. archives in 1966."[20]

I sent for the Justice Department press kit.

First, the packet contained a report, signed by Humes, Boswell, and Finck, on an examination of the autopsy photographs and X-rays they made in January 1967. "The undersigned physicians," they wrote, "have been requested by the Department of Justice to examine the X-rays and photographs for the purpose of determining whether they are consistent with the autopsy report.* This "Military Review" discussed what the pictures and X-rays showed in some detail, and concluded: "The photographs and X-rays corroborate our visual observations during the autopsy and conclusively support our medical opinion as set forth in the summary of our autopsy report."[21]

The next item in the press kit was a letter from Dr. Boswell to the Justice Department in February 1968.

Dr. Boswell noted that the autopsy findings "have been the subject of continuing controversy and speculation. Dr. Humes and I . . . have felt for some time that an impartial board of experts . . . should examine the available material. If such a board were to be nominated . . . it might wish to question the autopsy participants before more time elapses and

---

* Years later, I learned that in February 1967, a month after the Justice Department requested the doctors review the evidence, the Secret Service was requested to provide a summary of the chain of custody of the autopsy photographs, from the night of November 22, 1963, until they were turned over to the Kennedys in April 1965. That document was referred to by the House Select Committee in its report, and I obtained a copy of it in 1979, under the Freedom of Information Act. It is the basis for the information, provided in the text, about the processing of the photographs on November 27, 1963, at the Naval Photographic Laboratory. The four-page "Statement" was signed by Roy Kellerman, Robert Bouck, Edith Duncan, James Fox, and Inspector Kelley, on various dates in mid-February 1967.

memory fades. . . . Dr. Humes and I would make ourselves available. . . . I hope that this letter will not be considered presumptuous, but this matter is of great concern to us. . . ."[22]

Within a month, Ramsey Clark convened a panel of four doctors, headed by Russell Fischer, Maryland State Medical Examiner.*

The next item in the press kit was the sixteen-page Clark Panel report. The Clark Panel report contained two major surprises for anyone who had been following the case closely.

In the autopsy report, Commander Humes stated the entry in the back of the head was located "slightly above" the external occipital protuberance.[23]

The Clark Panel report said the entry at the back of the head was 100mm above the external occipital protuberance, nearly at the top of the back of the head—in the cowlick area, just behind the location where a man parts his hair.[24]

Upon seeing the 100mm measurement, my first reaction was to think it must be a typographical error, that the Panel must have meant 1mm or 10mm. All the previous autopsy information was consistent with Humes' statement.

In the FBI reconstruction, the agent simulating the President wore a patch low on the back of his head.[25] The Warren Report, discussing ballistics tests done at Edgewood Arsenal, referred to the autopsy location of the wound as "horizontal to the external occipital protuberance."[26] I had dug up an article in which Dr. Finck wrote in 1965, a year before he had seen the X-rays and photographs, that the fatal bullet "perforated the occipital bone."[27]

It soon became clear that 100mm was not a typographical error, that the Clark Panel actually placed the wound that much higher than Humes'

* The other doctors on the panel were: Dr. William H. Carnes, Professor of Pathology at the University of Utah, and a member of that state's Medical Examiner's Commission; Dr. Russell H. Morgan, Professor of Radiology at Johns Hopkins University, Baltimore, Maryland; Dr. Alan R. Moritz, former Professor of Forensic Medicine at Harvard.

The Clark Panel report was released on January 16, 1969, as part of the government's response to New Orleans District Attorney Garrison's subpoena of the X-rays and photographs. Garrison contended the autopsy photographs and X-rays would establish a conspiracy in Dealey Plaza by indicating, among other things, that there were shots from the front. The government contended the autopsy photographs would show no such thing, and filed the Clark Panel report.

Superficially, it might appear that the Clark Panel had been established to counter the Garrison subpoena, but that was not true: Garrison didn't file his subpoena until May 1968, whereas the Clark Panel was convened in February. I always suspected that Liebeler's memo, a copy of which went to Clark, and Liebeler's lobbying for an examination of the X-rays and photos, played a significant role in the creation of this panel.

autopsy description. Returning to the Military Review, it was also clear that Humes had noticed the difference, attributing it to fractures of the underlying bone and the elevation of the scalp by manual lifting. Humes said that photographs showed the wound "to be slightly higher than its actually measured site."[28] There was that word "slightly" again. "Slightly" seemed to expand or contract, depending on the circumstances.

The 100mm difference raised another question. If the entry, according to the autopsy, was a small hole situated beneath a large hole, and if the small hole had risen 100mm, what became of the big hole? Where was the exit now located?

The Clark Panel seemed to provide an answer. It described the damage as extending to "the midline of the frontal bone anteriorly," and that "throughout this region, many of the bony pieces have been displaced outward; several pieces are missing."[29]

In layman's language, the frontal bone was the forehead. This seemed to mean that the large hole, and the damage associated with it, was on the forward right-hand side of the head. Yet Humes, in describing the large hole, said it was "chiefly parietal" and extended "somewhat" into the temporal and occipital areas.

I resisted the idea that the words "to the midline of the frontal bone anteriorly" meant what they said—that the large head wound, on the autopsy photographs and X-rays, was further forward than the location described by Humes.

What finally persuaded me that this was indeed the case was a close rereading of the transcript of a CBS interview with Commander Humes in June 1967, shortly after Humes had seen the pictures. The interviewer was Dan Rather.

RATHER: About the—the head wound . . .

HUMES: Yes, sir.

RATHER: . . . there was only one?

HUMES: There was only one entrance wound in the head, yes, sir.

RATHER: And that was where?

HUMES: That was posterior, about two and a half centimeters to the right of the midline, posteriorly.

RATHER: And the exit wound?

HUMES: And the exit wound was a large irregular wound to the front and side—right side of the President's head.[30]

That was brand new. Humes had never said the large head wound went "to the front" before.

I noticed another thing. In the autopsy testimony, Humes had made it plain he could find no evidence of exit anywhere along the margin of the large hole, that his conclusion that the hole was an exit was based solely on deduction. Dr. Finck's notes, quoted in 1979 by the House Assassinations Committee, state: "No exit wound is identifiable. . . ."[31] Yet the January 20, 1967 report signed by Humes, Boswell, and Finck matter-of-factly reported that four photographs of the head wound "show . . . the margin of the exit wound; and also show the beveling of the bone characteristic of a wound of exit."[32]

This seemed improbable. The body ought to provide more information than photographs of the body. I pulled out the transcript of my interview with President Kennedy's Air Force Aide, Godfrey McHugh.

I had spoken with McHugh for over an hour on November 19, 1967. The purpose of that interview was to elicit information about the movements of the coffin. But during the call, McHugh volunteered that he had assisted in the photographing of Kennedy's body.

"He was a friend of mine," McHugh told me. "He was my President, he was a great gentleman, and I was obviously interested to know . . . I felt his hand, and I was holding his body several times when they were turning it and photographing it."

LIFTON: And you saw the wounds in the head then too?

MC HUGH: Oh yes; but they started fixing it up very well. You see, again, people keep on saying that his face was demolished and all; he was in absolute perfect shape, except the back of the head, top back of the head, had an explosive bullet in it and was badly damaged . . . and that had blown part of his forehead, which was recuperated and put intact, back in place . . . so his face was exactly as if he had been alive. There was nothing wrong with his face.[33]

The "top back" of the head was consistent with Commander Humes' statement that the wound was "chiefly parietal" but extended "somewhat" into the occipital. I tended to discount McHugh's statement that it "had an explosive bullet in it." No bullet was removed from the head, at autopsy; and I supposed McHugh meant that he inferred there had been an explosion, from the damage he saw. But what about the forehead being "recuperated and put intact, back in place?" In 1967, when I questioned him, there was no Clark Panel report, no Military Review, no reason to suspect the large wound was anywhere but on the top right side of the head, and extending to the rear—certainly no further forward than the leading edge of the parietal bone. That was the location of the coronal suture—about halfway between the eye and the ear.

LIFTON: When you say . . . his forehead had been put back in place, what do you mean . . . ?

MC HUGH: . . . the forehead, the bone of the forehead . . .

LIFTON: You mean the front [of the] head?

MC HUGH: The front. The top, the . . .

LIFTON: Top of the head.

MC HUGH: Top. No, not completely the top, the forehead . . .

LIFTON: The top right-hand side?

MC HUGH: No . . . well, it was done so quickly that you could hardly see it. The back of the head was all smashed in . . . but that explosion there loosened a flat bone on the forehead.

LIFTON: Forehead?

MC HUGH: Yeah. . . . You know, between the eyes, but high up . . . and his face was not—you could just see that crack there, and as soon as they put back that bone there, it was just like his face had never been hurt. His face was not hurt.

LIFTON: Where did they get the bone to put the bone back?

MC HUGH: It was brought back. They found it in the car.

LIFTON: I see. And you saw them putting the bone back?

MC HUGH: Well, we saw the whole damn operation.

LIFTON: I see. And they put that back in place before they took photographs?

MC HUGH: . . . I think they took photographs before, during, and after; they kept on taking photographs. They took photographs from the time they got the body out until it was put into the new casket . . . they will be seen someday, and it will show that many, many photographs were taken of the poor President's body while they were working on it.[34]

In November 1967 I was astounded at the suggestion there might have been skull reconstruction before the autopsy photography. But I had no information about what the pictures showed. Now, with the contradictory data emerging from the Clark Panel, I realized that here was a way for the autopsy photographs to be of John Kennedy's body, yet not to represent the body as it was seen by Humes.

I tried to get McHugh to define his terms. The forehead bone, he said, referred to a "semi-large bone, about the size of two fingers . . . that had been dislodged in the forehead."

LIFTON: When I say "forehead," I think of the region above my eyes. What do you mean by forehead?

MC HUGH: Well, I mean the region above my eyes, but quite a bit higher.

LIFTON: Top of the head, then.

MC HUGH: Top of the head, yes; let's call it top of the head.

LIFTON: As distinct from the back of the head.

MC HUGH: That's right.

I asked McHugh: "When you think of the head wounds, then, you think of, primarily, the top of the head, or primarily the back of the head?"

He replied: "Both. Ninety-nine percent the back, the top back of the head . . . that's the portion that had been badly damaged by the bullet."

I asked McHugh to define the back of the head: "The portion that is in the back of the head, when you're lying down in the bathtub, you hit the back of the head."

As for the bone being put back in, McHugh said: "Well, it was small, as I told you, no wider than two fingers. . . . It just looked like glass that breaks. You can take the same part and put it right back on."[35]

The notion that President Kennedy's head could be reassembled for the benefit of autopsy photography fit with the idea that there had been methodical removal of bone before the autopsy. But such "re-assembling" would make the autopsy photographs useless as a representation of the way the body was when Humes received it.

Consequently, when the Clark Panel report was released, and the reports of others who had seen the X-rays and photos became known, I began to realize that differences between what they reported and what Humes saw when he received the body might very well be explained by some sort of reconstruction of the head that took place after midnight.

In November 1967, after my conversation with McHugh, that was just a conjecture. In 1969, trying to understand why the Clark Panel descriptions of the head wounds differed from Humes', I began to give it serious consideration.

The second discrepancy concerned metal in the chest. Humes had testified "no metallic fragments were detectable by X-ray examination."[36] The Clark Panel, reporting on three X-rays which showed the lower neck, stated: "Also several small metallic fragments are present in this region."[37] How could these be the same X-rays? I turned back to the Military Review to find that Humes had ducked behind an adjective: ". . . X-rays taken during the autopsy . . . revealed no evidence of a bullet or of *a major portion* of a bullet in the body of the President. . . ."[38] (Emphasis added.)

A month after the Clark Panel report was released, Finck testified at the Shaw trial. Questioned about the conflict, he said: ". . . I don't recall seeing metallic fragments on the X-rays of this region of the neck. I don't recall. . . . This review was made by the radiologist. I am not a radiologist and a qualified man to look at the X-rays was the Bethesda radiologist. He did it at our request and he said there was no bullet remaining in the cadaver."[39]

The Bethesda radiologist, Dr. John Ebersole, had not been called as a witness by the Warren Commission, but he had signed a November 1, 1966 inventory saying that the X-rays he saw at the Archives that day were the same ones he exposed the night of November 22, at the morgue.[40]

Either these conflicts were the result of significant errors, or incompetence, on the night of November 22, or the X-rays at the Archives weren't the ones taken that night. Something was wrong.

In May 1969, four months after the Clark Panel report was released, Ramsey Clark spoke at UCLA. Afterward, at a meeting with students, I asked Clark whether he had ever heard of Liebeler's memorandum. Clark said he had never heard of Liebeler or his memorandum.* I asked Clark why the re-examination had been conducted at that particular time, and recorded what he said in a note to my own files that night: "He said the autopsy re-exam was totally under his jurisdiction . . . [that] the doctors had always been concerned about this matter, particularly Boswell; that he had had many conversations with Boswell about it, [and] that he, Clark, thought it unwise for the administration to go into an election year without anyone having examined this key evidence."

The report filed by the Clark Panel noted that the photographs and X-rays which had been examined "were listed in a memorandum of transfer, located in the National Archives, and dated April 26, 1965."[41]

The Clark Panel report was released on January 16, 1969. In August 1979, I obtained a copy of a Secret Service memorandum, under the Freedom of Information Act, which showed that on February 12, 1969, Mr. Harry R. Van Cleve, Jr., the General Counsel of the General Services Administration (which administers the National Archives) convened a meeting attended by James B. Rhoads, Archivist of the United States; a Justice Department lawyer; other Archives officials; and Secret Service Inspector Kelley (who wrote the memorandum for Secret Service files). Kelley wrote that Mr. Van Cleve "outlined the problem he wished to discuss," to wit, that the Clark Panel, by referring to the memorandum of transfer, had made a "gratuitous statement . . . and it would have been so much better if they had merely indicated what material they had examined."[42]

The problem, Van Cleve explained, was that although the Secret Service had transferred items 1 through 9 on the April 1965 document to the Kennedys, the Kennedys had not transferred everything to the Archives—specifically, certain articles described in item 9 were gone. This had been discovered in October 1966, at the time of the original donation. Van Cleve, Kelley reported, said that "a careful search was made . . . and they cannot be found in the Archives."[43] Included in item 9 were slides of tissue sections of the wounds. Also included was "1 stainless-steel container 7" in diameter $\times$ 8" containing gross material."[44] Inside the container, supposedly, was President Kennedy's brain.

What concerned Van Cleve, it seemed, was not what happened to the

---

* The record indicates otherwise. On November 16, 1966, Clark was sent a copy of Liebeler's memorandum. Within days, Justice Department attorney David Slawson wrote Clark a three-page memorandum about Liebeler's memo. (See Chapter 12, pp. 306–7.)

missing items, but what the Warren Report critics would say if they learned about all this—specifically, if they learned that this "Memorandum of Transfer" existed, and then obtained a copy and compared that inventory with the one published by the Clark Panel.

Wrote Inspector Kelley: "Mr. Van Cleve is concerned that writers like Weisberg or Mark Lane, when they learned that such an inventory existed, would demand to see the inventory and items covered by it. He indicated that he saw no legal reason how . . . this inventory could be kept from writers of this kind, and that when they learned . . . that some of the items on the inventory were not in the possession of the Archives, that this would lead to all sorts of speculation and accusation that the government was not being perfectly frank and open in handling this matter, and that it was further proof of the various conspiracies which these writers are alleging surround the assassination of President Kennedy. It is our opinion also that this is a distinct possibility."*[45]

The next day, February 13, 1969, Inspector Kelley went to see Dr. Burkley at his home. He wrote: "Dr. Burkley advised me that after turning all of this material over to Mrs. Lincoln he never saw nor heard anything about its disposition, and that he was surprised to hear that it was not with the remainder of the material. . . ." Dr. Burkley then telephoned Evelyn Lincoln. "He did this in my presence," wrote Kelley, "and Mrs. Lincoln told him that all of the material he turned over to her was placed in a trunk or footlocker; that it was locked, and that to her knowledge it was never opened nor the contents disturbed by her." Mrs. Lincoln said that "sometime after its receipt all of the material . . . was turned over to Angie Novello, Robert Kennedy's secretary."[47]

It was Angie Novello who, according to Van Cleve, had produced the key to the footlocker when the Kennedys donated the material on October 29, 1966.

Thus, it appeared that sometime between April 26, 1965, and October 29, 1966, the bins and footlockers containing the medical items had been culled of the brain and the slides.

When Kelley advised Van Cleve of the results, and suggested another person who might be questioned, Van Cleve "said he felt that the inquiry

---

* Inspector Kelley noted another problem. Item 9 in the inventory also referred to the "complete autopsy protocol of President Kennedy (orig. & 7 cc's)," yet the Secret Service had sent what purported to be the original, which it had in its files, to the Archives on October 3, 1967. Wrote Kelley: "This could raise the question about two original autopsy protocols. We, of course, were unable to resolve this discrepancy since we do not have access to the paper referred to in Dr. Burkley's inventory. We can speculate that what was described as the original autopsy protocol in the inventory might have been another ribbon copy of the original protocol or that it was merely mislabeled, but it does give an opportunity for writers to discuss the discrepancy."[46] This matter was never resolved.

would have to remain as it now stands; that perhaps we were borrowing trouble in exploring it any further."[48]

Thus, the seeds of controversy concerning the missing brain were planted; years later, they would sprout.*

---

* Moreover, although at the February 12, 1969 meeting, Van Cleve, according to Kelley, "indicated that he saw no legal reason how . . . this inventory could be kept from writers," the U.S. Archives did exactly that—withholding the April 1965 Memorandum of Transfer until 1974, when it was finally released after threats of a lawsuit by Harold Weisberg.[49]

CHAPTER 18

The Pre-Autopsy Autopsy

IN THE HALF YEAR following October 1966, when I discovered the Sibert and O'Neill statement about surgery, I immersed myself in books on forensic pathology, particularly chapters on head wounds. My first step had been to compare the Dallas and Bethesda descriptions of the President's head wounds, tabulating differences. At Dallas, the large wound was an egg-size hole at the right rear. At Bethesda, the autopsy surgeons described a hole nearly four times as large, at the top right side of the head. Now I realized there was another way of approaching the problem. I set out to scan the Bethesda data for damage not usually found in a gunshot case, damage which might indicate organized cutting.

The books made it clear that to a forensic pathologist, the scalp, the skull, and the brain represented three distinct entities; that to determine the cause of an injury, information from all three had to be combined, and that the wound margin was critical. It was there that the instrument of injury—whether it was a bullet, a knife, or a rock—left its signature.

I took a closer look at Humes' description of the scalp in the vicinity of the head wound.

Humes testified that the large hole was "devoid of any scalp or skull"[1]; but he noted, "the scalp was intact completely past this defect."[2]

Immediately following came one of the most intriguing passages of the autopsy report. Humes wrote that extending from the large hole atop the head, into the "more or less intact"[3] scalp, were four tears.

He listed them as "a," "b," "c," and "d," gave their lengths, their locations, their starting and ending points:

a. From the right inferior temporo-parietal margin anterior to the right ear to a point slightly above the tragus.

   b. From the anterior parietal margin anteriorly on the forehead to approximately 4cm above the right orbital ridge.
   c. From the left margin of the main defect across the midline antero-laterally for a distance of approximately 8cm.
   d. From the same starting point as c. 10cm postero-laterally.[4]

I translated Humes' verbal descriptions into a simple diagram. (See Fig. 28.)

These tears were strikingly symmetrical. Two emerged from the left side of the hole and traveled forward and left, and backward and left, respectively. The other two emerged from the right side, and they traveled forward and right, and backward and right.

The four tears delineated four symmetric flaps: a flap between tears "a" and "b," another between "b" and "c," and so on around the periphery of the hole. Would a bullet create such damage? Possibly. But the symmetry suggested that the scalp might have been parted by human design.

To get to the brain, the top of the skull would have to be removed. I wasn't sure exactly how that was done, but I knew that a saw was usually used, because Humes had volunteered, during his Warren Commission testimony: "We had to do virtually no work with a saw to remove these portions of the skull, they came apart in our hands very easily . . . as we moved the scalp about, fragments of various sizes would fall to the table. . . ."[5]

Was it possible that the large hole atop the head at Bethesda had been created, before the autopsy, to obtain access to the brain, to remove metal from authentic assassination bullets?

To test this hypothesis, I could think of only one approach: Consult

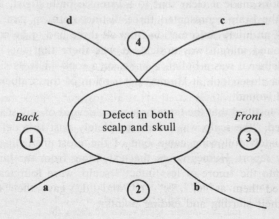

Figure 28.
Schematic drawing of the top view of four tears in Kennedy's scalp (a, b, c, d) which created four flaps (1, 2, 3, 4)

texts or articles on forensic pathology, with their profuse illustrations of gunshot injury, and compare the damage described at this autopsy with that normally reported in shootings with a rifle. The problem with this approach was that it was based on probabilities. Suppose I could show that four symmetrical scalp tears were not usually found in gunshot wounding.* That didn't prove they could never occur.

In mid-November 1967, I obtained an advance copy of Josiah Thompson's forthcoming book, *Six Seconds in Dallas*. It contained an important piece of information from his January 11, 1967 interview with Commander Boswell: "Commander Boswell told me that the President's brain was quite easily removed without recourse to surgery. . . ."[6]

That was brand new. The Warren Commission had heard no such testimony. Perhaps I was on the right track: Surgery wasn't required because surgery had already been performed.

I had spoken with Humes twice, on November 2 and 3, 1966. In the second conversation, I had informed him of the statement about head surgery in the Sibert and O'Neill report, told him about Liebeler's interest in the matter, and said Liebeler was drafting a memo upon which Humes might be asked to comment. In late December, Liebeler went to Washington and called Humes.[7] Humes refused to speak with him.[8] Liebeler called Boswell. Boswell did talk with him and on January 6, 1967, after Liebeler returned to Los Angeles, Liebeler sent Boswell his memorandum with a letter asking him for detailed comments.[9] On January 11, 1967, Thompson appeared for the interview with Boswell. When Thompson reached into his briefcase for the Sibert and O'Neill report, Boswell, said Thompson, "turned five shades of white . . . he physically blanched. . . ."[10]

Did Boswell believe that *Life* magazine, which owned the Zapruder film, which just two months earlier had called for a new investigation, publishing a cover story using frames to question whether Oswald was the lone assassin—did Boswell believe *Life* was about to take the next step, and raise the question of whether Kennedy's body had been altered? And did he think he was about to be questioned on the matter?

I reviewed what Thompson told me in October 1967 about his January 11, 1967 interview with Boswell: "On all sorts of points, he gave me information, when I don't think he knew he was giving me information. For example, in discussing the injury to the President's head, he pointed out that there was a lot more damage to the President's head than appeared in the autopsy. For example, that the skull was shattered on the left cerebral

---

* In my extensive reading, I was never able to find a case in which a rifle firing hard-jacketed ammunition produced a hole nearly a half foot across the top of the head, and in which four symmetric tears extended from the margins of the wound. The tearing seemed to be more random, and the wounds seemed to be smaller— more similar to the 2¾-inch hole at the right rear of Kennedy's head described by the Dallas doctors.

hemisphere, not just in the right."[11] Thompson told me that he asked Boswell how he knew that, because such information did not appear on the autopsy face sheet. "That's right, there was another autopsy face sheet," Thompson quoted Boswell as saying. "Yes, I'm sure there was another sheet, which had that measurement on it, and which had height, weight, and some other information. I'm sure of it."[12] Boswell's statement, if true, would mean that some of the notes made by the autopsy doctors have simply disappeared.

Thompson was unaware of the "head surgery" statement in the Sibert and O'Neill report, nor did he know about Liebeler's contacts with Boswell.

I thought Boswell's behavior in volunteering such information was significant. He was revealing to a journalist information that was not in the official autopsy report and that had not been given to the Warren Commission.

Two years later, Dr. Pierre Finck testified at the trial of Clay Shaw in New Orleans. Before the Warren Commission, Finck never hinted that the President's brain could be removed without surgery. But in New Orleans, when asked how much of the autopsy had been performed "by the time you got there," he volunteered: "As I recall, the brain had been removed. Dr. Humes told me that to remove the brain he did not have to carry out the procedure you carry out when there is no wound in the skull. The wound was of such an extent, over five inches in diameter, that it was not of a great difficulty for him to remove this brain, and this is the best of my recollection."[13]

Over the years, I accumulated additional detail to support my hypothesis. In 1975, I began to write this book. At the time, I had a conversation with writer Robert Blair Kaiser, who was interviewing me for an article in *Rolling Stone*, urging a re-opening of the Kennedy case. I had confided my hypothesis to Kaiser. Now I asked: How was I going to make such technical data readable? It seemed so abstruse, so dry. Kaiser listened to my description of what I believed had been done to the head and said: "You mean there was a pre-autopsy autopsy?"

I flinched. "Don't be ridiculous," I replied. "You're born once, you die once, and you only have one autopsy." I didn't like the phrase "pre-autopsy autopsy." It seemed a perversion of language and reminded me of "decoy ambulance." It made body alteration seem almost legitimate.

But the interchange planted a seed in my mind. The next day, I asked my friend Bernard Kenton, who was working in the Division of Clinical Neurology at City of Hope Medical Center, to get me an autopsy manual. Curiously, although I had studied books on forensic pathology, I had never looked at an autopsy manual. Now I had an idea.

Purely as a literary device, a way of making the data understandable to the reader, I planned to list all the steps normally taken to remove the brain; then I would go to the autopsy data—Humes' report, the autopsy testimony, Finck's testimony in New Orleans, anything available from the report of the Clark Panel, and make a comparison. How closely did the condition of President Kennedy's head, at the start of the autopsy, resemble the condition of a head after the standard autopsy procedure for removing the brain?

Reviewing the anatomic data from that standpoint, I was astounded. Excitedly, I telephoned my friend: "This is no literary device! It's as if an autopsy had already been performed on the head. That is a valid way of viewing the Bethesda data."

Here were the main points that I adduced in support of that hypothesis in 1976, supplemented by a few references that surfaced in 1979, in a published transcript of the September 1977 appearance of Humes and Boswell in a closed session with the House Assassinations Committee.

Removing the Skullcap: An Overview

The removal of the brain begins with the removal of the skullcap. The skullcap is more than just the very top of the skull. It is, approximately, that portion of the skull which would be covered by a baseball cap: the roughly hemispherical surface extending all the way from the middle of the forehead to the rearmost portion of the skull, and it includes both sides of the top of the head.

As a first step to remove the skullcap, the autopsy surgeon makes an incision from ear to ear across the top of the scalp. This permits the scalp to be parted in two great flaps, one of which is pulled back toward the rear (as one would pull back the hood of a windbreaker); the other, forward over the face (as one might pull forward and downward the upper portion of a full-face mask). This procedure exposes the entire skullcap. (See Fig. 29.)

Once the skullcap is exposed in this manner, it is removed by actually sawing it off. What is left is a large oval hole. The tools used to accomplish this—an electric saw, similar to a portable jigsaw; a chisel; a mallet; etc.—make the "operation" resemble more a piece of carpentry than the delicate procedures generally associated with the word "surgery." Nevertheless, removing a skullcap is "surgery"—standard autopsy surgery—and any pathologist who observed a body on which this appeared to have been done would properly refer to it as "surgery."

Removal of the Skullcap—A Step-by-Step Comparison

According to the Dallas descriptions, President Kennedy had an egg-size hole, about 2¾ inches, at the right rear of the head. At Bethesda,

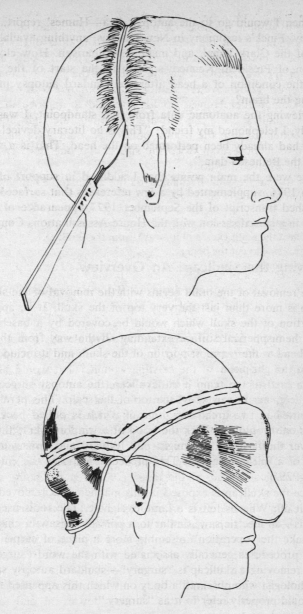

Figure 29.
Reflecting the scalp—first step in removing skullcap
    Diagrams from the autopsy manual of the Armed Forces Institute of Pathology illustrating how an ear-to-ear incision through the scalp is used to create two large flaps which, upon reflection, expose the entire skullcap. Dashed line on skull illustrates the recommended saw cut to remove skullcap.

according to Humes, the hole was much larger. It did not quite encompass the entire right side of the skullcap because the hole did not extend far enough forward—into the forehead area. It extended only about three-quarters of the way forward on the head, to the forward margin of the parietal bone.* To remove the skullcap in accordance with normal autopsy practice, Commander Humes would have had to remove the entire left side of the skullcap, and the forward portion of the right side—i.e., the part that extended into the frontal bone. He would have had to make a hole somewhat more than twice the size of the one that was present at the time he received the body.

Thus to remove what remained of the skullcap, Commander Humes would have had to:

1. incise the scalp;
2. reflect the scalp (i.e., pull it away) from the skull;
3. use a saw to cut the bone;
4. remove the bone.

There was reason to infer from the Bethesda protocol that each step, or a variant of it, had already been taken.

Incising the Scalp. Since, in this case, there was already a large hole in the head, Humes would have had to improvise, starting his scalp cuts somewhere on the periphery of the existing wound. That would have divided what remained of the scalp into flaps which, when pulled away from the existing hole, would expose what remained of the skullcap. When Humes received the body, he found that the tears divided the scalp, overlying what remained of the skullcap, into four flaps: one to the right side, one to the left, one to the front, and one to the rear. Although Humes described these tears in detail in the autopsy report, he never told the Warren Commission that the President's head, at the time he received the body, already had four flaps.

My reading in basic texts on autopsy procedure established the extent to which those four flaps made further cutting hardly necessary.

Consider, for example, the flap on the left, created by the two tears I thought exhibited the most suspicious degree of symmetry: Both began at the identical spot on the left side of the skull hole, both were of approximately equal length, and both ran off, according to Humes, "into the more or less intact scalp"[14]—one slanting downward and to the front, the other downward and to the rear. Together, they formed a large V-shaped

---

* The bone anterior to the parietal is the frontal bone—i.e., the forehead—but Humes' description mentioned nothing about the wound extending into the region of the frontal bone. The dividing line between the parietal bone and the frontal bone is the coronal suture. See Fig. 22, p. 315, for a diagram of the skull.

flap which could be reflected (i.e., pulled away) from the underlying bone to expose much of the entire left side of the skullcap.

A similar situation prevailed at the front of the skullcap, where a large flap resulted from the existence of scalp tears "b" and "c," the two which extended toward the front, on the right and left sides of the head, respectively. Normally, the forward expanse of the skullcap is exposed by pulling the anterior flap, created by the standard ear-to-ear incision, in a forward direction over the face of the deceased. Autopsy manuals specified how far forward the scalp should be reflected. Ludwig's *Current Methods of Autopsy Practice,* for example, recommended that it be ". . . reflected [forward] to a level 1 or 2cm above the supraorbital ridge."[15] (About ½ inch to ¾ inch above the eyebrows.*)

As in the case with the left side of the head, Humes described a condition suggesting the scalp already had been reflected toward the front. Radiating from the forward margin of the hole on the top right of the head, Humes found tear "b," ". . . extend[ing] . . . anteriorly [forward] on the forehead to approximately 4cm above the right orbital ridge."[16]

The scalp, it seemed, had already been reflected to within 2cm (¾ inch) of the location recommended in a standard autopsy manual.

If so, then hardly any further incising of the scalp was necessary to create flaps which could be reflected away to expose what remained of the skullcap; consequently, I was not surprised to find Humes had testified that, as the first step he took to remove the brain, he had ". . . extended the lacerations of the scalp which were at the margins of this wound down in the direction of both of the President's ears."[17]

Were Humes and Boswell aware that the four tears formed flaps? In 1976, I submitted an earlier draft of this manuscript to a criminal attorney well versed in forensic pathology. He suggested that I contact Humes and Boswell and ask that question. I kept procrastinating, but it became unnecessary in August 1979, when the House Assassinations Committee published the transcript of an appearance by both doctors in September 1977. Apparently, the passage of thirteen years had either lessened inhibitions or sharpened recollections. Boswell testified: "There were fragments attached to the skull or to the scalp and all three major flaps."[18] Humes testified: "And these flaps were not firmly attached, the[re] were bony fragments, floating around in the loose scalp."**[19]

---

* The supraorbital ridge is the curved and prominent margin of the frontal bone that forms the upper boundary of the orbit, the bony cavity in the skull which contains the eye.

** Although cosmetic considerations dictate that normally only a single ear-to-ear incision is made to reflect the scalp, the four tears Humes reported were adequate to expose the entire skullcap and provided a logical means for doing so without leaving the telltale sign of the standard autopsy incision. In fact, since the large hole at the top of the President's head was not observed at Parkland, and since the scalp was

And Boswell, describing one of the autopsy photographs which showed a flap, said: "And then we just folded that back and this back and an [a]nterior flap forward and that exposed almost the entire—I guess we did have to dissect a little bit . . . but not much, because this bone was all gone. . . ."[20]

In connection with the scalp tears, there was a curious silence, in both the autopsy report and testimony, on a related point. Like any tissue in the body, the scalp, when injured, can bruise. Curiously, the autopsy protocol never once said that the President's scalp was bruised in any way, yet Humes was careful to note other bruising he saw—in the area of the left eyelid, and over the right eye.

Most texts on forensic pathology have chapters on head injuries. *Glaister's Medical Jurisprudence and Toxicology* states: "Bruising of the scalp occurs in every case of head injury with the exception of incised wounds." A wound supposedly made by a bullet bursting through at over one thousand feet per second could hardly be called an "incised wound." *Glaister's* also notes that the scalp usually must be reflected to see the bruising, stating: "Bruises are frequently found . . . in the posterior part of the scalp below the occipital protuberance."[21] Humes testified he reflected the scalp in just that area to see the entry wound in the skull. Yet he reported no bruising whatsoever, describing the scalp as "intact" or "more or less intact."[22] The absence of bruising seemed significant. Texts on forensic pathology make clear that one way to tell whether a wound has been made antemortem or postmortem is to study tissue from the bruised area under a microscope. Such study can reveal whether a particular injury was made antemortem or postmortem by determining whether or not certain vital reactions took place. Almost every text has a section devoted to this subject of distinguishing antemortem from postmortem bruising. But here there was no subtlety whatsoever. Judging from Humes' report, there was no bruising at all—an indicator that the four symmetrically arranged tears had been made postmortem.

The Next Two Steps: Reflecting the Scalp and Sawing the Skull. Just because the scalp is incised to form a flap does not mean that the flap can

---

probably reflected away from the skull before that hole was created, I believed those four tears represented the remains of a series of longer incisions made as a first step to expose the skullcap for illicit surgery.

Since the two tears originating on the left margin of the hole began at the identical spot, this suggested they represented the truncated remains of two intersecting incisions. Specifically, the two "tears" on the left ("c" and "d") may originally have been continuous with the two "tears" on the right ("a" and "b"), but this must remain speculation since, as Humes noted, the entire portion of scalp corresponding to the hole found on the right side of the head was simply gone at the time of autopsy.

be lifted away from the skull, as a bedspread is lifted from a bed. Reflecting the scalp takes effort because the scalp is connected to the underlying skull by the subgaleal connective tissue. "Reflection is achieved," notes Wilson's *Methods in Morbid Anatomy,* "mainly by pulling and pushing."[23] Sometimes a considerable amount of force is required. "When the scalp is unusually unyielding," notes Rezek's *Autopsy Pathology,*

. . . the best maneuver is to stand at the head of the table . . . place each thumb under the flap . . . put the fingers on the exterior, pressing against the thumbs through the tissues and supinate the wrists with one's utmost strength.[24]

Another book warns the surgeon to be careful when forcibly pulling back the scalp with one hand, while using a sharp instrument, in the other, to sever the connective tissue: ". . . guard against [the scalp's] slipping, lest injury be done to the operator or to the subject."[25]

After the reflection of the scalp, the next surgical step normally necessary is the removal of the entire skullcap. By Humes' own description, over half the President's skullcap remained on his head—the entire left side and a portion of the right. To remove it, Humes should have had to do a considerable amount of work with a saw, and, as one autopsy manual notes, "sawing the skull is no easy task."

The difficulty is that the skull must be sawed through completely, but if the cut is too deep, the saw blade will damage the underlying brain. Furthermore, the saw cut, or cuts, must completely circumscribe the skullcap. Normally, an electric saw is used for this purpose. "If it is of prime importance to remove the brain as perfectly as may be," notes Wilson's *Methods in Morbid Anatomy,* "then one must use a hand saw, with which one can feel the depth of cut in a way scarcely possible with the electric saw." Whichever saw is used, the surgeon usually cuts almost, but not quite, through the entire thickness of the skull. Then, the skullcap is severed along the partial cut. "The remaining thickness of the bone," writes Wilson, "is cracked . . . by hammering a blunt chisel into the saw-cuts at intervals of two or three centimeters. The chisel acts as a wedge and splits the bone asunder."[26]

Once severed around its entire periphery, the skullcap cannot simply be lifted off. It must be pried loose, because it adheres, below, to the brain's outermost protective membrane, the dura mater. To obtain sufficient traction, some autopsy manuals recommend that a blunt hook be inserted into the saw cut. One describes this phase as involving "a judicious combination of pulling the skull-cap with one hand and using a dura elevator [a device resembling a small spatula used to separate the dura from the skull] or something similar with the other."[27] The fingers themselves can be used for this purpose, but "they must be well protected," advises one book, "as they are liable to slip and be abraded by the sharp edges of the bones."[28] "Where extreme care is indicated," notes Wilson, "the most sensitive dura elevators are the fingers. This way is slow and uncomfortable, [but] for a good result must be endured."[29]

Since, by Humes' own description, over half the skullcap remained, one would expect that Humes and Boswell would have to have exercised a considerable amount of craftsmanship during this stage of the autopsy, since the autopsy doctors certainly would not want to cause any further damage to the brain in a case of this importance.

Yet according to statements of Drs. Boswell and Finck, Dr. Humes found it unnecessary to perform surgery (and what has been described here *is* surgery) to remove the brain. How was that possible? Didn't the scalp adhere to the skull? And didn't Humes have to employ a saw and chisel to sever what remained of the skullcap? Once the skullcap was severed, wasn't the normal amount of effort necessary to remove it from the top of the head?

Humes described the situation as he found it in a few brief remarks in his Warren Commission testimony: "We had to do virtually no work with a saw to remove these portions of the skull, they came apart in our hands very easily . . . as we moved the scalp about, fragments of various sizes would fall to the table."[30]

Until I compared the way Humes found the body with the procedure normally employed to remove a brain I didn't appreciate the full significance of this testimony. But then I realized its clear implication: At autopsy, the remainder of Kennedy's skullcap must have been in the form of numerous individual pieces, which adhered neither to the scalp above nor to the dura mater beneath, pieces which just fell to the table, as Humes moved the scalp about.

A close inspection of the autopsy report and testimony revealed further detail supporting this conclusion. Humes reported the fragments were "numerous," ranging from 1mm to 10cm in size.[31] A ten-centimeter (3.94 inch) fragment represents a substantial piece of bone. It would take no more than two or three such fragments to comprise what remained of the skullcap. At one point, Humes referred to them as "these loosened portions of skullbone."[32] The fragmentation was so complex, and the skull pieces were in such disarray, that Humes found it difficult to determine which piece of bone came from what area of the head. He testified: "The fragments were so difficult to replace in their precise anatomic location."[33]

This contrasted sharply with the condition of the skull in Dallas. No one in Dallas reported four symmetrically arranged scalp tears, creating four large flaps. There was reason to believe that the President's skull had not yet been reduced to loose fragments. Dr. Malcolm Perry administered external cardiac massage, a relatively violent procedure. Again and again, he jolted the body, pressing sharply against Kennedy's chest, to compress the heart and force the circulation of blood. No pieces of skullbone fell to the emergency room cart.

My theory that what remained of the skullcap at Bethesda was completely fragmented raised an interesting question. Humes described the large "defect" as being on the right side. If so, then why wasn't it necessary to use a saw to remove the left side of the skullcap? Humes testified: "We had to do virtually no work with a saw. . . ."[34] Did Humes mean no work, or almost no work? In 1979, the House Assassinations Committee published excerpts of Dr. Finck's autopsy notes. Finck wrote: "Humes told me that he only had to prolong the lacerations of the scalp before removing the brain. No sawing of the skull was necessary."*[35]

But if so, if the left side of the skullcap could be removed without a surgical saw, wasn't that inconsistent with the autopsy description that the wound was situated only on the right side of the head? One possible answer was that the autopsy description was incorrect. That was supported by what Dr. Boswell told Josiah Thompson on January 11, 1967. Boswell, said Thompson, "pointed out that there was a lot more damage to the President's head than appeared in the autopsy. For example, that the skull was shattered on the left cerebral hemisphere, not just in the right."[38]

Boswell re-affirmed this ten years later in an interview with the House Assassinations Committee. Explaining a 10cm area he had marked off on the left side of the head, on his diagram of the skull, Boswell said: "This was a piece of 10 centimeter bone that was fractured off of the skull and was attached to the under surface of the skull. There were fragments attached to the skull or to the scalp and all the three major flaps."[39]

What all this suggested was that when Humes used the word "defect," he did not mean a hole in an otherwise intact skullcap, but rather a hole whose circumference was composed of other loosened fragments, and whose perimeter probably changed dramatically as he "moved the scalp about" and found that "fragments of various sizes would fall to the table."

I often wondered what held the fragments in place before Humes was given the body to examine. I concluded it must have been the additional blood-soaked wrapping on the body, reported by the FBI, but not mentioned by Humes. I guessed that after the skullcap was removed and access was had to the brain, pieces of the skullcap must then have been

* In an interview with the Forensic Pathology Panel of the House Assassinations Committee on September 16, 1977, Dr. Boswell said: "The scalp was so torn and lacerated that we never had to do any dissection there."[36] As Dr. Boswell was interviewed, each Panel member had in front of him a looseleaf notebook containing copies of the autopsy photographs, some of which apparently do show the flaps. Boswell emphasized that the photographs depicted the scalp as he found it: "The scalp was just laid over . . . just laid down, like so, without having done any dissection or anything."[37]

replaced on the left side, and held in place by the wrapping, leaving a large hole on the right, which crudely resembled a gunshot exit wound.

Analyzing the record in this fashion was slow and tortuous. Rudimentary yet compelling evidence that the skullcap must have been removed prior to autopsy came to me in February 1971, when I spent an evening with Secret Service Agent William Greer at his home in Rockville, Maryland. Greer told me that President Kennedy's head, at Bethesda, "looked like a hard boiled egg with the top chopped off."[40]

Greer's words were an excellent layman's description of what a head looks like at autopsy, after the skullcap has been removed.

Yet Humes never had to use a surgical saw.

My suspicion that the large hole at the top of the head was not a legitimate gunshot exit wound was supported by Humes' testimony that he could find no evidence of exit anywhere along the periphery. Humes testified: "A careful examination of the margins of the large bone defect [hole] at that point, however, failed to disclose a portion of the skull bearing . . . a wound of—a point of impact on the skull."[41] Dr. Finck's autopsy notes stated: "No exit wound is identifiable at this time in the skull. . . ."[42] Neither Humes nor Finck could find "outward beveling," beveling along the outside edge of the skull, which would have constituted definitive evidence of a bullet having emerged from within.

Both doctors concluded the large hole was an exit based on other evidence. Both made clear their conclusion was a deduction. Humes based his conclusion on the existence of a small entry wound, beneath the large hole: "This wound [at the rear] had to us the characteristics of a wound of entrance. . . . Having ascertained [this] to our satisfaction . . . we concluded that the large defect . . . in fact, would represent a wound of exit."[43]

Dr. Finck based his deduction on the beveled edge on one of the fragments of bone brought to the room. In his autopsy notes, Finck stated: "Most probably, these bone specimens are part of the very large right skull wound . . . mentioned above. This . . . wound is therefore an exit."[44] Humes also testified about the bone that was brought to the autopsy room. In the autopsy report, he cited the beveled edge as being a portion of a bullet wound "presumably of exit"[45] whose size he estimated at "2.5 to 3.0cm in diameter."[46]

Thus, the only direct evidence of exit from the President's head was not found on bone attached to the head at the time of autopsy, but on bone brought to the room later. In view of the role played by the bone fragments, their chain of possession was crucial.

The FBI only mentioned one fragment, said it arrived "during the latter stages of the autopsy," and was measured at 10 by 6.5cm (3.9 by

2.6 inches). Once I knew that the "removal" of bone was a part of the surgery necessary to take off the skullcap, Sibert and O'Neill's account of what was said when that bone was handed to Humes acquired increased significance: "Dr. Humes . . . was instructed that this had been removed from the President's skull."[47]

In January 1978, the FBI made available nearly one hundred thousand pages of previously withheld documents under the Freedom of Information Act. One document was a telegram sent by Sibert and O'Neill to the Dallas Field Office at 2:00 A.M. on November 23, summarizing the autopsy conclusions. The telegram referred to the bone fragment as "piece of skull measuring ten by six point five centimeters later flown in from Dallas Hospital. . . ."*[48]

Since no surgery was performed at Parkland Hospital, it was possible to dismiss the telegram as erroneous, but another view was that it represented a valid report of what the agents heard in the autopsy room, regardless of whether the information was true. The telegram could be explained if someone said that the bone brought to the room came from a Dallas hospital.**

Where did the bone fragments come from? When the FBI released its one hundred thousand pages, I hoped that they might contain that information, because the collection included numerous FBI reports and memoranda detailing the transmittal of evidence from Dallas to Washington, including such minutiae as what agent was carrying the evidence, what airline flight he was taking, who would be meeting him at the Washington airport, etc. Private researchers, and the staff of the House Assassinations Committee pored over these documents. The archive contained no record that any bone was sent from Dallas to Bethesda on the night of November 22, 1963. The House Assassinations Committee reported: "There is no evidence to show who sent these fragments to Bethesda."[51]

In March 1978, assassination researcher Art Smith interviewed Dr. John Ebersole, the Bethesda radiologist, then in retirement in Lancaster, Pennsylvania. Ebersole said: "I remember being called to the Commanding Officer's office, approximately between twelve and one o'clock, and being

---

* Although Humes testified before the Warren Commission that the bone fragments might have been found in the automobile, he wrote, in the autopsy report, that three pieces of bone were "received as separate specimens from Dallas."[49] In his autopsy notes, Dr. Finck described the arrival of the bone fragments this way: ". . . close to midnight, portions of cranial vault are received from Dallas, Texas."[50]

** This information, when joined with the Sibert and O'Neill statement that "surgery of the head area" was "apparent" and that Humes was "instructed that this had been removed," raised the question of whether Humes was under the impression that some sort of legitimate surgery preceded the autopsy—e.g., that an autopsy had already been started in Dallas.

told that the three fragments he had, and gave to me, had just arrived from Dallas."*⁵² If so, then it was Dr. John Ebersole who brought the bone fragments to the room.

It remains unclear how such bone fragments got to the office of any senior naval officer at Bethesda, or who sent them to the autopsy room with the explanation that they had "just arrived from Dallas."

Skull Fractures

How was the bone from the President's head detached? The usual autopsy surgery requires the use of a saw. Humes wrotes that he found the skullcap in numerous pieces. Was this a plausible result of a gunshot, or was a saw used to create them?

Humes' description of the fractures associated with the hole at the top of the head demanded an explanation.

Textbooks on forensic pathology state that when a skull is fractured by a sudden force, the fracture lines radiate from the point of impact. Their length and depth are indications of the magnitude of the applied force. In the autopsy report, Humes described the fracture pattern as follows:

Upon reflecting the scalp multiple complete fracture lines are seen to radiate from . . . the large defect [hole] at the vertex [the highest point on the head]. . . . These vary greatly in length and direction, the longest measuring approximately 19cm [7.5 inches].⁵³

A complete fracture is one in which the bone is entirely broken through. Multiple fractures are those in which there are two or more lines of fracture of the same bone—in this case, the skull—but the lines do not intersect. Nineteen centimeters is the entire width, or three quarters the length, of an average human skull.

Thus Humes stated that radiating from the hole at the top of the President's head was a series of large cracks—"complete fracture[s]" penetrating both tables of the skullbone—the longest over seven inches in length. Since fracture lines converge at the point of impact, and since in this case a series of such lines radiated from the large hole in the skull, there was no question an impact occurred somewhere within the periphery of that hole. But I asked myself whether the impact was from within to without, or from without to within. Humes implied the hole was made by an exiting bullet. I was skeptical, however, because (1) these fractures

* Dr. Ebersole did not say which "Commanding Officer" he was referring to, so it could have been one of three people: Capt. Robert O. Canada, the CO of Bethesda Naval Hospital; Capt. John Stover, the CO of the U.S. Naval Medical School; or Adm. Calvin Galloway, the CO of the National Naval Medical Center.

were associated with a large hole not seen at Parkland Hospital, and (2) according to Commander Humes' testimony, a "careful examination" of the entire margin of that large hole failed to reveal any specific evidence of exit.[54] The evidence that the hole was not made by the exit of a bullet at Dealey Plaza had to be reconciled with the fact of the fracture pattern— definitive evidence of impact. The two facts were not inconsistent: They suggested that the President received one or more violent blows at the top of his head.

An examination of the X-rays and photographs of the body taken at the autopsy was performed by a panel of four experts, the Clark Panel, convened by Attorney General Ramsey Clark in 1968. The Clark Panel reported that the fragmentation of the skull was so "extensive" that the photographs showed the contours of the head to be "grossly distorted."[55] Reporting on the X-rays of the skull, the panel stated it was fractured "bilaterally"[56]—that the fractures extended to both sides of the skull.

There are multiple fractures of the bones of the calvarium bilaterally. These fractures extend into the base of the skull and involve the floor of the anterior fossa on the right side as well as the middle fossa in the midline.[57]

The fossae are a series of bowl-like compartments in the front, middle, and rear of the skull, known as the anterior, middle, and posterior fossa, respectively. The floors of these fossae comprise the base of the skull, and are situated at different elevations within.*

In reporting that the fractures extended to the "floor of the anterior fossa on the right side,"[58] the panel stated that they extended down the right side of the skull and into the bones comprising the right eye socket. This was consistent with certain information in the autopsy report as well as in Boswell's skull diagram. Humes reported "abnormal mobility"[59] of the bone underlying the right supraorbital ridge. Boswell drew one long line, stretching across both sides of the skull in front, labeled with the number "19."[60] In the margin of the diagram appeared the notation, "globe right eye—fracture through floor,"[61] an apparent reference to a fracture through the floor of the right eye socket. (See Photo 27.)

Dr. John K. Lattimer, a New York City urologist and the first non-government doctor the Kennedy family permitted to examine the X-rays and photographs, graphically described the fracturing:

Radiating downward and outward from the margins of the large defect in the top portion of the skull there were several enormous cracks, some of which extended to the base of the skull, plus numerous others into the floor of the

---

* The anterior fossa is the highest, and the posterior, the lowest. The floor of the anterior fossa is composed of (among others) the bones which make up the roofs of the orbits, the bony cavities which contain the eyes. At the center of this fossa is the ethmoid bone, which forms part of the nasal cavity and rests atop a small bone, the vomer. (See Fig. 30.)

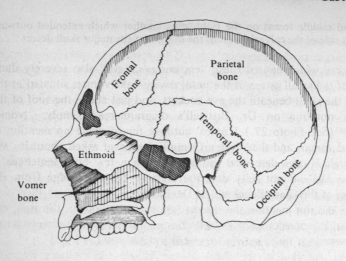

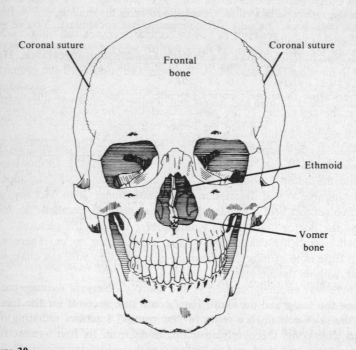

Figure 30.
Front and side views of skull illustrating location of vomer bone in nasal cavity.
On diagram filled out at autopsy, Boswell wrote: "vomer crushed."

anterior and middle fossas on the right, plus another which extended outward into the left side of the calvarium from the margin of the major skull defect. . . .[62]

The force which caused these "enormous cracks" also severely damaged one of the small bones of the nasal cavity—the vomer, situated at the midline of the skull beneath the eye sockets, and just above the roof of the mouth. A notation on Dr. Boswell's diagram read simply: "vomer crushed."[63] (See Photo 27.) Humes' autopsy report made no mention of the crushed vomer, and the Warren Commission never asked about it.

Although Humes described the fractures in a few brief sentences in the autopsy, he did not fully describe their severity, to judge from the descriptions of the Clark Panel and of Dr. Lattimer.

Humes did not mention the fracture through the floor of the right eye socket. Of the "enormous cracks" (Lattimer's term), Humes simply wrote that the fracturing "taxed satisfactory verbal description."

Dr. Michael Baden, the head of the House Committee's Forensic Pathology Panel, told me that Humes' procedure in stating the fracturing "taxed . . . verbal description" was highly irregular. "That's not part of forensic pathology," he said. "You've got to use vocabulary. You've got to describe what you see."[64]

In March 1964, before his Warren Commission appearance, Humes called in navy medical artist H. A. Rydberg and supervised the preparation of three medical drawings of the President's wounds to illustrate his testimony. Dr. Lattimer had noted that Rydberg's drawings were deficient in that they did not depict the severity of the damage. The fractures radiating into the base of the skull were simply not shown.

When Humes appeared before the Commission, he seemed aware of the inadequate nature of the drawings. He urged the Commission to examine the autopsy photographs, pointing out they were "far superior" to his "humble verbal description."[65] Commissioner John McCloy, at an executive session held a month after Humes testified, recalled "an indication by the doctor that . . . he would prefer to have the pictures . . . in connection with the charts that he was representing to us. There was a certain little note of minor inadequacy in connection with the chart which we had, without the pictures."[66]

There was another peculiarity: the sharply divergent damage patterns between the scalp and the skull. How could one account for the fact that while the skull contained a series of "enormous" fractures radiating out in various directions, the overlying scalp, aside from its four symmetrically arranged tears, was described as "intact," with no bruising reported?

How could all these apparently conflicting facts be reconciled?

Finally, this factor: Testifying before the Commission, Humes referred to brain injury described in the supplementary autopsy report as "superficial lacerations" on the underside of the brain in the area of the "left temporal and frontal lobes." He commented: "We interpret that these . . . contusions were brought about when the disruptive force of the injury pushed that portion of the brain against the relative[ly] intact skull. This has been described as contre-coup injury. . . ."[67] "Contre-coup" is the term used to describe a brain injury inflicted on one side of the brain from a force applied to the opposite side. Thus, a blow struck from the rear will cause "contre-coup" injury on the front, and vice versa.

Humes did not state, nor did anyone ask, why, if the President was struck from above and behind, contre-coup injury was found only on the underside of the brain, and not also on the anterior surface.

There seemed to be one way to explain all these facts. The fractures associated with the hole must be evidence of the mechanism employed to create it, of an act which must have occurred after the scalp was reflected, exposing the calvarium (the upper part of the skull) of the dead President. His skull must have then been violently crushed, like an egg.

The Brain

At autopsy, Commander Humes was able to extract only two tiny slivers of metal from President Kennedy's brain, slivers too small for use in ballistics examination.*

Why were there no bullets or sizeable fragments in the brain? I thought it was because they had been extracted by plotters who had first removed the skullcap. This made me wonder: Was the skullcap removed merely to probe the brain, or as a first step in removing the brain itself?

Even after the skullcap has been removed, the brain is still anchored inside the cranial vault by arteries, cranial nerves, protective membranes, and the spinal cord. The brain, in other words, is not like a ball which floats freely within the head and which might fall out through a hole in the top of the skull. Numerous connections must be severed; additional surgery must be performed.

Statements by the autopsy surgeons that surgery was unnecessary to remove the brain suggested not only that the skullcap had been removed, but that all structures holding the brain inside the cranial vault had also been severed.

An examination of the autopsy protocol revealed evidence that supported my surmise that surgery was unnecessary because it had already been performed.

* According to the autopsy report, one measured 7 by 2mm (approximately ¼ by ³⁄₃₂ inch), the other 3 by 1mm (approximately ⅛ by ¹⁄₃₂ inch).

"Falx Loose"

Once the roof of the skull has been removed, what lies exposed is not the brain itself but a tough, inelastic membrane: the dura mater (from the Latin "hard mother")—the outermost of the brain's three protective membranes. The autopsy surgeon then cuts the dura matter with scissors all along the edge of the skull hole. This is a required surgical step and, if surgery was unnecessary during the Kennedy autopsy, then the dura must have already been incised. (See Fig. 31.) In an appearance before the House Assassinations Committee in 1977, Dr. Boswell said: ". . . the dura was . . . completely destroyed. . . ."[68]

Along the midline of the dura mater, descending like a stiff curtain into the fissure separating the two cerebral hemispheres, is a vertical projection of the dura: the falx. At the front of the head, the falx is

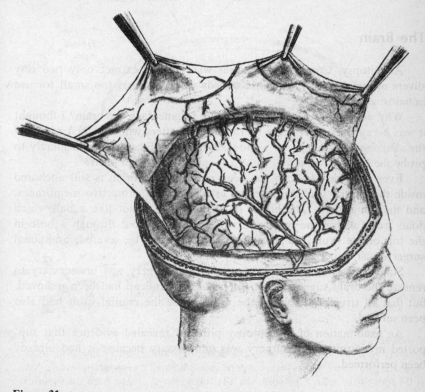

Figure 31.
Illustration showing the dome-shaped dura mater, which sheathes the brain.

attached to the ethmoid bone, which lies directly behind the nose; at the rear of the head, it is attached to the internal occipital protuberance. Running atop, but just inside, the sickle-shaped falx, between these two points of attachment, is a tubular blood-carrying channel—the superior sagittal sinus. This sinus extends, in semicircular fashion, from the front of the falx to the rear, and provides the means by which the falx is attached to the inside surface of the skull. The superior sagittal sinus is lodged in a corresponding groove in the skull—the sagittal sulcus. Like a curtain hanging from a rod, the falx descends from the superior sagittal sinus in the great cerebral fissure between the two hemispheres of the brain. (See Fig. 32.)

In a normal autopsy, after the skullcap has been pried loose, detaching the sagittal sinus—the "curtain rod"—from the skull groove which lodges

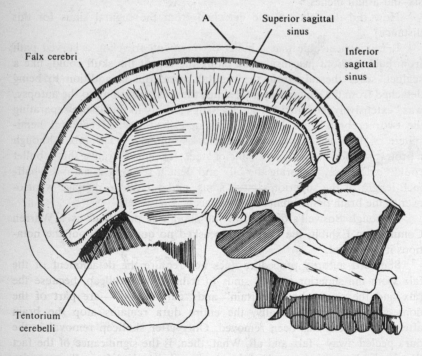

Figure 32.
Cutaway view of the head, showing the sickle-shaped falx, descending from its supporting structure, the superior sagittal sinus. Boswell's notation indicated that, at the time of the official autopsy, the falx was found detached from the superior sagittal sinus "from the coronal suture back" (from approximately point "A" on this diagram, toward the rear).

it—the sagittal sulcus—the dome-shaped dura mater is then cut away from the periphery of the skull hole, and the falx is detached from the ethmoid bone, its frontal point of attachment. This frees the entire dura mater—falx and all—so it can be subsequently pulled and peeled away from the top surface of the brain.

On Boswell's diagram of the skull, the following notation appears: "Falx loose from sagittal sinus from the coronal suture back." (See Photo 27.)

The coronal suture is the forward margin of the parietal bone, and marked the forward margin of the large skull hole described by Dr. Humes. As noted previously, the superior sagittal sinus extends, in semicircular fashion, from just behind the top of the nose to the internal occipital protuberance, its terminus at the back of the head. The distance between the coronal suture and the internal occipital protuberance is approximately six-and-a-half inches.*

How did the falx become detached from the sagittal sinus for this distance?

It was conceivable that a bullet or fragment, traveling a curved path from back to front just inside and along the top of the skull could, like a scalpel, sever the falx from the sagittal sinus. But in addition to being detached from the superior sagittal sinus, the falx, according to the autopsy, was "extensively lacerated." The falx hangs loosely in the fissure separating the two cerebral hemispheres. Humes described the left cerebral hemisphere of the brain, viewed from above, as "intact."[69] The falx, although a protective membrane, is not made of steel. It seemed strange that a bullet could "extensively" lacerate the falx and detach it along a six-and-a-half-inch length of the superior sagittal sinus, and yet do no damage whatsoever to the brain tissue immediately adjacent, on the left.

Although Boswell's diagram of the skull was published as a Warren Commission Exhibit, the Commission asked no questions about the notations it contained.

Standard autopsy procedure does not require the detachment of the falx from the superior sagittal sinus to remove the skullcap, because the falx and the sinus—both "curtain" and "curtain rod"—are part of the dome-shaped dura. Normally, the entire dura remains atop the brain after the skullcap has been removed. Only after skullcap removal is the dura peeled away—falx and all. What, then, is the significance of the fact that in the Kennedy case, the falx was found detached from the superior sagittal sinus "from the coronal suture back"?

The answer was, of necessity, somewhat speculative, for if a bullet

---

* This measurement was made on a standard adult skull of the type used by medical students.

did not create this damage, then what did? I attempted to understand what variant of standard autopsy procedure might have been employed. I concluded that an attempt was probably made to inspect the left side of the brain through a hole which, before it was fully enlarged, was located mainly on the right side of the skull.

Why would this have been done, and why would it result in the damage to the falx reported at the official autopsy? The purpose of any pre-autopsy inspection of the President's brain must have been to remove metal. Most of the small bullet fragments which remained were contained on the brain's right side. In attempting to reconstruct what occurred, I surmised that anyone involved in this affair would surely have been aware that the more extensive the damage created the more difficult it would be to attribute that damage to gunshot injury. Thus, the process of obtaining access to the brain probably began by removing only part of the skullcap—by enlarging the existing "Parkland wound" at the rear of the head toward the front of the head, thus exposing the right side of the brain. At some point, the question might have arisen as to whether, to retrieve all sizeable metallic fragments, it was going to be necessary actually to remove the brain from the skull. To do so would necessitate the removal of the entire skullcap. Thus, a more desirable alternative might have been to inspect the brain's left side through the rather large hole which, at that stage, already existed on the right side of the head.

The chief obstruction to any such examination would have been the falx. Descending like a stiff curtain between the two cerebral hemispheres, the falx would have prevented access to the left hemisphere of the brain through a hole in the right side of the skull. Indeed, to obtain such access, the falx would either have to be pierced and ripped away, or cut from its supporting structure—the superior sagittal sinus—so it could be pushed aside. The condition of President Kennedy's falx at the official autopsy—lacerated and detached from the superior sagittal sinus—was suggestive of maneuvers to permit visual inspection of the left side of the brain through a hole then centered on the right side of the skull—without the necessity of removing the entire skullcap. Without more information, the sequence of events which led to the falx damage observed at the autopsy cannot be reconstructed more precisely.

Almost every piece of information Dr. Boswell chose to record concerns damage closely related to the hypothesis that, before the official autopsy, surgery was performed to remove the skullcap. The navy autopsy report, drafted two days after Dr. Boswell drew his diagram, omitted much of the information on the diagram or alluded to it so indirectly that the picture of the head, painted in words chosen by Dr. Humes, bore little resemblance to its condition as depicted on the diagram drawn by Dr. Boswell.

Among the details noted by Dr. Boswell were:

— "vomer crushed" and "globe rt [right] eye-fracture through floor"—indicative of a blow struck from above;

— a 10 by 17cm area marked with the word "missing"—probably the true measurement of the enormous hole in both scalp and skull at the top of the head, dimensions considerably larger than the hole described by Humes;

— what appeared to be a 10cm fragment of bone on the left side,* presumably one of those which fell to the autopsy table when Humes "moved the scalp about";

— an oblique line, possibly corresponding to one of the scalp tears, on the left, and a similar one on the right;

— a series of notations at the rear of the head, probably concerning bone fragments;

— the notation about the falx being "loose" from the sagittal sinus.

Humes' autopsy report either omitted or modified most of these data. He made no mention of the crushed vomer or of the fracture of the globe of the right eye. In place of the 10 by 17cm area, marked "missing," he described a defect 13cm across. He made no mention of a ten-centimeter bone fragment, on the left, which Boswell said was fractured off and attached to the under surface of the skull—another indication of a force striking from above—or of the fact that this 10cm fragment, when joined to the 10 by 17cm "missing" area, comprised an irregular hole almost 20 by 17cm—almost 8 by 7 inches—easily three-quarters of the entire skullcap. The autopsy mentioned nothing about bone fragments corresponding to the one(s) shown by Boswell at the rear of the head, nor anything about the falx being "loose."

In his memorandum of November 8, 1966, Liebeler noted that the diagram "was made during the autopsy itself" and "form[s] a part of CE 397 [Warren Commission Exhibit 397—working papers of the Kennedy autopsy]. . . ." Liebeler suggested that additional sworn testimony be taken from the doctors, requesting "a general explication" of all "marks and notations." He suggested that when such additional testimony was taken, the doctors "should remark . . . upon the significance" of such notations as "vomer crushed."

After the skullcap has been removed and the dura laid back, the tops of both cerebral hemispheres lie exposed. With the tips of the fingers of the left hand, the surgeon gently raises the frontal lobes from where they rest on the floor of the anterior cranial fossa, the most forward of several bowl-like depressions which comprise the base of the skull. With a scalpel or scissors in the other hand, he begins the process of severing an assort-

---

* My interpretation was confirmed when Boswell appeared before the House Assassinations Committee (see p. 447).

ment of structures which connect the brain to other parts of the body. In these final stages, removing the brain is similar to disconnecting a complicated biochemical switchboard—one whose power lines are arteries, and whose message-carrying conduits are the cranial nerves.

The procedure begins at the front, where the olfactory bulbs (small outgrowths of the brain containing the cells governing the sense of smell) are freed from their attachment to the ethmoid bone behind the nasal cavity. Then the optic nerves leading to the right and left eyes are cut. At this point, the anterior portion of the brain is free from the floor of the skull. Since the body is lying on its back, the brain, under its own weight, will sag to the rear. To prevent the tearing of other structures which are still attached, the brain is supported with the palm of the left hand while it is tilted still further away from the floor of the skull, baring more of its underside, so additional connecting structures can be exposed and severed.

Autopsy manuals describe the procedure in detail, listing what needs to be cut and in what order. If the President's brain could be removed "without recourse to surgery," then none of this had to be done. All these structures must have been severed by the time Humes received the body.

The list includes the following:

1. the pituitary stalk;
2. the carotid arteries, which supply blood to the brain;
3. cranial nerves III, IV, V, and VI;
4. the tentorium—a horizontal shelf of dura mater separating the cerebellum from the cerebral hemispheres above;
5. cranial nerves VII, VIII, IX, X, XI, and XII;
6. the vertebral arteries.

I realized that none of these structures was so strong that it could not be cut by a bullet. But was it plausible that a single bullet could have severed them all?

The structures listed above are located at various points on the underside of the brain, and on both sides. The bullet could not be here, there, and everywhere—all at once. Did a shock wave cause all this damage? If so, why was it so selective? The left side of the brain was hardly damaged at all.

When all these connections have been severed, there remains one major structure holding the brain inside the cranial vault—the spinal cord, entering the skull through a hole in its base: the foramen magnum. (See Fig. 23.) Rezek's *Autopsy Pathology* describes this final step as follows:

Support and lift the brain again so as to expose the brain stem, and with a long knife transect the cervical cord [the upper part of the spinal cord] as low as possible making as transverse [horizontal] a cut as you can. The brain can now be lifted out, quickly inspected, weighed and set aside.[70]

Humes' autopsy report contained evidence which led me to suspect that he found the spinal cord already transected.

The "gross" findings of an autopsy consist of observations made with the naked eye. More information often is available from microscopic examination of tissues from selected areas of damage. In the supplemental autopsy report, Humes listed the various tissue sections he took, most of them from damaged areas of the brain. The fifth section (Item e) was "from the line of transection of the spinal cord."

The spinal cord must be severed to allow removal of the brain from the skull, but the autopsy surgeon does not normally make microscopic slides of incisions he himself makes. His mission at the time of autopsy is to investigate the cause of death—not the cause of his own incisions! Humes presumably had to make numerous incisions to remove other organs, including the heart, lungs, liver, spleen, kidneys, etc. He took no microscopic sections of the incisions to remove those organs.

The fact that Humes, in listing the microscopic sections, listed one "from the line of transection of the spinal cord," aroused my suspicions that the spinal cord was transected at the time Humes received the body.

Was it?

This issue is crucial. When an earlier version of this manuscript was submitted for review by a prestigious pathologist, he complimented me on the care with which I had assembled the data, and the accuracy of both the anatomical descriptions and the descriptions of the autopsy procedure. "The author has obviously done his homework very carefully," wrote the doctor, but he could not go along with the conclusion that the spinal cord had been transected. He wrote: "Despite my low opinion of military physicians, the fact that an experienced pathologist would have missed the implications of the spinal cord severance is incredible."

This pathologist's reaction made me realize that the issue of spinal-cord severance was fundamental. If it was severed, that was tantamount to saying the brain was lying free in the cranial vault, an irregularity so gross that if it was true, it demanded to be reported by the autopsy doctor in plain English. Dr. Charles Wilber, the Deputy Coroner of Larimer County, Colorado, told me in 1976 that if a civilian forensic pathologist had performed the autopsy at Bethesda and found the brain unattached inside the cranial vault, he would have "raised hell."[71] Dr. Michael Baden, the Chairman of the Forensic Pathology Panel of the House Assassinations Committee, told me in 1978: "If he [Humes] found the brain free in the cranial cavity, with the spinal cord already cut through, then that's grounds for saying 'Hey!', yelling, screaming, making a fuss about it. That would be grounds for looking into it. What you're saying is that somebody had previously cut through the brain."[72] Baden denied any such thing occurred, and cited, as one reason, the fact that Humes never reported anything so unusual.

Indeed he did not. After describing the large hole at the top of the head, the four scalp tears radiating from it, the associated fracturing, and the brain tissue that was "clearly visible," Humes wrote the following single-sentence paragraph: "The brain is removed and preserved for further study following formalin fixation."[73]

Humes' choice of language was interesting. Any knowledgeable reader would assume that when Humes said he "removed" the brain, it was understood that he, of course, removed it surgically. One would not think that the word "removed" signified that all the autopsy surgeon had to do was lift the brain out—without having to cut anything.

This example pointed up a problem which pervaded both the six-page autopsy report, drafted by Humes, as well as his Warren Commission testimony: Humes' statements about the President's body were broad enough to encompass prior surgery, even though they appeared to be completely routine.

What the doctors had told me, in effect, was that routine language was inadequate to describe such a gross irregularity, and since Humes went no further, at least not explicitly, then no such thing could have occurred.

But a closer look at the list of tissue sections Humes made, and the report he wrote about those sections, only aroused my suspicions further.

Seven sections were taken, labeled "a" through "g" in the supplementary autopsy report.[74] All but two—one of those being through the "line of transection"—were explicitly labeled as coming from damaged areas of the brain. For example, slide "a" was titled: "From the margin of the laceration in the right parietal lobe"; slide "d" was "from the contused left frontoparietal cortex."[75]

The report on the brain slides reads: "All sections are essentially similar and show extensive disruption of brain tissue with associated hemorrhage."[76]

A cut made with a surgical knife would not show "extensive disruption of brain tissue." In short, the slide report read as if the sections came from an area that was damaged by gunshot injury, supporting the view that Humes took the slide from an area of trauma. Yet its label implied that Humes had taken the section from a location where the spinal cord was "transected"—i.e., surgically cut.

An explanation was required as to why the slide should be labeled "from the line of transection of the spinal cord," and yet reveal, under the microscope, "extensive disruption of brain tissue." Did a bullet cut the spinal cord? Humes never said that in the gross autopsy report. Consequently, I was left to speculate in an attempt to reconcile the way the slide was labeled with what the slide report stated. Was the spinal cord damaged, but not severed, and did Humes make his line of transection in a damaged area? Or did Humes find the spinal cord transected and make a slide, properly labeled, of the "transected" area? The slides themselves could resolve this. But the slides, like the brain, are missing.*

Texts on autopsy procedure emphasize that if sufficient care is not exercised in removing the brain from the skull, both cerebral peduncles— structures on the brain's underside—can be torn. This can occur after structures holding the brain to the front of the head have been detached. At that point, if the brain is not properly supported, it will sag from its normal position in the cranial vault, resulting in excessive strain on the peduncles. Ludwig's *Current Methods of Autopsy Practice*, for example, warns: ". . . do not allow the brain to drop backward excessively since this will cause stretch tears in the cerebral peduncles."[77]

Curiously, Humes characterized the cut through the left cerebral peduncle not as a laceration, but as a "tear."

The Clark Panel, after examining photographs of the underside of the brain, reported that both peduncles were lacerated, and then went on to state their opinion as to the cause: "The peduncles have been lacerated, probably incident to the removal of the contents [i.e., the brain] from the cranium."[78]

In other words, the Clark Panel said the tears in the peduncles were man-made—indeed, that they were made by the autopsy surgeon!

But Humes, in reporting a "tear through the left cerebral peduncle,"[79] was describing the brain as he found it.

Could Humes have caused this damage? Much criticism has been directed at the navy autopsy proceeding because Humes, the chief surgeon, was not a forensic pathologist. Although this might be relevant in gauging his experience in evaluating gunshot wounds, both Humes and Boswell were professional pathologists and, as such, had conducted numerous autopsies during their careers—even if not in murder cases. It seemed unreasonable to me that the Director of Laboratories at Bethesda Naval Hospital and the Chief of Pathology at the Navy Medical School were so inept at basic autopsy procedure that they tore both peduncles on the President's brain upon removing it from the skull. What seemed more credible was that the man-made tears in the peduncles resulted from hurriedly performed pre-autopsy surgery.

This significant fact remained: A panel of experts convened by the U.S. Department of Justice to examine the Kennedy autopsy photographs evaluated the tears in the peduncles as having "probably" been made by the autopsy surgeon, in direct conflict with the testimony of the autopsy surgeon, who swore that that was the condition of the brain as he found it.

* The slides, like the brain, were part of entry 9 on the Memorandum of Transfer. See Chapter 17.

The problem came up during the investigation conducted by the House Assassinations Committee. Humes appeared before the Committee in September 1977, and Dr. John Coe, the Chief Medical Examiner of Hennepin County, Minnesota, and a member of the Committee's Forensic Pathology Panel, which examined the autopsy photographs, asked Humes to focus on the pictures showing the damage to the bottom of the brain.

Said Coe: "Dr. Humes, looking at photograph Number 46 [the brain, viewed from below], I am curious to know whether this destruction you feel is a post-mortem artifact in removing the brain [i.e., man-made damage], or was part of this, was caused by the bullet you think perhaps? . . ."

Humes replied: "No; well, I think it was partly caused by the bullet."

Responded Coe: "It was?"[80]

Dr. Coe seemed to respond as if he, like the Clark Panel, thought the damage was man-made.

Humes then said: "It was great—it was a tearing type of disruption that basically [you] had to go back to our description. The corpus callosum was torn, was it not Jay? [referring to J. Thornton Boswell, who was also present]. And the midbrain was virtually torn from the pons."[81]

In making the statement—"the midbrain was virtually torn from the pons"—Humes went further than he had in the autopsy report and his Warren Commission testimony. If the midbrain *was* torn from the pons, then that was tantamount to saying that the brainstem was severed—not at the normal, usual line of transection, perhaps (just above the foramen magnum), but about two inches higher.

The brainstem connects the spinal cord, which enters the cranial vault through a hole in the base (the foramen magnum), to the brain. The brainstem consists of three structures: The lowest is the medulla oblongata, cylindrical in shape and about one inch in length. Next comes the pons. Emerging from the pons are bands of nerve fibers which form the underside of the mid-brain, the third (and topmost) structure on the brainstem.

If the midbrain was torn from the pons, then the brainstem was severed; and if the previously listed structures had also been cut, the brain could be lifted from the cranial vault without severing the spinal cord.

Of course, Humes didn't say the midbrain was torn from the pons; he said it was "virtually torn." And so a fair translation would be that "virtually" no surgery was necessary to cut the spinal cord.

Brain Damage Described in the Supplementary Autopsy Report

Once the brain has been removed from the head, it is placed in a formalin solution to harden the tissues for ease of examination. On

December 6, 1963, two weeks after the assassination, the three autopsy doctors convened to examine President Kennedy's brain, and following their examination Humes wrote a report—the supplementary autopsy report—describing what he found.

In a highly unusual departure from standard procedure, the doctors did not section the brain—i.e., slice it like a loaf of bread. Humes said they did not do so "in the interest of preserving the specimen."[82] The doctors simply described what they saw, and that description comprises a major portion of the December 6, 1963 supplementary autopsy report, which was published in the Warren Report.

The supplementary autopsy report described "lacerations" presented in the context of gunshot wounding. However, if the evidence of pre-autopsy *access* to the brain is credible—e.g., the removal of the skullcap—then the brain damage could just as well represent cuts made to locate and extract metal. And my reading in standard texts on forensic pathology suggested that the damage described by Humes was not the standard damage expected.

One text, devoted entirely to forensic pathology of head wounds, described the brain wound to be expected in a gunshot case as "characterized by (a) a cone of destruction which consists of a focus of lacerated brain tissue immediately beneath the point of impact, and (b) a second portion of the wound or 'track' produced by the missile. . . ."[83] If the missile exits, says this text, the track will connect the two wounds. "There may be a slightly expanded terminal defect in the brain at this point but the other portions of the wound correspond to the penetrating wound."[84]

Another text states: "The most common lesion is a ragged cylindric tunnel through the brain substance, considerably larger in diameter than the caliber of the bullet. . . ."[85]

In the Kennedy case, the damage was different. There was not a typical bullet track connecting the entrance and the exit wounds. Instead, Humes described certain linear back-to-front patterns that extended extremely deep into the head, and in one case extended all the way from the back to the front. (See Chapter 10.) Since Humes was able to recover only two tiny slivers of metal, the question that repeatedly arose was: Where was the instrument of injury? How did a bullet, or even a fragment, going from point "A" to point "B" produce these particular lacerations? It seemed to me that the series of "lacerations" described by Humes, when joined with the evidence of pre-autopsy access to the brain, indicated that whatever damage originally existed had been modified by attempts to remove metal from the brain, not to mention the brain itself from the cranial vault.

Information on the brain was reported in two categories, corresponding to two distinct laboratory perspectives—the brain viewed from above, and the brain viewed from below.

The Brain Viewed from Above

Humes reported two lacerations in the brain viewed from above. One was directly at the midline; the other, parallel to the first but one inch to the right of the midline, extended "from the tip of the occipital lobe . . . to the tip of the frontal lobe."[86] It was the second laceration—the parasagittal laceration—which was a starting point for my own research. When I showed that to Dr. Abrams, in November 1966, he stated his belief it was damage made with a knife. When Liebeler read the description to a pathologist, it elicited the opinion: "Sounds like he was hit with an ax." (See Chapter 10 for a fuller discussion.)

The laceration at the midline was intriguing because it was suspiciously similar to one made during an autopsy. The brain is composed of two large hemispheres connected at the center by an ovoid, fibrous mass of tissue known as the "corpus callosum." (See Fig. 33.) Autopsy manuals and anatomy texts recommend that when the brain is removed from the head, the corpus callosum be severed, from back to front, since this facilitates examination of the brain. *Gray's Anatomy,* for example, notes that unless the corpus callosum is cut, "the medial surface cannot be examined. . . ."[87] (The medial surfaces of the brain are the adjoining surfaces of the two hemispheres.) The autopsy manual published by the Armed Forces Institute of Pathology recommends that after the brain has been removed from the skull, the autopsy surgeon "cut through the corpus callosum on each side to expose the lateral ventricles. . . ."[88] (The ventricles are cavities in the brain which contain cerebrospinal fluid.)

At the times Humes examined the brain, there was a back-to-front laceration through the corpus callosum, exposing the ventricular system. Humes testified:

. . . there was a laceration of the corpus callosum, which is a body of fibers which connects the two hemispheres of the brain to each other, which extended from the posterior to the anterior portion of this structure. . . . Exposed in this laceration were portions of the ventricular system in which the spinal fluid normally is disposed within the brain.[89]

The Underside of the Brain

The damage on the underside of the brain, according to the supplementary autopsy report, consisted of two lacerations—one, of unspecified length, which ran along the midline; another, joined to the first but angling off obliquely to the left, a three-quarter-inch tear severing the left cerebral peduncle.[90]

Both lacerations were deep within the head. In height, they were positioned just above the level of the cheekbone prominence (but below the bridge of the nose); in terms of distance behind the front of the head,

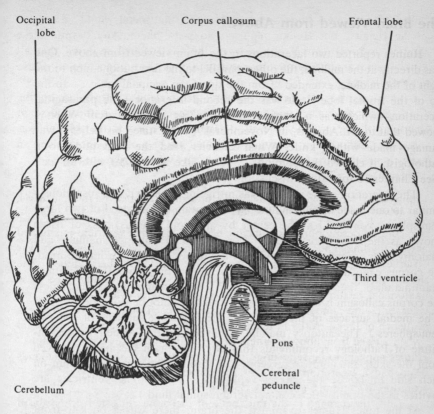

Occipital lobe · Corpus callosum · Frontal lobe · Third ventricle · Pons · Cerebral peduncle · Cerebellum

Figure 33.
Side view of brain illustrating relationship between the corpus callosum and the third ventricle (immediately beneath)

Humes said that when the brain was viewed from above, he found a back-to-front laceration through the corpus callosum (which exposed the ventricles), and that when the brain was viewed from below, he found a laceration through the floor of the third ventricle. Clearly, these two lacerations are connected to each other.

they are forward of the ear canals, but behind the bony prominence associated with the temple.* Their location, so deep within the head, raised the question of how they could possibly be caused by a bullet. (See Chapter 10.) If such damage on the brain's underside was caused by a

---

* These external reference points were arrived at in the following manner. Humes said the midline cut was located behind the mammillary bodies and the optic chiasm, and that the left cerebral peduncle was cut. In terms of the skull's interior, this places the midline cut behind the chiasmatic groove at about the location of the fossa which lodges the pituitary body. The cerebral peduncles emerge from the pons, which rests against the clivus of the sphenoid bone, immediately behind the fossa

bullet or a fragment, then one would expect that metal would be located in the vicinity. But Humes reported no metal there. And despite these injuries, located *below* eyebrow level, the Clark Panel reported that all visible metal fragments on the autopsy X-rays were concentrated above eyebrow level.[91]

The laceration of the left cerebral peduncle was attributed by the Clark Panel to damage made by the autopsy surgeon in the course of removing the brain. The laceration Humes described at the midline was interesting for another reason—it seemed to be nothing more than an extension of the one at the center of the brain "viewed from above."

Humes described it as:

a longitudinal laceration of the mid-brain through the floor of the third ventricle, just behind the optic chiasma and the mammillary bodies.[92]

Humes' description is significant because the third ventricle is situated at the midline, and when viewed from above, a back-to-front cut was observed through the corpus callosum (also situated at the midline). The third ventricle is located directly beneath the corpus callosum. Once these anatomical relationships are understood, it becomes evident that the two lacerations are almost certainly connected to each other. By describing a sequence of literal truths in technical language, some relating to the brain "when viewed from above," others to the brain "when viewed from below," Humes appears to be reporting, in technical language, that the President's brain had a laceration which, at the center, went completely through—from top to bottom!* (See Figs. 33 and 34.)

Thus, the damage to the underside of the brain consisted primarily of lacerations interpreted by a panel of experts to be man-made, supposedly by the autopsy doctor when he removed the brain, and a laceration that was an extension of one at the center, quite similar to one made at autopsy.

---

hypophysis. (The clivus is the backward and downward-sloping surface of the dorsum sellae, an upright square plate of bone which stands, like a domino, at the rear of the sphenoid and forms the posterior margin of the fossa hypophysis.) An examination of a laboratory skull establishes that these cuts are located above the floor of the middle cranial fossa, but below the floor of the anterior fossa. Thus, the following points outside the head were chosen: in terms of height, the cheekbone and the bridge of the nose; for distance behind the front of the head, the holes for the ears and the cheekbone.

* The key words in Humes' description are "through the floor of the third ventricle." Describing the brain "viewed from above," Humes reported the laceration through the corpus callosum penetrated so deeply that it "exposed . . . the interiors of the right lateral and third ventricles." Viewed from below, Humes reported a laceration, again at the midline (but not so stated explicitly) extending upward "through the floor of the third ventricle." Clearly, the third ventricle was exposed from above by the laceration through the corpus callosum, and from beneath by a cut through its floor.

What, When, and Where?

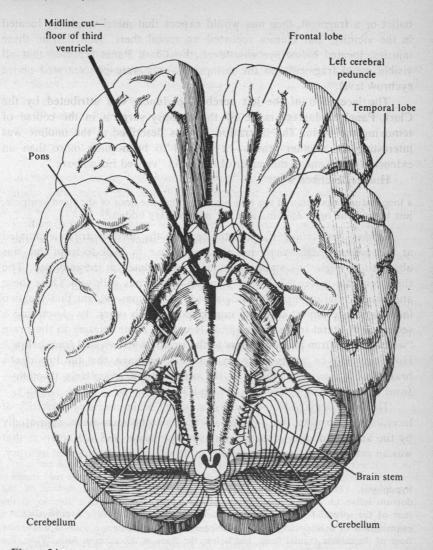

Midline cut—
floor of third
ventricle

Frontal lobe

Left cerebral
peduncle

Temporal lobe

Pons

Brain stem

Cerebellum

Cerebellum

Figure 34.
Brain viewed from below, showing location of midline cut described by Humes

An arrow marks the location of the midline cut through Kennedy's brain, described by Humes as being "through the floor of the third ventricle just behind the optic chiasm and the mammillary bodies." Humes did not give the length of this cut.

Extensive Loss of Brain Tissue

If pre-autopsy access was obtained to President Kennedy's brain, then the damage pattern observed at autopsy would consist of a number of components besides that originally created by the bullet: cuts made to remove the brain from the head, cuts made to explore the interior and locate metal, and absences of brain tissue removed in the course of extracting metal. Aside from the longitudinal lacerations previously described, a prominent fact about Kennedy's brain was that so much of the right side was simply gone.

The autopsy photographs of the brain were exposed on December 6, 1963, the day the doctors convened to examine the brain, and when Humes wrote the supplementary autopsy report. In that report, Humes stated: "There is considerable loss of cortical substance [brain matter] above the base [i.e., the bottom] of the laceration, particularly in the parietal lobe."[93] In May 1972, Dr. John Lattimer, the first non-government doctor to see the X-rays and photographs (in January 1972) published his own account in *Resident and Staff Physician*. Wrote Lattimer: ". . . approximately 70 per cent of the right cerebral hemisphere was missing, with only a torn and flattened portion of the base of the right hemisphere remaining."[94]

In retrospect, Commander Humes appears to have reported on this situation somewhat elliptically in his December 6 supplementary autopsy report. Is a one-sentence reference to "considerable loss" of brain material "above the base" of a laceration a fair description if more than two-thirds of the right side of Kennedy's brain was gone?

The Clark Panel's description was more informative, transforming Humes' "laceration" into a "canal" whose "roof" was "missing":

The right cerebral hemisphere . . . is transected by a broad canal running generally in a postero-anterior direction. . . . Much of the roof of this canal is missing. . . .[95]

In 1979, the Forensic Pathology Panel of the House Assassinations Committee reported: "On the right cerebral hemisphere is an anterior-posterior cylindrical groove in which the brain substance is fragmented or absent. This groove extends from the back of the brain to the right frontal area of the brain."[96]

Brain Damage: A Pattern of Withholding

How much of the right side of Kennedy's brain actually was missing on the night of the autopsy? The House Assassinations Committee commissioned a medical artist to make an exact copy of the photograph of the brain viewed from above. According to that photograph, Lattimer's description would appear to be borne out. (See Fig. 35.) But if so, then Commander Humes' description in the November 24 autopsy report was rather misleading, because Humes implied that the right cerebral hemisphere, while damaged, was present:

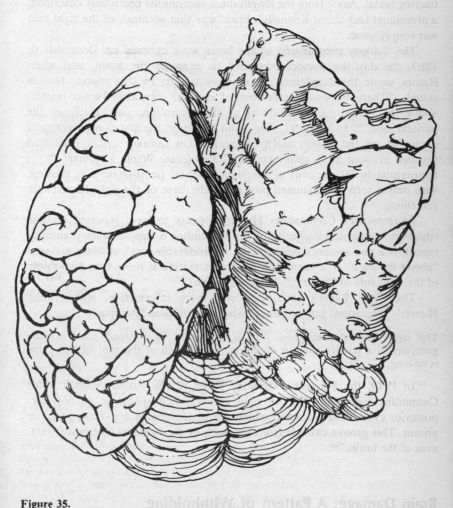

Figure 35.
House Assassinations Committee Exhibit F-302

A drawing done by Ida Dox of an autopsy photograph of the brain exposed on December 6, 1963. Note intact nature of cerebellum.

Clearly visible in the above described large skull defect and exuding from it is lacerated brain tissue which on close inspection proves to represent the major portion of the right cerebral hemisphere.[97]

The key word was "represent." If the December 6 photographs were credible evidence on this point, then what this passage appeared to say, at first reading, was not what it meant. The photographs showed that 70 percent of the right side of the brain was not there. Instead of saying so in his November 24 autopsy report, Humes employed the word "represent" in an ambiguous context—one which had the effect of obscuring the fact that so much brain material was missing. Indeed, the opposite was implied. Years later, when the autopsy photographs became available for inspection and revealed the enormous amount of missing brain tissue, one returns to the autopsy report only to discover the subtle ambiguity.*

The "pre-autopsy autopsy" concept offered a way of correlating a wide variety of technical data from the Bethesda autopsy within the framework of surgery performed to obtain access to the brain. My previous research concerning Dallas/Bethesda differences had persuaded me that both groups of doctors did not see the same wounds, that *something* happened to the body. The pre-autopsy autopsy evidence explained what happened, and

---

* This sentence can be read two ways, and it can be argued that 30% of the right side of the brain does "represent" the major portion of the right cerebral hemisphere. One of Webster's eleven definitions of "represent" is "to serve as a specimen, example, or instance of." Unfortunately, the effect of using such language— whether intended or not—was to obscure, if not totally hide, the startling fact that so much of Kennedy's brain was gone by the time the body was received in the Bethesda morgue on November 22, 1963.

The possibility exists that both descriptions are valid, and that a substantial amount of brain tissue was severed from the brain before the December 6, 1963 examination. In 1979, reporting on its own attempt to establish the chain of custody of the brain, the House Assassinations Committee said that the Bethesda doctors, after the autopsy, "placed the brain in a formaldehyde solution in a stainless-steel bucket and then deposited this in the closet of Admiral Galloway."[98] Since Humes' choice of language in both the November 24 and the December 6 reports would seem to indicate that the large amount of missing brain tissue was a problem being sidestepped on both occasions, my own conclusion was that the brain kept in Galloway's closet was the same brain examined and photographed on December 6, 1963.

After the December 6, 1963 examination, reported the House Assassinations Committee, the brain went from Bethesda to the White House. "Dr. Burkley stated . . . that Captain Stover gave him the brain in a white granite or stainless-steel bucket and that he personally transferred it to the White House where it was placed in a locked Secret Service file cabinet."[99]

The brain remained there, presumably undisturbed, until April 26, 1965, when the Secret Service transferred the stainless-steel container, along with the X-rays and photographs, to Mrs. Evelyn Lincoln at the National Archives, who, about a month later, and at Robert Kennedy's request, then transferred everything she received to Robert Kennedy's secretary, Angie Novello.[100]

why. It changed my view of body alteration from mere mutilation to organized cutting.

The Peculiar Testimony of Commander Humes

As I studied the medical evidence, I couldn't escape the fact that the source of much of my data indicating surgery had been performed was the autopsy report and testimony of Commander Humes. This gave Humes' words a most peculiar quality, making them subject to a number of interpretations. On the one hand, Humes appeared to be trying to tell the Warren Commission something; appeared, in fact, to be furnishing them evidence that the body had been altered. He supplied profuse and explicit detail about what he found, but counted on the presidential commission to draw the proper inference, to take the next step in a matter obviously beyond his authority.

At the other extreme, there was the possibility that Humes had not the slightest idea that anything was unusual about the autopsy. He simply recorded what he saw and honestly believed that all damage was the result of a gunshot injury. In that model, Humes was duped by a medical forgery. The details regarding surgery were in his testimony only because Humes was reporting what he observed. The chief difficulty with this interpretation was that, if the Sibert and O'Neill report was correct, one of the autopsy surgeons immediately made the evaluation that surgery had already been performed on the President's head, and said so. The FBI report recorded oral statements made in the autopsy room at the time of autopsy. Thus, as I discovered that the autopsy report and testimony contained specific indications that surgery *was* performed, it became more and more difficult to believe that the doctors were unaware that anything was amiss.

The third possibility was that Comdr. James Joseph Humes found himself in the midst of a perfectly incredible situation on the evening of November 22. The body of the President of the United States, as removed from the casket, gave every indication of having been surgically altered, and yet, when Humes or Boswell said something about it, it was made clear to them, perhaps by higher military authorities who were present, that no such thing had occurred—and would they please proceed with the autopsy. Given such an ambiguous situation, and knowing that the government was about to launch a major investigation, Humes might have behaved out of a combination of fear, self-preservation, bureaucratic impulse, etc., and tried to have it both ways. On the one hand, he would record in profuse detail the way the President's body appeared to him, but, on the other, set forth everything with a straight face in the context of gunshot wounds. Thus, regardless of what direction the investigation followed, Humes could never be accused of withholding information.

Over the years, I often speculated about the situation in which Humes found himself on the evening of November 22, 1963. The main issue, of course, was whether or not postmortem pre-autopsy surgery was performed on President Kennedy's body, not the psychology of Commander Humes. Nevertheless, Humes' behavior has always intrigued me because he was both the source of much technical information suggesting that the President's body had been altered, and the author of an autopsy report which ascribes everything to gunshot injury!

Often I returned to my tape recording of Commander Humes on November 3, 1966, particularly the part of the conversation when I kept pressing him, trying to elicit some comment. I had said: ". . . certainly, if an operation or if any kind of surgery was done to extract a bullet, or to do anything in the head before the body reached you, that doesn't mean there's anything sinister about it, but it does mean it certainly never came to the attention of the Warren Commission and it ought to have; that's probably a minimum statement you could make, if such a thing happened." Almost inaudibly, Humes had responded: "I certainly think it ought to have." [101] The conversation continued:

LIFTON: What's that?

HUMES: I certainly think it ought to have come to their attention.

LIFTON: I know, and I'm . . .

HUMES: [cutting in] like to know who, by whom it was done, and when, and where.

LIFTON: Right. . . . And certainly if you thought it had been done, wouldn't you have mentioned it to the Warren Commission?

HUMES: I would certainly hope I would.

CHAPTER 19

Certain Preliminary Examinations

FIVE MINUTES BEFORE *Air Force One* landed at Andrews Air Force Base, FBI Headquarters instructed agents Sibert and O'Neill, who were among those awaiting the plane's arrival, to "accompany the body to the National Naval Medical Center, Bethesda, Maryland, to stay with the body and to obtain bullets reportedly in the President's body."[1]

The agents reported that they immediately contacted James Rowley, the Director of the U.S. Secret Service, and told him of their instructions; and Mr. Rowley arranged seating for them "in the third car of the White House motorcade which followed the ambulance containing the President's body to the Naval Medical Center. . . ."[2]

In their report, agents Sibert and O'Neill described the arrival at Bethesda: ". . . the ambulance stopped in front of the main entrance, at which time Mrs. Jacqueline Kennedy and Attorney General Robert Kennedy embarked from the ambulance and entered the building. The ambulance was thereafter driven around to the rear entrance where the President's body was removed and taken into an autopsy room. Bureau agents assisted in the moving of the casket to the autopsy room."*[3]

Next came the two sentences in their report which led me to believe the agents had been prevented—at least for a time—from entering the room where the body had been taken.

A tight security was immediately placed around the autopsy room by the Naval facility and the U.S. Secret Service. Bureau agents made contact with Mr. Roy

---

* The choice of words in these two sentences raised the possibility that the FBI agents were deliberately distinguishing here between the removal of the "President's body" (the language in the first sentence) and the moving of the "casket" (the language in the second sentence). If so, it occurred to me that might have meant that these agents witnessed the body being taken into the hospital separately.

Kellerman, the Assistant Secret Service Agent in Charge of the White House detail, and advised him of the Bureau's interest in this matter.[4]

Where did this take place? To what entrance at Bethesda did the ambulance go? What doorway was cordoned off by a "tight security" that even the FBI could not pass?

In February 1971, I visited Bethesda, and one of my goals at that time was to explore the possibilities, to see whether the body, once inside the hospital, could have been moved to another location. I learned one thing for certain: Bethesda had only one morgue—at the back of the hospital, on a lower floor. It was on a Sunday morning when I retraced the steps of Sibert and O'Neill.

I walked from the front of the hospital to the back, to the loading dock. It was deserted. I ascended the ramp, pushed open the large doors, and entered the hallway. Just a few steps ahead, on the left, was a door leading to the morgue. It was locked. Just then, a phone rang in the morgue. A sailor came running down the hallway, thrust a key into the lock, and rushed inside to take the call. I took the opportunity and walked in. The hallway door opened to a vestibule, the anteroom to the morgue. Along one wall, resembling built-in filing cabinets, were the doors to several chillboxes, where cadavers were stored. I passed through the vestibule and, turning right, through a set of large swinging doors to the morgue itself. It was about fifty feet long. Off to one side were several rows of seats, arranged like bleachers, where spectators could sit and watch. This was where Sibert and O'Neill, Kellerman, Greer, and McHugh had sat on the night of November 22, 1963. At the opposite end of the room, past the bleachers, was a second doorway, which opened onto the same main hallway.

The history of November 22, 1963 had come from findings made in this room. I wondered whether the phone the sailor was using was the same one used that night to send messages to and from the room—when the Secret Service Chief called to tell Kellerman a bullet had been found; when the FBI agents called the laboratory to learn about the bullet; when McHugh called upstairs to tell the Kennedys on the 17th floor that the autopsy was taking longer than expected.

There were two autopsy tables in the room—the tops drilled with hundreds of holes so that fluids could be drained away to pipes underneath. This Sunday morning they were immaculate. I climbed up and sat on one of them. I wondered if it was the one used on November 22. I had the feeling I was sitting atop a chessboard on which, seven years before, a crucial game had been played.*

---

* I consider myself fortunate in having been able to get a personal look at the Bethesda morgue. In October 1968, author Jim Bishop was refused permission to see the room by Adm. Robert O. Canada, who was Commanding Officer of the Hospital

When the sailor got off the phone, I left. I came away haunted by the question that only grew more pressing over the next few years: Where could the surgery have been done?

Upon first interviewing the casket team in 1967, I had conjectured that the body must have been taken to another entrance, or taken in the proper entrance—perhaps even brought to the morgue—but then somehow, surreptitiously taken to an elevator, whisked to an upper floor, and then later returned to the morgue. But after my visit to Bethesda, I began to question all such scenarios.

Bethesda had only one morgue. When Sibert and O'Neill reported they assisted bringing the casket to "an" autopsy room, they must have referred to the room I visited. There was little, if any, possibility of confusion. They had escorted the Dallas casket to the doorway I stood in.

I began to consider the possibility that everything took place in one room—the Bethesda morgue—and that the key to this affair was not where the body was taken, but when the autopsy actually began—the official autopsy, that is.

Was that possible? That a "pre-autopsy" took place right in the autopsy room prior to the start of the official postmortem?

In 1975, I made a discovery in Humes' testimony that supported that theory. Humes' testimony never ceased to amaze me. I had often remarked to Liebeler that it had a biblical quality. It was possible to go back, reread it for the hundredth time, and still find something new, some little piece of information or turn of phrase subtle enough to have gone unnoticed, yet potentially of great significance.

Now it happened again. As I reread that transcript of Humes' March

---

on November 22, 1963, and was Commanding Officer of the Medical Center in 1968. What happened to Bishop was reported by Drew Pearson in October 1968: "Author Jim Bishop, who is gathering research for a book to be called *The Day President Kennedy Was Shot,* stopped by the Bethesda Naval Hospital the other day for a look at the autopsy room.

"The visit unsettled junior officers who scurried around with his request. Bishop . . . merely wanted to glance around the room so he could write a firsthand description.

"The Naval aides, after taking up his request with Rear Adm. R. O. Canada . . . came back with a turn-down.

"Bishop explained patiently that he sought no confidential information, that he would ask no questions, that he merely wanted to look at the room where the late President's body was brought.

" 'I only want to see the autopsy room. I don't want it done to me in there,' he said.

" 'Our commanding officer says you can't see it,' replied a Lieutenant firmly.

" 'Is it under security?' asked Bishop. 'Why is the Navy keeping the room secret?'

"The answer was still negative.

" 'Is it all right,' asked the author, 'if I look at the lobby on the way out?' "[5]

1964 appearance for perhaps the thousandth time, several words virtually sprang from the page.

Specter asked: "What time did the autopsy start approximately?"

Humes replied: "The President's body was received at 25 minutes before 8, and the autopsy began at approximately 8 P.M. on that evening. You must include the fact that certain X-rays and other examinations were made before the actual beginning of the routine type autopsy examination."[6]

What "other" examination had preceded the "routine type autopsy"? What was Humes talking about? Was I attempting to wring too much from those words? Or was Humes aware of some goings-on in that room prior to the autopsy, and had he inserted that language to protect himself?

I returned to the scene at the front of the hospital, when the ambulance with the Kennedy party arrived, and tried to account for the perceptions of each of three groups of participants: the Secret Service, the FBI, and the casket team.

I was now sharply aware that there was only one autopsy room, and that there was no chance of confusion about its location.

I already knew what happened to the casket team. There had been two ambulances, one called a "decoy," and considerable confusion. Two of the men talked of an ambulance chase. The *Washington Post* reported that Adm. Calvin Galloway had driven the ambulance from the front. Also at the front, Godfrey McHugh got into an extended debate with navy brass as to whether they could do the embalming at Bethesda.

The time frame for these events seemed well documented. Secret Service reports said the ambulance arrived from Andrews Air Force Base at the front entrance at 6:55. William Grigg, of the *Washington Star*, reported it remained there for twelve minutes after Jacqueline entered the hospital. That meant the ambulance drove off at 7:07, or a few minutes thereafter.* But the army casket-team report stated the honor guard brought the Dallas casket to the morgue at 8:00 P.M.

---

* Jacqueline may have taken a few minutes to enter the hospital, and whatever time she took must be added to 7:07. Grigg wrote: "She started up the walkway toward the front entrance of the hospital, then paused and turned back toward the ambulance. Then after a moment, she continued on into the hospital and . . . entered an elevator. . . . For at least 12 minutes after Mrs. Kennedy entered the hospital, the ambulance remained in the driveway. . . . Military officials, leaning on the open front door of the vehicle, apparently were not sure where the body should be taken. When word finally came, the crowds were pushed back and the ambulance took the President's body to an entrance at the far rear of the hospital."[7]

The *Washington Post* reported: ". . . the ambulance containing the coffin sat unattended for several minutes. A Navy cordon finally pushed the crowd back about 15 feet from the vehicle. Adm. Calvin B. Galloway, commandant of the medical center, pushed into the front seat and drove to the rear of the Hospital, where the body was taken inside."[8]

What happened to the Secret Service agents who were accompanying the body between 7:07 and 8:00? Greer's testimony wasn't useful. He simply said that he drove the ambulance from Andrews Air Force Base to Bethesda. He gave no estimate of how much time passed before the autopsy started, and in his 1967 conversation with me he made it clear that he thought the coffin had gone in the front door of the hospital.

Kellerman, who had ridden in the front of the ambulance with Admiral Burkley, provided more detail:

SPECTER: What time did that autopsy start, as you recollect it?

KELLERMAN: Immediately. Immediately after we brought him right in.[9]

Later in his testimony, he said: "Let's come back to the period of our arrival at Andrews Air Force Base, which was 5:58 P.M. at night. By the time it took us to take the body from the plane into the ambulance, and a couple of carloads of staff people who followed us, we may have spent 15 minutes there. And in driving from Andrews to the U.S. Naval Hospital, I would judge, a good 45 minutes. So there is 7 o'clock. We went immediately over, without too much delay on the outside of the hospital, into the morgue. The Navy people had their staff in readiness right then. There wasn't anybody to call. They were all there. So at the latest, 7:30, they began to work on the autopsy."[10]

Kellerman reported no delay outside the hospital. The tempo of his account seemed markedly different from that of the casket team; they reported a delay of almost an hour. Curiously, Kellerman made no mention whatsoever of the casket team. I returned to an old suspicion: that the Dallas casket entered the morgue twice—once at 8:00 P.M., and much earlier, when it was first driven to the rear.

I now wondered whether Kellerman had, perhaps, been a witness to a "pre-autopsy autopsy." How could he know the difference? Kellerman was a layman. He had gone to the morgue and described what he saw: "The Navy people had their staff in readiness right then. There wasn't anybody to call. They were all there. So at the latest, 7:30, they began to work on the autopsy."

What "navy people" and what "staff" were present at the autopsy which Kellerman testified was underway at 7:30? I checked the Secret Service report he had filed on November 29, 1963.

Kellerman said the motorcade arrived with a police escort at the front of the Naval Medical Center: "The body was immediately taken to the morgue. . . . William Greer and I remained in the morgue and viewed the autopsy examinations which were performed by Vice Admiral Gallway [sic], Commanding Officer, NNMC, Chief Pathologist Cdr. James Humes, Lt. Col. Pierre A. Finck . . . and J. Thornton Boswell, Cdr. Medical Corps, USN, together with the Naval Medical Staff. . . ."[11]

There were only three autopsy surgeons. Kellerman had named four.

He had added Galloway (misspelled "Gallway"), the same officer who, according to the *Washington Post*, was at the wheel of the ambulance.

Dr. Galloway was the first on Kellerman's list.

Could Kellerman have made an error, naming a superior officer who was present, but had done no surgery? I wondered about that. Also present were Adm. Edward C. Kenney, the Navy Surgeon General; Captain Canada, the Commanding Officer of the Hospital; and Captain Stover, the Commanding Officer of the Medical School, and Humes' immediate superior. All were doctors. All were there.

Yet Kellerman named Dr. Galloway. I guessed that when Kellerman entered the morgue, he might have been under the impression that Dr. Galloway either was or just had been doing autopsy surgery on the body of President Kennedy.

Kellerman's testimony also provided an upper limit for when the autopsy began: ". . . at the latest, 7:30, they began to work on the autopsy."[12]

A strange picture was now emerging of the time period between 7:10 and 8:00 P.M. The evidence suggested that while the casket team, confused by two ambulances, was looking for the ambulance with the Dallas casket, and before they found it and carried it inside the hospital at 8:00 P.M., the body was already inside Bethesda at the morgue. Also at the morgue was Secret Service Agent Roy Kellerman, present at what he believed was the autopsy, and FBI agents Sibert and O'Neill who had apparently followed the Dallas casket to the morgue entrance when it was first carried inside, but had then been barred from entering the autopsy room itself.

I returned to the situation of those two agents. How long had they been delayed? What had they been told?

Two puzzles now fused. Years earlier, certain typographical alterations in the Sibert and O'Neill report caught my eye. They were clearly visible on the printed page. In each case, it seemed, certain words or phrases in the report as originally typed had been erased. It appeared the standard secretarial "white-out" had been used. I had often wondered what the gaps might mean. Now, in light of my hypothesis of a pre-autopsy autopsy, and evidence the FBI might have been kept from the room, the gaps acquired a greatly increased significance. Deciphering what originally appeared seemed to provide clues as to what pretext might have been used to keep the FBI from the room—perhaps even justify the activity taking place inside.

A sentence just preceding the one describing the start of the autopsy looked like this:

Arrangements were made ... for the performance of the autopsy by   . the U. S. Navy and Secret Service. [13]

The blank was exactly six typewriter spaces wide. I denoted it by the block of letters "ABCDEF." Thus the sentence, as originally typewritten, was of the form:

Arrangements were made for the performance of the autopsy byABCDEFthe U.S. Navy and Secret Service.

I assumed that "A" and "F," as originally typewritten, were spaces; and that "E" was a comma. I guessed that the sentence, as originally typed, read:

Arrangements were made for the performance of the autopsy by BCD, the U.S. Navy and Secret Service.

This suggested that the name of some three-letter agency originally had been recorded in the Sibert and O'Neill report.

If so, that would mean that at Bethesda, Sibert and O'Neill had encountered individuals who purported to be representatives of another government agency, usually identified by three letters; that they had recorded that information in their report; and that the data had been stricken at some later date. I associated the erasure of the acronym with the evidence that Sibert and O'Neill had, at first, been barred from entering the autopsy room. I guessed they might have been told that either the CIA or a military intelligence agency was inside, involved in a "national security autopsy."

Another typographical change supported this idea. On the top of the next page the agents were describing the absence of bullets in the brain. Their report appeared as follows:

```
During the autopsy    inspection of the area of the brain,
two fragments of metal were removed by Dr. HUMES, namely,
one fragment measuring 7 x 2 millimeters, which was removed
from the right side of the brain.  An additional fragment of
metal measuring 1 x 3 millimeters was also removed from this
area, both of which were placed in a glass jar containing a
black metal top which were thereafter marked for identification
and following the signing of a proper receipt were transported
by Bureau agents to the FBI Laboratory.
```

Again, I counted the blanks. There was room for three more letters. I guessed the original sentence read: "During the autopsy preinspection of the area of the brain. . . ."

Thus, the Sibert and O'Neill report contained at least partial evidence of a purely typographical nature which correlated with my anatomic research, suggesting an event which took place before the official autopsy, an event originally mentioned by Sibert and O'Neill in their report, but then suppressed by these typographical alterations.*

---

* The logical problem with any theory of post-dictation typographical changes in this report is that "surgery of the head area" was not deleted. The only explanation that comes to mind is that the words were simply glossed over.

Medically, a "pre-autopsy autopsy" or a "national security autopsy" made no sense. You only have one autopsy. But given the bizarre events of that evening, I didn't think a "pre-autopsy autopsy" was any more unusual than a "decoy ambulance."

I carefully reviewed the remainder of the Sibert and O'Neill report, and found other typographical irregularities in paragraphs that described the autopsy itself and the findings being propounded by the doctors.

In each case, the fact that something had been changed was obvious. Gaps several characters wide existed where it appeared that something had been eradicated. In some cases, something else—taking up less space—had been typed in. There was nothing subtle about it. It was clear that the report had been rolled back into the typewriter. In each case, the question was: What had Sibert and O'Neill originally written, and why was it changed?

A related puzzle now came to the fore. Every FBI report has three dates: the date the investigation was performed, the date the report was dictated, and the date it was typed. It was not unusual to see reports where all three dates were the same. Yet in this case—the FBI report on the President's autopsy—only the first date was November 22, 1963. The other two were November 26, 1963. Did the agents actually wait four days to consult their notes and type up a report?

That had always seemed odd. It now appeared that Sibert and O'Neill were important witnesses not only because they had seen the autopsy but because of the information they might provide as to why four days passed before they wrote the report now in evidence, and why, even after that delay, the report was changed after it was typed.

Meanwhile, my attention focused on another issue.

Because Kellerman named Galloway as a fourth autopsy surgeon, and because the *Washington Post* named him as an ambulance driver, I took a closer look at reports of his behavior at the autopsy.

One irregularity in the autopsy was the incorporation in the "Clinical Summary" of a statement that three shots were fired, along with a news report quoting an eyewitness who said the shots came from the Texas School Book Depository. "According to available information," began the Clinical Summary, "the deceased . . . was riding in an open car in a motorcade during an official visit to Dallas. . . . Three shots were heard and the President fell forward. . . . According to newspaper reports (*Washington Post,* November 23, 1963), Bob Jackson, a Dallas *Times Herald* photographer, said he looked around as he heard the shots and saw a rifle barrel disappearing into a window on an upper floor of the nearby Texas School Book Depository Building."[15]

What made Humes focus on that information? Why did he include Bob Jackson's account in the autopsy?

The first glimmering of an answer came during Dr. Finck's 1969 testimony at the Shaw trial.

Question: "Doctor, I call your attention to page two, under the heading of 'Clinical Summary,' and I ask you to tell me the basis for your statement as part of your clinical summary that three shots were heard. . . ."

Replied Finck: "This is the information we had by the time we signed that autopsy report."

Question: "The information from whom, Doctor? . . . Who told you that three shots were heard? Who told you that?"

Reply by Finck: "As I recall, Admiral Galloway heard from somebody who was present at the scene that three shots had been heard, but I cannot give you the details of this."[16]

Asked once again about the source of the information, Finck replied: "During the autopsy of President Kennedy there were Secret Service Agent Kellerman in that autopsy room . . . Admiral Burkley, the personal physician of President Kennedy was present, and there was a third person whose name I don't recall who said to Admiral Galloway, who was there during the autopsy, that three shots had been fired. At the time we wrote this we had this information obtained from people who had been at the scene. . . ."[17]

Finck was asked: "Colonel, do you customarily take notice of newspaper articles in an autopsy report?"

"At times it is done," he replied.[18]

The prosecution kept pressing for further details. Finck added: "I personally talked to Admiral Galloway who was referring to a third witness present at the scene."[19]

At the Shaw trial, Colonel Finck provided one other piece of information about Admiral Galloway. Finck noted that the autopsy was signed in Galloway's office on Sunday. Questioned about the rear entry for the neck trajectory which, in the handwritten draft, had been modified with the phrase "presumably of," Finck testified: "As I recall, it was Admiral Galloway who told us to put [in] that word 'presumably.' "[20]

Another oddity concerned an instruction given to Humes, at the outset, by Surgeon General Edward Kenney. In the 1967 review of the autopsy photos, Humes wrote: "The Surgeon General of the Navy advised Dr. Humes that the purpose of the autopsy was to determine the nature of the President's injuries and the cause of his death."[21]

Every doctor knows that one purpose of an autopsy is to determine the cause of death. Kenney's instruction, therefore, and Humes' inclusion of it in his 1967 report, seemed entirely superfluous unless Humes viewed it as a restriction on the scope of his autopsy analysis—e.g., that it was *not* his duty to analyze postmortem damage to the body.

* * *

The next event in the development of my "pre-autopsy autopsy" hypothesis occurred in 1978, when the FBI released nearly one hundred thousand pages of documents. One was an account written by Sibert and O'Neill of their interview by Arlen Specter on March 12, 1964.[22]

The document was somewhat unusual. It was not a memorandum to file; rather, it was in the form of four pages of "Q" and "A" transcript.*

The document stated, in part:

Q: What was the time of the preparation for the autopsy at the hospital?

A: Approximately 7:17 P.M.

Q: What time did the autopsy begin?

A: Approximately 8:15 P.M.[23]

Here, in a document prepared by Sibert and O'Neill, "the time of the preparation of the autopsy" was reported as 7:17. The time of the first incision, 8:15, accorded with their November 26, 1963 report.

But what did "preparation for the autopsy" mean? Whatever it meant, the body must have been inside the morgue. Thus, Sibert and O'Neill were on record as stating there was a fifty-three-minute period between the time they entered the hospital and the time the autopsy began.

But what seemed most important was that when this document was joined with the casket team report, the combination provided documentary evidence of separate entries into the morgue, about forty-five minutes apart, by two groups of people, each believing it was with the coffin containing the body, and that the body was entering the morgue for the commencement of an autopsy.

It did not seem reasonable that this conflict in the record could be explained away as a mere arithmetic error. There seemed no way the FBI would have written 7:17 meaning 8:00 P.M., or that the casket team could have had the weird experience it reported, yet have entered the morgue at 7:17 P.M., just five or ten minutes after the ambulance pulled away from the front.

That neither group mentioned the other only strengthened my conviction that there must have been two separate entries.

Army files I later obtained under the Freedom of Information Act cor-

---

* A covering memorandum from FBI Assistant Director Al Rosen to Hoover's assistant Alan Belmont stated: "A detailed memorandum is attached setting forth the questions and answers that took place as best recalled by the Agents, it being noted they were not able to take detailed notes during the interview." Nevertheless, the format itself—i.e., a transcript—raises the possibility that the two agents in fact recorded the conversation, especially since at one point the transcript has one "Question" followed by another "Question," rather than an "Answer." That would be strange if the agents were simply constructing a "Q" and "A" based on memory.

roborated the time of 7:17. In his report, the "escort officer" to General Wehle stated that upon arriving at Bethesda, he "proceeded directly to the morgue . . . and made contact with the physicians who were to process the remains. . . ."[24] He said the autopsy began at "about" 7:14.* I assumed the army's "7:14" and the FBI's "7:17" referred to the same event, and for the purposes of my research used "7:17."

I now added the time of "7:17" to the chronology of events. (See Fig. 36.)

The chronology illustrated the relationship between the two separate entries of the Dallas casket into the morgue—the one corresponding to the FBI time of 7:17, and the one reported by the casket team at 8:00 P.M. Each group carried in the Dallas casket; neither group mentioned the presence of the other.

It was easy to understand why the casket team didn't know about the FBI entry. They were off somewhere chasing a decoy ambulance, making fruitless trips between the front and the back of the hospital looking for the ambulance with the Dallas casket.

What was not so easy to understand was how the Dallas casket got back outside the hospital and why, when it returned again, the FBI, already inside, didn't know about the 8:00 P.M. arrival of the casket team.

Another peculiarity: Where did Sibert and O'Neill get the hour "7:17"? Why wasn't it in their original report? Why was there evidence their original report had been altered? It was unreasonable to believe that, in March 1964, during a Warren Commission interview, an FBI agent would hark back nearly four months and recollect that something called "the preparation for the autopsy" began at "approximately 7:17." There had to be more to the story.

---

* On December 6, 1979, I filed a Freedom of Information Act request with the Military District of Washington requesting all documents pertaining to the handling of the body on November 22, 1963. Such documents were released to me in February 1980. The information quoted here is contained in an attachment to the report of Col. Phillipe P. Boas, the Provost Marshal. The escort officer is unnamed, but wrote: "At about 1914 hours the CG [Commanding General] arrived with his Aide. I was informed by the General to remain with him and that he would subsequently advise me as to the details of my responsibility for subsequent action. At about this time the postmortem examination of the remains was initiated."[25]

This report, incidentally, contradicts the information in Manchester's book that General Wehle and Lieutenant Bird waited together for the arrival of the navy ambulance. Bird's report says he arrived at 6:45. This report says Wehle arrived— apparently on a second helicopter—at 7:14. It is not clear how much of the confusion about ambulances Wehle witnessed, because documents show that upon his arrival at Bethesda, Wehle was asked to call the army Chief of Staff, General Earl Wheeler, "right away." General Wheeler wanted to tell him that with regard to the confusion at Andrews—i.e., whether Jackie would go to Bethesda in an ambulance or by chopper—"they were not blaming MDW at all."[26]

Time	Event	Source of Data
6:55	Ambulance arrives at front of hospital with Kennedys	Secret Service reports
7:07	Ambulance drives off	William Grigg in *Washington Star*, 11/23/63
	driven by Admiral Galloway	*Washington Post*, 11/23/63
	Confusion between two ambulances; ambulance chase	Interviews with casket team
	Two fruitless round trips between front and rear of hospital	Barnum's account, 11/29/63
	FBI follows an ambulance to rear entrance; assists with casket; prevented from entering a room	Sibert and O'Neill report
7:17	"Preparation for the autopsy"	Sibert and O'Neill interview with Specter, 3/64 (time corroborated by army report, which indicates autopsy commenced shortly after 7:14)
7:30	Kellerman gives this as latest time that autopsy began; names Galloway as fourth autopsy surgeon	Kellerman's testimony before Warren Commission
7:35	Humes says this is when he received the body	Humes' Warren Commission testimony
8:00	Casket team carries Dallas casket into morgue	Casket team report
8:15	First incision	Sibert and O'Neill report

Figure 36.
Chronology of events at Bethesda Naval Hospital

In 1978, I applied under the Freedom of Information Act directly to the FBI's Baltimore Field Office for documents relating to the autopsy.* I specifically pointed to the time, 7:17, which appeared in the March 1964 document released by headquarters a few months earlier, as well as to the language in the Sibert and O'Neill report which indicated the two agents might have been kept out of the room for a while. I spelled out exactly what I was looking for—a document which would give some explanation of what 7:17 meant, that would explain the "preparation for the autopsy."

It wasn't too long before my request was processed, and back came a previously unavailable document.

Dated November 26, 1963, the same day Sibert and O'Neill wrote their five-page 302 report on the autopsy, it was a memorandum to the Special Agent in Charge (SAC) of the Baltimore office:

* The Baltimore Field Office exercised supervisory control over the Hyattsville Resident Agency, to which Sibert and O'Neill were attached.

Date: November 26, 1963

To: SAC, Baltimore
From: SA's James W. Sibert and Francis X. O'Neill, Jr.
Subject: Assassination of President John F. Kennedy

Following arrival at the Naval Medical Center and preparation of the President's body for inspection and autopsy, to be performed by Dr. Humes, Chief Pathologist and Commander, United States Navy, Admiral Berkley [sic], the President's personal physician, advised that Mrs. Kennedy had granted permission for a limited autopsy and he questioned any feasibility for a complete autopsy to obtain the bullet which had entered the President's back.

At this point, it will be noted Dr. Humes, as the physician conducting the autopsy, stated it was his opinion that the bullet was still in the President's body and could only be extracted through a complete autopsy, which he proposed to do.

Special Agent Roy Kellerman, Secret Service, in conference with Special Agents Sibert and O'Neill, from an investigative and prosecutive* standpoint, advised Admiral Berkley that it was felt the bullet should be located.

At this point, Admiral C. B. Galloway, Commanding Officer of the National Naval Medical Center, Bethesda, Maryland, told Commander Humes to perform a complete autopsy.[27]

Several points should be emphasized about this memo:

The distinction made here between "inspection" and "autopsy" is significant, for the two words mean different things, and just how significant this distinction is can only be evaluated in the context of the agents' use of the same word, on the same date, in their report on the autopsy, and the typographical irregularity associated with it.

They had written: "During the autopsy [blank of four spaces—which I believed represented the prefix 'pre'] inspection of the area of the brain, two fragments of metal were removed. . . ."[28]

When that typographical irregularity, suggesting a pre-autopsy inspection, was joined with the fact that "inspection" was clearly distinguished from "autopsy" in the Field Office memorandum, and when those facts were, in turn, joined with "7:17" as the time of "preparation for the autopsy," it seemed to me reasonable to assume that another event had occurred preceding the autopsy—or at least that Sibert and O'Neill had believed that to be the case.

Other details provided corroboration for this idea. There was no indication anywhere in the record, other than this document, that the Kennedys tried to limit the autopsy in any way. The "Authorization for Post-Mortem," signed by Robert Kennedy, made no mention of any restrictions.

* In publishing this document on page 10 of volume 7—the first publication of this item anywhere—the House Select Committee made an error, and reproduced the word "prosecutive" as "protective."

But Burkley's statement, as reported by Sibert and O'Neill—that "Mrs. Kennedy had granted permission for a limited autopsy and he questioned any feasibility for a complete autopsy"—apparently did cause a delay. The delay terminated when Admiral Galloway "told Commander Humes to perform a complete autopsy."[29]

The possible implications of this "delay" emerged only when it was juxtaposed with the other seemingly incongruous information:

— the indications the FBI was kept out of the room;
— "7:17" as the start of the "preparation for the start of the autopsy," versus 8:15 as the time of the first incision;
— the distinction made between "inspection" and "autopsy";
— the casket team's futile search for the ambulance containing the Dallas casket, which it didn't carry into the morgue until 8:00 P.M.

In my view, all of this added up to some type of "off the record" occurrence in the morgue prior to the "official" first incision.

After considerable study of this November 26, 1963 Field Office memo, I began to realize that the irregularities in the Sibert and O'Neill documents—the dates they were written and the typographical alterations—told us something about the activities of these two FBI agents at the time. Eventually I came to view the Field Office document as a "memo to file" which explained in detail what had been deleted from their report. In short, it seemed likely that the two agents themselves had struck the prefix "pre" from that sentence in their report, and had written this Field Office memo to record what they now understood to be the explanation for the delay between the time they entered the hospital and the time the autopsy began.*

Other documents provided indications that Sibert and O'Neill were quite busy on November 26 and 27. They went to the White House and there interviewed Secret Service agents William Greer and Roy Kellerman, and recorded detailed information about their activities in Dallas. Moreover, their report of the Greer interview included some extraordinary in-

---

* Another question was why Sibert and O'Neill put some of their information in a Field Office memo, which ensured it would remain in the local Baltimore file, rather than include all of it in their 302 report, which would go to headquarters and beyond. The procedure was unusual.

Moreover, although their Field Office memo bore a slightly lower file number in the Baltimore FBI file than their report on the autopsy (the former was item 13b, the latter was item 31), there was internal evidence that it was written later. In the 302 report on the autopsy, Admiral Galloway was "Hollaway," and he was referred to as the Commanding Officer of the U.S. Naval Medical Center. In the Field Office memo, his name was spelled correctly, and the morgue was at the "National Naval Medical Center," the correct designation.

formation; that report concluded with William Greer's physical description —age, height, color of eyes.[30]

It certainly was not routine for the FBI to take such information from a fellow government employee who was not a "target" of investigation. Why then did Sibert and O'Neill treat Greer in that fashion? Other evidence suggested that these interviews with Kellerman and Greer may have been prompted by the trouble the two FBI agents experienced at Bethesda.*

In addition to interviewing Kellerman and Greer on November 27, Sibert and O'Neill also interviewed Gerald Behn, the Chief of the White House Detail of the Secret Service, apparently about how various items entered the mainstream of medical evidence.

Their line of questioning seemed to focus on events I found suspicious. Most provocatively: "Mr. Behn was questioned concerning the section of the President's skull"[33] which was brought in after the autopsy was in progress. On the previous day, Sibert and O'Neill said in their report that Humes had been "instructed" that it had been "removed" from the President's skull. Behn simply said that it had been found in the limousine. If Sibert and O'Neill thought the instruction to Humes was odd, they chose not to spell out their concern in these reports—but they did make a point of asking Behn where the bone had come from.

The precise source of Sibert and O'Neill's suspicions was not clear. But one thing seemed certain—that on November 26, the same day their report, with numerous typographical alterations, was put in the file, they had drawn up a Field Office memorandum explaining a delay at the start of the autopsy.

In July 1978 I realized that if I could see the original 302 report, it might be possible to actually see what had been typed originally. Under the Freedom of Information Act, I attempted to obtain access to the ribbon copy of the report. An FBI official in Washington assured me it was simply a matter of finding out whether the ribbon copy was kept in Baltimore, the office of origin; Dallas, the Field Office running the investigation; or Head-

---

* On November 29, 1963, Kellerman wrote a Secret Service report in which he noted that after *Air Force One* landed, he spoke with Secret Service Chief Rowley about the presence of the FBI at the autopsy: "At the airport, Chief Rowley advised me that two FBI agents, ˙Francis O'Neill, Jr., and James Siebert [sic], had been assigned to this case and to allow them into the morgue at the U.S. Naval Hospital. . . ." The final sentence of Kellerman's report said that on November 27 he had given Sibert and O'Neill "an oral statement along the lines of this report."[31]

Another possible indication of tension between the Secret Service and FBI agents at the autopsy can be found in an FBI document written by Agent O'Neill in December 1964. O'Neill wrote that he and Sibert "decided . . . to insure that one Bureau Agent and one Secret Service Agent would be present in the autopsy room at all times." To do this, wrote O'Neill, they "decided that SA Sibert would remain in the presence of SA William Greer, the President's driver, and SA O'Neill would remain in the presence of SA Roy H. Kellerman. . . ."[32]

quarters. I explained to him the reason for my interest—that I hoped, by examining the original, to find out what had been typed in the first place.

In November 1978 I received a call from the FBI telling me that no ribbon copy existed, that the report had been produced by mimeographing and that the original stencil had been destroyed.* This meant that the original document, which might have provided evidence that the Sibert and O'Neill report had been altered, no longer existed. The only way of finding out what FBI agents Sibert and O'Neill had originally written would be to question them in detail. That was obviously beyond the capability of a private researcher.

In a closed session before the House Select Committee on Assassinations in September 1977, Commander Boswell gave this account of what occurred at the start of the autopsy: "Initially Admiral Burkley said that they had caught Oswald and that they needed the bullet to complete the case, and we were told initially that's what we should do, is to find the bullet. Following the X-rays we realized that that was not possible, that there was no bullet there, except fragments, and at that point, Jim [Humes] and Admiral Burkley discussed it, and it was at that point that he agreed that we should continue and do a complete autopsy, which we then did."[35]

In public session, broadcast nationwide on TV on September 7, 1978, Commander Humes testified. He was asked the same question Specter had asked in 1964: "Approximately what time of the day or night did the autopsy begin?"

Replied Humes: "Well, the President's body, as I recall, arrived about 7:35, 7:40 in the evening and after some preliminary examinations, about 8:00 or 8:15."[36]

The 1964 answer, "certain . . . other examinations" had become "some preliminary examinations," but it was essentially the same.

There were two other men present at the autopsy who, as far as I knew, had never been interviewed. One was Calvin Galloway, and the second was

* This explanation was repeated in a letter dated November 17, 1978, which provided additional details: ". . . the Agent in Baltimore who located the documents and made the copies advised . . . that both of these documents had apparently been produced by some form of mimeograph process, where a master copy [stencil] was prepared, necessary corrections made on the master, and then the master was used to produce the number of copies needed. The master was then retained for a short period and destroyed. One of the copies produced from the master was initialed by the reporting Agents and placed in file." That copy, it was explained, served as the original. The FBI letter stated that in 1963, before the widespread use of Xerox machines, "it was fairly common to produce FD-302 forms in the above described fashion . . . particularly when more than the usual ten copies would be needed, and that other . . . forms in this particular Baltimore file were also produced in this fashion."[34]

Capt. Robert O. Canada. I intended to talk to them both, but I kept delaying. In 1972, Canada died suddenly while on a trip to Tokyo. In 1978, I called Galloway at his home in Annapolis. He was seventy-five. We spoke for almost an hour.

I asked Galloway if there was a pre-autopsy autopsy.

"There was only one autopsy. You can only do one autopsy," he said.[37]

I asked him if he had done any cutting during the autopsy. He said he had not. I told him the Secret Service report named him as an autopsy surgeon, and asked if he was wearing an autopsy gown. "No, I was not suited up. No, I was just in uniform."

When I asked him how he explained the FBI report that when the body was unwrapped, there had been surgery of the head area, Galloway replied: "I'm not aware of anything whatsoever that was done prior to the autopsy. Now what was done in Texas, I'm not familiar with that information, of course."

I noted that in Texas they certainly didn't start the procedure for removing the brain. Galloway replied: "They may have taken a couple of stitches, in the skin, to pull it together. I don't know."

I asked him if there were two ambulances. Galloway said there was only one ambulance. I asked if he had driven the ambulance from the front of the hospital to the rear. He said he was inside the ambulance, but that he was not the driver.

What about the FBI being kept out of the room? "The FBI people . . . imply in their report that they were kept out of the autopsy room for a while," I said.

Replied Galloway: "That's correct."

"What's that all about," I asked.

"Well, you just don't let a whole lot of unnecessary people into an autopsy. An autopsy is a very precise thing."

Galloway repeatedly said that the Warren Report was correct.

I told him about the conflicting chronological data—that the casket team carried in the casket at 8:00 P.M., whereas the FBI apparently followed an ambulance to the rear and entered the morgue, also with the casket, just prior to 7:17.

Galloway replied: "Well, from what I remember [this] is the first time we've had a President assassinated in a long time. He was a very popular President, and I can understand that, why, uh, there would be confusion in many people's minds. I try to reconstruct all of this in my own mind, but there's certain things that do not make any sense."

There was a major problem in my theory of a pre-autopsy autopsy (or pre-autopsy confusion, according to Galloway) at Bethesda. Following the evidence, I was led to believe that Sibert and O'Neill, having followed the navy ambulance, entered the hospital just prior to 7:17. From my interviews with the Military District of Washington casket team and their report I was led to believe that they, chasing an ambulance, finally located the right one, and brought in the Dallas casket at 8:00 P.M.

The problem, if both accounts were true, was obvious: Why didn't anyone see two separate arrivals? Why wasn't there a witness who, perhaps not knowing it was the same casket, thought he had seen two coffins? And if someone inside the hospital *did* see two arrivals, how was that explained?

My first hint of an answer came in October 1977. At that time, another Warren Report critic mailed me a newspaper clipping from the May 1, 1975 *Waukegan* [Illinois] *News-Sun*. Just a few weeks before, that newspaper had published a series of articles on the Kennedy case, because the Rockefeller Commission, investigating CIA activities, had recently announced it was going to enlarge its probe and investigate allegations of CIA complicity in the Dallas murder. After the articles had appeared, the paper received a call from a man who lived in Lake County, Illinois, and who had worked at Bethesda Naval Hospital on November 22, 1963. He had phoned the newspaper to tell of his experiences, but he didn't want his name used. Consequently, in the May 1975 article, the paper simply referred to him as the Lake County man.

"The Lake County man defends the autopsy as 'thorough' and 'well-done,' but doubts that all the necessary information was forwarded to the commission or made available to experts."

The paper reported: "He . . . questions the whereabouts of a memo he typed following the autopsy, at the direction of a secret service agent.

" 'The memo for the official record of the autopsy stated that four large pieces of lead were removed from Kennedy. They were not separate bullets but had jagged edges like shrapnel. There was more material than would come from one bullet, but maybe not enough for two,' he said. 'To my knowledge that memo was never made part of the commission report or any other report,' said the man.

"He [the Lake County man] recalled the scene at Bethesda. 'Several thousand people had gathered on the front lawn, waiting and watching. We had men stationed at every door and no one could use the elevators without special permission.

" 'We were scared to death. There had been rumors even then that a conspiracy was involved and no one was taking any chances. Kennedy's body was brought in through a back door in an unmarked ambulance. An official motorcade from the airport contained only an empty casket,' he said."

Here was exactly what I was looking for—someone at Bethesda who knew of two casket entries. It seemed to mate nicely with the experience of the casket team. They had been told two ambulances were used—one was a decoy for the press. This man, who had apparently seen an entry at the rear, was under the impression the casket at the front was empty.

Who was this man, and what had he seen? By 1977, I had about eight filing cabinets of information on the Kennedy assassination. In the file drawer devoted to the chain-of-possession problem, I opened a file on this witness. He didn't have a name. So I called him: "Lake County Informant." I knew that someday I would have to find him.

PART V

The X-rays and
Photographs: 1977-78

The X-rays and Photographs: 1971–78

The X-rays and Photographs: Circa 1971–72

THE FIVE-YEAR RESTRICTION that the Kennedy family had placed on the autopsy X-rays and photographs was due to expire on October 29, 1971, and I knew that when it did, forensic pathologists could apply to Burke Marshall, the Kennedy attorney, for permission to examine the evidence at the National Archives.

In December 1970, I began thinking ahead. Forensic pathology was a small profession, and the only forensic pathologist in the United States publicly identified with the critics was Dr. Cyril H. Wecht, the coroner of Allegheny County, Pennsylvania. Wecht had appeared on a 1967 CBS documentary, strongly criticizing the single-bullet theory. He was also quoted, on the program, as a proponent of the head-snap argument that the fatal shot struck from the front. In November 1967, after some interviews with the members of the casket team, I telephoned Wecht in Pittsburgh, introduced myself, told him I was working on a brand new theory dealing with the medical evidence, and would like his assistance when it was ready. Wecht said he would be glad to help.[1] Later that year, we met briefly when he was in Los Angeles and I found him articulate and friendly, and very outspoken in his criticism of the Commission. In December 1970, I telephoned Wecht and told him that I would like to come to Pittsburgh and give him a complete briefing.

Shortly after New Year's, 1971, I flew to Pittsburgh and spent the better part of a day in Wecht's office, going through my entire theory.

Dr. Wecht was both a lawyer and a doctor. I didn't have to explain that a body is evidence, or what it would mean to a legal investigation if someone altered that evidence before an autopsy.

Our meeting lasted about six hours; we covered the Sibert and O'Neill report, my conversation with Sibert and my theory that that FBI report recorded an oral utterance, and all the Dallas/Bethesda dichotomies concerning the throat and the head wounds.[2]

To my considerable surprise and puzzlement, Wecht was friendly, but completely noncommittal. He just sat there, listened, and at the end of our six-hour talk, suggested that I send him a written summary of the briefing.

That evening, I flew to New York. It was the first time I had been in New York City since 1964. I called Burke Marshall at his home on Long Island.

I told him I was a critic of the Warren Report, and a student of the medical evidence, and asked if he recalled a memorandum sent from Wesley Liebeler, a former Warren Commission attorney who was a professor at UCLA. No, said Marshall, he recalled no such memo. What was it about?[3]

I explained that it concerned a recommended course of action to be followed in evaluating the photographs and X-rays of the President's body. Marshall said he recalled no such memo. I explained that a page of the memo dealt with the statement in the Sibert and O'Neill report about surgery. Marshall said he had never heard of any such thing, and he ridiculed the FBI statement. I said that the record was clear that Hoover's position was that the statement was based on oral statements made by the autopsy doctors. Marshall told me that if an FBI agent said the moon was made of cream cheese, Hoover would undoubtedly stand behind that too.[4]

"Mr. Marshall," I said, "I want to know how the Johnson government came out of the Kennedy government." I told Marshall that, as a lawyer, he surely appreciated the significance of any evidence indicating the body had been altered.

Marshall told me that if he had received any memorandum even suggesting anything like that, he never would have shown it to Robert Kennedy.[5] Clearly, Marshall found the idea of body alteration ridiculous.

The next week, I went to Washington, D.C., and spent a month at the National Archives. Most Commission attorneys had left their files intact, and I was interested in studying these "working papers" of the Warren Commission. Most of the attorneys left behind papers occupying a few file folders contained in one box. When I asked to see Liebeler's files, the archivist brought out a cart with ten boxes. For weeks I studied these records. It was a fascinating experience. I was surprised to find that the Commission lawyers had recognized many of the issues the critics had "discovered," though the lawyers said nothing about them in public. I learned also that the Warren Commission's investigation was laid out for the lawyers by the time they reported for work in early January 1964.

When an author sets out to write a book, he makes an outline that governs the arrangement of his chapters. It was sobering to see that the outline for the Warren Commission investigation, centered on the hypothesis that Oswald was the lone assassin, was drafted within weeks of the assassination and handed to the lawyers when they reported for work. And that the outline for the Warren Report itself was drafted by late March 1964.[6]

That outline demonstrated that the Warren Commission's investigation was shaped by the medical and ballistic evidence—i.e., by the navy autopsy report and the FBI investigation of the sniper's nest.

Upon returning to Los Angeles, I mailed Wecht a series of sixteen memoranda summarizing the Pittsburgh briefing. I got back a perfunctory thank you, but no sign of approval or criticism.[7]

The next October, the five-year limit was up. Burke Marshall began receiving applications from private pathologists, but the first physician to whom Marshall granted access was not a pathologist at all—Dr. John Lattimer, a New York City urologist.

Lattimer emerged from the National Archives on January 7, 1972, and, by pre-arrangement, had a long interview with Fred Graham of the *New York Times*. The X-rays and photographs, said Lattimer, "eliminate any doubt completely" about the validity of the Warren Report's conclusions. Lattimer's pronouncements were carried in an exclusive page-one story in that Sunday's *Times*. Beneath a three-column headline, DOCTOR INSPECTS KENNEDY X-RAYS, was a picture of John Lattimer, his hand raised, pointing to the top of the back of his head, depicting the course of the fatal shot.[8] Lattimer went on network TV and radio talk shows to say there could be no doubt. He had sat at the window of the Depository; it was an easy shot. Oswald had assassinated the President. Period.[9]

The critics were outraged. By this time, several had good contacts in the press. Someone made it clear to Fred Graham that the Kennedys had selected a doctor who was not a forensic pathologist and had written articles revealing a severe bias. Dr. Wecht, then President of the American Academy of Forensic Sciences, told journalists that he considered Lattimer "unbelievably unqualified" in forensic pathology. The Kennedys had no business granting him access while refusing to act on Wecht's application. "I don't know what in the world possessed this fellow Lattimer to have the arrogance, the effrontery, to project himself into this. He's a urologist, a kidney-and-bladder man. By definition this is a guy who never moves above the belly button."[10]

Meanwhile, according to one source, the *Times* heard from forensic pathologists in Europe. Embarrassed editors put pressure on Graham, who in turn put pressure on Burke Marshall. Graham let Marshall know that if the Kennedys did not grant access to a bona fide expert from the critics, they would soon be reading about Marshall's refusal to do so in the *New York Times*.

May 1972: Lattimer Publishes

The first publicly available drawings of the autopsy X-rays and photographs appeared when Lattimer published his findings in an extensive article in the May 1972 issue of *Resident and Staff Physician.*

There was no question about it—the large head wound was unquestionably toward the front—as Lattimer wrote in the article: "on the front half of the right side of the top of the head."

The entry was high on the back of the head, "where the skull was starting to curve forward," wrote Lattimer, who commented that it was "obvious that this bullet came within a few centimeters of missing the President's head altogether."

Lattimer's drawings revealed something else—the President's occipital was intact. In other words, going up the back of the head, starting at the bottom, the first break was the entry wound, nearly four inches above the bottom of the back of the head. There was no trace of the wound the Dallas doctors had seen. It had simply disappeared.

Lattimer said that the photographs of the brain showed the cerebellum was intact. This was in direct conflict with what the Dallas doctors had seen. One after another had said the cerebellum was torn, herniated, macerated, or damaged.

Lattimer said that a roll of 120 film containing five exposures "had been spoiled by unrolling it in the light," and that he had been shown a document, along with the photographs, indicating "that this had been done deliberately by one of the agents present." There was no explanation, and Dr. Lattimer speculated that perhaps the agent "did not realize that photographs were being taken to assist in preparing an accurate autopsy report. . . ."[11]

That cried out for investigation. The collection of X-rays and photographs had to be examined by someone sympathetic to the critics' case.

Wecht Receives Clearance

On June 28, 1972, I returned to my apartment to find a telegram from a fellow critic: "Cyril's going in. Please call and brief at home . . . collect." I called Wecht and learned that Burke Marshall had called him to New Haven for an interview, and then granted him access. Wecht asked if I would assist him by preparing briefing materials, so that he could walk into the room and conduct an examination that addressed a wide range of issues as efficiently as possible.[12]

Wecht was bombarded with different views as to how to proceed. Some critics' expectations ran high. Distrust of the government's version was so great that many critics apparently believed that all that was necessary to prove shots from the front or that the rear entry in the neck was "low" was to have the evidence viewed by a sympathetic observer. In short, they still stubbornly believed that the problem was the psychology of previous investigators, not the evidence itself.

I was convinced otherwise. I advised Dr. Wecht that although he should, of course, make as many detailed observations as possible, the fundamental issue was authenticity: Was there any evidence of surgical alteration?

I said: "I think that the idea that one can look at photos—[and] announce on the steps of the Archives the solution to the assassination is oversimplified."

"I agree," replied Wecht. "That's not going to happen. There is not going to be anything dramatic that's going to enable me to say that the Warren Commission Report is absolutely incorrect, in terms of . . . the shooting."

Wecht's examination was the opportunity to adduce further data for my hypothesis; he seemed to agree: ". . . I certainly will be happy to reciprocate in your research afterward—you give me specific things, and I'll certainly tell you later on . . . what is there."[13]

Wecht's examination was scheduled for late August 1972; that left me about seven weeks. I spent most of that summer at the UCLA Biomedical Library preparing detailed briefing notebooks and consulting friends at the Medical Center whenever I needed assistance.

Years before, I had taken the medical information and indexed it to reflect differences between Dallas and Bethesda. Now I applied the same method to all information coming from Bethesda. What I wanted was a list of all differences in these two records of the body—the body as described by Humes in the autopsy report and testimony, and the body as portrayed by the X-rays and photographs.

Originally, my belief was that if the body was altered to deceive the autopsy surgeon, there would be no reason to falsify the X-rays and photographs. But the 100mm discrepancy in the height of the entry wound, reported by the Clark Panel, and the indications—from Lattimer's drawings, the Clark Panel's report, and Humes' CBS interview—that the large wound had moved forward, suggested that the X-rays and photographs at the Archives did not show the wounds described by Humes in the autopsy.

I trusted Humes and his ability to observe and report what he had seen. That trust had been the basis for my analysis of anatomic differences between Dallas and Bethesda, and now I extended it one step further—it became the basis for my distinguishing between these two Bethesda versions: what Humes saw with his own eyes, and what the photographs showed. The difference was substantial.

The autopsy photos and X-rays apparently represented a second Bethesda version of the head wounds. Both versions showed a back-to-front trajectory. But the "Humes trajectory" had the bullet entering at the bottom of the back of the head, and exiting from the top, but toward the rear, not the front. The X-rays and photographs indicated the bullet entered at the top and exited at the forward right side.

The difference was easily visualized: Looking at the President's head in profile from the right, everything seemed to have been rotated clockwise by about forty-five degrees. (See Fig. 37.)

I was now sufficiently sensitive to the concept of the body as "best evidence" to identify the fundamental issue, and it was not the exact spot the bullet entered the head or the trajectory angle. The issue was authenticity —whether the pictures and X-rays at the National Archives were the ones taken at the start of the autopsy.

I still resisted the notion they might not be, but still another mystery had been added to the other conflicting evidence.

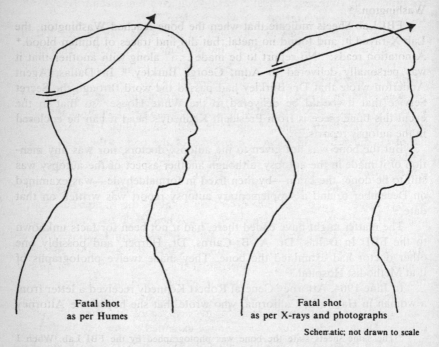

Fatal shot
as per Humes

Fatal shot
as per X-rays and photographs

Schematic; not drawn to scale

Figure 37.
Diagram showing two versions of the head trajectory

502

The Harper Fragment

At 5:30 P.M., Saturday, November 23, 1963, William Allen Harper, a Dallas college student, was taking photographs in the triangular grassy area located to the President's left at the time of the shooting, when he found what appeared to be a piece of human bone.[14] Harper took the fragment to his uncle, Dr. Jack Harper, at Methodist Hospital and he in turn brought it to Dr. A. B. Cairns, the Chief Pathologist of that hospital.[15] On Monday, November 25, Dr. Harper called the FBI and spoke with FBI Agent James Anderton.[16]

It is worth digressing to describe what took place behind the scenes, although this information wasn't revealed until the FBI released many documents in 1978. When FBI Agent Anderton notified the Secret Service, he was immediately instructed by Robert Bouck, the Chief of the Protective Research Section in Washington, that the bone fragment should be sent to the White House—"AND NO PUBLICITY WHATSOEVER," wrote Anderton in a November 25, 1963 Field Office memo.[17]

Meanwhile, FBI Assistant Director Alan Belmont called Dallas and instructed that the bone instead be sent directly to the FBI Laboratory in Washington.[18]

FBI Lab Sheets indicate that when the bone reached Washington, the Lab X-rayed it, and found no metal, but did find traces of human blood.* A notation reads: "No report to be made . . ." along with another that it was personally delivered to Adm. George Burkley.[19] In Dallas, Agent Anderton wrote that Dr. Burkley had passed the word through the Secret Service that it should be delivered to the White House "so that in the event this bone piece is from President Kennedy's head it can be enclosed in the autopsy reports."[20]

But the bone was not given to the autopsy doctors, nor was any mention of it made in the autopsy, although another aspect of the autopsy was still to be done: the brain—by then fixed in formaldehyde—was examined on December 6, and a supplementary autopsy report was written on that date.[21]

The matter might have ended there, had it not been for facts unknown to the FBI. In Dallas, Dr. A. B. Cairns, Dr. Harper, and possibly one other doctor had examined the bone. They made twelve photographs of it at Methodist Hospital.[22]

In June 1964, Attorney General Robert Kennedy received a letter from a woman in Hayward, California, who wrote that she hoped the Attorney

---

* The same sheets state the bone was photographed by the FBI Lab. When I applied under the Freedom of Information Act for those photos, the FBI said no such pictures were in the file.

General would someday run for President. She added, almost in passing, that in Dallas she had seen snapshots, taken at a hospital, of pieces of his brother's head.[23]

Robert Kennedy forwarded the letter to the Warren Commission, and Rankin's assistant, Howard Willens, immediately requested an FBI investigation.[24]

Now the FBI learned for the first time that pictures of the bone had been taken in Dallas; moreover, that Dr. Cairns had an opinion about its anatomic origin. The FBI report of a formal interview with Dr. Cairns in July 1964 states: "Dr. Cairns advised that he and Dr. Harper examined the bone. . . . Dr. Cairns stated the one specimen looked like it came from the occipital region of the skull. He said he . . . evaluated it purely from its gross appearance."*[25]

In 1972, I did not know the entire behind-the-scenes story of the Harper fragment. I knew only that a piece of President Kennedy's skull had been recovered in Dealey Plaza, that it was identified as occipital bone by a pathologist competent to make that determination. The implications were important.

If Cairns' identification was correct, the X-rays could not possibly be authentic, for nature provides us with only one occipital bone, and President Kennedy's occipital bone could not be lying on the grass of Dealey Plaza, and appear simultaneously in the X-rays of his skull taken that night at Bethesda. I explained this to Wecht, writing that the Harper fragment "was the medical equivalent of the legendary piece-of-a-dollar-bill which one carries to a rendezvous with an unknown person, where the trustworthiness of one's counterpart is vouched for by the fact that he can produce the other half. . . . [W]hen one goes to a rendezvous with one-half of a dollar bill, and the other party produces the *same* half, that can only mean one thing."[27]

A similar issue came up concerning the authenticity of the brain photographs. One Dallas doctor after another testified that the cerebellum—a structure at the bottom of the back of the brain—was damaged. It was "macerated," said Dr. Carrico;[28] "blasted out," said McClelland;[29] "present . . . on the cart," said Baxter;[30] "herniated from the wound," said Jenkins;[31] and "damaged and exposed," said Dr. Kemp Clark,[32] the neurosurgeon. Humes took a section from the cerebellum, and his report on that slide, and others from the brain, read: "extensive disruption . . . with associated hemorrhage."[33]

Yet Dr. Lattimer, having viewed photographs of the brain, reported: "The cerebellum appeared to be intact. . . ."[34]

---

* I was informed in 1972 by Robert P. Smith, an assassination researcher who had gone to Dallas, that a third physician, Dr. Noteboom, also saw the bone and held the same opinion.[26]

504

I trusted Lattimer's observation; but I also trusted those of the Dallas doctors, and Humes' ability to read a slide under a microscope.*

A question begged to be asked: Was the brain in the photographs President Kennedy's?

A similar question arose concerning the back wound, only here the issue was: Was the body that of the President? It was accepted that Dr. Humes probed the wound with his finger. But the Clark Panel stated: "Obviously, the cutaneous [skin] wound in the back was too small to permit the insertion of a finger."[36] Did that mean the wound was so shallow Humes had simply pressed the tip of his finger against it, but could not get beneath the surface? Or that the wound in the pictures wasn't the one Humes probed?**

I began to grapple with the question that for years I tried to avoid: the authenticity of the X-rays and photographs.

Concentrating on the head trajectory, I tallied up the differences between the condition of the head as reported by Humes, and what was reported in the X-rays and photographs, and displayed the data in a table. (See Fig. 38.)

The most striking difference between the two versions illustrated in the table was that in the X-rays and photographs the entire Dallas/Bethesda "overlap" had simply disappeared. No longer was there any hole, or any portion of a hole, at the right rear; and the underlying damage to the brain—the blasted cerebellum—had also disappeared. Moreover, the X-rays and photographs implied a back-to-front head trajectory that was more "reasonable," more plausible, than that described by Humes. The trajectory slanted downward and the periphery of the fatal wound displayed evidence of exit.

I began to form a hypothesis as to why photographs showing the body as described by Humes might have been removed from the record.

If, I reasoned, the wound as reported by Humes extended to the rear portion of the head, that gave support to the Dallas doctors' report of an exit at the rear of the head. Even if the Dallas wound was enlarged, the rearmost portion would still show characteristics of exit. So at least that rear portion would have to be modified before autopsy photographs. The

---

* Despite my trust in Lattimer's ability to report accurately what he saw, his bias against conspiracy theories and his tendency to minimize inconsistencies in the record were evident. For example, the complete sentence on the cerebellum read: "The cerebellum appeared to be intact despite rumors to the effect that cerebellar tissue was seen on the stretcher at the Parkland Hospital."[35] It was almost humorous that Dr. Lattimer would characterize the formal medical reports and testimony of the Dallas doctors as "rumors."

** All observers noted that no picture that showed the back wound also showed Kennedy's face, even in profile. And so when the Clark Panel reported that the back wound was higher than the throat wound, some critics suspected that the picture was of the back of another body.

	As per Humes et al.	As per X-rays and photographs*
Head (entry wound)	Low on back of head	High on back of head
Head (exit wound)	Top right side; parietal-occipital (no further forward than coronal suture)	Top right side, forward
Evidence of exit (i.e., beveled edge)	None	Present
Cerebellum	Blasted	Intact
Occipital bone	Blasted (piece missing; reported found in plaza)	Intact
Trajectory	Back-to-front (steeply upward)	Back-to-front (downward slant)**

Figure 38.
The condition of the head at Bethesda: Humes versus the X-rays and photographs

"modification" apparently was to erase that wound entirely—i.e., to "erase" it by somehow restoring the back of the head, at least on the pictures and X-rays.

Second, if the wound extended to the rear portion of the head, then a photograph would show two holes there—the small entry (which I believed was man-made) and the rear portion of the larger hole. That would probably look awfully peculiar. I hadn't forgotten Humes' strange testimony, in response to Dulles' question: "Scientifically, sir, it is impossible for it to have been fired from other than behind. Or to have exited from other than behind."[38]

If the President's head was nearly upright at the time the bullet struck, as it was in the Zapruder film, the trajectory of a bullet entering at the

* Although the entries in this table under "X-rays and photographs" were based on what was available in 1972 (the Military Review, the Clark Panel, and Dr. Lattimer's article), every one of them was confirmed by the panel of nine forensic pathologists who examined the same material for the House Select Committee in 1977–78.

** A panel of photographic experts from the House Select Committee examined the X-rays and photographs during the 1977–1978 investigation. Using the postmortem X-rays, the experts made precise measurements of the head wound locations. Their report states: "The entry point is 1.8 centimeters to the right of the midplane of his skull. The bullet passed forward through his head and exited at the right coronal suture at a point 11 centimeters forward of the entry wound and 5.5 centimeters to the right of the midplane. This exit point was 1 centimeter lower than the entrance wound, using as the exterior vertical reference a line drawn through the President's brow and upper lip. Thus the bullet was traveling 18.6° to the right relative to his midplane and 5.0° downward relative to his facial axis."[37]

bottom of the back of the head, and exiting on the side but toward the rear, would slant steeply upward. To achieve a downward slant, the artist —presumably at Humes' direction—had portrayed the President hunched far over. If the entry was on the top of the head, and the large hole was on the forward right side, then Kennedy could have been upright, and received a wound "from above and behind" on a downward slant.

Finally, the question of surgery itself. Humes testified he could find no evidence of exit anywhere along the periphery of the large hole. In his notes, made available years later, Dr. Finck said the same thing: "No exit wound is identifiable. . . ."[39] Yet the Military Review reported—and Dr. Lattimer confirmed—that evidence of exit was clearly visible on one of the photographs of the head wound. Because of this conflict I began to speculate that although the President's body, at autopsy, could be viewed as a medical forgery, the forgery might have been so imperfect that photographs of it could not be permitted to become evidence.

If I could go to the written record and develop evidence of organized cutting, what I later called the "pre-autopsy autopsy," wouldn't the photograph and X-ray record contain even more? On a photograph, a large hole with no evidence of exit might be interpreted as being rather similar to the removal of the skullcap, especially if extending from the periphery of the large hole were the four tears Humes described.

There must have been an effort made, somehow, to "sanitize" the pictures of the head.

This entire line of analysis was rather conjectural. But the existence of three mutually inconsistent and distinguishable records of the fatal shot was hard fact. I viewed these records as three lenses through which history could see the body of John F. Kennedy:

Lens 1 was the Dallas record. It showed a small hole at the front of the throat, a 5 by 7cm exit wound at the right rear of the head. This suggested that one or two shots struck from the front, and that something— a bullet or a fragment—exited from the rear.

Lens 2 was the Bethesda version reported by Humes. It showed two rear entry wounds, neither of which was seen at Dallas. In each case, the two wounds observed in Dallas became larger. Both trajectories inferred at autopsy were back-to-front.

Lens 3 was the Bethesda version of the photographs and X-rays. It showed a back-to-front trajectory, but a different one than that described by Humes. The bullet entered high on the top of the head, and blew out the forward right side.

Among these three versions, there were two groups of changes. I explained them as follows. The differences between versions 1 and 2— between Dallas and Bethesda-as-per-Humes—represented changes made on the body, on November 22, to reverse the direction of the shots. The differences between 2 and 3—between Humes' version and that depicted in the X-rays and photographs—represented a further modification to conceal evidence of surgery.

The three records comprised all the information about the fatal shot that was available to the public, published over a nine-year period, yet it reduced to three representations of the body at different points in time, between 12:30 P.M., CST, November 22, 1963, the moment of the shooting, and the time the X-rays and photographs were processed by the Secret Service on November 27, 1963, at the U.S. Naval Photographic Laboratory.[40]

Specter's Memoranda of April 30 and May 12, 1964

Reviewing the Warren Commission memoranda Arlen Specter had written to urge the Commission to examine the X-rays and photographs, I discovered that Specter seemed to be aware not only of the Dallas/Bethesda conflicts but of the two Bethesda versions as well.

Had Specter seen the autopsy photographs and X-rays? There was conflicting evidence. Jacob Cohen reported that on June 13, 1966, "Arlen Specter . . . told me that he had not seen any of these documents. . . ."[41] But shortly thereafter, Specter told a newsmagazine: "I was shown one picture of the back of the body which was represented to be the back of the President, although it was not technically authenticated."*[42] The Secret Service, in June 1966, issued a statement that the X-rays had been used to "brief" the Commission, and Inspector Tom Kelley told Harold Weisberg that he was the briefer, describing how he obtained the lightboxes and supervised the briefing.[44]

On the surface, Specter's memoranda seemed to be the writings of a lawyer pressing for the "best evidence," but if Specter had already seen the

---

* Specter seemed sensitive about even admitting he had pressed strongly to see the photos and X-rays, as evidenced by this interchange in a tape-recorded interview with Gaeton Fonzi in July 1966, when the Warren Report was first coming under major attack.

> FONZI: Did you ask to see the X-rays and photographs? [Long pause before Specter answers.]
>
> SPECTER: That question was considered by me, and the Commission decided not to press for the X-rays or photographs. Have I dodged your question? Yes, I've dodged your question. [Another long pause.] I don't want to dodge your question. . . . As the Assistant Counsel in that area, I was interested in every conceivable bit of evidence which bore on the issue of the direction of the bullet. . . . I think there were significant family wishes which were considered by the Commission in deciding whether it was necessary to see the photographs and the X-rays in order to come to its conclusions. I specifically leave out my personal attitude on the subject, because I don't think it's really your main factor.[43]

pictures, they could be construed differently, as reflecting suspicion about the autopsy testimony given the month before.

Specter had written two memos. The first was dated April 30, 1964, the day the Commission discussed the X-rays and photographs in executive session. Specter began by writing that the photos and X-rays were "indispensable." He listed three reasons why this was so: "1. The Commission should determine with certainty whether the shots came from the rear. . . . None of the doctors as Parkland Hospital in Dallas observed the hole in the President's back or the small hole in the lower portion of his head. With all of the outstanding controversy about the direction of the shots, there must be independent viewings of the films to verify testimony which has come only from Government doctors." Specter went one step further. The photos must be examined, he said, to verify "that the holes on the President's back and head had the characteristics of points of entry."

Specter's second point concerned the exact angle of the neck trajectory, as depicted on the artist's drawing. He noted the angle depended upon locating "precisely" the rear entry point, and that the artist's drawing showed only a slight angle of declination. "It is hard, if not impossible to explain such a slight angle . . . unless the President was farther down Elm Street . . . ," he wrote.

Specter's third point: "3. The Commission should determine with certainty that there are no major variations between the films and the artist's drawings."[45] Specter's language had a strange ring in 1972, as I tabulated the differences. Eight years earlier, supposedly not having seen the photographs, Specter wrote: "Some day someone may compare the films with the artist's drawings and find a significant error which might substantially affect the essential testimony and the Commission's conclusions."[46]

In view of Specter's prescient tone, I found it hard to believe he had seen just one autopsy photograph. It seemed implausible that Secret Service Inspector Kelley would play peek-a-boo with such crucial evidence.

More of Specter's foresight appeared in his second memo, dated May 12, 1964, after Earl Warren had instructed Rankin to have the photos and X-rays checked by a doctor, but not to include them in the record. Specter's memo was in the form of a checklist of what had to be done—not "if," but, in his language, "*when* the autopsy photographs and X-rays are examined. . . ." (Emphasis added) Among the items on Specter's numbered list: confirming the "precise location" of the two rear entries, the "precise area of the President's skull which was disrupted by the bullet when it exited . . . ," and a comparison between the X-rays and photographs and frame 312 of the Zapruder film "to determine for certain whether the angle of declination is accurately depicted in Commission Exhibit 388 [the artist's drawing of the head trajectory]." Finally, with regard to the two rear entries, Specter suggested that both wounds "should be examined closely in the photographs and X-rays to determine for certain whether they are characteristic of entrance wounds. . . ." Specter concluded the memo: "I suggest that we have a court reporter present so that we may examine Dr. Humes after the X-rays and photographs are reviewed to put on the record: 1. Any changes in his testimony or theories required by a review of the X-rays and films, and 2. Corroboration of the portions of all of his prior testimony which may be confirmed by viewing the photographs and X-rays."[47]

Specter's seeming awareness of the conflicts in the record cast the Glenn Bennett affair in a different light. Glenn Bennett was the Secret Service agent riding in the rear of the followup car, the only eyewitness to say he saw a bullet strike "about four inches down from the right shoulder," yet a photograph taken at the time showed him looking off in another direction.*[48]

I had always been mystified as to why, on May 14, 1964, Secret Service Chief Rowley, for no apparent reason, happened to pass along Glenn Bennett's handwritten account with a rather pointed letter: "There is forwarded herewith a copy of the original notes made by Special Agent Bennett . . . the significance of the attached notes is that they were prepared by SA Bennett on the President's plane during its return flight to Washington . . . before the details of President Kennedy's wounds became general knowledge."[49] (See Photo 10.)

Chief Rowley's letter was a departure from the usual procedure. Normally, the Secret Service and the FBI responded to specific Warren Commission requests for additional investigation. Chief Rowley's letter was related to no specific request, at least not any in writing. He had, apparently, simply dipped into Secret Service files and sent over some evidence that appeared to legitimize the back wound. Why?

Specter's memos of April 30 and May 12, 1964, put this entire matter in perspective. The sequence suggested that when Specter became aroused over the conflict between Dallas and Bethesda, and wrote memos which focused attention on the legitimacy of the wound, the Secret Service chief supplied more evidence—forwarding handwritten notes purportedly written before the autopsy, to indicate that the rear point of entry was legitimate.

It was impossible to know what Specter thought. He wrote only those two memos on the subject. But in June, Secret Service Chief Rowley forwarded another batch of reports, and one contained another eyewitness account—the report of Agent George Hickey, sitting next to Bennett at the right rear of the follow-up car.

Just as Bennett claimed to have seen the non-fatal shot strike, Hickey

---

* See Chapter 11 for a discussion of Willis picture number 5, which shows Bennett completely turned to his right.

was a Secret Service eyewitness to the fatal shot's striking, and at the "high" location shown on the photographs and X-rays. Wrote Hickey: "It looked to me as if the President was struck in the right upper rear of his head . . ." adding, in a statement that contradicted the Zapruder film, "the . . . impact . . . made him fall forward and to his left.*[50]

Specter's memoranda were a reminder of many things the Commission should have done but did not do. Both Bennett and Hickey should have been put under oath: Bennett to explain how he could see a bullet enter "four inches from the top of the shoulder" when he wasn't looking in that direction; Hickey to explain why he wrote a second report with a rephrased description of the rear impact to the head which accorded so closely with the X-rays and photographs. The Commission should have inquired as to how many Secret Service agents made notes on *Air Force One* describing the wounds, what happened to the original notebooks, and why so many of the reports were dated November 30, 1963. The Commission should have noticed that Kellerman's November 27 statement to FBI agents Sibert and O'Neill—that he saw the President reach behind his neck with his right hand to a point on his back,[54] a contorted movement that never took place according to the Zapruder film—was still another instance of a Secret Service account that legitimized a rear point of entry and, when considered in conjunction with Hickey's and Bennett's reports, suggested a suspicious pattern of Secret Service reporting.

Finally, the Commission should have strengthened its record by examining the X-rays and photographs and, as Specter suggested, recalled Humes and questioned him about the differences between his descriptions of the body and what the X-rays and photos showed.

It was all spilt milk. But now, in the summer of 1972, I was excited by the opportunity that seemed at hand—the chance to examine the X-rays and photographs.

Preparing for Wecht's examination, I set up a research notebook dividing the body into areas, listing questions to be asked about the pictures and X-rays, and suggesting the data to be taken which might provide answers.

One section was devoted to authenticity. Wecht himself seemed well aware of the problem. Many of the critics, he told me in July 1972, "are

* Hickey was one of a few Secret Service agents who had made two reports, one dated November 22, 1963, and a second dated November 30, 1963.[51] On the detail of where the shot struck the head, the second report, but not the first, is in striking agreement with the "high" location shown on the X-rays and photographs. In his November 22, 1963 report, Hickey wrote "I heard what appeared to be two shots and it seemed as if the *right side* of his head was hit. . . ."[52] Hickey's November 30 report described the location of impact as: ". . . in the *right upper rear* of his head. . . ."[53] [Emphasis added.]

very scared, and maybe quite properly, that they will give me materials which are substitutes. . . ." He said if I could think of ways of checking for validity, "by all means please let me know."[55]

Steven W. Bailey, a talented physical scientist, helped me respond to Wecht's request. We suggested that Wecht take detailed dental data to be used if access could someday be obtained to dental X-rays. They might help to verify whether the body was that of President Kennedy. Any gross inconsistencies might prove it was not. We suggested that Wecht group the pictures by camera perspective, so that we would know exactly which ones contained facial views undeniably of Kennedy. To test whether the X-rays were duplicate film rather than original, we obtained samples of each type from the Radiology Department at the UCLA Medical Center and made microphotographs of each. I asked that Wecht bring a microscope and check the grain size of the X-rays he was shown. My friend thought of a number of excellent tests to detect photo fakery—all based on the idea that such fakery, if it had occurred, would probably be imperfect, and a careful comparison of the photographs with one another, or with the X-rays, would pick up inconsistencies indicative of non-identical alteration. Bailey made an ingenious observation. He noted that Dr. Lattimer reported that two-thirds of the right side of the brain was gone, that all that remained was a torn and flattened base. Yet the X-rays, according to all reports, showed a trail of metal across the top of the head, from the entrance wound at the top back to the forward margin of the exit wound at the front.[56] How could that be? What was supporting the metal?

Another question was whether there was artwork on the films. The disputed wound locations and configurations pinpointed the locales where we urged a particularly careful examination.

As the sections of the notebook were completed, I mailed them to Wecht. On August 21, 1972, I flew to Pittsburgh.

En route, I began to wonder. The notebook addressed two possibilities: falsification by changes in the films, or falsification by the use of another body. There was a possibility I hadn't covered: the reconstruction of Kennedy's own body. I recalled what Godfrey McHugh had said when I asked if he saw the head wounds: "Oh yes, but they started fixing it up very well." And McHugh's description of how bone was put back on the head: ". . . like glass that breaks. You can take the same part, and put it right back on."[57]

Suppose it was Kennedy's body? Suppose there had been reconstruction, and reconstruction only. That might be almost impossible to detect. All tests directed at the body would come out negative for body substitution because it would have been John Kennedy's body. All tests to establish alteration of the films would likewise turn up nothing, because the photographs would in fact be authentic. Reconstruction of the body seemed the route to the perfect crime.

In Pittsburgh, a member of Wecht's staff met me and I was put up at Wecht's father's house. The next morning, Dr. Wecht picked me up and I accompanied him on his daily routine—blitz visits to each of his various professional addresses. Wecht was a law professor, had a private practice and lab, and was coroner. We reached the last office by racing through a side door in the Pittsburgh morgue, where several cadavers were in various stages of dissection, one being weighed on a scale.

Upon reaching Wecht's office, I learned that he had not read a page of my notebook. Wecht said he'd try to make time that day. I consoled myself with the hope that Wecht would be a quick study. There would be time on the flight to Washington and at the hotel. I was tense. This was the first time Burke Marshall had let a critic see this evidence; it might never happen again.

Wecht told me to wait in an office. I passed the time drafting a memo to be appended to the notebook dealing with the third possibility.

If pieces of bone had actually been shifted to "repair" the hole at the back of the head, that might show on the X-rays in the form of complete fracture lines—bone pieces totally circumscribed by through-and-through fractures. In the memo, I summarized the three possible methods of falsification and suggested priorities to be followed in conducting the inspection.

The day flew by with Wecht finding no time to study the material, and late in the afternoon we left for Washington.

Next morning, I met Wecht for breakfast and we proceeded to the Archives. After some perfunctory introductions in the office, Wecht took an elevator to an upper floor. Inside, on a table, were the photographs and X-rays of President Kennedy's body. Rather than wait outside in the hallway, I went to the main research room and read the State Department files on Lee Harvey Oswald.

Several hours later, Wecht emerged. I was on tenterhooks. I couldn't come right out and ask the questions I wanted because also present was another assassination researcher, Robert P. Smith, whom I had just met, and with whom I had not shared my research. The three of us went to lunch.

One of the first things both Smith and I inquired about was the document Lattimer had referred to about destruction of film at the autopsy by a federal agent. Wecht said he had been shown the document, an eleven-page inventory made out when the autopsy doctors had reviewed the photographs and X-rays on November 1, 1966 at the Archives. Wecht said Marion Johnson (the archivist supervising Wecht's review) wouldn't permit him to make a copy, but he had dictated what the report said into his recorder. The entry read: "One roll of 120 film (processed but showing no recognizable image) which we recall was seized by Secret Service agents from a navy medical corpsman whose name is not known to us during the autopsy and immediately exposed to light."[58]

I began asking questions about the wounds, and from the outset found it difficult to pin Wecht down on anything. The only definite statement I could get was that the large head wound did not extend into the occipital area, a contradiction of Humes' autopsy report.

During the afternoon session, it became quite obvious that Wecht had great difficulty reading the X-rays—that he couldn't find the entry wound reported by the Clark Panel or by Dr. Lattimer. There was no hole there at all, said Wecht.[59] I immediately went to a telephone and called Steve Bailey in Los Angeles, who nearly exploded upon hearing that Wecht was looking for a "hole." He informed me that on X-ray, the hole at the back of a sphere would merely appear to be a subtle shading. I passed this information back to Wecht. He was still not able to locate the entry wound.

I went to a store and bought a spool of thread. I tied two knots in it, one hundred millimeters apart. I went to the door of the examining room and handed it to Wecht, and told him to place one knot on the X-ray at the external occipital protuberance, and to swing an arc. Where the other knot crossed the skull, he could see the Clark Panel's "entrance wound." Wecht did this, and that was how he found the entrance wound in the back of President Kennedy's head.[60] To his recorder, he dictated:

This is a change in density which apparently is what is referred to in the previous panel as a "hole." This either takes imagination or some very sophisticated radiological expertise because it is difficult for me to consider this a hole. In any event, it has to be because it fits the measurements that they give about 100mm from the external occipital protuberance.[61]

This experience, among others, persuaded me that Wecht had difficulty reading the X-rays. He seemed, moreover, to have no inclination to pursue the issue of authenticity.

I had the feeling I was questioning a politician.

At one point, with the X-rays and photographs before him, Wecht had requested the archivist to bring him the artist's drawings! When they were brought, Wecht dictated page after page of notes on what they showed!

I could hardly believe what I saw. I was deeply disappointed, sorry for Wecht, and sorry for the entire research movement. It was clear that whatever his biases, Dr. John Lattimer had competence reading X-rays, and had collected a wealth of data. With my own eyes, I saw that "our" expert left much to be desired.

On the second day of his examination, the full picture emerged. In approaching me earlier, Wecht had said there would be no news conference, no public statements. We would gather the data. Now, he seemed preoccupied with a New York Times interview. I handled the liaison with Fred Graham, and was present when Wecht was interviewed on a drive to the airport.

Graham asked all the right questions, and Wecht said that the pictures and X-rays showed no shots from the front.

Then he stressed that he had not been able to see the brain or the pathological slides of the autopsy. That was true. Wecht couldn't see them because the Archives didn't have them, and the Archives didn't have them because the Kennedys had not donated that material to the Archives in the 1966 contract. Wecht had been told this months before; it was set forth clearly in letters he let me read.

Wecht emphasized the potential importance of these items—they might provide additional information, they might contain information contrary to the official version.

The following Sunday, Fred Graham's page-one *New York Times* article appeared: MYSTERY SURROUNDS FATE OF KENNEDY BRAIN.

The fact was that beyond the usual speech attacking the single-bullet theory, Cyril Wecht had found nothing that really challenged the official version. Lattimer had his story because he was there first. Now Wecht had his: The President's brain was missing.

Undoubtedly, the brain was essential, but, viewed in context, Wecht's approach struck me as 10 percent forensic science, 90 percent public relations.

August 25, 1972: A Conversation with John Stringer

Based on the inconsistencies concerning the head wound location, and the information that a Secret Service agent had seized certain autopsy film, I now decided to call the autopsy photographer, John Stringer. In what quadrant of the head did he see the large wound? Why was the film destroyed? All observers confirmed that there were no pictures in the collection of the bruised area atop the right lung. Yet Humes testified he had taken such photographs. Lattimer speculated that maybe those missing lung pictures were on the roll of destroyed film.[62] Was that so? I wanted to ask these questions of Stringer.

I telephoned him at his home in Maryland. He was perfectly friendly, but he didn't want to talk. He wanted me to go through official navy channels.

Finally, after an extended discussion of what we were going to talk about when I finally got official permission, we simply lapsed into a detailed discussion covering a wide range of topics.

Stringer said: "I helped lift him out of the coffin."[63] I asked him if he saw the honor guard, a multiservice casket-bearing team. "No," he replied. I asked again: a group made up of men from the Air Force, Navy, Marines, Army. Did he see any of that?

"Negative," he replied.

I asked Stringer about the photographs of the lung. Stringer confirmed that he made such photographs, saying: "We shot at least two of every-thing that was done." I asked him if that was what was on the roll of destroyed film. He said no. All photographs of the cadaver, he said, were made by him with the standard four-by-five camera.

What, then, was on the roll of 120 film? I asked. Stringer told me he thought the photographer, an assistant, had shot "some overall scenes"—pictures including not just the body, but pictures of the autopsy room, and the officers in the room, for historical purposes.

That such pictures would be destroyed was itself suspicious. But what was more interesting about Stringer's information was that the four-by-five pictures were supposed to include the pictures of the lung, because the pictures in the inventory agreed, in total number, with the number Sibert and O'Neill reported, but there were no pictures of the lung in the collec-tion. To make an analogy, it was as if someone left the grocery store with five apples, three oranges, and two grapefruit—and found later that the bag contained ten items, but the grapefruit were gone.

Something was wrong with the collection.

I turned to the wounds of the head:

LIFTON: When you lifted him out, was the main damage to the skull on the top or in the back?

STRINGER: In the back.

LIFTON: In the back? . . . High in the back or lower in the back?

STRINGER: In the occipital, in the neck there, up above the neck.

LIFTON: In other words, the main part of his head that was blasted away was in the occipital part of the skull?

STRINGER: Yes, in the back part.

LIFTON: The back portion. Okay. In other words, there was no five-inch hole in the top of the skull?

STRINGER: Oh, some of it was blown off—yes, I mean, toward, out of the top in the back, yes.

LIFTON: Top in the back. But the top in the front was pretty intact?

STRINGER: Yes, sure.

LIFTON: The top front was intact?

STRINGER: Right.*

---

* Just to make sure there was no question about what Stringer told me, I rephrased my question using the same description McHugh had used. "If you lie back in a bathtub, just in a totally prone position, and your head rests against the bathtub, is that the part of the head that was damaged?" I asked. "Yes," replied Stringer. I asked him about the part of the head which, in that position, would be straight up and down, the vertical part, the "top." Was that undamaged? Stringer replied: "I wouldn't say—undamaged, no. Some of it was gone . . . some of the bone."

This was the wound described by Humes, but not the wound shown by Dr. Lattimer, nor was it, to the extent I could get him to describe what he had seen, the wound described by Wecht.

Immediately, I called Wecht in Pittsburgh.

LIFTON: What's your reaction to the fact that the photographer who gets the body says that the main wounding of the skull is in the back of the head?

WECHT: Oh, I don't know. I don't know what he means by the back of the head. Certainly, more toward the back than the front. I don't know what the hell he means by the back of the head. You see, you gotta pin him down on that.[64]

LIFTON: Well, he said "occipital."

WECHT: Well, of course . . . occipital is not exactly a lay term, David, you know what I mean? I don't mean to insult anybody's intelligence, it's just not a word people use. They don't really know what they're saying when they [say that]; they know . . .

LIFTON: Yes, but assuming he did . . . that's what he means . . . that would be really great support for Parkland testimony. . . .

It was hopeless. Dealing with Wecht was like playing water polo with a greased watermelon.

But the next day, I decided to call Stringer again. Was it possible he didn't know what "occipital" meant?

LIFTON: Did you have medical training? When you used medical terminology, I was wondering if you just picked that stuff up or . . .

STRINGER: No. I've been trained in medical photography. I had taken anatomy and things like that. I have been in the field of medical photography now for over thirty years.[65]

LIFTON: In other words, you studied out of books like Grant's *Anatomy* or Gray's *Anatomy*.

STRINGER: Yes. Gray's *Anatomy*.

LIFTON: In other words, when you use medical terms, you're not just a layman whose main training is in photography, who happened to be called in that night. . . .

STRINGER: My major field is medical photography. I shot the autopsy on Forrestal. . . .

Stringer went on to explain that former Navy Secretary Forrestal had jumped out of one of the upper floors of the Bethesda tower.

The conversation with Stringer and a review of my November 1967 conversation with Brig. Gen. McHugh persuaded me that when President Kennedy's body was taken out of the coffin, the wound was perceived as being at the right rear of the head. I was a bit uncomfortable reconciling this with Humes, because Humes said the wound was chiefly parietal, and extending "somewhat" into the occipital area. In other words, Humes put the emphasis on the parietal bone, not the rear. But all this was incompatible with the back of the head being intact.

This raised a serious question. If Stringer remembered that the back of the head was blown out, and if these pictures showed the back of the head intact, how could Stringer walk into the National Archives on November 1, 1966 and sign the statement that these were the pictures he had taken? I asked him just that.

> LIFTON: What did you guys check for when you logged it into the Archives in 1966? . . . what test did you apply to make darn sure that the stuff that you were logging in was the stuff you exposed the night at the morgue?
>
> STRINGER: Well, I can't; I can't, since I didn't see it after it was developed. I can't actually say that everything was there. . . .

Stringer went on to explain that all he did was take the picture, remove the film holder, and immediately hand it to a Secret Service agent: ". . . all I had was the film holder . . . and gave it to somebody, so I mean . . . I don't know just what was the after-effects of it."

I asked if he kept any written records—for example, the batch numbers on the film he used. He said he did not. I asked if he was surprised, on November 1, 1966, at finding that the lung pictures were not in the collection.

Replied Stringer: "No, I can't say I was surprised or not. I don't actually remember the pictures I saw that . . . afternoon; it's been so long ago, and it was only a matter of an hour and a half."

Because the pictures in evidence did not agree, in a number of ways, with Humes' testimony, and because the lung pictures were missing, it was easy to speculate that the pictures shown Stringer at the Archives in 1966 weren't the pictures there in 1972. But, having spoken with Stringer, I rejected that idea. I trusted the integrity of the Archives. I found it implausible, furthermore, that those who altered the body between 1:00 P.M., CST and 8:00 P.M., EST on November 22, 1963, would wait until after 1966 to change the X-rays and photographs. Based on what Stringer told me, I resolved discrepancies between what Stringer said he saw on the body and what the pictures showed by looking to Stringer's psychology, and the rather cursory look he apparently gave the pictures in 1966. It was the "closure" phenomenon again. Stringer had worked for thirty years for the government. He just did his job; I doubted he looked for fraud.

A similar problem came up when I talked with Dr. John Ebersole, the radiologist. The Clark Panel said they saw metal in the chest. Humes testified there was no metal in the chest. At the Shaw trial, Dr. Finck said that Humes had relied on the radiologist. Yet here were X-rays which, according to the Clark Panel, showed metal.

On August 27, 1972, I called Ebersole.

I asked Ebersole whether he had kept a record of the numbers of the X-rays for his file.

"Not in this case, no," he said.[66]

I asked him how he had identified the film numbers.

"I had a light present in order to identify the film numbers," he replied. "The identifying numbers on the film."

I asked Ebersole whether he had seen metal that night.

EBERSOLE: I certainly did not see any that night, no.

LIFTON: Did not?

EBERSOLE: To the best of my knowledge, right now, I don't remember seeing any metallic fragments in the lung.

LIFTON: When you logged them in 1966, you did not examine them for medical-legal information?

EBERSOLE: No, I did not.

LIFTON: All you did was look at the numbers?

EBERSOLE: Yes.

Thus, Ebersole had logged in X-rays in 1966, which contained information that was contrary to his examination on November 22, and yet, like the photographer, had signed a document which said they were the X-rays he took.

I asked Ebersole when the autopsy actually started.

"To the best of my knowledge," he replied, "we actually started the autopsy formally about ten-thirty at night."

I was startled, and tried to hide it. I assumed Ebersole was just mistaken about the time.

"You were there when the body arrived in the coffin?"

"Yes, I was," he replied.

Trying to fix in my own mind a connection between the coffin opening as described by the photographer and Ebersole, I asked: "The photographer took it out?" since that was what Stringer told me.

"Hell, no," snapped Ebersole.

What to say next? Ebersole sensed my uneasiness and cut in to say that he didn't wish to answer any further questions, without identification.

I returned to Los Angeles convinced there was something wrong with the X-rays and photographs, aware it was not possible to analyze the evidence because of restrictions imposed in the Kennedy-Archives contract.

Meanwhile, Cyril Wecht gave a number of interviews to the press, saying that X-rays and photographs showed there was a conspiracy and that the CIA was probably involved.[67] Most of it was old wine in new bottles, allegations of conspiracy based on objections to the single-bullet theory. None of it dealt with authenticity. In our hallway conversations at the Archives, Wecht implied I was asking for too much, that "you'd need a whole team of experts."

Now, in interviews with the press, that theme cropped up. The Pittsburgh *Post-Gazette* reported: "Wecht said he planned to go to Yale University today to make a formal request of Burke Marshall . . . for a complete examination of the evidence by a team of experts in pathology, radiology, criminology and firearms. 'Let's have an honest and full review,' he said. 'Let's cut out the games.' "[68]

The next year, Wecht co-authored an article with Robert P. Smith. The X-rays and photographs, they said, "give every indication of being authentic," and "the available evidence, assuming it to be valid, gives no support to theories which postulate gunmen to the front or right-front."[69]

For all practical purposes, Wecht had closed off dissent about shots striking from the front or about inauthenticity. Nevertheless, he continued to present the public image of a dissenter.

He was a sheep in wolf's clothing.

CHAPTER 21

Changed Receipts

IN 1975, THE NATIONAL ARCHIVES made available critical evidence pertaining to the chain of possession of the autopsy X-rays and photographs: copies of the receipts made out by the autopsy personnel when the photographs were turned over to the Secret Service. These receipts took the form of transmittal memos, made to Secret Service Agent Roy Kellerman by Dr. John Ebersole, for the X-rays, and by Capt. J.H. Stover, Humes' superior and the CO of the Medical School, for the photographs. Also signing the photo memo was photographer Stringer and Floyd Reibe, Stringer's assistant.[1]

In both receipts, the numbers were changed from what was originally written. These changes were initialled on the receipts for the X-rays by Dr. Ebersole, and for the photographs, by Captain Stover.[2] A second copy of each receipt, completely retyped, containing no indication of change, was subsequently made out.* In each case the copy was formally "Certified to be a true copy" by both Rear Adm. Calvin Galloway, the Commanding Officer of the National Naval Medical Center, and Captain Stover. Also on the copied receipts was this notation: "Accepted and Approved. G.B. Burkley—Physician to the President."[3]

These receipts prompted me to fetch my 1972 notebook and turn to a section called "Picture Inventory," where I had gathered information concerning how many pictures had been exposed and how many were found in the collection by the Clark Panel. Now I wanted to know if the numbers on the newly released receipts—surely the best evidence as far as the number of pictures and X-rays actually created in the morgue that night—matched the totals reported by the Clark Panel.

---

* The signatures of the men who actually exposed the film—Reibe, Stringer, and Ebersole—did not appear on the retyped receipts.

They did not.

To understand the numbers involved, it should be kept in mind that each film holder contains two sheets of film.

The original receipt for the photographs contained one entry for black-and-white photographs, and one entry for color photographs.[4] The entry for color photos, as originally written, stated: "8 graphic film holders (4 x 5) containing 16 sheets of exposed Ektachrome E3 film."[5]

The "8" was crossed out, changed to "11," and that was initialed by Captain Stover.[6] But the number of film sheets—sixteen—was left unchanged.[7] The retyped receipt, countersigned by Stover, Galloway, and Burkley, read: "11 graphic film holders (4 x 5) containing 16 sheets of exposed Ektachrome E3 film."[8] (See Photo 29.)

Thus what was added was film *holders,* but *not film.*

A similar change was made in the case of the black-and-white film. The original receipt was made out for six film holders containing twelve sheets of exposed film.[9] The "6" was changed to "9," the change was initialed by Captain Stover, and the retyped receipt read: "9 graphic film holders (4 x 5) containing 12 sheets exposed portrait Pan film."[10]

However, the film in evidence did not consist of sixteen sheets of color film and twelve of black-and-white. In April 1965, according to the Clark Panel inventory, the Kennedys received from the Secret Service twenty color and eighteen black-and-white exposures.* This appeared to mean that more film was in the collection than was receipted for that night by the photographer and the radiologist.

In their report, FBI agents Sibert and O'Neill recorded numbers which they represented as "a complete listing of photographs and X-rays taken by the medical authorities of the President's body . . . the photographs were delivered to Secret Service undeveloped. . . ."[12]

---

* The Clark Panel report included an inventory which identified each picture by a number and grouped the pictures according to different views of the body. But the inventory was confusing. Two numbering systems were used for eighteen of the pictures, and black-and-white and color pictures weren't distinguished. Consequently, the total number of pictures in each category was unclear. Extracting this information from the Clark Panel report became a minor research project. I soon realized it was possible to ignore the "double numbering," and that the entire collection—brain photographs exposed on December 6, 1963, as well as autopsy pictures exposed on November 22—were intermixed and had been numbered 1 through 52. From information in news accounts and Marshall's letter of donation, I was able to infer that all photos numbered "25" and below were black-and-white, and all numbered "26" and above were in color. It also became clear that pictures 19 through 25 and 46 through 52 were the December 6 brain photographs—the former in black-and-white, the latter in color. From all this, I was able to conclude that the collection of autopsy photographs at the Archives consisted of (1) eighteen black-and-white photographs (numbered 1 through 18) and (2) twenty color photographs (numbered 26 through 45)—i.e., a total of thirty-eight. This analysis, based on the Clark Panel inventory data, was confirmed in the 1979 report of the House Assassinations Committee.[11]

The Sibert and O'Neill tally specified twenty-two color, and eighteen black-and-white, for a total of forty exposures, a figure that failed to agree with the number of exposures recorded on the receipts but came within two of matching the count made by the Clark Panel.*[13]

Humes' testimony did nothing to clear up the situation. When he was asked by Specter "precisely" how many photos were taken, he replied: "approximately fifteen to twenty in number, were made in total before we finished the proceedings,"[14] and when Specter asked again, for clarification, he repeated, "I would say they are in number fifteen to twenty."[15]

In analyzing this confusing array of figures, one fact stood out: The number of exposures now in evidence (thirty-eight, according to the Clark Panel) was ten more than the number recorded the night of the autopsy (twenty-eight, according to both the original and retyped receipts).

In short, the changes made on these receipts suggested that more pictures passed from the morgue to the Secret Service that night than had been officially exposed as part of the autopsy. This caused me to consider the possibility that, through the ruse of changing the number of holders, ten additional pictures had been added to the original twenty-eight, creating a hybrid collection of twenty-eight legitimate pictures and ten illegitimate ones. Another possibility was that a totally different thirty-eight-picture collection had been substituted for the original twenty-eight-picture collection.**

Changes also occurred in the case of the X-rays. The receipt originally read that eleven X-rays had been taken (a number which agreed with Sibert and O'Neill's list) but the changed receipt read fourteen X-rays, and fourteen were in evidence.[16]

None of this ever came to the attention of the Warren Commission, because they never conducted a formal examination of this evidence.***

The changes in these receipts pushed me in the direction of the recon-

* In addition, the Sibert and O'Neill figures agree exactly with the revised number of *holders* (eleven color and nine black-and-white) when those figures are doubled. This suggests that someone communicated to the FBI agents (either before they left the autopsy room, or by phone prior to November 26 when they wrote their report) the number of pictures that would ultimately be placed in evidence but which, of course, does not agree with the receipt made out that night and certified by Captain Stover.

** If this was the case, the obvious question arises: Why wasn't the number of pictures also changed to correspond with the revised number of holders? One possible answer might be that the people who exposed the original autopsy film were aware of the number of pictures they took and could not be expected to certify to a higher number. But the film holders were a different matter—a lower order of importance—and the same men might have paid less attention to them.

*** Despite the fact that the House Select Committee based its major conclusions on the photos and X-rays, and made claims for their authenticity, the Committee neither noted nor investigated the matter of the changed receipts.

struction hypothesis because changed receipts suggested substitutions or additions. On the other hand, it seemed unlikely that alterations in the photographs themselves would have affected the *number* of pictures in evidence.

A number of facts lying in public view, when put together, seemed to indicate that although the FBI agents left when they believed the autopsy was finished, they may have been mistaken.

FBI firearms expert Robert A. Frazier testified that he received the bullet fragments brought back by Sibert and O'Neill at 1:45 A.M.[17] Subsequently, a telegram prepared by Sibert was put out at 2:00 A.M.[18]

A reasonable estimate, therefore, was that the FBI agents arrived at the FBI Building at 1:30 A.M. Bethesda being about a twenty-minute drive from Washington, that would mean that Sibert and O'Neill left the morgue shortly after one o'clock.

The record contained evidence of a gap between the time Sibert and O'Neill left and the time the embalming started. In his November 30, 1963 report, Secret Service Agent Kellerman wrote: "After the completion of the autopsy and before the embalming I summoned SA Hill down to the morgue to view the body and to witness the damage of the gunshot wounds."*[19] Hill, in his own report, noted the time: "At approximately 2:45 A.M., November 23, I was requested by ASAIC Kellerman to come to the morgue to once again view the body. When I arrived the autopsy had been completed. . . ."[21]

Combining this information, it appeared there was a gap of about an hour and forty-five minutes between the time the FBI left the room (believing the autopsy was over) and the time Kellerman summoned Hill.

During this period, the body was on the table, but the embalming had not yet begun. What took place during this period?

A comparison of the Sibert and O'Neill account of the autopsy with Humes' testimony indicated that additional medical data were taken.

Sibert and O'Neill gave a chronological report of the autopsy, yet Humes' testimony contained facts which the two FBI agents did not report.

Sibert and O'Neill never reported that Humes found and examined an entrance wound at the back of the head. Second, Humes described in

---

* Before the Warren Commission, Kellerman testified: ". . . when the autopsy was about completed before the funeral directors were in, and it was my decision to get Mr. Hill down and view this man for all the damage that was done; so I went up to the floor where they were at and brought him down and he inspected the incisions." Specter asked: "What was your reason for that, Mr. Kellerman?" Replied Kellerman: "More witnesses, Mr. Specter; I think more to view the unfortunate happenings it would be a little better."[20]

detail a bruise atop the right lung—indeed, he testified photographs were taken of the bruise, and that was corroborated by Stringer when I spoke with him. Sibert and O'Neill were silent about Humes finding or examining such a lung bruise.

Whereas Sibert and O'Neill reported the arrival of one large piece of bone, Humes reported three pieces of bone; and in discussing his examination of them, reported: "Some time later on that evening or very early the next morning while we were all still engaged in continuing our examination. . . ."[22]

Earlier in his testimony he said the autopsy ended at 11:00 P.M. What then did Humes mean when he said that ". . . we were all still engaged in continuing our examination . . ."?

Exactly when did the autopsy end? According to Sibert and O'Neill, the end occurred when "Dr. Humes stated that the pattern was clear that the one bullet had entered the President's back and had worked its way out of the body during external cardiac massage and that a second high-velocity bullet had entered the rear of the skull and had fragmented prior to exit through the top of the skull."[23]

At that point, Sibert and O'Neill, according to their report, tallied up the film and left.*

The changed receipts and the indications that the FBI may have left the room early suggested a time in which additional autopsy photographs could have been taken, an idea first raised by McHugh's account. It was only a working hypothesis, but now I had a place for that activity on my time line. The three records of the event, corresponding to the three lenses, might be arranged as shown in Fig. 39.

The Bethesda autopsy was emerging as a rather fluid event, and the difficulty in pinpointing when it ended was similar to the problem concerning exactly when it began: What did Humes mean by "certain . . . other examinations were made before the actual beginning of the routine type autopsy examination"?[25] And what did Sibert and O'Neill mean by their statement that the body was brought to Bethesda for "inspection and autopsy";[26] that the "preparation" began at 7:17, but the autopsy began at 8:15, the time of the first incision?[27]

Autopsy A63-272 seemed to be an autopsy without a precisely fixed

---

* Sibert and O'Neill reported: "At the termination of the autopsy . . . personnel from Gawler's Funeral Home entered the autopsy room to prepare the President's body for burial. . . ."[24] Sibert and O'Neill departed, apparently believing the embalming was about to start and by 1:45 A.M. were at the FBI Laboratory in Washington. Yet at 2:45 A.M., Secret Service Agent Hill was summoned by Kellerman to view the wounds, and both Hill and Kellerman reported the embalming had not yet begun.

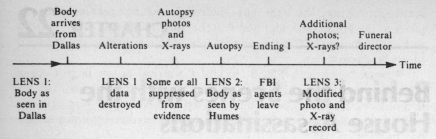

Figure 39.
Time line showing possible sequence of events resulting in three medical records of the assassination

beginning, which might hold the key to when alterations were made on the body, and without a precisely fixed end, which might similarly indicate when additional photos and X-rays were made.*

In short, I was beginning to suspect that what I called "Lens 3"—the photographic and X-ray record—was created sometime after midnight on November 22, 1963, and was intimately connected with the changes made on the receipts.

---

* On February 19, 1964, Arlen Specter turned in a preliminary report. In it, I found an indication that he may have been aware of problems at both ends of the time line. On page 80, he began his description of the autopsy: "A full autopsy was performed on President John F. Kennedy, starting at 8:00 P.M. (EST) (precise time of completion not listed). . . ."[28]

Did the adjective "full" suggest that Specter had some indication that prior to the start of what he called the official autopsy something less than a "full" autopsy had taken place? The FBI Field Office document which suggests a distinction between "inspection" and "autopsy," and explicitly states that Humes was not at first given permission for a full autopsy, is a Baltimore Field Office document; it was not made available to the Commission. Similarly, Specter's interview with Sibert and O'Neill, in which they talked of 7:17 as being the start of the "inspection," did not occur until March 12, 1964, about three weeks after Specter submitted his report.[29]

Behind the Scenes with the House Assassinations Committee

In 1974 I thought the Kennedy case was dead. But a resurgence of public interest was spurred by Robert Groden's optically enhanced version of the Zapruder film, which was seen on national TV in 1975, and shown to members of Congress. The impact of the film was so powerful that it ultimately led, in the fall of 1976, to the creation of the House Select Committee on Assassinations.

Like other Warren Report critics, I was intensely interested in this investigation. It was "our" investigation, an investigation that grew out of our movement, our books, our articles, our speeches and lectures. Only a handful of people in the United States had spent the time and money to study the Kennedy assassination in great detail. I daresay that every one wished that he could personally direct at least some part of the new inquiry. I felt I knew how to solve the case: Pursue the medical evidence.

But I was not in charge. The boss was Prof. Robert G. Blakey, a Cornell law professor hired in June 1977, after the Committee's leadership changed. The attorney in charge of the medical area was Donald Andrew Purdy.

Within a few months, word filtered out that a medical panel had been formed to examine the X-rays and photographs. The panel consisted of nine forensic pathologists. In September 1977, they had their first meeting. Information leaked out that the panel was going to find—on the basis of the X-rays and photographs—that President Kennedy was hit twice from behind. The Committee, it was said, would conduct tests to verify that the X-rays and photographs were authentic.

The Warren Report critics would never be able to say they hadn't been represented. For the panel included a dissenter, the Coroner of Allegheny County—Dr. Cyril H. Wecht.

I found the situation hopeless, and decided to confine my efforts to completing my book.

But what was going on behind the scenes?

On September 16, 1977, six members of the Forensic Pathology Panel met with Drs. Humes and Boswell in Washington. In one room were two of the doctors who had performed the autopsy, the photographs and X-rays they supposedly took, and professionals qualified to examine the evidence and ask the right questions.

The panel subsequently stated in its report published in 1979 that by September 18, 1977—two days after this meeting—"it became apparent that the members were in substantial agreement with respect to the interpretation of the evidence."[1]* At its first meeting, the Forensic Pathology Panel set the course for the Blakey investigation. President Kennedy had been struck twice from behind. That's what the photographs and X-rays showed; that's what this Committee would conclude.

The old house had been put on a new legal foundation. The much criticized autopsy report had been replaced by the autopsy photographs and X-rays. On several points, the transcript of the September 1977 closed session told the story.

1. Procedural Irregularities

One irregularity of the Kennedy autopsy was that it was incomplete. The doctors failed to examine certain organs, including the adrenal glands. By 1976, it was established that the charge made in the 1960 Democratic nomination fight—that Kennedy had Addison's disease—was true.**

It was not the Committee's function to investigate whether Kennedy did or didn't have the ailment. But it was within their prerogative to find out why mention of the adrenals had been deleted from the autopsy report. Did Robert Kennedy speak to Humes? Did Admiral Burkley? Exactly what happened?

The panel's questioning got off to an inauspicious beginning. "First of all," began Dr. Petty, "let me start with the question that was on the lips of everyone here and that is, did you or didn't you look at the adrenals?"

---

* Dr. Wecht, who was not present at this meeting, subsequently filed a dissenting report.

** Addison's disease is a failure of the adrenal glands. In 1977 Joan and Clay Blair, in their book, *The Search for JFK,* established by interviewing one of John Kennedy's doctors, Elmer C. Bartels, that Kennedy was diagnosed as an Addisonian in 1947.[2] In 1972, Dr. John Lattimer, based on his examination of the autopsy X-rays, which showed the adrenals, reported that "the President suffered from bilateral adrenal atrophy."[3]

Replied Humes: "I would ask . . . does that bear on your investigation of the event that took place that night?"

PETTY: No; all we were wondering was—we noticed that that was noticeably absent from the autopsy report.

HUMES: Since I don't think it bore directly on the death of the President, I'd prefer not to discuss it with you, doctor.

PETTY: All right. Fine. If you prefer not to, that's fine with me. We were just curious because normally we examine adrenals in the general course [of an] autopsy.

HUMES: I'd only comment for you that I have strong personal reasons and certain other obligations that suggest to me that it might not be preferable.[4]

The matter was dropped.

In February 1969, Dr. Pierre Finck testified at the Shaw trial in New Orleans that the organs of the neck were not examined, and that the doctors had been prevented from dissecting the back wound—the wound I suspected was false—by an unnamed army general.[5] In the closed session in 1977, Dr. Humes gave a contrary version. He said the decision not to dissect the neck was his alone.[6] The Committee did not confront Humes with Finck's statement, or cross-examine him. It interviewed Finck twice, but failed to publish either interview, thus sealing them for fifty years.* Humes said: "There was no question but we were being urged to expedite this examination as quickly as possible . . . did it harass us and cause difficulty, of course it did, how could it not?"[11] Humes implied the source of the pressure was Admiral Burkley, but he was not critical: ". . . he was the . . . physician to the President's family, [and] his concerns were, I think, very understandable . . . he was in hopes that the examination

---

* Finck's second appearance is made somewhat mysterious because the Committee noted that he, Finck, requested the interview, because he feared that what he had said the first time "may have been misunderstood."[7]

Another peculiarity of the record concerns Dr. Finck's autopsy notes. The House Assassinations Committee quoted from them in its report, but never reproduced them in full. For some unexplained reason, the only date associated with Finck's autopsy notes is February 1, 1965. The Committee repeatedly referred to them as being part of a letter addressed to Col. Joe Blumberg, head of the Armed Forces Institute of Pathology, on that date.[8] From the available information, it is impossible to know whether or not the notes are contemporaneous. Under the Freedom of Information Act, I requested the government copies of the notes from AFIP, the army, and the Department of Defense, to no avail. They are not on file.

Andrew Purdy, the House Assassinations Committee lawyer who handled the medical evidence, told me that the Committee obtained its copy from Dr. Finck himself, when he testified.

Finck's notes, as quoted by the House Committee, describe the large head wound as a "fronto-parietal-occipital wound,"[9] a hybrid lens 2/lens 3 picture.

But in June 1965, Finck published an article in *Military Medicine,* presumably

could achieve its goal in as expedient a manner as possible. . . ."[12] Dr. Boswell said: "Initially Admiral Burkley said that they had caught Oswald and that they needed the bullet to complete the case."[13] The House Committee failed to call Burkley to testify in public, and no transcript of any interview or depositions that may have been made in private were published.

2. The Harper Fragment

The Harper fragment was a 5 by 7cm piece of bone found on Dealey Plaza on November 23, 1963.[14] It was originally identified by Dr. A.B. Cairns, the Chief Pathologist at Methodist Hospital, as being occipital bone, an opinion concurred in by two other doctors.[15] Both in size and anatomic origin, the Harper fragment corresponded to the exit wound described by the Dallas doctors. The X-rays and photographs showed the occipital intact. If the Harper fragment was in fact occipital bone, then the X-rays and photographs could not be authentic representations of Kennedy's head as it was immediately after the shooting.

The Committee showed the pictures of the Harper fragment to Dr. Humes. He compared its periphery with the periphery of the wound shown in the photographs and said: "I don't see anything with quite the circumferential margins of these other[s]. . . . I don't think any of the borders of this fragment to me would coincide with this type of a wound of exit."[16]

About this time, Dr. J. Lawrence Angel, Curator of Physical Anthropology at the Smithsonian, arrived. Dr. Charles Petty, Chief Medical Examiner of Dallas, Texas, and a member of the panel, said: "We would like very much to have your expertise in identifying . . . this particular fragment . . . what part of the head . . . it came from. . . ."[17]

Dr. Angel's response was: "Well, it's clearly parietal bone, side left or right is not so easy." As evidence for this assertion, Dr. Angel said: "You can see one, two, or three markings for meningeal vessels on the

---

based on the notes he sent just weeks earlier to Colonel Blumberg, in which he described the head wound as a "temporo-parietal-occipital wound,"[10] a lens 2 description in agreement with the Bethesda autopsy.

Finck did not see the autopsy photographs until January 1967, a year and a half after the publication of the article. Did he change his notes from "*temporo*-parietal-occipital" to "*fronto*-parietal-occipital" at some time after he saw the autopsy photographs? One thing seems clear: Finck's original description of the head wound, as reflected in his June 1965 article, is *not* the same as the head wound described in the notes Finck showed the House Assassinations Committee, which were quoted in that Committee's 1979 report.

inner surface. . . ."* Based on that, he said the bone could fit into the huge hole "oh—around here." "Around where?" asked Petty.

Angel tried to describe the location; then he qualified his opinion: "At first I could see marks of sagittal suture here, but I don't think that's it." Dr. Angel discovered that what he had been calling a suture line wasn't a suture line at all.

Suture lines go completely through the bone, but Dr. Angel couldn't find a corresponding line on the photograph of the interior surface of the Harper fragment.

"Well, excuse me—it doesn't seem to show in the inside. I'm puzzled." Angel turned to the others: "Are you sure that's suture edge there?"

They were of little help. Boswell replied: ". . . we're not sure; we ask for your advice." Dr. Davis said: "That's why you're here, sir."

Dr. Angel then explained why his original idea was wrong. He said: "I thought these [referring to the grooves visible on the interior surface] were intermediate posterior branches of middle meningeal going up the side of the parietal here. . . ." He added: ". . . and I would have looked here for a trace of lambdoid suture." The lambdoid suture is an inverted V-shaped suture that marks the border of the occipital bone at the back of the head with the left and right parietal bones. If the Harper bone had contained lambdoid suture, it would be part occipital, part parietal, depending on where the suture line was.

Then Dr. Angel remarked: "Of course, I don't know what damage the skull showed and whether this has to be—but I'm not supposed to know this."

That was the essence of the matter. Dr. Angel's identification should have been based on anthropological evidence alone—not on knowledge of where the bone was "supposed" to fit. The Committee proceeded on a different basis. Dr. Baden said: "No, Dr. Angel; feel free to discuss this with Dr. Humes who did the autopsy. He'd be delighted to. . . ." Angel asked: "Is there a defect on the right that this would fit into?" Replied Humes, as if rewarding a good student bright enough to ask the proper question: "Good, Dr. Angel. Yes." Dr. Humes then asked that the X-rays showing the large skull hole be put up on the screen "for Dr. Angel's benefit."

Now the doctors suggested that the Harper fragment be moved toward the extreme forward part of the parietal bone, where the coronal suture marks the border with the frontal bone. "Could that be coronal suture?" asked Petty. Replied Angel: "I would have guessed that it might be. Again, I don't see any meningeal vessel markings, but . . . that's conceivable."

---

* Meningeal vessels are blood vessels which feed the brain, and the "markings" Dr. Angel referred to were the sulci, or grooves in the skull which lodge the vessels.

Dr. Angel now apparently realized that the X-rays showed that the hole actually extended into the frontal bone. "Oh, there was damage that far forward?" he said. Shown the lateral X-ray, he commented, "Yes, that's right." His immediate reaction: "Well, this then could be frontal perfectly well. It doesn't show the meningeal markings, and that's what made me unhappy about it . . . being, well—[the] photo makes more sense. . . ."

By this point, Dr. Angel had considered two distinct locations for the Harper fragment.

After some more discussion, Angel now came up with a third place for the Harper fragment, somewhere on the top of the head, in the parietal area. When Petty asked: "The Harper piece could be fitted posterior and slightly lateral, is that what you're saying?" he replied: "This is what I'm saying, yes, perhaps." A bit later he commented: "It's hard to do that—jigsaw puzzle—that's all I can say."

Dr. Petty admitted: "Well, it's terribly fragmented, and we can't really reconstruct it." Indeed, Dr. Petty seemed willing to settle for less: "Our ultimate question is, do you think this could well be part of the skull of the late President, referring now to the Harper piece?" Angel replied, "Yes."

The record indicated, then, that the Harper fragment was moved around on the head by Dr. Angel and members of the panel, trying to find a place for it within the hole that appeared on the photographs and X-rays. At different points, Dr. Angel indicated it might show lambdoid suture, sagittal suture, and coronal suture, corresponding, roughly, to the right rear, the middle (at the top), and the forward part of the head.

A month later, on October 24, 1977, Dr. Angel submitted his report. He described the perimeter of the hole seen on the photographs. "In order to approximate the position," he wrote, "it is necessary to define the gap. . . ," a sentence making the "jigsaw" method explicit. Then he drew three sketches—labeling the top view "deduced, not observed." "The Harper fragment photographs," he wrote, "show it as . . . coming mainly from the upper middle third of the right parietal bone."[18] Dr. Angel's report is noteworthy for the lack of any specific anthropological evidence uniquely identifying the bone. His memo states: ". . . vascular foramina on the inside and a faint irregular line on the outside indicate sagittal suture,"[19] but the transcript a month earlier shows he said: ". . . at first I could see marks of sagittal suture here, but I don't think that's it."[20]

Concluding his report, Dr. Angel attempted to relate the borders of the Harper fragment to the borders of the wound margin shown in the autopsy picture—borders which Dr. Humes said showed no relationship at all—using language such as one section "appears to fit," another "can fit," and a third area "may meet."[21]

This leaves the following question for history to decide: Whose identification of the Harper fragment is more reliable—that of Dr. A.B.

Cairns, who actually held the bone in his hand and examined it, and said it was occipital bone, an opinion concurred in by two other doctors who also saw the bone? Or the memorandum of Dr. Angel?

3. The "Incomplete" Bone Hole

In the artist's drawing of the skull that Humes prepared for the Warren Commission, the entry and exit were depicted as two separate and distinct holes, the entry being a small hole situated beneath the larger exit. However, on the diagram made in the autopsy room, Boswell made the following notation regarding that wound: "ragged, slanting," and an arrow that pointed upward and tilted slightly to the left.[22] (See Fig. 3, p. 78.) It was a puzzling notation, yet it seemed to fit with a statement that was written by Humes—but then crossed out—on the handwritten draft of the autopsy that the wound was "a lacerated wound tangential to the surface of the scalp."[23] Neither Humes' original description nor Boswell's "ragged, slanting" suggested a through-and-through wound, but in the absence of additional evidence the idea that the wound was anything but a through-and-through hole remained a suspicion.*

At the September 1977 meeting, Boswell was shown the diagram, and questioned about the various entries. Of the entry wound, Boswell said: ". . . there was a hole here, only half of which was present in the bone that was intact."[24] Then, referring to the smallest of the three fragments shown in the X-ray, Boswell added: "This small piece then fit right on there."[25] Later, he again described the entry as an incomplete hole: "There was a shelf and then a little hole, came up on the side and then one of the smaller of the two fragments in that X-ray, when that arrived, we were able to fit that down there and complete the circumference of that bone wound."[26]

Those fragments didn't arrive until after midnight. Until that time, the President's head did not show a separate entry hole, but simply a notch somewhere on the rear edge of a larger hole.

Dr. Finck's 1965 autopsy notes provide corroboration. Initially, he characterized the wound as "possibly of entrance," and wrote: "the skull shows a portion of a crater. . . ."[27]

The implications are threefold. First, when the President's body arrived there were not two separate holes, just one large hole in the head. Along the margin of the hole was a notch, what Finck called "a portion of a crater," what Boswell labeled "ragged, slanting" in his diagram, what he told the Committee was "a hole . . . only half of which was present." Thus,

---

* By "through-and-through hole," I mean a fully defined hole, surrounded by bone, whose circumference was complete.

the notion of a "little hole" beneath the big hole was merely a concept suggested by the navy drawing, implied by the Warren Commission testimony. It was not found on the body received for autopsy. Second, the autopsy doctors handled the situation in a way which could be charitably described as benignly misleading. Neither in their report nor testimony did they state that what they were calling an entry was anything but a separate and distinct hole. The drawing represented a reconstruction. But the X-rays and photographs, by all reports, show a separate and distinct hole. Hence, the third implication: If Boswell's information was accurate, if a complete hole did not exist until a small fragment arrived which "then fit right on there," then those X-rays could not have been made when the body first arrived. The fragments in question did not arrive until after midnight.*

4. The Chest Photographs

During the September 1977 session, Dr. Humes reaffirmed that he took photographs of the interior of the chest and the bruise atop the right lung. He said: "I distinctly recall going to great lengths to try and get the interior upper portion of the right thorax illuminated—what happened to that film, I don't know." The Committee had no answer either. Photographer Stringer told them what he told me—that he thought he took interior photographs of the chest.[28] The Committee reported: "Dr. Burkley, however, told the Committee that no one took any photographs of the interior of the chest. There is no evidence that such photographs exist."[29]

And that was the end of the Committee's investigation of the subject.

5. Destruction of Autopsy Notes

Before the panel, Humes gave an elaborate explanation for the burned notes. He destroyed them because they were bloodstained. While in the navy, he said, one of his duties had been to escort foreign naval medical officers to various locations in the United States. "I tried to teach them a little Americana," said Humes, who told how he took them to Greenfield Village, built by Henry Ford near Dearborn, Michigan, and to a court-

---

* This was strongly supported by Sibert and O'Neill's report that there were only eleven X-rays, and not fourteen. One possibility was that the three additional X-rays are of the bone fragment that arrived after Sibert and O'Neill left the morgue. If so, the question then arose as to how the three X-rays presumably taken when Sibert and O'Neill were present could possibly show a "complete" bone hole, if part of the circumference consisted of bone which arrived after they left.

house there which President Lincoln used to visit. In that courthouse was the chair from Ford's Theater in which Lincoln was sitting when he was murdered. "Now the back of that chair is stained with a dark substance," said Humes, "and there's much discussion to this day as to whether the stain represents the blood of the deceased President or whether it is Macassar [a hair dressing]." Humes said his foreign guests "were appalled that the American people would wish to have an object stained with the blood of the President on public display." Humes said he too was "amazed," that it bothered him. "It still does, to this day," he said. "And here I was, now in the possession of a number of pieces of paper, some of which unavoidably . . . were stained . . . with the blood of our deceased President. And I knew that I would give the record over to some person or persons in authority. . . ." Humes said he felt that "inappropriate . . . and it was for that reason and for that reason only, that, having transcribed those notes onto the pieces of paper that are before you, I destroyed those pieces of paper."*[30]

6. The Four-Inch Discrepancy

Perhaps the most important event recorded in the closed-session transcript was the protracted discussion concerning the location of the rear entry wound in the head. To understand what happened, it is necessary to understand what the autopsy pictures show. The Committee published exact replicas, made by a medical illustrator. They show the back of the head. Two hands hold the head, one forward, apparently holding the head by actually reaching inside the huge hole; the other, at the back, holding a ruler. Near the top of the ruler, centered in the photograph, is a small bullet entrance wound. At the bottom of the back of the head appears an artifact of some type, perhaps a spot of brain tissue. (See Photo 30.) The illustrated wound corresponds to a break in the bone shown on the X-rays—most readily visible in the lateral X-ray, which

* The "pieces of paper" to which Humes alluded was the handwritten draft of the autopsy, the autopsy which said the President was shot twice from behind, and the question, of course, is whether every fact recorded on the notes made it to the autopsy report. What happened in the case of Boswell's diagram is not reassuring. Boswell noted a ten-by-seventeen–cm area marked "missing"—those measurements were not mentioned in the autopsy. Boswell noted a 10cm bone fragment on the left side of the head—that was not mentioned. Boswell described the entry wound as "ragged, slanting"—not mentioned. These were just three examples of facts omitted from the autopsy report which would have vanished from history had that piece of paper been destroyed. If Boswell's notes were any guide, Humes' statement that he copied everything verbatim must be viewed skeptically.

shows an obvious discontinuity about four inches above the external occipital protuberance. (See Photo 31.)

The disagreement began when Dr. Petty showed the doctors the lateral X-ray and asked: "Is this the point of entrance that I'm pointing to?"

"No," replied Humes.

"This is not?" said Petty.

"No," replied Humes and Boswell simultaneously.

Petty asked: "Where is the point of entrance?"

Humes responded that it was "below the external occipital protuberance."

The transcript continued:

> PETTY: It's below it?
>
> HUMES: Right.
>
> PETTY: Not above it?
>
> BOSWELL: No. It's to the right and inferior to [below] the external occipital protuberance.
>
> HUMES: [It] precisely coincides with that wound on the scalp.[31]

By "that wound on the scalp," Humes designated a spot at the bottom of the back of the head that the others felt was merely brain tissue, or some other artifact. But Humes believed otherwise. "I'm quite confident," said Humes. "[I]t's just to the right and below by a centimeter and maybe a centimeter to the right and maybe 2 centimeters below the midpoint of the external occipital protuberance. And when the scalp was reflected from there, there was virtually an identical wound in the occipital bone."[32]

With that statement, there began a subdued but—if the transcript is any indication—somewhat tense argument. It went on for many pages.

The panel members seemed incredulous that Dr. Humes had chosen what they were convinced was an entirely incorrect location. Humes presumably picked the spot where he remembered the wound. Dr. Finck testified ten years before at the Shaw trial: "I don't endorse the 100 millimeters . . . I saw the wound of entry in the back of the head . . . slightly above the external occipital protuberance, and it was definitely not 4 inches or 100 millimeters above it."[33]

Petty began what was tantamount to a cross-examination. He noted the ruler in the picture seemed positioned to measure the upper location. But Humes denied that.

> PETTY: Then this ruler that is held in the photograph is simply to establish a scale and no more?
>
> HUMES: Exactly.
>
> PETTY: It is not intended to represent the ruler starting for something?
>
> HUMES: No way, no way.[34]

The doctors then referred to the brain photographs, and rebutted Humes by noting they showed the cerebellum intact, an unlikely condition if the bullet entered low on the back of the head, where Humes said it did.

Petty said: "We . . . wonder at the intact nature, not only [of] the cerebellum, but also [of] the posterior aspects of the occipital lobes . . . and this has concerned us right down the line as to where precisely the inshoot [entry] wound was, and this is why we found ourselves in a quandary, and one of the reasons that we very much wanted to have you come down today."[35]

The intact cerebellum contrasted sharply with the Dallas observations. Was the brain in the picture President Kennedy's? The Committee disregarded the Dallas testimony and tried only to reconcile the pictures with Humes' statements.

Dr. Coe made an inquiry regarding damage to the cerebral peduncles, visible on the underside of the brain.

> COE: Dr. Humes, . . . I am curious to know whether this destruction you feel is a post-mortem artifact in removing the brain, or was part of this . . . caused by the bullet you think perhaps?
>
> HUMES: . . . well, I think it was partly caused by the bullet.
>
> COE: It was?[36]

When Dr. Davis, looking at the photographs, stated his opinion the entry was at the top, Humes said: "No, no, that's no wound." Then, pointing to the place others thought was merely some brain tissue, he said: ". . . that was a wound, and the wound on the skull precisely coincided with it."[37]

Petty returned to the way the photograph was taken—the upper wound was centered, the lower one was not. The upper wound, not the lower one, was in focus. Petty said: "So on photograph No. 42, then . . . this photograph is not taken with the inshoot wound centered in the photograph? . . ."[38]

Humes kept returning to the body as he remembered it: ". . . I can assure you . . . there was no defect corresponding to this [the upper location] in the skull at any point, . . ." he told the panel. Referring to what the others were calling a bullet entrance wound, he said: "I don't know what that is. It could be to me clotted blood. . . . I just don't know what it is, but it certainly was not any wound of entrance."[39]

A bit later, Dr. Loquvam spoke up: "I don't think this discussion belongs in this record. . . . We have no business recording this. This is for us to decide between ourselves."[40] When Dr. Coe pointed out to Humes that other pathologists disagreed with him on the wound location, Loquvam interrupted again: "You guys are nuts. You guys are nuts writing this stuff. It doesn't belong in that damn record. . . . Why not turn off the record [the Committee was using a tape recorder] and explain to him and then go back and talk again?" Dr. Baden replied: "Well, our problem is not to get our opinions, but to get his opinions."[41]

Dr. Petty returned to the picture. "I think the biggest point in consideration here is that this is in focus here (pointing to [the] upper scalp area in question) and this is not in focus here (pointing to lower area) . . . therefore we must be looking specifically in that area." Dr. Davis wondered aloud whether the person taking the photographs was directed, or just took whatever he pleased. Humes cut in: "No, no. He was directed." Boswell added: "He was taking specific areas." The two men, apparently realizing the implications of what they said, each made a remark. Humes said: "A real problem." Boswell: "Yeah. I know."[42]

Humes then said: "I don't think the photograph permits us to say with accuracy where it is. . . ."

But Petty returned to the theme to point out that the lower spot was depicted only "incidentally . . . in photograph 15 and shows near the margin of the photograph down toward the hairline of the President. And again here on [photograph] No. 43 it shows the same thing."

Humes replied: "I object to your word 'incidentally.' "

Replied Petty: "Well, by that I mean it's not the subject of the center of the photographer's lens. . . ."

Dr. Baden said that he too thought the body was held "up specifically so that the photographer could get that point."

Humes replied: "Not that point. That is not the case." He went on: "I almost defy you to find [that] in the black and white. . . ."

Baden said: "We're not trying to be argumentative. . . ."

Humes said: "Nor I. . . ."

Baden said: "What we're trying to do is fully understand what you say and what you did."[43]

If Humes was correct, then the photographs he examined before the panel were not the photographs taken under his supervision at the autopsy. The Committee never raised the question. Humes made no such allegation. He simply argued that the pictures showed the wound he remembered, regardless of the fact that, according to his own testimony to the House Select Committee, they did not.

This standoff was captured in a final exchange. Earlier that day, Humes and Boswell had marked on a laboratory skull the location of the entry wound they remembered. (See Photo 33.) Dr. Baden asked: "In reviewing the skull [you marked] at this time and having review[ed] all of the films and incorporating our discussion, is that still a valid representation?"

Replied Humes: "Yes, I think so."

Baden reminded him: "Dr. Humes, this refers to the notation made on the skull. We are using it as an exhibit, and it is signed and initialed by you."

Humes wouldn't budge: "I believe that that's a reasonable representation."[44]

The September 1977 transcripts reveal the Committee's disinclination to resolve discrepancies. The adrenals question should have been settled; it wasn't. The Committee took no notice of Boswell's volunteered statement about what Burkley said at the outset of the autopsy—that the assassin had been apprehended "and that they needed the bullet to complete the case."[45] Burkley wasn't called as a witness in the public hearings, and all his contact with the Committee in private was unpublished, and so will remain sealed for fifty years. The Harper fragment was pushed around on the skull by a panel obviously trying to reconcile it with the hole shown on the X-rays and photographs. There is no indication that any credence whatsoever was given to the possibility the original identification might have been correct. Boswell's remarks that the original bone hole was incomplete were simply ignored, despite the fact that—aside from the four-inch discrepancy—that alone would disqualify the hole shown on the X-rays as being the one he described, and indeed, would mean that the X-rays, if of Kennedy's body, were made after a reconstruction. Humes' explanation of burned notes was simply accepted, without cross-examination. The panel members displayed no concern that photos he took were not in the collection, or that the ones at the Archives didn't show the wound as he remembered it. Indeed, the panel seemed to have treated Humes simply as a doctor who made a four-inch error. Legally, that was the problem to be solved. It was a problem because Humes had seen the body; they hadn't. Yet he wouldn't admit he was wrong. The panel was so sure he was wrong they wrote in their report: "The panel considered the value of disinterring the President's body to locate more precisely the various wounds. . . . The majority concludes that an examination of the body would fully support its conclusions. . . . Consequently, the majority of the panel decided against recommending disinterment."[46]

Most of these behind-the-scenes details were not available in 1977. The staff had signed oaths, subjecting themselves to legal action if they talked. But what did leak out was the Committee's general attitude, and a few incidents from another September 1977 meeting, when Robert Groden presented the Zapruder film to the panel. Upon seeing the President being slammed against the rear seat, one panel member said that things always move backwards when hit from behind. Action and reaction, he said. The meeting ground to a halt. It was one thing to posit a "jet-effect" theory, or even a neuromuscular theory. But this particular "expert" was making one statement after another that completely contradicted Newton's laws, which he apparently didn't understand. Even defenders of the Warren Report couldn't take it. An argument began. After fifteen minutes, Groden was asked to leave the room. He recalled the scene as he walked out—several panel members trying to give their colleague a lesson in elementary physics, while Dr. Wecht, over in the corner, was shaking his head sadly from side to side.

My next contact with the Committee came in March 1978, and was prompted by an article that appeared in the Philadelphia papers.

CHAPTER 23

Allegations of Dr. John Ebersole

DR. JOHN EBERSOLE was called to Washington to testify before the House Assassinations Committee on March 11, 1978. A brief wire-service account appeared saying that he completely agreed with the findings of the Warren Commission.

About a month later, Paul Hoch sent me an article published in the *Philadelphia Inquirer* the day before Ebersole testified. Dr. Ebersole was quoted about the confusion at the autopsy because the doctors didn't know about the wound in the front of the throat. That confusion, he said, led him to X-ray the body repeatedly: "The X-rays that were taken that night and interpreted by me were for one purpose and one purpose only—prior to the start of the autopsy, because of the lack of finding of an exit wound [where the bullet or bullets left the body], it was felt that a bullet might still be in the body."[1]

Ebersole then explained why he had been under the impression the hole at the throat was merely a tracheotomy incision: "Later we found a wound of exit in the neck that had been neatly sutured by a surgeon in Dallas. That caused some confusion early on because we thought that it was from a tracheotomy. But it was the exit wound."[2]

". . . neatly sutured by a surgeon in Dallas. . . ."?

The simple fact that the wound was sewn up was evidence that someone had intercepted the body between Dallas and Bethesda. No one in Dallas had sutured a wound. When I spoke with Dr. Kemp Clark in 1966, he was under the impression that the tracheotomy tube remained in place when the President's body left Parkland Hospital.*[3] He assured me that

* I explained to Clark that this was not the case, which he said he did not know at the time of our November 1966 conversation.

no surgery of any kind had been done—Clark even said that no bandages had been placed on the head, in Dallas, to sop up blood.

Ebersole's observation raised the question of whether there had been a deliberate attempt to foist off a bullet wound at the autopsy as a tracheotomy incision, by actually sewing it shut. The autopsy report ought to have noted the sutures in the section on gross description of the body. The report made no mention of any such thing.

Finally, if the hole was sutured, that again raised the question of the legitimacy of the autopsy photos. As far as I knew, those photos did not show the hole sutured. So if the body was received that way, the question was: When were the sutures broken, and when were those pictures taken?

Shortly after reading the Ebersole allegation, I telephoned the House Select Committee and asked to speak with Michael Ewing.

Ewing was a Warren Report critic who wrote a book with Bernard Fensterwald. Politically, he was well connected, and had married the daughter of a U.S. Senator. I had been in touch with Ewing before and found him to be an effusive talker, a person who projected the air of an insider. Months before, when most of the critics were concerned about the direction apparently being taken by the Committee, Ewing, who had no official status yet, was at pains to assure me that the Committee would do an honest job and destroy the single-bullet theory. In the preface to his book, he had written: "We do not demolish the single-bullet theory for the one hundred and first time. We believe that responsible critics have done this in spades over the past several years."[4]

Now, Ewing had been hired; the word was he was close to Blakey because they shared an interest in fighting organized crime.

Within the first ten minutes, it became clear that now that he was affiliated with the Committee, Ewing's views had shifted markedly.

In the same facile way he had assured me the Committee would be shooting down the single-bullet theory once and for all, he told me the single-bullet theory was the Bible. One theme that ran through Ewing's conversation was that the Dallas doctors were liars. He continually referred to them as "those goddamn doctors." A month earlier, he had told me that, with respect to the wounds, "their stories are changing. . . . They are on about their fifth version right now." He said, "They all seem to be blowing whichever way the wind is going."[5]

Coming from Ewing, it was an interesting comment, and extremely difficult to counter since Ewing, supposedly, was speaking from authority. I had no way of knowing what the doctors were telling the Committee. When the hearings were published over a year later, they showed that some of the Dallas doctors were not contacted, and the Committee published verbatim interviews with only two, neither of whom changed his story from what he had told the Warren Commission in 1964.

Ewing then told me the Committee had "definitely" shot down the notion of any shots striking from the front. "I've always thought that was baloney," he said. "That's been my bias."[6]

When I brought up the matter of planted ammunition, Ewing immediately responded that it was also possible to believe in flying saucers, that Kennedy wasn't in the car, that perhaps he wasn't assassinated.

Then I turned to the main topic. I told him about Ebersole's statement that the throat wound was sutured. Ewing told me that he had never heard of that before. "Nobody in Dallas sutured that wound," I said. He assured me: "I never heard of it." After another speech about how Oswald was guilty, I said: "Look, Michael, if you think there's no conspiracy, you've got a responsibility of finding out who sutured the throat wound." "I agree," he replied.

"You can't walk in there and say 'I'm a little biased that there's no shots from the front,' and find that the body arrived with the throat wound sewn up."

"Absolutely," he replied.

I asked how the Committee was going to deal with the head-snap. "Oh, well, I think we'll just go with spasms. It's mysterious, it's strange, but we'll have to conclude it happened, because we don't have anything from the front. Strange things do happen."[7]

Nothing was done. In its report published a year and a half later, the Committee said nothing about the matter and in a disservice to history, it failed to publish the March 11, 1978 deposition with Dr. Ebersole, thus causing it to be sealed, under congressional rules, for fifty years.

After speaking with Ewing, I immediately set out to gather more information. First, I had to find out the source of the story—who had interviewed Ebersole? Did a tape exist? Soon I learned that the *Philadelphia Inquirer* story was a condensation of a much longer one done in Dr. Ebersole's hometown newspaper, the *Lancaster* [Pennsylvania] *Intelligencer-Journal*.

I contacted reporter Gil Dulaney, who sent me the story which had appeared on March 9, 1978, two days before Ebersole went to Washington. The headline was: BREAKS 15-YEAR SILENCE ON KENNEDY X-RAYS, CITY RADIOLOGIST DID AUTOPSY X-RAYS ON BODY AT BETHESDA. Most of the story was a straight interview and, clearly, Dr. Ebersole, a supporter of the lone-assassin theory, was not aware of the implications of the suture information, nor for that matter of the implications of the description of the head wound. Ebersole was quoted as follows: "When the body was removed from the casket there was a very obvious horrible gaping wound to the back of the head."[8] That description was the same as what McHugh and Stringer told me—it was totally inconsistent with what the photographs showed, according to all reliable reports.

As to the sutures, the story described how Ebersole repeatedly took X-rays of the body, unaware that the hole at the front was a bullet wound.

" 'We could not find any exit wound. . . . There was, however, at the base of the throat a very neatly sutured, neatly sewn, opening that we interpreted initially as a surgical wound.'

"The radiologist said it appeared someone had done a tracheotomy on Kennedy and then, after death, removed the tube from Kennedy's throat and sewn up the incision."[9]

The story then described how the autopsy personnel discovered that the sutured hole was really a bullet wound: "Around 11:00 or 11:30 P.M. on the night of Nov. 22, 1963, those doing the autopsy on Kennedy got in touch with medical officials who had treated Kennedy in Dallas and it was only then that they realized that the hole that had been sewn up in Kennedy's throat was actually the bullet's exit wound." Ebersole was then quoted: " 'They did a tracheotomy and then removed the tracheal tube after death and surgically repaired the wound, post-mortem.' "[10]

Reporter Gil Dulaney apparently did not realize the implications of the information volunteered by Ebersole. Dulaney told me how the interview had come about. One night, after Ebersole was called to testify, Ebersole's wife called him up and said: "My husband took the X-rays of John Kennedy. And he's going to be called up to the House Assassinations Panel. Would you like to interview him?"[11]

I asked Dulaney if he would share his original transcript with me, and he read portions of it to me on the phone. Dulaney's quotes in the article were verbatim from the transcript.

Soon I learned of another, even more detailed interview. Shortly after the Dulaney story appeared, Art Smith, a schoolteacher from nearby Chester, Pa., telephoned Ebersole and obtained an in-person interview with permission to use a tape recorder. Smith made his tapes available to me.

Smith's interview was on March 28, 1978, and lasted well over an hour. Ebersole left no doubt that the throat wound was sutured.

At great length, Ebersole explained why he had repeatedly X-rayed the body, and why he had used a portable machine rather than bring the body to the X-ray department: ". . . we were looking for a metal slug that you can pick up with any old X-ray machine. Again, I think . . . that probably is a point I want to really emphasize—the X-rays were taken not because we thought they would add anything to the overall story—", and now Ebersole pounded the desk as he talked, "where is the round that caused this wound of entrance [i.e., the entry at the rear of the neck] and no wound of exit? Even after dissection, the pathologist did not find it, and an agent, a non-medical person, asked me to take the X-rays again, in order that he could be convinced there wasn't a slug there."

Ebersole explained how the matter was cleared up: ". . . somewhere in the course of the evening we were in communication with Dallas, and determined that there had been a wound of exit at the throat, which had been sutured. That, to me, solved the problem. There's no need to take any more X-rays, or anything else. We have a wound of entrance, and now, historically, we have a wound of exit. Remember the sutured wound we saw . . . [it] looked as if someone had done a tracheotomy and perhaps sewed it up. It was neat. It was surgical. Certainly, in my eyes, it was."

When the interviewer related Dr. Perry's description of the wound as an entrance, Dr. Ebersole—in the spirit of one professional disagreeing with another—said: "That's his privilege. To my knowledge, what I saw was certainly a wound of entrance in the back; and later on, an explanation was given for why we didn't identify a wound of exit." Raising his voice for emphasis, he continued: "It had been dickered with. Through a surgeon's knife, or sewing up, or tracheotomy; it certainly had been changed from whatever it was. Which is unavoidable if they are going for a life-saving thing like a tracheotomy."[12]

Of course, years later, it might seem foolish to expect to hide a wound that way, but such a judgment enjoys the benefit of hindsight—specifically, the knowledge that Perry had talked to the press and that his statements about the throat wound were on the wire services. All that was true, but that afternoon, poor communications could well have given rise to a situation in which an attempt had been made to hide the wound entirely.

This, once again, brought up the question of whether the back wound had been placed low by "mistake," and it added an entirely new dimension to Dr. Burkley's failure to mention the existence of the throat wound to the Bethesda doctors and his omission of it from his own report. Now the problem was compounded by another: How could Burkley fail to be aroused by the existence of sutures?

Still another dimension to the "sutured wound" issue: The FBI was given President Kennedy's clothes within twenty-four hours, and its own documents prove the FBI Lab had examined them by the morning of November 23, 1963. Yet despite that, the FBI omitted from its December 9, 1963 report any pictures of the clothing, or any mention that the President's clothing showed a bullet hole at the front of the throat. This had always seemed peculiar. But when joined with Dr. Ebersole's suture allegation, it raised the question of whether there wasn't a plan afoot in the early hours to actually hide a bullet wound. The first Dallas Field Office report to state that the President's clothing had a hole at the front was dated December 23, 1963, and the first Summary Report to do so was dated January 13, 1964.

Once I had gathered together Smith's tapes, Dulaney's article, and the portions of his original transcript read over the phone, it became clear that Dr. Ebersole's information was important for still other reasons.

The head wound. According to the interview published on March 9,

1978, Ebersole told Dulaney: "The front of the body, except for a very slight bruise above the right eye on the forehead, was absolutely intact. It was the back of the head that was blown off."[13]

Two days later, Ebersole was in Washington, saw the X-rays in evidence, and identified them as the ones he took. When Ebersole met with Art Smith on March 28, he said: "The back portion of the head . . . the back part of the head, was reasonably intact." Referring to Dulaney's article, Smith continued the questioning:

SMITH: That was a misquote?

EBERSOLE: Yes. Misquoted. I, really, ah, I may have said that—what I meant was, the side.[14]

I contacted Dulaney who agreed to read to me from his own transcript of a tape he had made of his interview made before Ebersole went to Washington and saw the X-rays: ". . . when the body arrived, and when it was removed from the casket, there was a very obvious horrible gaping wound at the back of the head. . . ." Another quote: "Later on in the evening, between midnight and 1:00 A.M., a large portion of the skull was sent up from Dallas . . . that represented the back portion of the skull."*[15]

The entry wound. Showing him Warren Commission Exhibit 388, the drawing of the head trajectory, Smith asked Ebersole if he saw the small entry wound at the back of the head. Replied Ebersole: "*I* didn't. No . . . Now when I say I didn't see a wound there doesn't mean it wasn't there. I'm not a pathologist. My business was to take the X-rays."**[16]

Finally, Ebersole's response brings up a peculiar event that took place in March 1964.

If my theory was correct, the X-rays in the possession of the Secret Service were not the ones Ebersole took. Ebersole recalled how he was first shown the X-rays now in evidence.

"Roughly within a month of the autopsy, I was called by Captain James Young, who was on the White House medical staff, and asked if I could, from the skull X-rays, furnish life measurements."[17] Ebersole was told that these data were needed by a sculptor who was going to do a bust of John F. Kennedy. Ebersole went to the White House Annex, was shown the films, and drew some pencil lines on the X-rays—lines which remained on the X-rays in evidence. When he finished, he provided the measurements to Dr. Young.

Dulaney related that Ebersole told him he "believes that the sculptor ultimately did not require the measurements he took, that he relied instead

* Boswell's diagram of the skull shows what could be fragments at the rear of the skull.

** Ebersole's comment was, of course, consistent with Boswell's September 1977 statement about an incomplete bone hole. (See Chapter 22.)

on Kennedy's hat size and photographs taken of the President while he was still alive."[18]

The incident raised serious questions in my mind as to whether Ebersole had been called in to look at the X-rays in order to see how he would react should it be necessary to call him as a witness before the Commission.

Listening to the Smith tapes, I had mixed feelings about Ebersole. He was humble about the role he had played that night, repeatedly stressing that he was just a radiologist. Many times, when Smith would confront him with facts at variance with the official version, Ebersole would carefully distinguish between his opinion about what happened in Dallas, and what he could testify to based on personal observation. About his own beliefs, Ebersole made no secret: that the President was struck twice from behind, and that the public just had a hard time accepting the fact that a lone assassin could wreak so much havoc on society.[19] Ironically, Dr. Ebersole unwittingly provided damaging information that went to the heart of the matter of whether the body arrived unaltered, and whether the X-rays he took were the ones in evidence.

CHAPTER 24

House Select Committee: 1978 Public Hearings

I FIRST SAW PERFECT REPLICAS of the autopsy photographs on September 7, 1978, when the House Select Committee began public hearings on the medical evidence. WETA in Washington employed me as a commentator for its coverage of the hearings, which was aired nationwide on PBS. Entering the main hearing room about an hour early, I saw a large poster-sized exhibit showing the back of John Kennedy's head. In the picture, two hands held a ruler. The rear of the head was intact, except for a small bullet hole near the top.

It was a photograph of House Committee Exhibit F-36. Behind it were two others, one of the throat wound, another of the back wound.* The drawings were not schematic representations like the ones prepared under the direction of Commander Humes, but precise reproductions made from the original autopsy photographs by Ms. Ida Dox, a medical illustrator. Ms. Dox told me later of the effort involved. So precise were the drawings of the back of the head, with every hair in place, she said, that the archivist who watched her at work said he could not tell the difference between the photograph and the drawing.

The back of the head was intact. My research made me painfully

* No drawing was published of any of the autopsy photographs taken from the front or right side, photos which showed the full extent of the fatal wound, because those photographs would necessarily include a partial view of Kennedy's face. Ms. Dox testified that one such drawing was in fact prepared. Some months later, Blakey told me why he decided not to release it: Despite efforts to crop the picture so that it showed only the wound, what remained was a picture which, Blakey felt, was too recognizable and therefore too shocking. Thus, fifteen years after the murder, considerations of taste prevailed to prevent public disclosure of this vital evidence—a picture of the fatal wound itself.

aware of the sharp contrast between this picture on the one hand and both the autopsy report and the Dallas testimony on the other.

After Ms. Dox testified, the Committee called Dr. Lowell Levine, a forensic dentist. Levine had studied the X-rays of the skull and compared the dental work with X-rays of President Kennedy's teeth. He testified there was "absolutely no question" that the X-rays in evidence were of the skull of the late President.[1] His report stated: "It is further my opinion that the unique and individual dental and hard tissue characteristics which may be interpreted from Autopsy Films 1, 2, 3 could not be simulated."[2]

The next witness was photo expert Calvin McCamy. McCamy testified that by checking the batch numbers, he had ascertained that the films in evidence were manufactured in 1963. He also testified that he had checked the photographs themselves: "We found no disturbing of the surface of the film . . . nothing taken away . . . or added . . . no evidence of any cutting or pasting or construction of a montage, in short, found no evidence whatsoever of any such faking."[3]

He added that he had viewed the pictures that were taken from the same angle stereoscopically—a procedure that would have revealed even minor differences, as might exist if there had been imperfect art work. There were none. It was clear that the Committee had charged the experts with considering extreme possibilities. At one point McCamy testified: "Suppose . . . we take the possibility that someone substituted a body and that it was not the body of the President. Viewing these photographs stereoscopically provides the best kind of view because you can observe not only lateral dimensions but dimensions in depth, so it provides the best kind of view for identification."[4] McCamy testified that on the basis of his analysis, it was "extremely unlikely" the pictures were of a substituted body, or pictures which had been altered in any way.[5]

Dr. Baden took the stand. Speaking for the Forensic Pathology Panel, he testified that President Kennedy had been struck twice from behind. Much testimony was devoted to an error Baden claimed the autopsy doctors had made in locating the rear point of entry on the head. They had placed it four inches too low, he said, perhaps because they had written the autopsy report based on memory.[6]

Representative Preyer asked Baden: "How do you account for that when [they] actually saw the body . . . and [you] did not?" Replied Baden: "In general, the doctors who perform [an] autopsy have a better opportunity to make valid observations than those who come later, but in this instance, the photographs taken . . . and the X-rays taken . . . provide sufficient evidence for the panel members to arrive at valid . . . independent conclusions."[7]

Baden's testimony covered a wide variety of detail and took the better part of a day. Then came the high point of the hearings. Blakey announced: "It would be appropriate now, Mr. Chairman, to call Captain Humes." A jowly, tired-looking man stood up. Humes was now a professor of pathology at Wayne State University and Vice-President of Medical Affairs at St. John's Hospital in Detroit. Congressman Louis Stokes administered the oath. From the broadcast booth, all I could see directly was Humes' back. I watched his face on a small TV monitor screen. The Committee interrogator was Deputy Chief Counsel Gary Cornwell. (See Photo 36.)

Humes began: "I was summoned from my home late in [the] afternoon of that day by the Surgeon General of the Navy and the Commanding Officer of the Naval Medical Center, and the Commanding Officer of the Naval Medical School,* and much to my surprise, was told that the body of the late President was being brought to our laboratories and that I was to examine the President and ascertain the cause of death."[8]

Then came a question about when the autopsy began. Replied Humes: "Well, the President's body, as I recall, arrived about 7:35, 7:40 in the evening and after some preliminary examinations, about 8 or 8:15."[9] Humes had told the Warren Commission: after "certain . . . other examinations."[10] He included the same detail, just changing "certain other" to "some preliminary."

Cornwell asked: "About what time of the night was the autopsy finally concluded?"

Replied Humes: "Oh, I would estimate around midnight."[11]

Cornwell proceeded to say that, as Humes knew, the panel had reviewed his autopsy report, had spoken with him "on one prior occasion," and that there was ". . . one possible major area of disagreement, and that is with respect to the location of a bullet wound in the back of the President's head. . . ."[12]

Cornwell asked if it wasn't the case that there was "one and only one bullet wound to the back of the President's head, that it did enter in the rear, exited the front. Is that report accurate on those three points, to the best of your knowledge?"

"Absolutely," replied Humes.[13]

Cornwell showed Humes the Ida Dox drawing which was the exact replica of an autopsy photograph of the back of the head.** Cornwell edged into the controversy. "Our panel of forensic pathologists, of course, were not present during the autopsy, did not have access to the body, and, therefore, you and your colleagues who were there are in a unique position to provide testimony as to the nature of the wounds. . . ." Cornwell then noted that Humes had been examined once before by the House Select Committee, and picked out a spot at the bottom of the back of the head

---

*Respectively, Adm. Edward Kenney, Adm. Calvin Galloway, Capt. John Stover.

** There were four such photographs—two black-and-white (numbered 17 and 18) and two in color (numbered 42 and 43).

as the entrance wound. Cornwell read one excerpt after another from the transcript to indicate that Humes had steadfastly maintained that what Cornwell referred to as a "small droplet" at the bottom of the picture was the wound of entry.

All this was news to me. I had no idea that Humes had been called, and was surprised to learn that he had maintained his position in 1977.

Cornwell went through the same points Dr. Petty had enumerated in the closed session which would indicate that the lower position was the artifact, the upper position was the wound: the focus of the pictures, the way the ruler was held, etc.

The time had come for Humes to make a public retraction.

Cornwell asked Humes if he had had "a greater opportunity" to review the photographs "and if, after doing so, you have a more well-considered or a different opinion or whether your opinion is still the same; as to where the point of entry is?"

"Yes, I think that I do have a different opinion," replied Humes, but he said he had several comments to make before answering the question: "I go back further to the original autopsy report which we rendered, in the absence of any photographs of course. We made certain physical observations and measurements of these wounds. I state now those measurements we recorded then were accurate to the best of our ability to discern what we had before our eyes."[14]

I was electrified. That was the Commander Humes I knew from the twenty-six volumes of the Warren Commission: ". . . to the best of our ability to discern what we had before our eyes"—Humes had a way of saying things which were either perfectly obvious or extremely dramatic, depending on their context.

Now Humes returned to the Ida Dox drawing and the X-ray. And he didn't retract. He did concede that the bullet wound was at the upper location—not the lower location—but he then maintained that the upper location was the location he described in the autopsy report. "We described the wound of entrance in the posterior scalp as being above and to the right of the external occipital protuberance," said Humes.* "And it is obvious to me as I sit here . . . that the upper defect to which you pointed, or the upper object is clearly in the location of where we said approximately where it was . . . therefore, I believe that is the wound of entry."[16]

Humes then said that he attributed its apparently higher location to underlying skull fractures and the positioning of the head for the photo, "making some distortion of anatomic structures to produce this picture."[17]

* The autopsy report said the wound was located "2.5cm laterally to the right and slightly above the external occipital protuberance."[15]

He said the lower item which he had previously identified he had identified "erroneously" and "would not fit with the original autopsy findings."[18]

But it was the X-ray which was the source of measurement—four inches above the external occipital protuberance. Humes was now asked to step up to the enlargement of the X-ray and identify the wound. This he did, commenting that it was a "pleasure" to have such materials. "I didn't have anything of this kind formerly,"[19] he said. Cornwell asked Humes to describe in words the spot to which he was pointing.

Humes did not back down. "Well, in this approximate area would be about where the external occipital protuberance would be, the knob we can feel in the back of our head. This would be above it." By way of explanation he added: "There is a great enlargement here, so it looks considerably further away than it would be on a standard size film or on the skull. . . ."[20]

"If I might add, and more importantly, I had the opportunity, which none of the gentlemen had to do, to examine the President's skull from the inside when the brain was removed, with great care. There was one, and only one, wound of entrance."[21] Humes said its exact location had embroiled them in "somewhat of a semantic discussion."[22]

The X-ray of the head seemed to show large skull fragments. Commenting on them, he made a curious remark: ". . . this bullet was so disrupt[ive], those fragments I think could virtually be any place."[23] It was a strange remark considering that "those fragments" comprised most of the skullcap.

Cornwell then came to the fundamental question—that the panel had measured the wound on the X-ray and that they placed it at "approximately 10 centimeters above [the] external occipital protuberance. Would that discrepancy be explainable?"

Humes balked: "Well, I have a little trouble with that; 10 centimeters is a significant—4 inches." Humes then added: "I go back to the fact there was only one, period."[24]

That night the newspapers headlined that the autopsy doctor had admitted that he made a four-inch error. But did he admit that? I didn't think so. Humes stubbornly maintained that the wound depicted in the evidence was the one he described that night, suggesting that the enlargement on the X-ray might make it appear higher, and specifically stating, when confronted with the 100mm measurement: "I have a little trouble with that. . . ."

The rest of Humes' testimony was over in a few minutes. Humes told how he had called Dallas and learned about the throat wound, how it was decided that a committee of three couldn't write the report, "so I assumed the responsibility," and that he had burned the notes because they were bloodstained.[25]

One interchange seized my attention. This testimony seemed significant because of the possibility that a reconstruction was photographed and subsequently used as evidence. Humes said he stayed in the morgue to assist the morticians:

CORNWELL: During that period, were there efforts made to reconstruct the President's head?

HUMES: Yes, indeed.

CORNWELL: Would it be accurate to state that those efforts entailed handling of the head over a long period of time?

HUMES: Very accurate.[26]

Chairman Stokes asked Humes if he had anything to say; he was allowed five minutes to make a statement. Humes said he was "quite elated" that the findings of all the panels that had examined the autopsy X-rays and photographs "in such great detail, are in basic accordance with what we originally ascertained to be the situation. We are pleased by that.

"Our testimony before the Warren Commission is quite lengthy, as I am sure some of the Committee members are aware. However, I feel it also was hampered by our inability . . . to never have seen, after about midnight of that night, the X-rays, to never have seen at any time until a year or two after the Warren Commission the photographs which we made."*[27]

He closed by saying: "I will be pleased to answer any other questions from you, sir, or any other members of the Committee."[28]

But there were no questions.

Liebeler's question came back to me: "Humes can measure, can't he?"

When Humes left the stand, I went over and sat down beside him.

The Committee had tried to impeach his testimony, which stood in the way of their analysis. He should have had legal representation.

Sitting next to him, I could see that Humes' hands were trembling.

I asked him: "Dr. Humes, why don't you have a lawyer?"

He replied: "I don't need a lawyer. I have nothing to hide."

I said: "Dr. Humes, do you remember me? I called you up in 1966 and asked you about a statement in the FBI report that when the body was unwrapped there had been surgery of the head area, namely, in the top of the skull."

"No," he said. "I don't know who you are. I don't know of any such statement."

"Dr. Humes," I said, "in your testimony you said that prior to the autopsy there were 'certain preliminary examinations.' What did you mean by that?"

* Humes first saw the pictures on November 1, 1966, after the Kennedy donation. He saw them again on January 26, 1967, when he wrote the report referred to previously as the "Military Review."

Humes was obviously agitated; and my questions were not having a calming effect. He replied he meant taking the body out of the coffin, and taking the autopsy photographs. That's what he meant by "certain preliminary examinations." I was not persuaded.[29]

I said nothing more, and returned to the WETA booth.*

Soon the day's hearings were recessed. Watching this unfold was upsetting. I had spent years researching the case that the body had been altered, and was aware of the effort it took to explain the details of this hypothesis, even to a willing listener. Yet at heart the matter was simple. Now I was in Washington, and before my eyes another investigation was going down the same garden path. There is a peculiar feeling one gets in Washington. You see familiar senators and congressmen walking in the hallway or in the lunchroom. The government isn't distant. The levers of power are at hand. They can be pushed; events can be changed, or so it seems.

I went down to the floor where Andrew Purdy was standing.

Purdy had been a critic of the Report while at the University of Virginia. He knew the issues well. He also knew who I was, and that I was writing about the assassination.

I had decided to keep my distance from the Committee because I suspected their motives and methods. I believed they were creating the appearance of thoroughness. I felt I might be used, and didn't want my material discredited by a Committee dealing in appearances, not substance. But I felt some guilt about the course I was following, and now it came to a head.

I went over to Purdy and introduced myself. He seemed to remember me. I pointed to the large poster-sized exhibit showing the neck wound from the front and emphatically said: "That's not the way the body looked in Dallas. The wound wasn't that large. The body's been altered, and if you people don't address that question, you're not going to get anywhere with your investigation."

Purdy looked perplexed. He asked me: "Why would anybody enlarge the wound?"

"Andy," I said, "the body is evidence, and by altering the wounds, basic facts were changed."

Purdy seemed not to comprehend. I told him this was *the* fundamental issue and I wanted to speak with him before I left Washington.

The next day, Friday, September 8, began with the testimony of Dr.

---

* Two days later, Humes was questioned by Paul Hoch. Humes told Hoch: "I wish they'd asked some more questions. . . . I was surprised at the Committee members. . . . They sort of had a golden opportunity, you know. I was there, but they didn't choose to—and it didn't bother me one way or the other. Whatever pleased them, pleased me."

Petty, another member of the panel. Petty's presentation was primarily devoted to a rebuttal of Dr. Wecht's testimony of the previous day that the single-bullet theory wasn't tenable.

One point he made bore on my theory that the back wound had been situated "low" by mistake and was actually below the wound at the front of the throat. The day before, Dr. Baden said the panel placed the wound "a bit lower, almost 2 inches lower" than Humes did on the navy drawing.*[30] Petty testified that the bullet traveled through the body "in a somewhat upward direction anatomically speaking."[34] Here was testimony that the back wound was lower than the throat wound, and despite the explanation that Kennedy was bending forward, Petty's statement supported my theory that the back wound had been placed "low" by mistake, and that the photographs in evidence were in fact authentic.

Next came Larry Sturdivan. Anyone wishing to claim Kennedy was shot only from the back must account for the backward head-snap. Sturdivan was the Committee's answer. He provided a film of the assassination of a goat. In slow-motion film, he demonstrated that shooting a goat in the head could cause its neck to arch backwards and limbs to splay outward. This hardly explained what happened in Dallas because the Zapruder film showed that Kennedy went limp like a rag doll. No one even questioned this discrepancy, and it was precisely this sort of performance by the Committee that made me wonder about their motives.**

---

* Dr. Baden testified that X-rays showed the first thoracic vertebra was fractured[31]—completely new information. Humes had testified he could find no fractures.[32] I assumed the fracture was caused either when a false back wound was created or by the impact of a bullet from the front. Defenders of the Warren Report had cited lack of fractures as evidence that a bullet could (1) traverse the neck undamaged, and (2) traverse the neck without wobbling, thus creating a small exit wound.

Representative Preyer asked: "Could . . . the pristine bullet have nicked President Kennedy's vertebra and still have left the neat, clean exit wound in the throat?"

Baden replied with a hairsplitting argument: "Yes, sir. Usually, when a bullet strikes something of substance, it will begin to wobble, but as a bullet wobbles, there are times when it will be aligned in a straight-on directional course . . . it may have begun to wobble after it came out from the neck."[33]

** By this time, my view of the headsnap had changed considerably, and I no longer subscribed to the theory of a forward high-angle shot to explain the double motion. My revised view was inextricably linked to new information I had obtained bearing on the authenticity of the film.

In 1971, I was permitted to study, in the L.A. offices of Time-Life, a 35mm print made from what Time-Life called the "camera original" of the Zapruder film. To my surprise, I found that those frames showed the large head wound situated toward the right front, not at the rear of the head as reported by the Dallas observers. The rear of the head gave the appearance of having been "blacked out"— or of having been in deep shadow.

I also discovered splices on the film which had never been mentioned by Time-

Finally, on Friday afternoon, came the Committee's most potent scientific witness—Dr. Vincent Guinn, a nuclear chemist from the University of California at Irvine.

The three pieces of ammunition which linked the rifle to the assassination were found outside anyone's body—bullet 399 on the stretcher, and Commission Exhibits 567 and 569, the two large fragments found in the car on Friday night, November 22, at the White House garage.

But also in evidence were pieces of metal too tiny to be compared under the ballistic microscope, pieces allegedly found inside the bodies of the victims. They were Warren Commission Exhibit 843, two metal fragments removed from the brain (and the only metal removed from Kennedy's body at the autopsy), and Warren Commission Exhibit 842, the fragments removed from Connally's wrist.

The fragments were too small for ballistics tests, and the FBI, within twenty-four hours of the shooting, had done the routine spectrographic examination. Flame spectrography was used: a destructive test in which a tiny sample is burned and the color of the flame compared with known standards to reveal chemical composition. The results reported on November 23, 1963 were inconclusive. All the FBI could report was that the lead in the different samples was "similar,"[36] which is something like saying the "2" in "102" is "similar" to the "2" in "42"—not very enlightening. Several months later, at the request of the Warren Commission, the FBI attempted neutron activation analysis: a non-destructive test in which two samples to be compared are bombarded by neutrons and their radioactive

---

Life. I then began exploring the possibility that the Zapruder film itself had been altered sometime before it became Warren Commission evidence in 1964, perhaps even before it went to Life on November 23, 1963. (Life purchased the film on November 25, 1963, for $150,000.) But alteration of the film required a film laboratory with the sophisticated apparatus normally used by Hollywood to create "special effects." Was the original Zapruder film at some point taken to such a laboratory? Officially, the film went only from Zapruder to Kodak in Dallas; then to the Jamison Film Co. in Dallas, where three prints were made (two for the Secret Service, and one for Zapruder); then back to Zapruder, and then to the vault at Life. I suspected it had taken a secret detour, but I could find no direct evidence to prove that.

Then, in 1976, among records released by the CIA under the Freedom of Information Act, Paul Hoch found CIA item 450, a group of documents indicating that the Zapruder film was at the CIA's National Photo Interpretation Center (NPIC), possibly on Friday night, November 22, 1963, and certainly within days of the assassination. NPIC is one of the most sophisticated photo labs in the world.

The CIA documents indicate that the film, when at NPIC, was not yet numbered as it was later by the FBI Laboratory. CIA tables of frame numbers arranged in a multiple-column format bearing such headings as "frames on which shots occur" and "seconds between shots" explores various three-shot interpretations of the film. One document refers to the existence of either a negative or a master positive—and calls for the striking of four prints from that item: one "test print," and a second group of

characteristics compared. That can reveal what trace elements—minor impurities—exist, and in what concentrations; and that, in turn, permits a conclusion about the probability of common origin.

The FBI found the results inconclusive. It was not possible to tell, said their expert, from which of the larger bullets any of the smaller fragments might have come.

The critics were suspicious because the existence of those tests was not revealed until the 1970s, and the actual data themselves—FBI Laboratory worksheets—were not released until 1975, after a series of lawsuits under the Freedom of Information Act.

Critics believed that if the work was done properly it would immediately became apparent that Warren Commission Exhibits 399 and 842 (the metal from Connally's wrist) were different, and that would disprove the single-bullet theory.

Vincent Guinn was hired to do such tests. The Archives sent a courier to his laboratory at UC, Irvine, where he had a nuclear reactor. Guinn made measurements of the lead and antimony content of the bullets and found that 399 and the metal in the sample box labelled "CE 842" were statistically indistinguishable—which, in the language of the chemist, meant that they were identical.[37]

In early 1978, word leaked that the Committee had done this work,

---

three prints. The total job, it indicated, would take seven hours. The making of four prints is significant—that number is exactly what existed in Dallas: an original, and three prints made from that original.

In 1976, I interviewed Herbert Orth, the photo chief at *Life*. Orth believed the film never left his custody in 1963. Yet the CIA documents establish that it, or a copy, was worked on at the CIA's film lab in Washington. Indeed, the figures used in the CIA documents to describe the time intervals between shots—"74 frames later" and "48 frames after that"—are identical with those used in the first *Life* article about the film (*Life*, 11/29/63, "End to Nagging Rumors: The Six Critical Seconds"). Was the CIA supplying *Life* with data? Or did the agency have the film later, and was it reading *Life* for its information?

In my view, previously unreported CIA possession of the Zapruder film compromised the film's value as evidence: (1) the forward motion of Kennedy's head, for one frame preceding frame 313, might be the result of an altered film, and if that was so, it made the theory of a forward high-angle shot (see Chapter 2) completely unnecessary; (2) an altered film might also explain why the occipital area, where the Dallas doctors saw a wound, appears suspiciously dark, whereas a large wound appears on the forward right-hand side of the head, where the Dallas doctors saw no wound at all. Dr. Paul Peters, one of the Dallas doctors quoted in this book, when shown color blowups made from the Zapruder film frames depicting these wounds, wrote: "The wound which you marked . . . I never saw and I don't think there was such a wound. I think that was simply an artifact of copying Zapruder's movie. . . . The only wound I saw on President Kennedy's head was in the occipitoparietal area on the right side."[35]

and Blakey was repeatedly citing it as proof of the validity of the single-bullet theory.

But meanwhile, information of another sort became available. Audrey Bell, the operating-room nurse who had actually handled the metal from Connally's wrist on November 22 and given the fragments to a Texas Highway Patrolman, was interviewed by *Dallas Morning News* reporter Earl Golz. "She said she recalled seeing four or five bullet fragments being placed in a glass," wrote Golz, who pointed out that only three fragments were supposedly in evidence, according to the Commission. The issue, of course, was whether more metal had been removed from Connally than could have come from the base of bullet 399.[38] Upon hearing this, I asked Golz to reinterview her and ask her about the sizes, because it was often claimed they were no bigger than dust particles. Nurse Bell said: "No, they weren't dust particles because we wouldn't have been able to have taken those out. . . . They were larger than dust particles. They were small fragments . . . anywhere from 3 to 4mm in length by a couple of mm wide. . . . They were identifiable fragments."[39] Audrey Bell's description was quite inconsistent with the three grains, at most, missing from the base of 399.

With respect to the other fragments in evidence, there was also a problem. In 1969, the Secret Service sent documents to the National Archives that hadn't been released to the Warren Commission. One was an FBI receipt for "a missile removed . . . by Commander James J. Humes . . . on this date." The receipt, dated November 22, 1963, was issued to Capt. John Stover, Humes' superior, and signed by FBI agents Sibert and O'Neill.[40]

In May 1970, shortly after the release of the receipt, I wrote a letter to the FBI requesting an explanation. Back came a reply which didn't answer the question. I sent a follow-up letter. Several days later, I returned to my apartment and was surprised to find a note on the door from an FBI agent: "Please call John Morrison at FBI, Los Angeles. . . ." I called, and had a lengthy conversation noting that this receipt didn't seem to be for anything in the evidence. Morrison told me that according to head-quarters officials, the receipt for "a missile" was actually for the two tiny fragments removed from the brain. After that phone call, the FBI sent me a letter stating that in plain English.[41]

Thus, in the case of the brain fragments, there were irregularities associated with the documentation which recorded how they originally became evidence, and Nurse Bell's recollections raised similar questions about the Connally wrist fragments.

Guinn testified his tests showed that the brain fragments came from one of the two missiles found in the car, and that Commission Exhibit 842 came from the bottom of bullet 399, where some lead was missing.[42]

I cornered Guinn in the hallway afterward to question him further. He had testified that the fragments he measured didn't match in weight the ones the FBI had tested in 1964.[43] He also testified that although the FBI had been unable to draw a conclusion from their 1964 data, his analysis demonstrated that those samples, too, supported his conclusion. Guinn said he assumed the 1964 samples were from bullet 399, but he didn't know what had become of them.[44]

I asked Guinn about the legitimacy of the fragments as evidence, and whether he could have been fooled. He admitted: "Possibly they could take a bullet, take out a few little pieces and put it in the containers, and say: 'This came out of Connally's wrist.' And naturally, if you compare that with bullet 399, they'll look alike. I have no control over those things. I have to believe that these are honest people."[45]

Guinn talked about another matter bearing on the legitimacy of the fragments in the sample boxes. He told how he opened one box—Q-15, supposedly metal from the windshield—to find it completely empty. "What did you do?" I asked. He said that he carefully examined the interior of the sample box with a magnifying glass, but nothing was there.[46]

Guinn's work played a major role in convincing the Committee that bullet 399 had struck Connally's wrist—hence, that Kennedy and Connally were struck by the same bullet.

If this were an ordinary murder case, I could accept that. But in light of the evidence that the body had been altered, and the numerous irregularities concerning the chain of possession on the fragments, what Guinn's testimony showed me was the naiveté of the critics—myself included—in believing that plotters would plant bullets, but leave genuine fragments in the FBI sample boxes, thereby leaving their scheme at the mercy of spectrographic tests.

It was also another instance of the Committee's less-than-thorough investigation. They never called Audrey Bell as a witness.

By Friday afternoon, September 8, the critics had had their day in court, and lost. There was a certain inevitability to this process. What I had seen in the last two days was a rerun of the debate between the critics and the Warren Commission which had been going on since 1964. The debate had a predictable structure: the head-snap versus the autopsy findings; or the Dealey Plaza eyewitnesses versus the autopsy findings; or the Dallas doctors versus the autopsy. But whereas in the mid-1960s defenders of the Report said Humes couldn't have lied, now they said photos and X-rays couldn't lie. In both instances, suspicion had been focused on the investigators. But the problem wasn't the investigators, it was the evidence.

On Saturday morning, September 9, 1978, two days after Humes testified, I called Purdy at his office. Speaking with a member of the staff of the House Assassinations Committee was strange, because they had been instructed to accept information, but were supposed to give no feedback whatsoever. At the hearing room, I had forcefully asserted the existence of changes on the body, but had not mentioned a key piece of evidence—the statement about surgery in the Sibert and O'Neill report. Now I told Purdy about that statement.

It was my strong impression that until that conversation, Purdy hadn't the faintest notion that such a statement was in that FBI report. I told him that there was much anatomic information in the record to indicate that the body had been altered, and that I'd like to come up to his office and review it with him.

Purdy said that given what the autopsy photographs showed, what I was really saying was that "somebody rebuilt the back of his head." I replied that certainly some such thing must have occurred before photography, but that the fundamental change between Dallas and Bethesda was a little hole becoming a much bigger hole.

Throughout the conversation, which lasted about a half hour, Purdy seemed ambivalent, expressing a strong interest on the one hand, but playing devil's advocate on the other—as if he had already come to terms with the divergent Dallas descriptions, and that for some reason that just wasn't strong enough evidence.

I told Purdy that I had a manuscript which set forth the medical data, and that I'd like to show it to him. Purdy agreed to see me and asked me to call him back to arrange a meeting.

I returned to where I was staying and prepared briefing notes.

When I called Purdy, he said he would not meet me. Time was not a factor, he said. It was "too risky" because I was with the media. I could misrepresent the meeting. I could say he had said something.

"Put me on inquiry notice," Purdy said. "What's 'inquiry notice'?" I asked. He replied: "You've got to send me something so that I'll have to act on it, something that would make me look bad if I don't."

I turned to my briefing notes and proceeded through every single point on the telephone, to make sure that he understood what I was talking about.

On Monday, September 11, the House Committee presented the testimony of acoustics expert Dr. James Barger, who testified about the most striking new development in the House Committee's investigation. As a result of the efforts of a group of Dallas researchers, the Committee learned of the existence of a tape recording of Dallas Police radio transmissions, and the researchers' analysis that it contained the sound of the shots. The Committee located the original tape and sent it to Dr. Barger's firm—Bolt Beranek and Newman. In August 1978, Dr. Barger went to Dallas and conducted an audio reconstruction of the assassination. Guns were fired from two locations—the Texas School Book Depository and the grassy knoll—and the echoes were compared with the sounds heard on the tape.

Barger's conclusion was that the tape contained the sounds of four shots—and that the third one appeared to come from the grassy knoll.[47]

I could see what was coming next—the Committee now had audio evidence that a shot came from the front, but medical evidence that the shots came from the rear. The Committee was going to conclude that the President was shot by Oswald, but that another shooter had fired and missed.

Before leaving Washington, I spoke with another Committee attorney, Belford Lawson, III, in charge of the Committee's investigation of the Secret Service planning for the President's Dallas trip. For about thirty minutes, at a table in the House cafeteria, I explained my medical alteration theory, pointing out the implications with respect to the trip planning. The route had been charted by Secret Service officials. The same agency had custody of the body. If the body was altered, the sequence of events leading to Kennedy's making the trip to Dallas and the selection of the route ought to be subject to new scrutiny. Lawson sat, sphinx-like. I asked if he understood what I was saying. He said he understood "exactly" what I was saying. Then he gave me a weak handshake and an extremely formal reply that if I had anything more to say I should make an appointment to see someone on the Committee.

I flew back to New York. On October 13, I spoke with Michael Ewing for almost two hours and explained the surgery hypothesis in considerable detail. Ewing said the Committee was doing a great job. He claimed that the Dallas doctors were "a bunch of liars."

The next week, I called the House Select Committee again to talk with Ed Lopez, a member of the staff. To my surprise, Professor Blakey answered the phone. We talked for almost an hour. I went through my theory again. Blakey is a thoughtful person. But it was also clear that we had differing views. "If this case proves one thing," said Blakey, "it proves that oral testimony, observational testimony, by people, is generally unreliable. And what you have to do is get a hard core of what I could call scientific evidence, real evidence." Wesley Liebeler would have called it "best evidence." In considerable detail, Blakey explained why he believed the Dallas observations could be discounted, why it was possible to discount even Humes' testimony.

When he was through, I said: "Professor Blakey, all you have is a theory as to why there is error in the observations." My theory, I said, "addressed the conflicts directly."

Blakey said he was openminded, that it was the eleventh hour, but he would be glad to read my manuscript.

Blakey left little doubt about how he viewed the conspiracy issue. "The dynamite's in the fourth shot," he said more than once. I told Blakey the "dynamite" was if any shots struck from the front and were removed before the autopsy. He disagreed: "I find it much easier to suppose the shot from the front missed than to suppose that it hit." He told me: "You've got a rough uphill road to run to convince me that the underlying material is inauthentic."

"I'm sitting here as a writer," I said. "You have the power to call in Sibert and say: 'Why did you write down "surgery of the head area"? And why did you tell Lifton in 1966 "The report stands"?' "

"I sure do," he replied.

"You guys can break that conspiracy," I said. "There was something at Bethesda that night called a pre-autopsy inspection of the skull, and if you would call the right witnesses, and I really mean this, Professor Blakey, you could crack that aspect of the case. You could prove that the body was altered."

Blakey said that if I would send him "raw material," he would be willing to evaluate it. "I wouldn't do it in a public hearing necessarily—there's all kinds of places you can do it. . . . The main thing I'd do is put them under oath."

The next morning I had the most detailed conversation of all with a member of the House Committee's staff, speaking for more than two and a half hours with Ed Lopez, a Cornell law student who, I had been told, was close to Blakey. I asked Lopez to take notes, and I went through most of the manuscript in detail. Lopez was clearly sympathetic, but his authority was limited.

I soon decided that for better or worse I was not going to send my manuscript to the House Select Committee. I had now spoken with five people on the Committee, including the General Counsel. They had the basic idea, and I felt that if they really wanted to pursue it, they could. Certainly they were not in the position of the Warren Commission who, it could be argued, were genuinely deceived because they had never even considered the possibility. But I had the impression the Committee was dealing in appearances—they were anxious to be able to say they had considered everything, and I did not want my manuscript to become a hostage to that process.

This impression was strengthened in a conversation I had with Lopez shortly thereafter. Lopez told me he had spoken with Purdy, and that Purdy did not take the idea of body alteration seriously. "Exactly what did he say?" I asked. Lopez said Purdy thought the idea was impossible, that the whole world would have to be involved. He said Purdy exclaimed: "Now *that's* what I call a conspiracy."

In December 1978, there was a new development in the area of conspiracy. The press had largely downplayed the acoustics analysis because Barger had hedged his testimony, saying that it was only a 50-50 probability there was a fourth shot. The 50-50 probability came from the fact that the position of the motorcycle had only been estimated within eighteen feet. The Committee hired two additional consultants, Dr. Mark Weiss and

Ernest Aschkenasy, who performed a more refined analysis. Using scale drawings, they computed the predicted echo pattern of Dealey Plaza. Then they compared the predicted echoes with the impulses of the "fourth" shot on the tape. Their conclusion, leaked to the press several days before their testimony, was that the probability was not 50 percent, but 95 percent that the fourth sound was a gunshot-like noise emanating from the grassy knoll.

Those hearings were held on December 29, 1978, and were broadcast live by the Public Broadcasting Service.

I sat at the press table as Counsel Blakey delivered the opening statement. For all its faults, the House Select Committee had come a long way from the Warren Commission's view of the case. It was a strange transformation. Blakey read the litany of the grassy knoll witnesses, the same witnesses rejected by the Warren Commission in 1964, taken seriously now by the General Counsel of a House Select Committee. I could see Blakey's hands tremble as he read the statement.

I had a sense that this rather conservative man knew he was opening a Pandora's Box.

Why were the grassy knoll witnesses credible now? Because the "best evidence" was the tape; the tape could not be denied.

Then followed, for several hours, the testimony of experts Weiss and Aschkenasy—explaining their charts and diagrams, saying that the analysis was simple to understand, that it could be "understood by anybody who has ever heard an echo."[48]

Some of the congressmen resisted. Congressman Edgar asked: "Dr. Weiss, are you aware of the phenomenon that exists out on the open sea when ships are trying to locate the port and they hear a forghorn in the distance? Are you aware . . . that occasionally the sound from that foghorn directs the ship in a false direction, as opposed to the accurate direction of seeking a safe harbor, and, in fact in some instances those ships wind up on the rocks and go in exactly the opposite direction of where they should go?"

The metaphor was clear. Dr. Weiss answered simply, "No, sir, I am not,"[49] and the audience exploded with laughter and applause.

The experts had tested the tape against Dealey Plaza with only two assumed shooter locations. With more extensive tests, it could well be that other information on the tape might represent the sounds of additional shots. Blakey himself said to more than one researcher that there might be more than four shots on the tape, but he treated that statement as an "investigative hypothesis." I thought it was a good one.

When the hearing recessed, I buttonholed Andrew Purdy and asked what he had done with the "head surgery" information I had passed on in September. Purdy told me he had spoken with FBI Agent Sibert. "He disagrees with your theory," said Purdy.

"Well then, why did he say there was surgery in the FBI report he wrote?" I asked.

"He says that that was just an initial impression. He said he thought there had been surgery because when the body first arrived, the hole in the top of the head was so big, before they brought in the bone fragments."

"Andy," I said, "that's not what he told me. I spoke to him in November 1966, that's twelve years ago. I read him the statement twice, and he said: 'The report stands.' And I have a tape of that. Also, are you aware that there are FBI documents in that hundred thousand pages that indicate that Hoover took the position that the statement was based on oral statements made in the autopsy room? Did your research staff get those for you?"

Purdy was clearly miffed. "No," he replied. "Look, David, why didn't you bring that to my attention? I can only look into it if you bring it to my attention."[50]

To the House Committee the fourth-shot evidence could have been a radical door-opener; but it was used merely as a perturbation on the Oswald-did-it theory.

Blakey announced that in view of the fourth-shot evidence, he had gone back to his medical panel—that they insisted there was no question about it, only two shots struck from behind.

I thought the fourth shot cried out not for a re-examination of the "medical evidence"—photographs and X-rays—but for an examination of the authenticity of that evidence. But neither Blakey nor anybody else on the Committee had the slightest inclination to pursue such an investigation.

In early January 1979, the House Committee released its findings— four shots, probably a conspiracy, probably a Mafia plot. Much of the press comment was derisive.

Editorials criticized the Committee for having wasted the taxpayers' money. One newspaper suggested its report be filed in the wastebasket. The *New York Times*, apparently not challenging the acoustics evidence, objected to the word "conspiracy." "The word is freighted with dark connotations of malevolence. . . . 'Two maniacs instead of one' might be more like it."[51] The *Washington Post* said: ". . . leave the matter where it now rests, as one of history's most agonizing unresolved mysteries."[52]

Blakey and many members of his staff stayed on for six months, putting together a report that was promised first in February, then March, and was finally published in July 1979.

Watching the House investigation unfold, I had the feeling I was watching a play I had seen several times before—in Liebeler's class, in the working papers of the Warren Commission, in numerous debates between defenders and critics of the Warren Report. The script was taught in law school. It was an argument about authority. If you understood the concept of "best evidence," the outcome was predictable.

There were basically three representations of the body: the Dallas version and the two Bethesda versions—what I called the three lenses. The Warren Commission had looked at the body through the Dallas lens and through the first Bethesda lens, invoked the concept of best evidence, and rejected the Dallas version. Now this Committee had looked through the third lens and concluded that the X-rays and photographs superseded everything that preceded them.

The lawyers talked as if they had based their conclusions on the body. They had not. The body was buried at Arlington.

Like the smile on the Cheshire cat, all that remained were the stories told by three lenses.

PART VI

1979: The Coffin/Body Problem

1979: The Coffin/ Body Problem

CHAPTER 25

The Lake County Informant

DURING THE SPRING OF 1979, I was writing the final chapters of this book, aware that there were certain loose ends in my theory that I needed to investigate.

I had evidence, but no proof, of where the body might have been altered. I tended toward the theory that the alterations took place in the Bethesda autopsy room because of information I had accumulated that the body had been brought to the morgue considerably earlier than the start of the official autopsy. I had developed evidence of two separate and distinct entries of the same Dallas casket into the morgue.

The motorcade from Andrews Air Force Base pulled up at Bethesda at 6:55.* Mrs. Kennedy got out and went directly into the hospital. The *Washington Star* said that for twelve minutes after Mrs. Kennedy went inside, the ambulance stayed at the hospital's main entrance. The *Post* reported that officers gathered at the door of the ambulance, that Admiral Calvin Galloway got inside, and drove away. In conversation with me, the Admiral denied that he drove, but admitted he was in the ambulance.

The ambulance therefore pulled away at about 7:07.

The evidence for what followed came from two different sources: FBI agents Sibert and O'Neill, and members of the Military District of Washington casket team. Each group reported entirely different experiences. The FBI agents reported they followed the ambulance to the rear, and that the "preparation for the autopsy" began at 7:17.[1] The casket team told me of a mixup between two navy ambulances—one referred to as the "decoy"—

---

* This is the time mentioned in Secret Service reports. *Washington Star* reporter William Grigg gave the time as 6:53, and the AP used that time too. 6:55 will be used henceforth in this book.

and an ambulance chase, which culminated with their carrying in the casket at 8:00 P.M.

Were there then two separate casket entries, one at 7:17 and another at 8:00?

The most promising lead to an answer seemed to be the May 1975 story in the Waukegan *News-Sun,* sent to me by a fellow-critic, Wallace Milam, of Dyersberg, Tennessee. The Lake County informant, whoever he was, had apparently witnessed the arrival of the body at the back door. He said the ambulance that arrived at the front was empty. I thought he must be wrong.

But probably the Lake County man had seen the Sibert and O'Neill arrival. His evidence might be helpful.

In fact, by the time I set out to find the Lake County man, I had worked out in my mind an entire theory about the account he would provide.

The language used by FBI agents Sibert and O'Neill to describe the entrance of the body at the rear of Bethesda Naval Hospital was subject to the interpretation that the body had been brought in separately from the casket. Their description consisted of two sentences—the first said "the body" had been brought inside; the second, that Bureau agents assisted with "the casket."* But I couldn't be sure that my interpretation was correct. It was possible that in writing their report, Sibert and O'Neill had simply used "the casket," in the second sentence, as a synonym for "the body" in the first. But, if the Lake County man's account clearly conflicted with the casket team's about the details of the entry—e.g., if he said he had seen President Kennedy's body carried in on a stretcher, followed by some federal agents assisting with the Dallas casket—that would have confirmed my interpretation of the FBI report. The result would be corroboration for my chronological analysis, which indicated that the Dallas casket entered Bethesda twice—shortly before 7:17 P.M., and again at 8:00 P.M.

This, then, was my expectation for the account the Lake County informant might provide.

It was May 1979. Time was slipping by. Suppose I couldn't find the Lake County man?

That month, I called Art Petersen, who had written the story four years before. Petersen had no recollection of the man's name, and did not recall what rank he held at the hospital, but he assured me that he was

---

* The agents had written that after Jacqueline and Robert Kennedy left the ambulance at the front, "The ambulance was thereafter driven around to the rear entrance where the President's body was removed and taken into an autopsy room. Bureau agents assisted in the moving of the casket to the autopsy room."[2]

credible. Petersen had met with him for several hours, had kept no notes of the interview, had no tape recording.

A few days later, Petersen called back. He had found a notation in a file—the man's name was Dennis David. He had lived in a farming town nearby, but had moved. Petersen told me he thought he was in a small farming community in a midwestern state.

I called Information, only to find there were innumerable people by that name, and over five hundred such "small farming communities." Since Petersen's information was about four years old, it seemed it would be an extravagant stroke of luck if I found the man.

Then I had a stroke of luck of a different kind. About that time, I met someone who could get current addresses from military personnel records. A check produced the name, address, and telephone number of Dennis Duane David—who lived in a town I had never heard of, in an area whose code I had never dialed.

On July 2, 1979, I placed the call. A clear and friendly voice with a Southern accent answered. I identified myself, said that I was writing a book on the events of November 22, and that the reporter for the *Waukegan News-Sun* had given me Mr. David's name.

Dennis David was perfectly friendly. He was willing to tell me whatever he remembered. He told me that he retired from the navy as a Lieutenant Commander in the Medical Service Corps. On November 22, he said, he was a First Class, or E6, Petty Officer.

Dennis David was an editor of training manuals for Hospital Corpsmen, affiliated with the U.S. Navy Medical School, Bethesda.

Regarding November 22, 1963, he said: "On that particular night, I was Chief of the Day for the Medical School."

When he heard about the assassination, he went to the office of the Master at Arms and sat there, listening to the radio with Dr. Boswell.

At about 5:00 or 5:30, he said, the radio announcer reported that Kennedy's body was being flown in from Texas, and would be taken to the Medical School.

To this point, Dennis David's recollection was accurate. I had the AP teleprinter output, and at 4:56, AP had announced the body was being brought to Bethesda. I told him about that, and asked him to continue.

"That was the first indication that we had that it was even coming here," he told me. He said that he looked at Dr. Boswell, "and I made some comment, I said—'Boy, you're in for it tonight . . . the rest of us are too.' Because, you know, I'm not that stupid. I had an idea what kind of security was going to be involved."

Dennis David said that the Chief of the Day for the Medical Center command was in touch with him within fifteen minutes, and that Secret Service agents were at the hospital. "They called us together. . . . I was asked to get a certain number of people to help guard the doors, to stand at the elevators, to act as roving patrols to keep sightseers and other morbid people out." He also said he made telephone calls to various members of the morgue crew "to call them to come in."

He said he did not watch the arrival at Andrews Air Force Base on TV: "I didn't have the time."

At some point, David received notification "that the ambulance with the body was arriving at the morgue. And we went down there, and then it was taken off and placed in the morgue facility."

I asked David how the body was brought in. He replied: "In a casket."

I was disappointed. I had pinned my hopes on the possibility that the body and the casket had parted ways at the back door. But as Dennis David continued, I grew uneasy. The casket entry he described didn't sound like the casket team's, and it didn't sound like Sibert and O'Neill's either.

Dennis David said he had called "seven or eight sailors" to help unload the casket. He stood there watching the unloading. Did you actually help? I asked. "No. I had several men doing that. I was Chief of the Day. I was supposed to be the supervisor. . . . I was standing off to one side, watching the casket being brought in, and then followed it into the morgue facility."

Sibert and O'Neill made no mention of sailors unloading a casket.

I asked the obvious question: "How do you know that the official motorcade from the airport contained only an empty casket?"

Dennis David replied that he didn't actually see the second ambulance arrive at the back, but that the first ambulance had the body. That's how he knew the second one was empty.

I said: "There's a casket team that actually carries in the casket . . . the official casket with all the regalia, the ceremonial team, the Fort Meyer group."

"Right," he said.

"You're saying they carried in an empty casket."

"Yes," he said.

Still I didn't understand why he said that. He spoke very matter-of-factly about it. I couldn't understand his basis for that statement.

"But they come in the same back door, don't they? . . . Both caskets passed through the same entrance into the hospital?"

"As far as I know," he replied.

At my request, David repeated his story. As he did, I noticed that he said the casket that actually held the body "had come in through the back gate . . . which was located over there by the Officers' Club."

He assured me that when this ambulance—this "first" one—arrived, all the senior officers were present: "Dr. Boswell, who was the Officer of the Day, and Dr. Humes, plus the chief of the Bureau of Medicine and

Surgery was there, and the Chief of the Army and the Chief of the Air Force Medical Departments were already there, at the morgue."

Dennis David repeated quite matter-of-factly that there were two caskets, that the second one was empty.

"I was told by the doctor that the body was in the first casket."

"Oh, I see," I said, trying to be mellow. "Which doctor said that to you?"

"Dr. Boswell."

"Boswell said the body was in the first casket?"

"Yep."

"In other words, Boswell knew there were two caskets?"

"Right."

"He told you this, then?"

"Well, he told me . . . that the body came in the casket, the one when I was down there, which was the one that came in the back gate. . . ."

Now I was thoroughly confused. What did Dennis David mean by "the back gate"? He repeated it more than once—that the first casket came in an ambulance, "that one [that] came in the back gate." That didn't sound like Sibert and O'Neill. They followed a navy ambulance from the front.

I fastened on the layout of Bethesda. "Just so I get this straight. Let me start with some of the geometry of Bethesda. When you say 'the back door,' it came in through the back door, we're talking about the morgue jetty, are we not?"

"Yes."

"Okay. But when you say 'it came up through the back way,' you mean something else . . . or do you? In other words, the first one that arrived didn't enter from the main entrance of the hospital. It didn't come in through the main gate. Is that what you mean?"

"Right."

"It came in through another area?"

Dennis David now drew me a verbal map. (See Fig. 40.)

The front of the National Naval Medical Center faces Wisconsin Avenue, which runs north and south. David said that there was also a back, or east, entrance to the grounds. He couldn't remember the name of it, but it ended in "Road." (A map and a telephone check with Bethesda later established that it was Jones Bridge Road.) David continued that the road from the east entrance ". . . comes in from the back gate, and goes by the Officers' Club, and then comes down by the barracks, and up the little hill, and then goes around into the morgue entrance, and ends up at the jetty there [at the back]. . . . And that's what I'm talking about 'coming in the back way.' The *other* ambulance came up Wisconsin Avenue proper . . . the front entrance of Bethesda."

Things were beginning to clear up. David was speaking of two ambu-

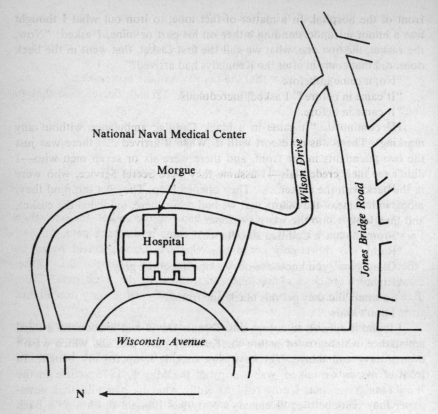

Figure 40.
Grounds of National Naval Medical Center, Bethesda, Maryland

lances coming onto the grounds of the National Naval Medical Center by two separate entrances. But this didn't fit the report of Sibert and O'Neill or the evidence of the casket team.

Dennis David explained that the navy ambulance "came in . . . the front entrance of Bethesda. And then went on around, and went back. And I was not there when it came in. It was—I don't know—fifteen, thirty minutes *after* the other casket had arrived."

When Dennis David first made this statement—that the casket entry he had witnessed occurred *before* the navy ambulance carrying the Dallas casket arrived at the front entrance, it confused me. I didn't understand what he was talking about. To this point, I had assumed that, whatever took place, all the arrivals at the morgue entrance at the rear of the hospital took place *after* the motorcade with the Dallas casket arrived at the front of the hospital. In a matter-of-fact tone, to iron out what I thought was a minor misunderstanding either on his part or mine, I asked: "Now, the casket, the first one, what we call the first casket, that went in the back door, did that come in after the Kennedys had arrived?"

"No, it came in before."

"It came in before?" I asked, incredulous.

"It came in before."

He continued: "It came in a black Cadillac ambulance without any markings. There was no escort with it. When it arrived . . . there was just the two attendants in the front, and there were six or seven men who—I didn't see their credentials—I assume they were Secret Service, who were in the back with the casket. . . . They opened it up. They got out, and they, along with some of the sailors that we had down there, unloaded the casket, and they took it into the morgue proper."

"From the black Cadillac ambulance?"

"Right."

"Okay. Now, you know the navy ambulances are gray."

"Right."

"So where did they get this black one from?"

"I don't know."

I found it difficult to accept this. Dennis David had introduced a third ambulance, which arrived before the Kennedy party did, and which wasn't even a navy ambulance. Yet he wasn't making it up for my benefit. In front of me, as we talked, was a copy of the May 1, 1975 article in the *Waukegan News-Sun*. I now read carefully what he had told that newspaper four years before: "Kennedy's body was brought in through a back door in an unmarked ambulance. An official motorcade from the airport contained only an empty casket. . . ." Until now, I had never paid attention to the words "unmarked ambulance."

"You are a personal witness to the black Cadillac ambulance?" I asked.

"Right."

"And that ambulance—the black Cadillac ambulance—is distinct and different from the Kennedy ambulance? We'll call it the 'navy ambulance'?"

"Right."

"That was escorted in by the military casket team?"

"Right. From the front. *It* came in the front . . . that's the one that came in from the Wisconsin Avenue entrance."

Throughout the conversation, Dennis David kept referring to the vehicle he saw as a black Cadillac "ambulance." Later, he explained what he meant by "black Cadillac ambulance": "I'm sure you've seen a number of funerals with the black hearse in front. That's what it was, if you want to call it a hearse. I've always called it an ambulance."

David gave me further details about the black Cadillac "ambulance."

"There were just two attendants—a driver and another attendant. . . . It seems to me that they were both wearing white smocks . . . there was no indication it was a military vehicle because, well—that was one of the things that seemed strange kind of at the time. I didn't know why, but— there were just these six, seven—seven or eight—big men in the back with the casket, who were in civilian clothes. . . . I assumed they were Secret Service."

The motorcade arrived at 6:53–6:55. The FBI reported preparation for the autopsy started at 7:17. The casket team carried in a casket at 8:00 P.M.

When did this happen? Why a third vehicle?

My first reaction was that he must be wrong about the sequence of arrivals. But if that was his error, then his account still conflicted with the one I had obtained from some members of the casket team. They had seen two navy ambulances, but no *hearse*. Was it possible they didn't see two ambulances, but one ambulance and a hearse?

"I don't doubt your story or anything," I said, "but I was wondering— is it possible the Kennedy ambulance arrived at the front, and then for a security measure, they put it [the body] into a black Cadillac ambulance *after* it reached Bethesda? In other words, how do you know that the black Cadillac ambulance arrived at the back before the Kennedy ambulance arrived at the front if you're at the back?"

"Okay. I see what you're saying. All right. *After* I was down at the [back], after the black ambulance was there, *then* I went back up to the front of the Naval Medical Center . . . [to] the Commanding Officer's office . . . and other areas [which] were on the second floor. And if you've walked into the Navy Medical Center, you know there's a huge rotunda, and the second floor is kind of on a balcony; and there's a couple of offices back to the [west] of there. I was in the office, and was standing there looking out toward Wisconsin Avenue, when the motorcade with the navy ambulance in the lead came in the front gate. This was like fifteen or twenty, thirty minutes *after* the black ambulance had arrived."

As calmly as possible, I asked: "You're telling me that you actually witnessed this up on the second floor?"

"Up on the second floor. Yes, looking out a window . . . in an office."

"I see. so you actually witnessed the arrival with the motorcycles and the whole business."

"Yes. Up there."

"Did you watch Jackie get out of the ambulance with Robert Kennedy?"

"I was standing right on the second floor balcony when Mrs. Kennedy came through the door of the front entrance of the Naval Medical Center."

I began to understand that my time scale, and my preconceptions, had prevented me from understanding the story he was telling me.

No wonder Dennis David "knew" the coffin was empty. He didn't have to remember the exact times. He relied on his recollection of the sequence. If a coffin with the body arrived at the back before the Kennedy motorcade with the Dallas casket arrived at the front, the body obviously was not in the Dallas casket.

There was more to his story. David told me that the men he worked with discussed the matter. He distinctly recalled having one conversation. "It was one of the federal agents that made the statement, that said something—or someone said about 'Why two caskets?' and 'Why the rigmarole?' And some federal agent said some statement to the effect—'Deception in case anybody attempted to hijack [the body]' or 'To keep things a little more in control.' I'm not sure exactly what he was getting at at that time."

"Sure, I understand," I answered. "Now, was this statement made to you?"

"In my presence," replied Dennis David. "Not directly *to* me. . . . Somebody else said something, some of the other kids that were there at the time knew that there was two caskets also, and because they were involved in this, and they made that comment; and were told that the reason was they [the authorities] were afraid maybe . . . somebody might try to kidnap it, or it might be—delays. People might gather round and delay the traffic. Arguments of this type."

The implications of David's story, I found, were easiest to grasp by visualizing the casket's journey from Dallas to Bethesda and examining the sequence of scenes in reverse order.

The final scene showed the motorcade under full police escort, with the navy ambulance in the lead, coming down Wisconsin Avenue and arriving at the front of the National Naval Medical center. Driving was William Greer. Sitting beside him were Secret Service agents Roy Kellerman and Paul Landis. Sitting on Landis' lap was Adm. George Burkley.[8] The journey from Andrews to Bethesda took about forty-five minutes.[4] FBI Agents Sibert and O'Neill were in the third car behind the ambulance.[5] The car immediately behind the ambulance contained Dave Powers, Kenneth O'Donnell, and Larry O'Brien.[6] No one reported any stops. Seven people were in the ambulance. In the back, Jacqueline Kennedy, Robert Kennedy, and Godfrey McHugh sat next to the casket. If David's account was correct, that casket was empty. But an empty casket upon arrival at Bethesda meant that the casket placed aboard the ambulance at Andrews Air Force Base must have been empty. That brought up the preceding scene.

There, the casket was put aboard the ambulance at Andrews Air Force Base. Secret Service agents carried the casket from a yellow army cargo lift at the left rear of the aircraft, to the ambulance, a distance of about fifteen feet. That brief journey was broadcast live on national TV. It was then, according to members of the honor guard, that Secret Service agents prevented them from carrying the casket. Manchester reported that it "wobbled wildly."*[7] An empty casket at Bethesda meant an empty casket was taken off that lift.

Going backwards, the next scene was the brief vertical journey from the top position of the lift to the bottom. It took place in the eye of national TV: Jacqueline Kennedy, her hand clutched tightly in Robert Kennedy's, standing next to the casket, surrounded by Kennedy aides.

The coffin on the lift came from just inside the rear door, in the tail compartment. That scene began when *Air Force One* rolled to a halt. The rear port door was opened. Outside the plane, the lift was rolled up, then was slowly raised. Standing atop it was Lt. Sam Bird, his gloved hand in a salute. Inside the airplane, Godfrey McHugh and the others struggled with the coffin, moving it from its berth the few feet to the port door, then taking it off the airplane and putting it on the lift. That too was on national TV. An empty casket at the top of the lift meant that the casket on the airplane must have been empty.

Jacqueline Kennedy, Larry O'Brien, Kenneth O'Donnell, Dave Powers, Godfrey McHugh—all rode in the tail compartment. All were near the coffin, drinking scotch, reminiscing, crying.

Kennedy's wife and closest associates established an ironclad chain of possession of the casket.

If David was correct that the casket was empty at the Bethesda front entrance, it must have been empty on takeoff from Dallas.

The result followed logically, but I could barely believe it. Dennis David's account implied the body had been surreptitiously removed earlier in the day. When? Where? How could that be?

It was with relief that I returned to a more mundane matter: David's experiences in typing up a receipt for bullet fragments. The 1975 story read: "He also questions the whereabouts of the memo he typed following the autopsy, at the direction of a Secret Service agent. The memo for the official record of the autopsy stated four large pieces of lead were removed. . . ." Dennis David explained to me what happened.

"Sometime in the evening, one of my superiors . . . came with a Secret Service man. And he said: 'Denny, you work in the Administrative Offices. You can type, can't you?' I said 'Yes.' 'Do you have a clearance?' And I

---

* In his December 10, 1963 report, Lieutenant Bird wrote that when the team "moved forward to secure the casket [it] was disrupted by a host of agents moving forward pushing the team out of the way. The agents then placed the casket in an awaiting navy ambulance."[8] NBC videotapes of the event clearly show that although the casket was carried by Secret Service agents, at least two men from the military casket team managed to play a role. Sailor Hubert Clark is seen, his back to the camera, as the casket was taken from the lift; and as it was put into the ambulance, photographs show Air Force Sergeant Gaudreau reaching inside to help.

said, 'Yes. I have up to and including Secret clearance.' And the Secret Service man then says, 'Well, I want you to type this memo.' And we went into what was my office then—the Administrative Office . . . at that time—and I sat down and typed this memo. Exactly what it said, I don't even remember, [but] to the effect that these pieces of lead had been removed from . . . and there was a description—so many centimeters high, so many centimeters long, so many centimeters thick, etc. . . . And so I typed that memo for the Secret Service man. And I don't remember even whose signature I typed on it."

I asked him if "Kellerman" or "Greer" rang any bells. He said he had no recollection, that even when he talked to Art Petersen in 1975, too many years had passed.

But David was certain that there were four pieces of metal, and that each was identified by size.

David said the memo was "One page—a half sheet" on a five-by-eight memo form.

He said that he kept no copies. "I just typed it on an original . . . and handed it to the Secret Service agent. And he made some comment about, 'This is considered classified material. Secret.' Or something to that effect."

David said the closest time estimate he could give for this was sometime between 10:00 P.M. and midnight.

I now returned to the sequence of coffin arrivals. I wanted to know more about the basis for his belief that there were in fact two separate coffins.

David told me: "Early the next morning, some time around three thirty, four o'clock in the morning . . . a bunch of us who had been involved in this were sitting down in the galley having coffee. And someone made the comment that: 'Hey, did you know there were two caskets?' I said 'Yes.' And then somebody else said: 'Yeah, but the second one was empty.' And I said, you know, I said, 'Which one are you talking about?' They said, 'The one that came in on the motorcade, the one with all the traffic.' He said the actual body came in the first one, which didn't have any trappings on it, and came up Fourteenth Street and came in the back gate. Now, you know, these were some of the boys who had been down there. But I didn't pursue it any further than that. I didn't ask him if they were there when it was opened, or anything—but why would they have any reason to lie? They weren't involved other than just being down in that morgue area."

I asked Dennis David what the first casket looked like.

"It was a gray metal casket," he replied. "Just a gray, fairly plain, gray plain metal casket."

I told him the Dallas undertaker had given the Kennedys a fancy bronze casket. "It was definitely not a polished bronze casket?"

"No, it wasn't," replied David. "It was a gray metal casket I saw."

I asked him whether he knew of anyone who said he saw the two caskets at one spot, side by side. He replied he did not.

He repeated again that he was certain the first casket arrived before the Kennedys arrived because of the sequence, the type of vehicle, and its point of entry.

"I know that one came in the back gate," he said, "and then twenty, thirty minutes later—I'm not exactly sure, but I was upstairs—and I saw the other ambulance come in, the one with the motorcade which had the gray navy ambulance. And then I walked out on the rotunda. I was looking down from the second floor into the entranceway of the Naval Medical Center lobby when Mrs. Kennedy came in. . . . And there was the Secretary of Defense, and a few other dignitaries, a whole bunch of people."

I asked Dennis David when was the last time he saw the first casket.

"When it went through the doors into the morgue," he said.

David said he had put sailors around various parts of the hospital. He said he knew of no incident where the FBI was kept out of the autopsy. (That incident, which Galloway had confirmed, seemed to be peculiar to the 7:17 FBI arrival.)

David told me that although he had no first-hand knowledge, it had always been his impression that the autopsy started just after the coffin arrived.

I returned to the question of how much time passed between the arrival he described at the back and the one he witnessed at the front. The number he mentioned was thirty minutes. He conceded it might be less— perhaps fifteen minutes. That would place the arrival of the black Cadillac hearse at about 6:40.

I asked him to describe who was present when the first casket arrived. He said the Surgeon General of the navy was present. "He was there. [And] Dr. Humes had already arrived and was waiting. And Dr. Boswell stayed in the Pathology Lab after the . . . first casket had arrived. They stayed down there. In fact, they were there."

If Dennis David was correct, it meant that the navy officers who ran the autopsy all knew that the body had arrived in a black hearse. "You saw them there?" I asked.

"Yes," he replied.

"You saw Humes and Boswell when the first casket arrived?"

"Right."

"No question about that?"

"Right. And, let's see, there was one other man that was in there would have been John Stover, Captain Stover, who was the Commanding Officer of the Medical School."

"But . . . the ones that you can personally . . . assure me that you saw there were Boswell and Humes?"

"Humes and Boswell; and there were a couple of other people—I don't remember who they were."

The information David gave me was completely at variance with anything I had heard before. We were not in a courtroom, but I knew I had an obligation to try to shake him.

"I was going to ask you a bottom line question. . . . I know that all this is somewhat indistinct, but I know that some of it's very vivid too . . . there's some details you obviously will never forget that night."

"You're right," he said.

"I'm going to ask you this. Assuming there were two ambulances . . . is it possible that you're incorrect about that happening before the second coffin [arrived]? . . . that . . . what I'm getting at is—is it possible that the Kennedy party arrived, that you were up there, saw that, that they shifted the ambulances around, or whatever, and transferred the coffin to this black ambulance; that it pulled up at the rear, and that you witnessed that at the rear. And *then* the second coffin arrived. But that in recollecting it years later, you seem to think that you were upstairs and saw the full [motorcade] arrive down Wisconsin Avenue, that you saw that happen after the first casket came in, when in fact you first saw the Kennedy casket come in on Wisconsin Avenue, and *then* witnessed the arrival of two coffins, spaced thirty, or what it was in minutes, apart?"

David's answer was simple: "No. It's vivid as hell, because of some of the conversations later on. And I was talking, we compared notes, just in the sense I've already told you. No. I would stand absolutely firm on the fact that the black ambulance arrived well before—that is, with enough time to be distinctive between the two. The black ambulance was there, and I saw it arrive, and then I went back up front, and I saw the gray navy ambulance come in with the motorcade off Wisconsin Avenue. That is definite."

I assured Dennis David that I knew he was being careful in relating what he remembered. "I'm just trying to shake you." I asked: "If there's a weakness in the story, where would it be?"

David replied: "I couldn't say definitely that Kennedy's body was in the black ambulance. But I do know that the black ambulance with the casket—with a casket—came in, and that subsequently, later, the navy ambulance came in."

"You can definitely state the sequence?" I asked.

"Yes."

He also assured me that the casket he saw being brought in didn't appear to be empty. "I witnessed the casket being taken off the hearse. . . .

They were seven or eight men that carried that casket in then. It obviously wasn't just an empty casket, because it was much heavier than that, the way they were handling it. Because an empty casket—seven or eight men could bounce around with no problem. This one was heavy enough, you could see the strain on them. There was obviously something in it."

I had a very difficult time coming to terms with what David told me. I really did not want to believe his account. It upset a tidy world I had inhabited for more than ten years.

What Dennis David's account ultimately meant was that the body was secretly removed from the Dallas casket earlier in the day—sometime before takeoff in Dallas. This was completely at variance with my entire conception of the event. I had believed that because of Jacqueline Kennedy's insistence on remaining with the coffin, conspirators couldn't possibly have removed the body before its arrival at Bethesda. I had believed that the history of the Kennedy assassination was rewritten during the thirty-minute time lapse between the casket's arrival at the front and its trip to the back of Bethesda Naval Hospital.

But if David's account was correct, plotters had obtained access to the body before *Air Force One* left Dallas.

I now had to admit that I not only had no idea when the body was removed from the Dallas casket—I didn't even know how it got from Dallas, Texas, to Washington, D.C. It just showed up at the rear of Bethesda Naval Hospital in a black hearse.

There are many facets to the Kennedy assassination mystery: Oswald's trip to Mexico, his stay in New Orleans during the summer of 1963 and his activities on behalf of the Fair Play for Cuba Committee, his murder in the basement of Dallas Police Headquarters, and many others. No one person can study all in detail. The record is too voluminous. Different researchers have pursued them—as avocations. I had devoted myself, for years, to study of the medical evidence. The "medical evidence" was a euphemism. My central insight was that the body was the key to the case. I felt certain it was altered, and confident I had the evidence to prove it. Moreover, because of my interviews with the casket team, I thought I knew when the body was altered.

In other words, my conception of who the guilty parties must be, in general terms, was based on my belief that I had narrowed down the theft of the body and its alteration to a specific locale and a specific time frame, the National Naval Medical Center, Bethesda, between 7:00 and 8:00 P.M.

I thought I could answer the classic question: Who had the means and the opportunity?

Now in the middle of what I thought was well-known territory, there appeared another enormous unknown.

I fought back a desire to reject David's account out of hand. I knew that it required corroboration, and that meant searching for people who had been at Bethesda that night, other "extras" on the stage set of history, other "Dennis Davids" who were out there, somewhere in America, who might have vital information whose significance they didn't comprehend.

Meanwhile, in July 1979, I gave his account a conditional acceptance. Suppose it was true; what would that mean? In that spirit, I began to re-evaluate everything I knew—or at least thought I knew—so well. It was a painful experience. It meant revising my own revisionist history of the Kennedy assassination at a very late date.

I began at Bethesda.

The Ambulance Chase Revisited

Central to my theory about an altered body was the research I had done and interviews I had conducted with the men of the Military District of Washington casket team. I was fond of saying that the accounts of these witnesses "broke" the chain of possession on the President's body. If the body wasn't in the casket, they did no such thing. They broke the chain of possession on the *casket*. The body was already inside the hospital.

Therefore, the first re-interpretations I made ran along these lines: that the purpose of the ambulance chase was not to steal the body from the casket, but temporarily to regain possession of the empty casket, so that the body—already inside the hospital—could be put back inside it. That would permit the casket team, and Gen. Godfrey McHugh, to carry the Dallas casket into the hospital at 8:00 P.M., with the body—now altered—inside, and witness a coffin opening prior to the start of the official autopsy.

The chronology remained the same. It was merely the purpose of the ambulance chase that changed.

The FBI Experience Revisited

By their account, the FBI followed the "correct" ambulance and escorted the Dallas casket to the autopsy room just prior to 7:17. Their report indicated they were kept out of the autopsy room for a while, and "7:17," in their version, was the time of the "preparation for the autopsy."[9]

Previously, I had believed that the FBI was kept out of the room because they could not be permitted to enter during the "pre-autopsy autopsy"—i.e., while the body was being altered.

If Dennis David's account was correct, that idea had to be discarded. Now, it appeared that the reason the FBI could not be permitted to enter the morgue was that they were escorting a casket which they assumed contained Kennedy's body, but which was in fact empty. They could not be permitted inside because Kennedy's body was already there. They would immediately have seen it, and would have known the Dallas casket was empty.

If Dennis David was right, the notion that the pre-autopsy autopsy took place in the Bethesda morgue between 7:17, when the FBI arrived at the door, and 8:00 P.M., when the casket team carried in the Dallas casket, had to be discarded. What went on between 7:17 and 8:00 was the re-introduction of the body into the Dallas casket, and somehow—I hadn't the vaguest idea how—the re-introduction of the casket back into the navy ambulance, so that Godfrey McHugh et al. could carry in the Dallas casket with the body inside, at 8:00 P.M.

Therefore, the "preparation for the autopsy," which Sibert and O'Neill reported to the Commission (the "pre-autopsy" inspection indicated in their own report and Field Office memo), appeared to have been merely a cover story given to the FBI agents to delay them at the door and prevent them from learning that the body had preceded the casket—not a cover story used to conceal alterations to the body being made inside the room.

This seemed to mean that the pre-autopsy procedure was done either at Bethesda, *before* the FBI arrived at the morgue door (i.e., before the motorcade even arrived at the front of the hospital, if the body arrived early enough), or before the body even reached Bethesda. In July 1979, I had no theory. I was just grappling with the problem.

The 7:35/8:00 P.M. Anomaly Re-evaluated

Humes testified he received the body at 7:35.[10] The casket team report said they brought in the Dallas casket at 8:00 P.M.[11] Putting these together, I had concluded that the casket team carried in an empty casket.

That meant that everyone who helped bring in the Dallas casket at 8:00 P.M. had to be prevented from actually entering the autopsy room, for they would have seen that the body was already there—i.e., that the casket they carried was empty.

While I tended to accept this theory over the years, there were some serious drawbacks to it. First, although General Wehle told me he did not enter the autopsy room, and therefore did not see a casket opening, I had no evidence of a concerted effort to keep the other people out. Godfrey McHugh never talked about being kept out, and both he and one member of the casket team, James Felder, insisted they had witnessed the coffin opening. McHugh would never give me any details, so I had been reluctant to accept his statement. But Felder was adamant—he said he saw the

Dallas casket opened. I had simply set his account aside. I assumed he must have been wrong.

Now I realized the Dallas casket could have been opened at the Bethesda morgue at 8:00 P.M., and inside—if Dennis David's account about the "early" arrival was correct—could have been the altered body of John F. Kennedy.

In short, I now realized that the 7:35 "time of arrival" given by Humes, and the 8:00 time of arrival given by the casket team, probably referred to the same event.

I realized that there *was* an entry in which the Dallas casket arrived with Kennedy's altered body inside. I wasn't sure whether this occurred at 7:35, 7:45, or 8:00—but it did occur. Which time was correct? Because the "7:35" came from Humes' testimony, whereas "8:00 P.M." came from the written report of the casket team, I tended to accept 8:00 P.M. as the time for that occurrence, and I tentatively concluded that Humes must have made a twenty-five-minute error.

In developing a theory to account for all this testimony, it soon became apparent that if David's account was correct it was necessary to postulate three separate coffin entries to the morgue area. Those three entries, the evidence for each, and my interpretations, were:

#1   *Time:* About 6:45.*

Event: Black Cadillac hearse arrives; a half dozen men in plain clothes carry in plain metal coffin.

Evidence: The account of Dennis David.

Interpretation: This coffin contains President Kennedy's body, and this marks the first entry into the hospital. (It was not clear to me, after interviewing Dennis David, whether the body had been altered by this time.)

#2   *Time:* Between 7:05 and 7:17.

Event: Navy ambulance, which carried Jacqueline and Robert Kennedy and led the procession from Andrews Air Force Base, is driven from the front of the hospital to the rear.

Evidence: Secret Service reports state the ambulance arrived at the Bethesda front entrance at 6:55, and the *Washington Star* reported it remained there for at least twelve minutes after Jacqueline Kennedy went inside the hospital.

FBI agents Sibert and O'Neill report they escorted the casket in this ambulance to the morgue entrance. Their report states that a "tight security" was "immediately" thrown around the room by the Secret

---

* I use 6:45 instead of 6:20 or 6:30 because of analysis of how the body arrived in Washington, to be discussed later.

Service and the navy, and implies they were prevented from entering. They had to locate Secret Service Agent Kellerman, and when they did (how much time passed is not clear), they "advised him of the Bureau's interest in this matter."[12] Sibert and O'Neill reported the "preparation for the autopsy" began at 7:17.[13]

During this period, the Military District of Washington casket team reported "considerable confusion as to where the body would be taken"; Lieutenant Bird said the team followed an ambulance to the rear and found it empty; James Felder and Hubert Clark described an ambulance chase; George Barnum, in his 11/29/63 account, reported two fruitless round trips to the rear before being re-united with the proper ambulance, which they subsequently escorted to the morgue.[14]

Interpretation: While the casket team is deliberately led astray, the empty Dallas casket is brought to the morgue.

#3   *Time:* 8:00.

Event: Assisted by General McHugh, the six-man MDW casket team brings the Dallas casket to the morgue. Godfrey McHugh and James Felder say they were present when the coffin was opened.

Evidence: The casket team report and the accounts of those men cited above: General Wehle, General McHugh, et al.

Interpretation: The casket team is "permitted" to find the "correct" ambulance and the President's body is brought to the Bethesda morgue, in the Dallas casket, for the official autopsy. The body has already been altered.

This interpretation of the evidence was based on what was seen outside the hospital, and outside the autopsy room. What was the perspective of someone inside the autopsy room?

If this interpretation was correct, an observer inside the autopsy room throughout the period from 6:45 to 8:00 would have seen the following:

He would have seen the body brought in, the first time, in the plain metal casket. He would have seen it removed from the casket and placed on the autopsy table or a stretcher or other surface.

Perhaps he would have been aware of the arrival of Sibert and O'Neill outside the room. He might have heard them told that they could not enter, that they must find Roy Kellerman, Assistant Special Agent in Charge of the White House Detail of the Secret Service. He might have heard Sibert and O'Neill protest.

Next, he would have seen the body transferred into the Dallas casket, which was then taken back outside and put into the "correct" ambulance. (I had no witness outside to such an event, but logic dictated that the body must have left the autopsy table after it arrived the first time, if it was in the Dallas casket which was brought in by the casket team at 8:00 P.M.)

Next, my hypothetical observer in the autopsy room would have seen

Photo 28. White House Press Secretary Malcolm Kilduff points to right temple in answering question at Parkland Hospital press conference as to where the bullet struck Kennedy.

From: CAPT J. H. STOVER, Jr., MC, USN
Commanding Officer
U. S. Naval Medical School
To: Roy H. Kellerman
Assistant Special Agent in Charge
United States Secret Service

The following items of photographic material were placed in the custody

of Mr. Roy H. Kellerman, Assistant Special Agent in Charge, United

States Secret Service, 22 November 1963 at the Morgue, U. S. Naval

Hospital, Bethesda, Maryland:

(a) 8 graphic film holders (4 x 5) containing 16 sheets of exposed

Ektachrome E3 film

(b) 8 graphic film holders (4 x 5) containing 12 sheets exposed

Portrait Pan film

(c) 1 roll 120 Ektachrome E3 exposed film.

To my personal knowledge this is the total amount of film exposed on

this occassion.

It is requested the film holders be returned or replaced.

J. H. STOVER, Jr.
CAPT, MC, USN
Commanding Officer
U. S. Naval Medical School

John T. Stringer Jr.
Photographer

Rec. by: Roy H. Kellerman
U. S. Sect Servi
11-22-63

Photo 29. Receipt for photos and X-rays, with handwritten changes

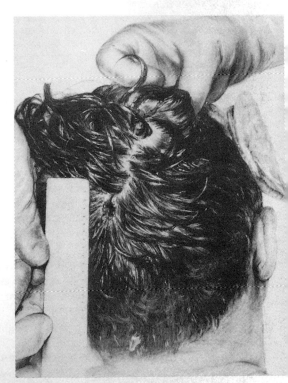

Photo 30. House Assassinations Committee Exhibit F-48—medical drawing that is an exact replica of autopsy photograph of the back of President Kennedy's head

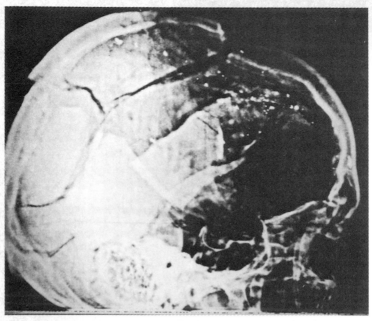

Photo 31. House Assassinations Committee Exhibit F-53—lateral X-ray of President Kennedy's head (electronically enhanced)

Photo 32. House Assassinations Committee Exhibit F-56—antero-posterior X-ray of President Kennedy's skull (electronically enhanced)

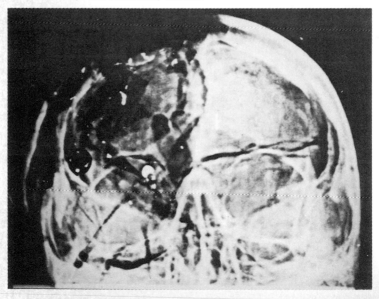

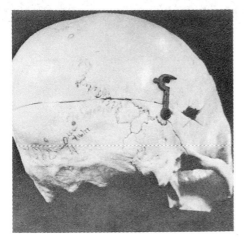

Photo 33. Photograph of laboratory skull initialed by autopsy doctors at location where they said they saw entry wound. The higher mark, without initials, is where the Committee's experts said X-rays and photos showed entry wound.

Photo 34. FBI/Commission reconstruction of assassination in May 1964. FBI agent wears patch on head at location of entry wound.

Photo 35. House Assassinations Committee Exhibit F-36—medical drawing by Ida Dox, an exact replica of autopsy photograph showing anterior throat wound

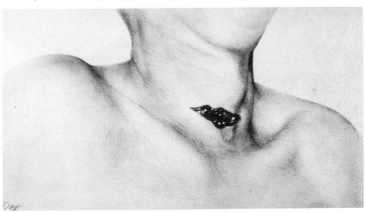

Photo 36. Dr. James Humes as he appeared on TV, testifying before House Assassinations Committee, September 7, 1978

Photo 37. Paul O'Connor, about 1963

Photo 38. James Curtis Jenkins, about 1963

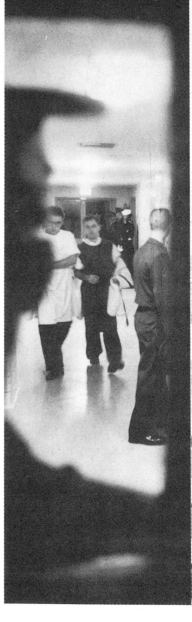

Photos 39 and 40. Life photographer Bob Phillips went out to Bethesda and took a series of photographs while hiding behind a door, in a stairwell in the corridor outside the Bethesda morgue.

39. A stretcher either being taken into or out of the morgue. When published in *Life,* the picture's caption stated that this stretcher was used to carry President Kennedy to the morgue. But persons I interviewed said the *Life* caption was incorrect—that this was the stretcher they were told was used to bring a stillborn baby to the morgue.

40. Phillips shot this photo right past the ear of a guard who was attempting to block his view. It shows X-ray technicians Jerrol Custer (left, in white lab coat) and Ed Reed (right, carrying his lab coat).

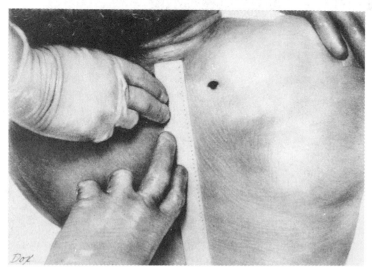

Photo 41. House Assassinations Committee Exhibit F-20—medical drawing by Ida Dox, an exact replica of autopsy photograph showing entry wound in right upper back

Photo 42. Photographs taken by White House photographer Cecil Stoughton from the front door of *Air Force One,* showing Secret Service agents carrying President Kennedy's coffin aboard the plane.

A, Roy Kellerman struggles with coffin. At the bottom of the ramp can be seen Larry O'Brien (wearing glasses), General Clifton (in uniform), Jacqueline Kennedy, Mary Gallagher, and Kenneth O'Donnell (in front of man with hand to face). The man in glasses with tousled hair is Admiral Burkley. Immediately to the right, Dallas Police Chief Jesse Curry.

B, Among the agents carrying the coffin up the ramp are Richard Johnsen (profile in glasses), who had been given bullet 399 at Parkland Hospital.

C, Jacqueline Kennedy ascends ramp.

A

B

C

D

Photo 43. The swearing in of President Johnson
LBJ, Ladybird, et al. wait for Jacqueline Kennedy
before beginning the ceremony. In the foreground is
Judge Sarah Hughes. To her left is Malcolm Kilduff.
In background (left to right) are General Chester
Clifton (in uniform), Chief Curry (in glasses),
Congressman Homer Thornberry (in tie, to right of
Johnson), Secret Service Agent Lem Johns (profile
behind Thornberry), and Congressman Jack Brooks.

B, Swearing in begins when Mrs. Kennedy arrives.
At left, in bowtie, is Congressman Al Thomas. To
right of Jacqueline is Congressman Jack Brooks,
and to right of him is Admiral George Burkley.

C, After ceremony, Johnson and Ladybird speak
to Mrs. Kennedy. Then Johnson turns to his wife
(D), looks up *(E),* and gets a wink and a smile from
Congressman Thomas.

F, Johnson has turned around and requests that
the plane leave for Washington immediately. Those
visible include General Clifton (at extreme left),
Merriman Smith (in corner, to left of Presidential
seal), Secret Service Agent Jerry Kivett (back of
head to seal), Dr. Burkley (in profile, holding
glasses), Bill Moyers (behind Burkley), Liz
Carpenter, and Kennedy aide Dave Powers, barely
visible at the extreme right.

E

F

*(Photographs by Cecil Stoughton, White House
photographer)*

the Military District of Washington casket team, and Godfrey McHugh, arrive with the Dallas casket and the body for the start of the official autopsy.

I referred to this as the "three-entrance" casket scenario: the first casket enters once with the body; the second casket enters twice, once to get the body, the second time for the official entry.

This was a hypothesis. My principal evidence for it was the account of Dennis David. I thought that if I could obtain the accounts of enough people in the vicinity of the morgue, I might be able to work out the details of what had happened.

Dennis David's account made me aware of a fallacy in my earlier approach to this problem. Previously, I had supposed the President's body was stolen, altered, and then replaced in the Dallas casket—all at one general location. Now I realized that the body could have been stolen at "A," altered at "B," and re-introduced into the Dallas casket at "C," and that "A," "B," and "C" might represent entirely different locations. I had never looked at the problem that way before because I never had any reason to believe the President's body and the Dallas casket parted ways before the casket reached the doorstep of Bethesda Naval Hospital.

If David's account was true, the re-introduction of the body into the Dallas casket was a logical and necessary inference, but the details surrounding such a maneuver remained unclear. Furthermore, David's testimony raised other, even more profound questions: when was the body stolen? How did it get from Dallas to Washington? And where was it altered?

The chain-of-possession problem itself now demanded a redefinition.

I took out files I hadn't looked at in years, and chronologies I had made more than ten years earlier to search for an answer. I began with this central fact: If David's account was true, the body was not in the Dallas casket when *Air Force One* took off from Love Field.

I began looking for time intervals when something might have happened. The possibilities quickly narrowed. Just as the trip from Andrews Air Force Base to Bethesda was uninterrupted, with Jacqueline Kennedy always beside the coffin, the trip from Dallas' Parkland Hospital to Love Field was uninterrupted, and attended.

At 2:04, the Dallas casket made its departure from Parkland Hospital, after an argument between Secret Service agents and Kennedy aides, who wanted to depart immediately, and Dallas County Medical Examiner Earl Rose, who demanded an autopsy be performed in Dallas.[15] The casket was rolled out to the loading platform and placed in a cream-colored hearse. Hundreds of spectators watched. National TV networks covered the event. Jacqueline Kennedy, Admiral Burkley, and three Secret Service agents climbed into the hearse. One agent drove. They arrived at Love Field at 2:14.[16]

Pictures published in *Life* magazine showed the casket being brought up the ramp of the airplane by Secret Service agents.[17] Seats had been removed at the rear of the plane.[18] The casket was placed inside at 2:18.[19] Judge Hughes arrived at 2:30 to swear Johnson in.[20] The oath was administered at 2:38.[21] At 2:47, *Air Force One* was airborne.[22]

There were, it seemed, only two periods of time when the body could have been taken from the casket. One possibility was that the body was removed from the casket after it had been put inside at Parkland Hospital, and that Jacqueline Kennedy had escorted an empty casket from the hospital to the airplane. The second possibility was that President Kennedy's body was removed from the Dallas casket during the events surrounding the swearing in of Lyndon Johnson.

Both possibilities were extraordinary.

But if David's account was correct it made little difference whether the body was somehow withheld from the coffin at Parkland, altered, and secretly flown to Washington, or somehow taken off *Air Force One,* altered, and flown to Washington.

The body must have been stolen at "A," altered at "B," and returned to the Dallas casket at "C." The "A-B-C" algorithm remained essentially the same regardless of where the theft took place. "C" was Bethesda. "A" was Dallas—either Parkland Hospital or Love Field. And "B"—the exact location of the alteration of the body—seemed a fact beyond any reasonable hope of discovery.

Did this "A-B-C" algorithm explain the sequence of events on November 22, 1963? That depended upon whether Dennis David's account was true.

CHAPTER 26

The Recollections of Paul Kelly O'Connor

AFTER I INTERVIEWED DENNIS DAVID on July 2, 1979, I immediately began looking for corroboration. David had not been able to remember the names of any of the sailors who were on the loading dock when the black hearse arrived. I read him the list of men in the autopsy room included in the Sibert and O'Neill report, but he couldn't recall the names of the medical technicians either. He had emphasized that he had never entered the autopsy room itself. He was not a medical person. He did give me the name of another man, Laurence Webb, who, he said, might have been there that night. After much effort, I finally tracked Webb down. He had kind things to say about Dennis David, that he was a truthful and reliable witness. But no, Webb was not on duty that night. However, he recalled the name of J. S. Layton Ledbetter, who was Chief of the Day for the Medical Center command. (David had been Chief of the Day for the Medical School command.)

I began to search for Ledbetter. I talked with telephone companies all over the South, and driver's-license bureaus in various states. I was determined to find him.*

Meanwhile, I anxiously awaited the publication of the House Select Committee's report.

A government report can be a gold mine of information. What might this one contain? What would it say about who was at Bethesda that night? What would it say about surgery? What would it say about the allegation of Adm. David Osborne?

---

* I located Ledbetter in September 1979. As discussed in Chapter 16, he provided information about the arrival of two ambulances.

The Osborne Allegation

About June 1978, some of the critics who were in touch with the staff of the House Select Committee found out that a serious allegation had been made by a naval officer, David P. Osborne who, as Chief of Surgery at Bethesda Naval Hospital, had attended the Kennedy autopsy. Admiral Osborne had retired as Deputy Surgeon General.

Admiral Osborne alleged that at the start of the autopsy he saw an intact bullet roll from clothing on the President's body and onto the autopsy table.

When I learned of Osborne's assertion, I wondered if there had been a scheme to plant an intact bullet at Bethesda.

Already in the record was a curious receipt, executed by FBI agents Sibert and O'Neill, dated November 22, 1963. It was made out to Capt. J. H. Stover, Jr., the Commanding Officer of the U.S. Naval Medical School, Humes' immediate superior, and it read: "We hereby acknowledge receipt of a missle [sic]* removed by Commander James J. Humes, MC, USN on this date."[1]

This receipt was never given to the Warren Commission. The Secret Service sent it directly to the National Archives in 1969.[2] As previously noted, when I learned of its existence, I immediately wrote a letter to the FBI in Washington. What bullet corresponded to this receipt? I asked.[3] An ambiguous reply came back.[4] After I wrote a second letter,[5] I returned to my apartment one day and found a note on the door from an FBI agent asking me to call him.

The FBI agent told me that the receipt was for the two tiny slivers of metal removed from the brain. On the phone, I reviewed with him all the reasons why that seemed unlikely: the receipt was for "a missile"; moreover, Sibert and O'Neill had reported that the two slivers "were placed in a glass jar containing a black metal top which were thereafter marked for identification and following the signing of a proper receipt were transported by Bureau agents to the FBI Laboratory."[6]

It seemed unlikely to me that two FBI agents would receive a glass jar containing two slivers of metal and issue a receipt for "a missile removed by Commander James J. Humes . . . on this date."[7]

When I pressed further, the FBI agent said: "They've told you all they're gonna tell you about that."[8] I then wrote a letter to Director Hoover requesting that he state, in writing, what his agent had told me on the phone, and back came a crisp two-sentence letter informing me that the Sibert and O'Neill receipt was for the metal that became evidence under the designation "Warren Commission Exhibit 843"—i.e., the fragments from the brain.[9]

* This misspelling will be corrected in subsequent references.

I still had my doubts. I suspected there might have been confusion among the conspirators during the twenty-four hours following the assassination as to whether the bullet was to originate from a stretcher at the Dallas hospital or from the environs of the autopsy room.

This idea first occurred to me about 1975, when I was shown the transcript of an interview another critic had conducted with the man who found the bullet at Parkland Hospital—Darrell Tomlinson, the hospital's senior engineer. Tomlinson claimed that after midnight on the night of the assassination—between 12:30 and 1:00 A.M. on November 23, 1963— he was awakened by a phone call from the FBI. They wanted to speak to him about the bullet. Tomlinson said that they "told me to keep my mouth shut . . . [about] what I found." Tomlinson didn't amplify on what was said. The FBI's instruction, he said, was: "Just don't discuss it." Tomlinson added: "And they have a way of making a believer out of you."[10]

Yet by the following Tuesday the bullet and Tomlinson were receiving dramatically different treatment at the hands of the authorities. Tomlinson said he was called to the office of O. P. Wright, the Chief of Security at Parkland, to whom Tomlinson had surrendered the bullet on November 22, to meet Gordon Shanklin. Shanklin was the head of the FBI's Dallas Field Office, and one of the most important men in the Kennedy assassination investigation. Tomlinson said he was shown the bullet and asked if it was the same one he found.

And there was another anomaly. O. P. Wright wrote a long report about the day's events—more than three pages, single-spaced. He even described how a nurse came to him with Kennedy's wristwatch, how he made arrangements for its return to the President's family, via the Secret Service.[11] Yet Wright never mentioned that he was handed an assassination bullet, and that he had given it to a Secret Service agent. When I called Wright in the summer of 1966 and asked him about this omission, he refused to discuss the matter. Perhaps he honestly forgot to mention this bullet in his report. But O. P. Wright should have been knowledgeable about matters of evidence. Later I learned that, before he went to work at Parkland Hospital, O. P. Wright had been Deputy Police Chief of Dallas.

Tomlinson's late night phone call from the FBI and O. P. Wright's failure to mention the bullet in his report made me wonder if perhaps there was a period that Friday night when the role assigned to this bullet was still unclear, when its "origin" had not yet been decided upon, a period when someone was actually considering the possibility of concealing the fact that it came from a Dallas stretcher.

This idea made Admiral Osborne's assertion particularly interesting. For his statement raised the possibility that a bullet matching the Bethesda back wound had been planted with the body, that he had seen that bullet, but evidence of its existence had subsequently been suppressed, and the receipt originally issued for it had been assigned to the two fragments from the brain.

All this was conjecture. The staff member of the Committee who originally circulated the report about Osborne soon circulated another: that Osborne was wrong, that he had admitted he was wrong, and that we could read a full account in the Committee's report.

I was also interested in seeing what the report would say about Sibert and O'Neill's statement that there had been "surgery of the head area," which I had brought to the attention of Andrew Purdy in September 1978, at the time of the public hearings, and to the attention of Chief Counsel Robert Blakey about six weeks later.

I obtained a copy of the House Committee report as soon as it was available. Volume 7 contains a staff report devoted to the medical evidence. It was the work of Andrew Purdy and Mark Flanagan.

Upon flipping through it the first time, I was delighted to find a list of everyone who was in the autopsy room.[12] The Sibert and O'Neill report contained such a list; next to each person's name was his function. But there were nine names in that report for which no function was listed. I knew who three of them were—Ebersole was the radiologist, Boswell was one of the autopsy doctors, and "Raihe," whose name was misspelled, was the photographer's assistant. That left six people who were an utter mystery. The House Select Committee report contained a complete list, apparently from an official source, which even included middle initials—extremely useful when hunting for someone.

Also, the functions of the people were listed, including the six whose jobs were previously unknown: Jerrol F. Custer and Edward F. Reed were X-ray technicians; Jan Gail Rudnicki, James Curtis Jenkins, and Paul K. O'Connor were laboratory technologists; and James E. Metzler was a hospital corpsman third class.

Neither Dennis David nor Ledbetter was listed. Apparently the Committee had only secured the names of those inside the room, those who saw the body and had a medical function at the autopsy.

I turned to the question of pre-autopsy surgery. Not only had I discussed my theory with Andrew Purdy and Robert Blakey, but during the same period I had also spoken to Ed Lopez, a staff member reportedly close to Blakey, who seemed sympathetic to the idea, as well as to Michael Ewing, and to Belford Lawson, who was in charge of the Secret Service area. So I fully expected to find something on the subject in the staff report.

The Committee "Deals" with Pre-Autopsy Surgery

I found that Andrew Purdy and Mark Flanagan had indeed dealt with the surgery matter. At the beginning of chapter four, the report stated: "The various accounts of the nature of the wounds to the President differ significantly. As revealed in section 2 of this volume, 'Performance of the Autopsy,' eyewitness descriptions of the wounds, as described by the staff at Parkland Memorial Hospital, differed from those in the autopsy report, as well as from what appears in the autopsy photographs and X-rays. Further, the reports of FBI agents Sibert and O'Neill referred to 'surgery' of the head area being evident when the body arrived for the autopsy, yet no surgery of the head area was known to have been performed."[13]

The report continued, a few paragraphs later: "If the autopsy doctors are correct, then the Parkland doctors are incorrect and either lying or mistaken. It does not seem probable that they are lying. . . . On the other hand, it does seem possible that the Parkland personnel could be mistaken. . . ."[14]

The next paragraph summarized and dismissed my theory: "The theoretical possibility also exists that both Parkland and the autopsy personnel are correct in their observations and that the autopsy photographs and X-rays accurately reflect the observations of the autopsy personnel. This could have occurred if someone had altered the body while in transit from Parkland Memorial Hospital to Bethesda Naval Hospital. This possibility, however, is highly unlikely or even impossible. Secret Service agents maintained constant vigilance over the body from Parkland to Bethesda and stated that no one alter[ed] the body. Second, if such alterations did occur, it seems likely that the people present at the autopsy would have noticed them; in which case they are now lying about their observations . . . this does not appear likely."[15]

And two paragraphs later, after acknowledging that the Parkland doctors reported a large gaping wound at the rear of the head which did not appear on the autopsy photos, the report says "it appears more probable that the observations of the Parkland doctors are incorrect."[16]

The Purdy/Flanagan investigation had several footnotes.

The sentence that Secret Service agents maintained "constant vigilance" over the body was tagged with footnote number 7, which read: "Outside Contact report, William Greer, Dec. 4, 1978 . . . ; Outside Contact report, Roy H. Kellerman, Dec. 1, 1978."[17]

What was an "Outside Contact report"? I soon learned that the House Select Committee conducted much of its investigation by telephone, because the Committee had access to free telephone service—i.e., a government WATS line. After speaking to a witness on the telephone, the lawyer or researcher would prepare an "Outside Contact report" on what was said.

Thus, the record indicated that on December 1, 1978 Purdy and/or Flanagan called up Roy Kellerman, now retired, and asked him whether anybody could have altered the body; then, three days later on December 4, 1978, one or both of them called up William Greer and asked the same thing. No, Kellerman and Greer replied, that could not have happened, they had exercised "constant vigilance." This, then, was the House Select

Committee's "chain-of-possession" investigation. After reading it, I couldn't resist pulling from my files the transcript of my conversation with William Greer in November 1967. Greer had told me then that he didn't know how the President's body got inside Bethesda Naval Hospital. He continually maintained that he thought it was taken in through the lobby, and told me that I should call Dr. Burkley if I wanted to know for sure—that there ought to be no mystery attached to that question.[18]

On another page of volume 7, buried in a footnote, was the revelation that four days after I spoke to Blakey, the Committee had obtained an affidavit from FBI Agent Sibert. This footnote—the only evidence of a direct investigation of the surgery matter—read: "In their report, Sibert and O'Neill also stated that surgery had been performed on the head area prior to the arrival of the body at Bethesda Naval Hospital. The committee concludes that this report was in error. In an affidavit to the committee, Sibert acknowledged that the statement that head surgery was performed was determined 'not to be correct following detailed inspection.' See affidavit of James Sibert, October 24, 1978 . . . JFK Document No. 012806."[19]

The Committee had obtained an affidavit from Sibert on what was perhaps the most important issue in the entire investigation—the integrity of the body at the time of autopsy—and chose to mention it only in a footnote, and even then quoted only seven words of the affidavit.

Nevertheless, I found some solace in the fact that those seven words were, in fact, consistent with my conclusion that an oral utterance had been made at the outset of the autopsy that there had been "surgery of the head area, namely, in the top of the skull."

The Committee stated: "Sibert acknowledged that the statement that head surgery was performed was determined 'not to be correct following detailed inspection.' "[20] I believed Sibert was boxed in by events. In 1978, he could not maintain his report was simply erroneous—i.e., that the "surgery" statement was *his* mistake—because in 1966, as a result of my telephone call to him and my subsequent correspondence with the FBI, headquarters had gone on record that the statement about head surgery was based on information "orally furnished" by the autopsy doctors.[21] Moreover, an entire series of FBI memos attested to the accuracy of information reported by Sibert and O'Neill (see Chapter 12).

In light of Sibert's 1978 position—in effect, that his report about what the doctors *said* was accurate, but that they themselves then determined they were wrong—the following question now demanded an answer: If Sibert heard either Humes or Boswell state that there had been surgery of the head area at the outset of the autopsy, and if that allegation—obviously serious—had then been determined to be incorrect after a "detailed inspection," why did Sibert and O'Neill include the incorrect allegation in the report they dictated on November 26, 1963, but not the refutation? That seemed incongruous, to say the least.

But all that was beside the point. The House Select Committee ought to have put Sibert and O'Neill under oath and questioned them, and made the transcripts of those interviews available. Instead, someone had telephoned Sibert, an affidavit was drawn up, mailed in, and that was the "denial" of surgery.

I found this aspect of the Committee's report particularly frustrating.

I now turned to Admiral Osborne's assertion. The report prepared by Purdy and Flanagan consisted of numbered paragraphs. The Osborne allegation was reported in paragraph number 84, and refuted in paragraph 85. Paragraph 84 stated: "In a committee telephone interview with Admiral Osborne, another issue arose. He stated that he thought he recalled seeing an intact slug roll out from the clothing of President Kennedy and onto the autopsy table when personnel opened the casket and removed the clothing from the body of the President."[22]

The refutation was based on the conclusion that Osborne must have recollected incorrectly because President Kennedy was unclothed at the time of the autopsy, and Osborne had said the bullet rolled out from "the clothing of President Kennedy."[23] The clothing reference, implied the report, meant Osborne's memory was unreliable. As the report put it, Admiral Osborne had stated "he thought he recalled seeing . . ." the slug.[24] The report noted that no one else who was present when the body arrived— neither Paul O'Connor nor James Jenkins, the two technologists who had assisted in moving the body from casket to autopsy table—had seen any such slug.

I studied the refutation closely: "The committee reviewed thoroughly all documents and recontacted those persons who moved the body of the President from the casket onto the autopsy table and then prepared the body for examination. Paul K. O'Connor, who along with James Jenkins had the duty of preparing the body for the autopsy, said the body had arrived at about 8:00 P.M. and was wrapped in a body bag. . . ."[25]

I blinked. Stared at the statement. Read it again.

". . . the body . . . was wrapped in a body bag. . . ."

A body bag? I knew what that was. Who could not? How many times had I watched newscasts of the Vietnam war, where the dead were removed from the battlefield in body bags.

Nobody had put Kennedy in a body bag in Dallas, at least not while Jacqueline Kennedy was in the room. He had been wrapped in sheets, and put in an expensive bronze coffin. A piece of plastic was used to line the coffin.

Yet here, in the same government report that denied surgery, which relied on a superficial statement from a Secret Service agent that "vigilance" had been exercised concerning the President's body—here was a statement which, if true, actually supported the idea of pre-autopsy surgery and, at least indirectly, supported the account of Dennis David! He had seen the body arrive in a plain metal casket. O'Connor's statement now raised the possibility that inside that casket was a body bag containing the President's body.

It was a stroke of luck for me, as well as a commentary on the ineptitude of the investigation, that I should find such significant evidence in a report published by the House Select Committee. If I had not had the experience in 1966 of first reading the FBI report about "surgery of the head area" in Epstein's paperback book, which could be bought in any drugstore or supermarket, I would have been more surprised. But I now knew how government bureaucracies worked and I understood how critical evidence about the machinations of November 22 could make its way, unnoticed, into an official government publication. Just as Sibert and O'Neill had reported "surgery of the head area" without realizing its implications, so Andrew Purdy and Mark Flanagan of the House Select Committee had received, and reported as fact, the information that President Kennedy's body had arrived at Bethesda in a body bag without realizing the implications of that information.

On August 20, 1979, I called Andrew Purdy in Philadelphia. I wondered if he had any idea what he had written in volume 7. And I wondered where in the United States O'Connor lived. I had to talk to him.

I began by asking Purdy if he had ever heard of Dennis David.[26] No, he had not. Then I told him that before publishing my book, I would like to speak with as many of the people in the autopsy room as I could find. Although Purdy did not accept my hypothesis that the body was altered, he was helpful. He did his best to recollect the home town of each person, and said he would call Mark Flanagan and that he, too, would help. I asked him how he had located people in the room, and he told me of a file in the navy's Bureau of Medicine and Surgery, which contained useful information. Purdy explained that when he had first tried to contact the people in the autopsy room, he had been met by a stone wall. They refused to talk because in November 1963 they had been directly ordered to keep silent. Purdy said that it took the Committee months to arrange cancellation of this order. A high Defense Department attorney, Dianne Seimer, initially had ruled against the Committee's request. Blakey had had to ask Congressman Louis Stokes, Chairman of the Committee, to meet with Secretary of Defense Harold Brown. It was only then that Seimer's decision was overturned. At that time, the Bureau of Medicine and Surgery was instructed by higher authority to send out letters to each person in the autopsy room—all those who had been forbidden to talk in November

1963, subject to threat of court martial—stating that they could now speak with this Committee. This had been done, said Purdy, and there was a very interesting file on it somewhere in the government.

We argued about the surgery matter, and Purdy maintained that there was no evidence to support the conclusion that the President's body had been altered between Dallas and Bethesda. The X-rays and photos were the final word. Contrary observations were simply in error. Purdy talked the language of "best evidence."

I turned to paragraph 85. I read it slowly to Purdy, as if it were just a detail in the refutation of the Osborne allegation.

"Andy," I asked, "did he say 'body bag'?"

"If that's what I wrote, that's what he said," said Purdy.

"Andy," I asked, "do you know what a body bag is?"

Purdy really wasn't sure. He had just written down what O'Connor had told him. A body bag, I explained, was a rubberized bag, standard equipment for the removal of the victims of combat or disaster.

"The President's body," I said, "was *not* put in a body bag in Dallas."

Purdy grew flustered and defensive. He said that just because O'Connor said "body bag," that didn't mean there *was* a body bag.

Now we went over the matter in detail. Purdy explained that he had gone personally to interview O'Connor in the southern United States, and that he had interviewed Jenkins too. The two men were related—brothers-in-law, he thought. He cautioned me that one of them—he was not sure which—was "spooked" about speaking about the assassination; that I should tread carefully. And he also cautioned me not to ask leading questions just to wring some words from a witness to support my theory.

Purdy wasn't hostile. He was helpful, and I had many conversations with him as my investigation progressed. We agreed to disagree about the alteration of the body. It was, to some extent, a rerun of my relationship with Liebeler thirteen years before, on a smaller scale. Liebeler had taught me how to play the "best evidence" game.

But I was confident that if President Kennedy's body left Dallas in a sheet but arrived at Bethesda in a body bag, their "best evidence" game was over.

Interviewing Paul O'Connor

One of the first things I did after speaking with Purdy was to write to the Defense Department to request the file Purdy spoke of.

Then I set out to find Paul Kelly O'Connor.

He had moved—Purdy's recollection wasn't all that clear—and I spent many hours on the telephone calling "O'Connors" in a number of cities. Finally the middle initial matched. I had found the right O'Connor.*

It was August 25, 1979, when I placed the call.

I identified myself as a writer doing a book for publication, who had just learned of his name through the House Select Committee report. O'Connor was cheerful, and said he would be glad to help. "I got a pretty good memory of that night," he remarked.[28] I began by asking for some background information. O'Connor told me that on November 22, 1963, he and James Curtis Jenkins—distantly related because their wives were cousins—were in Bethesda's laboratory school, studying to become medical technologists. "And we rotated in different departments—pathology, hematology—and my duty station was pathology. And I assisted the prosectors or the pathologists in all the autopsies that were done. And it just so happened that was a Friday night, and I was on duty that night, so that's the reason I was there."

O'Connor told me how he first heard that Kennedy had been shot. "We were at school that morning, we had taken a break, and I happened to pass the security shack, which is in the hospital area, and everybody was transfixed watching TV. I poked my head in and found out that the President had been shot. Then we found out later he had passed away. They cancelled all school, and had everybody just report to their duty station. We had no idea that he was coming, or anything like that. So I reported to the morgue. . . ." O'Connor said that Admiral Galloway came to the morgue. "He told us that we were now confined to the morgue—he told us both, both Jenkins and I—that we had an important visitor coming in that night. Of course we knew who it was then."

Later that afternoon, about 5:00 or 6:00 P.M., "the morgue started filling up with people—generals, admirals, you name it, they were there. And the body came in at eight o'clock on the dot, the body was . . . you know, the shipping casket came in with the body."

"The who came in?" I asked, trying to reconcile an eight o'clock entry with what I thought I heard him say about the type of casket that came in.

"The shipping casket. The shipping casket."

"Yeah, right," I replied, as if I understood.

"They brought him in, and we put him on the table. . . ."

I knew what a shipping casket was—it was certainly not the four-hundred-pound ceremonial casket that Kennedy's body left Dallas in, and for which the Government was billed almost $4,000. But before pursuing that, I decided to clear up another matter. O'Connor said "eight o'clock." What was the basis for that statement? I asked. "Because I recorded it in

---

* A complicating factor was that his name was spelled correctly (O'Connor) in the section on the Osborne allegation, but incorrectly (O'Conner) in the official list of autopsy witnesses.[27]

the log," he replied. He went on to explain that inside the autopsy room was an ordinary, general issue logbook, in which were recorded the times of all the autopsies that took place at Bethesda. O'Connor told me it was simply called the "Autopsy Log," and that he supposed the log had been preserved by the Navy Department. Repeatedly during our conversation O'Connor said that he had logged in the time as 8:00 P.M.

"Okay, now you say 'shipping casket.' What do you mean by 'shipping casket'?" I asked.

"Well, I used to work in a funeral home as a kid," explained O'Connor, "and a shipping casket is nothing but a cheap casket. It was a kind of pinkish gray, and it's used, for example, say a person dies in California and he wants to be buried in New York. They just bring him in a casket like this, and they ship him to New York, and they bury him. It's nothing fancy. It's just a tin box. . . ."

I asked O'Connor for more detail about the casket's color.

"It was kind of a slate-type gray, and a kind of light pinkish color on the edges," he said.

"I see. I see," I replied. "And when you opened it up, how was he wrapped?"

"He was in a body bag," replied O'Connor.

"Now when you say 'body bag,' what do you mean by 'body bag'?" I asked.

"Okay. A body bag is nothing but a rubber bag that bodies are put into, say in a disaster, or something like that, where a lot of people are killed. They bring these bags in. An air crash disaster. It's a heavy rubber bag with a zipper on it. They zip up the body . . . it's a standard body bag used in disasters."

"Is that the kind of body bag they talked about in Vietnam, when they brought soldiers back?" I asked.

"It was the same."

"Was it absolutely the same?" I asked.

"Just about. Yeah, I'd say—they're just about all the same. They're used for just that one purpose, and that's it . . . it's a rubber bag . . . just a regular zippered bag. . . ."

"In other words, it was nothing makeshift or ad hoc?" I asked, exploring the possibility that the sheet of plastic used to line the Dallas casket might be confused with a body bag.*

---

* The twenty-six volumes contained some information about how President Kennedy's body was wrapped in Dallas. The reports of Nurses Diana Bowron, Pat Hutton, and Doris Nelson, and orderly David Sanders all mentioned that a plastic mattress cover was used. Nurse Hutton said it was used "to line the coffin."[29] Nurse Bowron said the President's body was "placed . . . on a plastic sheet in the casket."[30]

To verify that President Kennedy's body was not put inside the mattress cover,

"No," he replied, and his answer to my next question made it clear that the possibility of O'Connor's being confused was remote.

". . . how many years did you work in a funeral home?" I asked.

"Oh, since I was about fourteen; I went through high school working in funeral homes."

"What was your job at the funeral home?" I asked.

"I did everything."

"You mean at fourteen years old, Mr. O'Connor, you were preparing bodies and . . . ?"

"Well, I was assisting. You see, I came from a very very small town in Indiana. The funeral home had the whole ambulance service for the whole county. And we did ambulance service, and I also helped with bodies, and preparing [them]. . . . I was just kind of a like a 'gofer.' I went for this, I went for that, I cleaned up. I went on ambulance runs. . . ."

I told O'Connor that when I was that age, I could barely put a worm on a hook.

"Well," he said, "I always wanted to go into the Navy Hospital Corps, I always liked medicine, I enjoyed it."

O'Connor described the body bag from which he removed the President's body. "We unzipped the whole bag. . . . The zipper runs right down the middle of the bag, all the way down to the feet."

"From head to toe?" I asked.

"Right."

"How was he wrapped inside there?"

"He was naked, and he had a sheet wrapped around his head."*

I contacted Aubrey Rike, one of the two employees of O'Neal's Funeral Home who put Kennedy's body inside the casket.

Rike had vivid recollections of the events of that day. He told me that the plastic was merely used underneath the body, to keep blood away from the satin lining of the coffin. Rike was emphatic that the body had not been put inside the mattress cover. When I inquired whether a body bag had been used, Rike was incredulous that I would even ask such a question: "A body bag . . . a 'crash bag'? No way," he said.[31]

* On November 26, 1963, Robert Bouck, of the Protective Research Section of the Secret Service, issued a receipt to Dr. George Burkley for a number of items obtained from Burkley on that date. The fourth item on the "Bouck receipt" was: "One receipt dated Nov. 22, 1963, for bed sheet, surgical drapes, and shroud used to cover the body in transit."[32] It was not clear who signed this particular receipt, but the Bouck document, dated November 26, 1963, was evidence that the receipt existed as of that date. After speaking with O'Connor, my attention immediately focused on the word "shroud." No "shroud" was put on the body in Dallas—just sheets. I suspected the "shroud" was a euphemism for the body bag, and it made me wonder about the Secret Service's handling of that document.

On May 2, 1978, I had applied to the Secret Service, under the Freedom of Information Act, for this receipt. On May 16, 1978, I received this response: "A

O'Connor's version was good evidence that President Kennedy's body did not arrive at the autopsy room in the Dallas casket, and later in our interview, he used the following phrases to describe the shipping casket: its weight was "maybe one-hundred-fifty pounds." It was "a regular old metal casket," he said, "the cheapest kind . . . just a cheapie . . . a cheap metal thing."

I asked him how it opened: "It's a cheap casket, and it's got what looks like aluminum head screws, and you undo the screws, as I remember, on the right side . . . [it] lifts up on the left. . . . And inside is the body —the body bag."

I decided to ask O'Connor about what the body looked like, and exactly what "preparation for the autopsy," which the Committee said was his function, consisted of.

"We set up the instruments to examine the body—scissors, knives, saws."

Then he added: "In most cases, we remove the brain for gross anatomy."

"Sure," I said, wondering what was coming next.

"But he didn't have any brains left."

I stiffened. This was new. I could almost sense what was coming next.

"What do you mean?" I asked.

"The wound in his head was terrific. It was about—oh, I'd say, eight by four inches."

"What did you say—eight by four inches?"*

"Yes," replied O'Connor. He then asked: "Do you know anything about anatomy?"

"Yeah, I sure do. I had to study it for this project."

"The wound was in the occipital-parietal area . . . clear up around the frontal area of the brain. . . ."

To follow what happened next in the conversation, it is essential to understand that O'Connor believes the Warren Report, and didn't have any suspicions at all about the condition of the body or its method of arrival at Bethesda. He simply had not studied the matter.

"I think what happened is he got hit when he fell over [O'Connor

---

search of Secret Service records failed to surface this document." On July 24, 1978, I wrote asking if they had a document which explained why that item and two others were not in the file. My letter stated: "I am requesting any memorandum or internal record created when the Secret Service first became aware that it did not have any of the above three items, and when it made the absence of these items a matter of record in its own files." On August 2, 1978, the Secret Service replied: "The Secret Service file does not contain any documents which make reference to why the file does not have the documents you requested."

* Boswell's diagram of the skull showed an area 10 by 17cm marked "missing." 10 by 17cm is 3.9 by 6.8 inches, very close to the dimensions provided by O'Connor.

meant, he later explained, that the President must have been bending forward] . . . the bullet must have ricocheted off, and entered at the back of the head and then came out the front of the head. It blew all of his brains out—literally."

"When you say 'blew his brains out'—I mean, I know the expression in English. But when [you] say he didn't have any brains in there, did you have to go through the medical procedure to remove the brain?" I asked.

"No, sir," replied O'Connor. "There wasn't anything to remove."

"What do you mean by that?" I asked.

"The cranium was empty," he replied.

"The cranium was empty," I stated flatly—not quite a question. If O'Connor was right, there was no question but that the body was altered prior to its receipt at Bethesda.

O'Connor described what remained as "bits of brain." But most of it was gone, "blown out," he said. "I would imagine it got blown all over the car."

I asked: "What about the lobes of the brain?"

"Nothing was left," he replied.

"In other words, the cranium, for all practical purposes, had been eviscerated?"

"It was gone," said O'Connor. "Everything was gone. There were bits of brain matter laying around inside the cranium, but other than that, that was it."

"There was no other brain matter in there?"

"No, sir."

"Were you surprised to see that much damage?" I asked.

"Yes, I was."

O'Connor was describing a cranium which, for all practical purposes, was the same as one after the skullcap and the brain had been removed, although it was clear from our conversation that he perceived the damage as coming from a gun.

To obtain more information, I pretended not to understand the full implications of what he had said.

"Do you normally, in an autopsy—is it your job as a 'prepper' of the body, if I can call you that, or a preparer of the body—[to] do the medical procedure yourself to remove the brain?"

"Yes, I do," he replied.

"In other words, you usually cut off the . . . roof of the skull?"

"Right."

"And you found that you didn't have to do that here?"

"Yes, right. That's right."

"Did you have the duty of telling that to Boswell?—'There's no brain in the cavity.' "

"Boswell and Humes saw it," replied O'Connor.

"And what was their reaction to that?" I asked.

"Oh, they were—everybody was really aghast, you might say."

"That there was no brain in there?"

"Yes. Well, not only that, but the severity of the wound, I guess."

I was determined to get the most precise information possible about his recollections. I wanted to understand how he reconciled what he had seen that night with certain facts about the autopsy which were in the public record.

One was the brain.

I told O'Connor that there was something called a Supplementary Autopsy Report. "And they weighed a brain—and they do have a report on a brain, describing it. Where did they get that brain from?"

"I don't know," he replied. "That's another thing. I've heard about that too, and that's very puzzling, because there was no brain on the body, near the body, or in the casket, or anything that I know of. They might have weighed pieces of matter, but they—I don't know how they come up with a brain."

"What about the skullcap itself," I asked, "the pieces of bone? Other than that eight-by-four-inch hole, were they still there?"

"No, they were gone," he replied. "They were blown away. There was a great big hole. You see, after they got done looking and taking pictures, and whatever they were supposed to do, they filled the cranium with plaster of paris."

LIFTON: You mean this is after the autopsy?

O'CONNOR: Yes.

LIFTON: You mean they filled the cranium with plaster of paris . . . so that it would have substance.

O'CONNOR: Right. And . . . if he was a bald-headed man, they would have been in trouble . . . and they took and combed his hair. And his hair just happened to be combed in that direction. He had a lot of hair, and they just—they were able to hide the wound.

O'Connor had worked in a funeral home in his teens. He paid close attention as the undertakers went about their work.

O'Connor accepted the official version that the President was struck in the head from behind. I asked if he saw the entry wound.

"No, there was no hole, really," he replied.

"What do you mean?" I asked.

"Well, there was just a great big massive hole in the skull. That was the only thing that was there. There was no round definition showing that the bullet had entered. It was just a great big blown-out piece of the skull."

O'Connor said that the huge hole he saw was "all on the right side. . . ."

"What about the scalp above that area?" I asked.

"It was laid back, that's all . . . just laid back, you know, torn. That's about the only thing I can say."

I asked O'Connor about the left side of the brain.

"Well, the left side of his brain was gone," he replied, "and as you looked in, there was just nothing inside the cranium."

"Even on the left side?" I asked.

"That's right," he replied.

"I know you're not a doctor," I said, "but how did the left side of his brain get out of there?"

"Must have been the force of the impact just sucked it all out. I don't know, blew it all out. It was just torn to pieces."

"I see, but it was not in there?"

"No . . . just little pieces, bits and pieces."

O'Connor told me that after leaving the navy, he had been a Deputy Sheriff in Brevard County, Florida for a while.

"Now, have you ever seen a gunshot wound case like that before?"

"I wouldn't say exactly like that. I've seen some massive gunshot wounds, yes, but that was, the way that he was falling, and the way that the bullet struck him, was a kind of unique thing—a freak thing, you might say. . . . I expected to see a wound, but I didn't expect to see something that massive."

I turned to the wound in the throat. O'Connor described it as "a great big hole in his larynx. . . . They said they tried to do a tracheotomy—it was already blown open. I don't know how they could have done anything with it . . . there was nothing. The esophagus was laid open. . . ."

It is rather obvious that if someone has no brains left in his head, he cannot be alive. Yet it was well known that Dr. Perry had performed a tracheotomy. I was curious to know what O'Connor thought about that.

"Well," he said, "I'm sure if they saw him, like we saw him, there wasn't any hope at all of them doing anything."

"How do you explain the fact that all the Dallas doctors [according] to all these news stories . . . did a tracheotomy. How do you explain all that?" I asked.

"I don't," he replied. "I can't explain that. I don't think they really went through as much as they said they went through because, as I said, he was dead."

O'Connor added: "He was just like he was brought out of a battlefield."

O'Connor's statement that the tracheotomy seemed incongruous in view of the condition of the head reminded me of the Warren Commission testimony of Dr. Malcolm Perry, who performed the tracheotomy, and who received a telephone call from Humes on Saturday morning.

That was the phone call in which Humes said he learned, for the first time, that what he had believed was a tracheotomy was actually a surgical incision over a bullet wound. Perry described how the call began: "He [Humes] inquired about, initially, about the reasons for my doing a tracheotomy. . . ."[33] Humes was apparently curious about the other life-support measures as well. Perry testified: "He subsequently called back . . . and he . . . inquired about the chest tubes, and why they were placed. . . ."[34]

As a pathologist and Director of Laboratories at Bethesda, Humes of course knew why tracheotomies were done, and why chest tubes were placed. Humes' questions to Perry, I now believed, reflected his own state of mind on Saturday morning, as he attempted to reconcile the evidence of a massive, obviously mortal wound with the incisions left by the Dallas doctors' resuscitative measures. Humes must have been confused.

O'Connor gave me his impression of Humes' demeanor at the time he first saw the head wound. "He was scared to death," he said.

O'Connor told me that he, too, was "afraid," and I asked him why.

"Well, I was just a junior enlisted guy . . . and around these big admirals and everything. And I just decided to keep my mouth shut."

O'Connor discussed a number of other matters.

The time of arrival. O'Connor insisted that the shipping casket arrived at 8:00 P.M. on the dot, and that he had entered that information in the autopsy log. I tried hard to locate that log. Other men I subsequently interviewed told me that the log was taken from the room that night—that "every scrap of paper" connected with the autopsy was confiscated. Subsequently, the National Personnel Records Center in St. Louis, after several searches in which I supplied "accession numbers" given me by officials at the National Naval Medical Center, reported: "Disposition of the requested autopsy log is unknown to this center."[35]

My own conclusion was that the events witnessed by Paul O'Connor probably occurred at least an hour earlier than 8:00 P.M. O'Connor also told me that the President's body left the morgue at 5:30 in the morning, although the casket team record established that it left at 4:00 A.M.

The mode of arrival. O'Connor was under the impression that the shipping casket in which he said the body arrived was brought to Bethesda by helicopter. I questioned O'Connor closely about the basis for this belief. He told me: "I heard the helicopter, for one thing . . . then they rushed the body in. And then they sealed off the morgue, and they had marine guards all over the hallway. . . ."

O'Connor explained that the heliport at Bethesda was at the front of the hospital, and that he would not have heard a helicopter landing there because the morgue was at the rear of the hospital.

I could only speculate that O'Connor was an earwitness to a helicopter that landed somewhere at the back of the hospital, perhaps near the parking lot by the Officers' Club, and if that helicopter brought the body in, that its cargo was then transferred to the hearse reported by Dennis David.

This was most hypothetical. But O'Connor was quite definite about the role helicopters played in getting the body to Bethesda, and he told me about conversations he had had with others that week.

"I remember hearing somebody say that they saw three helicopters, for the express purpose, you know, of decoying the people."

I told O'Connor about the "decoy ambulance," and asked if he knew anything about that. He said he did not. But firmly entrenched in his memory were recollections—admittedly imprecise—about one or more "decoy helicopters." I was to hear about the decoy helicopter from other witnesses.

By far the most important part of O'Connor's account was his statement that President Kennedy's body arrived at Bethesda in a body bag inside a shipping casket, and his observation that the body arrived without the brain. From the first statement, I concluded that O'Connor had received the same plain casket that Dennis David saw plainclothesmen carry to the morgue door. From the second, I concluded that the President's body had not been altered at Bethesda Naval Hospital, but beforehand.

In short, Paul O'Connor's account provided strong corroboration for the account given by Dennis David.

After speaking with O'Connor, I began to try to arrange events in the autopsy room along a time line. For example, I found O'Connor perfectly credible when he said the throat wound was unsutured when the body arrived. I also found Ebersole credible when he said it *was* sutured at what *he* thought was the outset of the autopsy. I thought they made their observations at different times.

In 1972, when I spoke with Ebersole, the first question I asked was: "When did the autopsy begin?"

Ebersole replied: "To the best of my knowledge, we actually started the autopsy formally about ten-thirty at night."[36]

This suggested to me that sometime that evening, prior to what Dr. Ebersole thought was the start of the autopsy, the throat wound had been sutured.

Time-line analysis had been a great aid in determining what happened to the body between Dallas and Bethesda. After speaking with O'Connor, I began to realize that the same technique probably would be necessary to reconcile conflicting accounts of various Bethesda witnesses, all of whom were convinced they attended "the" autopsy.

I placed O'Connor at the very beginning of the Bethesda time line. If he was correct, he had opened the casket in which the body arrived. I believed him when he said: "I was the one that took the sheet off his head."

At that moment, the throat wound was unsutured and the body had no brain.

CHAPTER 27

The Recollections of
James Curtis Jenkins, et al.

AFTER I SPOKE WITH O'CONNOR, I realized that the men who played ancillary roles at the autopsy—the lab technologists, the X-ray technicians —might possess valuable information. I resolved to locate and interview as many as I could.

Meanwhile, I had applied to the Defense Department for the file of documents pertaining to the order issued by Surgeon General Edward Kenney on November 22 that required all personnel present at the autopsy to keep silent. Within two months I had the entire file.

The "Order-Not-to-Talk" File

Thirteen men—the three autopsy doctors, the radiologist, the photographer, the medical illustrator, a hospital corpsman, two laboratory technicians, two X-ray technicians, Galloway's secretary, and a naval officer of whom I had never heard—were subject to the order.

Capt. John H. Stover, Humes' superior and the Commanding Officer of the U.S. Naval Medical School at Bethesda (which administered the morgue), issued a confirming written order to each man. The document to laboratory technician James Jenkins, dated November 26, 1963, read:

1. You are reminded that you are under verbal orders of the Surgeon General, United States Navy, to discuss with no one events connected with your official duties on the evening of 22 November–23 November 1963.
2. This letter constitutes official notification and reiteration of these verbal orders. You are warned that infraction of these orders makes you liable to Court Martial proceedings under the appropriate articles of the Uniform Code of Military Justice.

Immediately beneath was a "First Endorsement," which read:

1. Above orders received this date.
2. I have read and fully understand them and am aware of the disciplinary action possible in the event that I disobey these orders.

James Curtis Jenkins signed the document on November 27, 1963. Similarly dated signatures appeared on all the other "First Endorsements" in the file.

Below the first endorsement was a second endorsement—from Stover to Galloway, reading: "Forwarded to you this date for retention in your files."

The order was effective. When, at the outset of the House Committee's investigation, Purdy called these witnesses, they refused to speak with him.

Purdy contacted the appropriate officials in BuMed in September 1977. They in turn contacted Admiral Burkley on September 22, 1977. A navy memo stated that Burkley said "that he, as the White House Physician, had given the order."[1] The navy memo noted: "RADM [Rear Admiral] Kenney's role in the transmission of this order is still not clear."[2]

The roadblock was finally dismantled, and in March 1978, identical letters were sent to each person who received the original order.*

The first paragraph of that letter reminded the recipient of the order of November 1963. The second stated that the House Select Committee was conducting an investigation and that "You are advised that the Department of the Navy interposes no objection to you, should you wish to do so, discussing with designated members of the Select Committee's staff, matters pertaining to the autopsy. . . ."

On Sunday, September 23, 1979, before I received the file, working with information provided by Purdy and Flanagan, I found James Curtis Jenkins.

Interviewing Jenkins

From the beginning of the conversation, it was clear that I was speaking to someone still deeply affected by what he had witnessed at Bethesda

---

* Dianne Seimer, an Assistant General Counsel of the Defense Department, interposed a major roadblock to the lifting of the order. The file showed that on November 3, 1977, after clearances had been arranged from the navy medical department, Ms. Seimer overruled them and refused to rescind the orders. Ms. Seimer wrote: "All of the records, notes and other materials related to the autopsy were delivered by the navy to the White House physician, Dr. George G. Burkley. The Department of Defense has no such documents or materials in its possession at this time.

"The record with respect to the autopsy is complete and has been preserved intact. Under these circumstances, the Department cannot rescind the order to personnel who were involved in the autopsy prohibiting disclosure of any information about the autopsy acquired in the course of their official duties."

sixteen years before. Jenkins was nineteen at the time. He told me that except for the House Committee's representative Purdy and staff investigator James Kelley, he had spoken to nobody about the autopsy. That Sunday, he and I talked almost three hours.

I had hoped to confirm O'Connor's "body bag" story. Jenkins told me that he didn't remember how the President was wrapped. It was a detail that made little impact on his memory. He did recall the casket: "It was *not* a really ornamental type thing . . . it was kind of a plain casket. . . ." "Awful clean and simple" was another of his descriptions, and he added: "As a matter of fact, it was not something you'd expect a President to be in. . . ."

Jenkins insisted that he had put a brain in formaldehyde that night—and that he had gone through the procedure of "infusing" it. After listening to his account, I wondered whether a brain had simply been brought to the room, or whether Jenkins had found it in the cranial vault.

It was clear that the perceptions of Jenkins and O'Connor, and their corresponding recollections, were different. Certain details which made a deep impression on O'Connor made none whatsoever on Jenkins, and vice-versa. It was as if the two men were tuned to different frequencies. What was central to Jenkins' whole experience that night was his conviction, from looking at the President's head, that the fatal shot struck from the front.

Jenkins did not see an entry wound on the front of the head. But the large hole in the head—i.e., what the Bethesda autopsy report called the exit defect—was situated toward the rear. The general way the fragments were distributed—the way scalp with bone attached seemed to have been exploded outward and to the rear—convinced Jenkins that the shot must have come from the front.

Jenkins had had previous experience with gunshot injuries to the head. Before he went to laboratory school at Bethesda, he had been a hospital corpsman stationed at Cecil Field, Florida. One night he was called to the front gate. A civilian, dressed in white clothes—thought to be a sailor—was seriously injured. He had been shot by a relative armed with a .30-.30. The whole front right side of his face, said Jenkins, "had been taken off."

Jenkins, knowing nothing about trajectories or ballistics, had assumed he had been shot from the front. But it was explained to him that in fact the individual had been shot from the rear. Jenkins learned then how a bullet behaves when hitting a skull. The bullet "enters small" and "goes out big." It was explained to Jenkins why a bullet injures a skull that way—that upon entry it punches a small hole in the bone, but that as it traverses the relatively hollow skull cavity, it begins to wobble, and produces a much larger wound upon smashing against the opposite surface.

Jenkins put aside the unpleasant experience. But he absorbed the lesson. One of his ambitions was to be a doctor. His outlook, he explained to me, was "totally scientific."

So on the night of November 22, 1963, James Curtis Jenkins stood at the autopsy table, "touching elbows," as he put it, with "the army officer" (as he recalls Finck) who was the specialist in ballistics. And based on his previous experience, and seeing Kennedy with a huge hole in the head—Jenkins said that "at last one-third of the skull was gone when Kennedy was brought in"—a hole which extended toward the rear, and with fragments that seemed to be hanging on, and which seemed to have been exploded toward the rear, Jenkins formed the opinion that President Kennedy had been shot in the head from the front.

Since Jenkins didn't see a frontal entry wound, he assumed that it had been blown away when the bullet struck, and he concluded that the bullet must have struck from the right front.

But then, the next day, said Jenkins, "I found out that supposedly he was shot from the back. I just, you know, I just couldn't believe it, and have never been able to believe it."

He said: "I was very surprised by the conclusion . . . it was really kind of shocking to me. I guess I accepted it because of the circumstances I was in. . . . But, I mean, I didn't accept it as being fact."

It was clear, from speaking with Jenkins, that he was very frightened by the experience. Jenkins spoke of the autopsy with care and precision. He was different from the other personnel I hunted down on this project. He was a keen observer. He eventually spent several years in a Ph.D./M.D. program at the University of Mississippi. He never completed the program, but went to work with medical instrumentation. It was obvious that what happened on November 22, 1963, was a turning point in his life.

He left the autopsy room convinced, from the appearance of the head, that President Kennedy had been shot from the front, only to find—from the next day's newspapers—that President Kennedy had supposedly been struck in the head from the rear. "It frightened me," he said. "I did not discuss it with anybody for many many years, but I followed it very closely. . . . I eventually discussed it with my wife."

I questioned Jenkins closely about how he perceived the "order not to talk."

LIFTON: . . . did you feel that the order not to discuss it was related to the fact that what you saw was different than what you were reading in the newspapers?
JENKINS: Yes, I did.

Jenkins told me of his first introduction to the order regarding silence.

He had remained in the morgue all night, he told me, and didn't leave until nine o'clock the next morning.

LIFTON: You stayed up all night?

JENKINS: Yes.

LIFTON: How come? . . . what happened after five that you would still be up?

JENKINS: I had to clean up the morgue.*

Jenkins told me: "After we got it cleaned up, we were told to wait till nine o'clock for Captain Stover, who was the Commanding Officer of the Medical School there; and we were taken to his office, and we were told, verbally, that we were to discuss this with no one—not even our immediate family—under penalty of, you know, such and such. . . ."

Jenkins' voice stuttered and faltered as he said the word "penalty."

". . . and that orders would be issued officially, subsequently, which they were."

Frankly, I identified in a very personal way with Jenkins. He had had the same problem with the body—and how its appearance clashed with what he had been taught—that I had had with the Zapruder film and my beliefs about the backward motion of the head.

But one thing puzzled me. Didn't Jenkins know that night that the surgeons drew the conclusion that the shot came from the rear?

I asked him this. He said that no such conclusion was drawn at the time of the autopsy. His description of what was said at the autopsy table was different from anything I had found in the official record created by Humes, Finck, Boswell, Sibert and O'Neill.

"There were no conclusions that night," said Jenkins. Jenkins described what he heard as "discussions." "There were some speculations—discussions—between the three physicians, with a couple of other people—I don't know who they were. They seemed to be in charge, or seemed to be some type of authority." Jenkins didn't know who these civilians were, but they came up again and again in his account. As to the doctors' discussions about the fatal shot, he said: "There were some discussions, questions asked, and things of that nature. But it was all kind of in a manner of—you know, searching for a conclusion, as opposed to drawing a conclusion."

Jenkins told me the role the civilians played. It had made a vivid impression. There was "temperament," "anger," and "rumblings," said Jenkins. "The people running around in civilian clothes . . . had a pre-concluded idea, and . . . because it was not panning out, you know, they were *very*—there were a lot of animosities, to be quite frank with you . . . there were very short tempers. Things of that nature." Jenkins told me it "was not obvious, but there were rumblings. . . ."

---

* In a re-interview some months later, O'Connor told me that he and Jenkins had to "get down on our hands and knees" and clean up the entire morgue after the autopsy.

Jenkins had great difficulty even discussing it.

"You mean—'tensions'?" I asked.

"Yes," he replied, "that you kind of feel." Jenkins said it was his impression that "animosity" was "directed toward the people doing the autopsy—you know, Dr. Humes, Dr. Boswell, and Dr. Finck. . . ."

Jenkins elaborated on what he recalled of the discussions: ". . . you know, this would be found, and somebody would say, 'No, that's not right; can't be . . . ,' that type of thing. 'That's not possible.' To the point that, at the time, I felt like Dr. Humes and Commander Boswell were being— were getting irritated, or sometimes I even felt like—and this was my opinion, I don't know how they felt about it—that . . . someone was chastising them."

Jenkins said the source of the irritation in the room was the civilians he had described, but he could not identify them: "I don't know what they were, or who they were, what their functions were, or anything of that nature." He had been preoccupied with the medical details of the examination, and didn't remember much about them. "Civilians are just totally a blank to me . . . there were a lot of discussions among the civilians themselves as to what had happened, where the bullet had come from— and to be quite honest, I was not at that time concentrating on any of these conversations." Jenkins told me he was "purely interested" in the autopsy itself, the examination of the body. "I was there to hand him [the doctor] instruments, to do odd things for him, get him things, make sure the specimen bottles are there, take down weights, things of that nature."

When I told Jenkins that according to the official record there were only about five men in civilian clothes present at the autopsy—Sibert, O'Neill, Kellerman, Greer, and O'Leary—he was incredulous. "There were only five civilians there?" he asked. "No, that's not true. . . . I can't give you a definite number," he said, adding that he knew many more were present, and that they were sitting in the "gallery."

Jenkins had vivid recollections about the controversy concerning the neck trajectory. The wound at the front of the throat, throughout the autopsy, he said, was assumed to be a tracheotomy. Yet, said Jenkins, the civilians who seemed to be in charge seemed to be trying to get Humes to conclude that a bullet passed from back to front through the body. Jenkins had a clear recollection that that wasn't possible. He remembered very clearly Humes' probing the back wound with his little finger. "What sticks out in my mind," Jenkins told me, "is the fact that Commander Humes put his little finger in it, and, you know, said that . . . he could probe the bottom of it with his finger, which would mean to me [it was] very shallow." He had another recollection. After the body was opened and the organs removed, Jenkins watched the doctors probe it again. "I . . . I remember looking inside the chest cavity and I could see the probe . . . through the pleura [the lining of the chest cavity]. . . ."

LIFTON: Explain that to me. You could see the probe that he was putting in the wound? You could see it through the pleura?

JENKINS: You could actually see where it was making an indentation.

LIFTON: . . . an indentation on the pleura.

JENKINS: Right . . . where it was pushing the skin up. . . . There was no entry into the chest cavity . . . it would have been no way that that could have exited in the front because it was then low in the chest cavity . . . somewhere around the junction of the descending aorta [the main artery carrying blood from the heart] or the bronchus in the lungs. . . .

LIFTON: Did you hear Humes say he could feel the bottom of it with his finger?

JENKINS: Yes, I did.

I told Jenkins that Humes testified that he found a bruise atop the upper lobe of the lung, and that was the evidence for the bullet going all the way through. Jenkins told me he had no recollection of any such bruise being examined the night of the autopsy.

I was unwilling to believe that Humes made that up out of whole cloth; and, anyway, photographer Stringer told me he had photographed it.

I asked Jenkins what conclusions he had expected the autopsy report to state based on what he saw while he was there. He said he assumed the report would have concluded that the President had been shot once in the back from behind—"and that they could not find the bullet"—and that the second shot, to the head, came from the front.

I asked Jenkins how he explained the autopsy report that was written. Jenkins minced no words. He said that Humes was a "super-military type of person"—not in the sense that he was authoritarian, but that he was concerned with his next promotion and his career in general. "He was the type of individual that would do anything anybody above him told him to do . . . my personal feeling is that he was probably directed to write the autopsy report." Jenkins told me he has always assumed such "directions" came "from someone outside the hospital."

I said that the chain of command was short—Humes' senior officers were Stover, C.O. of the Medical School; Galloway, C.O. of the Medical Center; and Kenney, the Surgeon General. "And then you're either at the Joint Chiefs of Staff or orders from the White House." Jenkins replied: "I didn't say that; you did."

It was obvious that he had given the matter some thought, and he was not comfortable discussing it.

Jenkins' statement that the "Friday night conclusion" regarding the neck trajectory was different from the autopsy report was not new. That was the old "non-transit/transit" conflict between the FBI report and the navy autopsy. But the statement that the doctors did not come to a firm conclusion about the head shot, that their discussions were tentative, was new. To evaluate that, and much else Jenkins said, it is necessary to make a brief digression.

The Autopsy Conclusion Regarding the Head Shot

It was well known that according to the record one or more pieces of bone were handed to Commander Humes at the morgue on November 22, 1963. There is a conflict as to how many pieces were involved—the FBI agents reported one large section, Humes testified there were three. In any event, X-rays were made of the three. Sibert and O'Neill reported that night, in an FBI telegram, that the bone fragment had been "flown in from [a] Dallas hospital."[3] Later Gerald Behn, Chief of the White House Detail of the Secret Service, told Sibert and O'Neill it came from the automobile.[4] Humes testified he wasn't sure. Ebersole told researcher Art Smith that around midnight he was called to the commanding officer's office and given the bone fragments and told they had arrived from Dallas.[5] The House Committee concluded: "There is no evidence to show who sent these fragments to Bethesda."[6] The record is clear that until these fragments arrived, the autopsy surgeons had found no evidence of either an entrance or an exit wound on the head. Humes testified that after a "careful examination" of the wound margin, he could find no evidence of exit on the skull itself.[7] Finck's autopsy notes state the same thing: "No exit wound is identifiable at this time. . . ."[8]

With regard to an entrance wound in the head, Finck's notes and Boswell's statements at a 1977 closed session of the House Committee made clear that no such entrance wound existed until after midnight. Colonel Finck's autopsy notes state that along the bottom edge of the large hole in the head was "a portion of a crater."[9] Boswell said it wasn't until after the bone fragments arrived that he was able to take one of the smaller pieces and "fit that down there and complete the circumference of that bone wound."*[10] Until those bone fragments arrived, what the doctors called an entry wound was nothing more than a notch at the rear end of a large hole.

---

* The drawing made by Dr. Boswell at the autopsy table supports his later testimony. At the bottom of the back of the head are several numbers, almost certainly referring to bone fragments that were used to reconstruct the rear portion of the head. And at the bottom of the sketch, Boswell actually drew a small half-moon shaped figure, showing just such a "notch," probably his own attempt to illustrate how the notch became a hole. (See Photo 27.)

Since the record is unequivocal that Humes did not have these bone fragments until after midnight, it is obvious that, until that time, he not only had no evidence of exit, he had no separate entrance wound. This fact supports James Jenkins' statement regarding the tentative nature of the conclusion drawn about the head wound, in that no conclusions could have been drawn until those bone fragments arrived.

Two other factors also support Jenkins. Secret Service Agent Roy Kellerman testified: "Just for the record, I wish to have this down. While the President is in the morgue, he is lying flat. And with the part of the skull removed, and the hole in the throat, nobody was aware until they lifted him up that there was a hole in his shoulder. That was the *first* concrete evidence that they knew that the man was hit in the back first."[11] (Emphasis added.)

Kellerman said the autopsy had been underway "for quite some time"[12] before the rear shoulder entry wound was discovered.*

Kellerman's testimony that the hole in the shoulder was the "first concrete evidence" that the President "was hit in the back first" clearly supports Jenkins' assertion that the doctors could draw no conclusions about the direction of the fatal shot from the initial appearance of the head.

Finally, there was the report filed by Sibert and O'Neill. I read Jenkins the following passage: "Dr. Humes stated that the pattern was clear that one bullet had worked its way out of the body during external cardiac massage and that a second high-velocity bullet had entered the rear of the skull and had fragmented prior to exit through the top of the skull."[13]

LIFTON: . . . you didn't see anything like that taking place?

JENKINS: No. That is something that I definitely would have remembered.

Jenkins insisted that the discussions were speculative—always limited to possibilities.

On this point, Sibert and O'Neill's report contained typographical alterations which suggested that the version in the record had been revised from some earlier version.

For example, the report contains this typographical anomaly:

---

* There is a conflict in the record between Kellerman's testimony and Sibert and O'Neill's Baltimore Field Office memorandum. Sibert and O'Neill wrote that before the autopsy began those concerned—the doctors, Kellerman, and Sibert and O'Neill—discussed whether a full autopsy was necessary "to obtain the bullet which had entered the President's back." Thus, according to that memorandum, the back wound had been observed *before* the autopsy began. Yet, according to Kellerman, it was discovered *after* the autopsy was underway. Sibert and O'Neill, despite their memorandum, also stated in their report that the back wound was not discovered until "the latter stages" of the autopsy.

```
On the basis of the latter two developments, Dr. HUMES
stated that the pattern was clear   that the one bullet had
entered the President's back and had worked its way out of the
body during external cardiac massage and that a second high
velocity bullet had entered the rear of the skull and had
fragmentized prior to exit through the top of the skull.
```

On the second line of the foregoing sentence, it appears that something two characters wider was originally written in the space now occupied by the word "clear." Was the word originally "unclear"?*

Jenkins told me that when the body arrived in the autopsy room, at least a third of the skullbone was not attached. Fragments, he said, were in the coffin. Some were attached to the scalp.** "I would say the parietal and occipital section on the right side of the head—it was a large gaping area, even though, I think, as we put it back together, most of the skull, the bone itself was there. It had just been crushed, and kind of blown apart, toward the rear."

When I asked Jenkins to describe more graphically where the wound was, he replied: "I'm laying my hand on the back area of my skull. And my hand is probably five to six inches from the span of my little finger to the tip of my thumb. So if I spread my fingers and put my hand back there, that probably would be the area that was missing." Jenkins said, regarding all the bones that were either attached to the scalp or in the casket: "When they put it back together, it would probably have been about the size of your fist—which was an actual hole missing." Jenkins said that "the hole that they came in with was, like I said, would have probably covered at least a third of his total head area."

That comported with O'Connor's estimate of 8 by 4 inches, and Boswell's diagram notation of 10 by 17cm.

When I told Jenkins that the autopsy photographs showed that the back of the head was essentially intact, except for a small bullet entry

---

* The autopsy conclusion that the bullet exited the head at a particular location was based on the doctors' placement, on the head, of a piece of bone which showed beveling. Jenkins told me the doctors tried several possibilities but reached no firm conclusion. The paragraph in the Sibert and O'Neill report which describes that activity—the first full paragraph on page 5—appears to have been altered: The final sentence expressing the conclusion was retyped and lengthened by several words.

** The official version is that the bone fragments were brought to the autopsy room later. In a closed session before the House Select Committee, Humes may have made a slip of the tongue. He said: ". . . the only extra piece of bone brought to us then—that was contained *in the casket that brought the President to us*—was a piece of bone that was brought to us later on that evening. . . ."[14] (Emphasis added) This may indicate that his spontaneous recollection of the way the bone fragments arrived was different than the official version.

wound at the top, he was incredulous. "That's not possible. That is totally —you know, there's no possible way. Okay? It's not possible."

Jenkins account suggests that President Kennedy's body, even though altered, was not altered sufficiently to create the unambiguous appearance of a shot from the rear.

Central to his experience is his belief that the President was shot in the head from the front, and that that fact was covered up from the start. Throughout our conversation, it seemed that Jenkins was still frightened. He told me that on a number of occasions he had "considered trying to put this in my own words, because I wanted—I wanted to have it down . . . for history." He didn't necessarily want to publish it. "I wanted to put it down on paper in my own words, not so much for anybody else to know. . . . I wanted to say what my feelings, what my conclusions were, before they were published from some other source. . . ." But he never carried through such a plan, and now his memories of that night were getting fainter with each year. He told me he had considered consulting a hypnotist to strengthen his recollections.

I thought: How extraordinary to have seen the actual event occur, to have formed conclusions, and then watch history unfold another way. "That's a very interesting story," I said.

"It's a realistic thing to me," he said. "The fact is that my feelings of credibility, what I've been told, because of this . . ." His voice trailed off. He began again: "Every time there seems to be something of importance that affects the nation, and I'm told one way by the government, I'm skeptical about it. Because this was probably the most significant thing that had happened in this country in God knows how long, and my feelings are that the people themselves were just—well, to be quite frank—lied to about it, and for what reason I have no idea. I don't want to speculate on that—those type of things. If it's happened in something this important, this dramatic—I had almost wished that I had not been there. . . ." His voice trailed off.

Jenkins and the House Committee

One Sunday afternoon in 1978, Jenkins received a phone call from Andrew Purdy, who identified himself as a lawyer with the Assassinations Committee. Jenkins told Purdy that he would be happy to talk with him, if he had proper identification. He also requested that the interview be conducted in his congressman's office.

Purdy came to Jackson, Mississippi, where Jenkins was a student at the time, to interview him, accompanied by staff investigator James P.

Kelley. Purdy showed his identification card, Kelley flashed a badge, they retired to the office for an interview of some three-and-one-half hours.

No tape recording was made. No stenographic record was made. Jenkins thought that Kelley might have made a few handwritten notes. Jenkins told me that it quickly became apparent that Purdy and Kelley were not interested in what he had to say. "They seemed to only want me to answer their questions," said Jenkins. "I did feel a little intimidated."

LIFTON: Did you tell Purdy . . . that you thought, from what you saw that night looking at the cadaver, that the President had been shot in the head from the front?

JENKINS: Well, you know, they were not really interested, to be quite frank . . . as to what my opinions were. It was all a matter of— we're going to ask you these questions—you answer them, to your knowledge; and that's all I want. Never an opinion. . . .

LIFTON: . . . did you ever sit down and say, "Hey, look guys, I'm answering your questions, but I think you should know that that night, here's what I thought"?

JENKINS: Every time I would get into that avenue, Mr. Kelley would kind of change the conversation back to, you know, force the conversation back—and as a matter of fact, most of the questions that I answered were asked by them.

Jenkins told me that after the session in the congressman's office, Purdy took him to the University of Mississippi Law Library, got out a copy of the Warren Report, and reviewed the "facts" of the case with him.

"Purdy was asking me: 'Would I be surprised if I knew that there was a hole, a bullet hole in the top of the cranium?' And I said 'Yes.' " Jenkins explained to me there wouldn't have been any skull there at all—at the position Purdy was referring to.

Jenkins recalled: "I told him 'Yes, I would be *very* surprised,' and then he showed it to me."

What Purdy showed Jenkins were the Dox drawings depicting the wound.

My own reaction to what Jenkins told me was mixed. I was pleased that Purdy and Flanagan had taken steps to see that the navy order was rescinded; I was grateful for the help they had provided me in locating the witnesses. But I also felt none of this should have been necessary—that the Committee should have published depositions or tape recorded interviews with these witnesses. Now, upon speaking with them myself, I was learning that no such records had even been created,* that these uniquely

* The Committee's records are sealed at the Archives for fifty years, but when they become available, what will be there, in the case of these autopsy witnesses, are the Outside Contact reports written by Purdy and Flanagan. But one exception is

valuable witnesses had been handled in a casual way that indicated little awareness of what they had to contribute.

The X-Ray Technicians: Custer and Reed

My conversation with Jenkins whetted my appetite to speak to every single person who had been in the morgue on November 22, 1963. Using the navy file, and information from Purdy and Flanagan, I found the two X-ray technicians, Edward Reed and Jerrol F. Custer. (See Photo 40.)

Reed was a twenty-year-old in 1963. He told me that he relied on the location of the large head wound—"more posterior than anterior"—in forming the opinion that the President was shot in the head from the front. He said that about six months passed before he realized that the official version of the autopsy conflicted with his own opinions.

> LIFTON: Personally, how did you come to terms with that, or what was your reaction to it?
> REED: It was hard for me to believe it.[15]

I asked Reed whether at any time that evening he had seen a small entry wound on the rear of the head.

"No," he replied.

Despite these opinions, Reed didn't react strongly to the situation. He vividly recalls being called into the Admiral's office the next day and told he could not talk about what he had seen, subject to court martial, but he assumed that was standard procedure for a case of this type, and didn't have a theory that anyone was trying to hide anything.

One other observation Reed made about the wounds seemed pertinent. He told me: "It wasn't like a tracheotomy, a normal tracheotomy. It was a lot larger."

Jerrol Custer was the other X-ray technician at the Bethesda autopsy. Custer told me the President's head wound was enormous—"I could put both of my hands in the wound. Okay?"—and that he believed he had been shot from the front. "Let me tell you one thing. If you ever have gone hunting, you know as well as I do, when a bullet goes into the body, it goes in small and comes out big. Okay? Well, that is exactly how the skull looked. Okay? . . . from the front, to the back."[16]

Custer said that he held this view in November 1963, but when the

---

the case of Richard Lipsey, General Wehle's aide. Lipsey insisted that Purdy tape record his interview, and Lipsey also made his own tape of the interview for his records.

official version was publicized, he simply shrugged it off. I asked him why. He replied: "For the reason that I was only a little lowly X-ray technologist. Okay? And all of these so-called experts were saying that this didn't happen. I just figured—well, maybe I could be wrong."[17]

I questioned him about the Bethesda entry wound:

LIFTON: Did you personally see an entry wound at the rear of the head, at any place?

CUSTER: No.

LIFTON: You did not?

CUSTER: No.

Custer also told me that when he saw the throat wound, it did not look like a standard tracheotomy incision. He said that based on what he saw at Bethesda he thought the President had been shot from two directions, with the head shot coming from the front.

He said that he exposed, and returned to the morgue, X-rays showing that the rear of the President's head was blown off.

Custer had a vivid recollection of signing the order not to talk, and reacted negatively when the House Select Committee called him, and without any identification, expected to question him by phone. He told me he never received the letter they said had been sent out, and, when they called, he got off the phone quickly—not really confident they were who they said they were.

The most important thing I learned from Custer occurred at the end of our conversation.

One of his vivid recollections on November 22 was that he saw Jacqueline Kennedy.

"Where?" I asked.

"Right there at Bethesda," he replied.

"Yes, but where? Where would you see her?"

"She was coming in through the main entrance. She was going up to the towers."

"You saw Jacqueline Kennedy when she arrived, you mean?"

"Yes, definitely. I had passed her. I had passed her and I had my arms full of film, and in fact what struck me is she still had that dress on."

"Had you already taken any X-rays?"

"Oh, definitely. This was even the second or third trip."

Custer explained that to develop the X-rays, he had to take them from the morgue to one of the upper floors, and so had to pass through the lobby area. A Secret Service agent escorted him. "I remember her coming in and being surrounded by reporters, and then there were Secret Service men, and they were pushing the reporters out of the way. As they pushed them out of the way, I remember seeing her come through. . . . I can't remember what color dress, but I remember I saw the bloodstains on it . . . and the Secret Service guy behind us said: 'Come on, let's go.' For some reason, he didn't want people to know—you know—what we were doing."

Custer said that he saw Jacqueline from a distance of ten or fifteen yards. "I saw her, because she stuck out like a sore thumb." He continued to the hallway and took an elevator upstairs to get his films processed.

Here was the strongest evidence that the President's body was at Bethesda before Jacqueline got there. She entered the hospital no later than seven o'clock. Outside the hospital door stood the navy ambulance, with the Dallas casket. Yet Custer already had in his hands X-rays of President Kennedy's body.

CHAPTER **28**

The Clandestine Intermission Hypothesis

IN QUESTIONING WITNESSES who were at Bethesda the night of the autopsy, I asked each person the same series of questions: Where were you when you first heard the President was assassinated? Tell me how you found yourself involved in the autopsy of President Kennedy. Where were you when you first saw the body, or the coffin containing the body? Were you on the loading dock or inside the autopsy room? What is your recollection of how the body got to Bethesda? Did you see a coffin? What kind of coffin was it? Did you see a coffin opening? How was the President's body wrapped? Who was there?

Most of the witnesses fell into two groups—those who said that President Kennedy was brought to the morgue in a ceremonial casket by the Military District of Washington honor guard, and those who reported they saw a plain metal casket, or who recalled that Kennedy was inside a body bag, and noted the presence of previously unreported plainclothesmen.

Had this been an ordinary case, the choice of which witnesses to believe would have been left to the jury. But this was no ordinary case. I thought there was reason to believe that the body was carried into the morgue more than once.

There were, if my chronological analysis was correct, three episodes that must have taken place in the area of the morgue:

1. arrival of the body, in a shipping casket, for the first time;
2. appearance of Sibert and O'Neill outside the door of the morgue, accompanying the Dallas casket which, unknown to them, was empty;
3. the Dallas casket's entry into the morgue a second time, with Kennedy's body inside.

Why didn't witnesses to the first entry also see the second?

There was no problem with the group that came in later. They would have had no way of knowing about the earlier coffin opening in the same room, unless they were told about it. The problem was with the group that was there from the start. I called them "audience 1." Why didn't "audience 1" see events connected with the removal of the body from the table, and the arrival of the second group—the McHugh group, whom I called "audience 2"?*

An observer who remained in the room throughout the period would have witnessed the President's body removed from the autopsy table, replaced in the Dallas casket, and the second entry into the autopsy room.

Why was there no evidence of such an observer?

Struggling with this problem, I again questioned my assumption that everything took place in one room. Perhaps there were two morgues. Perhaps one group of witnesses saw certain events in one room; another group saw other events in another room. Two groups could have seen different events, but not each other.

But this didn't work. I had personally inspected the morgue facilities at Bethesda, and I knew there was no "second morgue."

Once again I went through the testimony of each member of audience 1. Jenkins told me that at one point he had been sent to get a laboratory specimen jar.[1] Perhaps he was absent when audience 2 arrived. Custer left the morgue to carry the X-rays upstairs, escorted by a Secret Service agent.[2] That might account for him.

But what about Sibert and O'Neill? I wasn't sure when they entered. All I knew was that they reported 7:17 as the time of the "preparation for the autopsy" and that they had apparently been kept out of the morgue for a while.[3] But even if they were in the hallway, they would have seen the coffin's entrance, exit, and its re-entry; and once inside the morgue, could hardly have been sent on errands.

---

* I couldn't always be sure which ones were in audience 1 and which were in audience 2, but it did seem clear from the evidence that O'Connor and Jenkins were in audience 1; that Floyd Reibe, the photographer's assistant, was in audience 1; that Stringer was probably in audience 1; that Drs. Humes and Boswell were in audience 1; that Captain Stover, according to Dennis David (who said he was definitely there when the black hearse arrived) was in audience 1; that Custer, because of his description of seeing Jacqueline when he was carrying X-rays upstairs, must have been in audience 1. Sibert and O'Neill apparently joined audience 1 at 7:17. Kellerman appears to have joined audience 1 shortly before 7:30; and Greer, assuming he remained with Kellerman, was probably there too.

In audience 2 were Godfrey McHugh; any members of the honor guard who went into the morgue and watched the coffin being opened, or assisted; Humes and Boswell, again; Admiral David Osborne; Colonel Finck, who arrived after the autopsy was underway; and Dr. John Ebersole who, Humes told me, was not present when the body was brought in. (Ebersole told me in 1972 that he thought the autopsy began formally at 10:30. His account will be discussed later.)

On September 3, 1979, discussing this problem with an associate, I blurted out: "What I need is evidence that *everybody* was asked to leave the room!"

I had no sooner spoken those words when I remembered a passage in the Sibert and O'Neill report.

I consulted the document. Sure enough, the two agents wrote:

The President's body was removed from the casket in which it had been transported and was placed on the autopsy table, at which time the complete body was wrapped in a sheet and the head area contained an additional wrapping which was saturated with blood. Following the removal of the wrapping, it was ascertained that the President's clothing had been removed and it was also apparent that a tracheotomy had been performed, as well as surgery of the head area, namely, in the top of the skull. *All personnel with the exception of medical officers needed in the taking of photographs and X-rays were requested to leave the autopsy room and remain in an adjacent room.* [Emphasis added.]

Upon completion of X-rays and photographs, the first incision was made at 8:15 P.M.[4]

I realized this required a change in my view of when Sibert and O'Neill were permitted to enter the room. Their report indicated they had been kept out for an unspecified period of time. Previously, because I thought the body was altered at Bethesda, I had supposed that period might have lasted thirty or forty minutes. Now, because of the information provided by O'Connor, I had good reason to believe the body came to Bethesda already altered, and I realized it was totally unjustified to infer that Sibert and O'Neill had been kept out of the room that long.

Sibert and O'Neill were probably kept out for no more than three or four minutes—just long enough for the Dallas casket they were escorting to enter the anteroom to the morgue.

While they waited, Sibert and O'Neill could no longer see the casket—but neither could men inside the morgue proper, since the anteroom is closed off both from the autopsy room and from the hallway. (See Fig. 41.)

When the two agents were permitted to enter, they would have seen the casket—probably in the anteroom—and the body on the autopsy table. Prevented from entering immediately, they were thereby prevented from discovering that the casket they had escorted to the door was empty—that the body was already inside the morgue.

Sibert and O'Neill may nevertheless have learned, at this point, that the casket which they brought to the door—i.e., the Dallas casket—was not the casket in which the body had arrived at the morgue. I noted that they wrote in their report: "The President's body was removed *from the casket in which it had been transported* and was placed on the autopsy table. . . ." (Emphasis added.)[5]

Those words—"from the casket in which it had been transported"—seemed superfluous, unless Sibert and O'Neill were aware by November 26,

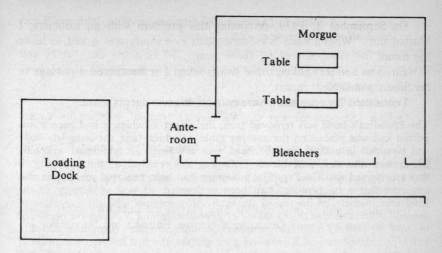

Figure 41.
Sketch of the morgue at Bethesda Naval Hospital

1963, when they dictated their report, that the casket "in which [the body] had been transported" was to be distinguished from another casket. Those words supported the idea that the shipping casket reported by O'Connor and some of the others was still in the room at the time Sibert and O'Neill entered.

This interpretation permitted Sibert and O'Neill to be inside the morgue within a few minutes of 7:17. Roy Kellerman testified that 7:30 was the latest the autopsy could have begun, that when he arrived at the morgue, "The navy people had their staff in readiness right then. There wasn't anybody to call. They were all there."[6]

I could understand why Kellerman seemed impressed with the rapidity with which the navy staff had convened. Dennis David's account convinced me that the body arrived at the morgue about 6:45, which meant that Kellerman actually entered the room a good thirty to forty minutes later.

Thus, by 7:30, Kellerman, Sibert and O'Neill, and those who had seen the body arrive in the shipping casket—O'Connor, Jenkins, et al.—were all inside the morgue.

Following the evidence chronologically from that point, it now seemed clear what must have happened.

Inside the hospital the following situation existed:

1. the body lay on the table inside the morgue;
2. in the vicinity of the morgue entrance stood the Dallas casket—brought to the morgue door by the FBI;

625

3. upstairs was Jerrol F. Custer, X-ray cassettes in hand, with the Secret Service agent who escorted him.

From the viewpoint of all these people—Kellerman and Sibert and O'Neill, who had just arrived, and those already in the room—the autopsy had already started.

Outside the hospital was Godfrey McHugh.

Outside the hospital was the Military District of Washington casket team.

This was the group who thought they had escorted Kennedy's body to Bethesda in the navy ambulance.

The casket team was trying to escort the casket to the autopsy room, but they couldn't find the ambulance.

The most vivid account of how they passed the next fifty minutes was the one written by Coast Guardsman George Barnum, on November 29, 1963:

"We were following an ambulance . . . as we arrived at the rear entrance to the hospital, by the morgue, we were informed that the casket had not been driven there. We then jumped back into the pickup and returned to the front of the hospital. There were so many people that the instructions were still confusing and we were told to return again to the rear. We did so and once again [were] informed that the casket was not there. We returned again to the front and this time . . ."[7]

"This time," according to Barnum, the ambulance with the Dallas casket inside finally arrived.

The MDW team escorted it inside, and their report says this occurred at 8:00 P.M.[8]

Thus, about fifty minutes passed between the time the navy ambulance first pulled away from the front entrance (carrying an empty coffin, according to my analysis) and the time the MDW casket team carried the Dallas casket into the morgue at 8:00 P.M. At that time, it once again contained the body, if the accounts of audience 2 are to be believed.

Why didn't audience 1 see the second entry? And how were they prevented from seeing that the body left the autopsy table after it first arrived (i.e., in the shipping casket)?

The report written by the two FBI agents suggested an answer. They wrote: "All personnel with the exception of medical officers needed in the taking of photographs and X-rays were requested to leave the autopsy room and remain in an adjacent room."[9]

The taking of autopsy X-rays might have been an excuse to clear the room; more precisely, the excuse given to Sibert and O'Neill. Perhaps other persons were sent out for other reasons. But the Sibert and O'Neill report seemed to me good evidence that that was how they were induced to leave, and that they were under the impression that others left at the same time.

I called this period during which audience 1 was gone from the room a "clandestine intermission"; "clandestine" because the purpose was hidden. The chronology indicated that it was during this period that the casket —with the body now inside—reappeared back outside the hospital. (See Fig. 42.)

If the coffin entry described by the witnesses of audience 2 was to be accepted, during the clandestine intermission the body must have then been put back in the Dallas casket, and the casket must have been rolled through a door and put back into the ambulance, so that the ambulance could reappear to be reunited with the casket team.

The account of George Barnum meshed nicely with this hypothesis. According to Barnum, the casket team was told to leave the front of the hospital twice. The first time would have been when the team lost the Dallas casket. The second would have been when the ambulance with the Dallas casket was re-introduced to the front of the hospital. Thus the casket team would have been prevented from witnessing the re-appearance of the ambulance. When they returned to the front of the hospital the second time, they would simply have found it there, and chalked the whole experience up to innocent confusion.

It was unclear exactly how the casket was moved from inside the hospital back outside. That might have taken place at the morgue entrance. Or perhaps the casket was put on a dolly and rolled to another entrance, where it was put back into the ambulance.

My research has turned up no eyewitness to such an episode. However, Paul O'Connor told me that there was talk going around the hospital the next week about an "empty casket" that was rushed into the emergency area at some point.[10] The "empty casket" could have been the Dallas casket with Kennedy's body inside, on its way to a rendezvous with the navy ambulance.

Perhaps it was during this period that the coffin was damaged.* McHugh told me he didn't notice any damage until he brought the casket into the hospital through the rear entrance.

My analysis indicated that when McHugh and the casket team escorted the Dallas casket to the morgue at 8:00 P.M., events must have unfolded along these lines. First, McHugh, General Wehle, and his aide, Richard Lipsey, would have been unaware that this was the second entry for that casket—and unaware that the body had arrived at Bethesda before they did.

At the 8:00 P.M. entry, the body would have been taken out of the casket, placed on a stretcher, and rolled inside the morgue. It would then have been transferred back to the autopsy table.

Following the 8:00 P.M. morgue entry, audience 1 could be told that the period for taking X-rays was over and that they could return to the

---

* See Chapter 16 for discussion of damage.

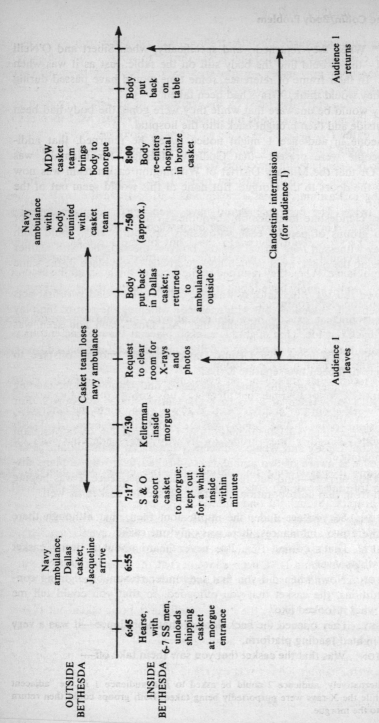

Figure 42.
Time line for clandestine intermission hypothesis

morgue.* When they returned—and specifically, when Sibert and O'Neill returned—they would find the body still on the table, just as it was when they left. In their frame of reference, some time would have passed during which, they would think, X-rays had been taken.

They would be unaware that while they were gone, the body had been taken outside and then brought back into the hospital.

Someone in audience 1 might notice, when he returned, that additional people were present—that Godfrey McHugh, for example, was present. Or that the Military District of Washington casket team was now guarding the doors to the morgue. But none of this would seem out of the ordinary.

This "clandestine intermission" hypothesis offered an explanation for how two groups of people, each witnessing separate events, could both think they witnessed *the* "arrival" of the body at the morgue, with neither group seeing the other, even though both "arrivals" took place in the same room.

Viewed this way, the autopsy was like a play which had two first acts for two separate audiences, but with everyone watching the rest of the play together, neither group knowing that the "Act One" each had seen was different.

Of course, someone like Dennis David was far enough offstage to know there had been two separate arrivals.

Before I understood the time sequence, I had trouble understanding why David's knowledge of "two caskets" wasn't shared by others. For example, on August 30, 1979, I spoke to Richard Lipsey, General Wehle's aide. Army documents I later received under the Freedom of Information Act state that Lipsey and Wehle's helicopter landed at Bethesda at 7:14.[11]

Lipsey was aware of two ambulances—he had heard those plans discussed at the airport—and before I understood the sequence, I was hoping to obtain from him corroboration of perhaps a second casket, as well.

LIFTON: So you are under the impression, then, that although there were two ambulances, there was only one casket.

LIPSEY: That's correct . . . I've never heard about a decoy casket whatsoever.

LIFTON: Now, when did you first see, under reasonable lighting conditions, the casket that you offloaded, so that you could tell me what it looked like?

LIPSEY: They opened the back door of that ambulance—it was a very lighted loading platform.

LIFTON: Was that the casket that you saw them take off—

---

* Alternatively, audience 2 could be asked to join audience 1 in the "adjacent room" while the X-rays were purportedly being taken. Both groups could then return together to the morgue.

LIPSEY: [interrupting] That was the *only* casket.

LIFTON: It was the big heavy Dallas casket?

LIPSEY: Yes, it was the *only* casket.

LIFTON: Well, let me ask you—was it a big four-hundred-pound monster?

LIPSEY: Well, we had one hell of a time getting it out. . . . I remember two or three of us grabbed it before the whole honor guard got right there; and we were trying to hoist it out of there, and we had a hell of a time moving it.

LIFTON: It was not an ordinary shipping casket . . . to ship a body from one location to another air freight?

LIPSEY: No. . . . I can assure you, that while I may have not been in the room when they took the body out, that is the *only* casket, and I can swear on a stack of Bibles that is the only casket that entered those doors. If another one came in, it had to come down the mail chute. . . .[12]

It didn't come in the mail chute. It just came in earlier.

In April 1980, I interviewed Humes' superior, Capt. John Stover. Stover referred to the casket in which the body arrived as a "transport coffin."[13] When I asked him whether he meant "shipping casket," he said it "could be," but that he did not remember. Stover said that he was involved in making "arrangements for security measures," but he did not know whether there had been two ambulances.

"I can easily believe that there may have been such an arrangement," he told me, "but I don't know that of my own knowledge."

On a number of points, Captain Stover's memory was very fuzzy, and he reminded me how many years had passed since November 22, 1963. But on one subject, Stover gave me a positive answer: "I think there was a body bag," he said. "I remember seeing a body bag. . . . I think I remember seeing a body bag peeled off."

Stover seemed quite certain about this, which means that corroboration for O'Connor's account comes from the man who was Dr. Humes' commanding officer.*

James E. Metzler

The notion that there were two coffin openings at the Bethesda morgue is strongly supported by the experiences of James E. Metzler. I interviewed him at length in November 1979, and just as Paul O'Connor had strong and vivid recollections of the arrival of the President's body

---

* When I told Captain Stover about the Secret Service receipt for a shroud, he said that was probably a receipt for the body bag.

in a shipping casket, Metzler was an eyewitness to, and apparently a participant in, the arrival of the body inside the Dallas casket. Metzler was a hospital corpsman, third class. He was in the room for only five or ten minutes; he was then asked to leave. His account is important for another reason: It provides concrete evidence of a group of men, in civilian clothes, who were keeping very careful track of who was entering and leaving the room. This group, between six and ten in number, was stationed in the anteroom to the morgue, where the chillboxes were.

Metzler told me he was in lab school at the time: ". . . clinical lab and blood bank they called it . . . you had to stand what they called 'watch' in the navy . . . you had a choice between a fire watch in the barracks or you could be on the morgue watch, which was doing autopsy, helping the pathologist. I chose that because it was . . . more interesting than watching the barracks at night. . . ."[14] Metzler explained that after the coffin arrived, he did not remain inside the room for more than five more minutes. He said he told the House Select Committee: "I was just there for maybe about five or ten minutes when they brought in President Kennedy . . . we got a call from upstairs—they said they were bringing him in by decoy around the back.* So I went out back and sure enough, there was the honor guard.

LIFTON: Were you outside on the loading dock when he arrived?

METZLER: I went out to the door, yes . . . the honor guard was there. They brought in the casket . . . by the time I got to the door I believe they were just about coming in. . . . The honor guard brought it in and they had to leave. And then I helped put him on the table—there was maybe about five of us that helped put him on the table. . . .

LIFTON: How was the body wrapped?

METZLER: He was all in a sheet. His head was wrapped in a sheet. . . .

LIFTON: Was it a ceremonial coffin or a shipping casket?

METZLER: . . . it was dark brown, I believe it had handles on the side of it. It would be something that you'd see at a viewing. . . .

LIFTON: It was not the kind of casket you'd use in a disaster situation? To ship a body from New York to L.A.? Something like that?

---

* By this point in my research, I had heard so many accounts from different witnesses about "decoy ambulances" and "decoy helicopters" that I had become jaded. I asked Metzler what he meant when he said they were "bringing him in by decoy." He replied: "You see, they had a helicopter somewhere. . . . ," and he went on to say that some sort of measure was used to keep people away from the area when the body was brought in. He was not specific, and his information was based upon what he heard during the next few days. Metzler also told me that it was general knowledge, the next week, that the Kennedy party arrived *after* the body.

METZLER: It's not a rubber bag or a metal box, if that's what you mean.

LIFTON: That's what I meant. It was a regular viewing casket, or what I call a ceremonial coffin?

METZLER: Yes.

LIFTON: What you see in a funeral home for a viewing?

METZLER: Exactly.

Metzler told me that inside, the body was wrapped in two sheets—one around the entire body, another around the head.

Metzler said that he was then requested to leave: "The pathologist told me I could go—they had everything they needed."

He told me that the people who would be assisting in the autopsy were "the people that came from upstairs that were on lab watch." And that, he said, would be O'Connor, whom he repeatedly referred to as having been there earlier, before he got there. But Metzler never indicated that O'Connor was present at the coffin opening that he witnessed—i.e., the Dallas, or ceremonial, coffin.

As to his own experience, he said: "They hadn't started the autopsy yet. They were just about to begin."

What happened when Metzler walked out the door is significant. The autopsy room, remember, has two doors—both of which open onto the hallway. Standing in the hallway facing the room, the door on the left is next to the rear entrance, near the loading dock. If you open that door, you do not enter the morgue area itself, but a small anteroom, where the half-dozen chillboxes are located, along with a desk and a phone. Big double doors open from that anteroom into the morgue itself—with its amphitheater and the two autopsy tables.

As Metzler left, he had to walk through the anteroom. There he encountered a group of men in plainclothes.

METZLER: . . . seemed like almost ten of them. . . .

LIFTON: In that little—?

METZLER: Small room, yes.

During our conversation, Metzler told me he had always assumed they were FBI, but he really did not know for a fact which government agency they represented.

Whoever they were, they had what Metzler referred to as a "roster."

"Well, the FBI men didn't come in—they were out in the refrigerated thing. So when I left, they asked me for my identification, and I gave it to them, and they saw that my name was not on the list to be in the room, because I had been in the room before they came.

"They had a roster—who should be there. You know how they are. . . .

"I guess they were guarding who comes in and who goes out—security, part of it. . . . Because when I came out into the refrigerated room, this one guy says, 'What's your name?' and I told him, and he looked down at his list and he said, 'Let me see your ID card,' and they looked at that —there's a picture on it, of course—[and] they said, 'His name isn't on the list.' And the other guy steps across the door, so you can't open the door, you know, it [was] really kind of spooky. . . ."

LIFTON: The point is they wanted to make sure you didn't leave?
METZLER: Right.
LIFTON: Until they knew who you were?
METZLER: Exactly.
LIFTON: And did the guy take out a pad and write your name down?
METZLER: Yes, he wrote down my name.

In evaluating Metzler's experience, it was essential to place him correctly on the time line, and so I questioned him carefully about what he meant by "honor guard." Metzler said he actually walked out onto the loading dock: "I went out first of all, maybe to help them bring it in, but I didn't know the honor guard was there. They had plenty of people to bring him in. There was an admiral there with the honor guard. [The admiral could have been Burkley, Galloway, or Kenney.] I don't even remember how many stripes he had above the wide gold stripe—at least two [a vice admiral] . . . he was there with the honor guard when they brought him in."

LIFTON: When you say "honor guard," do you mean men from different services joined in one group, or do you mean all marines?
METZLER: No, I think this was the bunch that used to take care of the funeral duties for any President, heads of state, you know, from all [the] different branches. I'm pretty sure that's who it was.

Metzler added: ". . . there was so much brass there, it was unbelievable. I never saw so much brass in my life—not only inside the room, but around the hospital . . . high-ranking officers . . . like this one admiral who came in, and there were others—I think I saw another admiral and someone who was possibly from the army, who was maybe general staff . . . out in the corridors in the hospital."

When Metzler left the room, the first thing he did was go upstairs and tell one of the officers in charge that his name wasn't on the list because, he said, he didn't want him to get in trouble.

One final point about Metzler's experience. He thought that when the sheet was taken off, you could see a brain, or part of a brain inside the cranial vault.

It was also his impression, from the way the wound was located toward the back of the head, that President Kennedy must have been shot in the head from the front. He wasn't adamant about it, and when he read later that the official autopsy concluded otherwise, he simply assumed he had been wrong.

Metzler left the hospital and returned to the barracks. He vividly recalls: "Chet Huntley was on the news as I walked in, and he said: 'I'm afraid at this time we don't know where President Kennedy is, and if we did know, we wouldn't tell you anyhow.' "

The Civilians in the Ante-Room

From my interview with Metzler, I concluded that he was a witness to the arrival of the Dallas casket escorted to the morgue by the honor guard; that the Dallas casket definitely contained the body of President Kennedy; that the body was transferred from the Dallas casket to the autopsy table in Metzler's presence; and that the body may have contained a brain—or a portion of a brain—by that time.

But what I found most fascinating about Metzler's experience was his encounter with the group of about ten men in plainclothes who were in the morgue anteroom.

When Metzler first described it, I thought it must have been Sibert and O'Neill. But upon reflection, it seemed clear that could not be the case.

First, Sibert and O'Neill had no security function whatsoever at the Bethesda autopsy—their sole function, according to their report, was "to obtain bullets reportedly in the President's body." In an internal FBI document, they wrote: "We were instructed solely and specifically to obtain any bullets which might have been in the President's body and take them to the FBI Laboratory. This was our purpose for being present at the autopsy."[15] In other documents, they refer to it as their "primary purpose."

Sibert and O'Neill therefore would not be determining who should be entering or leaving the autopsy room. That was simply not their prerogative.

Second, Metzler said the men took the information off his ID card. Sibert and O'Neill's list contains many misspellings; and there are no navy ID numbers.[16]

Who were these men, and what were they doing? Like everyone else, within three or four days, Metzler was asked to report to Admiral Galloway's office and sign a statement that he would not talk about what he had seen or heard that night, subject to court martial. It is my belief that the men Metzler saw, and the roster he saw them working with, are the source of information for the "order not to talk" file, which the House Select Committee learned of during its investigation, and which I obtained under the Freedom of Information Act.

Metzler's experience makes clear that extremely tight security was maintained on the autopsy room, that very careful records were kept of who was inside. It would appear that those whose names were recorded were then called into the Admiral's office and asked to sign a statement.

None of this would seem out of the ordinary were it not for the fact that the evidence suggests that *two* coffin openings took place, that the body was brought to the room twice, once in a shipping casket and once in a ceremonial casket.

All conspiracy theories of the Kennedy assassination suffer from the fact that it is possible to document acts, but the existence of the actors must be inferred. In this case, the issue is whether there was a degree of stage management to the Bethesda autopsy and, if so, who were the ubiquitous "they."

To say the least, Metzler's experience shows the extent to which the high-ranking officers at the National Naval Medical Center were keeping track of who was inside the room. Beyond that, however, if there were two separate casket openings, Metzler may have bumped into some of the stage managers on his way out of the morgue.*

The people Metzler encountered in the anteroom could have been the group Dennis David saw in the black hearse. But there is another possibility.

J. S. Layton Ledbetter was the Chief of the Day of the Medical Center command. He was one of those aware that the body was at the hospital before the navy ambulance arrived. He talked of Bethesda as a ship: "I saw the navy ambulance pull in, and I was let known that it was already aboard."[18] Ledbetter told me he was sure there were two ambulances— that he witnessed their arrival. But that wasn't the original plan. ". . . I'm not sure on the ambulances. I know there was two helicopters involved. One never did land; and the other one, I think, was a decoy. . . ." But even ambulances and helicopters were not central to his experience.

---

* As he looked back, sixteen years later, Metzler wasn't frightened by what he recalled of that night, even though he believed that from the way the President's head looked, he must have been shot from the front. When I spoke with him, as with the others, I tried to say little, if anything, of what I had learned from anyone else.

Metzler, a friendly type, remembered one man from that period. He asked: "Did you speak with someone named Jenkins? . . . I liked him. He was from the South."

"Yes, Mississippi," I replied.

"Yes, and he said he wanted to be a doctor after he got out; and I never heard from him since. I wondered if he ever did in fact become a doctor."

"Why do you ask that?" I said.

"I thought he'd be a good doctor," said Metzler. "It just seemed like . . . he would be good at it. . . . When you work with people, side by side, you can tell when there's somebody next to you that has a feel for what's going on. . . . You know, you just have a feeling about some people—some people have it, some don't. He seemed to have it."[17]

He reported for work about ten minutes before 4:30, when the Officer of the Day watch began. Just as he walked in the door, he took a phone call from "downtown" telling him the President's body would be coming to Bethesda. And while he was taking the call, three Secret Service agents showed up in his office. "I answered the phone. The White House wanted to speak to the Officer of the Day, and . . . these three gentlemen walked up to me and they said: 'Are you Chief Ledbetter? Do you have the Chief of the Day watch today?' And I said, 'Yes, sir. I do. Can I help you?' He said: 'We're Secret Service men receiving the body of President Kennedy back here, and . . . there's already twenty-six of us here on the compound.' They identified themselves."

Ledbetter told me he had personal contact with only those three, and "a few more" later on, but that they made clear that from that point forward, it was a Secret Service operation.

The Secret Service men seen by Ledbetter at 4:20 P.M. are as unknown to the official records of the investigation as the so-called Secret Service agents on the grassy knoll. Assuming they were authentic, the only conclusion I could draw was that Chief Rowley had sent a contingent of operatives to Bethesda, but never chose to reveal that to the Warren Commission or the FBI.* None of which would be necessarily important, were it not for all the strange goings-on at Bethesda.

Ledbetter said he referred the group of agents to the Administrative Duty Officer, and arrangements were made for the handling of the autopsy.

When I joined Ledbetter's account of the arrival of agents at 4:20 with Metzler's account of encountering plainclothesmen in the morgue with a roster, I concluded that someone made arrangements for an autopsy in which the identity of each participant—the photographer, the lab techs, the X-ray techs—was carefully recorded. In short, the group in the anteroom was not just keeping track of the comings and goings to and from the room. Ledbetter's information makes clear that by 4:30, two and a half hours before the body got to the hospital, agents, probably working with naval officers, made detailed arrangements as to who would conduct the autopsy. That fitted with O'Connor's account. He said Admiral Galloway himself came to the morgue, told them they would be confined to the morgue, and that they were expecting "an important visitor."[19]

Floyd Albert Reibe

On the navy list was one Floyd Albert Reibe, the photographer's assistant. Back in 1972, Commander Stringer told me that the roll of

---

* The Warren Commission records mentions only five Secret Service agents at Bethesda. They all traveled on *Air Force One:* Clint Hill, who escorted Mrs. Kennedy to Bethesda; Paul Landis; Roy Kellerman; William Greer; and Muggsey O'Leary.

film which was destroyed during the autopsy—"seized by Secret Service agents and exposed to light"—was taken by Reibe. Stringer also said then that Reibe had taken "scene" photographs which would show people in the room.

I contacted Reibe on November 26, 1979. I wanted to know what coffin opening he witnessed, where he would fit on the time line. In 1979, Reibe, then forty-three, was a medical technician working with nephrologists on artificial kidney research. On November 22, 1963, he was a student at the school of medical photography at the U.S. Navy Medical School. He became involved in the Kennedy autopsy, he explained, because "I was the duty photographer that night."[20]

Reibe first learned that President Kennedy was being brought to Bethesda when one of the superior officers called him and "told me to get everything I needed down to the autopsy room." Reibe called medical photographer John Stringer, a retired naval officer employed as a civilian at the hospital.

Reibe said that he was inside the morgue when he first saw the coffin. He said the coffin was brought in by men "in civilian clothes, with a military guard."

I asked him what kind of casket he saw. Reibe's spontaneous response was to utter the word "bronze," but then he immediately retracted and said he saw a bronze-type casket somewhere that night, and maybe he was thinking of the fancy casket that Kennedy was put in later that evening.

I asked Reibe to distinguish between a viewing casket and a shipping casket, and his immediate response was: "This was not a viewing casket—it didn't open halfway . . . the whole lid came off. . . ."

> LIFTON: . . . it wasn't the kind you'd use in a funeral home for a fancy burial?
> REIBE: No. I don't think it was. In fact, I'd swear it wasn't.

Reibe said the coffin had "turnbuckles on it, if I remember right," that the entire top came off, and that there were some sort of screws—"something like thumbscrews were on there. They just take them off and pick the lid up. . . ." Reibe's description was fairly close to O'Connor's. I asked him how the body was wrapped.

> LIFTON: . . . was he in any kind of bag or anything, or in a sheet?
> REIBE: I think he was in a body bag.
> LIFTON: A body bag.
> REIBE: Yes, a rubberized bag. . . .

Reibe said it was a dark bag that opened with zippers. He said that his recollection was "vague."

As to how the body arrived, Reibe was one of those who thought it had come in by helicopter—not of his own knowledge, just what he had heard later.

Most surprising was his description of the pictures he took that night, for that description varies significantly from what the pictures now in the official collection show. Reibe said that pictures of the back wound were taken when Kennedy was lying on his stomach.

LIFTON: You took pictures of him when he was on his stomach?
REIBE: On his stomach, right.
LIFTON: No question about that?
REIBE: No.

There are no pictures in the present collection of Kennedy lying on his stomach. The picture of the back wound shows Kennedy lying on his *back* with his right shoulder tilted up away from the table.*

Reibe also said he thought he took about six pictures—"I think it was three film packs"—of internal portions of the body. Again, there are no such pictures in the official collection.

The official pictures show that Kennedy's head and shoulders were resting on a towel, clearly labeled "Bethesda Naval Hospital." I asked Reibe if there was any kind of cloth or anything else under the body. He replied that he didn't think so, adding, "They don't normally do that when they do an autopsy."[22] I asked why, and Reibe explained how an autopsy table is constructed. It has two levels, to facilitate the draining of fluids: "You got the upper part and it's got hundreds of holes in it for any fluid to go ahead and drain down and almost out of sight; but if you put a sheet or a cover, something like that [under the body], it would all stay up at the top."

While I realized that in evaluating Reibe's recollections it was necessary to consider the fact that these events took place sixteen years ago, I could not discount them for that reason. He had, after all, been there.

Reibe's account supported Jenkins' assertion that no firm conclusions were drawn about the bullet trajectories. He told me: "It seemed to me a couple of them [the autopsy doctors] might have been a little bit confused, and I think they were just going to go over the results later on and come up with their conclusions." That, said Reibe, was just his "impression."

Reibe talked about the security surrounding the room when he was inside. At one point, he recalled, he needed a battery pack or a roll of film for one of the cameras. He went to the door. One of the instructors from the Medical School was outside, and the instructor was escorted on the errand by a Secret Service agent. Reibe recalled the man's name. Sure

* The medical consultants for the House Select Committee on Assassinations criticized the pictures because of the inadequate way they were posed.[21]

enough, he was on the list kept by those in the anteroom: Robert William Rittmeyer, one of the senior instructors at the school of medical photography. "He went out and got the battery pack, and he brought it back down, and it was passed through the doors."

As for the order not to talk, Reibe remembered it vividly. In fact, when he first began speaking, he told me ". . . this is all still top secret. I mean it's all classified. I really don't think I can comment on it." Before Reibe would speak with me, I had to convince him that the order had been rescinded, which I did by reading him the paragraph on that point from the House Select Committee.

The file shows that Reibe signed his statement ("I have read and fully understand them and am aware of the disciplinary action possible in the event that I disobey these orders. . . .") on November 27, 1963; and his description of the circumstances surrounding that statement was interesting: "Captain Stover called down and told Mr. Stringer that he and myself [were] to come on up, and I think just about everybody who was at the autopsy that night was up there—all navy personnel, and he explained to us the Secrecy Act, and [word] came down from the White House, [they] wanted this kept top secret and nobody must talk about it. . . ."

LIFTON: He actually used the words "the White House"?
REIBE: Yes.

Reibe explained that he assumed the procedure was legitimate, and the purpose was to prevent gossip about the wounds.

What was the level of awareness of the FBI and of Commander Humes about the goings-on at Bethesda? There is evidence in the record to indicate that both were aware of peculiar happenings. However, just because something is peculiar doesn't mean it will strike a given individual as sinister. And it is easy to pass off something that is, in fact, sinister with the label "security." The casket team was told the "decoy ambulance" served a security function. Dennis David was told that *security* was the reason for two caskets, and why the one at the front was empty. And that same codeword, *security*, to my surprise, cropped up in the testimony of Commander James Humes.

I made this discovery within an hour of formulating the clandestine intermission hypothesis. I returned to the record to see whether Humes had mentioned anything—given any hint—about the strange goings-on at the outset of the autopsy, other than his statement that the autopsy began "after certain other . . . examinations . . ." and, to the House Committee, after "some preliminary examinations."

Specter questioned Humes about the beginning of the autopsy:

SPECTER: Tell us who else in a general way was present at the time the autopsy was conducted in addition to you three doctors, please?

HUMES: This, I must preface by saying it will be somewhat incomplete. My particular interest was on the examination of the President and not of the security measures of the other people who were present.[23]

He continued: "However, the Surgeon General of the Navy was present at one time or another. Admiral Galloway, the Commanding Officer of the National Naval Medical Center; my own Commanding Officer, Captain John H. Stover of the Naval Medical School; Dr. John Ebersole, one of the radiologists assigned to the Naval Hospital, Bethesda, who assisted with X-ray examinations which were made. These are the chief names, sir, that I can recall."[24]

Thus, Humes is on record as saying there were "other people . . . present" whose function was "security measures," but he never elaborated, and the phrase has laid buried in the transcript all these years. It is an innocuous phrase, and only comes to life when joined with an account like Ledbetter's or, more important, James Metzler's, who was an eyewitness to a roomful of men with a roster in the anteroom to the morgue.

In November 1979, I called Humes and asked him how the body arrived. His spontaneous recollection was that it had arrived in "a hearse."[25] I will always regret that I did not ask Humes the color of the vehicle. Instead, I asked: "Was that a hearse or a navy ambulance?" Humes immediately backed off, saying it made no difference, that he really had no recollection.

Before the House Select Committee in closed session, Humes, describing the beginning of the autopsy, said that he had put on his scrub suit, and then went out from the morgue to the loading dock to "await the arrival of the people accompanying the body." He then immediately rephrased the sentence, and made an explicit statement that the body had *not* yet arrived when he went to meet the escort at the loading dock: "And as I came out of the morgue in my scrub suit before the President's body arrived. . . ."[26]

Humes' friend of twenty-five years, Admiral Osborne, was a Captain and Chief of Surgery at Bethesda the night of November 22. Osborne was not present when the body arrived. He told me that it has always been his understanding that the body arrived in a hearse.*[27]

Although I did not ask Osborne the source of his information, I thought it reasonable to infer that it came from his friend, Dr. Humes.

---

* Osborne elaborated, saying he believed that the "undertakers" who brought Kennedy to Bethesda had a contract with the navy for handling deaths which occurred in the hospital.

The FBI Agents' Level of Awareness

There is reason for believing that Sibert and O'Neill became aware that President Kennedy's body was at the morgue before they arrived. First, there is the sentence they wrote that the body ". . . was removed from the casket *in which it had been transported*. . . ." (Emphasis added.)[28] Those words led me to wonder whether Sibert and O'Neill had somehow learned that the President's body had arrived in some casket other than the Dallas casket. My chronological evidence indicated that the body was at the Bethesda morgue before they reached the room. The question was: Did they become aware of that? The report of the interview they conducted the following Wednesday at the White House with Gerald Behn, Special Agent in Charge of the White House Detail of the Secret Service, contains evidence that they did.

Sibert and O'Neill's trip to the White House the next week had always seemed a puzzle to me. Two agents from the Hyattsville Resident Agency —a tiny offshoot of the Baltimore Field Office—had gone to the White House and had questioned senior officials of the Secret Service: Gerald Behn, Special Agent in Charge of the White House Detail; William Greer, the driver of the limousine; and Roy Kellerman, in charge of the Dallas trip. Moreover, in a departure from routine procedure when obtaining information from a fellow government employee, Sibert and O'Neill took a complete physical description of Greer.[29]

Their questioning of Behn also seemed peculiar. The first page of their report consisted of three paragraphs. The second began: "Mr. Behn was questioned concerning the section of the President's skull, which was brought to the National Navy Medical Center at Bethesda . . . after the autopsy was in progress. . . ."[30] Behn said it came from the car.

The third paragraph began: "Behn was likewise questioned concerning the location of a bullet which had been found on a stretcher at Parkland Hospital. . . ."[31] I could not understand why Sibert and O'Neill were questioning Behn about a matter like that, since Behn, who hadn't been in Dallas, would have had no direct information, and it was a matter of record that the bullet was turned over to the FBI at 8:50 P.M. on November 22, 1963, by Secret Service Chief Rowley.

But the first paragraph was the most mysterious. Sibert and O'Neill omitted the question they asked. But here was the answer:

Mr. Gerald A. Behn, Special Agent in Charge, White House Detail . . . was interviewed at his office and advised that during the President's visit to the State of Texas, then Vice President Johnson would always arrive at the next city to be visited ahead of the President and would join in the party awaiting the President's arrival. This was accomplished by the use of two Jets: Air Force I, which carried the President, and Air Force II, carrying the Vice President. On departing from a city, Air Force I would first take off followed by Air Force II which would thereafter pass Air Force I in flight, cruising at a faster speed, thus allowing the Vice President to arrive prior to the President and be with the greeting party.[32]

Gerald Behn thus described what the pilot of *Air Force One*, Jim Swindal, later described to me as "leapfrogging." But what does "leapfrogging" have to do with the medical evidence? What question did Sibert and O'Neill ask to elicit this response?

The answer, I believed, could be found in the first three lines of the Sibert and O'Neill report on the autopsy, in an obvious typographical alteration:

```
At approximately 3 p.m. on November 22, 1963, following the
President's announced assassination, it was ascertained that
Air Force One, the President's jet, was returning from Love
Field, Dallas, Texas, flying the body back to Andrews Air Force
Base, Camp Springs, Maryland. SAs FRANCIS X. O'NEILL, JR.
and JAMES W. SIBERT proceeded to Andrews Air Force Base to
handle any matters which would fall within the jurisdiction
```

The original spacing between "Air Force" and "the President's jet" was seven characters wide. In other words, the report, as originally typed, apparently read:

. . . it was ascertained that Air Force ABCD, the President's jet, was returning from Love Field. . . .

What was "ABCD"?

One possibility was that what had originally been written there was the numerical designation for *Air Force Two*, whose plane number is 86790 but, in Secret Service reports, was often abbreviated to 6790.

Thus, it was my theory that the Sibert and O'Neill report, as originally typed, read that the body was aboard "Air Force 6790, the President's jet. . . ." It should be noted that 6790 was Lyndon Johnson's jet, and he was now "the president."

This typographical alteration suggested there had been a change in Sibert and O'Neill's understanding as to which plane carried the body from Dallas. When that was joined with the questioning of Behn, it seemed reasonable to believe that Sibert and O'Neill, baffled by the sequence of events they had witnessed at Bethesda, were at a loss to understand how the body got from Dallas to Washington and arrived at Bethesda before they did.

Exactly what Sibert and O'Neill asked Gerald Behn at the White House on November 27, 1963, must remain a matter of speculation. But they did record the response—a response which suggests they may have been told that the body was aboard *Air Force Two,* and that *Air Force Two* passed *Air Force One* in flight.

Does this recorded response mean that they asked why the body arrived at Bethesda before they did?

The FBI questioning of Gerald Behn; the account of Dennis David, who witnessed the arrival of the body in a black hearse before the Kennedy party arrived; the account of Paul O'Connor, who received the body in a body bag inside a shipping casket; and Jerrol Custer, who saw Jacqueline Kennedy entering the hospital as he was passing near the lobby with X-rays of the body—all this supported the idea that President Kennedy's body arrived at Bethesda before the 6:55 P.M. arrival of the navy ambulance containing the Dallas casket. Which meant that the Dallas casket, at 6:55 P.M., was empty.

The clandestine intermission hypothesis was my way of explaining how events were manipulated so that that same casket could be carried into the hospital at 8:00 P.M., and contain President Kennedy's body at that time.

There is corroborative evidence from James Jenkins of two coffins in the vicinity of the Bethesda morgue on November 22.

Jenkins told me that except for one brief period, he was in the morgue throughout the autopsy. His absence occurred at the outset of the autopsy, when he was sent on an errand with a Secret Service escort.

Since Jenkins claims he was present during the taking of X-rays, this errand could have taken place when the body was replaced in the Dallas casket, taken outside the hospital, and brought back inside in the Dallas casket.

But it occurred to me that when Jenkins returned, he would have seen the Dallas ceremonial coffin in the anteroom of the morgue. How could he have accounted for it?

When I asked him to recall any irregular procedures, he remembered that no one was supposed to know Kennedy's body was inside Bethesda. He added: "As a matter of fact, they went to the extent of bringing . . . a Lieutenant Colonel, or a Major, or something of that nature from the Air Force that was to be buried at Arlington, that was brought into the morgue, and stayed overnight in the morgue. And in the morning, whenever the caskets went out, I think his went out first. . . ."[33] Jenkins told me that the Air Force officer "was actually brought in a coffin. His coffin actually set in the little entrance room there where we did all the logging stuff for the whole night."

The accounts given by Manchester and by several witnesses I talked to indicated that the Dallas casket, and the Dallas casket alone, stood in the anteroom during the autopsy.[34]

The coffin Jenkins thought belonged to "an Air Force Colonel" must have been the Dallas casket.

Godfrey McHugh may have also seen two caskets. Having brought Kennedy's body to the anteroom in the Dallas casket, he may have seen the shipping casket upon entering the morgue, and made the assumption that it was to serve as Kennedy's burial casket.

Manchester reported that McHugh called upstairs: The casket was "cheap and thin . . . ," the family should secure a better one. Manchester, knowing only about the $3900 Dallas casket, wrote: "The casket was neither cheap nor thin."[35]

If the authorities were playing a shell game, everything they did must be questioned. For instance, how was "the brain" brought to the morgue?

It will be recalled that Paul O'Connor said the President's cranial vault was empty. Yet Jenkins remembered infusing a brain.

Was a brain brought to the morgue separately from the body?

Jenkins recollected another incident, an episode involving a stillborn baby.[36] Manchester wrote about the stillborn baby too, based on his interview with Lt. Sam Bird. "After his men had lowered the casket to a wheeled gurney he shepherded them into the corridor and mounted guard. Two Navy corpsmen passed, rolling a litter. Nothing appeared to be on it except a small lump wrapped in sheeting. 'What's that?' he inquired. 'Baby. Born dead,' one mumbled. The lieutenant whispered, 'Oh.' "[37]

Was the "stillborn baby" a ruse to get a brain into the morgue?

This could explain why Paul O'Connor vividly recollected opening the shipping casket and seeing an empty cranium, while James Jenkins recalled being given a brain to infuse with formaldehyde.

In March 1980, a researcher assisting me telephoned Bethesda Naval Hospital. She explained that she had a problem with a family estate, which revolved around the claim that a baby had been stillborn at Bethesda on November 22, 1963. Officials at Bethesda checked the log of deaths at the hospital and reported that no baby was stillborn at Bethesda Naval Hospital on November 22, 1963.

As for the "Air Force Colonel" story, the same researcher requested that the burial records of Arlington National Cemetery be checked to determine what military personnel may have been buried the day after Kennedy's death. On April 4, 1980, R. J. Costanzo, Superintendent of Arlington National Cemetery replied: "There were no interments on 23 November 1963."[38]

CHAPTER **29**

The Assertion of
Adm. David P. Osborne

IN MAY 1975, after thirty-four years of service, Rear Adm. David P. Osborne retired from the U.S. Navy as Deputy Surgeon General. On November 22, 1963, Dr. Osborne held the rank of Captain, and was Chief of Surgery at Bethesda Naval Hospital.

The House Select Committee reported Osborne's assertion that he "thought he recalled seeing an intact slug roll out from the clothing of President Kennedy and onto the autopsy table" at the outset of the autopsy.[1]

The Committee rejected this because "no one else recalled anything about the discovery of a missile." The Committee also noted that the President's body was unclothed at the outset of the autopsy.[2]

They reported that Admiral Osborne had been recontacted, advised of these objections, and "then said that he could not be sure he actually did see a missile."[3]

I telephoned Admiral Osborne in October 1979 and, after receiving a letter from my publisher, he agreed to speak with me.

He came to the morgue that night because he was an old friend of Humes, whom he referred to as "Jim."

Admiral Osborne told me that when he arrived at the morgue, the casket had not yet been opened. "It was a very elaborate casket," he told me, "as one might expect." It had not yet been opened, he said, and in fact Humes was insistent that the casket *not* be opened until everyone had arrived.[4]

"We were all standing there . . ." Osborne told me. "There was quite a delay before the casket was opened, actually, because they were waiting for everyone to arrive that Jim wanted to be there. . . ."

"Everyone" included Dr. Pierre Finck. "Jim didn't want to start until

Colonel Finck got there. . . ." Admiral Osborne told me that the delay lasted "at least fifteen, twenty, thirty minutes—something in that neighborhood."

There were other men present, he said, "urging that everything be rushed and done as quickly as possible, and get it over with. . . . Jim was insisting that he wanted to get additional help."

At some point—it is not clear from Finck's testimony whether it was before he had arrived—the casket was opened. And it was then, according to Osborne, that a "reasonably clean," "unmarred" bullet fell from the clothing that he said was around the body. "The bullet was not deformed in any way," Osborne told me.

He said that he and the Committee had gotten into a "disagreement, not really a disagreement, but I told them that this was the way I remembered it, and they said: 'Well, it must be wrong, because the Secret Service testified that [the] bullet was found in the hospital in Parkland, and brought back to Washington.' And so I said: 'Well, if that's true, then they brought it to the morgue, because I had that bullet in my hand, and looked at it.' "

I was startled to hear Osborne say he held the bullet. The Committee reported only that he "thought he recalled seeing" the slug.[5]

"You had the bullet in your hand?" I asked.[6]

"That's right," he replied.

"You actually held it, Admiral?"

"That's right," he said again.

"Did you tell the Committee that?"

"Yes," he said.

When I asked Osborne if the bullet had any blood on it, he replied: "No, it was reasonably clean."

Was bullet 399 at Bethesda? There is a clear chain of possession on bullet 399—the only "intact" bullet in this case—from Parkland Hospital to the FBI Laboratory. It traveled from Dallas to Washington in the pocket of Secret Service Agent Richard Johnsen, of the White House Detail. At 7:30 P.M., Johnsen gave the bullet to Secret Service Chief Rowley, at the Executive Office Building.[7] At 8:50, Rowley sent it to the FBI Laboratory.[8] The bullet was not at Bethesda; at least it was not supposed to be. If, however, it was, that would mean that no decision had yet been made as to where the bullet would be "found." In any event, Osborne's impression that the bullet might have come from Parkland Hospital was not a legitimate explanation for its presence at Bethesda.

Osborne and I discussed the matter further. "Who else held the bullet in their hand besides you, by the way?" I asked. "Do you remember?"

"Several people had it," said Osborne. "I know the Secret Service had it."[9]

"Have you ever talked to Humes about the question of whether he had a bullet there—a whole bullet that night?"

"No, I tried to call Jim after you called me, but he's been out of town. I haven't been able to get ahold of him. I wanted to talk to him before I talked to you. . . ."

I now read to Admiral Osborne the paragraph in the report in which his assertion was rejected, where it was passed off as something which "he thought he recalled seeing."

Osborne replied: "Well, as far as I'm concerned, that's a lot of malarkey, because there was a bullet there, and it was totally intact. What happened to it, I don't know, but the Secret Service took it. Let me call Jim Humes when I can catch him, and talk to him about it, and see what I can jog out of his memory and see why there's this discrepancy before we go on."

Later, I came back to the matter again. Osborne again said he would be sure to contact Humes on it, to resolve the matter, "because I just can't see any reason for it, and I don't understand it."

Still later, I returned to the matter again, pointing out to him the seriousness of the assertion—that the bullet in question never became evidence.

"Well, the bullet existed," he replied. "I'm sure of that. The only concession I made to the Committee when they called me was the fact that they led me to believe that the FBI or Secret Service had carried that bullet back and deposited it somewhere at the headquarters or something or other, and that it didn't fall out of the clothing at Bethesda. And I told them on the phone that I wouldn't argue that point too much, as to whether they'd carried it back, or whether it fell out of the clothing. As I remembered it, it fell out of the clothing, but I know that it was there because I saw it . . . it fell out on the table, and I think everybody spotted it. All of us were right there. We spotted it at the same time, essentially."

As soon as I could, I telephoned Humes, and apparently reached him before Admiral Osborne did. He apparently did not know that Osborne had been interviewed by the Committee. When I told him of the basic allegation, Humes replied: "I don't know where he got that. . . . You mystify me with that story."[10]

Dr. Humes told me that Dr. Osborne was "a super nice guy." I asked him how long they had known each other. "Dr. Osborne and I have been friends for twenty-five years," said Humes.

The conflict was so irreconcilable that I was forced to ask Humes: "I was curious whether he [Osborne] is getting on in years. . . ." Humes interjected: "No, he's a very bright, intelligent man. I don't know what he's talking about."

But then Humes made a remark that I found rather curious; it was almost a concession. "Well, they found a bullet in Dallas, and whether they brought it there [Bethesda] or not, I can't tell you. I don't even remember that . . . I don't know. It was not my problem, at that point."

Then Humes said: "Certainly no bullet came with the wrappings of the President." And I wondered: What did Humes mean by "wrappings"—the sheet that was there when the body came in? Or the clothing that Osborne insisted that he saw? Did someone change the "wrappings"?

Following these conversations, I reviewed the Osborne assertion from the standpoint of the record.

The FBI receipt was dated November 22, 1963, and was issued by Sibert and O'Neill to Capt. J.H. Stover, Humes' superior. Its exact wording was: "We hereby acknowledge receipt of a missile removed by Commander James J. Humes, MC, USN on this date."[11]

This receipt apparently remained in Admiral Burkley's possession until November 26, 1963. On that date, Burkley gave the receipt for a missile, along with the autopsy report and other related paperwork (i.e., a copy of the navy order not to talk, the receipt for film holders, the receipt for surgical drapes and shroud) to Agent Robert Bouck, head of the Protective Research Section of the Secret Service.[12]

Upon receipt of these items, Bouck issued a receipt to Admiral Burkley on Treasury Department letterhead. The seventh item on this "Bouck receipt" was the FBI receipt, listed as "one receipt from FBI for a missile recovered during the examination of the body."[13]

Inexplicably, Bouck never gave the Warren Commission the FBI receipt itself. And despite the existence of the Bouck receipt in the Commission's files—an official Treasury Department document alluding to an FBI receipt for a missile—there is no indication the Commission ever took notice of that, or investigated the matter. The critics first learned of the FBI receipt when Bouck's receipt, which was an unpublished Warren Commission document, came to light in 1966.

In 1969, after critic Harold Weisberg threatened to go to court to sue the Secret Service, under the Freedom of Information Act, for the items of evidence listed on Bouck's receipt that were not at the National Archives, the Secret Service turned over a file of documents to the Archives, and the FBI receipt for "a missile" was among them.

Subsequently, when I questioned the FBI about the receipt, they took the position that the receipt was for the two tiny fragments Humes said he removed from the brain—that that was the only metal Sibert and O'Neill brought back to the FBI Laboratory.[14]*

---

* Curiously, in the autopsy report, Humes referred to the two tiny fragments, saying: "These are placed in the custody of Agents Francis X. O'Neill, Jr. and

Until Admiral Osborne's statement, then, the record shaped up as follows:

1. there was, on the one hand, a receipt for a "missile," but no "missile" in evidence corresponding to that receipt;
2. there was a jar containing two tiny metal fragments, but no receipt that seemed applicable to that jar; yet the FBI stated, in their own report, that they had executed a "proper receipt" for these two fragments.[18]

Therefore, until the Osborne assertion, the natural conclusion was that the receipt for two fragments was simply worded badly.

The Osborne assertion cast everything in a new light. It raised the possibility that there was an incident at the outset of the Bethesda autopsy —or at least at a coffin opening which was witnessed by Admiral Osborne—at which a bullet, which looked like bullet 399, fell from the vicinity of the body.

James W. Sibert, . . . who executed a receipt therefor (attached)."[15] But no receipt was "attached."

There is evidence indicating that at some point the authorities may have had an informal conference of sorts to decide how to explain this receipt, which reached the National Archives in 1969.

My correspondence with the FBI about the receipt occurred in 1970, and at that time, I attached to my letter a copy of the Bouck receipt I obtained from the National Archives. I drew in a small arrow, pointing to the seventh item on the Bouck receipt. The FBI assigned a file number to my correspondence.

Years later, I directed a request, under the Freedom of Information Act, to the Secret Service for the original Secret Service copy of the Bouck receipt. I had been told by a staff member of the Senate Select Committee on Intelligence that the Secret Service files were in disorder, and that certain items were missing.

Shortly thereafter, I received from the Secret Service what purports to be their official copy of the Bouck receipt.[16] Immediately, I noted something appeared odd, because although the document was originally in the possession of the Secret Service, and although my request was directed to the Secret Service, the document I received had, in the lower right-hand corner, an FBI file number.

I requested Robert Ranftel, a researcher in Washington, to go to the FBI files and find out what FBI file number was on that Bouck receipt. In other words, I wanted to know why the Secret Service was issuing a document which apparently came from an FBI file.

Ranftel excitedly called back to inform me that the FBI file number was the one assigned to my correspondence.

In short, what the Secret Service now has in its files, as the supposedly "official" copy of the Bouck receipt, came from my files. It is a Service Service copy of an FBI copy of my copy of an Archives copy.

When I explained this to the Secret Service Freedom of Information Act officer, he replied: "Your comment reference the copy of the 'Bouck' receipt which was forwarded with our letter of May 16, 1978 may be correct."[17] I asked the Secret Service if their files reflected any liaison with the FBI over my requests about this matter. They claim they do not.

I now realized that if Admiral Osborne was correct—if he saw this bullet and held it in his hand—that did not necessarily mean that the bullet was brought back to the FBI Laboratory. Indeed, Osborne was firm on who had the bullet: "I know the Secret Service had it," he told me.[19] Did they keep it?

Osborne's account raised the possibility that the bullet existed, that it was at Bethesda, that the FBI typed a receipt for it, but that the missile was not surrendered to the FBI—that Secret Service agents brought it back to Secret Service headquarters, where it was turned in to the FBI Laboratory as a bullet which was found on a Dallas stretcher.

Such an incident, if it occurred, would be a major irregularity in the handling of this item of evidence. It suggested to me a last-minute change in the role the "intact" bullet was to play in this affair—i.e., where it was supposed to have originated. Certainly that was supported by the post-midnight call to Darrell Tomlinson in Dallas, telling him not to discuss the bullet.*

Because neither Humes nor Boswell ever spoke of such an incident, Osborne's assertion required corroboration. I was most surprised to discover corroboration in the report filed by FBI agents Sibert and O'Neill of their questioning of Secret Service Agent Gerald Behn, the Special Agent in Charge of the White House Detail.

The Sibert and O'Neill interview of Gerald Behn on November 27, 1963 was extraordinary because it appears that the two agents were questioning Behn about three matters pertaining to the autopsy, all dealing with how evidence reached the mainstream of the investigation.[20] The first question was not listed, but the answer had to do with *Air Force Two* passing *Air Force One* in flight. My conclusion was that the first question probably was: Why was the body there before we were?

The second question was listed: "Mr. Behn was questioned concerning the section of the President's skull, which was brought to the National Navy Medical Center at Bethesda, Maryland, after the autopsy was in progress."[21] On Friday night, according to the telegram they sent at 2:00 A.M., Sibert and O'Neill had apparently been told the bone was "flown in from [a] Dallas hospital."[22] On November 27, 1963, Behn told them it was found in the car.[23]

And the third question, considered in the light of the Osborne assertion, now made sense: "Behn was likewise questioned concerning the location of a bullet which had been found on a stretcher at Parkland Hospital in Dallas and which had been turned over by the Secret Service to an Agent of the Federal Bureau of Investigation for delivery to the FBI Laboratory."[24]

Sibert and O'Neill's wording was precise. They were not questioning

* See discussion, p. 591.

Behn about which stretcher the bullet was found on in Dallas. They were questioning him on the bullet's "location."

I believed they must have asked: What was a bullet, which we were subsequently told originated on a Dallas stretcher, doing at the Bethesda morgue?

In view of Osborne's account, the receipt issued by Sibert and O'Neill which matched the bullet but not the fragments, and Sibert and O'Neill's questioning of Gerald Behn about "the location" of the bullet, it seemed reasonable to believe that the incident reported by Admiral Osborne did in fact occur. The bullet must have been at Bethesda, and the Secret Service probably took possession of it, explaining to Sibert and O'Neill that the missile had been found in Dallas, and would be delivered to the FBI Laboratory.

Since the receipt in question was issued to Capt. John Stover, the Commanding Officer of the U.S. Naval Medical School, and Humes' immediate superior, in April 1980 I contacted Stover. I went directly to the point, told him about Osborne's allegation, the Committee's position, and Osborn's insistence he saw the bullet in the room—indeed, that he held it in his hand. Stover confirmed the bullet was in the Bethesda morgue. "It seems to me that the one they found in Dallas they brought up. . . . I think it was in a brown paper envelope." Stover said he was unaware that Osborne had held the bullet. Stover said he himself had not. He said he associated the bullet with a brown paper envelope—"one of those slim ones with the opening across the narrow end."[25]

I asked Stover about the receipt he signed. He said: "I'm not sure that that's [the] complete round that you're talking about—it's the thing I may or may not have signed the receipt for." Then he added: "I signed a receipt for some fragments."

Stover was not questioned about the matter by the Committee. He told me his entire contact with the Committee was one or two phone calls.

What was ironic about the Committee's handling of this affair was its reliance on Paul O'Connor and James Jenkins to refute Admiral Osborne. Neither of them, said the Committee, "could . . . recall any foreign object, specifically a missile, being discovered during the autopsy. . . ."[26] But what Purdy and Flanagan didn't know at the time they conducted their investigation was that what Paul O'Connor meant by the "opening of the coffin" was the arrival of Kennedy's body in a body bag inside a shipping casket, whereas what Admiral Osborne called the "coffin opening" was the opening of a ceremonial casket after a delay of some time while Humes was waiting for "everyone" to be there." Moreover, the Committee staff seems to have been unaware of the powerful corroboration provided Osborne by the Sibert and O'Neill interview of Behn.

My own appreciation for the Osborne assertion grew when I put the various events on a time line.

The Military District of Washington casket team brought in the casket at 8:00 P.M.[27] Osborne witnessed a casket opening sometime afterward.[28] At 8:50, Secret Service Chief James Rowley turned in the bullet and said it had been found on a Dallas stretcher.[29] Sometime after that, he made a call to Bethesda and told Kellerman that the bullet had been found on a Dallas stretcher.[30] Between eleven and twelve o'clock, according to Sibert and O'Neill, they called the FBI Laboratory and first learned that a bullet had been found on a stretcher.[31]

The question that had always seemed strange was why, if the Secret Service had the bullet since 2:00 P.M., they had not notified the FBI Laboratory until 8:50 P.M. *Air Force One* has radiotelephones. The FBI could easily have been notified that a bullet had been found and would be delivered after the plane landed. *Air Force One* landed about 6:00 P.M. Special Agent Johnsen's memo indicates it wasn't turned over to Rowley until 7:30.[32] Why a ninety-minute further delay before Rowley was told about the bullet? And why another one-hour-and-twenty-minute delay until 8:50, when the FBI was notified?[33]

This peculiar behavior on the part of Secret Service officials in the handling of this item of evidence only enhanced the credibility of the account of Admiral Osborne.

Osborne's account and Stover's corroboration implied the incident was witnessed by others at Bethesda who had chosen to say nothing about it. These would have included Dr. Humes and Dr. Boswell, and Sibert and O'Neill, who omitted it from their report on the autopsy.

Humes' statement to me was not an outright denial. Rather, it was consistent with the view that the bullet was not connected with the body on which he was preparing to do an autopsy.

"Well, they found a bullet in Dallas," he said, "and whether they brought it there or not, I can't tell you. I don't even remember that . . . I don't know. It was not my problem, at that point. . . . Certainly no bullet came with the wrappings of the President."[34]

What did Humes mean when he said: "It was not my problem, at that point"?

I never called back Osborne to find out what explanation Humes provided when he called. The conflict is irreconcilable. Still I have wondered about the conversation that must have passed between these two men who have been friends for twenty-five years, when the only alternatives are that one of them imagined he held a bullet, or the other has chosen to remain silent about the incident during the course of all previous government investigations.

PART VII

Synthesis

The X-rays and Photographs Reconsidered

The X-rays and Photographs Reconsidered

THE EVIDENCE UPON WHICH the Warren Commission relied in arriving at its conclusion that President Kennedy was struck twice from behind was the testimony of Cmdr. James Joseph Humes. But the evidence upon which the House Select Committee on Assassinations relied—and the evidence on which future historians will rely—is the X-rays and photographs at the National Archives.

The following question, therefore, is important. Why, if the body was altered to create the appearance of wounds inflicted from behind, was it necessary to falsify the X-rays and photographs? My answer was that if the body was a "perfect" medical forgery, it would not have been necessary.

That, apparently, was not the case. The alterations were so imperfect that, as the body lay on the Bethesda autopsy table, some witnesses thought it appeared the President had been shot in the head from the front. According to the Sibert and O'Neill report, some doctor actually recognized and stated that surgery of the head area had been performed. If Paul O'Connor was correct and the body arrived without a brain, it was easy to understand why the doctor made that observation.

Neither evidence of shots from the front nor evidence of pre-autopsy surgery could be permitted to become part of the photo and X-ray record of the Bethesda autopsy. The first would establish "two gunmen" in Dealey Plaza, evidence contradicting the "lone-assassin" scenario being fabricated; the second, and more dangerous, would establish a plot to alter the body.

Therefore, to the extent that such evidence existed—to the extent that the body was altered imperfectly—those imperfections had to be eliminated from the photo and X-ray record.

The fact that there is a definite divergence between the condition of the head as described by Humes, and the condition of the head as shown in the photographs and X-rays, supported my theory that just such changes were made, and such imperfections eliminated.

Humes wrote in his autopsy report that the President's fatal wound was "chiefly parietal," but extended "somewhat" into the "occipital area." It seemed to be an enlarged version of the wound observed at Dallas. Humes wrote that beneath the rear margin of this hole was a bullet entry wound. And the gunshot trajectory he posited entered at the bottom of the back of the head and blew off the top of the head. For the sake of analysis, I called Humes' description of the wounds, and the corresponding trajectory, a view of the body through "Lens 2." (See Chapters 17 and 20.)

The autopsy photographs and X-rays showed a different back-to-front trajectory. The large head wound was on the forward right side of the head. It did not extend to the rear. The rear portion of the skull, the occipital area, was intact, except for a small bullet entry wound near the top of the head, at the back. That entry, nearly four inches above the external occipital protuberance, was in the parietal bone. The gunshot trajectory depicted in those photographs entered the top back of the head, and appeared to have blown out the forward right side. I called this portrayal of the wounds, and the corresponding trajectory, a view of the body through "Lens 3."

The Lens 2/Lens 3 contrast went beyond an inconsistency between what Humes reported and what the photographs showed. There was a clear divergence between what Humes reported he saw on the body and what most of the autopsy witnesses said they saw. Most disturbing about the Bethesda witnesses was not their opinion that the shot came from the front—that was a matter of opinion, and opinions might vary—but that so many failed to see the bullet entrance wound at the rear Humes said was there.

Neither Custer nor Reed, the two X-ray technologists, saw it. They both thought the shot came from the front.[1]

James Jenkins thought the shot came from the front; he didn't see the entry wound.[2]

Dr. Ebersole didn't see it.*

Even those who went along with the notion that the shot somehow struck from the rear and blew off the rear half of the head didn't see the entry wound. O'Connor didn't see it.** And Admiral David Osborne, Humes' friend of twenty-five years, didn't see it either.***

---

* See p. 546 for Ebersole's remarks.

** Paul O'Connor told me: "Well, there was just a great big massive hole in the skull. That was the only thing that was there. There was no round definition showing that the bullet had entered."[3]

*** Admiral Osborne told me: "It blew the whole back and top of his head off.

The notion that all these bystanders—Jenkins, Custer, Reed, O'Connor, Osborne, Ebersole—simply missed the entry wound was improbable. It was even more improbable when considered in the context of the photographs. The entry wound was not something located on the photographs after a search with a magnifying glass. The photographs were posed to depict the entry—a ruler was placed up against the head, the camera was pointed at the wound. Any one of these bystanders present when the pictures were taken should have seen the entrance wound depicted in the photographs. But they didn't. And they didn't see the entry Humes described either (about four inches lower). Indeed, they observed no entry whatsoever. And some of them—e.g., James Jenkins—were convinced that the bullet came from the front and blew out the back of the head. Most of the Bethesda witnesses I interviewed gave a description of a rear exit that resembled the Dallas doctors' description, only the wound they described was much larger than the egg-size exit seen in Dallas.

If a photographic record had been made which showed the head wound described by these Bethesda observers—e.g., Jenkins, Custer, Reed, O'Connor, and even Osborne—the testimony indicates those photographs probably would have been interpreted to show a gunshot exit wound at the rear of the head.

But the photographs and X-rays in evidence—Lens 3—showed no such data.

How was that accomplished? What was the source of these photographs?

. . . It appeared that the bullet hit low in the occiput of the back of the head and entered the skull there and then traversed a portion of the brain and then hit the inside of the top of the skull toward the rear also and blew a good portion of that part of his skull right out. . . ."[4]

I asked: "Did you actually see the little entry at the bottom of the back of the head?"

"Couldn't see the entry," he replied. "That tissue was all pretty much blown away. . . ." I gathered that Osborne based his conclusion that the bullet struck from the rear on an interpretation of where it hit the inside of the skull on the way out. I asked him how the bullet could enter from the rear and blow out the rear of the head. He said: ". . . he had to be leaning forward, and the bullet had to hit him in the lower—right behind, you know, that little lump in the back of your head there. . . ." Osborne was referring to the external occipital protuberance, where Humes said there was an entrance wound. Again, I asked Admiral Osborne if he saw that wound. He replied: "Well, the pieces were all blown apart, so it didn't make one tiny little hole in the bone—no. . . . It blew that portion of the skull into several pieces.

LIFTON: I see. So you didn't actually see an entry wound, per se, but it's inferred that it was somewhere towards the bottom of that big hole—or something like that?

OSBORNE: It had to be. Otherwise it couldn't have hit the inside of the skull where it did.

They were placed in the National Archives by Robert Kennedy in October 1966. Kennedy received the photographs from the Secret Service in the spring of 1965. The Secret Service claimed they were authentic, that they came from the Bethesda morgue on the night of November 22, 1963. They were supposed to depict the body as it was at the outset of the official autopsy.

In my interviews with Godfrey McHugh in November 1967, he gave vivid descriptions of what seemed to be reconstruction, carried on in his presence while photographs were taken. On this information and the changes made on the receipts,* I based a theory that the pictures had been created sometime after midnight in the morgue.

After the House Committee report was published, I modified that hypothesis. I still believed the pictures were based on a reconstruction, but not one necessarily made after midnight.

Before presenting my own analysis, it is worth examining briefly what the Committee did.

The House Committee investigation strengthened my basic theory, because a reconstruction hypothesis is only one of several ways the photographs and X-rays could have been faked, and the House investigation, because of the approach it adopted, eliminated the other possibilities.

In its report, the Committee spelled out in detail a possibility of fraud it took seriously and went to great lengths to disprove. "Some . . . theorists," said the Committee, "suggest that the body shown in at least some of the photographs is not President Kennedy, but another decedent deliberately mutilated to simulate a pattern of wounds supportive of the Warren Commission's interpretation of their nature and significance. As outlandish as such a macabre proposition might appear, it is one that, had the case gone to trial, might have been effectively raised by an astute defense anxious to block the introduction of the photographs as evidence. In any event, the onus of establishing the authenticity of these photographs would have rested with the prosecution."[5]

The Committee accepted that burden and commissioned experts in anthropology, radiology, and photography to analyze the collection and prove that the body was that of John F. Kennedy.

The authenticators compared the X-rays with X-rays of President Kennedy taken in life. They concluded: "To summarize, the skull and torso radiographs taken at autopsy match the available ante-mortem films of the late President in such a wealth of intricate morphological detail that there can be no reasonable doubt but that they are indeed X-rays of John F. Kennedy and no other person."[6]

Similar testing was done in the case of the photographs.

The House Select Committee, accepting the report of the authentica-

* See Chapter 21.

tion experts, made the following statement: "From the reports of the experts' analyses of the autopsy photographs and X-rays, the evidence indicates that the autopsy photographs and X-rays were taken of President Kennedy at the time of his autopsy and that they had not been altered in any manner."[7]

This statement can be broken down into three parts:

1. that the victim shown is John F. Kennedy;
2. that the pictures were taken "at the time of his autopsy";
3. that the photos and X-rays "had not been altered in any manner."

I accepted the Committee's conclusions that the victim shown was John F. Kennedy, and that the photos and X-rays were unaltered. I did not believe the Committee established that the pictures and X-rays in evidence in fact depicted the body as it was at the time it arrived at the Bethesda morgue—specifically, at the time Paul O'Connor, as the House Committee itself states, received the body of John F. Kennedy in a body bag.

If one accepts the Committee's conclusions that the pictures are of John F. Kennedy, and that the pictures and X-rays are unaltered, then—to account for the Lens 2/Lens 3 problem—one is driven to posit reconstruction. There is no other possibility.

The Committee's experts made the following comments about the "deficiencies" in the collection:

"1. They are generally of rather poor photographic quality.

"2. Some, particularly closeups, were taken in such a manner that it is nearly impossible to anatomically orient the direction of view.

"3. In many, scalar references are entirely lacking, or when present, were positioned in such a manner to make it difficult or impossible to obtain accurate measurements of critical features (such as the wound in the upper back) from anatomical landmarks.

"4. None of the photographs contain information identifying the victim; such as his name, the autopsy case number, the date and place of the examination."[8]

The Committee's experts passed off these "shortcomings" as the result of "haste, inexperience and unfamiliarity with the . . . rigorous standards generally expected in photographs to be used as scientific evidence."[9] And it went on to point out: ". . . under ordinary circumstances, the defense could raise some reasonable and, perhaps, sustainable objections to an attempt to introduce such poorly made and documented photographs as evidence in a murder trial. Furthermore, even the prosecution might have second thoughts about using certain of these photographs since they are more confusing than informative. Unfortunately, however, they are the only photographic record of the autopsy."[10]

A more accurate statement might be "the only surviving record." John Stringer had been a photographer for twenty years. It was not his practice to take pictures of "poor photographic quality," or pictures where it is "nearly impossible to anatomically orient the direction of view."

The authenticators' own comments suggested to me reconstruction of the body performed hastily in the Bethesda morgue, and photographs taken by persons who lacked the appropriate expertise.

A body of circumstantial evidence from the Committee's own technical data supported the reconstruction theory.

Item: The string of metallic fragments visible in the X-rays of the head.

Dr. Lattimer said of the brain photographed on December 6, 1963, that two-thirds of the right side was gone.[11]

Along the top right side of the X-rays of the head was a string of some nineteen metallic particles, forming a gunshot track from back to front.[12]

The question was: What supported these particles? They could not have been suspended in midair inside the cranial vault.

Their location appeared inconsistent with the amount of tissue missing from the brain.

Item: The radiologist's report.

Dr. David O. Davis, of the George Washington University Medical Center, filed a report with the Committee in which he commented on the string of metallic fragments. "These fragments extend inferoanteriorly [downward and toward the front] across the entire skull and actually project (on other images that I have seen) in a fashion that suggests that the large fragment is outside the intracranial space. Presumably this represents a metallic fragment in the scalp, although this cannot be accurately determined from this particular examination."[13]

Later in his report, in the section designated "Conclusion," Dr. Davis wrote: "It is not possible to totally explain the metallic fragment pattern that is present [because] some of the metallic fragments located superiorly in the region of the parietal bone, or at least projecting on the parietal bone, are actually in the scalp. The frontal view does not give much help in this regard and it is impossible to work this out completely."[14]

Andrew Purdy told me that Dr. David O. Davis was the finest of the radiologists the Committee consulted, that he analyzed the X-rays carefully, and took the time to explain his interpretations at his Georgetown office.

I believed the report he wrote supported the conclusion that some of the metallic fragments cited by the Committee as evidence of a gunshot track were in fact *not* inside the skull. As Davis himself said, the largest projected "outside the intracranial space."[15]

Item: Humes' reaction to the X-rays.

Dr. Humes did not find any such metallic fragments at the time he conducted the official autopsy—this, despite the presence on the X-rays of metal which projected outside the intracranial space, and one large metallic fragment which, according to Dr. Davis, is "embedded in the outer table of the skull," and Dr. Davis' assertion that "some of the metallic fragments . . . are actually in the scalp."[16]

In the closed session before the Committee, Humes said: "Most of the fragments that we recovered were grains of sand type fragments." Referring to the fragments strewn in the pattern of a bullet track on the X-rays, he said: "I don't recall them of that size."[17]

Item: The fragmentation of the skull.

When I first saw the enhanced X-rays in Washington, it struck me that the entire cranium appeared to be composed of bone fragments fitted together.

After visiting radiologist Dr. William Seaman at Columbia Presbyterian Hospital, Purdy wrote an Outside Contact report: "He found inferences difficult to draw from the extensive damage to the top of the skull, which includes overlapping skull pieces. . . ."[18] Dr. Davis' report focused on one such fragment: "This fragment is displaced from its normal position as indicated by overlap of the infer[ior] and posterior aspects of the fracture fragment. . . ."[19] Dr. Davis wrote: "There is a displaced fragment or fragments in the right frontal and parietotemporal region, with some overlap of the bone."[20] Dr. Norman Chase of NYU Medical Center said, according to Purdy's report, that it was "unclear exactly what happened to the top of the skull because of the extensive damage. . . ."[21]

Item: The late-arriving bone fragments.

The record is clear that Commander Humes was not provided the bone fragments until after midnight. One of those fragments showed "beveling," and constituted the only direct evidence of exit of a bullet from the President's head. Humes testified that after "careful examination," he could find no such evidence on the skull itself.[22] Yet the autopsy photographs showed bone, on the skull, that revealed a beveled edge.[23]

How could pictures exposed at the start of the autopsy contain evidence which Humes did not see on the body?

Similarly, Dr. Boswell told the Committee that until the bone fragments arrived, there was no separate entrance wound. But then by fitting one of the fragments into the rear portion of the large head defect he was able to "complete the circumference" of a smaller wound.*[24]

The X-rays, however, showed a "hole"—or at least a complete break in the bone. How could the X-rays depict the skull at the outset of the autopsy if they show a wound whose circumference was composed of bone that didn't arrive until after midnight?

Item: No autopsy photographs show the brain inside the head.

---

* In other words, the manipulation of late-arriving bone fragments created a separate entrance wound which was originally just a "notch" at the rear of the large head defect.

I had expected the photographs and X-rays of the autopsy to show the brain inside the head. The brain ought to have been in the cranial vault at the start of the autopsy, and I believed that if it had been removed for the purpose of extracting metal—i.e., as part of the illicit pre-autopsy surgery—it would have been re-inserted for the purpose of autopsy photography. Yet I could find no evidence in the House Select Committee's report that any of the pictures showed the brain inside the head.

The authenticators' report made clear that the photographs of the body fell into five categories: left front, right front (called left and right lateral by the Committee), top view, rear view, and cranial cavity.[25]

The Committee's report stated that in the pictures which showed the interior of the cranial vault the brain has been removed. The rear-view pictures could also be eliminated. One of those photographs, reproduced as a Dox drawing, obviously did not show any of the cranial vault. Three categories remained: the left front, the right front, and the "superior view" (top view).

Did any of these show the brain inside the head?

In 1979, after the House Select Committee report was published, it became known that the photographs and X-rays had somehow been surreptitiously copied, possibly during the course of the House investigation.*

Subsequently, I was provided an opportunity to see these materials. The copies were poor black-and-white reproductions.

Surprisingly, I did not find them particularly shocking. In fact, I found the Zapruder film showing President Kennedy being murdered more shocking.

The pictures showed the President's head resting on a towel that said "Bethesda Naval Hospital."

For all rear views of the body (i.e., the pictures used to depict the wound in the shoulder and in the head), the body was apparently rolled over to one side. It was tilted at an angle with the right shoulder lifted up away from the autopsy table. Gloved hands are visible holding the body in place.

My preconception of the collection was that it consisted of numerous pictures from numerous angles. That was not the case. There were only five poses and within each group the pictures were practically indistinguishable. The Committee discussed this in its report, but its significance wasn't clear to me until I saw the pictures themselves.

The black-and-white films, according to the Committee's experts, were

* I first learned in August 1979 that a private party was offering the pictures for sale when a network news reporter called me for assistance in preparing a story about this. That story was never aired, but the same information was published on August 29 in the *New York Times*.

"virtually duplicates" of the color pictures. Consequently, the Committee's experts ignored them. Even among the color prints, the Committee found six instances of identical photographs. When the number of pictures was adjusted by eliminating black-and-white and identical color pictures, the collection was reduced from thirty-eight to fifteen photographs.*

My own examination of these pictures indicated that the brain was not identifiable from the left side or the right front.

One category of the original five remained: the "superior views."

In these pictures, the President lay on his back, and the camera was apparently aimed horizontally along the top of his body, from behind. His nose rises like a distant mountain peak.**

I peered at the black-and-white versions of these photographs, wondering if the brain was visible. I couldn't see a thing—not even the wound. It was impossible to tell whether or not the brain was shown in those pictures. They seemed almost useless.

At home that evening, I reread the authenticators' report, and discovered I wasn't the only one who found those pictures of little use. The Committee's experts wrote: "From the standpoint of pathological interpretation, the least informative photographs are those of group 3, which provide a superior view of the head and shoulders. This is because the scalp has neither been shaved nor reflected from the cranium, procedures which would possibly have shown some of the crucial details of the cranial trauma. In these photographs, a portion of the victim's forehead and nose are shown from above."[28]

I called Dr. Michael Baden, who was in charge of the Committee's Forensic Pathology Panel, and had spent many hours analyzing the collection, writing the panel's report, and preparing to testify that these pictures demonstrated that President Kennedy had been struck by two shots from behind.

I asked Dr. Baden if *any* picture in the whole collection showed the large hole with the brain inside the head.

Baden said that was a good question, that he did not know the answer. (Apparently he had never looked at the problem that way before.)[29]

Based on my own examination and the Committee's record, it appears that such pictures do not exist. The hole shown in the photographs is not large enough for an entire brain to be removed. If the brain was not inside

---

* These figures are mine, not the Committee's, but are based on information from the Committee's report. One of the Committee's authenticators, Frank Scott, in discussing which photographs could be used for stereo viewing, tabulated the identical and non-identical views.[26]

** The Committee listed six such photographs, but its own report found two instances of duplication within this group, reducing the total to four supposedly original color negatives.[27]

the head, then the wound shown in the photographs must be a reconstruction, because at some point it had to be big enough for the brain to have been removed.

It will be the ultimate irony of the Committee's investigation, if my tentative conclusion proves true, that a group of forensic experts failed to notice this peculiarity of the Bethesda photographic record—that it contains no picture of the brain inside the head.

This, then, was the basis for my belief that the autopsy photographs showed a reconstructed body. If this was the case, when and where could it have been done?

I concluded that when the body arrived at Bethesda, it had been altered, but no photographic and X-ray record had yet been created. I based this on my analysis of how the body got from Dallas to Bethesda, which persuaded me there was insufficient time both to alter the body *and* to create the necessary photo and X-ray record.

If I was right, the conspirators faced a serious problem—the reconstruction had to be performed, and the X-rays and photographs had to be taken, in the morgue at Bethesda. But by the late fall of 1979, I had interviewed many witnesses to the Kennedy autopsy and became convinced, on the basis of detailed questioning, that none saw any photography taking place after midnight, during the period the funeral director was doing his work.* By a process of elimination, I concluded that the pictures, assuming they were in fact made in the Bethesda morgue, must have been made *before* the autopsy. If so, then the order in which events occurred was:

1. the arrival of a body crudely altered—and without a brain, if O'Connor's account was correct;
2. reconstruction of the head for X-rays and photographs;
3. the autopsy.

Was there time to do such reconstruction and photography before the autopsy began?

The Y-Incision: When Was It Made?

At the start of an autopsy, a Y-incision is made to remove the organs from the trunk of the body. The Kennedy autopsy photographs show no

---

* This caused me to re-evaluate my November 1967 conversation with Godfrey McHugh. He vividly recollected, and described in considerable detail, activity which appeared to me to be reconstruction preceding the photography. But his brief reference that photos were taken "from the time they got the body . . . until it was put into the new casket"—a remark which led me to infer post-midnight photography—was probably in error.

Y-incision—and they should not. If they did, that would prove they were "post-autopsy" photographs—i.e., pictures of reconstructions.

If the head was to be reconstructed for the autopsy photographs, it would have been necessary to do that before the Y-incision was made. Stated differently, the Y-incision could not be made until the photography was completed.

It therefore struck me as more than a coincidence that there was an argument at the outset, in which Humes said he wanted to do a "full autopsy," but his military superiors denied him the authority to do so. While this argument proceeded, the Y-incision was postponed.

How long did this period last, and what happened in the interim?

On November 26, 1963, Sibert and O'Neill wrote: "Following arrival at the Naval Medical Center . . . Admiral Burkley, the President's personal physician, advised that Mrs. Kennedy had granted permission for a limited autopsy and he questioned any feasibility for a complete autopsy. . . ."[30]

The Committee reported that Sibert said, in his interview, "that he, too, had the impression that the Kennedy family was somehow transmitting step-by-step clearances to the pathologists. . . ."[31] The Committee said that photographer John Stringer "likewise recalled some discussion at the beginning of the autopsy concerning the scope of the autopsy. He said he believed Dr. Burkley played a central role in the discussions and seemed to be acting on behalf of the Kennedy family. He specifically recalled Dr. Burkley indicating to the doctors that they should not conduct a full autopsy, saying, '. . . [you] shouldn't do a complete one if [you] don't have to.' "[32]

There is evidence to indicate that these discussions lasted for an hour, possibly two, and that during this time work may have been done on the body, and that this work was photographed.

When I asked Dr. John Ebersole in 1972 when the autopsy began, he replied that it didn't get underway "formally" until 10:30.[33] This was consistent with Sibert and O'Neill's statement to Specter that the call to the FBI Laboratory regarding the bullet was made between 11:00 P.M. and midnight.*[34]

Additional corroboration for the time lapse came from Dr. Finck. He testified in 1969 that when he arrived at Bethesda, the only available X-rays were of the head. He requested additional X-rays: "I requested them, and we waited, I would say, an hour or more for these whole body X-rays. . . ."[35]

Dr. Ebersole said that when he saw the body, the throat wound had been sutured.[36] Dr. Ebersole has made clear, in interviews, that this

---

* The FBI agents were under the impression that the autopsy began at 7:17, with an "inspection" or "preparation," whereas 10:30 was the "beginning" for Dr. Ebersole.

observation applies to the body as it was at the start of the autopsy, which, if his recollection is accurate, means sometime after ten o'clock. Someone explained to Ebersole that this wound had been sutured by a Dallas surgeon. This explanation was false, but that is beside the point. The sutures are good evidence that someone worked on the body prior to what Ebersole called the start of the autopsy, i.e., prior to 10:30 P.M. And there is more.

When I spoke to Paul O'Connor, he told me that the morticians who worked on the body were "undertakers from New York."[37] I explained to O'Connor that, according to the record, the morticians who worked on the body were from the respected Washington firm of Gawler's. "Well, somebody told me they were from New York."

When I recontacted O'Connor several months later, after realizing the possible significance of what he had told me, he retracted the story, believing he had simply made an error. Did he?

Dennis David said that the body was originally brought to Bethesda in a hearse, and that with the men in plainclothes were two men in smocks.[38]

Admiral Osborne told me that it was always his impression that the body was brought to Bethesda by the undertaker who had the navy contract.*[39]

Honor guard member James Felder told me he distinctly recalled the coffin they carried in at 8:00 P.M. was opened by an undertaker.[40]

Godfrey McHugh talked about how they started "fixing him up . . . pretty quick."[41] And so did Jenkins.[42] Such speed in repairing the head would appear inconsistent with the long delay during which Humes was prevented from starting a full autopsy.

John Van Hoesen, of the Gawler firm, sat in the bleachers in the autopsy room. He told me: "When we got up there, nothing had been started; then we had to wait for the autopsy; and then, periodically, more pictures were being taken—you know, different angles and so forth; where the entry was, and so forth; this angle, and that angle. . . ."[43]

Finally, there is Admiral Osborne's recollection. He witnessed a coffin opening and recalls the corpse being clothed.[44] The Committee used this feature of Osborne's story to reject Osborne's other recollection that, when the body was unwrapped, a bullet fell from the clothing.[45] Osborne's recollection of clothing, far from being a reason for rejecting his account, may in fact be an important clue: that, prior to the coffin opening Osborne witnessed, people may have been working on the body under the guise of legitimate undertaking procedures.

The indications of reconstruction and Hoesen's recollection that the body was photographed "periodically" prompted me to contact Capt. John Stover in April 1980 and ask him why the numbers were changed on the

* Gawler's did not have the navy contract.

receipts for photographs which he had signed. Stover had also initialed the changes.

> LIFTON: Do you have any recollection of what incident occurred that they were initialed and changed on the receipt?
>
> STOVER: No, I don't. It seems to me that the photographer, and I guess it was Mr. Stringer at the time, came back in. I think he wasn't satisfied with some of the shots and decided that he wanted some more. He was back in there more than once, I believe. In other words, the pictures were't taken all at one time. As I remember it, he did return to shoot a couple of extra shots.[46]

When did the picture-taking stop and the "full autopsy" begin? All that is known is that after a considerable delay, Admiral Galloway, according to Sibert and O'Neill, gave Humes permission to perform a full autopsy.[47]

The entire autopsy, from beginning to end, took much longer than expected.* If Ebersole was correct that it got underway at 10:30, that would mean almost two hours passed between the time the casket team carried in the Dallas casket and the time the Y-incision was made.**

Sibert and O'Neill reported that "upon completion of X-rays and photographs"—when they returned to the morgue—the X-rays which had been taken and returned showed that the head and brain "disclosed a path of a missile which appeared to enter the back of the skull and the path of the disintegrated fragments could be observed along the right side of the skull. The largest section of this missile as portrayed by X-ray appeared to be behind the right frontal sinus. The next largest fragment appeared to be at the rear of the skull at the juncture of the skull bone."[50]

Although that paragraph contains a rather skimpy description, enough detail is provided to infer that these X-rays were probably the lateral and A-P (anterior-posterior) X-rays of the head examined by the Clark Panel, now at the National Archives, and which were originally given to Robert Kennedy by the Secret Service. Those X-rays existed, and were put up on the morgue lightbox before the "latter stages" of the autopsy described by Sibert and O'Neill on the night of November 22, 1963.

This was one of the most unexpected results of my analysis—that

---

* Army documents from MDW dated November 22 state: "Gawler's has confirmed their instructions. They will receive the body following the autopsy, which is estimated to take approximately one hour."[48]

** The Sibert and O'Neill report states: "The first incision was made at 8:15."[49] If this refers to the Y-incision, it is completely inconsistent with the evidence cited here that the permission for a full autopsy was not granted for at least an hour, and either the Sibert and O'Neill report is in error, or there was a typographical alteration to change the time. Only a formal investigation with the power to subpoena the agents and question them under oath could resolve this question.

Lens 3, the photo and X-ray record, preceded Lens 2, the written autopsy description, in real time. In short, the X-ray and photo evidence which has superseded the written autopsy report, and dominated the record, was not fabricated days, weeks, or years after November 22, 1963, as part of a "coverup," but was created on the night of November 22, 1963, before the official autopsy got underway, and probably in conjunction with the plan to alter the President's body.*

The Puzzle of the Ruler

Two trajectories tied the crime scene (i.e., the sniper's nest) to the body—the head trajectory and the neck trajectory. My analysis indicated that, in the case of the head trajectory, a more plausible record was created for the benefit of the medical camera and X-ray tube than was created for Humes' own eyes. Stated differently, the head as examined by Humes was an *imperfect* medical forgery; but, as reconstructed for the photos and X-rays, it was a perfect medical forgery.

The head trajectory, based on wounds described by Humes, was "imperfect" because the large head wound extended to the rear of the head, and the entry wound was at the bottom of the back of the head, making the trajectory implausible because it sloped upward. But the photo and X-ray record of the head showed a trajectory which entered at the top rear of the head, and exited on the forward right side.

The neck trajectory had its corresponding imperfections, its plausibility problems.

As explained in the Trajectory Reversal chapter,** the back wound was apparently made too low, because the trajectory fabricated was nothing more than a shallow impact, to be associated with a bullet found on a

---

* That necessitated an additional assumption: that the reconstruction of the head must have been disassembled before the beginning of the official autopsy. By "disassembled," I mean the removal of any mechanical devices—e.g., tape, thread, etc.—which held the head together. Furthermore, if the pictures were made before the autopsy, then the incident of the late-arriving bone fragments had to be re-interpreted. Formerly, I believed their belated arrival was evidence of post-midnight reconstruction and photography. But if a reconstruction *preceded* the autopsy, the post-midnight arrival of bone that appears in the autopsy X-rays would be circumstantial evidence of disassembly of that reconstruction before Humes started the official autopsy. Just as the bone fragments would be necessary in the pictures and X-rays to create the proper appearance, they would have to be supplied to Humes so that he could draw the corresponding conclusion based on the body itself.

One other point: If the pictures were made before the autopsy, the changed receipts may indicate substitution, rather than additional, photography.

** See Chapter 14, 374–76.

stretcher. This apparently was the result of the plotters' failure to account for the throat wound.* The solution to this problem was to "raise" the back wound, thus creating a transiting trajectory.

In 1966–67, when the controversy first erupted and the photos and X-rays were unavailable, I conjectured this was accomplished by pressuring Humes to change his written autopsy report. But that conjecture raised a serious question.

Humes might be pressured, some hours after the autopsy was over, to change an autopsy conclusion, but a "low" back wound, once created, could not be made to disappear. And so I wondered: If the autopsy photographs became available, what would they show at the "low" location?

Would the wound be there? Could it have been concealed?

I thought that if there was one place on the photographs where there might have been retouching, this would be it—the spot where Hill and Sibert and O'Neill saw the "low" back wound, the same spot indicated by the clothing holes.

I anxiously awaited reliable information as to what the pictures showed. The first official report came from the Clark Panel in 1969. It said the back wound was higher than the throat wound. But from that report it was impossible to know what was depicted at the "low" location.

Over the years, contradictory information abounded as additional examiners viewed the photographs.** In August 1972, I asked Dr. Wecht, after he examined the photographs, what he saw at the "low" location. He said it was impossible to see anything there because a ruler was lying along the body to the right of the spinal column. I wondered about that ruler.

In 1978, I saw the Ida Dox drawings—each of them an exact replica of one of the autopsy photographs—at the House Assassinations Committee public hearings. Two things immediately struck me about the Dox reproductions of the autopsy photograph showing the back wound: The wound

---

* An alternative theory was that the plotters' failure to account for the throat wound was deliberate—i.e., that they planned, in the early hours, to pass the wound off as a tracheotomy incision, and nothing more.

** The Clark Panel said it was higher than the wound in the front of the throat.[51] Dr. Werner Spitz, who saw the pictures for the Rockefeller Commission, said it was lower.[52] Dr. John Lattimer said the wound was so high, and the trajectory sloped downward so steeply, that if the throat wound was an entry, and the bullet had been going in the other direction, the assassin would have to have been on the floor of the car.[53] Even the experts on the House Select Committee couldn't agree on exactly where the wound was located. Dr. Baden said its location, with respect to the throat wound, depended on the body's posture.[54] From his testimony, Dr. Petty seemed to have arrived at the conclusion that, posture aside, the wound was lower than the throat wound. He testified the bullet had traveled in an anatomically upward direction, even though it was going downward in space.[55]

seemed to be higher than the throat wound, and the ruler seemed to be in a peculiar place. (See Photo 41.) In the autopsy report, the non-fatal wound was recorded as being at "14 centimeters below the tip of the right mastoid process" (the bony protuberance behind the ear).[56] This implied that such a measurement was made at the time of autopsy. But in the picture, the ruler was not placed alongside the wound, nor did it extend up to the right mastoid process.

The ruler was simply held against the body, to the right of the spinal column. It covered the spot where Sibert and O'Neill and Hill and the clothing holes indicated the wound was located.[57] I wondered whether the ruler was being used to cover a "low" back wound from the eye of the camera.

If so, that would be the solution to the "low"/"high" conflict that had permeated the debate for years, but it would also have certain implications. It would mean that by the time these pictures were taken—i.e., by the time the "Lens 3" record was being constructed—the plotters knew very well that the hole at the front of the throat had to be accounted for as a gunshot wound.

In short, if the ruler concealed a "low" back wound, that would be evidence of the plotters' intention, by the time these pictures were made, to change the autopsy conclusion from non-transit to transit.*

Of course, once the ruler was removed, there then would have been two holes on the rear surface of the body, and Humes would have to be given an explanation for the second defect (the lower one). He may have been told that this lower wound (which Clint Hill described, based on a 2:45 A.M. observation, as an "opening" in the back)[58] was made by the Dallas doctors for some reason. This line of reasoning made me re-evaluate the question Humes asked Perry: Did you make any wounds in the back?

Humes may not have been asking Perry whether the bullet entrance wound cited in the autopsy report was man-made, but trying to satisfy himself why there was a second defect in the back. According to notes made when Dr. Wecht was looking at the pictures, there was a bloody spot on the ruler ". . . at a point approximately 3cm below the other [shoulder] wound."**[59]

The only way to establish unequivocally that the ruler in the picture concealed a second defect on the back would be to exhume the body.

* It would be a matter of speculation whether, at that early hour, the timing problem was also spotted—i.e., whether the purpose of the change was merely to account for the throat wound, or to lay the foundation for the single-bullet theory.

** Dr. Wecht's notes continue: "It is a heavy blood stain, the kind of stain one would wash away before determining whether or not there is a hole beneath it."[60]

Nevertheless, circumstantial evidence supports this theory. My own investigation has turned up two accounts indicating that a transiting neck trajectory was being discussed on Friday night.

In his November 29, 1963 account, Coast Guardsman George Barnum wrote that as the men were having sandwiches and coffee sometime after midnight, Admiral Burkley came in and talked to them, and said three shots had been fired, that the President had been hit by the first and third, and he described the trajectories of the two that struck: "The first striking him in the lower neck and coming out near the throat. The second shot striking him above and to the rear of the right ear, this shot not coming out. . . ."[61] Although Barnum's report was incorrect on the head shot not exiting, both points of entry are those shown in the autopsy photographs, and the neck trajectory was the "transiting" conclusion to be found in the official autopsy report Humes wrote later that weekend.*

James Jenkins told me that during the autopsy, when the "civilians" were practically arguing with Humes, they put the idea to him that the bullet entered at the rear, exiting through the tracheotomy incision, and that that bullet went on to hit Connally.**[62]

The evidence indicates that in the case of both the head and the neck, photographs and X-rays showing the body as a "perfect" medical forgery were created on Friday night at Bethesda, before the Y-incision was made.***

Once the "best evidence" had been created, it didn't matter that other, conflicting information also existed. It was inevitable that the lawyers running such investigations would rely on the X-rays and photographs, and posit various theories to explain divergences between that medico-legal record and any other.

When presented on a time line, the three medical records of the

* Barnum's account also raises this question: why Burkley, speaking informally, described a transiting trajectory, yet in filing his medical report on November 22, omitted any mention of the throat wound.

** Unfortunately, Jenkins never made a written record, and so it is easy to discount his recollections by claiming he was influenced by what he later read in books and magazines.

But having spoken with him, I didn't believe that was the case. Jenkins did *not* follow the case and, in fact, until I spoke with him in September 1979, did not know a bullet wound at the front of the neck had been observed in Dallas. Jenkins kept referring to it as the "tracheotomy incision," and couldn't understand why those "civilians" in the autopsy room kept claiming that a bullet exited there.

*** This statement is based on the assumption that all the pictures in the official collection were made at essentially the same time. Of course, one can't preclude the possibility that some of these pictures—i.e., the photos of the back posed with the ruler—may have been made after the Y-incision, because the Y-incision wouldn't show in photographs taken from the rear.

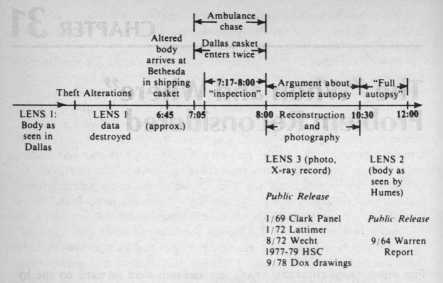

Figure 43.

shooting, all based on the President's body as seen at different points in time, appeared as in Figure 43.

The alteration of the body was the first in a sequence of steps to falsify the autopsy conclusions. Until the X-rays and photos had been created and the autopsy concluded, the foundation for a false version of history had not been laid.

By midnight, that was accomplished. The "best evidence" existed tying the sniper's nest at the Texas School Book Depository to the body of President Kennedy.

In Dallas, at 11:26 P.M. CST (12:26 EST), Lee Harvey Oswald was charged with the assassination.[63]

CHAPTER 31

The "When and Where" Problem Reconsidered

FOR MORE THAN THIRTEEN YEARS, my research went forward on the hypothesis that President Kennedy's body had arrived at the front of Bethesda Naval Hospital unaltered, and had been altered during the fifty minutes before the autopsy, at the time of the events connected with the ambulance chase.

My interview with Dennis David on July 2, 1979 completely upset that hypothesis, and I began to re-analyze the data. In mid-July 1979, when the report of the House Assassinations Committee was released, I discovered the statement published in that report that President Kennedy arrived at Bethesda in a body bag. In a few weeks I interviewed Paul O'Connor, and other men who were in the autopsy room. From these interviews, as well as a re-analysis of documents, I developed a substantial case that President Kennedy's body arrived at Bethesda before the Dallas casket. If O'Connor was correct that the body came in without a brain, then it had already been altered.

It seemed that President Kennedy's body had been stolen at "A," altered at "B," and re-introduced into the Dallas casket at "C."

"C" was Bethesda. If the accounts of Dennis David, Paul O'Connor, et al. were correct—if the body arrived separately from the Dallas casket —it must have been removed from the casket before *Air Force One* was airborne. "A" had to represent Dallas, either Parkland Hospital or Love Field.

President Kennedy's death was announced at 1:30 P.M. CST by Press Secretary Malcolm Kilduff.

Secret Service Agent Clint Hill had approached Parkland Hospital administrator Jack Price for help in obtaining a casket. Price's assistant Steve Landregan called Vernon O'Neal's funeral home, and at 1:40 Vernon

O'Neal arrived at Parkland in a hearse with the four-hundred-pound Elgin Brittania casket.[1]

Vernon O'Neal had the contract for part of the ambulance service in Dallas. Two of his employees, Aubrey Rike and Dennis McGuire, were already at Parkland Hospital, because they had brought in a man who had an epileptic seizure about five minutes before the President arrived.[2]

The casket was wheeled into Trauma Room One, where Vernon O'Neal, assisted by Aubrey Rike and Dennis McGuire, put the body inside.

At 1:58, according to Secret Service reports, the casket was wheeled from the emergency room and put aboard the O'Neal hearse.[3]

The time period between 1:40 and 1:58, when the coffin left, was one of two periods in Dallas when the body could have been taken from the coffin, but the records indicated that Jacqueline Kennedy was always with the coffin, and implied that Aubrey Rike was also present. In March 1980, I contacted Rike and went through the events of the day.

In considerable detail, Rike explained how he and "Peanuts" McGuire lifted the President, wrapped in sheets, into the coffin. The casket had been lined with a piece of plastic; "a heavy plastic sheet that they use for bed-wetters and things."

Rike told me that during the time he was there, Mrs. Kennedy came in twice—once to put a ring on her husband's finger, and a second time, after the coffin was closed. "She came back later on—and it was me, and Peanuts, and the Catholic priest, and her was in there by ourselves."

LIFTON: Now once you put him in the casket, who closed the casket?
RIKE: Mr. O'Neal.
LIFTON: Now what happened next—did you stay there?
RIKE: Me and Mr. O'Neal did. . . . We had to stay in the room, they wouldn't let us out of the room, once we put him in. . . .[4]

The "they" Rike was referring to were Secret Service agents. Rike described the argument in the hallway. Seventeen years later, he remembered it vividly. "I was scared to death," he said. "I was scared all the time I was there. . . . Dallas wanted to do an autopsy. The government wanted the casket out. The government said 'take it out'; Dallas said 'bring it back.' You know, we'd start pushing, and somebody would grab us, and push us back, and pull the casket back. You'd have to see it to believe it."

LIFTON: You never left the room from the time you put the body in the casket until the time the casket left the hospital?
RIKE: No, no; you wouldn't have either, if you'd been there. You'd been as scared as we were. . . . I felt safe in there. If you'd been there, no kidding, it was the most unorganized, scary type situation I have ever been in in my life. I'm a policeman now, and I've been up against all kinds of stuff.[5]

It seemed impossible that anything could have happened between the time Aubrey Rike put the President's body inside the casket and the time the casket was wheeled out.

Then, in full view of reporters, the casket was wheeled to the hearse, and put inside. Jacqueline Kennedy climbed inside and sat next to the casket.

The Secret Service commandeered the O'Neal hearse and drove to the airport.

At 2:14, the hearse arrived at the plane. Secret Service personnel and *Air Force One* staff helped carry the casket up the ramp. The scene was photographed by White House photographer Cecil Stoughton. Secret Service reports stated the casket was in place at 2:18. At 2:47, *Air Force One* was airborne.[6] (See Photos 42A–C.)

Aboard Air Force One 2:18 to 2:47

It was not possible to evaluate what happened aboard *Air Force One* without studying the confused circumstances in which both the new President and Mrs. Kennedy, and their respective staffs, went aboard the same airplane.

The situation was first described in detail in 1966–1967 in Manchester's book, *Death of a President*. The Kennedys went to the airport having no idea Lyndon Johnson was aboard *Air Force One*. Finding him already there was their first surprise. Their second was learning that their departure would be delayed because President Johnson was waiting for a judge to swear him in.[7]

At 2:30, Judge Sarah Hughes arrived. Everyone went amidships to the stateroom. Cecil Stoughton took photographs of the assembled group. At 2:38, the oath was administered.[8]

At 2:47, *Air Force One* was airborne.

Could the body have been removed between 2:18 and 2:47?

Air Force One was a Boeing 707 jet, identical to those used in commercial service, except for its interior. (See Fig. 44.)

The rear port door opened on the tail compartment. Normally, these were the quarters for Secret Service agents and White House staff. On the return to Washington, four of the six seats normally there were removed, and the coffin was placed against the port side of the plane, just forward of the rear door.

Immediately forward of the rear staff area was the Presidential bedroom. A narrow corridor led from the rear staff area, past the bedroom, to the stateroom. The stateroom, in which Johnson was sworn in, functioned as the President's office. In front of the stateroom was the "passenger section" of *Air Force One*—formally called the "Press and Staff Area." It contained about eight rows of seats, and tables with electric typewriters.

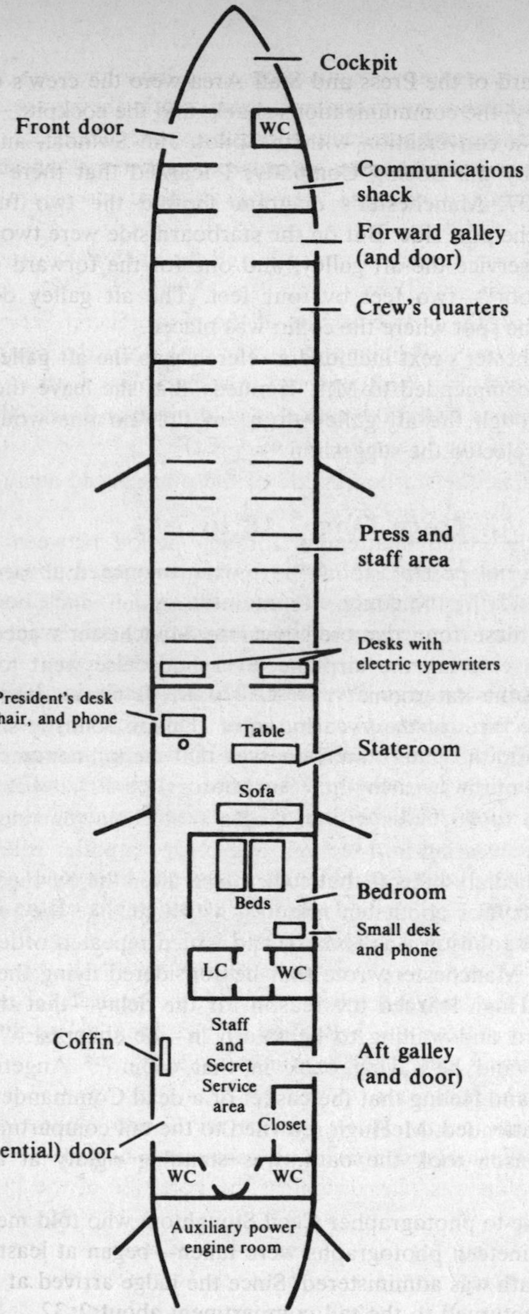

Cockpit
Front door
WC
Communications shack
Forward galley (and door)
Crew's quarters
Press and staff area
Desks with electric typewriters
President's desk chair, and phone
Table
Stateroom
Sofa
Beds
Bedroom
Small desk and phone
LC
WC
Staff and Secret Service area
Coffin
Aft galley (and door)
Closet
Rear (presidential) door
WC
WC
Auxiliary power engine room

Figure 44.
Diagram of the interior of *Air Force One*

Forward of the Press and Staff Area were the crew's quarters, the forward galley, the communications shack, and the cockpit.

From a conversation with the pilot, Jim Swindal, and from drawings provided by the Boeing Company, I learned that there were four doors on the 707. Manchester's diagram showed the two full-size passenger doors on the port side. But on the starboard side were two additional doors —one to service the aft galley, and one for the forward galley. Each was a "half door"—two feet by four feet. The aft galley door was directly opposite the spot where the coffin was placed.

Manchester's text included a reference to the aft galley door. Malcolm Kilduff recommended to Mrs. Kennedy that she leave the plane, with the coffin, through the aft galley door, so that no one would see her. Mrs. Kennedy rejected the suggestion.[9]

In Dallas, the starboard side of the plane faced away from the airport fence, and toward *Air Force Two*.

Was the coffin unattended for any period between 2:18 and 2:47? The answer depended upon the movements of four people—Jacqueline Kennedy, Godfrey McHugh, Kenneth O'Donnell, and Larry O'Brien.

Only these four mattered because Manchester's account made plain that, upon entering the airplane, everybody else went to the staff cabin, forward of the stateroom.[10]

The pictures of the swearing-in of Lyndon Johnson showed everybody crowded into the stateroom. I guessed that the tail compartment was empty at the time of the swearing-in. (See Photos 43A–F.)

I soon found I was wrong. Godfrey McHugh remained with the coffin during the swearing-in. McHugh had played a major role in the argument about immediate takeoff that took place after the Kennedy party boarded the aircraft. For about ten minutes, McHugh, like the rest, remained unaware that Johnson was aboard, and issued repeated orders to the pilot to take off.[11] Manchester wrote that he considered flying the plane himself.[12] When McHugh learned the reason for the delay—that the new President was aboard and waiting to be sworn in—he snapped: "I have only one President, and he's lying back in that cabin."[13] Angered by Johnson's behavior, and feeling that the casket of a dead Commander-in-Chief should not be unattended, McHugh returned to the tail compartment, and at 2:38, when Johnson took the oath, was standing rigidly at attention, by the casket.

I spoke to photographer Cecil Stoughton, who told me that his picture-taking—nineteen photographs were taken—began at least five minutes before the oath was administered. Since the judge arrived at 2:30, I supposed McHugh returned to the tail compartment about 2:32.

The critical period was 2:18 to 2:32. It appeared, from the public record, that the coffin was then unattended.

Godfrey McHugh was in the forward part of the aircraft.

Jacqueline Kennedy was in her bedroom. After entering the plane, she was escorted there by Ladybird Johnson, and the Johnsons then stayed with her and expressed their condolences. Manchester, based on his interview with Jacqueline, wrote that Johnson told her the judge wouldn't arrive for an hour. The result was that when they left, she stayed in the room.[14]

Kenneth O'Donnell and Larry O'Brien were called to the stateroom by Johnson. This is described in both O'Brien's memoir and in his Warren Commission testimony.[15] During these conversations, O'Donnell urged immediate takeoff. Johnson replied that Attorney General Robert Kennedy had recommended by telephone that the oath be administered before takeoff from Dallas. O'Donnell was incredulous that Robert Kennedy had recommended that course of action. He wrote that Robert Kennedy later denied giving Johnson that advice.[16]

Secret Service Agent Jerry Kivett, of the Vice-Presidential detail, wrote in his report: "The Vice-President and Mrs. Johnson attempted to console Mrs. Kennedy in the State Room where she was. It was cleared of all personnel [with the] exception of Vice-President, Mrs. Johnson, Mrs. Kennedy, ASAIC Youngblood, and a member or two of the White House staff, exactly who I cannot recall."[17]

When I first read Kivett's sentence, I didn't understand it. Ladybird and Lyndon Johnson visited Mrs. Kennedy in the bedroom, not the stateroom. There seemed to have been no reason for the bedroom to be "cleared of all personnel." Only Mrs. Kennedy was there in the first place.

If, however, Kivett was forward of the stateroom door, in the rear part of the Press and Staff cabin, under instructions to let no one pass, the sentence might make sense. It might mean that during the period when the Johnsons were visiting Mrs. Kennedy in the bedroom, the rear part of the plane—from the forward stateroom door back—was "cleared of all personnel." In ignorance of their actual location, Kivett might well have written that the Johnsons were extending their condolences to Mrs. Kennedy "in the State Room where she was."

Probably, the "member or two of the White House staff" referred to O'Donnell and O'Brien.

The statement by a Secret Service agent aboard *Air Force One* that any area of the plane at the rear was "cleared of all personnel" during this particular time period seemed significant.

If my analysis was correct, the President's body was inside the Dallas casket when it was put aboard *Air Force One* at 2:18, but was no longer inside the casket at 2:47, as the plane rolled down the runway.

How Was the Body Transported?

How did President Kennedy's body get from Dallas, Texas, to Washington, D.C.?

I considered three possibilities:

1. that it was aboard *Air Force Two;*
2. that it was aboard some other plane of which I had no knowledge;
3. that it was aboard *Air Force One,* but not in the Dallas casket.

The *Air Force Two* possibility was suggested by the change in the Sibert and O'Neill report and the questioning of Gerald Behn by Sibert and O'Neill on November 27, 1963. It was not clear what questions Sibert and O'Neill put to Behn, but the response they recorded was that *Air Force Two* passed *Air Force One* in flight. That interchange, added to the typographical alteration in the first three lines of their report, concerning what plane the body was on, suggested that possibly it had been put aboard *Air Force Two.*

There was a relationship between any theory of how the body got from Dallas to Washington, and where it was altered. Secret Service reports indicated that *Air Force Two* left Dallas at 3:15, and arrived in Washington at 6:30.[18] If the body was taken off *Air Force One* between 2:18 and 2:32, that left almost forty-five minutes in Dallas to account for. The *Air Force Two* hypothesis and the possibility that the body had been altered in Dallas were inextricably intertwined.

Another factor fueling my speculation concerning *Air Force Two* was a rumor circulated that afternoon, reported as fact by AP at 2:18, that a Secret Service agent had been killed in connection with the assassination.[19] I wondered whether the story was a cover story to account for an extra body going back to Washington on some plane.

In February 1980, I spoke with Col. Joe Sofet of *Air Force Two*, and the flight engineer, Deroy Cain. The object of these telephone interviews was to establish whether there was any reason for believing that they had taken back anything resembling a body bag, or a shipping casket, or had been asked to hold the plane for any reason. Deroy Cain told me that the plane was not held for any reason, that nothing was put aboard at the last minute. He said he had never heard the dead Secret Service agent story, and characterized the notion that anything was surreptitiously put abroad *Air Force Two*, just before takeoff, as "bull." "I would know," he said. "I'm the flight engineer. I'd have to know something like that." Cain also said that he closed the baggage holds.[20]

Sofet expressed surprise at my line of questioning. He too had never heard of the dead Secret Service agent story, and didn't recall the plane being held for anything to be placed aboard.[21]

I rejected the *Air Force Two* hypothesis.

It was always possible to postulate that there was some aircraft we did not know about which had flown the President's body from Dallas to Washington. Since Sofet stayed at Love Field until 3:15, I asked him if he saw any other military aircraft taking off from Love Field. He said he did not. For a while, I postulated that perhaps the body was flown in a private plane to Carswell Air Force Base and put aboard a supersonic jet. That would fit with the original time of arrival listed in the Sibert and O'Neill report—5:25.*[22]

Other evidence, however, seemed to diminish the importance of the 5:25 time. Documents indicated that time was logged in by the Military District of Washington, shortly before *Air Force One* took off.**[23] I concluded it must have been an erroneous "ETA." Moreover, I found that time was announced on the NBC network.[24] It seemed innocent.

That President Kennedy's body was removed from the casket and hidden somewhere on board *Air Force One* in a body bag seemed the only remaining possibility. Disguised as luggage, it might have been put in the baggage hold, or in the forward galley area.

The House Select Committee reported physical evidence of rough handling of the body. The Committee's authenticators faced the problem of proving that pictures of the body which did not show the face were in fact of the same body as those which did show the face. They took note of certain abrasions on the President's upper back: "3 narrow parallel marks approximately 3 centimeters in length which appear to be slight skin abrasions. These marks and stains are situated several centimeters lateral to the back wound and do not appear to be directly associated with it. It is possible that they were made in the course of handling and lifting of the body. There is also a 3 by 5 centimeter area of discoloration at the base of the neck in the right area which apparently represents either a slight contusion or some post-mortem lividity."[25] These marks appeared in both sets of pictures. In view of the possibility that they might in fact be evidence of rough handling of the body, I found the Committee authenticators' evalutions—based on a concern the body wasn't Kennedy's—rather ironic: "Such minor and random details are also the kind of characteristics that would likely be overlooked in any attempted hoax."[26]

This question remained: If the body was hidden aboard *Air Force One*, how did it get to Bethesda, and where could it have been altered?

* The flight time for *Air Force One* between Dallas and Washington was two hours, fifteen minutes. That would indicate an average speed of 535 mph. If the body were taken to Carswell Air Force Base and left by about 3:15 (4:15 EST), it would be possible for it to arrive in Washington at 5:25 only if it were flown aboard a supersonic jet at an average speed exceeding 1000 mph.

** I obtained the Military District of Washington file on the Kennedy assassination in March 1980, under the Freedom of Information Act.

Dennis David said he was told the black hearse he saw coming from the rear gate had come down Fourteenth Street. A check of a map of Washington showed that a few miles away was Walter Reed Army Medical Center.

The Walter Reed Evidence

I was aware, from two sources, that there had been radio instructions from the plane, to arrange an autopsy at Walter Reed.

Radio transmissions aboard *Air Force One* were taped by the U.S. Army Signal Corps. In 1964, William Manchester learned that such a tape existed. He was not permitted to listen to it, but he was shown a transcript.

In 1975 a Warren Report critic, Fred T. Newcomb, tracked down the only transcript known to exist—at the LBJ Library.

At one point, Secret Service Agent Roy Kellerman, in a conversation with Secret Service headquarters, said: "Arriving Andrews 6:05. The body will go to Walter Reed. Have an ambulance from Walter Reed to take the body there."[27]

At another point, Rear Adm. George Burkley called General Heaton, Surgeon General of the Army: "General Heaton, this is Admiral Burkley. Did you contact MDW in regards to taking care of the remains of President Kennedy taking him directly to Walter Reed? Probably Mrs. Kennedy will also be going out there. We will clarify that later."[28]

Then, Gen. Chester Clifton, the senior military aide, got on the radiotelephone connection: "This is General Clifton. We do not want a helicopter to go to Bethesda Medical Center. We do want an ambulance and a ground return from Andrews to Walter Reed, and we want the regular post-mortem that has to be done by law under guard performed at Walter Reed. Is that clear?"[29]

Was this just another example of confusion that day?

In March 1980, grappling with this problem, I applied under the Freedom of Information Act for certain Air Force documents. Back came pages from the official Air Force history of the 1001st Air Base Wing, written in December, 1963, which stated: ". . . the body of the slain President was removed to Walter Reed General Hospital. . . ."[30]

I began seriously to consider the possibility that in fact the body did go to Walter Reed. There was only one way possible—via helicopter.

Walter Reed is just 13.3 miles from Andrews. At 150 mph, a standard helicopter speed, the trip would take 5.2 minutes. Thus, if the body was immediately put aboard a helicopter, it would be at Walter Reed at 6:05, and that would leave about thirty minutes for alterations, and then a quick

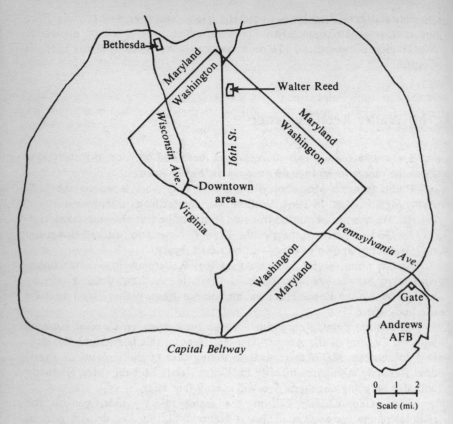

Figure 45.
Map showing locations of Andrews Air Force Base, Bethesda Naval Medical Center, and Walter Reed Army Medical Center

helicopter hop to the rear grounds at Bethesda, for rendezvous with the hearse, or just a short ride to Bethesda.* (See Fig. 45.)

But that would require an immediate helicopter take-off. Was there evidence of a helicopter take-off near *Air Force One* when it landed?

I had an excellent collection of tape recordings made that day, in storage in Los Angeles. I remembered that they included one of the Andrews arrival. An associate sent it to me.

---

* From the map, it would appear the distance between Walter Reed and Bethesda was about five miles, and that the travel time, by car, was perhaps eight minutes. But I retraced the route by car and found that the winding roads extended that time considerably. It took me about fifteen minutes.

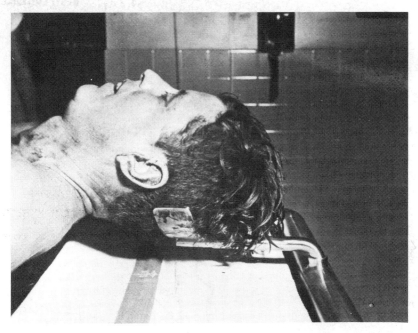

Autopsy Photo 1.
Left lateral view of President Kennedy's head

Autopsy Photo 2.
View from the top of the head, shows the abdomen. Note: No Y incision has yet been made, which establishes that at least this photo was taken at the outset of the autopsy.

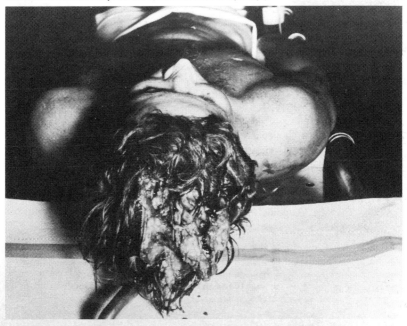

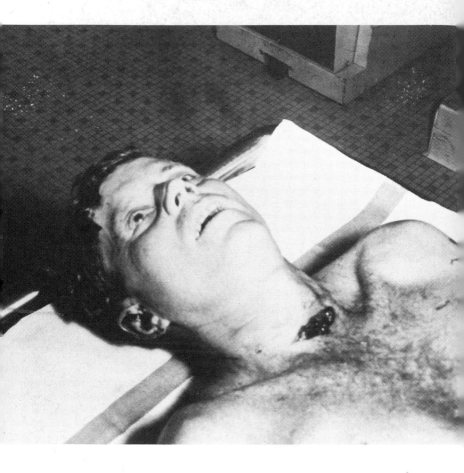

Autopsy Photo 3.
Full face view, from forward right-hand side. Note the large throat wound, which is supposed to be the tracheotomy incision made by Dr. Perry. Original wound was 3–5 mm. (See p. 275). Perry told me his incision was "2–3 cm." (p. 238) The wound described in the autopsy report is 6.5 cm. (Under oath, Humes testified it was "7–8 cm.") and had "widely gaping irregular edges." Also note the right forehead area: according to the A-P and lateral X-rays (see Photos 31 and 32) the bone is completely gone, at least as far down as the area of the right eye socket. The bone is not gone on the photographs.

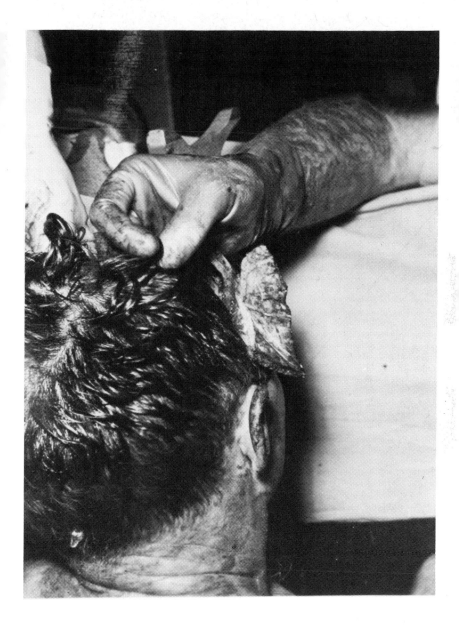

Autopsy Photo 4.
Rear view of head. Gloved hand positions head. Large flap of scalp and bone on forward right side, allegedly associated with large exit wound. Ruler, white area at lower left, is partially visible here but shown fully on Dox drawing (Photo 30). Dox drawing was made from a similar but not identical autopsy photo. Rear entry wound, a major feature of Dox drawing, is not discernible on this picture. Why, is unclear.

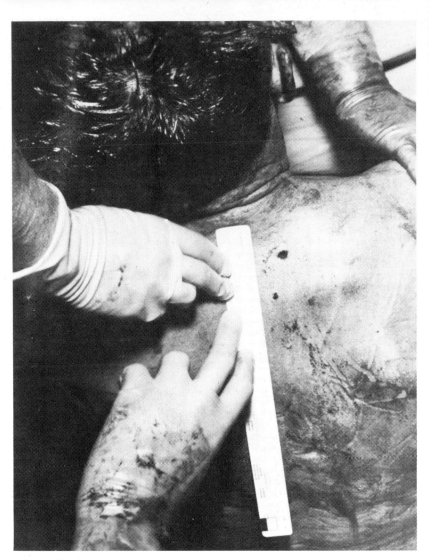

Autopsy Photo 5.
Rear view of Kennedy's body. Note the extensive post-mortem wrinkles and abrasions not portrayed on the Dox drawing of the same photo (Photo 41). Also note the ruler, which as positioned seems unrelated to the way the back wound is measured in the autopsy report: the distance between the wound and the right mastoid process, the bony point behind the right ear. But the ruler *does* cover the area on the body where the FBI reported a "low" back wound. (See p. 163, on the "low"/"high" conflict, and p. 668, "The Puzzle of the Ruler.") Also note that the back of the head, reported blown out by the Dallas doctors, appears intact in these pictures. (See also photo 30, the Dox drawing of another autopsy photo of the back of the head.)

Autopsy Photo 6.
Facing page, top: View of the top of the head. This picture, which would normally be expected to show the brain inside the head, at first appears to show a confusing mass of brain tissue and hair. On closer inspection, it appears to show a mechanical device inside the head. (See Autopsy Photo 6A, and discussion on pp. 661–663.)

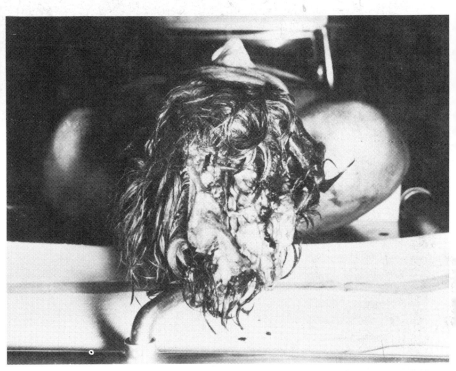

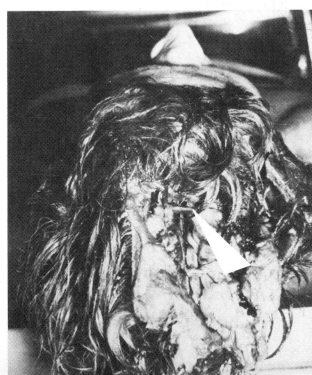

Autopsy Photo 6A
Enlargement showing what appears to be a clip or device inside the head. (See arrow)

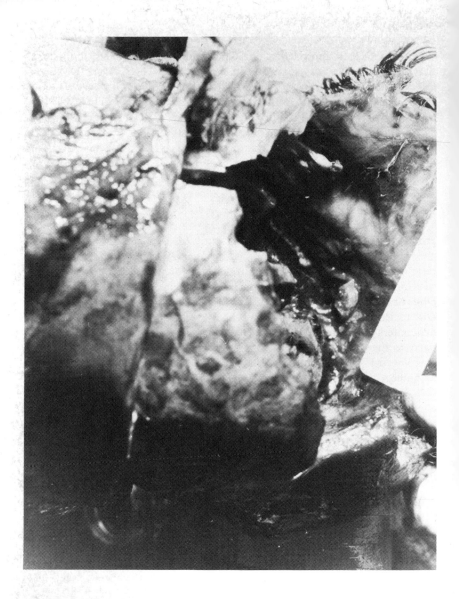

Autopsy Photo 7.
Interior of cranium. Officially titled by House Select Committee ''Anterior-superior [view] of cranial cavity. Brain removed.'' In the official collection, no picture exists showing the brain inside the head. (See pp. 661 663) Note semicircular notch in bone. House Select Committee placed great emphasis on this notch, citing it as medico-legal evidence of exit. Humes, however, testified that he examined entire periphery of wound and could find no evidence of exit. (See p. 248)

As six o'clock approached, the CBS anchorman reminded the listener that *Air Force One* was soon due in Washington. Then, Harry Reasoner, looking at his monitor, said: "This is film or tape of that arrival." A voice in the background spoke: "Live. Live." Reasoner: "It is live. It is live. Right now. Of the plane coming in."[31]

At that point, a technician threw a switch, and the audio came from Andrews Air Force Base. The announcer was saying: ". . . this is one of the most unique and tragic moments in the history of Andrews Air Force Base. The field that is used for welcoming the arrival of presidents and kings and prime ministers and men like Khrushchev and all the rest at this time it has the sad but still historic journey. . . ."

It was difficult to hear the announcer because, thundering in the background, could be heard the turning rotor of a helicopter, accelerating, growing louder. There was nothing ambiguous about the sound. A chopper took off from very near *Air Force One*. By timing the tape, I established that the chopper took off within ninety seconds of the arrival of *Air Force One*. At 6:09 EST the Associated Press "A" wire reported that as *Air Force One* taxied to a halt, "the Presidential helicopters flew in close to it." Those helicopters could not be the Presidential helicopters that carried the Johnson party to the White House, because when *Air Force One* landed they were standing still on the port side of the plane. Indeed, ten minutes later the announcer, describing them, said, "Their rotors have not yet turned." A helicopter hovering near *Air Force One* when it arrived may well have been captured on network TV tapes. The NBC log, published commercially, carried this description of the scene: "The Presidential jet is seen arriving, along with an Army helicopter." [32]

In 1976, I had been able to locate copies of the *Air Force One* tapes themselves. I now gave them a very close examination.*

To understand the implications of what was said on the tapes, I found it useful to review the record about the arrangements to send President Kennedy's body to Bethesda for autopsy.

In the report he submitted to the Warren Commission, Burkley described his conversation with Mrs. Kennedy on the plane: "Throughout the plane trip, Mrs. Kennedy sat in the vicinity of the coffin. . . . I spoke to her while kneeling on the floor so I would be at the level of her face rather than leaning forward and expressed complete desire of all of us and especially of myself to comply with her wishes, stating that it was

---

* Interpretation of the tapes is hampered by the fact that they have been edited. A voice at the beginning says so. More than one channel was used from *Air Force One,* but the tapes include no information as to which transmissions come from which channel, or the order in which they were originally made, although there is a general pattern established from Love Field takeoff to the Andrews landing. Attempts to locate the whereabouts of the original tape recordings—attempts made by several researchers, including myself—have so far proved fruitless.

necessary that the President be taken to a hospital prior to going to the White House. She questioned why and I stated it must be determined, if possible, the type of bullet used and compare this with future material found. I stated frankly that I had no preference, that it could be any hospital, but that I did feel that, if possible, it should be a military hospital for security measures. The question was answered by her stating that she wanted the President taken to Bethesda Naval Hospital."[33]

There was actually little choice. There were two military medical establishments in Washington—Bethesda and Walter Reed—and because John Kennedy was a former naval officer, Bethesda became the hospital which served his needs from the day of his inauguration.

A month after the inauguration, he was assigned a navy doctor. Professional military journals of the time recorded the fact that Bethesda was now the Presidential hospital.*

In view of these circumstances, then, it was predictable that Mrs. Kennedy would "choose" Bethesda.

But those same factors made all the more peculiar the various radio transmissions from *Air Force One*. The activity seemed to center around attempts on the part of Burkley and Maj. Gen. Chester Clifton to reach Surgeon General of the Army Leonard Heaton to arrange for an autopsy at Walter Reed.

At no time do the tapes show an attempt to contact the Navy Surgeon General. The radio operator on board *Air Force One* called the White House to ask for a phone patch. The White House was called "Crown."

AF-1: Crown, Air Force One.

CROWN: This is Crown, go ahead.

---

* *The Army-Navy-Air Force Register and Defense Times,* on February 25, 1961, carried an article by Jack Virden: BETHESDA LIKELY TO BE *THE* HOSPITAL FOR VIPS. "One of the by-products of the power struggle now going on in Washington with the advent of a new regime is the reestablishment of the Bethesda Naval Medical Center as THE hospital for the real VIPs to go for relief from their aches and pains and the other afflictions that plague all who are mortal. . . .

"The Presidential Suite, up on the 17th floor, is all ready. Redecorated and furnished in French Provincial, yet!" The French Provincial, of course, was a gesture toward Jacqueline, but the National Naval Medical Center was very much Kennedy's hospital. Virden noted that "for almost 20 years," Bethesda had played "second fiddle" to Walter Reed, because the last Navy President was FDR. "It's just one of the facts of political life," he wrote, "that our last two presidents have been Army types. It was only natural they went to Walter Reed when they were ailing."

Manchester noted that Burkley arranged to have a helipad built on the lawn in front of the hospital, should quick access be required. But Virden noted: "If President Kennedy continues in the bouncing good health he now exhibits the Navy may have gone to all the expense and trouble of readying a suite for him at Bethesda for nothing."

It was ironic that Kennedy's first trip to Bethesda would be for an autopsy.

AF-1: OK, we need a patch with Surgeon General of the Army, Heaton . . . we want a patch with General Heaton—H-E-A-T-O-N —the Surgeon General.

CROWN: Roger, Roger. That's General Heaton, the Surgeon General of the Army.

AF-1: That is correct.

CROWN: Roger. Roger, stand by. [pause] Air Force One, [this is] Crown. Stand by please. We're reaching the General now. . . .

But the switchboard couldn't find Heaton immediately. That led to these transmissions:

CROWN: Air Force One, this is Crown. . . . General Heaton is at Walter Reed. . . . You'll have to stand by just a moment. . . . It will take about a minute to reach him.

AF-1: Crown, Roger. Try to get General Heaton. And in the meantime, try to get the Deputy Surgeon General. We'll talk to either one . . . this is very important. . . .

CROWN: Roger. I'll put an "emergency" on it; and we'll get him as soon as possible. . . .

Meanwhile, Dr. Burkley came to the radio room and came on the line.

BURKLEY: This is Dr. Burkley.

CROWN: Dr. Burkley, this is Crown. . . .

BURKLEY: This is Dr. Burkley; I want to get in touch with General Heaton, or General Heaton's deputy.

CROWN: Dr. Burkley, this is Crown. We're working as fast as possible trying to get the call through for you. He is at Walter Reed. We're unable to locate. We're still searching. Over.

BURKLEY: The deputy must be at the General's office, over in the main navy building.

CROWN: Roger, Roger. If you'll stand by, we'll try and reach him.

Before Burkley reached Heaton, another series of transmissions occurred between Roy Kellerman, aboard the plane, and Gerald Behn. There were clearly conflicting messages as to where the body was to go. "Duplex" was Behn.

BEHN: This is Duplex. This is Duplex.

KELLERMAN: Arrival Andrews, 6:05. Stand by. An ambulance from Walter Reed furnished, to transport body. Over.

BEHN: Arrangements have been made for a helicopter for the Bethesda Naval Medical Center.

KELLERMAN: Stand by, Jerry. I'll have to get Burkley here.

BEHN: OK.

Burkley then came on the line:

BURKLEY: Duplex . . . this is Dr. Burkley. What arrangements have been made with regard to the reception of the President?

BEHN: Everybody aboard Air Force One, everyone aboard Air Force One, with the exception of the body, will be choppered to the Naval Medical Center at Bethesda. Over.

BURKLEY: The body will be choppered, or will it go by ambulance to the Navy Medical Center?

BEHN: Will be choppered. Will be choppered.

Burkley then told Behn: "I have called General Heaton and asked him to call the Military District of Washington with regard to this. Will you call him and cancel the—supposed to have it go to Walter Reed. I didn't know these arrangements were already made. . . . The body is in a casket, you know, and it will have to be taken by ambulance and not by chopper."

Behn replied that he would contact Capt. Tazwell Shepherd, Kennedy's naval aide, who was at the White House.

The next transmission on the tape was between Burkley and Heaton.

BURKLEY: General Heaton, this is Admiral Burkley.

HEATON: Yes, Burkley.

BURKLEY: Air Force One.

HEATON: Yes. [pause] I read you, Admiral Burkley.

BURKLEY: Hold for a minute, please, General Clifton is here.

CLIFTON: This is General Clifton.

HEATON: Yes, General Clifton.

CLIFTON: [part apparently missing; tape picks up] Two: We do not want a helicopter for Bethesda Medical Center. We do want an ambulance, and a ground return from Andrews to Walter Reed; and we want the regular postmortem that has to be done by law under guard performed at Walter Reed. Is that clear? Over.

HEATON: That is clear, General Clifton. You want an ambulance and another limousine at Andrews and you want the regular postmortem by law done at Walter Reed.

CLIFTON: That is correct.

But then, later on the tape, when Heaton repeated these arrangements to Burkley, Burkley replied: "General Heaton, will you kindly hold? There have been some arrangements *already* made which [one word unintelligible] will have to clear that before we make any further [sic]."

Apparently, Capt. Tazwell Shepherd, at the White House, was making arrangements for Bethesda. At one point, one of the radio operators said: "He would like to get on and talk to Air Force One, when General Heaton is finished. It might be possible for us to put him up on a conference [call], so that they could all make the arrangements together. I understand that Captain Shepherd, the naval aide, has made some arrangements also. . . ."

Meanwhile, Clifton was in touch with Secret Service White House Detail Chief Gerald Behn:

CLIFTON: Duplex, this is Watchman. Over.

BEHN: Go ahead Watchman, this is Duplex. Over.

CLIFTON: Duplex, this is Watchman. I understand that you have arranged for a mortuary-type ambulance to take Mrs. Kennedy to Bethesda. Is this correct?

BEHN: Watchman, it has been arranged to helicopter, helicopter, the body to Bethesda.

CLIFTON: This is Watchman. That's OK, if it isn't after dark. What about the First Lady? Over.

BEHN: Everybody else aboard, everybody else aboard—arrangements have been made to helicopter into the South Grounds [of the White House].

CLIFTON: This is Watchman. Are you sure that the helicopter operation will work? We have a very heavy casket.

BEHN: According to Witness [Captain Shepherd], yes.

CLIFTON: This is Watchman. Don't take a chance on that. Also have a mortuary-type ambulance stand by in case the helicopter doesn't work.

BEHN: That's affirmative.

Clifton then began giving instructions to Behn as to where he wanted ramps placed when *Air Force One* landed. The only two exits previously mentioned in the record were the left front, where a ramp was placed at the door just aft of the cockpit, and the left rear, where the lift truck was rolled up, and Mrs. Kennedy and the casket deplaned.

Clifton made arrangements for a third exit point, for the "First Lady."

CLIFTON: Now, some other instructions; listen carefully. We need a ramp—a normal ramp with steps, put at the front of the aircraft, on the *right* hand side just behind the pilot's cabin, in the galley. We are going to take the First Lady off by *that* route. Over. Do you understand? (Emphasis as spoken.)

BEHN: I receive, affirmative.

CLIFTON: Also, on the right rear—no, no, the left rear of the aircraft, the left rear of the aircraft, where we usually dismount, debark, we may need a fork-lift rather than a ramp . . . too awkward. We may need a platform to walk out on, and a fork-lift to put it on. Is that possible? Over.

BEHN: We will try for the fork-lift.

Later, Clifton summed it all up for Behn:

CLIFTON: Duplex, this is Watchman. I say again. On the right front, a ramp for Mrs. Kennedy. On the left rear, if possible, a fork-lift for the casket; and on the left front, near the pilot, a normal ramp. And the normal press arrangements . . . has everybody got that clear? Over.

BEHN: That is affirmative.

If the instructions given in these transmissions were followed, then in addition to what the reporters and the rest of the nation saw on TV—a ramp at the left front and a lift at the left rear, where the Kennedy party deplaned—a ramp was also put on the starboard side at the front galley door. Did the body come off the plane via that exit, and leave by the helicopter so clearly audible on the network tape?*

There were a number of other items of evidence indicating that President Kennedy's body may have gone to Bethesda via Walter Reed.

In July 1979, I spoke with Commander Boswell, who was extremely hostile to being interviewed, denied all the major allegations of my research, and assured me: "You can take everything I said as gospel." But Boswell did answer this question:

* In July 1980, I conducted a detailed tape-recorded interview with General Clifton in his office in Washington, D.C. I brought with me the Air Force tapes, the transcript available from the LBJ Library, and a more detailed transcript I had made. When he began perusing the transcripts, General Clifton said he did not know why there had been a change of plans from Walter Reed to Bethesda: "To this day I don't know where the authority for the change came [from], because when I was on the phone telling them [we] were going to Walter Reed, that was what I had been told by Johnson or one of his staff."

Then General Clifton examined the transcripts in detail. He said there was no need actually to play the tapes. He said that whatever was on the tape about the body going to Walter Reed reflected arrangements he had made based on instructions received from others. Clifton said he was in the forward part of the aircraft, near the communications shack, and had little personal contact with the Kennedy party at the rear of the plane. He said he would assume the Walter Reed information came from either Kenneth O'Donnell or the Secret Service. I could not investigate further because O'Donnell died in 1977, and the Secret Service told me it was their policy to refuse interviews with its agents.

The record indicates that Bethesda arrangements may have been made, in part, by Capt. Tazwell Shepherd, Kennedy's loyal and devoted naval aide. Shepherd's code name, "Witness," is referred to by Gerald Behn in connection with making arrangements to fly the casket by helicopter to Bethesda, and the airplane's radio operator, as noted in the text, also makes a reference to Shepherd trying to make arrangements. After studying the transcripts, Clifton told me he believed it was Tazwell Shepherd who made the Bethesda arrangements, and suggested I contact him. I spoke with Shepherd in August 1980. He had no recollection of making any arrangements concerning the autopsy or the transportation of the body.

With regard to the ramp for the exit of the First Lady, General Clifton said he

LIFTON: How did you learn that the body would be brought to your hospital?

BOSWELL: I was called by the Deputy Director from the Armed Forces Institute [of Pathology]. . . . The President's physician was on the airplane, and he radioed to Washington, and the information either came directly to Walter Reed, or indirectly through some other communication means, to Walter Reed, to Captain Bruce Smith, who was the Navy Deputy Director at the AFIP [Armed Forces Institute of Pathology, at Walter Reed Army Medical Center]. And he notified me that they were coming directly to Bethesda.[34]

Re-examining Burkley's November 27, 1963 report, I was surprised to find that after describing how he conversed with Jacqueline Kennedy on bended knee—the conversation in which she chose Bethesda—he wrote: "Arrangements were made on the ground for departure to Walter Reed Army Hospital or Bethesda Naval Hospital, as the case may be."[35]

It wasn't clear what Burkley meant by "as the case may be," since by his own report, Jacqueline had chosen Bethesda.

I found an additional piece of evidence at the LBJ Library in Austin, Texas, in the "Presidential Diary" file for November 22, 1963, which contained the raw notes used to make up the diary. While aboard *Air Force*

---

believed he assumed Mrs. Kennedy might wish to avoid the press, and that was why arrangements were made for a ramp on the starboard side at the forward galley door.

I questioned Clifton at some length as to whether he had any knowledge of the President's body having been removed from the coffin, perhaps as a security measure. Clifton said he had no such knowledge. I asked him if he had heard any talk along those lines from any of the Secret Service agents aboard *Air Force One*. He said he had not. I asked if he knew of the use of multiple ambulances in connection with the transportation of the body, with one being used as a decoy. "There was no decoy," he said.

One item in the MDW files released to me in 1980 is a log kept at the army's funeral operations center. This log contains entries indicating that, with regard to the Andrews arrival, General Wehle was assigned "responsibility for security" at 5 P.M., and that it was agreed that "MDW will be on guard of the remains throughout." The log indicates that at 5:30 P.M., word was passed that President Kennedy's body (assumed to be in the Dallas casket) was going to Bethesda Naval Hospital. At that time, one army official notified Admiral Galloway "advising them to provide a security cordon around the heliport at the Bethesda Naval Center, expecting arrival of the remains at approximately 1830 hours [6:30 P.M.]."

Ten minutes later, at 5:40 P.M., the log reflects that the same army official had just spoken with General Clifton by radio telephone at 5:30, and "that President Kennedy will be taken directly to Bethesday [sic] Naval Hospital."

In our interview, General Clifton said that by the time the plane landed, he knew that the body was going to Bethesda, and participated in making those arrangements.

One returning from Dallas, Lyndon Johnson's personal secretary, Marie Fehmer, made chronological notes. Among other things, she recorded Johnson's conversations with Robert Kennedy about whether he should be sworn in, and various activities aboard the plane. The notes were made on a typewriter. But as the plane came in for the landing, Ms. Fehmer apparently removed the sheet of paper and a final entry, made in her own hand at the time of the plane's landing, read: "5:58 Arr Andrews—Body w/Mrs. K to Walter Reed."[36]

Ms. Fehmer of course knew that at the rear of the plane Jacqueline Kennedy was deplaning with the casket. Her note seemed to indicate that she must have heard, or been told, that "the body" was going to Walter Reed.*

---

* In July 1980 I mailed Mrs. Andrew Chiarodo, the former Ms. Fehmer, a copy of the notes she made while aboard *Air Force One*. In a subsequent telephone conversation, we discussed the 5:58 "Walter Reed" entry. "The handwriting is mine," Mrs. Chiarodo said, adding that the notes were probably contemporaneous—that her usual practice was to look at her watch before writing down a notation as to time. But she could not recollect why, at 5:58, she might have written that the body would go to Walter Reed. "I'm sure someone told me," she said, "but . . . I have no way of remember[ing] who."[37]

CHAPTER 32

The Assassination as a Covert Operation

ON NOVEMBER 24, 1963, the *Washington Star*'s editorial concluded: "The desolation Americans have felt since Friday afternoon is made more complete by our knowledge that such an act of murder has no rational relationship to the course of American politics, policy or history. . . . the American political assassin has invariably presented a problem in personal mental health rather than one in political conditions. . . . The final horror of the violent death of an American President is that in our system assassination is a political irrelevancy. That is also our consolation."[1]

Like the writer of that editorial, I immediately assumed that weekend that the President's killer must have been a lunatic. When the authorities produced the name of the lunatic, I went about my business as a student paying little attention to the assassination until the following September, when the Warren Report was published. Then I met critics who viewed the Report as a pack of lies.

But it wasn't until a year later, when I barged into Wesley Liebeler's office, that my course was set. I was drawn into debate with Liebeler, who insisted that the Commission and its staff were honest. That tension between opposites forced me to look at the evidence itself, not the motives of the investigators, to resolve the contradictions, and that in turn led to my discovery of evidence indicating the President's body had been altered.

If someone had told me on November 22, 1963 that I would spend fifteen years of my life on the Kennedy assassination, I would have said the thought was ludicrous. No doubt I would have taken the same position when I bought my copy of the Warren Report in September 1964, and when I first met Liebeler in October 1965; but on October 23, 1966, when I found the statement about surgery, I began a period of research and writing which in fact has lasted ever since.

What are the results? The record revealed a break in the chain of possession of the President's body between Dallas and Bethesda. I believe I have shown that President Kennedy's body was secretly altered between the time of his murder and the time of the autopsy, which began some six and a half hours later and thirteen hundred miles away, at Bethesda, Maryland. I believe I have shown that the body, at the time of the official autopsy, was a medical forgery, and that the facts ascertained by examining the body at Bethesda were therefore not a valid guide to the details of the shooting.

Why was the body altered? Altering the body provided a means of hiding basic facts about the shooting. Surgery on the wounds changed the bullet trajectories and concealed the true locations of the shooters. Bullet retrieval insured that bullets and bullet fragments from the weapons that actually murdered the President would not reach the FBI Laboratory. If the navy autopsy is viewed as the first in a sequence of federal investigations, then it could be said that the results of that investigation—results on which all others relied—were manipulated through the alteration of the body.

Another reason for altering the body was to introduce a false assassin. The assassination of an American President is an extraordinary crime. It would necessarily set off major investigations. The plotters would be in a vulnerable position if their chief protection against discovery was that the shooters had made a successful getaway. Their protection would be significantly increased if they could deflect all investigations by providing a false solution, a false perpetrator. And that is the other side of the body-alteration coin—that it was done not just to destroy data, but to fabricate data; not just to hide the true facts, but to introduce false facts; in short, to fabricate evidence against a scapegoat, a patsy.

Still another aspect. The assassination of an American Chief of State is a political crime. People would want to know not only who killed the President, but why. Those who altered the body were in a position to provide an answer of sorts to that question. By creating the appearance that President Kennedy's death was the work of a lone and embittered man, it was denuded of political meaning. The events of November 22, 1963 were made to appear to be a historical accident, one which resulted from the chance convergence of a lone malcontent and a target of opportunity.

How a false assassin was introduced in this case can be understood by considering what alteration of the body did to the legal record. The dichotomy in the evidence between the Dallas and Bethesda views of the body corresponds to a split in the Warren Commission's evidence between the sniper's nest data, on the one hand, and the grassy knoll data, on the other.

Alteration of the body suppressed evidence of shots from the front. If the body was altered in accordance with the trajectory-reversal scheme, plotters must have put a rifle and a sniper's nest behind and above the motorcade, but shot Kennedy from the front. Such falsification of the circumstances of death was integral to the crime.

Consequently, the record contains traces of what actually happened (i.e., shots from the front), but it also contains evidence of a false appearance (i.e., shots from behind).

These two patterns co-exist in the evidence and represent two different pictures of the Kennedy assassination.

Pattern One	Pattern Two
Gun found on sixth floor	Smoke seen on grassy knoll
Three shells	Smoke smelled
Three pieces of ammunition	Footprints in mud behind fence
1 bullet found on stretcher	Cigarette butts
2 pieces in car	Sounds heard from knoll
Three sounds heard	Head-snap
Sniper seen at window	Dallas medical observations
Bethesda autopsy conclusions	

The Warren Report set forth Pattern One. It is the case Dallas District Attorney Henry Wade would have prosecuted at Oswald's trial, the case for the assassination as a historical accident.

Pattern Two is the case of the Warren Report critics. It is their evidence of conspiracy, evidence of a "second shooter."

Many observers have combined these two patterns and posited the existence of a conspiracy of two shooters—Oswald and an accomplice.

The link between these two patterns is the President's body, and the two views of the body correspond to the two patterns in the other evidence concerning how the shooting occurred. But the shooting, however it occurred, happened only one way. The body was in only one condition at any particular point in time.

The legal reaction to the record is important. To the eyes of any lawyer, Pattern One consists of the "best evidence." Pattern Two consists of what might be termed "second-best evidence." In the debate that has surrounded the Kennedy assassination for some fifteen years, the proponents of Pattern One have had the better case because they could point to the rifle, the shells, the ballistic data. Most important, Pattern One was firmly grounded in the autopsy report. The proponents of Pattern Two pointed to the filmed head snap and the Dallas clinical observations and were driven to a theory that the autopsy doctors lied about the direction of the shots.

But one thing I learned from Liebeler's class, and which was driven home by many debates between defenders and critics of the Warren

Report over the years, was that if you accepted the discipline of the law, the divergence between these two patterns vanished. A lawyer saw only the "best evidence" and disregarded Pattern Two, which he dismissed as "loose ends" with a series of pat explanations.

The denigration of the grassy-knoll evidence as the province of conspiracy mongers, fantasists, and paranoids persisted until 1978, when the House Assassinations Committee found acoustics evidence, on a Dallas police tape, which appeared to establish a shooter on the grassy knoll. It was the acoustics evidence which finally caused the Committee to credit the accounts of the grassy knoll witnesses. The electronic impulses recorded on a dictabelt, rather than the affidavits of Dealey Plaza witnesses, qualified as "best evidence" of whether the sound of a shot in fact came that day from the grassy knoll.

I didn't have to wait for the acoustics data. Once I developed evidence that the body was altered, I felt confident I knew why there were two patterns in the record. The reason was not the explanation given so often in Liebeler's class: that life is untidy, that there are always "loose ends," that we can't know the truth. The two patterns resulted from events that happened one way, followed by the fabrication of evidence to make them appear to have happened another.

Legally, only Pattern One mattered. But if the body was altered, an inversion took place. The primacy of Pattern One was destroyed. Observations of the President's body at Bethesda were impeached as evidence of what happened in Dealey Plaza. The Dallas doctors' observations, the medical evidence of Pattern Two, then became the "best evidence," the only accessible guide to what happened. The evidence in Pattern One emerged as the artifacts of a disguise.

The Dallas doctors' observations indicated that President Kennedy was struck from the front. But the identity of those shooters is less important than the structure of the plot that disguised them. The disguise centered around the alteration of the body, and the disguise itself revealed the nature of the plot. By substituting artifact for fact, both on John Kennedy's body and at the Texas School Book Depository, the disguise created the appearance that the President was murdered by a lone malcontent.

This clandestine substitution of appearance for reality, this sleight of hand with the "best evidence," convinced me that the proper way to view the assassination was as a covert operation. The camouflage of body alteration disguised a political murder as a historical accident.

Covert operations are not new to the U.S. government. The targets of such operations as we know about were foreign governments and officials. The Church Committee concluded, upon evidence published in its report, that CIA officials plotted the murder of foreign officials. One cable CIA Headquarters sent to Havana inquired whether a particular Cuban agent was, according to the Church Report, "sufficiently motivated to risk 'arranging an accident' involving Raul Castro."[2] In reply, the agent "agreed to take a 'calculated risk,' limited to possibilities that might pass as accidental."[3]

This is not to say that the CIA murdered Kennedy, but that the modus operandi existed. Clandestine operators had developed and refined it over many years. Central to it is the art of disguise.

Camouflage is the art of concealing the fact that you have concealed something. In this case, the first—and fundamental—concealment was of the fact that Kennedy was shot from the front. That was concealed by alterations of the body. The second concealment was of the fact that the body was altered.

Former CIA Inspector General Lyman Kirkpatrick has said that the ideal covert operation is one which is secret "from inception to eternity."[4]

Allen Dulles wrote about the malfunctionings of even well-planned covert operations, "the little slips or oversights which can give away the whole show."[5]

"Mishaps, whatever their cause and nature, can be divided into those which reveal or 'blow' the existence of an undercover operation . . . and those which simply cause the operation to fail or malfunction internally. . . . Minor mishaps in intelligence have a nastiness all their own. One can never be quite certain whether they were damaging or not. . . . Most of them have to do with losses of 'cover', with partial or temporary exposure. . . . Minor mishaps may expose any of a number of elements that point to espionage. They may in many cases simply show that something out of the ordinary is going on, and whether this is interpreted as espionage and is therefore damaging depends in great measure on the innocence or sophistication of the beholder, whether he is, let us say, a policeman or a landlord or just a passerby."[6]

My research turned up examples of the loss of cover. Consider a few points in the record in this case.

• At Bethesda, Dennis David, the Chief of the Day at the Medical School, saw the arrival and unloading of a black hearse. He knew there were two ambulances, that the second one arrived empty. He saw it arrive after they unloaded the first one. He assumed it was a legitimate security measure.

• James Felder, the army sergeant on the casket team, remembered two navy ambulances. One was a "decoy." Hubert Clark, the sailor on the team, also remembered the decoy ambulance. Neither perceived the decoy ambulance as sinister.

• Paul O'Connor, a medical technician at the Bethesda morgue, said he opened the coffin when it was first brought in. It was a shipping casket. He told me the President's cranial vault was empty. As he put it, the bullet "blew all of his brains out—literally." O'Connor had no idea of the significance of what he saw. When I pointed out to him that the casket taken off the plane was elaborate and quite unlike the "tin box" he opened, he remarked that yes, he really hadn't noticed that until now. O'Connor believed the Warren Report.

• Jerrol Custer remembered the X-rays he helped take—and will forever remember passing within fifteen yards of Jacqueline Kennedy as he walked across the Bethesda lobby with the X-rays of her husband's body in his hands. She had just entered the hospital after leaving the ambulance, parked out front, which contained the Dallas casket, and supposedly the body. The experience raised no puzzlement in his mind.

• FBI agents Sibert and O'Neill reported surgery of the head area. The erasures in their report and the Baltimore Field Office memorandum they filed that distinguishes between "inspection" and "autopsy" suggest they were told there had been a pre-autopsy inspection. Apparently they passed off the whole matter as a delay before Commander Humes was authorized by military superiors to perform a full autopsy. Sibert seemed to believe it was a minor irregularity, and had no trouble filing an affidavit for the House Select Committee denying there had been surgery of the head before the body reached Bethesda.

Each of these persons witnessed a fact or facts that didn't fit the official version of the event. Each one accounted for the anomaly with little difficulty. None of them thought himself a witness to a clandestine operation involving the murder of a President.

Those who did suspect a conspiracy didn't relate it to what they themselves saw. Medical technician James Jenkins was certain the Warren Commission was wrong about the direction of the bullet that struck the head, because the large hole was at the back of the head. He remained deeply troubled ever after. It shaped his view of the government. But he had no suspicions that the body might have been altered. Custer felt the head shot came from the front. So did X-ray technician Edward Reed. Hubert Clark believed a conspiracy murdered the President in Dallas, but when I asked him whether the ambulance chase he witnessed at Bethesda might be related to it, he didn't understand what I was driving at.

As Allen Dulles noted, interpretation depends on the innocence or sophistication—and the vantage point—of the beholder.

In a way, we are all beholders. We are beholders of the historical records of Record Group 272 at the U.S. National Archives—the records of the Warren Commission investigation—and also of the recollections of people such as Jenkins, and Felder, and O'Connor, and David, and Clark.

We must come to terms with that record.

Record Group 272 is bifurcated. The Dallas observers saw one thing; the Bethesda observers saw another. It contains a motion picture film of the assassination which appears to show the shooting taking place in a way that contradicts the autopsy report.

What lessons do we learn from the record? Do we conclude that people can't observe what takes place before their eyes? That they can't describe what they see? Do we dismiss the congruences of the elements of Pattern Two—the Dallas doctors' observations, the grassy-knoll witnesses—as mere coincidence?

In our judgments, shall we be innocent or sophisticated?

Former CIA Chief Allen Dulles apparently favored innocence. At the Commission's third executive session, he handed out paperback copies of a book about previous assassinations. Said Dulles: "It's a book written about ten years ago giving the background of seven attempts on the lives of the President. . . . It's a fascinating book, but you'll find a pattern running through here that I think we'll find in this present case."[7]

The pattern Dulles expected to find does exist. It is Pattern One. Dulles went on to say that except for the Truman assassination attempt "these other cases are all habitual, going back to the attack on Jackson in 1835."[8] McCloy cited the Lincoln assassination and retorted: "The Lincoln assassination was a plot." Replied Dulles: "Yes, but one man was so dominant that it almost wasn't a plot."[9] At a later meeting, Dulles suggested that the Commission involve itself in "studying previous cases of assassination attempts . . . particularly in the United States. . . . There is a pattern that runs through that, you know. It is rather interesting, I have been studying that a good bit myself. . . ."[10]

I myself think that a sophisticated appraisal of the evidence must force one to the conclusion that there was a plot involving the executive branch of the government to remove Kennedy from office and, by fabricating the evidence of Pattern One, make his death appear a historical quirk of fate.

Any plot must have required considerable planning. It is implausible that the plotters decided on the night of November 21, 1963 to shoot the President in Dallas the next day and alter his body. A foundation must have been laid. Some government officials must have been recruited into the plot. That recruitment represents a covert politics of sorts that must have taken place during the thousand days of John Kennedy's presidency.

And that is the final importance of the body as evidence. Pattern One may tell us what appeared to have happened; and Pattern Two may tell us what actually happened. But these are mere details. The fusion of these two patterns tells us where to look for those who manipulated this event.

The Secret Service furnished the bodyguards—controlled the trip planning, controlled the security at the moment of the shooting, controlled the speed of the car. The Secret Service had physical custody of the body, the clothing, the bullets, the limousine. The Secret Service had in its custody the X-rays and photographs taken at Bethesda. It would hardly be possible to implement the modus operandi described here without the involvement of some Secret Service personnel. And that is just the beginning. Others had to be involved.

The question for any future investigation must be the identity of those involved. Only a new investigation can answer that question, but that job will not be easy. The "national security" cover-story ruse may have created a situation in which some government employees unknowingly participated in the falsification of evidence, yet believed they were acting in response to legitimate orders. Some may have believed they were involved in a "benign" conspiracy, carried out for reasons of state. Others may believe that irregularities or oddities regarding the movement of the body were part of a legitimate security operation. Determining each person's state of knowledge is critical. Moreover, a prosecutor would face the problem of distinguishing among at least three separate conspiracies:

1. to murder the President;
2. to alter the body;
3. to hide the fact that the body was altered.

It is my personal belief that none of the three autopsy surgeons or other autopsy personnel was involved in a plot to murder the President, nor was any of them involved in a plot to alter the body. Moreover, I do not say that any person mentioned in this book was knowingly involved in any conspiracy or illegal activity. It is entirely possible that any number of people thought they were acting honorably and in the line of duty in not disclosing that the body was altered.

But the fact remains that the body was altered, and that it did not make an uninterrupted journey from Dallas to Bethesda, and this should be the logical starting point for any future investigation.

Will such an investigation ever take place?

That depends on the political climate. Is the nation ready to face its past?

The problem is not logical, but psychological. If the different descriptions of Kennedy's head wounds—and the stories of the decoy ambulance and of Dennis David and of Paul O'Connor—if these were part of the murder of a foreign dictator, most people would accept them. It is easy to believe that the palace guard of a banana republic could be penetrated, that policemen could be bought. But it is difficult to accept the idea that such things can occur in our own country.

It is easy to believe that Oswald "had help." It is not easy to believe that the coffin the nation watched being unloaded from *Air Force One* was empty, that even then plotters in another place were fabricating a false history by altering the best evidence—the President's corpse.

Wesley Liebeler discussed the psychological barrier with me many years ago. He said: "You require people to accept the notion that somebody is playing around with Kennedy's body. David, I might as well tell you now—I mean, nobody will believe it." He referred to my research as "an exercise in epistemology . . . you know, I don't think you really comprehend the kind of thing you're dealing with."

"What about the evidence?" I asked. What would happen when I published a documented account showing that the legal record itself contained evidence the body was altered?

"Well, I don't think that anybody will ever believe anything you say," replied Liebeler.

"Why not?" I asked.

"Because it's relatively unbelievable. You know . . . there comes a point where, after all, the emperor may rely on his power to demand that he is clothed. And this is not only a function of power; it's also a function of relative probability, and a concession to the shortness of life."

Liebeler continued: "The unconscious notion that the emperor will be clothed is a very powerful notion to rely on. . . . Let me put it this way: Even if you were right, which I don't think you are, I think I could beat you in the argument."

"How?" I asked.

"Because of the presumption that the emperor is clothed."

This position, in my opinion, represents a cynical view of our society. It presumes the gullibility and timidity of the electorate, and the absolute sanctity of vested authority. It is a view that I do not want to accept. Yet I must concede that even if there is a new investigation, it is unlikely that the architects of this plot can be identified or brought to justice. But that is not the point. The disguise they erected must be torn down, and it must be done officially. *That* would be the most important outcome of a new investigation. If we cannot have justice, perhaps we can at least have the truth.

At present, the disguise erected by the plotters not only conceals their identity, but some fundamental truths about our country. It hides the fact that some time during Kennedy's thousand days, a secret veto was cast on his presidency and his life.

Epilogue to 1982 Edition

There has been no official reaction to *Best Evidence*. Perhaps that was to be expected. The House Assassinations Committee concluded there was a conspiracy, but the Justice Department has yet to reopen the case. It has merely asked the National Academy of Sciences to review the acoustics evidence that appears to indicate a shot from the front. The NAS panel has yet to issue its report.

But there have been a number of developments that bear directly on the thesis advanced in *Best Evidence*. For example, additional witnesses have come forward. Within a week of the publication of *Best Evidence* and a *Time* Magazine story about it, Donald Rebentisch of Coopersville, Michigan, a petty officer stationed at Bethesda on November 22, 1963, told his local paper, the *Grand Rapids Press,* that the two-ambulance story published in *Time* was not news to him—he had been telling his family the same story for years. He stated that President Kennedy's body was not in the gray navy ambulance, which carried Mrs. Kennedy and the ceremonial casket and which arrived at the front of the hospital. Instead, the body had arrived at the back of the hospital in a black unmarked hearse. *Grand Rapids Press* reporter Jerry Morlock told me about Rebentisch before his story ran on the wire services, and I was able to interview Rebentisch before he read *Best Evidence.* He provided corroboration for Dennis David's account by recalling that he had helped unload the first casket, an ordinary shipping cakset, and that it had arrived at the back before the gray navy ambulance arrived at the front. Rebentisch said that *after* unloading the first casket, he went upstairs to the lobby area of Bethesda where he saw Mrs. Kennedy, who had just arrived in the navy ambulance, waiting for the elevator.

Reporter Morlock found other witnesses who knew that two caskets had been used at Bethesda that night. "It was common knowledge," said one. Like the witnesses I had interviewed, these new witnesses told Morlock the two-casket scheme was used as a security measure.

Rebentisch's account ran on both wire services, the weekend of January 23, 1981. Subsequently, in March 1981, the Canadian Broadcasting Company made arrangements for me to participate in a TV interview of Rebentisch at his home in Michigan for a program that was broadcast in Canada in mid-April. I thought him honest and straightforward, and he seemed concerned that events he had personally witnessed were not in the official story.

In the course of the CBC project, additional evidence was uncovered. This evidence related to the thesis that when *Air Force One* landed at Andrews Air Force Base, a helicopter on the starboard side—the side hidden from public view because the TV cameras were on the port side—played a crucial role in the transportation of the body from Andrews to some unknown location. The pivotal question is whether a helicopter was really there, on the starboard side. In Chapter 31, I set forth a pattern of evidence indicating it was: an audio tape which recorded the sound of a chopper taking off within 90 seconds of the arrival of *Air Force One;* an entry in an NBC-TV log indicating that a helicopter could be seen hovering alongside Air Force One when it landed; and radio transmissions from officials aboard the plane en route to Washington arranging for a ramp to be put against the forward starboard side, at the galley door, and for helicopter transportation of the body from Andrews Air Force Base. It was my thesis that the President's remains, probably in a body bag, were secretly removed from the forward starboard area of the plane and put aboard the helicopter.

In the course of working on the Rebentisch story, CBC producer Brian McKenna located unedited film footage of the arrival of *Air Force One* at Andrews. The film was taken from the port side of the plane, and it contains a soundtrack. In viewing it, one can, as the noise from *Air Force One's* engines dies down, hear the whirring rotor of a chopper. Just under the belly of the plane, on the starboard side, the chopper's blinking lights can be clearly seen where the forward galley door is located (and where the ramp had been called for). As the film winds on, the chopper's lights move away from the side of *Air Force One,* and the helicopter prepares to take off.

David Lifton
12/6/81
Los Angeles, California

log indicating that a helicopter could be seen hovering alongside Air Force One when it landed; and radio transmissions from officials aboard the plane en route to Washington attributing force enough to be put against the forward starboard side, at the galley, where the helicopter transportation of the body from Andrews Air Force Base, was my thesis that the President's remains, probably in a body bag, were secretly removed from the forward starboard area of the plane by helicopter.

In the course of working for the Huntsville store, CBC producer Brian McKenna located unedited film footage of the arrival of Air Force One at Andrews. The film was taken from the port side of the plane, and it contains a soundtrack. In viewing it, one can, as the noise from Air Force One's

Afterword
by
David S. Lifton

Many readers of this book have written to ask why any conspirators would have planned the chaotic events I have described. "How could anyone know they could get the body out of the coffin on *Air Force One*?" I am asked. At my talks about this book, some student almost always asks: "How come the plotters used a coffin that was so different? How come there is a body bag in Bethesda, but no body bag in Dallas?"

I often respond, "What you are really asking is: 'How come this wasn't a perfect crime? Why is there evidence?' " The answer is that what happened wasn't what was intended to happen. The assassination was elegant in conception, but bungled in execution. In a future work, I intend to lay out my inferences about what was planned. To state it as simply as possible: President Kennedy's body was never supposed to have left Dallas unaltered. However, the plotters lost control of the body. The reason for that loss of control was a major accident: the shooting of Governor Connally. This led to circumstances which precluded the alteration of President Kennedy's body in Dallas. The result was that the theft of the body and its alteration were done in a hurried and brutal manner.

In 1981, I received a letter from Maryland radio journalist Mark Crouch saying he knew someone who had a set of the autopsy photographs, the same photographs that were at the National Archives. He subsequently introduced me to James K. ("Jack") Fox, formerly a photographer with the Intelligence Division of the U.S. Secret Service. Documents from the House Assassinations Committee establish that Fox was one of a few officials who had access to the photographs. On three occasions, he supervised their processing. According to Fox, shortly after the assassination he was told by Secret Service Agent Roy Kellerman: "Here, make a set of these for yourself. They'll be history someday." Fox showed me the pictures he had, and later I was able to obtain a set.

Viewing them, I was again horrified at the ghoulishness of a plot that would desecrate the body of John F. Kennedy. Again I confronted the question: How does one deal with this material without appearing to be insensitive? My immediate reaction was that these pictures should never be published. Over the years, my attitude has changed. The pictures are evidence—at this point, the closest thing to the best evidence—and unfortunately the issue of respect for the living is in conflict with justice for the dead.

I publish the photographs here with great reluctance, but with the realization that it is an absolute necessity: These pictures go to the heart of this book. Most people will have difficulty looking at them. So did I. All of us prefer to remember the President in life. We prefer to remember him with his right hand raised, at his inauguration, inspiring the country with his message of hope. We prefer to remember him at the zenith of his life, for his thousand days were a special time for this country. But these autopsy photographs are also a part of those thousand days, also a part of the public record, and the American people have a right to see them.

The autopsy photographs show two holes, presumably of entry, on the rear of the body, and two larger holes, presumably of exit, at the front: one at the front of the neck, the other at the top of the head. I resolved to take the pictures to Dallas and show them to the doctors and nurses at Parkland who attended President Kennedy. My purpose was to ask them—especially regarding the tracheotomy wound at the front of the throat and the nearly intact condition of the back of the head—"Is this what you saw?"

In December 1982 I showed the pictures to Dallas Nurses Audrey Bell and Doris Nelson, both of whom were primarily involved with Governor Connally's medical treatment but who also saw President Kennedy. Doris Nelson told me the tracheotomy was not the one she remembered: "Looks a little large to me . . . [it] shouldn't be that big," she said. When I told her Humes testified it was 7–8 cm. (about 3 in.), she said: "It wasn't any 7–8 cm. [It was] just wide enough to get the trach tube in." She looked at Photo 30 and Autopsy Photos 2, 4, and 5 and shook her head from side to side: in Photo 30 and Autopsy Photo 4, the back of the head is largely intact; she remembered a large wound there.

Audrey Bell was emphatic on the same point. The wound she saw was so localized at the rear that, from her position on the right hand side, with Kennedy lying face up, she couldn't see *any* damage. She described walking into the room, seeing Kennedy face up on the cart, and expressing puzzlement to Dr. Perry: *Where was the wound?* Perry pointed to the back of the President's head and moved the head slightly in order to show her the wound. On the subject of the tracheotomy incision shown in the photographs, Ms. Bell was equally firm. "Looks like somebody has enlarged it," she said. "You don't make trachs that big. Not if you've got as much experience as Perry has. If you've got a brand new intern, who has never done one before, you may get one botched up and get it too big. But not when you've got a man of Perry's experience doing one."

Two weeks later, in January 1983, I returned to Dallas with fellow researcher Pat Valentino for another round of interviews.

Our first appointment was with Dr. Marion Jenkins, the anesthesiologist. Jenkins began the conversation with criticism of Kennedy's failure to provide air cover at the Bay of Pigs. He told us he failed to see why people didn't believe the Warren Report.

Regarding the head wound: In his November 22 report, Jenkins (the only Dallas doctor who typed a detailed report) stated "the cerebellum protruded from the wound"—an observation clearly placing the skull wound at the back of the head. (See pp. 322–323) Jenkins now said that whatever the Warren Report said was correct, and that whatever the photographs showed was fine with him.

Jenkins, whose observation regarding a protruding cerebellum supported an exit wound at the rear, and who, in his testimony, specifically implied a head shot from the front, now maintained that there was an entry wound somewhere on the President's back. No such wound was reported by anyone at Parkland Hospital. (See pp. 192–3) "I didn't say I saw it," said Jenkins. "I probed it." Jenkins made no mention of any such shoulder or back wound in his November 22, 1963, report. His first mention of it was fifteen years later in a 1978 letter to Dr. John Lattimer, who in turn mentioned it in a letter he wrote to *Time* magazine after *Best Evidence* was published. Both Dr. Peters and Dr. Jones expressed surprise that Jenkins had never made any mention of this wound to them. Moreover, Jenkins claimed he didn't remember what he had testified to. When I confronted him with his own testimony, he responded with remarks such as: "Well, if you say so. I haven't read the testimony."

The Jenkins interview was a disappointment. The autopsy photographs clearly conflicted with his 1963 report and testimony, but he seemed willing to rationalize any inconsistency. "This whole controversy would make a good novel," he said and asked: "If there was a conspiracy, why hasn't anybody come forward?"

Back at my hotel, I was astonished to receive a call from Dr. Kemp Clark, the neurosurgeon in attendance, whose reputation for animosity towards assassination researchers was well known. To my surprise, Clark was both cordial and cooperative in his willingness to see me the next day. Clark apparently had spoken to Jenkins and it seemed clear to me that he wanted to see the pictures.

The next day began with an appointment with Dr. Peters. Peters had testified to the Warren Commission that the large head wound was in the right occipital-parietal area (See Chapter 13). Now, shown the autopsy photos, Photo 30, and the head X-rays (Photos 31 and 32), he reacted with considerable surprise. he told me he could have sworn the wound was at the *back* of the head. Yet, on the photos there was no large wound there, and the wound (as shown on the X-rays) was in the *fronto*-parietal area. As to the tracheotomy incision, Peters admitted it was rather large, but commented that it was made under emergency conditions. I could see Dr. Peters grapple with the conflict between what the pictures showed, and his memory of events some twenty years earlier. It drove home a point: The body might be the best evidence, but if the body was altered, that played havoc with the very human measuring system, one's own memory.

I spoke next with Dr. Ronald Jones. Dr. Jones testified to the Warren Commission that he thought Kennedy was shot from the front, with the bullet exiting the rear of the head. Now, faced with the pictures, Dr. Jones had to deal with what was, apparently, reality. "If you brought him in here today, I'd still say he was shot from the front," said Jones. Nevertheless, he deferred to the pictures.

Then I kept my appointment with Dr. Kemp Clark, the neurosurgeon who had pronounced Kennedy dead. The cordial Dr. Clark who had called me the previous day had vanished. His opening remark set the tone: "Well, I guess the only person who got anything out of this deal was Specter," (referring to Arlen Specter, father of the Single Bullet Theory, who went on to become a U.S. Senator). Clark refused to let me open the envelope containing the pictures. Apparently he had thought about it overnight and had changed his mind. He was unmoved by any pleas about history, truth, etc. "If you think the body was altered after it left our charge," he said, "then I suggest you speak to the Secret Service about that."

On January 8, 1983, I visited with Nurse Trish Gustaffson, (formerly Nurse Patricia Hutton). On November 22, she met the presidential limousine in the parking lot and ran with the stretcher carrying the President to the emergency room. She had placed a bandage against the wound at the back of the head. She was unequivocal: The large throat wound shown in the photographs was not the tracheotomy incision that she saw in the emergency room on November 22, 1963 ("It doesn't look like any that I've taken part in, let me put it that way.") and the head wound was at the back, not as shown in the pictures. "I was standing behind him when I was putting pressure on the head," she said, "and it was right in front of me. It wasn't around the side and up on top." Shown the large hole on the forward right hand side depicted in the X-rays (Photos 31 and 32), she exclaimed: "No way!"

One doctor I didn't see in 1983 was Dr. Malcolm Perry, the man who performed the Dallas tracheotomy. Shortly after President Kennedy's body left Parkland Hospital, Dr. Perry held a news conference at which he stated—three times—that the President was shot in the throat from the front. (See pp. 61–62) The wound was "3–5 mm," he told Humes the morning after the shooting. In 1966, Dr. Perry told me his incision through that wound was 2–3 cm. (See p. 238) In 1979, researcher Robert Groden, a consultant to the House Assassinations Committee, was present at an unofficial, privately arranged meeting when Dr. Perry was shown an autopsy photograph clearly showing the throat wound. Dr. Perry looked at the picture, shook his head from side to side, and then, on the condition that he not be quoted, gave his reaction: The tracheotomy was too large; it was not the trach he had made. He said the throat wound in the picture was "larger, expanded" and that his was "neater." Dr. Perry said the head wound was not the way he remembered it either, and that the picture published in *Six Seconds in Dallas* (a picture prepared by Dr. McClelland and similar to my Figure 20 [left side]) was much closer. Of Dr. Perry's reaction, Groden said: "It was one of the most vivid memories I have of this case. I knew it was important. I knew it was historic."

Groden first told me of the meeting with Perry shortly after it occurred. He has honored Dr. Perry's confidence these many years, but has now given me permission to quote what Dr. Perry said in 1979 because Dr. Perry has recently told the television program *Nova* that he sees no discrepancy between the tracheotomy incision he made and the tracheotomy wound depicted on the Dox drawing (i.e., the artist's rendition of an autopsy photograph showing the throat wound. See Photo 35).

The "Clip"

In early 1983, Mark Crouch called to say that, in enlarging the photos, he had found evidence of a metallic-looking clip of some kind inside the head. It was visible in the top view. Soon, additional enlargements arrived. There did appear to be something in the head (See Autopsy Photo 6A). I have not, however, been able to determine what it is. But its presence brought to mind a question posed by House Assassinations Committee counsel Andrew Purdy when I told him about my body-alteration evidence back in 1978. If the

Dallas doctors were correct, he asked, then "How do you explain the fact that, in the pictures, the rear of the head is back on?" Here for the first time seemed to be evidence, in the autopsy pictures themselves, of reconstruction.

Post Mortem Abrasions

In its report the House Assassinations Committee noted the existence of post-mortem abrasions on the President's body (p. 680). These abrasions are clearly visible in photographs showing the rear view of the body, but are entirely absent from the Dox drawing (Compare Photo 41 with Autopsy Photo 5). I was startled by them. With regard to some of these abrasions, the Committee's report speculated: "It is possible that they were made in the course of the handling and lifting of the body." These abrasions may well be evidence of the unorthodox manner in which President Kennedy's body was transported from Dallas to Washington.

X-ray/Photo Mismatch

In an ordinary autopsy in a gunshot case, photographs and X-rays would be exposed at the outset and would comprise the official record of what the wounds looked like when the body was presented to the forensic pathologist. Exposed at the same time, those photographs and X-rays should be entirely consistent. In this case, a serious mismatch exists between the photographs and the X-rays of the head.

I have shown the lateral and A-P X-rays (see Photos 31 and 32) to four radiologists, who all agree that the large hole in the head is on the forward right-hand side and extends at least to the top of the right eye socket.

However, the *photograph* (see Autopsy Photo 3) shows no such huge hole. The hole, if one goes by the photographs, is apparently located in the *top* of the head.

This startling mismatch between the photographs and the X-rays is evidence that they were not exposed at the same time and suggests some sort of reconstruction. Supporting that idea is the nature of the damage shown on the X-rays. They show a series of bony fragments and overlapping skull pieces, which are puzzling. Even the House Committee's own radiology experts had difficulty interpreting them (See p. 661). These X-rays (particularly the lateral X-ray) prompted one radiologist I spoke with to ask, "What's holding the head together?"

As previously stated, my first reaction on seeing these autopsy photographs was that they should not be published, but over the years my attitude has changed. I have come to believe they are as much a part of President Kennedy's thousand days as his inaugural pictures, that they provide the closing bookend to Camelot. John Kennedy was a man I deeply respected, but it's time for the whole business of the President's body and its alteration to be demystified.

Yes, the pictures are shocking, but they are also evidence. They support, on the most fundamental level, the premise that President Kennedy's body was altered. This, in turn, is evidence that there was a covert plan to falsify the circumstances of his death and make it appear that he was shot by a lone assassin using a bolt action rifle. These so-called "facts" shield an enormous transfer of power, and the ultimate issue is whether the assassination was a covert action in which the Vice President became President under circumstances that appeared accidental, a quirk of fate.

It is time for the public to see this evidence and render its own verdict.

These autopsy photographs are crucial to understanding what happened to the body, and the body is crucial to understanding what happened to the office of the Presidency in November, 1963.

Did [Kennedy] have a premonition of tragedy—that he who had set out to temper the contrary violences of our national life would be their victim?

Last June, when the civil rights riots were at their height and passions were flaring, he spoke to a group of representatives of national organizations. He tolled off the problems that beset him on every side and then suddenly, to the astonishment of everyone there, suddenly concluded his talk by pulling from his pocket a scrap of paper and reading the famous speech of Blanche of Spain in Shakespeare's *King John*:

> *The Sun's o'ercast with blood;*
> *Fair day, Adieu!*
> *Which is the side that I must*
> *go withal?*
> *I am with both; each army had*
> *a hand,*
> *and in their rage, I having*
> *hold of both,*
> *They whirl asunder and dismember*
> *me.*

As reported by James Reston in the *New York Times*, November 23, 1963.

709

November 22, 1963

12:30 P.M. CST	JFK shot in Dallas motorcade
12:34–12:38	Police transmissions pinpoint sniper's nest
12:38	JFK arrives at Parkland Memorial Hospital
12:45	Police broadcast description fitting Oswald as that of "suspect"
1:00	JFK pronounced dead
1:12	Police find sniper's nest at Depository
1:18	Police learn Officer Tippit shot
1:25 (approx.)	LBJ leaves for airport
1:30	Press Secretary Malcolm Kilduff announces JFK's death
1:55	Police arrest Oswald as suspect in shooting of officer
sometime between 1:00 and 2:00	At Parkland Hospital, Secret Service Agent Johnsen handed bullet found on stretcher
2:04	JFK's body leaves hospital in Dallas casket
2:14	Hearse carrying casket arrives at *Air Force One*
2:18	Casket placed aboard plane
2:20 (approx.)	Dallas doctors' press conference—Dr. Perry says throat wound an entry wound
2:30	Judge Hughes arrives at Love Field; boards *Air Force One*
2:38	LBJ sworn in
2:47	*Air Force One* airborne
5:58–6:02 EST	*Air Force One* arrives Andrews Air Force Base
6:10	Jacqueline and Robert Kennedy depart in navy ambulance for Bethesda Naval Hospital

6:45 (approx.)	Dennis David observes arrival of black hearse at rear entrance with plain metal casket, accompanied by 6–7 men in plain clothes
6:45 (approx.)	Shipping casket brought into morgue; Paul O'Connor reports JFK's body wrapped in body bag; no brain inside head. O'Connor recollects this occurred at 8:00 P.M.
6:55	Navy ambulance arrives at Bethesda front entrance Jacqueline Kennedy enters hospital
6:55–7:05	Dennis David and Jerrol Custer (carrying exposed X-ray film) see Jacqueline Kennedy enter hospital
6:55–??	McHugh argues with admirals
6:55–7:05	Military officials confer at door of ambulance
7:05	Ambulance drives off
	—casket team loses ambulance; chase according to Clark and Felder; two fruitless roundtrips to rear, according to Barnum; confusion caused by two ambulances
	—FBI accompanies Dallas casket to morgue entrance
	—FBI prevented from entering morgue
7:17	Time of preparation for autopsy, according to FBI
7:30	Kellerman's estimate of latest time body arrived at morgue and autopsy began
8:00	Casket team carries in Dallas casket, assisted by McHugh
8:15	Time of first incision, according to FBI
8:50	Secret Service gives bullet 399 to FBI lab
10:00	Two bullet fragments found in car
10:30	Autopsy formally begins, according to Dr. Ebersole, who saw the throat wound sutured
11:00–12:00 midnight	Sibert and O'Neill telephone headquarters from morgue; informed of bullet found on Dallas stretcher
12:00 midnight	Humes states autopsy results—two shots from rear

November 23, 1963

12:26 A.M. EST	Oswald charged in President's assassination
1:45	Sibert and O'Neill bring metal fragments to FBI lab
2:00	Sibert and O'Neill teletype autopsy results to Dallas
3:56	Jacqueline Kennedy accompanies body to White House
6:00	Chicago FBI find Oswald's order for rifle at Klein's
6:30	FBI Agent Drain arrives in Washington with rifle
9:00	FBI receives clothing from Secret Service
sometime that morning	FBI lab matches gun and bullets

Sunday, November 24, 1963

11:21 A.M. CST	Oswald shot by Jack Ruby in Dallas
12:20 P.M. EST	Humes completes autopsy report after burning earlier draft
6:00 P.M.	Humes brings autopsy report to Burkley at White House

Monday, November 25, 1963

Galloway transmits "sole remaining copy" of autopsy to Burkley at White House

JFK's funeral

Tuesday, November 26, 1963

FBI agents Sibert and O'Neill dictate report on autopsy and memo to Baltimore field office file

Secret Service Agent Robert I. Bouck issues receipt to Burkley for autopsy report and related material

Wednesday, November 27, 1963

FBI agents Sibert and O'Neill interview Secret Service agents Kellerman, Greer, and Gerald Behn at the White House

Friday, November 29, 1963

LBJ creates Warren Commission

Subsequent Events

12/9/63	FBI issues Summary Report
12/20	Secret Service sends autopsy report to Warren Commission
1/13/64	FBI issues Supplemental Report
3/12/64	Sibert and O'Neill interviewed by Arlen Specter
3/24/64	Commander Humes testifies to Warren Commission
9/27/64	Warren Commission Report released
11/24/64	Twenty-six volumes of Warren Commission Hearings released
3/65	Salandria critique of medical evidence published in *Liberation*
4/26/65	Secret Service transfers autopsy photos, X-rays, brain, and slides of tissue sections to Robert Kennedy
5/31/65	Epstein interviews Liebeler; obtains FBI reports
5/66	*Inquest* published; implies Commission changed autopsy
8/66	*Rush to Judgment* published; Sibert and O'Neill report published
10/24/66	Lifton-Liebeler meeting regarding "surgery" statement in FBI report

Chronology

SOURCES

Two recently published bibliographies provide a useful guide to the massive amount of material now available on the John F. Kennedy assassination. A bibliography compiled by the Library of Congress for the House Assassinations Committee was published in volume 12 of the Committee's hearings. The bibliographic data is given twice—once arranged chronologically, the other alphabetically. An even more extensive bibliography has been compiled by University of Wisconsin history professors Lloyd J. Guth and David R. Wrone. Their work—*The Assassination of John F. Kennedy: A Comprehensive Historical and Legal Bibliography, 1963–1979* (Westport, Conn.: Greenwood Press, 1980)—includes 5,000 sources, contains a 60-page introduction and a complete listing of all related *New York Times* stories for the past 15 years, and lists documents that have become available as a result of suits filed under the Freedom of Information Act.

What follows is a highly selective listing of my own primary sources.

Records of the Warren Commission Investigation

Upon completing its work, the Warren Commission turned its records over to the U.S. National Archives, where it is stored as Records Group 272. A printed inventory is available at the Archives. The testimony of 552 witnesses and a substantial portion of documentary evidence were published in the 26 volumes of Hearings and Exhibits. Upon publication in 1964, the entire set was made available for $76. They now have the status of rare books but are available in most major libraries. Much unpublished data can be found in Records Group 272, including FBI and Secret Service reports; material declassified since 1964; the transcripts of the Executive Sessions; and the working papers of the Commission, including internal memoranda and correspondence files with other government agencies.

Sources

Records of the House Select Committee on Assassinations

These consist of twelve volumes of transcripts of the 1978 public hearings, and staff reports covering various areas of the investigation. Unlike the Warren Commission, the House Committee left no working papers for public scrutiny. Moreover, much of its evidence is unpublished—the footnotes in its staff reports refer to documents that are unpublished and therefore, under Congressional rules, will remain sealed for fifty years.

A useful guide to the twenty-six volumes of the Warren Commission Hearings and Exhibits as well as the House Assassinations Committee Report and its supporting volumes is *Master Index to the JFK Assassination Investigations* by Sylvia Meagher and Gary Owens (Metuchen, New Jersey: Scarecrow Press, 1980).

Materials Obtained Under the Freedom of Information Act (FOIA)

These sources include approximately 100,000 pages of FBI documents released in 1977 and 1978 (and now available on microfilm) and the following items, which I obtained as a result of my own FOIA requests:

1. documents pertaining to the autopsy in the FBI's Baltimore field office;
2. documents pertaining to the autopsy photos and X-rays from the Secret Service;
3. documents from an Air Force history;
4. a file maintained by the navy's Bureau of Medicine and Surgery pertaining to the gag order on those who attended the autopsy;
5. documents from the Military District of Washington pertaining to the movements of the coffin on November 22, 1963.

Network Tapes and Wire Service Records

These materials were particularly useful for reconstructing the flow of information on November 22, 1963. My personal collection consists of substantial segments of uninterrupted broadcasts aired that afternoon on all three networks. Available at the National Archives, as part of Records Group 272, are many reels of tape from local Dallas radio stations. Of particular value has been the time-stamped AP and UPI "A" wire copy, which I obtained from wire service executives in 1971. The Warren Commission "audio visual project," part of Records Group 272, contains a useful compilation of interviews as well as assorted inventories and chronologies. In working with these materials, the published version of the NBC-TV log, *There was a President* (New York: Ridge Press, Random House, 1966) is useful.

Newspapers

The New York Times index provides a convenient way of tracing the evolution of the debate concerning the Kennedy assassination. I have also drawn

715

upon the microfilm records of both Dallas papers, the *Times-Herald* and the *Morning News*, for November 1963. The JFK Memorial Collection, a ten-reel collection available on microfilm from the Microphoto Division of Bell and Howell, has been a valuable source of reporting from many other papers.

Dallas Police Radio Tapes

These tape recordings, which I obtained from a Dallas researcher, provide a chronology of the unfolding police department investigation.

Books and Magazine Articles

Of the numerous books and articles that have been published, the following have most significantly influenced the shape of the debate concerning the findings of the Warren Commission:

Books

Epstein, Edward J., *Inquest*. New York: Viking Press, 1966. An account of the functioning of the Warren Commission, joined with a theory that the Commission changed the autopsy report for political reasons.

Lane, Mark. *Rush to Judgment*. New York: Holt, Rinehart, and Winston, 1966. A defense brief for Lee Harvey Oswald.

Manchester, William. *Death of a President*. New York: Harper and Row, 1967. The only book about the assassination to come from the Kennedy camp and an invaluable source of information ranging from details about who was running the bureaucracy to Jacqueline Kennedy's personal reactions.

Meagher, Sylvia. *Accessories After the Fact*. New York: Bobbs-Merrill, 1967. An exhaustive comparison between all major statements in the Warren Report and the underlying evidence as published in the twenty-six volumes; implies a theory that the Warren Commission deliberately covered up the truth.

Popkin, Richard. *The Second Oswald*. New York: Avon Books, 1966. An essay on the autopsy and a theory of whether an Oswald look-alike was deployed as part of a plot.

Thompson, Josiah. *Six Seconds in Dallas*. New York: Bernard Geis, 1967. An analysis of the medical evidence and a reconstruction of the shooting in terms of three assassins. Excellent graphics.

Weisberg, Harold. *Whitewash*. (Hyattstown, Md.; self-published, 1966). A carefully researched, although somewhat shrill, attack on the Warren Report.

Weisberg, Harold. *Post-Mortem* (Frederick, Md.; self-published, 1975). Provides a convenient appendix of many of the medical documents available at the National Archives.

Articles

Cohen, Jacob. "The Warren Commission Report and Its Critics." *Frontier*, November 1966.

Sources

————— "What the Warren Report Omits: Vital Documents." *The Nation*, July 11, 1966.

————— "Conspiracy Fever." *Commentary*, October 1975.

Cohen's articles comprise a rebuttal to the Warren Report critics because he focuses on deficiences in all theories about shots from the front.

Fein, Arnold L. "JFK in Dallas: The Warren Report and its Critics." *Saturday Review*, October 22, 1966. A well-reasoned review of the first critical books.

Feldman, Harold. "Fifty-two Witnesses: the Grassy Knoll." *Minority of One*, March 1965. The first published article devoted to the "grassy knoll" witnesses.

Fonzi, Gaeton. "The Warren Commission, Arlen Specter, and the Truth." *Greater Philadelphia Magazine*, August 1966. A journalist/critic's interview with Arlen Specter after the publication of *Inquest*.

Knebel, Fletcher. "A New Wave of Doubt." *Look*, July 12, 1966. The establishment's answer to Epstein's book.

Lattimer, John, M.D. "Observations Based on a Review of the Autopsy Photographs, X-rays, and Related Materials of the Late President John F. Kennedy." *Resident and Staff Physician*, May 1972. Lattimer's revelations and analyses of the autopsy X-rays and photographs contained the first published diagrams of the X-rays.

Lifton, David, and Welsh, David. "The Case for Three Assassins." *Ramparts*, January 1967. My own "three assassin" model of the shooting, originally drafted in May and June of 1966, and then rewritten after I had many of the "surgery" insights described in this book.

Salandria, Vincent. "The Warren Report?" *Liberation*, March 1965. The first detailed criticism of the Warren Commission medical evidence and of the single-bullet theory.

USNWR staff. "The Truth About the Kennedy Assassination: Questions Raised and Answered." *U.S. News and World Report*, October 10, 1966. Arlen Specter defends at length the Warren Report and his work on the Commission.

Shaw Trial Transcript

In 1967, New Orleans District Attorney Jim Garrison announced he had "solved" the assassination and charged New Orleans businessman Clay Shaw with conspiracy. I was among those who soon came to view Garrison's conspiracy theory, which generated numerous headlines, as a farce. However, a number of important witnesses testified, and the transcript of Dr. Pierre Finck, one of the three autopsy doctors, is an important addendum to the Warren Commission legal record.

Interviews

My own interviews, conducted mostly on the telephone, have provided an important source of information. They are listed below.

Name	Function/Position Held on November 22, 1963*	Date of Conversation
James Altgens	Assassination eyewitness	11/1/65

* Unless other dates provided.

Dr. Michael Baden	Forensic pathologist and consultant to House Assassinations Committee, 1977–1978	11/8/79
George Barnum	Coast Guardsman on MDW casket team	8/20/79
Dr. Charles Baxter	Dallas physician who treated Kennedy	11/8/66
Lt. Samuel Bird	Officer in Charge, MDW casket team	11/25/67
Robert Blakey	General Counsel, House Assassination Committee, 1977–1979	10/20/78
Dr. J. Thornton Boswell	Commander, USN; Chief of Pathology, U.S. Navy Medical School; one of three autopsy surgeons	7/5/79
Dr. George Burkley	Rear Admiral, USN; White House physician	11/19/67
Deroy Cain	Flight Engineer, *Air Force Two*	3/4/80
Dr. Charles Carrico	Dallas physician who attended Kennedy	11/8/66
Timothy Cheek	Member, MDW casket team	11/19/67
Marie Fehmer Chiarodo	Secretary to Lyndon Johnson	9/4/80
Hubert Clark	Sailor on MDW casket team	12/19/67
Dr. Kemp Clark	Dallas physician who attended Kennedy	11/9/66
Chester Clifton	Major General, USA; aide to the President	7/15/80
Jerrol Custer	X-ray technician at Bethesda autopsy	9/30/79 10/7/79
Dennis Duane David	Chief of the Day, U.S. Naval Medical School, National Naval Medical Center, Bethesda	7/2/79
Vincent Drain	FBI agent, Dallas field office	7/27/80
Dr. John Ebersole	Radiologist at Bethesda autopsy	8/27/72
James L. Felder	Sergeant, USA; member of MDW casket team	11/20/67 12/16/67
Dr. Calvin Galloway	Rear Admiral, USN; Commanding Officer, National Naval Medical Center, Bethesda	6/4/78
Richard Gaudreau	Sergeant, USAF; Member of MDW casket team	8/26/79
William Greer	Secret Service agent; driver	11/20/67 1/18/71
Paul Groody	Dallas undertaker who buried Oswald	7/29/80
Dr. James Humes	Commander, MC, USN; Director of Laboratories, U.S. Navy Medical School, National Naval Medical Center, Bethesda; one of three autopsy surgeons	11/2/66 11/3/66 9/7/78 11/9/79
James Curtis Jenkins	Laboratory technologist at Bethesda autopsy	9/23/79

Sources

Dr. Ronald Jones	Dallas physician who attended Kennedy	11/10/66
J.S. Layton Ledbetter	Chief of the Day, Medical Center Command; National Naval Medical Center, Bethesda	9/25/79
Richard Lipsey	Lieutenant, USA; aide to General Wehle	8/30/79
Dr. Robert McClelland	Dallas physician who attended Kennedy	11/9/66
Godfrey McHugh	General, USAF; aide to President Kennedy	11/19/67
Burke Marshall	Kennedy family attorney, 1966	1/6/71
Douglas Mayfield	Spec. 4, USA; member of MDW casket team	12/16/67
James Metzler	Hospital corpsman third-class; U.S. Naval Medical School, Bethesda; was present at start of autopsy	11/25/79
Paul K. O'Connor	Laboratory technologist at Bethesda autopsy	8/25/79
Dr. David Osborne	Captain, MC, USN; Chief of Surgery at Bethesda Naval Hospital	11/4/79
Dr. Malcolm Perry	Dallas physician who attended Kennedy	10/27/66
Dr. Paul Peters	Dallas physician who attended Kennedy	11/12/66
Donald A. Purdy	Lawyer on House Assassinations Committee in charge of the medical evidence, 1977–1979	8/20/79
Edward Reed	X-ray technician at Bethesda autopsy	11/25/79
Floyd A. Reibe	Assistant to medical photographer at Bethesda autopsy	11/26/79
Aubrey Rike	Ambulance driver; assistant to Dallas undertaker Vernon O'Neill	3/11/80
James Sibert	FBI agent at autopsy	11/2/80
Joe Sofet	Lieutenant Colonel, USAF; pilot of *Air Force Two*	3/4/80
Dr. John Stover	Captain, MC, USN; Commanding Officer of U.S. Naval Medical School, Bethesda	4/13/80
John Stringer, Jr.	Medical photographer at autopsy	8/25/72 8/26/72
James Swindal	Colonel, USAF; pilot of *Air Force One*	3/4/80
John Van Hoesen	Washington undertaker	3/25/80
Philip Wehle	General, USA; Commanding Officer of the Military District of Washington	4/9/67

AN EXPLANATION OF NOMENCLATURE WITHIN THE NUMBERED REFERENCES

Citations in this book use a series of abbreviations, all of which are listed in alphabetical order following these few words on their usage.

References to the Warren Commission Report, or more simply the Warren Report, are indicated by the abbreviation "WCR," followed by a page number (e.g., the notation WCR, p. 540).

Documents in the twenty-six volumes of the Warren Commission Hearings (WCH) are cited either by page and volume number (e.g., 22 WCH 325 means page 325 of volume 22) or by Warren Commission Exhibit number (e.g., WCE 362). Warren Commission documents stored in Records Group 272 at the National Archives are cited by their "CD" number; thus, CD 1245, p. 3, means Warren Commission Document 1245, page 3. Material in Records Group 272 is sometimes cited by its file location; for example, RG 272, E-52, means Records Group 272, Entry 52.

Medical documents commonly referred to include the Bethesda Autopsy Report (BAR), available in the Warren Report or volume 7 of the House Assassinations Committee Report; the Supplementary Autopsy Report (SAR); and the Sibert and O'Neill FBI report (S&O). The Sibert and O'Neill report corresponds to CD 7, pp. 280–85.

The House Assassinations Committee hearings are abbreviated HAC; references to it take the form 7 HAC 45, meaning page 45 of volume 7. References to the report volume (HACR) take the self-explanatory form HACR, p. 45.

Documents released by the FBI under the Freedom of Information Act will usually be listed by their FBI document numbers (e.g., FBI 62-109060-427).

The Shaw Trial is abbreviated "ST" and pages in the transcript of the testimony of Dr. Finck will, for example, be listed as ST, Dr. Finck, 2/24/64, p. 64.

Abbreviations of cited newspapers and books appearing in the bibliography will simply be based on their full titles.

My own transcript of various tape recordings will be indicated by "AT," for Author's Transcript, followed by the subject matter being transcribed (e.g., AT—AF-1 is my own transcript of tape recordings made of radio transmissions between *Air Force One* and Washington on November 22, 1963).

A complete List of Abbreviations follows.

LIST OF ABBREVIATIONS

AAF	*Accessories After the Fact* by Meagher. See Sources.
AP	Associated Press
AT-AF-1	Author's Transcript of tape recordings of radio transmissions made between *Air Force One* and the Pentagon.
AT-DPT	Author's Transcript of Dallas Police Tape
AT-Lb/Lane	Author's Transcript of Liebeler-Lane debate, UCLA, 1/25/67
AT-Lomax	Author's Transcript of Liebeler on Lomax show, taped 10/23/66 in Los Angeles
AT-TI	Author's Transcript of public discussion of Warren Report at Theatre of Ideas, 9/30/66, subsequently broadcast on Pacifica radio stations
BAR	Bethesda Autopsy Report
BG	*Boston Globe*
CPR	Clark Panel Report
CD	Commission Document
DMN	*Dallas Morning News*
DOP	*Death of a President* by William Manchester. See Sources.
DTH	*Dallas Times-Herald*
E-	Refers to "Entry number" in Records Group 272
FBI	Refers to FBI number used to identify documents made available through Freedom of Information Act
FWP	*Fort Worth Press*
HAC	House Assassinations Committee
HACR	House Assassinations Committee Report
HP	*Houston Post*
LAT	*Los Angeles Times*
MDW	Military District of Washington, D.C.
MIR	Military Review. Report of the three autopsy documents after review of the autopsy photos and X-rays in January 1967. Published in *Post-Mortem*. A public document available at Justice Department.

NA	National Archives
NMS-Report	NA report of inspection by naval medical staff (11/1/66) of X-rays and photos of JFK autopsy
NYHT	*New York Herald Tribune*
NYT	*New York Times*
PSB	*Philadelphia Sunday Bulletin*
PM	*Post-Mortem.* See Sources.
RG	Records Group, usually used to signify Records Group 272
REP	File designation for RG-272 documents
RSP	*Resident and Staff Physician.* Refers to article by Dr. John Lattimer in May 1972 issue. See Sources.
RTJ	*Rush to Judgment* by Lane. See Sources.
S&O	The Sibert and O'Neill FBI report on the Bethesda autopsy
SAC	Special Agent in Charge (head of any FBI field office)
SAR	Supplementary Autopsy Report (See discussion above.)
SLPD	*St. Louis Post-Dispatch*
SS	Secret Service
SSD	*Six Seconds in Dallas* by Thompson. See Sources.
ST	Shaw Trial. See Sources.
UPI	United Press International
USNWR	*U.S. News and World Report*
WCE	Warren Commission Exhibit
WCES	Warren Commission Executive Session
WCH	Warren Commission Hearings
WCH-LaEx-2	Lawrence Exhibit 2 in the 26 volumes
WCH-PrEx	Price Exhibits in volume 21 of the 26 volumes
WCH-SyXA	Sawyer Exhibit A in volume 21 of the 26 volumes
WCR	Warren Commission Report
WDD	*Where Death Delights* by Marshal Houts (New York: Coward McCann, 1967)
WP	*Washington Post*
WST	*Washington Star*

NUMBERED REFERENCES

Part I THE PUZZLE

CHAPTER 1
Entering the Labyrinth (pp. 3–32)

1. WCR, p. 89
2. WCR, p. 90
3. 17 WCH 48
4. FBI 62-109090-472
5. *Life*, 10/2/64
6. WCR, p. 71
7. 6 HAC 124
8. 8 HAC 128
9. 2/27/65, "News Conference," KNBC, Los Angeles
10. 18 WCH 19
11. WCE 917
12. WCE 1024, passim
13. WCE 1974
14. WCE 705
15. WCE 705, 1974, and Sawyer Exhibits A and B (21 WCH 388–97, 398–400)
16. 12 WCH 329
17. 22 WCH 395
18. *Newsweek*, 11/28/66, p. 19
19. 17 WCH 48
20. 2 WCH 373
21. 17 WCH 33, 36
22. cf. 17 WCH 31 (last paragraph) and BAR, p. 2
23. 24 WCH 212
24. 6 WCH 246
25. 6 WCH 245–46
26. 6 WCH 230
27. 19 WCH 485
28. 22 WCH 833
29. 22 WCH 836
30. Filmed interview of Simmons by Mark Lane, 3/28/66, as quoted in RTJ, p. 40
31. Filmed interview of Dodd by Mark Lane, 3/24/66, as shown in film, RTJ
32. Taped interview of Walter Winborn by Barbara Bridges, 3/17/65; Taped interview of Winborn by Stewart Galanor, 5/5/66
33. Taped interview of Thomas Murphy by Stewart Galanor, 5/6/66
34. 6 WCH 338; 22 WCH 662
35. 22 WCH 685
36. 6 WCH 388
37. 24 WCH 521
38. 24 WCH 229; 3 WCH 204, 209
39. 24 WCH 204
40. 24 WCH 205
41. DTH, 11/22/63
42. RTJ, pp. 56, 422
43. 6 WCH 294
44. 6 WCH 206–7, 212–13
45. 7 WCH 572
46. 24 WCH 219
47. 24 WCH 213
48. 7 WCH 560
49. 6 WCH 286
50. 6 WCH 288
51. *Texas Observer*, 12/13/63
52. 19 WCH 502–43
53. 19 WCH 530
54. 7 WCH 109
55. WCR, p. 76
56. Ibid.
57. AAF, pp. 45–64
58. WCR, p. 120; WCE 773
59. WCR, p. 81; 20 WCH 174

60. 20 WCH 366; also, author's audio tape
61. Audio tape, analyzed by George O'Toole, *The Assassination Tapes* (New York: Penthouse Press, 1975), p. 125
62. Author's audio tape from sound-track of UPI newsfilm
63. NYT, 11/23/63
64. 7 WCH 510
65. 7 WCH 557
66. 7 WCH 576
67. Author's memo, 10/12/65, first interview with Liebeler
68. 18 WCH 19
69. 18 WCH 19–24
70. SSD, pp. 216–18
71. Letter, Liebeler to Rankin, 10/13/65
72. Ibid.
73. Author's memo, 10/12/65, first interview with Liebeler
74. Author's memo, 11/30/65, interview with Liebeler, Note 1 re: first meeting
75. Letter, Rankin to Liebeler, 10/21/65
76. Letter, Redlich to Liebeler, 10/18/65
77. Ibid.
78. Ibid.
79. Letter, Rankin to Liebeler, 10/21/65
80. Compare WCE 2114 with Secret Service photos of May 1964 re-enactment
81. Letter, author to another critic, 11/6/65
82. Ibid.
83. Letter, Redlich to Liebeler, 10/18/65
84. Author's memo, 11/1/65 conversation with Altgens
85. Ibid.
86. 20 WCH 493
87. 20 WCH 489–95
88. Author's memo, 11/20/65 conversation with Hill
89. *Paris Match*, 11/27/65
90. Author's memo, interview with Liebeler, 11/30/65

CHAPTER 2
The Head Snap (pp. 33–54)

1. Author's memo on interview with Allen Dulles, 12/7/65
2. *The Nation*, 1/27/64, pp. 86–89; WCES, 1/27/64, pp. 128–82; Memo, Redlich to Rankin, 2/11/64, NA, RG 272, E-25
3. BG, 4/25/75
4. BAR, p. 3
5. 6 WCH 33
6. 2 WCH 141

7. BAR, p. 4
8. WCR, p. 86
9. 6 WCH 136
10. 6 WCH 74
11. 6 WCH 71
12. 6 WCH 11
13. 6 WCH 25
14. 6 WCH 48, 71, 74, 11, 25, 35, 6, 42 respectively; 2 WCH 128
15. 6 WCH 25
16. *Liberation*, 3/65, p. 29
17. BAR, p. 4
18. *Liberation*, 3/65, p. 27
19. *Liberation*, 3/65, p. 31
20. 6 WCH 56
21. 6 WCH 37
22. 6 WCH 71
23. 6 WCH 67
24. 6 WCH 50
25. 18 WCH 731
26. 18 WCH 765
27. WFAA-TV interview, as shown in documentary film *Rush to Judgment*
28. 19 WCH 490
29. SSD, p. 103
30. Ibid.
31. SSD, p. 102
32. *New York Daily News*, 11/24/63
33. HP, 11/23/63
34. 6 WCH 294
35. 6 WCH 292
36. RTJ, p. 56
37. 18 WCH 801
38. 20 WCH 353
39. UPI "A" Wire, 2:47 EST
40. Author's tape of NBC broadcasts
41. WCR, p. 527
42. 6 WCH 35
43. 6 WCH 48
44. 6 WCH 51
45. Ibid.
46. PSB, 11/24/63
47. NYT, 11/23/63
48. SSD, p. 275
49. *Ramparts*, 1/67, p. 89

CHAPTER 3
The Throat Wound:
Entrance or Exit? (pp. 55–69)

1. WCR, p. 90
2. 2 WCH 362
3. UPI "A" wire, 3:10 CST
4. NYT, 11/23/63
5. WCR, p. 90
6. AP "A" wire, 2:40 CST; UPI "A" wire, 3:10 CST; NYT, 11/23/63
7. DMN, 11/24/63, p. 11
8. WCR, p. 519

9. 6 WCH 141
10. Ibid.
11. SLPD, 12/1/63, p. 16
12. 6 WCH 141, 143
13. BG, 11/24/63, p. 9
14. Interview of Dr. Shaw by Martin Steadman, NYHT News Service, as published in HP, 11/29/63
15. SLPD, 12/1/63, p. 16
16. 6 WCH 9
17. 3 WCH 362
18. 6 WCH 55
19. 6 WCH 37
20. 3 WCH 373
21. 3 WCH 375
22. 3 WCH 379
23. 3 WCH 377
24. 3 WCH 378
25. Ibid.
26. CD 678
27. CBS News Inquiry, "The Warren Report, Part II," 6/26/67
28. RTJ, pp. 53, 422
29. WCE 1415; WCR, p. 91
30. SLPD, 12/1/63, p. 16
31. Ibid.
32. SLPD, 12/10/63, p. 1
33. SLPD, 12/18/63, p. 1
34. Ibid.
35. Ibid.
36. Ibid.
37. SLPD, 12/18/63, p. 6
38. Ibid.
39. NYT, 12/6/63
40. NYT, 11/27/63
41. NYT, 12/6/63
42. UPI, "A" wire, 3:10 CST
43. DMN, 11/24/63, p. 11
44. BG, 11/24/63, p. 9
45. NYT, 11/27/63
46. SLPD, 12/1/63
47. NYT, 12/6/63
48. Ibid.
49. SLPD, 12/18/63
50. 3 WCH 362
51. Ibid.
52. 3 WCH 373
53. 6 WCH 42
54. 6 WCH 55
55. Ibid.

CHAPTER 4
The Zapruder Film and the
Timing Problem (pp. 70–96)

1. WCR, p. 97
2. WCR, pp. 97, 194
3. WCR, pp. 105–6
4. WCR, p. 106

5. *Inquest*, p. 43
6. 5 WCH 155
7. 4 WCH 116
8. 4 WCH 132–33, 135–36
9. 4 WCH 147
10. 5 WCH 171–72
11. Ibid.
12. WCR, p. 105
13. WCR, p. 19
14. NYT, 11/27/63
15. WCR, p. 19
16. WCR, p. 87
17. WCR, p. 106
18. Ibid.
19. WCR, p. 92
20. 2 WCH 366
21. 18 WCH 760
22. WCR, p. 111
23. 2 WCH 100
24. 2 WCH 143
25. 2 WCH 127
26. 2 WCH 93
27. WCE 397
28. Ibid.
29. 2 WCH 93
30. 2 WCH 127
31. ST, 2/24/69, p. 120
32. WP, 12/18/63, p. A-3
33. NYT, 12/18/63, p. 27
34. NYT, 1/26/64, "Twelve Unanswered Questions," p. 68
35. WCR, p. 88
36. Ibid.
37. Ibid.
38. Ibid.
39. Ibid.
40. 2 WCH 361
41. 2 WCH 368
42. CD 1, p. 18
43. CD 107, p. 2
44. CD 1, p. 18; CD 107, p. 2
45. *Inquest*, p. 206
46. Fletcher Knebel, "A New Wave of Doubt," *Look*, 7/12/66
47. TI, 9/30/66
48. WCES, 12/16/63, pp. 11–12
49. WCES, 11/23/63, p. 12
50. WCES, 1/21/64, p. 20
51. *Inquest*, p. 61
52. RTJ, pp. 65–66
53. *Inquest*, p. 34, quoting "Portrait of the Assassin" by Gerald Ford and John Stiles, p. 20, in turn quoting WCES, 1/27/64, p. 139
54. *Inquest*, p. 62
55. Robert Groden, "A New Look at the Zapruder Film," *Rolling Stone*, 4/24/75, p. 35
56. Vincent Salandria, "The Separate

Connally Shot," *The Minority of One*, 4/66

57. Ibid.
58. 3 WCH 428–29
59. 3 WCH 430
60. ST, 2/22/69, p. 151
61. 2 WCH 374–75
62. 2 WCH 376
63. 2 WCH 382
64. 4 WCH 113–14
65. WCR, p. 95
66. 4 WCH 109
67. WCR, p. 95
68. 6 WCH 130
69. 6 WCH 131
70. 6 WCH 132
71. 6 WCH 134
72. 3 WCH 389
73. *Ramparts*, 1/67, p. 86
74. NYT, 11/23/66, p. 25
75. *The Nation*, 7/11/66
76. Ibid.

CHAPTER 5
The Sibert and O'Neill Report and the Emerging Controversy (pp. 97–119)

1. *Inquest*, p. 132
2. Ibid., pp. 14–15
3. Ibid., p. 92
4. Ibid., p. 22
5. Ibid., p. 7
6. Ibid., p. 98
7. Ibid., pp. 97–98; 5 WCH 258
8. Ibid., p. 96
9. Ibid., pp. 96–97
10. *Inquest*, p. 96
11. Ibid.
12. Ibid., p. 97
13. Ibid., pp. 15, 27
14. Ibid., p. 24
15. Ibid., pp. 137–38
16. Ibid., pp. 146–47
17. WCE 1974, p. 96
18. *Inquest*, p. 135
19. Liebeler memo, 9/6/64, re: galley proofs of Chapter IV of the Report, p. 20, NA, RG 272, *REP* files
20. Ibid., pp. 21, 24
21. Ibid., p. 25
22. *Inquest*, p. 147
23. 8 WCH 235
24. CD 7, pp. 281–85, hereafter abbreviated "S&O"
25. S&O, p. 5
26. S&O, p. 4
27. Ibid.
28. Ibid.
29. S&O, p. 5

30. Ibid.
31. Letter from Dr. Richard Popkin, *New York Review of Books*, 10/6/66
32. *Inquest*, p. 116; see also, pp. 50, 62
33. WCES, 12/16/63, p. 12
34. Fletcher Knebel, "A New Wave of Doubt," *Look*, 7/12/66
35. Ibid.
36. Ibid.
37. Ibid.
38. AT-TI, 9/30/66
39. Ibid.
40. Ibid.
41. Ibid.
42. Ibid.
43. Ibid.
44. Ibid.
45. Ibid.
46. Ibid.
47. Ibid.
48. Ibid.
49. Ibid.
50. Ibid.
51. Ibid.
52. Ibid.
53. Ibid.
54. Ibid.
55. Ibid.
56. Letter, author to Sylvia Meagher, 10/13/66
57. NYT, 10/23/66
58. Letter, author to Sylvia Meagher, 10/13/66
59. Letter, Hoover to Liebeler, 10/19/66, FBI 62-109060-4232
60. Memo, Rosen to DeLoach, 10/19/66, FBI 62-109060-4228, p. 4
61. Ibid., p. 5
62. Same as note 59
63. Letter, Sylvia Meagher to author, 10/9/66
64. Ibid.
65. Ibid.
66. Letter, author to Sylvia Meagher, 10/13/66
67. "Commission Critic Lane Announces He Will Sue UCLA Prof. Liebeler," UCLA *Daily Bruin*, 10/14/66
68. *Time*, 11/25/66, p. 34
69. Letter, author to another critic, 10/20/66

CHAPTER 6
Redefining the Problem: The Autopsy as "Best Evidence" (pp. 120–46)

1. Edward Bellamy, *Looking Backward: 2000–1887* (New York: Vanguard Press, 1926), p. 205

Numbered References

2. Ibid., pp. 208–9
3. 15 WCH 699
4. Ibid.
5. 2 WCH 141
6. WCR, p. 50
7. *Inquest*, p. 15
8. Author's memo, interview with Lie-beler, 11/30/65
9. WCR, p. 110
10. *Inquest*, 148–51
11. *Inquest*, p. 149
12. *Inquest*, pp. 150, 219
13. WCR, p. 19
14. *Inquest*, pp. 54–88
15. BAR, p. 3
16. 18 WCH 744
17. Letter, author to another critic, 10/20/66
18. WCR, p. 19
19. Liebeler at Stanford, 10/17/66, as recorded by KZSU
20. Ibid.
21. 2 WCH 349
22. 2 WCH 349–50
23. 2 WCH 350
24. Ibid.
25. 2 WCH 351
26. 2 WCH 366
27. 2 WCH 369

28. RTJ, p. 61
29. "The Vital Documents," *The Nation*, 7/11/66, p. 47
30. Ibid.
31. Official Secret Service statement issued to Hoch on 6/21/66
32. Gaeton Fonzi, "The Warren Commission, the Truth, and Arlen Specter," *Greater Philadelphia Magazine*, August 1966
33. Ibid.
34. USNWR, 10/10/66, p. 53
35. Ibid.
36. Same as note 19
37. USNWR, 10/10/66, p. 58
38. Ibid.
39. BAR, p. 6
40. 2 WCH 371–72
41. Letter, 10/19/66, Liebeler to UPI
42. Ibid.
43. USNWR, 10/10/66, p. 53
44. "Open for Discussion," 9/10/67, KTLA, Los Angeles
45. AT-TI, 9/30/66
46. "Newsmakers," 11/27/66, KNXT, Los Angeles
47. Fonzi, op. cit., p. 82
48. Ibid.

Part II   A NEW HYPOTHESIS

CHAPTER 7
Breakthrough (pp. 149–80)

1. Arnold Fein, *Saturday Review*, 10/22/66
2. S&O, p. 5
3. CD 1, p. 18
4. NYT, 12/18/63; WP, 12/18/63
5. CD 107, p. 2
6. *Inquest*, p. 17
7. 2 WCH 361–64; BAR, pp. 4–5
8. CD 371
9. Fein, op. cit., p. 43
10. CD 1, p. 18
11. "Kennedy Autopsy Report," WP, 12/18/63, p. A-3
12. "Kennedy Autopsy Reveals First Wound Wasn't Fatal," WST, 12/18/63, p. A-9
13. *Inquest*, p. 47
14. AAF, p. 138
15. BAR, p. 3
16. BAR, pp. 3, 5
17. Interview with Bill Burrus, March 1978
18. "Kennedy Shot Entered Back," DTH, 12/12/63

19. SLPD, 12/18/63, p. 1
20. WP, 5/29/66
21. Same as note 46 for Chapter 4
22. 2 WCH 373
23. WCE 397
24. 2 WCH 373
25. S&O, p. 4; 2 WCH 143
26. 2 WCH 362
27. S&O, p. 3
28. RG 272, E-52
29. S&O, p. 4
30. ST, Finck, 2/24/69, p. 120
31. S&O, pp. 4–5
32. Fein, op. cit., p. 44
33. S&O, p. 4
34. S&O, p. 5
35. 2 WCH 361–62
36. "Overwhelming Evidence Oswald Was Assassin," USNWR, 10/10/66, p. 49
37. Ibid.
38. "A New Wave of Doubt," *Look*, 7/12/66
39. *Liberation*, 3/65, p. 18
40. 2 WCH 362
41. WCR, p. 88
42. 2 WCH 367

43. WCR, p. 89
44. S&O, pp. 4, 5
45. 2 WCH 143
46. 2 WCH 93, 127
47. WCR, p. 92
48. WCE 397
49. BAR, p. 3
50. WCE 385, 386, 388
51. BAR, p. 6
52. WCE 397
53. WCE 397, passim
54. BAR, p. 2
55. 7 HAC 258
56. SLPD 12/18/63, p. 6
57. S&O, p. 1
58. Ibid.
59. S&O, p. 3
60. Ibid.
61. Ibid.
62. Ibid.
63. 2 WCH 371–72
64. S&O, p. 3
65. S&O, p. 4
66. BAR, p. 4
67. 2 WCH 81
68. RTJ, p. 59
69. RTJ, p. 58
70. 2 WCH 360
71. Ibid.
72. S&O, p. 3
73. S&O, p. 5
74. Ibid.
75. S&O, p. 3

7. 6 WCH 3
8. 6 WCH 4
9. 2 WCH 143
10. 2 WCH 103
11. Ibid.
12. 21 WCH 216, 242
13. WCR, p. 642
14. S&O, p. 4
15. 2 WCH 364
16. Ibid.
17. WCE 397 (17 WCH 33)
18. Ibid.
19. BAR, p. 3
20. WCE 397 (17 WCH 38)
21. Ibid.
22. BAR, p. 4
23. SLPD, 12/18/63
24. Ibid., p. 6
25. Ibid., p. 1
26. 3 WCH 365
27. Ibid.
28. Ibid.
29. WCR, p. 76
30. WCR, pp. 79–80; 18 WCH 798–800
31. WCE 2003, pp. 131–35
32. S&O, p. 4
33. 2 WCH 351
34. 2 WCH 352
35. Ibid.
36. Ibid.
37. 2 WCH 81
38. Ibid.
39. S&O, p. 1
40. Ibid.

CHAPTER 8
Emergence of a New
Hypothesis (pp. 181–206)

1. WCR, pp. 19, 86–87
2. ST, Frazier, 2/22/69, p. 151
3. "The Louis Lomax Show," video-taped 10/23/66, aired 10/27/66; all quotes from transcript of author's tape
4. 2 WCH 355
5. 2 WCH 356
6. Ibid.

CHAPTER 9
October 24, 1966—A Confrontation
with Liebeler (pp. 207–32)

1. 2 WCH 78
2. 2 WCH 102–03
3. S&O, p. 3
4. S&O, p. 1
5. LAT, 5/30/66
6. Same as note 32 for Chapter 6
7. USNWR, 10/10/66, p. 50
8. NYT, 2/5/64

Part III   A SEARCH FOR NEW EVIDENCE

CHAPTER 10
The Liebeler Memorandum
(pp. 235–70)

1. BAR, p. 3
2. Ibid.
3. Ibid.

4. 2 WCH 352, 353
5. WCE 397 (17 WCH 46)
6. 2 WCH 361
7. Telephone Conversation with Liebeler, 11/2/66
8. Telephone Conversation with Humes, 11/2/66

9. Telephone Conversation with Sibert, 11/2/66
10. Telephone Conversation with Liebeler, 11/3/66
11. 2 WCH 360
12. 2 WCH 379–80
13. 2 WCH 353
14. 2 WCH 352
15. BAR, p. 4
16. 2 WCH 354
17. 2 WCH 371
18. 2 WCH 141; *see also* 18 WCH 742
19. CD 7, p. 286
20. 2 WCH 360
21. Telephone Conversation with Liebeler, 11/3/66
22. SAR, p. 1; 2 WCH 356
23. 2 WCH 356
24. Ibid.
25. SAR, p. 1
26. Telephone Conversation with Humes, 11/3/66
27. Telephone Conversation with Liebeler, 11/3/66
28. Telephone Conversation with Liebeler, 11/4/66
29. S&O, p. 5
30. 2 WCH 81
31. 2 WCH 354
32. S&O, pp. 3, 5
33. 2 WCH 367
34. Liebeler memo, 11/8/66, Justice Department file 129–11, section 14, item 5, p. 2
35. Ibid., p. 4
36. Ibid., p. 5
37. Ibid., pp. 3, 13
38. Telephone Conversation with Liebeler, 11/8/66
39. Same as note 34
40. Same as note 38
41. Letter, Lifton to Hoover, 11/9/66, FBI 62-109060-4269

CHAPTER 11
The Tracheotomy Incision:
Dallas vs. Bethesda (pp. 271–94)

1. Telephone Conversation with Dr. Baxter, 11/8/66
2. Telephone Conversation with Dr. Jenkins, 11/8/66
3. Telephone Conversation with Dr. Carrico, 11/8/66
4. Same as note 1
5. Telephone Conversation with Dr. Peters, 11/12/66
6. Telephone Conversation with Dr. McClelland, 11/9/66
7. Ibid.
8. Ibid.
9. Telephone Conversation with Dr. Jones, 11/10/66
10. Same as note 1
11. Same as note 2
12. Same as note 6
13. Same as note 9
14. Telephone Conversation with Dr. Akin, 11/8/66
15. cf. 2 WCH 361 and BAR, p. 3
16. BAR, p. 3
17. Same as note 6
18. Same as note 5
19. Same as note 9
20. 3 WCH 361
21. 6 WCH 9
22. WCE 397
23. 6 WCH 15
24. 6 WCH 42
25. 6 WCH 9
26. Ibid.
27. 3 WCH 369
28. 3 WCH 362
29. 6 WCH 9
30. 6 WCH 42
31. 6 WCH 54
32. Ibid.
33. 6 WCH 32
34. BAR, p. 3
35. 2 WCH 362
36. 6 WCH 42
37. BAR, p. 3
38. 3 WCH 370
39. 6 WCH 42
40. Ibid.
41. 2 WCH 363
42. 6 WCH 42
43. Same as note 5
44. Same as note 6
45. BAR, p. 3
46. WDD, p. 57
47. WCR, p. 88
48. BAR, p. 4
49. WDD, p. 57
50. Ibid.
51. Ibid.
52. ST, 2/24/69, p. 147
53. ST, 2/24/69, pp. 149, 152
54. BAR, p. 5
55. 2 WCH 363
56. 2 WCH 363
57. 3 WCH 360
58. 3 WCH 360; 6 WCH 3
59. 3 WCH 370
60. 6 WCH 70
61. 6 WCH 54
62. 6 WCH 47
63. 3 WCH 371

64. 6 WCH 28
65. Ibid.
66. NYT, 11/27/63
67. 6 WCH 32
68. 6 WCH 51
69. ST, Dr. Finck, 2/24/69, p. 120
70. Ibid., p. 15
71. Ibid., p. 128
72. S&O, p. 4
73. 2 WCH 369
74. 6 WCH 17
75. 7 HAC 83
76. Ibid.
77. 7 HAC 192
78. 18 WCH 760
79. Ibid.
80. WCE 2112
81. Ibid.
82. Ibid., Letter, Rowley to Rankin, 5/14/64
83. Ibid.
84. FBI interview of Kellerman by Sibert and O'Neill, 11/27/63; CD 7, p. 7
85. 6 WCH 17

CHAPTER 12
An Oral Utterance (pp. 295–307)

1. FBI 62-109090-472
2. 5 WCH 99
3. FBI 62-109060-4269
4. NYT, 11/26/66
5. Ibid.
6. 6 WCH 17
7. S&O, p. 3
8. 2 WCH 349
9. S&O, passim; see also 7 HAC 8, list based on HAC inquiry; and WCE 1126 for Admiral Kenney and Captain Canada
10. Telephone Conversation with Liebeler, 11/27/66
11. Telephone Conversation with Dr. Clark, 11/9/66
12. Telephone Conversation with Dr. McClelland, 11/9/66
13. FBI 62-109060-4244, p. 1
14. Ibid.
15. Ibid., p. 2
16. FBI 62-109060-4269
17. FBI 62-109060-4270, p. 1
18. Ibid., p. 2
19. Ibid.
20. Ibid.
21. Ibid., p. 1
22. FBI 62-109060-4123, pp. 2, 8
23. Ibid., p. 2
24. Ibid., p. 5

25. Ibid.
26. FBI 62-109060-4143, p. 2
27. Ibid., p. 2
28. FBI 62-109060-4116
29. FBI 62-109060-4239, p. 1
30. FBI 62-109060-4209
31. FBI 62-109060-4235, p. 2
32. Ibid.
33. FBI (Baltimore) 89-30-262, p. 3
34. Ibid., p. 1
35. FBI (Baltimore) 89-30-267, p. 1
36. Sanford Ungar, FBI (Boston: Little, Brown and Co., 1976), p. 279
37. Church Committee (Senate Select Committee on Intelligence Activities, 94th Congress), vol. 6, p. 182
38. Justice Department file 129-11, Section 14, item 4
39. Ibid.

CHAPTER 13
The Head Wound:
Dallas vs. Bethesda (pp. 308–37)

1. BAR, p. 3
2. Telephone Conversation with Dr. Paul Peters, 11/12/66
3. S&O, p. 5
4. BAR, p. 3
5. WCE 397 (17 WCH 46)
6. Interview with William Greer, 1/18/71, Rockville, Maryland
7. BAR, p. 4
8. 2 WCH 141
9. 18 WCH 742
10. Ibid.
11. 2 WCH 141
12. Declassified testimony of Jacqueline Kennedy, p. 6815, NA, RG 272
13. 2 WCH 82
14. Theodore White, In Search of History (New York: Harper & Row, 1978), pp. 521–22
15. 21 WCH 216
16. 6 WCH 136
17. 6 WCH 6
18. 3 WCH 361
19. 6 WCH 54
20. 17 WCH 6
21. 6 WCH 11
22. 6 WCH 65
23. 6 WCH 33
24. Ibid.
25. Ibid.
26. Ibid.
27. 6 WCH 71
28. Same as note 2
29. Ibid.
30. Ibid.
31. RTJ, p. 56

32. CD 1395, p. 50
33. 6 WCH 35, 37
34. 6 WCH 21
35. 6 WCH 56
36. Telephone Conversation with Dr. Ronald Jones, 11/10/66
37. 6 WCH 11
38. 6 WCH 50
39. 6 WCH 67
40. Same as note 2
41. DMN, 11/24/63
42. BG, 11/24/63
43. Transcript 1327-C of Perry and Clark news conference, 11/22/63, LBJ Library
44. WCE 392 (WCR, p. 518)
45. 2 WCH 351
46. BAR, p. 4
47. 2 WCH 369
48. 2 WCH 356
49. 6 WCH 6
50. 3 WCH 361
51. BAR, p. 3
52. Ibid.
53. Ibid.
54. CBS News Inquiry: "The Warren Report, Part II," 6/26/67
55. Telephone Conversation with Dr. Boswell, 7/5/79
56. Same as note 54
57. 17 WCH 46
58. 2 WCH 351
59. 6 WCH 33
60. SLPD, 11/24/63
61. Same as note 2
62. WCE 392 (WCR, p. 530)
63. 6 WCH 48
64. Same as note 43
65. 17 WCH 9–10
66. WCE 392 (WCR, p. 518)
67. 6 WCH 20
68. 6 WCH 26
69. 6 WCH 41
70. 6 WCH 6
71. 6 WCH 33
72. Same as note 2
73. 7 HAC 302
74. BAR, p. 4
75. 17 WCH 15
76. 6 WCH 71
77. Same as note 2
78. Ibid.
79. BAR, p. 3
80. BAR, p. 4
81. 2 WCH 81
82. WCE 392 (WCR, p. 523)
83. 17 WCH 15
84. Kilduff press conference, 11/22/63, Transcript 1327B—LBJ Library
85. 20 WCH 353

86. *See*, for example, KLIF, Reel 11, NA, RG 272
87. WCE 885, frames 277–96; also 1 HAC 438, reprint of article by physicist Luis Alvarez, demonstrating how Brehm's clapping rate can be used to compute camera speed
88. *John Kennedy Assassination Film Analysis*, Itek Corporation, Lexington, Mass., 5/2/76, p. 80
89. 2 WCH 352
90. BAR, p. 3
91. 2 WCH 81
92. WCR, p. 86
93. 6 WCH 20
94. Taped interview of Arlen Specter by Gaeton Fonzi, July 1966
95. New York: Putnam, 1974, Reprint ed., Bantam, 1976, p. 227
96. SSD, p. 111

CHAPTER 14
Trajectory Reversal:
Blueprint for Deception (pp. 338–79)

1. S&O, pp. 4–5; CD 107, p. 2
2. 2 WCH 143
3. Richard Lewis and Lawrence Schiller, *The Scavengers and Critics of the Warren Report* (New York: Delacorte Press, 1967), p. 149
4. "The Lingering Shadow," reprint by DTH of AP article published 6/25/67
5. Jacob Cohen, "The Warren Commission Report and Its Critics," *Frontier*, November 1966, p. 16
6. Appearance on radio program as quoted in PM, p. 394
7. CD 1, p. 18
8. SSD, pp. 201, 214
9. WCES, 1/27/64, p. 193
10. CD 107, pp. 2–3
11. Ball-Belin Report #1, 2/25/64, p. 35, NA, RG 272, E-27
12. WCE 1434
13. WCR, p. 152
14. Ibid.
15. Ibid.
16. WCR, p. 151
17. 3 WCH 227
18. WCR, p. 152
19. Ibid.
20. 6 WCH 392
21. WCR, p. 154
22. WCE 3076 (CD 1526)
23. Ibid.
24. WCR, p. 600
25. WCR, p. 162
26. 7 WCH 59; WCE 2003, p. 91
27. WCR, p. 613

28. Same as note 60, Chapter 1
29. Same as note 62, Chapter 1
30. 1 WCH 468
31. WCR, pp. 119–20
32. WCR, pp. 119–22
33. WCR, p. 123
34. KLIF radio, Reel 20, NA, RG 272, E-19
35. WFAA-TV, Reel 2, NA, RG 272, E-19
36. WCR, p. 123
37. Ibid.; WCE 2637
38. Letter, Liebeler to Rankin, 8/28/64, FBI 62-109090, section 19; Letter, Hoover to Rankin, 9/1/64, RG 272, E-25
39. WCE 3145
40. 4 WCH 262; CD 5, p. 161
41. The card—WCE 630, 645; Latona—6 WCH 7
42. Telephone Conversation with Jack Moseley, 7/28/80
43. Telephone Conversation with Vincent Drain, 7/27/80
44. Telephone Conversation with Paul Groody, 7/29/80
45. CD 5, pp. 159–61
46. FWP, 11/25/63; WCH-PrEx 32, pp. 5–6
47. Stevenson—WCE 2167; Wade—WCE 2169, p. 14
48. WCE 2168
49. WCR, p. 628
50. WCR, pp. 145–46
51. 5 HAC 676–77
52. 5 HAC 680
53. CD 80
54. Ibid.; WCE 2011, p. 4
55. 18 WCH 800; CD 320; SS 656
56. 2 WCH 103
57. Ibid.
58. 2 WCH 99
59. Ibid.
60. 2 WCH 99–100
61. S&O, p. 4
62. S&O, pp. 4–5
63. CD 320, SS 656
64. Memo, Hoover to Johnson, FBI 62-109060-433, p. 2
65. FBI 89-69-29
66. FBI 105-82555-95
67. WCR, p. 79
68. WCE 1974, p. 165
69. AT-DPT; WCE 1974, p. 166; WCH-SyXA
70. Droke House (Anderson, S.C.), 1969, pp. 305–64
71. WCH-LaEx-2 (5 HAC 618); 6 WCH 299, 302
72. WCE 1974, p. 166

73. Ibid.
74. WCH-LaEx-2 (5 HAC 618)
75. 6 WCH 302
76. 6 WCH 306
77. WCE 1974, p. 24
78. CD 329, p. 16
79. 6 HAC 109
80. Letter, Hoover to Rankin, 11/12/64, NA, RG 272, E-11
81. Same file as in note 80
82. Ibid.
83. 6 WCH 322
84. WCE 1974, p. 170
85. Ibid.
86. Ibid., pp. 24, 170
87. 7 WCH 535
88. SS records—CD 3, p. 44; HACR, pp. 183–84; other encounters—6 WCH 312; 7 WCH 107
89. SLPD, 12/1/63, p. 16
90. Interviews of Stavis Ellis and H.R. Freeman by Gil Toff, 4/21/71 and 4/22/71 respectively, conducted in connection with research for *Murder from Within,* by Fred T. Newcomb and Perry Adams, (Santa Barbara, Ca.: self-published, 1974)
91. CD 80, SS 310
92. WCR, p. 77; memo, Rankin to Hoover, 3/18/64; memo, Rankin to Rowley, 3/18/64; memo, Hoover to Rankin, 3/23/64; NA, RG 272, E-22
93. CD 80, p. 2
94. WCR, p. 77; 5 WCH 69
95. Ibid.
96. 2 WCH 96
97. Robert P. Smith, "Report of Interview of Mr. Bill Ashby, Concerning Presidential Car," 2/16/72
98. CD 107, p. 5
99. CD 80, p. 2
100. Same as note 3, p. 17
101. Jacob Cohen, "Conspiracy Fever," *Commentary,* October 1975, p. 39
102. Same as note 4
103. TI, 9/30/66
104. 6 WCH 220–221
105. "Certificate of Death," signed by Dr. Burkley, E-52, RG 272
106. Ibid.
107. WCE 1126
108. *Newsweek,* 12/5/66
109. UPI "A" Wire

CHAPTER 15
Winter 1966–67 (pp. 380–86)

1. Telephone Conversation with Josiah Thompson, 10/30/67

2. Memo by Arlen Specter, "Interview of FBI Agents Present at Autopsy," 3/12/64, JFK 4-1 file, NA, RG 272
3. BAR, p. 4
4. Same as note 2
5. AT-Lb/Lane
6. Ibid.
7. Ibid.

Part IV   WHAT, WHEN, AND WHERE?

CHAPTER 16
Chain of Possession:
The Missing Link (pp. 389–422)

1. 18 WCH 744 (WCE 1024)
2. 2 WCH 349
3. *Look*, 2/21/67, pp. 47–48
4. Ibid., p. 48
5. DOP, p. 391; 18 WCH 757 (Landis); 18 WCH 744 (Hill)
6. DOP, p. 391
7. *Look*, 3/7/67, p. 51
8. WCR, p. 59
9. WCR, p. 819, note 277
10. 18 WCH 744
11. WCR, p. 59
12. S&O, p. 3
13. 18 WCH 744 (Hill), 757 (Landis)
14. 2 WCH 349
15. S&O, p. 3; 2 WCH 349
16. S&O, p. 3
17. S&O, p. 1
18. Ibid.
19. Victor S. Navasky, *Kennedy Justice* (New York: Atheneum, 1971), p. 82
20. S&O, p. 1
21. WCE 1126
22. Ibid., p. 7
23. *Newsweek*, 4/10/67
24. DOP, pp. 241, 355, 389; MDW— Bird Report
25. DOP, p. 389
26. Ibid.
27. Ibid.
28. DOP, p. 390
29. Ibid.
30. Ibid.
31. Ibid.
32. Ibid.
33. Attachment to 12/9/63 "After Action Report: President Kennedy's Funeral," from the Provost Marshall, to ANCS-SE; MDW file obtained under Freedom of Information Act.
34. MDW—Bird Report; DOP, p. 390, implies 6:30
35. DOP, p. 399
36. DOP, p. 397
37. Ibid.
38. S&O, p. 1
39. 18 WCH 744
40. DOP, p. 398
41. 18 WCH 744 (Hill); 18 WCH 757 (Landis)
42. DOP, p. 398
43. Ibid.
44. Ibid.
45. Ibid.
46. DOP, pp. 660, 669
47. DOP, p. 661
48. Telephone Conversation with General Wehle, 4/9/67
49. DMN, 11/26/63, p. 15
50. Telephone Conversation with Timothy Cheek, 11/19/67
51. DOP, pp. 430–31
52. Telephone Conversation with Godfrey McHugh, 11/19/67
53. Telephone Conversation with William Greer, 11/20/67
54. Telephone Conversation with Dr. George Burkley, 11/19/67
55. WCE 1126, p. 7
56. Same as note 54
57. Telephone Conversation with James L. Felder, 11/20/67
58. MDW—Bird Report, 12/10/63
59. Ibid.
60. Ibid.
61. 2 WCH 349
62. MDW—Bird Report, 12/10/63
63. 18 WCH 744 (Hill); 18 WCH 757 (Landis)
64. Same as note 57
65. S&O, p. 1
66. 2 WCH 349
67. MDW—Bird Report, 12/10/63
68. S&O, p. 3
69. Telephone Conversation with Captain Samuel Bird, 11/25/67
70. Major Eugene Bickley, "Memoires of the JFK Funeral: Epilogue—What Happened to the Pallbearers?" *Soldiers*, November 1964
71. Telephone Conversation with Douglas Mayfield, 12/16/67
72. Ibid.
73. Tape recorded interview with James Felder, 12/16/67, Los Angeles

8. Article by Lawrence Olsen, UCLA *Daily Bruin*, 2/2/67
9. LAT, 10/4/74
10. Memo, Rankin to Liebeler et al., 12/1/66, Richard Russell Library, University of Georgia; also available with Dulles papers at Princeton University

74. Telephone Conversation with Hubert Clark, 12/19/67
75. S&O, p. 1
76. DOP, p. 399
77. Same as note 52
78. Telephone Conversation with Richard Gaudreau, 8/26/79
79. Telephone Conversation with Barbara Gaudreau, 8/26/79
80. Telephone Conversation with George A. Barnum, 8/20/79
81. Personal memorandum of George Barnum, 11/29/63 .
82. Ibid.
83. WST, 11/23/63, p. A-3
84. Ibid.
85. WP, 11/23/63, p. A-11
86. Ibid.
87. CD 371
88. WCR, p. 546
89. 1 HAC 311
90. Telephone Conversation with Richard Lipsey, 8/30/79
91. Telephone Conversation with J.S. Layton Ledbetter, 9/25/79
92. Telephone Conversation with Godfrey McHugh, 4/30/78
93. S&O, p. 1
94. Ibid.
95. 2 WCH 349
96. MDW—Bird Report, 12/10/63
97. DOP, p. 399
98. Same as note 73

CHAPTER 17
The X-Rays and Photographs:
1963–69 (pp. 423–35)

1. S&O, p. 3
2. S&O, p. 5
3. Kellerman—18 WCH 727; Humes—BAR, p. 6 and 2 WCH 351, 372
4. WCES, 4/30/64, p. 5881
5. Ibid.
6. Memo, Specter to Rankin, 4/30/64, "Autopsy Photographs and X-Rays of President John F. Kennedy," JFK 4-1 file, NA, RG 272
7. WCES, 4/30/64, p. 5882
8. Ibid.
9. 2 WCH 371
10. WCES, 4/30/64, p. 5884
11. Earl Warren, *The Memoirs of Earl Warren* (New York: Doubleday, 1977), p. 371
12. Ibid.
13. "The Clamour Rises for Kennedy X-Rays," *London Observer*, 8/7/66
14. Letter, Robert Kennedy to Dr. Burkley, NA, RG 272, E-52
15. 7 HAC 27
16. NYT, 11/2/66, p. 1
17. USNWR, 11/14/66, p. 81; *Newsweek*, 11/14/66, p. 28
18. Telephone Conversation with Liebeler, 11/27/66
19. *Newsweek*, 11/14/66; NYT, 11/5/66
20. LAT, 1/17/20
21. MIR, p. 5
22. Letter, Dr. Boswell to Atty. Gen. Ramsey Clark, 1/26/68
23. BAR, p. 4
24. CPR, p. 11
25. *See*, for example, photos published in *Newsweek*, 11/14/66, p. 28
26. WCR, p. 585
27. Lt. Col. Pierre Finck, "Ballistic and Forensic Pathologic Aspects of Missile Wounds. Conversation Between Anglo-American and Metric-System Units," *Military Medicine*, June 1965, p. 551
28. MIR, p. 3
29. CPR, p. 10
30. Same as note 54, Chapter 13
31. 7 HAC 122
32. MIR, p. 4
33. Telephone Conversation with Godfrey McHugh, 11/19/67
34. Ibid.
35. Ibid.
36. 2 WCH 361
37. CPR, p. 13
38. MIR, p. 4
39. ST, Dr. Finck, 2/24/69, p. 214; 2/25/69, p. 29
40. NMS-Report, 11/1/66
41. CPR, p. 5
42. Memorandum for file, 2/13/69, by Thomas J. Kelley, Assistant SS Director
43. Ibid., p. 1
44. Memorandum of transfer, 4/26/65, NA
45. Same as note 42
46. Ibid.
47. Ibid., p. 3
48. Ibid.
49. PM, pp. 281–88, 405

CHAPTER 18
The Pre-Autopsy Autopsy
(pp. 436–74)

1. 2 WCH 353
2. 2 WCH 352

3. BAR, p. 3
4. Ibid.
5. 2 WCH 354
6. SSD, p. 109
7. Telephone Conversation with Liebbeler, 1/4/67
8. Ibid.
9. *See* Chapter 15 for text
10. Telephone Conversation with Josiah Thompson, 10/30/67
11. Ibid.; SSD, p. 110
12. Ibid.; SSD, p. 201
13. ST, Finck, 2/24/69, p. 50
14. BAR, p. 3
15. Jurgen Ludwig, M.D., *Current Methods of Autopsy Practice* (Philadelphia: W.S. Saunders, 1972), p. 158
16. BAR, p. 3
17. 2 WCH 354
18. 7 HAC 253
19. 7 HAC 264
20. 7 HAC 246
21. Edgar Rentoul and Hamilton Smith, eds., *Glaister's Medical Jurisprudence and Toxicology*, 13th ed. (Edinburgh and London: Churchill Livingstone, 1973), p. 298
22. 2 WCH 352; BAR, p. 3
23. Robert Wilson, *Methods in Morbid Anatomy* (New York: Appleton-Century-Crofts, 1972), p. 46
24. Philipp Rezek and Max Millard, *Autopsy Pathology: A Guide for Pathologists and Clinicians* (Springfield, Ill.: Charles Thomas, 1963), p. 52
25. Henry W. Cattell, *Post-Mortem Pathology* (Philadelphia: J.B. Lippincott Co., 1905), p. 225
26. Wilson, op. cit., p. 47
27. Ibid.
28. Cattell, op. cit., p. 227
29. Wilson, op. cit., p. 47
30. 2 WCH 354
31. BAR, p. 4
32. 2 WCH 355
33. 2 WCH 371
34. Ibid.
35. 7 HAC 135
36. 7 HAC 245
37. Ibid.
38. Telephone Conversation with Josiah Thompson, 10/30/67
39. 7 HAC 253
40. Interview with William Greer, 1/18/71, Rockville, Maryland
41. 2 WCH 353
42. 7 HAC 122
43. 2 WCH 352
44. 7 HAC 122
45. BAR, p. 4
46. Ibid.
47. S&O, p. 5
48. FBI 62-109060-459
49. BAR, p. 4
50. 7 HAC 122
51. 7 HAC 13
52. Interview of Dr. Ebersole by Art Smith, 3/28/78, Lancaster, Pennsylvania
53. BAR, p. 4
54. 2 WCH 353
55. CPR, p. 7
56. CPR, p. 10
57. Ibid.
58. Ibid.
59. BAR, p. 2
60. WCE 397 (17 WCH 46)
61. Ibid.
62. RSP, p. 62
63. WCE 397
64. Telephone Conversation with Dr. Baden, 11/8/79
65. 2 WCH 369
66. WCES, 4/30/64, pp. 5882–83
67. 2 WCH 356
68. 7 HAC 247
69. SAR, p. 1
70. Rezek, op. cit., p. 70
71. SAR, p. 1
72. Telephone Conversation with Dr. Charles Wilbur, 9/26/76; with Dr. Baden, 11/8/79
73. BAR, p. 4
74. SAR, p. 1
75. Ibid.
76. SAR, p. 2
77. Ludwig, op. cit., p. 160
78. CPR, pp. 7–8
79. 2 WCH 356; SAR, p. 1
80. 7 HAC 247
81. Ibid.
82. SAR, p. 1
83. Cyril B. Courville, M.D., *Forensic Neuropathology: Lesions of the Brain and Spinal Cord of Medicolegal Importance* (Mundelein, Ill.: Callagan & Co., 1964), p. 49
84. Ibid.
85. Thomas Gonzales, Morgan Vance, Milton Helpern, and Charles Umberger, *Legal Medicine: Pathology and Toxicology*, 2nd ed. (New York: Appleton-Century-Crofts, 1954), p. 424
86. SAR, p. 1; 2 WCH 356

87. Roger Werick and Peter Williams, eds., *Gray's Anatomy*, 35th British ed. (Philadelphia: W.B. Saunders, 1973), p. 926
88. Armed Forces Institute of Pathology, *The Autopsy* (Washington, D.C.: 1951), p. 32
89. 2 WCH 356
90. SAR, p. 1; 2 WCH 356
91. CPR, p. 11
92. 2 WCH 356
93. SAR, p. 1
94. RSP, p. 57
95. CPR, p. 8
96. 7 HAC 129
97. BAR, p. 4
98. 7 HAC 25
99. Ibid.
100. 7 HAC 26–27
101. Telephone Conversation with Dr. Humes, 11/3/66

CHAPTER 19
Certain Preliminary Examinations
(pp. 475–94)

1. S&O, p. 1
2. Ibid.
3. Ibid.
4. Ibid.
5. New Orleans States-Item, 10/11/68
6. 2 WCH 349
7. WST, 11/23/63, p. 3
8. WP, 11/23/63, p. A-11
9. 2 WCH 100
10. 2 WCH 102–3
11. 18 WCH 726–27
12. 2 WCH 103
13. S&O, p. 3
14. S&O, p. 4
15. BAR, p. 2
16. ST, Dr. Finck, 2/24/69, p. 99
17. Ibid., pp. 99–100
18. Ibid., p. 107
19. Ibid., p. 114
20. ST, Dr. Finck, 2/25/69, p. 4
21. MIR, p. 1
22. FBI 62-109060-2637
23. Ibid., p. 2
24. Same as note 33, Chapter 16
25. Ibid.
26. Narrative dated 11/22/63, author not indicated, in MDW file
27. FBI (Baltimore) 89-30-13B
28. S&O, p. 4
29. Same as note 27
30. CD 7, pp. 5–11
31. CD 7, p. 286
32. 18 WCH 726–27
33. 7 HAC 263
34. Letter, McCreight (FBI) to Lifton, 11/17/78
35. 1 HAC 324
36. Telephone Conversation with Adm. Calvin Galloway, 6/4/78

Part V THE X-RAYS AND PHOTOGRAPHS: 1971–78

CHAPTER 20
The X-Rays (pp. 497–520)

1. Telephone Conversation with Dr. Wecht, 11/26/67
2. Memo, Lifton to file, re: 1/6/71 meeting with Wecht
3. Telephone Conversation with Burke Marshall, 1/6/71
4. Ibid.
5. Ibid.
6. Memo, J. Lee Rankin to staff, 1/13/64, NA, RG 272, E-20; *See* E-25 for assorted outlines of WCR; also, REP files.
7. Letter, Wecht to Lifton, 3/8/71
8. NYT, 1/9/72
9. Ibid.; PM, pp. 388–92
10. "'Unbelievably Unqualified' Doctor Called Unfit to Judge JFK Data," *Chicago Daily News*, 1/11/72
11. RSP, 5/72
12. Telephone Conversation with Wecht, 6/29/72; 7/6/72
13. Telephone Conversation with Wecht, 6/29/72
14. CD 5, p. 150
15. CD 1395, p. 50
16. FBI 89-43-479
17. Ibid.
18. Ibid.
19. FBI lab sheets, 11/27/63; FBI 62-109060, Attachment to Airtel cited in note 20.
20. Airtel, SAC, Dallas, to FBI Director, FBI 62-109060-60, p. 2
21. SAR
22. CD 1395, p. 46
23. CD 1395, p. 44
24. Letter, Rankin to Hoover, 7/3/64, NA, RG 272, E-25
25. CD 1395, p. 50
26. Letter, Robert P. Smith to David Lifton, 7/20/72, summarizing recent conversations with Drs. Noteboom, Cairns, and Harper in Dallas
27. Letter, Lifton to Wecht, 7/10/72
28. 6 WCH 6

29. 6 WCH 33
30. 6 WCH 41
31. 6 WCH 48
32. 6 WCH 20
33. SAR, p. 2
34. RSP, 5/72, p. 57
35. CPR, p. 15
36. RSP, p. 57
37. 5 HAC p. 35
38. 2 WCH 360
39. 7 HAC 122
40. 7 HAC 23
41. *The Nation*, 7/11/66, p. 46
42. USNWR, 10/10/66, p. 53
43. PM, pp. 285, 555
44. Tape of interview of Arlen Specter by Gaeton Fonzi, July 1966
45. Memo, Specter to Rankin, 4/30/64 "Autopsy Photographs and X-Rays of President John F. Kennedy," JFK 4-1 file, NA, RG 272
46. Ibid.
47. Memo, Specter to Rankin, 5/12/64, "Examination of Autopsy Photographs and X-Rays of President Kennedy," JFK 4-1 file, NA, RG 272
48. 18 WCH 760; Willis slide 5
49. WCE 2112
50. 18 WCH 762
51. 18 WCH 765, and 18 WCH 761–64
52. 18 WCH 765
53. 18 WCH 762
54. CD 7, p. 5
55. Telephone Conversation with Wecht, 7/6/72
56. RSP, 5/72, p. 57
57. CPR, p. 11; RSP, 5/72, p. 43, item H
58. NMS-Report, p. 11
59. Memo, Lifton to file, "Report on Wecht Autopsy Review of August 23–24, 1972," pp. 44–45
60. Ibid., p. 45
61. Wecht notes, p. 12
62. Same as note 59, pp. 49–50
63. Telephone Conversation with John Stringer, 8/25/72
64. Telephone Conversation with Dr. Wecht, 8/25/72
65. Telephone Conversation with John Stringer, 8/26/72
66. Telephone Conversation with Dr. Ebersole, 8/27/72
67. "Pathologist Finally Sees John Kennedy Autopsy Report; Wounds Show There Had to Be More than One Assassin," *Los Angeles Free Press*, 12/22/72; "'Robert Kennedy Was Killed Because He Planned New Probe in JFK's Death,' Says Top Lawyer-Pathologist," *National Enquirer*, 10/15/72, p. 3
68. "Wecht Blames More than One Gunman in JFK Slaying," *Pittsburgh Post-Gazette*, 8/28/72, p. 3
69. Cyril H. Wecht and Robert P. Smith, "The Medical Evidence in the Assassination of President John F. Kennedy," *Forensic Science Gazette* (Dallas, Texas: Southwestern Institute of Forensic Sciences, September 1973)

CHAPTER 21
Changed Receipts (pp. 521–26)

1. Item 1(E), NA, RG 272, E-52
2. Ibid.
3. Ibid.
4. Ibid.
5. Ibid.
6. Ibid.
7. Ibid.
8. Ibid.
9. Ibid.
10. Ibid.
11. 7 HAC 46–47; *see also* lists on pp. 49 and 51
12. S&O, p. 5
13. cf. S&O, p. 3, with CPR, p. 5
14. 2 WCH 349
15. Ibid.
16. Same as note 1
17. 5 WCH 73
18. FBI 62-109060-459
19. 18 WCH 727
20. 2 WCH 100
21. 18 WCH 744
22. 2 WCH 354
23. S&O, p. 5
24. S&O, p. 3
25. 2 WCH 349
26. FBI (Baltimore) 89-30-13B
27. FBI 109060-2637, p. 2; S&O, p. 3
28. Memo, Arlen Specter and Francis Adams to J. Lee Rankin, "Comprehensive Memorandum on Phase I . . ." 2/18/64, REP 3 files, NA, RG 272
29. FBI (Baltimore) 89-30-1313

CHAPTER 22
Behind the Scenes with the House Assassinations Committee (pp. 527–40)

1. 7 HAC 76
2. Berkeley Medallian, 1976, Chapter 44

3. RSP, 5/72
4. 7 HAC 243
5. ST, Dr. Finck, 2/24/69, pp. 118–19; 2/25/69, p. 6
6. 7 HAC 262
7. 7 HAC 77
8. 7 HAC 111, 122, 135
9. 7 HAC 122
10. Same as note 27, Chapter 17
11. 7 HAC 261
12. 7 HAC 264
13. 7 HAC 263
14. CD 5, pp. 150–51; CD 1269
15. CD 1395, p. 50; see note 26, Chapter 20
16. 7 HAC 245–46
17. 7 HAC 247
18. 7 HAC 228–30
19. 7 HAC 229
20. 7 HAC 248
21. 7 HAC 229
22. WCE 397 (17 WCH 45)
23. 17 WCH 36
24. 7 HAC 246
25. Ibid.
26. 7 HAC 260
27. 7 HAC 113
28. 7 HAC 12; Telephone Conversation with Stringer, 8/25/72 and 8/26/72
29. 7 HAC 12
30. 7 HAC 257–58
31. 7 HAC 246
32. Ibid.
33. ST, Dr. Finck, 2/24/69, p. 192; 2/25/69, p. 23
34. 7 HAC 246
35. 7 HAC 259
36. 7 HAC 247
37. 7 HAC 251
38. 7 HAC 252
39. 7 HAC 254
40. 7 HAC 255
41. Ibid.
42. 7 HAC 260
43. 7 HAC 260–61
44. 7 HAC 261
45. 7 HAC 263
46. 7 HAC 177

CHAPTER 23
Allegations of Dr. John Ebersole
(pp. 541–47)

1. Jack Severson "Celebrity in Their Midst," *Philadelphia Inquirer*, 3/10/78
2. Ibid.
3. Telephone Conversation with Dr. Kemp Clark, 11/9/66
4. Bernard Fensterwald and Michael Ewing, *Concidence or Conspiracy*? (New York: Zebra Books, 1977), p. 14
5. Telephone Conversation with Michael Ewing, 4/23/78
6. Telephone Conversation with Michael Ewing, 6/78
7. Ibid.
8. *Lancaster* [Pa.] *Intelligencer Journal*, 3/9/78
9. Ibid.
10. Ibid.
11. Telephone Conversation with Gil Dulaney, 8/7/78
12. Taped interview of Dr. John Ebersole by Art Smith, Lancaster, Pa., 3/28/78
13. Same as note 8
14. Same as note 12
15. Same as note 11
16. Same as note 12
17. Ibid.
18. Same as note 11
19. Same as note 12

CHAPTER 24
House Select Committee:
1978 Public Hearings (pp. 548–66)

1. 1 HAC 152
2. 1 HAC 173
3. 1 HAC 176–77
4. 1 HAC 179
5. Ibid.
6. 1 HAC 306
7. 1 HAC 300
8. 1 HAC 324
9. Ibid.
10. 2 WCH 349
11. 1 HAC 324
12. 1 HAC 324–25
13. 1 HAC 325
14. 1 HAC 327
15. BAR, p. 4
16. 1 HAC 327
17. Ibid.
18. Ibid.
19. 1 HAC 328
20. 1 HAC 328–29
21. 1 HAC 329
22. Ibid.
23. Ibid.
24. Ibid.
25. 1 HAC 330
26. 1 HAC 331
27. 1 HAC 310
28. Ibid.

29. Author's memo, 9/7/78, re: conversation with Humes earlier that day
30. 1 HAC 233
31. 1 HAC 199
32. 2 WCH 364
33. 1 HAC 305–6
34. 1 HAC 377
35. Letter, Dr. Paul Peters to Wallace Milam, 4/14/80
36. 24 WCH 263
37. 1 HAC 504, 554–55
38. DMN, 4/1/77
39. Letter, Earl Golz to Lifton, 10/25/79, transmitting interview notes
40. NA, RG 272, E-52, item 1(c)

41. Letter, Hoover to Lifton, 7/10/70, FBI 109060-6947
42. 1 HAC 555
43. 1 HAC 562
44. Ibid.
45. Taped interview with Vincent Guinn, 9/8/78
46. Ibid.
47. 2 HAC 17–105; HACR, pp. 66–72
48. 5 HAC 588
49. 5 HAC 609
50. Lifton memo, 12/29/78, re: conversation with Purdy that day
51. NYT, 1/7/79
52. WP, 1/6/79

Part VI THE COFFIN/BODY PROBLEM

CHAPTER 25
The Lake County Informant
(pp. 569–88)

1. FBI 62-109060-2637, p. 2
2. S&O, p. 1
3. 18 WCH 744; DOP, p. 391
4. 18 WCH 744
5. S&O, p. 1
6. 18 WCH 744
7. MDW—Bird Report, 12/10/63
8. Ibid.
9. Same as note 1
10. 2 WCH 349
11. MDW—Bird Report
12. S&O, p. 1
13. Same as note 1
14. See Chapter 16
15. DOP, pp. 294–307
16. 18 WCH 743–44
17. *Life*, 11/24/67
18. 18 WCH 744; DOP, pp. 266, 276, 309
19. 18 WCH 744 (Hill)
20. 18 WCH 775 (Johns)
21. 18 WCH 744 (Hill)
22. Ibid.

5. Letter, Lifton to Hoover, 7/1/70, FBI 62-109060-6947
6. S&O, p. 4
7. Same as note 1
8. Telephone Conversation with FBI Agent John Morrison, 6/26/70
9. Letter, Hoover to Lifton, 7/10/70, FBI 62-109060-6947
10. Telephone Conversation with Darrel Tomlinson, by Ray Marcus, 7/25/66
11. WCH-PrEx 29, p. 2
12. 7 HAC 8
13. 7 HAC 37
14. 7 HAC 38
15. Ibid.
16. 7 HAC 39
17. 7 HAC 42
18. Telephone Conversation with William Greer, 11/20/67
19. 7 HAC 19
20. Ibid.
21. FBI memo, Rosen to DeLoach, 11/6/66
22. 7 HAC 15
23. Ibid.
24. Ibid.
25. 7 HAC 15
26. Telephone Conversation with Andrew Purdy, 8/20/79
27. cf. 7 HAC 15 and 7 HAC 8
28. Telephone Conversation with Paul K. O'Connor, 8/25/79
29. WCH-PrEx 21
30. WCH-PrEx 12
31. Telephone Conversation with Aubrey Rike, 3/11/80
32. CD 371
33. 6 WCH 16
34. Ibid.

CHAPTER 26
The Recollections of
Paul Kelly O'Connor (pp. 589–606)

1. NA, RG 272, E-52, item 1(c)
2. The title of E-52, as cited in Archives inventory for RG 272
3. Letter, Lifton to Hoover, 5/12/70, FBI 62-109060-6932
4. Letter, Hoover to Lifton, 5/22/70, FBI 62-109060-6932

35. Letter, Chief, Navy Reference Branch, NPRC to Lifton, 1/7/80
36. Telephone Conversation with Dr. John Ebersole, 8/27/72

CHAPTER 27
The Recollections of
James Curtis Jenkins et al.
(pp. 607–21)

1. "Summary of Events Concerning Contacts Between HAC and Navy Medical Department; prepared by Lt. Comm. Robert E. Broach, 9/29/77"; BuMed file obtained under FOIA
2. Ibid.
3. FBI telegram, FBI 62-109060-459
4. CD 7, p. 286
5. Taped interview of John Ebersole by Art Smith, 3/28/78
6. 7 HAC 13
7. 2 WCH 353
8. 7 HAC 122
9. 7 HAC 113
10. 7 HAC 260
11. 2 WCH 103
12. Ibid.
13. S&O, p. 5
14. 7 HAC 244
15. Telephone Conversation with Edward Reed, 11/25/79
16. Telephone Conversation with Jerrol Custer, 9/30/79
17. Telephone Conversation with Jerrol Custer, 10/7/79

CHAPTER 28
The Clandestine
Intermission Hypothesis (pp. 622–44)

1. Telephone Conversation with James Jenkins, 9/23/79
2. Telephone Conversation with Jerrol Custer, 10/7/79
3. FBI 62-109060-2637, p. 2; S&O, p. 1
4. S&O, p. 3
5. Ibid.
6. 2 WCH 103
7. Memorandum by George Barnum, 11/29/63, p. 3
8. MDW—Bird Report
9. S&O, p. 3
10. Telephone Conversation with Paul O'Connor, 8/25/79
11. MDW file, same as note 24, Chapter 19

12. Telephone Conversation with Richard Lipsey, 8/30/79
13. Telephone Conversation with John Stover, 4/13/80
14. Telephone Conversation with James Metzler, 11/25/79
15. FBI 62-109060-2637, p. 1
16. S&O, p. 2
17. Same as note 14
18. Telephone Conversation with J. S. Layton Ledbetter, 9/25/79
19. Telephone Conversation with Paul K. O'Connor, 8/25/79
20. Telephone Conversation with Floyd Reibe, 11/26/79
21. 7 HAC 46
22. Same as note 20
23. 2 WCH 349
24. Ibid.
25. Telephone Conversation with Dr. Humes, 11/9/79
26. 7 HAC 261
27. Telephone Conversation with Adm. David Osborne, 11/4/79
28. S&O, p. 3
29. CD 7, pp. 10–11
30. CD 7, p. 286
31. Ibid.
32. Ibid.
33. Telephone Conversation with James Jenkins, 9/23/79
34. DOP, p. 432
35. DOP, pp. 430–31
36. Same as note 33
37. DOP, p. 399
38. Letter, 4/4/80, R. J. Costanzo (Superintendent, Arlington National Cemetery) to Sarah Holland

CHAPTER 29
The Assertion of
Adm. David P. Osborne (pp. 645–52)

1. 7 HAC 15
2. Ibid.
3. 7 HAC 16
4. Telephone Conversation with Admiral Osborne, 11/4/79
5. 7 HAC 15
6. Same as note 4
7. 18 WCH 800
8. CD 7, p. 288
9. Same as note 4
10. Telephone Conversation with Dr. Humes, 11/9/79
11. NA, RG 272, E-52
12. CD 371
13. Ibid.

14. Letter, Hoover to Lifton, 7/10/70, FBI 62-109060-6947
15. BAR, p. 4
16. Letter, Secret Service to Lifton, 5/16/78
17. Letter, Secret Service to Lifton, 8/2/78
18. S&O, p. 4
19. Same as note 4
20. CD 7, p. 286
21. Ibid.
22. FBI 62-109060-459
23. CD 7, p. 286

24. Ibid.
25. Telephone Conversation with John Stover, 4/13/80
26. 7 HAC 15
27. MDW—Bird Report, 12/10/63
28. Same as note 4
29. CD 7, p. 288
30. 2 WCH 99
31. FBI memo, Rosen to Belmont, 3/12/64, FBI 62-109060-2637, p. 2
32. 18 WCH 800
33. CD 7, p. 288
34. Same as note 10

Part VII   SYNTHESIS

CHAPTER 30
The X-Rays and
Photographs Reconsidered
(pp. 655–72)

1. Telephone Conversation with Jerrol Custer, 10/7/79; with Ed Reed, 11/25/79; *see* Chapter 27 for direct quotes
2. Telephone Conversation with James Jenkins, 9/23/79; *see* Chapter 27
3. Telephone Conversation with Paul O'Connor, 8/25/79
4. Telephone Conversation with Admiral Osborne, 11/4/79
5. 7 HAC 46
6. 7 HAC 45
7. 7 HAC 4
8. 7 HAC 46
9. Ibid.
10. Ibid.
11. RSP, p. 57
12. CPR, p. 11; RSP, pp. 43, 56
13. 7 HAC 223
14. 7 HAC 224
15. 7 HAC 223
16. 7 HAC 222, 224
17. 7 HAC 251
18. 7 HAC 322
19. 7 HAC 223
20. 7 HAC 224
21. 7 HAC 282
22. 2 WCH 353
23. MIR, p. 4; 7 HAC 118
24. 7 HAC 260
25. 7 HAC 49
26. 7 HAC 70
27. 7 HAC 51, 70
28. 7 HAC 49
29. Telephone Conversation with Dr. Baden, 11/8/79

30. 7 HAC 10
31. 7 HAC 9
32. Ibid.
33. Telephone Conversation with Dr. John Ebersole, 8/27/72
34. As recorded by Sibert and O'Neill, in their memo re: interrogation by Specter, FBI 109060-2637, p. 2
35. ST, Finck, 2/25/69, pp. 15–16
36. See discussion in Chapter 23
37. Telephone Conversation with Paul O'Connor, 8/25/79
38. See Chapter 26, passim
39. Telephone Conversation with Admiral Osborne, 11/4/79
40. Telephone Conversation with James Felder, 11/20/67; taped interview with Felder, Los Angeles, 12/16/67
41. Telephone Conversation with Godfrey McHugh, 11/19/67
42. Telephone Conversation with James Jenkins, 9/23/79
43. Telephone Conversation with John Van Hoesen, 3/25/80
44. 7 HAC 15
45. 7 HAC 15–16
46. Telephone Conversation with Captain Stover, 4/13/80
47. 7 HAC 10
48. MDW file, memo dated 11/22/63 Item 11, time dated 5:10 EST
49. S&O, p. 3
50. Ibid.
51. CPR, p. 9
52. Dr. Spitz on "Lou Gordon Show" aired in Los Angeles on 5/17/75
53. "Doctor Inspects Kennedy X-rays," NYT, 1/9/72, p. 40
54. I HAC 231
55. I HAC 377
56. BAR, p. 3

57. HAC, JFK Exhibit F-20 (*see* photo section of this book)
58. 2 WCH 143
59. Wecht notes, p. 44
60. Ibid.
61. Personal file memo of George Barnum, 11/29/63
62. Telephone Conversation with James Jenkins, 9/23/79
63. WCR, p. 198; *see also* WCE 2003, p. 168

CHAPTER 31
The "When and Where"
Problem Reconsidered (pp. 673–90)

1. 18 WCH 743 (Hill); DOP, p. 291; WCH-PrEx 7, p. 4
2. CD 1245, p. 7
3. 18 WCH 743 (Hill)
4. Telephone Conversation with Aubrey Rike, 3/11/80
5. Ibid.
6. 18 WCH 744
7. DOP, pp. 313–14
8. 18 WCH 744; AP "A" wire, 2:50 CST; UPI reported 2:39; see UPI "A" wire, 3:53 EST
9. DOP, p. 348
10. DOP, pp. 309–10
11. DOP, pp. 313–16
12. DOP, p. 313
13. DOP, p. 316
14. DOP, p. 317
15. 7 WCH 470; Lawrence O'Brien, *No Final Victories* (New York: Doubleday, 1974; reprint ed., Ballantine, 1976), p. 165
16. 7 WCH 454; Kenneth O'Donnell and Dave Powers, *Johnny, We Hardly Knew Ye* (Boston: Little, Brown and Co., 1972; reprint ed., Pocket Books, 1973), pp. 38–39; cf. DOP, pp. 415–16
17. 18 WCH 780–81
18. 18 WCH 738 (Roberts), 749 (Ready)
19. AP "A" Wire, 2:14 CST; SS denial at 4:33 EST
20. Telephone Conversation with Deroy Cain, 3/4/80
21. Telephone Conversation with Lt. Col. Joe Sofet, 3/4/80
22. S&O, p. 1

23. MDW file, log kept by Major Dwight Adams, Funeral Operations Center, entries 5 and 6, 11/22/63
24. NBC-TV broadcasts at 3:32 P.M. and 3:48 P.M., as recorded in published version of log, *There Was a President* (New York: Ridge Press, Random House, 1966), pp. 21–22
25. 7 HAC 49–50
26. 7 HAC 50
27. "Tape Transcription, Monitored from AF-1," Special File on the Assassination of John F. Kennedy, LBJ Library, p. 5
28. Ibid.
29. Ibid.
30. U.S. Air Force, History of the 1001st Air Base Wing, 7/1/63–12/31/63, p. 120
31. AT-CBS network broadcast
32. Same as note 24, 6:00 P.M. broadcast
33. WCE 1126, p. 6
34. Telephone Conversation with Dr. Boswell, 7/5/79
35. WCE 1126, p. 6
36. Presidential Diary, "Backup file," 11/22/63, LBJ Library
37. Telephone Conversation with Marie Chiarodo, 9/4/80

CHAPTER 32
The Assassination as a
Covert Operation (pp. 691–99)

1. *Washington Star*, 11/24/63
2. U.S. Congress, Senate Select Committee to Study Governmental Operations with Respect to Intelligence Activities. *Alleged Assassination Plots Involving Foreign Leaders.* S. Report 94–465, 94th Congress, 1st session 1975, p. 73
3. Ibid.
4. Thomas Powers, *The Man Who Kept the Secrets* (New York: Knopf, 1979), p. 82
5. Allen Dulles, *The Craft of Intelligence* (New York: Harper and Row, 1963), pp. 205–6
6. Ibid., pp. 209, 211
7. WCES, 12/16/63, pp. 51–52
8. Ibid., p. 52
9. Ibid.
10. WCES, 1/21/64, p. 11

Name Index

Casket team (*continued*)
  and McHugh assisting with coffin, 412
  members of, 398
Central Intelligence Agency, 364, 556
Chain of command, U.S. Navy, 298, 417–418, 613
Chain of possession, body, 227–228
  allegation of continuity on, 400, 412–413, 420
  coffin unattended, 677–678
  definition of, 397
  initial discovery of break in, 392
  possible break on *Air Force One*, 588, 675–678
  possible break at Parkland, 588, 674
  re-evaluation of, 587–588
  See also Ambulance chase
Chronological analysis, 208–209
  See also Time-line analysis
Clandestine intermission hypothesis, 627–629, 643
Clark Panel. *See* X-rays and photographs; Wounds
"Closure" phenomenon, 397, 422, 518
Clothing holes, 76–77, 154–155, 163, 197, 203, 218, 344, 545
  authenticity of, 283
  caused by head shot fragment, 348–349
Coffin, "Air Force colonel's," 643–644
Coffin, Dallas
  acquisition of, 673–674
  and allegation of front-door entry at Bethesda, 401, 479, 594
  arrival of at Andrews, 390, 393–394
  arrival of at Bethesda, 220
  arrival of at morgue, 391–392, 406–407, 478, 631, 633
  as center of attention, 205
  constantly accompanied at Parkland, 674–675
  damage to, 399, 400, 405, 411, 627
  departure from Parkland of, 582
  description of, 598, 644
  and dispute over removal from Parkland, 389–390, 674
  empty, 492, 570, 572–573, 575, 577–578
  and "empty casket" rumor at Bethesda, 579, 627
  and flight from Dallas to Andrews, 578
  loading of on *Air Force One*, 588
  and multiple-entry hypothesis, 484–485, 492, 624–626
  placement of in *Air Force One*, 390, 675
  plastic lining in, 595, 599–600, 674
  and ride from Andrews to Bethesda, 577
  and ride from front of Bethesda to rear, 391; *see also* Chain of possession, body; Ambulance chase
  and ride to Love Field, 390, 675
  unloading of from *Air Force One* at Andrews, 577–578
Coffin entries. *See* Autopsy, coffin entries
Coffin-opening, witnesses to, 396–397, 408, 515, 519, 584–585
Coffin, shipping, 579–580, 598–599, 601, 609, 629, 637

Concealment of other assassins, 123
Conspiracy
  barriers to acceptance of, 334
  and case against Oswald, 352–359
    gun-victim connection, 357–359; Oswald-gun connection, 353–355; Oswald-victim connection, 355–357
  and inferences from head surgery, 179–180
  plot structure of based on trajectory reversal, 350; *see also* Body alteration
  possible Secret Service involvement in, 370
  relative importance of different types of, 182
  view of media on, 222
  viewed as random events, 696
Contre-coup injury, 454
Covert operations, 694–695

Dallas Police radio transmissions, 365–369
  description of Oswald in, 369
  and unknown witness, 365–368
Death of a President, 389, 390–396, 675–577
Dulles/Humes interchange, 176–177, 188, 248, 250, 506

"Emperor's New Clothes" metaphor, 23, 699

Federal Bureau of Investigation
  and conclusion of Oswald's guilt, 362
  and Hoover's public statement on controversy, 296–297
  and Hoover's public statement urged by White House, 306
  and internal documents regarding head surgery, 301–305
  Summary Reports, 346, 377
    conflict of with autopsy report, 83–84; criticism of, 85, 109; omission of from Warren Report, 162
Forensic pathology
  and entry and exit bullet wounds, 248
  and gunshot wounding of brain, 465
  and skull fracturing, 450, 453
  See also Autopsy, procedure
Fourth shot. *See* House Select Committee on Assassinations, acoustics evidence of
"Friday-night" information. *See* Twin transmission line model

Harper fragment
  conflict of with X-rays, 504
  discovery of, 316, 503
  examination of, 316–317, 503–504
  FBI handling of, 503
  identification of by HSCA, 530–533
Head-snap
  and acceleration of car, 121
  and conservation of momentum, 121
  and explanation of double motion, 51–53, 555
  ignored in Warren Report, 6
  initial discovery of, 6
  as neuromuscular reaction, 122, 555
  physicists' explanations for, 96
  reaction of Allen Dulles to, 34

reaction of Richard Feynman to, 48–50, 122
as reported in *Life,* 7

Hearse, black
arrival of at morgue, 574–576, 580–581, 605
occupants of, 575–576
witnesses to, 580–581

Helicopter
casket team rides in, 394–395, 399, 408
decoy, 605–606, 636
General Wehle rides in, 394, 485
as mode of arrival for body, 605–606
as possible transport for body bag, 682–683
takeoff of near *Air Force One* at Andrews, 682–683

Hickey, George, report of alleging witnessing fatal shot strike, 510–511

House Select Committee on Assassinations
acoustics evidence of, 560–561, 563, 694
authentication of X-rays and photographs by, 549, 658–663
conspiracy conclusion of, 564
criticism of photographs by, 638, 659
informed of body alteration, 554, 560–562
interview of James Jenkins, 617–619
medical panel of, 527
and meeting with autopsy doctors, 528–530; verification of X-rays and photographs by, 528
radiology report of, 660–661
reliance on X-rays and photographs by, 655
report of
on body alteration, 592–595; on chain of possession, 593–594; and list of persons attending autopsy, 592
report of skin abrasions on body, 680
testimony
of Ernest Aschkenasy, 563; of James Barger, 560–561; of Vincent Guinn, 556–558; of James Humes, 549–553; of Charles Petty, 554–555; of Larry Sturdivan, 555; of Mark Weiss, 563

Humes, James J.
and Arlen Specter, 77, 144, 203–204
forbidden to talk, 4, 65
and telephone call to Malcolm Perry
back wound as man-made, 283, 287; as reason for changed autopsy report, 160–161
testimony of as "best evidence," 124

Inquest
autopsy report alteration hypothesis in, 84–87, 98–99
"political truth" conclusion in, 86–87

Johnson, Lyndon B.
abdominal surgery of, 261
swearing-in of, 588, 677
visit with Jacqueline Kennedy on *Air Force One,* 678

Kellerman, Roy
alleged witnessing of reaction to back wound, 286

Kennedy, John F.
and Addison's disease, 528
position of in limousine, 4, 58–59, 65–66
possible means of transporting body of, 679–680
pronouncement of death of, 389

[illegible] New York City, 3–4
lecture by at UCLA, 5–6

"Lens" metaphor, 423, 507–508, 526, 529, 565, 656, 657, 667–668

Liebeler, Wesley J.
concern of over X-rays and photographs, 142
conversations
with Joseph Ball, 223–224; with pathologist, 217; with Richard Russell, 241; with Arlen Specter, 224
course on Warren Commission by, 114–116
criticism of Warren Commission by, 99–100
and debates with Mark Lane, 112, 383–384
and impressions of Mark Lane, 113, 118, 426
interrogation of witnesses by, 20–21
on Louis Lomax TV show, 185–190
and meeting with Ray Marcus, 386
memorandum of 9/6/64, 100–101
memorandum of 11/8/66, xviii, 380–381, 426–427, 433, 459, 498
distribution of, 288, 298, 381; drafting session for, 262–264; final draft of, 267–269; first draft of, 266; reaction to, 385
proposed book by, 113–114, 116, 186
reaction of to Sibert and O'Neill report, xvii–xviii, 214–215, 291, 294
as source of documents for *Inquest,* 84–85

Lifton, David S.
acceptance of Warren Commission's integrity, 137
belief in falsification of autopsy report, 75
bullet-planting hypothesis, early, 346
changed autopsy report, analysis of, 161–164
changed autopsy report, hypothesis of, 211
confrontation with Allen Dulles, 34–36
conversations
with Morris Abrams, 199–201; with James Altgens, 29; with Michael Baden, 453, 461, 663; with George Barnum, 414–415; with Charles Baxter, 272; with Samuel Bird, 407; with Robert Blakey, 561–562; with J. Thornton Boswell, 319, 688; with George Burkley, 401–402; with Deroy Cain, 679; with Charles Carrico, 271–272; with Timothy Cheek, 399; with Hubert Clark, 408–413; with Kemp Clark, 300–301; with Chester Clifton,

General Index

"Low/high" conflict, 163–164, 191–192, 195, 203, 210, 344–345, 374–377, 668–671

National Naval Medical Center. *See* Bethesda Naval Hospital
Neutron activation analysis, 556–557
Non-transit, evidence for, 79–80

Occam's Razor, 142
Oswald, Lee H.
  behavior and whereabouts of
    after leaving Texas School Book Depository, 351–352; in Texas School Book Depository, 4, 350–352
  denials of crime by, 20, 352
  identification by witness, 355–356
  proficiency with rifle, 100–101
Oswald, Marina, 99–100

Palmprint on rifle, 13, 354–356
Patterns of evidence, 693
Planted-bullet hypothesis, 90–94
Pre-autopsy autopsy. *See* Body alteration
Press conference, Parkland, 59–62, 161, 271

Radio transmissions. See *Air Force One*, radio transmissions; Dallas Police, radio transmissions
Ramparts magazine, 37–38
  author's relationship with, 268, 333–334
  and "The Case for Three Assassins," 38, 95
Reconstruction of head, 430, 432, 523–524, 553, 658, 663–664, 668
Re-enactment of assassination, 65, 76
Rifle, Mannlicher-Carcano
  minimum firing time, 71
  photograph of Oswald with rifle, 355

Secret Service
  accompanying body, 593–594
  and alleged possession of bullet 399 at autopsy, 646
  memorandum by regarding metal recovered from body, 578–579
  in morgue anteroom, 631, 632–636
  possession of physical evidence by, 94, 198, 211–213, 224, 284, 359–361, 363, 697
  and presence of "agents" on grassy knoll, 369
  and rumor of death of agent in Dallas, 679
  visit to Parkland doctors by, 64–65, 156, 166, 195–197, 221–222, 238, 286
Sibert and O'Neill
  barred from autopsy room, 392, 475–476, 491, 583–584, 623
  interviews
    with Gerald Behn, 250, 489, 641–642, 650–651; with William Greer, 488–489, 641; with Roy Kellerman, 488, 641; with Arlen Specter, 484
  level of awareness of, 641–643
  memorandum of 11/26/63, 486–487
  receipt for missile, 558, 590, 648–649

report of
  additional head wrapping, 171, 174, 447; agents assisting with coffin, 171, 206, 392, 475; arrival of *Air Force One* at Andrews, 475; arrival of motorcade ambulance at Bethesda, 475; autopsy trajectory conclusions, 102; delay in dictating, 202, 482; early departure of agents from autopsy, 525; as evidence against late change in autopsy report, 106; existence of, 101; failure to pursue head surgery report, 177; and "low/high" conflict, 102; observation of head surgery, 171–172; observation of tracheotomy, 172, 348–349; omitted from Warren Report, 162; reaction to, 381; as source of FBI Summary Reports, 103–106; "surgery" statement attributed to autopsy doctors, 296–297, 301–305, 328; "surgery" statement overlooked, 295–296; typographical alterations, 480–482, 489–490, 615–616, 642; wrapping of body, 171, 297
  role of at autopsy, 297, 634
Single-bullet theory
  objections to
    alignment of victims, 73–74; separate hits, 71–72; testimony of John Connally, 73; trajectory through President Kennedy, 74–75
  origin of, 213
  plausibility of, 67–68
  timing problem of, 70–71, 288
Smoke, on grassy knoll, 9–10, 15–16, 189–190
Sniper's nest, 4, 9
  attention drawn to, 365–367
  delay in discovery of, 367–368
"Stillborn baby" story. *See* Brain, possible entry into autopsy room
"Sunday-night" information. *See* Twin transmission line model

Theatre of Ideas, 84, 109–112
Three-assassin model, 38, 70, 151
Time-line analysis
  Bethesda, 606, 622–623
  Dallas-Bethesda, 671–672
Timing problem. *See* Single-bullet theory, timing problem of
Tracheotomy tube flange, 273–274
Trajectories
  and double-hit hypothesis, 334–335
  of fatal shot, 317, 329, 656, 668
  initial opinion of Dallas doctors regarding, 39–43
  of non-fatal shot, 161, 360–361, 381, 555, 612–613, 668–669, 671
    angle of, 75–76; belated inference about, 162–163; evidence of transit of, 382
Trajectory reversal, 338–344
  and case against Oswald. *See* Conspiracy
  concept of, 281–282
  and planted bullets, 343
  and plot structure. *See* Conspiracy

753

Now You Can See Best Evidence

BEST EVIDENCE, THE RESEARCH VIDEO

DAVID S. LIFTON presents dramatic interviews with eyewitnesses involved in JFK's autopsy originally filmed during research for this book. After years of silence — enforced by military order — these important witnesses speak for the first time on videocassette. Includes autopsy photographs and x-rays with startling new analysis, plus archival footage and rare photographs.

1990. Color and B&W. Approx. 37 min., VHS. Only $14.95.

Also available is COLLECTORS SET, featuring BEST EVIDENCE, THE RESEARCH VIDEO and BEST EVIDENCE, the recent book. Receive both for $29.95.

Please send me:

TITLE				TOTAL
BEST EVIDENCE, THE RESEARCH VIDEO	$14.95 ea.			_____
BEST EVIDENCE COLLECTORS SET	$29.95 ea.			_____
	Subtotal	$		_____
$2.00 Shipping & Handling 1st item				_____
Other $ per additional				_____
CA residents add 8.25% sales tax				_____
	TOTAL	$		_____

Name _____

Address _____

City/State/Zip _____

___ Check or money order enclosed payable to BE VIDEO

___ Charge my: ___ Visa ___ MasterCard

Card # _____

Signature _____ Exp. Date _____

Complete and mail to BE VIDEO
11500 W. Olympic Blvd., #400
Los Angeles, CA 90064

Please do not send cash. Allow 4-6 weeks for delivery. Offer valid in U.S.A. only.

Now You Can *See* Best Evidence
BEST EVIDENCE: THE RESEARCH VIDEO

DAVID S. LIFTON presents dramatic interviews with eyewitnesses involved in JFK's autopsy, originally filmed during research for this book. After years of silence—enforced by military order—these important witnesses speak for the first time on videocassette. Includes autopsy photographs and x-rays with startling new analysis, plus archival footage and rare photographs.

1990 / Color and B&W / Approx. 35 Min. / VHS Only / $14.95

Also available as a COLLECTORS' SET featuring BEST EVIDENCE: THE RESEARCH VIDEO with BEST EVIDENCE paperback book together for only $24.95.

- -

Please send me:

TITLE	QUANTITY	PRICE	TOTAL
BEST EVIDENCE: THE RESEARCH VIDEO	————	$14.95 ea.	————
BEST EVIDENCE COLLECTORS' SET	————	$24.95 ea.	————

Subtotal: $————

$2.00 Shipping & Handling 1st tape

plus 75¢ each additional: ————

CA residents add 6.75% sales tax: ————

TOTAL: $————

Name ————————————————————————

Address ————————————————————————

City/State/Zip ————————————————————

———— Check or money order enclosed payable to BE VIDEO

———— Charge my ————Visa ———— MasterCard

Card # ————————————————————————

Signature ———————————————— Exp. Date ————

Complete and mail to: BE VIDEO
11500 W. Olympic Blvd., #400
Los Angeles, CA 90064

Please do not send cash. Allow 4–6 weeks for delivery. Offer valid in U.S.A. only.

FINE WORKS OF NON-FICTION
AVAILABLE IN QUALITY
PAPERBACK EDITIONS FROM
CARROLL & GRAF

☐ Anderson, Nancy/WORK WITH PASSION $8.95
☐ Asbel, Robert/THE PIZZA GOURMET $10.95
☐ Asprey, Robert/THE PANTHER'S FEAST $9.95
☐ Athill, Diana/INSTEAD OF A LETTER $7.95
☐ Bedford, Sybille/ALDOUS HUXLEY $14.95
☐ Barton, Peter/CLOUDBURST IN THE... $10.95
☐ Blaise, Peter/JROCOTL $14.50
☐ Bizardel, .../PIERRE LOTI $10.95
☐ Blythe, Ronald/THE STABLES OF PARADISE $9.95
☐ Bramson, Robert/THE WILDER SHORES OF
  LOVE $8.95
☐ Bowen, John/IN THE LAND OF NYX $7.95
☐ Bunyan, John/PILGRIM'S WAY $10.95
☐ Carr, John Dickson/THE LIFE OF SIR ARTHUR
  CONAN DOYLE $9.95
☐ Brice, Virginia Sorma/THE FAMILY HUNTER
  $9.95
☐ WORLD HISTORY OF CLASSICAL MUSIC $12.95
☐ Cherry-Garrard/THE WORST JOURNEY IN THE
  WORLD $13.95
☐ Coffin, Robert/JUSTICE AT NUREMBURG $11.95
☐ Cooper, Duff/OLD MEN FORGET $10.95
☐ Cooper, Lady Diana/AUTOBIOGRAPHY $13.95
☐ De Jonge, Alex/THE LIFE AND TIMES OF
  GRIGORII RASPUTIN $10.95
☐ Edwards, Anne/SONYA, THE LIFE OF
  COUNTESS TOLSTOY $8.95
☐ Ellington, John/THE GENE FACTORY $8.95
☐ Faison, Nigey/THE WAY OF A
  TRANSGRESSOR $9.95
☐ Garbo, Martin/TRAITORS AND HEROES $10.95
☐ Gill, Brendan/HERE AT THE NEW YORKER $12.95
☐ Godwin, Stephen & Sky, Kathleen/THE BUSINESS
  OF BEING A WRITER $8.95
☐ Gelenbeck, Peter/HOW TO WIN AT ROTISSERIE
  BASEBALL $8.95
☐ Green, Julian/DIARIES 1928-1957 $9.95

FINE WORKS OF NON-FICTION AVAILABLE IN QUALITY PAPERBACK EDITIONS FROM CARROLL & GRAF

- ☐ Anderson, Nancy/WORK WITH PASSION $8.95
- ☐ Arlett, Robert/THE PIZZA GOURMET $10.95
- ☐ Asprey, Robert/THE PANTHER'S FEAST $9.95
- ☐ Athill, Diana/INSTEAD OF A LETTER $7.95
- ☐ Bedford, Sybille/ALDOUS HUXLEY $14.95
- ☐ Berton, Pierre/KLONDIKE FEVER $10.95
- ☐ Blake, Robert/DISRAELI $14.50
- ☐ Blanch, Lesley/PIERRE LOTI $10.95
- ☐ Blanch, Lesley/THE SABRES OF PARADISE $9.95
- ☐ Blanch, Lesley/THE WILDER SHORES OF LOVE $8.95
- ☐ Bowers, John/IN THE LAND OF NYX $7.95
- ☐ Buchan, John/PILGRIM'S WAY $10.95
- ☐ Carr, John Dickson/THE LIFE OF SIR ARTHUR CONAN DOYLE $8.95
- ☐ Carr, Virginia Spencer/THE LONELY HUNTER: A BIOGRAPHY OF CARSON McCULLERS $12.95
- ☐ Cherry-Garrard/THE WORST JOURNEY IN THE WORLD $13.95
- ☐ Conot, Robert/JUSTICE AT NUREMBURG $11.95
- ☐ Cooper, Duff/OLD MEN FORGET $10.95
- ☐ Cooper, Lady Diana/AUTOBIOGRAPHY $13.95
- ☐ De Jonge, Alex/THE LIFE AND TIMES OF GRIGORII RASPUTIN $10.95
- ☐ Edwards, Anne/SONYA: THE LIFE OF COUNTESS TOLSTOY $8.95
- ☐ Elkington, John/THE GENE FACTORY $8.95
- ☐ Farson, Negley/THE WAY OF A TRANSGRESSOR $9.95
- ☐ Garbus, Martin/TRAITORS AND HEROES $10.95
- ☐ Gill, Brendan/HERE AT THE NEW YORKER $12.95
- ☐ Goldin, Stephen & Sky, Kathleen/THE BUSINESS OF BEING A WRITER $8.95
- ☐ Golenbock, Peter/HOW TO WIN AT ROTISSERIE BASEBALL $8.95
- ☐ Green, Julian/DIARIES 1928–1957 $9.95

Available from fine bookstores everywhere or use this coupon for ordering.

Carroll & Graf Publishers, Inc., 260 Fifth Avenue, N.Y., N.Y. 10001

Please send me the books I have checked above. I am enclosing
$_____ (please add $1.00 per title to cover postage and
handling.) Send check or money order—no cash or C.O.D.'s
please. N.Y. residents please add 8¼% sales tax.

Mr/Mrs/Ms _____

Address _____

City _____ State/Zip _____
Please allow four to six weeks for delivery.